KT-394-693

INDEPENDENT TRAVELLERS

AUSTRALIA

THE BUDGET TRAVEL GUIDE

Gareth Powell

Thomas Cook
Publishing

Published by Thomas Cook Publishing,
a division of Thomas Cook Tour Operations Limited
PO Box 227
The Thomas Cook Business Park
15–16 Coningsby Road
Peterborough PE3 8SB
United Kingdom

Telephone: 01733 416477
E-mail: books@thomascook.com

Text:
© 2005 Thomas Cook Publishing

Maps and diagrams:
© 2005 Thomas Cook Publishing

ISBN 1 841574 93 7

Head of Publishing: Chris Young
Production/DTP Editor: Steven Collins
Project Administrator: Michelle Warrington
Cover design and layout: Studio 183, Thorney,
Peterborough
Maps by Polly Senior Cartography, Lovell Johns Ltd,
Studio 183 Ltd
Editorial and layout for 2006 edition: 183 Books,
Thorney, Peterborough
Editor: Deborah Parker
Project Manager: Stephen York
Proofreader: Stuart McLaren

Text typeset in Book Antiqua and Gill Sans
using QuarkXPress
Printed and bound in Italy by Legoprint S.P.A.

For all Australian advertising enquiries please
contact:

Michael VanDerMolen
Michael Maya & Co Pty Ltd
50 Church Street, Albion Park
NSW 2527, Australia
Tel/fax: +61 (0)2 4257 3518
Mobile: +61 (0)412 518 927
E-mail: mmcoasia@1earth.net

First edition (2000) and additional
chapters (2005) written and researched
by: **Gareth Powell**

Book Editor, 2006 edition:
Ian Connellan

Update research for 2006 edition:
Ian Connellan, Gillian Manning

Transport information:
Peter Bass, Editor
Thomas Cook Overseas Timetable

With thanks to Belinda Moore and
Linda Bass for their contributions.

All rights reserved. No part of this
publication may be reproduced, stored
in a retrieval system or transmitted, in
any form or by any means, electronic,
mechanical, recording or otherwise, in
any part of the world, without the
prior permission of the Publisher. All
requests for permission should
be made to the Publisher at the
above address.

*Although every care has been taken in
compiling this publication, and the
contents are believed to be correct at time
of printing, Thomas Cook Tour Operations
Limited cannot accept responsibility for
errors or omissions, however caused, or
for changes in details given in the
guidebook, or for the consequences of any
reliance on the information provided.*

*The opinions and assessments expressed
in this book do not necessarily represent
those of Thomas Cook Tour Operations
Limited or those of the Thomas Cook UK
Limited group of companies.*

INDEPENDENT TRAVELLERS

AUSTRALIA

THE BUDGET TRAVEL GUIDE

Cork City Library
WITHDRAWN FROM STOCK

Other titles in this series include:

Independent Travellers Britain and Ireland
The Budget Travel Guide

Independent Travellers Europe by Rail
The Inter-Railer's and Eurailer's Guide

Independent Travellers New Zealand
The Budget Travel Guide

Independent Travellers Thailand, Malaysia and Singapore
The Budget Travel Guide

Independent Travellers USA
The Budget Travel Guide

BISHOPSTOWN
LIBRARY

5223051

SHARE YOUR EXPERIENCE

Have you had a great, interesting or even awful experience while travelling in Australia? Or do you have a helpful tip to pass on, that no guidebook seems to mention? We'd love to hear from you – and if we publish your experiences in the next edition we'll be happy to send you a free copy of the guide!

Write to the Series Editor, *Independent Travellers Australia*, Thomas Cook Publishing, PO Box 227, The Thomas Cook Business Park, 15–16 Coningsby Road, Peterborough PE3 8SB, UK, or e-mail books@thomascook.com.

THE AUTHORS

Gareth Powell was born in Wales and started his career working in circuses. After a spell in the regular British army he moved into journalism and publishing. In England he started Mayflower Books and was the publisher of *Fanny Hill* which resulted in a charge under the Obscene Publications Act. He emigrated to Australia where he started, among other magazines, *Pol*. In Hong Kong he started *Discovery* for Cathay Pacific, which he published for ten years.

He is the author of several books, including *The Practical Traveller*, *My Friend Arnold's Guide to Personal Computers*, *My Friend Arnold's Guide to Camcorders* (all Allen and Unwin), *The Book of Fax* (Philips), and *Touring Australia* and *Signpost New Zealand* (Thomas Cook). He has been a journalist most of his working life. He has a house in Sussex and in Sydney, and spends much of his time travelling, either in aircraft and by train or electronically on the internet. Returning to *Independent Travellers Australia*, he wrote two more chapters for the 2005 edition. He is currently working on a book entitled *So You Want to Emigrate to Australia?*

Gareth would like to thank Tom, 'who taught me much about Australia'.

Ian Connellan is a Sydney-based journalist, photographer and editor. After several years as a senior writer and book editor for *Australian Geographic,* he turned to writing guidebooks and has since co-authored bicycle-touring guides to Australia, Britain and Ireland. In 2000 he compiled the first edition of Thomas Cook's *Time For Food – Sydney*. Ian has worked on each of the six annual revisions of *Independent Travellers Australia*.

PHOTOGRAPHS

Thomas Cook Publishing wishes to thank Ethel Davies for supplying the photographs (to which she holds the copyright), with the exception of those indicated below.

Colour section pp. 96–97
Telstra Tower, Australia Capital Tourism
Canberra Parliament Building, Spectrum Colour Library
Gum tree and Three Sisters, Blue Mountains, Caroline Jones
Colour section pp. 192–193
Little Penguins, Penguin Parade®
Brisbane by night, Tourism Queensland
Colour section pp. 328–329
Snorkelling on the Great Barrier Reef, Tourism Office, Tourism Queensland
Sea lion, South Australian Tourism Commission
Colour section pp. 424–425
Wolf Creek Meteorite Crater, Photo Index
Uluru; Valley of the Winds, Kata Tjuta, David Hancock/Skyscans
Perth Swan Bells Tower, Elizabeth Czitronyi/Alamy

Cover photograph
Male Aboriginal, portrait, Pete Turner/Getty Images

Legend for Town Maps

Main Road & slip road	─(1)─
Mall	PITT STREET MALL
Other road	
Footpath	
Railway	+++++++++++
Monorail route/ station	●──
Tram or light rail route/station	●──
One-way street	↖
Bus station	🚌
Ferry route	— — — —

Parking area	P
Place of interest	● Art Gallery
Information centre	ℹ
Hospital	⊕
Police station	●
Post office	✉
Hotel	CARLTON Ⓗ
Park	
Library	📖
Golf course	⛳
Built-up area	

View point	☀
Place of worship	△

Tasmania Map

Major route	═⟨1⟩═
Minor road & track	
Footpath	════════
International/ other airport	✈ ✈
Place of interest	● Liffey Falls
Peak	▲ 466 m

HELP IMPROVE THIS GUIDE

This guide is updated each year. The information given in it may change during the lifetime of this edition and we would welcome reports and comments from our readers. Similarly we want to make this guide as practical and useful as possible and are grateful for any comments, criticisms and suggestions for improving future editions.

A free copy of this guide will be sent to all readers whose information or ideas are incorporated in the next edition. Please send all contributions to the Series Editor, *Independent Travellers Australia*, Thomas Cook Publishing, at PO Box 227, The Thomas Cook Business Park, 15–16 Coningsby Road, Peterborough, PE3 8SB, UK, or e-mail books@thomascook.com.

CONTENTS

GENERAL INFORMATION

ROUTES & CITIES

INTRODUCTION

The price of getting to Australia has dropped dramatically over the past few years, so that you no longer have to take out a mortgage on your house to be able to afford to visit. But, yes, it is a long way away, and from Europe you will be enjoying – if that is the right word – some of the longest flights in the world. Is it worth it? Certainly. That is why visitors keep coming back again and again.

This book is not a comprehensive guide to Australia. It is a guide to Australia for 'soft backpackers' – that is, travellers who would like to see as much of the country as cheaply as possible, but still with some style and comfort.

When talking to travellers, however long they have been exploring the country, you find that there are parts of Australia that none of them – not one – has ever seen. But neither is any one of them dismayed at the fact. There is only so much of Australia that the traveller can see at one time, and you have to be selective. And so is this book. Thus, Fraser Island is in because almost every traveller coming to Australia is hell-bent on visiting that magical island. On the other hand, you will find little about Lithgow or Wangaratta or a hundred other towns because, in the main, the traveller goes through without stopping or bypasses these places.

From looking at the destinations provided by the long-distance bus companies, and from my own travelling experience, the following routes seem to be the most popular:

Sydney–Brisbane (including Newcastle, Coffs Harbour, Byron Bay, Surfers Paradise)
Brisbane–Cairns (including Fraser Island, Airlie Beach, Magnetic Island, Great Barrier Reef)
Cairns–Alice Springs via Townsville and Tennant Creek (including Uluru)
Alice Springs–Darwin via Tennant Creek (including Katherine, Kakadu tours)
Alice Springs–Adelaide
Adelaide–Melbourne via the Great Ocean Road (including Apollo Bay)
Melbourne–Sydney via Canberra
Adelaide–Perth (including Albany)
Darwin–Perth (including Monkey Mia, Broome, Carnarvon)
Tasmania.

Even those driving around Australia – as opposed to taking a bus – seem to stick to the basic bus routes that backpackers follow. There are stops and areas on these bus routes that may not be interesting to everyone. For example, towns such as Gympie, Childers and Bowen on the east coast are just fruit-picking towns and would not interest anyone who isn't on a working holiday.

TRAVELLING ON A BUDGET

Australia loves travellers on a budget. You could even say Australia adores them: it is almost as if the whole country was set up specially for happy wanderers who need to watch their pennies. There are three main reasons for this.

Australia has a long and honoured tradition of people travelling light. In the early days they were called – and in some places they still are – swaggies. That is because they carried their baggage in a blanket roll across their shoulders and this was called the swag (possibly derived from thief's cant in England). These swaggies were not tramps in the English tradition. They were itinerant workers, with perhaps the nearest equivalent being a hobo in the United States. They travelled from town to town following seasonal work. They were utterly independent and the relationship with the boss was ever a meeting of equals. If the boss wanted to fire a swaggie – downsize in the modern parlance – the phrase, 'It's a nice day for travelling, but', would be used and there would be little embarrassment on either side. (That 'but' on the end means nothing. It is a sort of sentence ending. Strangely enough, you also find it in Canada.) So the tradition of travelling light and inexpensively is an old and honourable one.

WEBWISE

When collecting information on Australia, you may want to bypass the tourist offices unless you can conveniently call in, and go straight to the huge amount of facts and advice on the internet. For a useful one-stop site, try **www.budgettravel.com**.

Then there is the odd circumstance of the country pub. In Australia the word pub means both a bar – quality varying wildly – and hotel. It was the law in Australia for nearly a century that every pub had to offer inexpensive accommodation. Would you want to stay there? Probably not, unless you like the idea of being serenaded to sleep by slightly tipsy Crocodile Dundees, each blessed with a tin ear and brass lungs. But that idea of inexpensive accommodation in every town has been passed down directly to the motels of Australia. They are one of the glories of the country.

Another strand that makes Australia so attractive for the money-wise (that sounds so much better than budget) traveller is that a few years ago the country suddenly found that it could make money out of the intelligent traveller working within a tight budget. Indeed, it is one of the major sources of tourist revenue. The backpacking boom in Australia has been something to watch over the past ten years. Suddenly every state government and many business people realised that here was a seriously viable business. In the beginning there were, admittedly, some rough edges. There were backpacker hostels in Sydney, for example, where you would not house your dog. But competition and some legislation drove the undesirables out of the business. Now backpacker hostels are very, very inexpensive and, in many cases, more than acceptable to the soft backpacker.

INTRODUCTION/HOW TO USE THIS BOOK

WHEN TO GO

Whatever budget you are travelling on, there is one firm rule – try to avoid travelling to Australia over Christmas, the New Year, the whole of January and much of February, unless you will be staying with relatives and the accommodation is free. And even then it might not be such a good idea. The main school holidays in Australia are in January and most Australians think that it is a great idea to let Christmas slide into the New Year and then have their annual holiday in January. Universities stay out an extra month. This is also the hottest part of the year, which can make some places pretty uncomfortable.

Plainly there are still lots of Australians left in, say, Sydney, but many hotel and motel rooms around the country will be fully booked with holidaying Australians and, as always in times of scarcity, prices go up. From Christmas to 1 February it can be totally impossible to find accommodation at the last moment. Anyone, for example, who would like to spend that period in Lorne in Victoria had better start thinking a year ahead. At any other time of the year, with minor exceptions, you will never have any problems booking accommodation as you go.

HOW TO USE THIS BOOK

Independent Travellers Australia provides you with expert advice on 56 different routes, regions, towns and cities, each in its own chapter. Reflecting the tremendous variety of the country, as well as its almost daunting size, these chapters vary in their approach, each featuring the best way to see and enjoy that part of the country.

Because Sydney is the most popular arrival point, that is where this book also starts. It then journeys south to explore the cities and countryside of New South Wales, ACT (Australian Capital Territory), South Australia and Victoria before embarking on the long route up the coast to Brisbane and Queensland. A further route sets

DRIVING ROUTE

Once out of Sydney the freeway climbs Mt Colah and Mt Ku-Ring-Gai, past Bobbin Head and Berowra and through Cowan, then drops down to cross the Hawkesbury River at Mooney Mooney. The road then climbs out of the valley with Brisbane Water on the right and continues to the turn-off for Gosford (85 km). Beyond Gosford, Hwy 1 takes the inland route to Newcastle (156 km from Sydney).

▲

ROAD DETAILS
Route details and approximate cumulative mileages given.

PRICES

The price indications given below (Australian dollars) have been used throughout this book. Please bear in mind that prices do fluctuate – these symbols have been given for guidance. Occasionally we mention accommodation, food and highlights that are very expensive (shown $$$$+); these are included if the attraction is an unmissable one or in case you want to splash out on a special treat.

Accommodation

$	=	under $30
$$	=	$30–50
$$$	=	$50–80
$$$$	=	over $80

Based on standard double room, no meals but including all taxes.

Food

$	=	under $7
$$	=	$7–12
$$$	=	$12–20
$$$$	=	over $20

Based on the price of a mid-range main course.

Highlights

If an admission charge is made:

$	=	under $6
$$	=	$6–12
$$$	=	over $12

KEY TO ICONS

◈	Rail Services
◈	Bus Services
◈	Car
◈	Ferry Services
i	Information
◈	Accommodation
◈	Food and Drink

PUBLIC TRANSPORT DETAILS

Timetables for the routes have been extracted from the *Thomas Cook Overseas Timetable* (OTT); see p. 54. Special symbols used in the timetables are explained below.

①	Monday
②	Tuesday
③	Wednesday
④	Thursday
⑤	Friday
⑥	Saturday
⑦	Sunday
ex	except, e.g. 'ex 6' means does not operate on Saturdays
Ⓐ	Monday to Friday
Ⓒ	Saturday, Sunday and holidays
r	stops by request
u	stops to pick up only
s	stops to set down only
t	stops on highway, does not go into town

off inland for Alice Springs and Uluru (Ayers Rock). Perth, the main city on the west coast, is the starting point for discovering the vastness of Western Australia, with routes south to dairy country and the national parks of the south-west coast, and inland to Kalgoorlie and the goldfields. Another major route takes you north towards the Great Sandy Desert, beyond which lie Broome, Darwin and the true outback. Last, the book visits Tasmania and its magnificent national parks and wilderness areas.

Most chapters are accompanied by a map, showing the route or city and the stops described in the text. For driving routes the exact route is detailed, town by town, with stopovers and the most important attractions, together with price ranges, opening hours and other details. Cities or attractions which are worth longer stops each include detailed information on how to get there and get around, and how to make the most of your time. All chapters give suggestions for budget-friendly lodgings and places to eat, as well as how to find local entertainment highlights. Throughout the book you will see notes and tips in the margins. These provide added information, suggest places to stop en route or day trips from the main destination, tell you about interesting facts, or recommend an onward route connecting this with other chapters.

CAIRNS — COOKTOWN
OTT Table 9071

Service	◈	◈	◈	◈	◈	◈	◈	◈
Days of operation Special notes	①⑤⑦ A	②④⑥	Daily	Daily	Daily	Daily	Daily	Daily
Cairns..................d.	0600	0600	....	0700	0900	1130	1330	1800
Port Douglas..........d.	0700	0700	0700	0830	1030	1300	1500	1930
Daintree Town........d.			r		r	....	....	....
Daintree Ferry........d.			0750	0905	1130	....	....	....
Cape Tribulation......d.		0845	0900	1000	1300	....	....	....
Cooktown...............d.	1115	1200	....	....	....	....	....	....

Special notes:
A–This service operates via Lakeland.

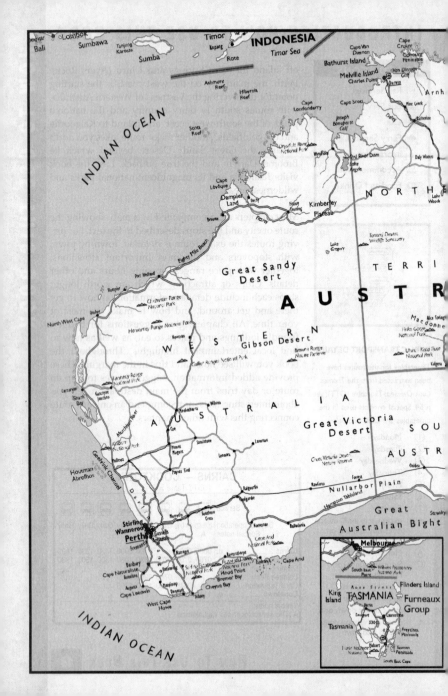

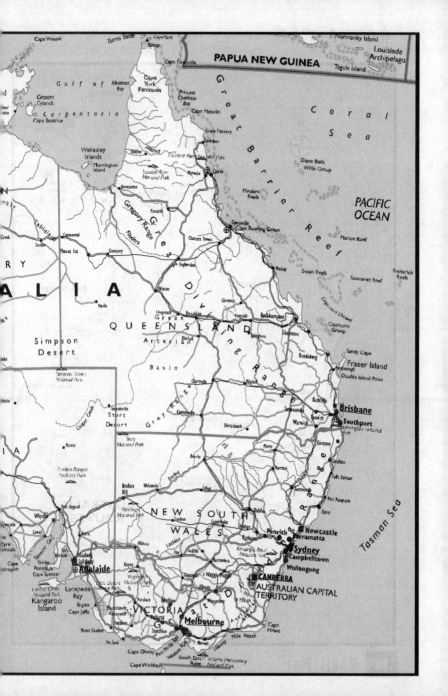

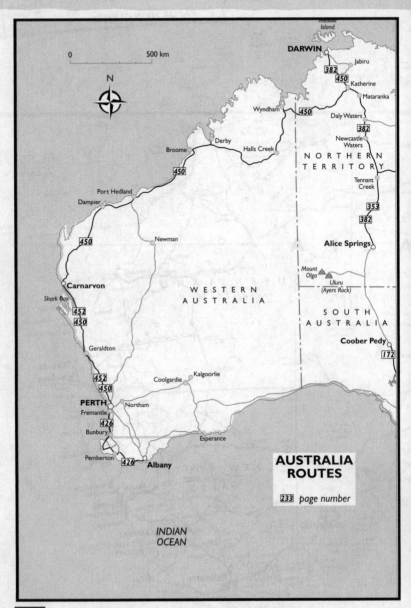

0   500 km

N

DARWIN
Melville Island
Jabiru
382
450
Katherine
Mataranka
Wyndham   450   Daly Waters
382
Newcastle Waters
Derby   Halls Creek
Broome   **N O R T H E R N**
450   **T E R R I T O R Y**
Port Hedland   Tennant Creek
Dampier   353
382
450   Newman
Alice Springs
Mount Olga   Uluru (Ayers Rock)
W E S T E R N
A U S T R A L I A
Carnarvon
Shark Bay   **S O U T H**
452   **A U S T R A L I A**
450
Geraldton   **Coober Pedy**
172
452   Coolgardie   Kalgoorlie
450
PERTH   Northam
Fremantle   426
Bunbury   Esperance
Pemberton   426
Albany

AUSTRALIA ROUTES

233 *page number*

INDIAN OCEAN

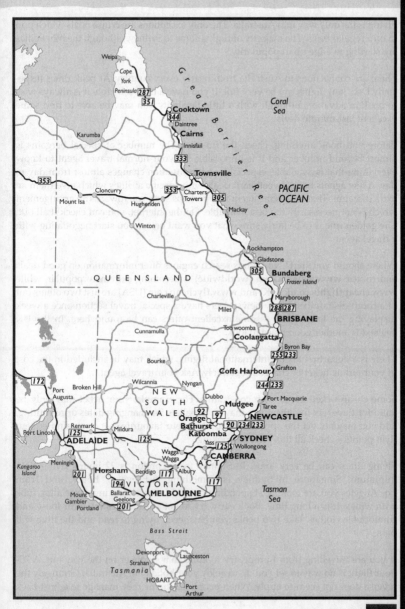

Flying is the only way into Australia. The only exceptions are cruise boats which pop in on a regular basis. The majority of flights come to Sydney, although the other cities are starting to edge up in popularity.

There are connections to Australia from nearly every country. At peak times (especially Dec/Jan) flights can be very full. If you have a tight schedule it is always wise to book in advance, although with a little flexibility you may be able to find some excellent last-minute deals.

Before you book anything, check the internet. The number of special bargains is almost beyond number and it is impossible for your normal travel agent to know everything that is available, especially as the situation changes almost from day to day. A few agents have 'sweetheart' deals with specific airlines which give them an extra discount. That means the agent will perhaps steer you towards an arrangement which is not necessarily the best available. On the internet, you can check it all out. The golden rule is to be fairly sure what you want before you start negotiating with a travel agent.

Where should you start? Numerous search engines offer information on good deals and routes: **www.expedia.com** (worldwide) is becoming extremely popular, while **www.cheapflights.co.uk** (UK) and **www.flycheap.com** (USA) are just two others out of a countless number. Many newspapers have a special travel section once a week displaying the latest deals – some excellent offers can be found here. In the UK Teletext is another good place to look.

There is a departure tax on international flights, which may be included in the cost of your airline ticket or charged separately. Ask your travel agent.

Some cheap tickets come with constraints. For example, your ticket may only be valid for three/six months; there may be penalties for changing dates or re-routing, and you may not get the opportunity to book your favourite seat or obtain frequent flyer points – check all this prior to booking.

Flying times can be very long. To Sydney from London is 22 hours' flying time minimum. Singapore to Sydney is something just over 7 hours, and from Los Angeles you are looking at spending over 13 hours sitting in a large alloy tube with wings. It is a long time. Book early, try to get a seat allocated, wear loose and comfortable clothes, take two books you have been dying to read and the time will pass.

If you are travelling from Europe, try to build in a stopover on the way out. A 25-hour flight is no way to set you up to enjoy your holiday in Australia. (Strangely the reverse does not seem to apply. When people get home they manage to adjust back to the old, familiar timetable very quickly.) From Europe the possibilities of a stopover are many, with Thailand, Malaysia, Singapore and Hong Kong making the front running. Of those, Thailand is by far the cheapest, and a good choice for your outward stopover if you are travelling on a budget.

Most airports have trolleys, which are free of charge for inbound flights, but there is a small hire charge for outbound passengers. Airport porters are alleged to exist. This may well be the case, but they are an endangered species and possibly only nocturnal; I have never seen one.

PAINLESS AIR TRAVEL One way of making your travel easier is to use a series of checklists to make sure you have covered the essentials.

● *Which airline are you flying with and where is it going?*
This is more important than you might imagine. Airlines have a cosy arrangement called code share. You are flying to Sydney and are booked on Airline X. The problem is that, no matter what the ticket says, Airline X does not, as yet, fly to Sydney. What it does is code share with another airline. There is nothing at all wrong with the other airline, but it is a little disconcerting if your ticket says Airline X, the flight code is Airline X and yet you find yourself on another airline's aircraft. Some of the code-sharing arrangements are between very disparate airlines – there are some airlines one would not wish to fly with even at half price.

So before you finally make the booking cross-examine the agent to make sure that you will actually fly with the airline that you are supposed to be booked on, or at least an acceptable substitute.

● *Are there any stops?*
If you are flying a long distance you certainly do not want to be hanging around airports more than you need. Nothing is more irritating than thinking you are going directly to Sydney only to find you are going to Melbourne first. There you will spend well over an hour in a waiting room at Melbourne airport when you have better things to do with your life.

Airlines, for obvious reasons, do not make much of the fact that a flight is not direct. They do not advertise it in large letters. You need to check carefully. Watch out for anything that is called a technical stop. This is precisely the same as a normal stop in that it extends your journey by at least an hour. The airlines believe that because no passengers are getting on and off the technical stop makes little difference. It does – to the passenger. An hour added to your journey on the homeward run stretches into infinity.

KEEPING THE COSTS DOWN

The cost of travelling breaks down into three areas: those costs totally outside your control, those you can partly control and those where you make decisions.

Costs outside your control include, for example, flying around Australia. Although there are different categories of fares they are fixed.

Costs you can partly control include those incurred in hotels. The published rate for a room, called the rack rate in the trade, is the opening stage in the bargaining process. Unless the hotel is booked solid, rack rates can normally be negotiated. They are discounted as a matter of course for corporate accounts, tour packagers and members of certain travel clubs. Weekend discounts are common in city hotels.

The same applies to hire car rates. There is a fixed basic rate and then a raft of special offers floating somewhere below. Getting those discounts may only require that you be a member of a frequent flyer program.

You will often find that costs included in a package beat anything you can arrange yourself. A good example is flight stopovers. Many airlines offer a deal with a hotel room thrown in for a few nights. There is no way you could match that price by booking each part separately.

Costs you can completely control: there are very few cities in Australia where any form of locomotion can beat walking – in Sydney, for example, walking is often faster than any other means of getting around. Plan all your activities so that you can walk to where you want to go. It is healthy, you meet a better class of person, and you save a lot of money. Your only investment will be a small map which you get at the tourist information office whenever you arrive at a destination. Mostly these maps are free.

If you cannot walk to your destination, because of distance or weather, use public transport.

Do not make interstate or international telephone calls from a motel or hotel telephone until you have ascertained the charges.

A great way of managing your expenses is, on your first week, to write down everything you spend, including little treats, souvenirs, etc. Then break down those costs into categories. Many travellers find that their biggest costs are food and accommodation, which can easily be reduced – eat in a fancy restaurant once a week instead of every night (go to the supermarket and buy food to cook yourself). Rather than stay in a hotel room every night, try staying in a dormitory occasionally – choose the right place and you can meet some interesting people, and save a lot of money. Camping can also be a truly great experience. Control your finances well, and you can spend more time seeing more of the country, while still living comfortably.

● *Can you rearrange the trip to be cheaper/more convenient/more desirable?*
It is tempting to take the first itinerary or fare offered. It is more intelligent to shop around or change your itinerary to take advantage of reduced-fare offers. The internet is superb in helping you do this. You can spend a happy hour juggling around possibilities to see which is the best mix of convenience and low cost.

● *Can seats on the aircraft be booked ahead?*
Some airlines allow you to book specific seats prior to check-in, while others allocate seats only on check-in on a first-come-first-served basis. Check with the airline when booking, and be prepared to check-in early.

● *Have you let the carrier know your meal requests?*
Meal requests are useful. I, for example, am a flying vegetarian, because experience has shown that on some airlines vegetarian meals are fresher and better presented than other meals.

● *Is your passport up to date?*
Airlines will not carry you unless your passport is valid, because in most countries, by law, they then have to fly you back at their own expense. To avoid a last-minute panic, allow plenty of time to send off for a new passport if necessary – holiday times, computer glitches and work-to-rule by passport office staff are causes of delay.

● *Do you have enough nostrums and medicaments to keep you healthy on your travels?*
Injections and vaccinations are not needed for travel to Australia. Medicines are not universally the same, so if you are taking any prescription medicines, try to take enough for the whole of your trip (see p. 46). Take the prescription along in case.

● *A final travel checklist*
About three days before you leave, do a final check:
  ● Money – small cash, some traveller's cheques
  ● Tickets
  ● Credit cards in credit
  ● Confirm bookings
  ● Check suitcase is not broken
  ● Clothes clean and ready to pack
  ● Sufficient film or digital storage for camera and check all batteries.

When travelling, at every port of call, at every check-in and check-out, I recite a magic mantra: 'pamcam'. It is not Sanskrit. It is an acronym for 'passport, airline tickets, money, credit cards, address book and medicines'. Keep getting 'pamcam' right and you will have no problems.

Insurance

You can insure against almost any mishap that can happen on your travels – including loss of cash up to $500. Travel insurance should include provision for cancelled or delayed flights and weather problems, as well as immediate evacuation home in the case of medical emergency. If you are ill in Australia you will have the very best of medical care, but it can be expensive if your holiday is disrupted and you need special treatment. The only way to get over that worry is to have medical cover. Thomas Cook and other travel agencies offer comprehensive policies. Insurance for drivers is covered in more detail under Travelling by Car, p. 27.

● *Limit packing*

Don't over-pack. It is so easy to overload your suitcase or backpack with clothes for every occasion and a few extras for luck. Whether you're staying in hotels or backpacking you'll still be lugging your possessions around for most of your trip. Don't forget that the airline baggage allowance is only 20 kilograms on some routes, and remember you'll probably want to bring things back with you when you return.

Entry Formalities All travellers, except New Zealand citizens, must obtain a visa before travelling. Visas may be a stamp or label in a passport, although many tourists and short-stay business visitors obtain an Electronic Travel Authority (ETA), an electronic record authorising your travel into Australia. Passport holders from 33 nations – including most European nations, the USA and Canada – are eligible to apply for ETAs. Visas are issued for three to six months and extensions are generally okay if you're a genuine traveller.

Working holiday visas are available for 18–30-year-old single people from Canada, Denmark, Germany, the Republic of Ireland, Japan, Korea, Malta, the Netherlands, Norway, Sweden and the UK. You cannot apply for a working holiday visa once you have arrived in Australia – you have to do it abroad, or in your home country. There's also a temporary residence programme, which allows certain categories of people to live and work in Australia temporarily.

Vaccinations are not required unless you have come from or visited a yellow fever infected country or zone within six days prior to arrival, which is unlikely. No other health certificates are needed to enter Australia.

Backpackers

A number of travel companies provide services aimed at backpackers and other independent travellers, offering accommodation and travel packages (usually involving HI or other similar networks of hostels) plus bus, rail or air passes. And they often give discounts on these services – surf the net to see what is available. In the UK, the Travellers Contact Point (tel: 020 7243 7887; www.travellers.com.au) sells travel passes, and offers mail holding and forwarding services – useful if you are planning a longer stay.

You can tell people until you are blue in the face how big Australia is, and they still do not believe you. They ask if they can go on an afternoon's trip to Uluru (Ayers Rock) from Sydney. They decide it would be a good idea to drive across the whole country to Perth. They take the bus from Darwin to Cairns to catch a flight and wonder why they walk funnily for days afterwards.

This is a big country. It is almost as big as the continental United States minus Alaska, and 50 per cent bigger than Europe without counting the old USSR. She's a beaut country, as they say, but she is a hell of a size. To give you some exact figures: from the most northerly point, Cape York, to Wilsons Promontory in Victoria is 3180 km (3680 to the southern tip of Tasmania). Measured from east to west, Australia is somewhere around 4000 km.

With a population of about 20 million and a land mass of 7,692,000 sq km, Australia is a very empty country. Just 1 per cent of Australia's land mass accounts for 84 per cent of the total population – the majority living along the east coast. The only two cities to even know what a proper traffic jam is are Melbourne and Sydney – traffic jams are relatively tame affairs elsewhere. Sydney to Perth is roughly the distance from London to Moscow, and there is not an awful lot in-between. In fact the only towns you pass through worth seriously talking about are Broken Hill and Port Augusta – unless you are thinking of Iron Knob as an important destination. Gazetteers list 4768 towns in Australia. However, by applying a 'sacred and profane test' – that is, if a town does not have a church and a pub and, say, 500 people, it does not count – there are fewer than 850 towns in the whole country.

Getting from one place to another therefore requires some thought. If you have all the time in the world, the easiest way to see a lot of the country is to buy or hire a car and drive everywhere. Some of the drives will be long and boring, and the price of petrol is rising, but you can set your own timetable.

Without the luxury of limitless time, the best bet for seeing the most of Australia is to hire cars from the second-echelon firms (see p. 27) on an as-needed basis, and to use either the internal airlines or the buses to connect the major destinations. That way you have the best of both worlds. The easiest way to operate is to let someone else – a pilot or a bus driver – do the driving while you sit back and have a snooze.

TRAVELLING BY AIR

No matter what decision you make about how to get around the country, it is worth noting that for Australians flying is the only way to go between cities if any distance is involved, and in Australia that is almost every time. An amazing 80 per cent of long-distance trips by public transport are made by air.

TIME ZONES

There are three time zones in Australia:

Eastern Standard Time (EST) covers New South Wales, the Australian Capital Territory, Victoria, Tasmania and Queensland, and is 10 hours ahead of Universal Time Coordinated (UTC).

Central Standard Time (CST) covers South Australia and the Northern Territory and is 9.5 hours ahead of UTC.

Western Standard Time (WST) covers Western Australia and is 8 hours ahead of UTC.

This becomes confused in the summer months when all states move to daylight-saving time (clocks forward one hour) except Western Australia, the Northern Territory and Queensland, so there can be different clock times in one time zone.

You can fly almost anywhere within Australia, not just between the major cities but out to Uluru (Ayers Rock) and even to the Great Barrier Reef. Flights connecting small country towns tend to be expensive because they serve a captive market. Often, it can work out cheaper to fly to the nearest large town and pick up a car. To reach Byron Bay, for example, it is possible to fly from Sydney up to nearby Lismore or Ballina. But it's less expensive to fly that bit further, to the Gold Coast airport at Coolangatta, and then hire a car to drive back through Tweed Heads and over the border between Queensland and New South Wales to Byron Bay.

BEST FLIGHT DEALS

Australian flyers welcomed another discount carrier to the market in May 2004: Jetstar, wholly owned by Qantas. Jetstar mainly links the big eastern cities (Sydney, Melbourne, Brisbane) with popular holiday destinations, such as Tasmania and Queensland's Gold Coast and Tropics. It also operates some services to Avalon airport, which is closer to Geelong than Melbourne. Qantas still flies to all but a couple of Jetstar's destinations.

There's little doubt that Jetstar has its only real competition, Virgin Blue, sharpening its pricing pencil. A check of internet sites – where you'll find the lowest ticket prices for Australian domestic travel – reveals that Jetstar and Virgin Blue prices are very low and very similar. Qantas's cheapest prices ('Red-e Deals') still look good compared to full-fare tickets, but they're consistently more expensive than the discount carriers.

You generally need to buy on the internet at least a day before flying, and the conditions for the cheapest ticket are usually as flexible as iron girders. But there are some real bargains out there. Start searching at www.virginblue.com.au, www.jetstar.com.au or www.qantas.com.au.

TRAVELLING BY BUS AND RAIL

Within cities, most public transport is fine. Melbourne has its trams. Sydney has an excellent bus system interconnecting with the ferries and the railways. Most of them run pretty much on time. In Sydney, for example, the figure for buses being on time is around 97 per cent and for ferries it is better than 98 per cent. Almost every city in Australia has an Explorer bus that follows a circular route: visitors can get on and off as they wish at points of interest.

RAIL AND BUS PASSES

Various useful rail passes are available. Rail Australia offers the **Austrail Flexi Pass**, which allows economy-class travel country-wide over 15 or 22 days within a 6-month period. Prices are $862.40 (15-days) and $1210 (22 days). The **Great Southern Railway Pass** provides six months of unlimited travel on all GSR routes. Adults $590; students/backpackers $450 (available to members of major recognised Backpacker organisations and students with a valid ISIC card). Other passes are the **East Coast Discovery Pass** and **Backtracker Rail Pass**. Details can be found on the Rail Australia website, www.railaustralia.com.au. Passes can be purchased before reaching Australia, or can be obtained from most CountryLink travel centres in Australia (tel: 13 22 32, www.countrylink.info) – upon proof that you are a bona fide overseas traveller. In the UK they are available through International Rail, tel: 08701 201 606, and the Gold Medal Travel Group, tel: 0870 606 4012.

Other passes allow travel on more restricted areas of the rail network. The **Sunshine Rail Pass** offered by Queensland Rail (Queensland Rail Travel Centres or tel: 07 3235 1122, www.traveltrain.qr.com.au) has options for 14, 21 or 30 days' travel and ranges in price from $335.50 to $487.30 for economy-class travel. Transwa offers a **Southern Discovery Pass**, allowing 28 days of travel on trains and buses south of Perth and Kalgoorlie for $155.20. This can only be purchased from Transwa on arrival in Perth (tel: 1300 662 205; www.transwa.wa.gov.au).

Australia's largest interstate coach company is Greyhound Australia. It offers two main passes: the **Aussie Explorer Pass** and the **Aussie Kilometre Pass**. For the Explorer Pass you choose from 17 pre-set travel routes. You can stop off as often as you like, and the passes are valid from 1 to 12 months depending on which you choose; they cost between $104 and $2288. For the Kilometre Pass you choose your own itinerary, and can backtrack and stop off as often as you like. You purchase your travel in 1000-km blocks ranging from 2000 to 20,000 km. The Kilometre Pass is valid for 12 months and costs from $300 for 2000 km to $2200 for 20,000 km. Discounts are available for students, seniors, YHA, Nomads and VIP (backpacking card) members and ISIC card holders. Some Explorer Passes include additional tours and these can also be purchased using some of kilometres from the Kilometre Pass. To contact Greyhound, tel: 13 14 99; see www.greyhound.com.au or e-mail info@greyhound.com.au. To purchase the passes outside Australia, tel: +61 7 4690 9950.

TRAVELLING AROUND AUSTRALIA

The rail system connecting the cities of Australia is not the best in the world. However, rail travel has its advantages. You can get up and walk around on long journeys, most trains have some sort of refreshments available, and some are quite interesting – such as the high-speed tilt train, which operates in Queensland between Brisbane and Cairns. There are also some great train journeys – the Indian-Pacific, covering the massive stretch Sydney–Adelaide–Perth, takes two to three days and is an amazing experience. The Ghan, which runs from Adelaide to Darwin via Alice Springs, is a spectacular journey through the interior to the tropical Top End.

Coaches or long-distance buses – which are less expensive than the train and widely available – are by far the better option. But a long bus journey is only for the young. If you are past the age when you find nine hours' bus travel exciting, then explore flying to your destinations or break the journey up into easy sections.

One of the most popular routes for tourists, for example, is Sydney to Cairns. It's a long way (nearly 3000 km), and the bus journey takes 46 hours. But a bus pass which allows unlimited stops, enabling you to do the journey in several short hops, will give you the opportunity to spend time at places on the way up. The bus companies offer a variety of special fares and passes to members of the YHA, and some similar organisations, students and seniors.

HIKING

Hiking – bushwalking – is a wonderful way to see the countryside and is perfectly safe, providing you follow some basic rules. The biggest dangers are from fire, and from getting lost. The best way to be safe is to avoid dense scrub and heavy vegetation during periods of high bushfire danger. Observe all fire bans religiously. The most vulnerable parks have indicators at the entrance; these are also to be seen along some main roads. Warnings are also given in newspapers and on the radio. When the indicator tells you that there is high or extreme fire risk, consider some other activity. If you are in a car and you get caught in a bushfire, the most sensible thing to do is to wind up all the windows and stay there until the fire passes. Petrol tanks rarely explode.

HITCH-HIKING

Do not even think of doing it. In all parts of the world this is a most dangerous way of getting around, and Australia is no exception. No matter what your sex and no matter what your belief in your invulnerability, you are putting yourself at serious risk hitch-hiking. The converse holds true – never pick up hitch-hikers on the road.

When walking in the bush, dress correctly. You may think that shorts would be cooler, but lightweight, full-length trousers will protect you from bites, scratches and the sun. You need solid footwear – not thongs and sandals – and you should wear a shirt with long sleeves that can be rolled down when needed.

If you are not an experienced bushwalker stick to the trails and marked paths, or arrange to join a guided group. The various state National Park management bodies have laid out a network of trails covering almost every national park in Australia and you will never be bored. And if you stick to the paths, you will never be lost.

TRAVELLING BY CAR

Australians always harp on about the need for a serious new road-building programme. In the main this is clever PR by the road hauliers who have managed to get the government to abandon the railways so that most freight goes by road. Having achieved that, they start another campaign to say that the roads are not good enough for the traffic they carry.

Almost any visitor over 18 can drive in Australia on his or her own national driver's licence for the same class of vehicle. You are told that you must carry your licence and your passport when driving, but the police are not stuffy about the latter provided you have sufficient identification. On the internet there are several sites offering an International Driver's Permit for a silly amount of money. Do not be conned: your regular driver's licence is fully accepted in Australia.

HIRING A CAR

The big operators such as Hertz, Avis and Europcar (www.Hertz.com, www.avis.com and www.deltaeuropcar.com.au) are present at every airport of any size in Australia. Second-echelon hire car companies exist in every big city but never have offices at the airport. This requires some explanation.

Business travellers come off the aircraft, walk up with their folding suit bag over their arm and ask for their pre-booked car. Within minutes, they are handed an envelope with the keys to the car and the insurance documentation and are directed out to the car park where a clean, new, air-conditioned saloon with automatic gearbox and full petrol tank awaits them.

Unfortunately this is not the cheapest way of hiring a car. The company is paying serious money for the airport concession, and if you hire from the airport you are paying for a car that will be very new and meticulously maintained.

There are many advantages in hiring through a second-echelon car company. First, the car will be far less expensive. It will invariably be on a flat rate with no mileage charge. The downside is that the car will be somewhat older and will have covered a fair distance. But it will typically have air-conditioning, an automatic gearbox and power steering and, most important, it is very unlikely to break down. You could arrange to have your car delivered to the airport, but it is better to take the airport bus – not a taxi – into town, check into your motel and collect the car later. This way, you do not have to worry about the drive in from the airport, which can be difficult especially after a long flight.

There are many places you may want to drive where four-wheel drive is an attractive option – or even a necessity. The lower age limit is usually 25 for hiring a four-wheel drive vehicle, although it is only 21 on Fraser Island.

General tips for car hire

- An automatic gearbox will make life much easier.
- You must have your licence with you and present it when you pick up the car. A valid credit card is also necessary for security.
- If you have a companion who is going to drive, make sure both names are listed on the hire form, otherwise the insurance cover will not be valid.
- Before you drive off, find out who to call if the car should break down. Breakdowns, although rare, do happen.
- Get the hire company to provide you with any maps that are available.

When you hire a car you are given a form full of small print which you are asked, nay instructed, to sign on the spot. General legal opinion appears to be that much, if not most, of the contract is unenforceable, because (a) the clauses are in a typeface that is something less than easily legible; (b) the implications of the clauses are not verbally explained; and (c) pressure is applied to make you sign the form on the spot and not give careful consideration to its contents.

None of this matters very much providing you take full collision insurance. While the company is almost certainly making a profit on this extra insurance, the peace of mind from knowing that you are fully covered outweighs the extra cost. If you do not take out the extra insurance, you are totally responsible for the car and you must make quite sure that all defects – especially in the bodywork – are listed on the form and accepted by the renter.

Buying a Banger

In most major cities there are companies that specialise in the sale of cars for the budget traveller. Sometimes these can be a great bargain, sometimes not.

Buying an old banger has its advantages – you can take it on dirt roads or through the odd stream and not worry about the knocks and bumps; you can also sell it again at the end of your trip. There are also disadvantages – it is a lot more likely to break down (which may cost you more in the long run).

This, in theory, can be done. In practice, all you want to do is to get away, so the best bet is always to take the extra insurance.

Important note: Many hire cars in Australia are not insured if you go on an unmade road. You need to check this very carefully indeed if you intend to explore in any serious way – Australia has a lot of dirt roads.

Fuel

Although not as cheap as in the United States, the price of petrol is cheaper than that in Britain. That makes a big difference if you are driving around Australia. And the fact that speed limits, very low speed limits, are strictly enforced, means you get better consumption. Leaded petrol has almost totally been banned and all hire cars use unleaded grades. Prices are by the litre. Australia has fewer petrol stations than it once had – there has been a recent culling. They all accept credit cards. Some of them offer forecourt service which is a pleasant change. Almost all of them also run a store as part of the complex, offering everything from milk to magazines.

Tolls

An increasing number of roads and highways in Australia are toll roads, especially in Sydney and Melbourne. Toll motorways are still avoidable in Sydney – barely – although journeys are shortened if they're used. Important tolls to remember are the $3.00 charge for crossing Sydney Harbour Bridge or going through the Harbour Tunnel (only imposed on southbound traffic), the Gateway bridge linking Brisbane airport with the Gold Coast, and the new private CityLink tollway system in Melbourne which affects almost all major highways around the city. This CityLink system has its fees charged electronically and invisibly, which means that every car must carry a special card on its dashboard with credit registered on it to be able to use these roads. Hire car companies in Melbourne will sell you day passes to enable you to use the network.

Rules of the Road

When you drive in Australia, slip your brain into a lower gear. There are no superhighways and many of the main roads of Australia are two-lane highways with passing places – that is, you drive single file until you come to a passing place which may well be 20 km away. In these circumstances a tranquil approach and an understanding of the virtues of meditation come in particularly useful.

This lack of multi-lane racetracks has a plus side. The accident rate in Australia is relatively low and generally is falling. In 1972 there were 26.59 fatalities per 100,000 of the population. By 1998 that had dropped to 9.4. The figures have been dropping

TAXIS

There are always taxis for hire which are inexpensive and well regulated.

Sydney uses cabs far more than any other city – twice as much as Melbourne. The waiting times for cabs called over the telephone are accepted as being some of the best in the world. Eighty-five per cent of passengers are collected within ten minutes of making the call. There is a slight problem at around 1500 which is changeover time for drivers, but it is never serious.

Although cab drivers do not pass the stringent locality tests of, say, London cab drivers they are tested and can find most places. They are also very strictly regulated as to dress and manners. The suggestion that you are even thinking of filing a complaint will sort out any problem immediately. I have never had a problem of any sort in any cab in Australia – and that is in a long career as a journalist where a cab is a tool of the trade.

fairly steadily with some occasional blips in the wrong direction. The reasons for the improvement in the figures are many. Random breath testing is carried out all the time, and if you have been drinking you will eventually be caught. Visitors to the country imagine it is a law that is sketchily enforced. Not a bit of it. There are regular campaigns throughout Australia and on a long trip you can expect to be stopped and have your breath checked at least once or twice.

The speed limit is generally 100 kph on the open road and 60 kph in town (about 62 mph and 37 mph), although 50 kph (31 mph) is increasingly common in towns. There are some carriageways where you can speed up to 110 kph (just under 70 mph) – and that is it. (The Northern Territory, p. 362, has its own rules, which is why it has the worst accident rate in Australia.) There is very little tolerance regarding speed limits. They are regarded as absolutes – speed and you will be nicked. It is illegal to have a radar detector of any kind, and the police use plain cars, spotter planes, speed cameras and radar guns which can read forward or back.

At the same time as the authorities have been getting tougher, cars are becoming safer and drivers more safety conscious. So driving in Australia is pretty safe provided, if you are a European, you adjust to the different speed and, if you are almost any nationality other than British, you get used to being on the left-hand side of the road.

Seat belts must be worn by all passengers at all times in all cars, with the single exception of taxis, and even that will probably change in the near future. Infants must travel in approved infant-carriers. Up to the age of four, children are allowed to travel in a properly fitted child car-seat, and after that they must wear seat belts. All new buses must be fitted with seat belts and where available these must be worn.

Most of the road signs follow international practice and most of the rules are those you have been used to. There is only one exception and that is in central Melbourne. At some intersections where there are tramlines as well as a two-way road system, to turn right you move to the left-hand lane first. Melburnians are happy to sit down and explain to you the mad logic of this system, which is called the hook turn. It can lead to exciting moments for the novice driver and much enjoyment for the Melburnian spectators.

In short:

- Never drive when you are tired. It is difficult enough to adjust to a new car and a new landscape without adding this extra burden.
- Do not speed.
- Do not drive if you have had more than a glass of wine or so.
- Work on the basis that all other drivers are as mad as cut snakes. This is undoubtedly true in the Northern Territory outside the few major towns.

OUTBACK DRIVING

If you are driving in the Northern Territory and parts of Queensland you will come across road trains – trucks with three or four trailers. In dry weather they leave a cloud of dust behind them which can reduce your visibility to almost zero. Overtaking them is not easy and you need a long clear stretch of road before you should even think of doing so. It is better to stop, take a rest and then drive on. Driving across the Nullarbor Plain towards Perth you may be dazzled by the lights of an oncoming truck. Get used to it: the road is so straight that it sometimes takes five or ten minutes to meet and pass. The most dangerous times for hitting animals are dawn and dusk. Keep a special look out for them and reduce your speed. Hitting a full-grown kangaroo at speed is a very serious accident and 'roo bars' are worse than useless.

Make sure you know the route and that you have discussed it with locals. The police are, as always, a mine of useful information. If you are seriously 'going outback' on unmade roads into the desert, you must carry essential supplies, especially water, fuel and basic spare parts. You simply cannot have too much water: 20 litres a head is a good rule as this could last you up to a week with care. The heat of the day in Australia will mean that you will be running with the air-conditioner set on high most of the time. Although this technology has improved tremendously in the past few years, it still means that your fuel consumption will be relatively high, so fill your tank. If you break down, stay with your vehicle. It provides shade and is a good target for a search party.

All of this sounds somewhat forbidding, though this is not the intention. Australia is a very easy country to drive around and the locals think nothing of covering very long distances in a day – 1000 km being not uncommon.

CROSS-COUNTRY ROUTES

If you look at a map you will see a road that runs right around the whole of mainland Australia. This is Highway 1. It is known as the Pacific Highway in parts and in some stages along its route is given other names by the locals.

If you leave Sydney and head north, you immediately find yourself on Highway 1 which will take you to Newcastle then up the coast – Port Macquarie, Coffs Harbour, Byron Bay – and then Tweed Heads. You are now moving out of New South Wales into Queensland, still on Highway 1.

From there it goes up the coast through Surfers Paradise to Brisbane, then on from that delightful city through Bundaberg and Rockhampton where it crosses the Tropic of Capricorn. Now the Great Barrier Reef is about 100 km out to sea on your right-hand side and seems to follow the contours of the highway as it heads north.

You go on through Townsville to Cairns. Then Highway 1, unable to tackle the Daintree River, sharply turns to the west and nips across the Gregory Range to Normanton and the Gulf Country. It runs along the Gulf of Carpentaria and through places like Borroloola which are unknown to anyone except outback Australian travellers, and then follows through to Daly Waters which takes you down through Mataranka to Katherine. There are those who would argue that the stretch from Normanton to Katherine is not truly Highway 1. As roads go it has its deficiencies. Indeed, in most countries it would not be considered a country road. But this is Australia and it is Highway 1.

From Katherine, once again certain of its identity, Highway 1 zooms over to Willeroo and Timber Creek and just bypasses Wyndham. (If you have never heard of these towns, don't let it worry you: they are not major centres of civilisation.)

Then the road jinks south and goes through Turkey Creek and over the McIntosh Hills until it reaches Halls Creek, where it heads out to the west coast of Australia at a magical place called Broome. Then it runs along the Eighty Mile Beach and skirts the Great Sandy Desert on its way to Port Hedland.

From there to Dampier and through two totally forgettable outback farms (Minilya and Boologooro) to Carnarvon, Highway 1 then heads dead south as it makes its way through Geraldton and, with a sigh of relief, drops down to Perth. It has come right around the top end of Australia from the east coast to the west.

From Perth it swings down to the bottom of Western Australia and then to Esperance where it kinks back inland to Norseman. Now it takes a deep breath and hurtles across the Nullarbor Plain – a Latin name meaning no trees – until it is in South Australia where the first serious sign of civilisation is Ceduna. From there it continues east to Port Augusta before turning south to the wonderful city of Adelaide and then along the coast past Kingston SE – the odd initials differentiate it from another Kingston – to Melbourne. From this queen of a city the road hugs the coast as it goes through Bairnsdale and Orbost to reach Eden, which is in New South Wales and is a very fair name for a most pleasant spot. Then it is a gentle stroll north again through Narooma, Berry, Wollongong and ... what is that on the horizon? Sydney yet again.

That gives you the basic infrastructure of the road system – a not very well drawn lasso around the main island of Australia called Highway 1. Along the way its quality varies widely. There are much quicker ways to do some of the component parts of the journey – no one would ever drive from Melbourne to Sydney on Highway 1, for instance, unless they had plenty of time to spare. But it does go right the way around Australia, with the sole exception of Tasmania – which has a wonderful road system (lots of scenery, few cars) of its own.

Right down the centre a road that bisects the oval of Highway 1, from Darwin at the centre top end through Alice Springs to Adelaide at the centre bottom, is Highway 87. It has been around in one form or another for some time but as a sealed road it has only been operating in the last 15 years or so. (Nearly the same can be said about Highway 1.)

Where do all the other main roads run? The answer is that there are not that many. Within Victoria and, to a lesser extent, New South Wales, there is a network of interlinked roads. But Victoria is, relatively, a small state and New South Wales, although much larger, is not in the size race with Western Australia. Even in New South Wales, once you get past Orange the roads are few and far between. There are, indeed, different ways of running inland to get from, say, Sydney to Cairns. One way is to take Highway 71 from Dubbo through to Bourke. After that you are 'back of Bourke', which is the Australian way of saying that a place is seriously deep in the wild country. The road then crosses the border into Queensland and goes through Cunnamulla, Charleville, then down to Torrens Creek and on to Cairns. Highway 39 does the same sort of thing but runs closer to the sea, going through Narrabri on the New South Wales side and then over to Queensland and Goondiwindi, then towards Gladstone where it peters out when it hits Highway 1.

The point here is that, once you are outside urban areas, you simply do not have the choice of roads you get when you drive in, say, Europe or New England. If you want to get from Newcastle to Port Macquarie you have one road that you can take, unless you want to cut inland on country roads and substantially extend your journey. In any move from one major place to another your choice will have been made for you by the fact that there is only one logical route.

ABORIGINAL AUSTRALIA

No one is certain how many Aboriginal people inhabited Australia when the First Fleet set up shop at Sydney Cove in 1788. Popular estimates range from 300,000 to 500,000, but it's widely conceded that the number could have been considerably more. Aboriginal people had lived here for up to 60,000 years, possibly longer. When the Europeans arrived, they made up more than 200 distinct language groups (600–700 dialects were spoken) that ranged over defined traditional lands. While none had a written language, each group (usually referred to as a 'tribe' for convenience) had particular creation, or 'Dreamtime', stories and ceremonial beliefs that had been celebrated and perpetuated for millennia through oral tradition, dance and art.

The importance of traditional stories to Aboriginal people can't be overstated, nor can non-Aboriginal people expect to easily understand them. They weren't all serious stories – some were simply entertainment for children – but many explained the origins of a language-group's traditional lands, or country, and others detailed codes of behaviour. In the same way that Christians accept Bible stories and Muslims follow the teachings of the Koran, Aboriginal people took their traditional stories to be literally true. The messages, they believed, had been passed down from the ancestors. Critically, they also helped to answer the same spiritual questions that most belief systems purport to address: they explained how people came to be there, why their land and its creatures looked as they did, why certain acts or types of behaviour would not be tolerated, and what might be expected after death.

Stories were recorded – often as simple symbols that masked complex meanings in cave and bark paintings, or in oral tradition – and were passed along in dance or song. The renowned 'songlines' of certain groups recorded landscape features vital for defining a group's territory, or for navigation or survival – the location of water-

GETTING IN TOUCH WITH ABORIGINAL CULTURE

The best starting point for information on Aboriginal cultural tours is the Australian Tourism Commission (tel: 1300 361 650; www.australia.com) or, if you already have a destination in mind, the relevant state tourism body – most have indigenous programmes. If you're visiting a community on Aboriginal land you'll very likely need a permit, and state tourism bodies can advise on where to obtain these. Take the time to learn the basics of community protocols before visiting Aboriginal lands; it could mean the difference between a good visit and a great one.

The Australian Cultural Network (www.acn.net.au), Aboriginal Australia (www.aboriginalaustralia.com) and Aboriginal Tourism Australia (www.aborginaltourism.com.au) websites provide links to several operators that run Aboriginal cultural tours, and are also a good starting point if you're interested in Aboriginal art, crafts and books.

holes in the desert, for instance. Traditional beliefs and stories survive in some parts of Australia. The ancient ceremonies are still practised, and elders (men and women) retain the old knowledge, both practical and sacred.

After the arrival, better described as an invasion, of Europeans, Aboriginal people fought fiercely for their lands, employing guerrilla tactics to attempt to overcome a well-armed adversary. The settlers showed little understanding of Aboriginal feelings. Random shootings and sometimes massacres were commonplace; flour distributed to Aboriginal people, and sometimes their waterholes, were poisoned; European diseases exacted an unknown toll. The first several decades of contact between Aborigines and whites were characterised by this kind of brutal laissez-faire. The country was simply too big, and communication too difficult, to ensure compliance with any orders from colonial capitals.

From the later 19th century until the 1960s, the principal feature of Aboriginal 'protection' was the establishment of reserves, usually managed by missions. There's a bitter-sweet irony in Aboriginal people being 'given' lands they'd always known to be their own, and being 'cared for' by white missionaries who, in all likelihood, wouldn't have survived for more than a few days alone in the bush. Aboriginal and Torres Strait Islander people weren't granted Commonwealth voting rights until 1962, and it took a 1967 referendum – passed by a huge majority – to finally give them status as citizens. The first tract of traditional Aboriginal land – belonging to the Gurindji people, in the Northern Territory – was handed back in 1975, and other land returns followed. But it was 1992 before the High Court's judgement in the Mabo case overturned the doctrine of terra nullius – the legal fiction that Australia in 1788 was an empty land – and enshrined indigenous title to land in the common law.

Reconciliation between black and white Australians has been a feature of political and community life for more than a decade. In 2000, people throughout the country – 500,000 in Sydney alone – marched in support of reconciliation. But practical steps to give all Aboriginal and Torres Strait Islander people the same opportunities in education, employment and health as other Australians remain, at best, a hope.

ACCOMMODATION

MOTELS In Australia motels are less expensive and more salubrious than those of the United States. Typically they provide inexpensive, squeaky clean, plainly designed accommodation perfect for Australians on the move. There is no town, no matter how mean or humble, that does not have a motel. And all the motels are immensely affordable. During the holiday season, which lasts from the week before Christmas to 1 February, you will find motel rooms in popular places to be very expensive – but only by Australian standards.

Every motel provides you with equipment to make tea and instant coffee. Without exception they are air-conditioned. Without exception they supply you with a tablet of soap that would not work up sufficient lather for a well-endowed ant – carry your own. Without exception they will serve breakfast to your room if you ask. Do yourself a favour, however, and do not ask: motel breakfasts are not the glory of Australia. Otherwise motels in Australia are, by and large, pretty marvellous.

They are also almost all the same. They are constructed from brick or breeze block, and typically are single- or at most two-storey. The manager is normally the owner, frequently a couple. The motel may be a member of a group-selling organisation, but most are individually owned with the owners on the premises.

Although almost all motel owners have plenty of local knowledge, you should take their advice on routes and sightseeing but not on restaurants. As far as laundry is concerned you will find that almost all motels will offer laundry and ironing facilities, possibly at a small charge. Far and away the most comprehensive and up-to-date listing of motels is found on the AAA Tourism website: www.accommodation guide.com.au.

BACKPACKER HOSTELS AND YOUTH HOSTELS The backpacker hostels throughout Australia have found that there is a major market for people who would like a clean private room with air-conditioning and en-suite facilities at a reasonable price. So the name 'hostel' can be misleading. However, despite the wide availability of private rooms, hostels still consist of predominantly dormitory beds. These dormitories can range in size with anything from 4 to 20 beds to a room.

Hostels can vary – some provide towels and linen while in others all you'll find is a base sheet to place a sleeping bag on – although most will rent 'doonas' (duvets) for a small additional fee.

Online enquiries and bookings for backpacker hostels grow in sophistication each year. All but the tiniest hostels have their own websites, and many hostels are associated with larger organisations. If you join an umbrella group such as YHA (about 140 hostels in Australia), or become a member of the Hostelling International group, or VIP Backpackers (about 130 Australian hostels), you can make savings on hostel accommodation, transport (including the long-distance bus companies), clothing and equipment and various services – for example, adventure tours. Both YHA (www.yha.com.au) and VIP (www.vipbackpackers.com) have online booking services, while the Backpackers Ultimate Guide (BUG) site (www.bugaustralia.com) has extensive listings (sensibly arranged under state and town headings), and some very useful independent reviews.

CAMPING, CARAVANS AND CAMPER VANS (RVs) There are campsites throughout Australia and, almost without exception, in all the national parks. In some cases the only way to see a national park is to hike in, camp and explore from there. Camping outside designated sites may be forbidden; when in doubt check with a ranger before you enter the park. Camping gear can be hired from the YHA and several camping stores. For some of the more popular sites such as Kakadu and Wilsons Promontory it is necessary to book in advance.

Although RVs can be hired, most travellers tend to use hostels or motels. Despite this there are plenty of caravan and trailer parks, frequently supplied with power points, and shower and toilet facilities. Britz Australia, www.britz.com, is one of the most popular rental companies, and, depending on availability, flexible travellers may be interested in 'vehicle relocation'. Drivers must be over 21.

CHARACTER AND CONDUCT

There are serious attempts to gloss over Australia's convict heritage. It is claimed that most of those sent to Australia were deported for stealing a silk handkerchief or, at worst, a sheep. This simply is not true. Australia also received hardened criminals who had committed crimes that would, even to this day, give you pause for thought when you read about them. And the soldiers sent to guard the prisoners were not, in truth, much better. The officers were not from good regiments and were not averse to criminal endeavour to line their own pockets.

The police are not popular. (A 1990s royal commission showed that the police of New South Wales were corrupt beyond belief. No Australian was in the slightest surprised at this revelation.) Strangely, the result has not been a large amount of crime, but simply a culture that has no time for class distinctions. Being rich is fine. Being up yourself – full of your own importance – is totally unacceptable.

When I originally heard the following I put it down to urban myth, but have since been able to confirm it in every detail. A bishop was paying a visit to a vicar in a small Queensland town. The bishop was dressed for the part with a hard collar and the scarlet shirt which is the mark of his rank. The vicar was in his usual open neck shirt and blue jeans. He took the bishop for lunch to his normal café. The waitress said to the vicar, 'G'day, Bert, the usual?' The vicar nodded assent. Then she turned to the bishop and said, 'And what will little Robin Redbreast be having?'

You should not expect servility at any level in Australia. When Bob Hawke was prime minister of Australia – and for much of that time the most popular prime minister the country has ever known – you called him Bob. Everyone called him Bob. Is there another country in the world where the head of state is called familiarly by his first name? In international hotels you will sometimes find the level of service which you find in, say, a European grand hotel. The person offering that is unlikely to have been resident in Australia for very long.

Most visitors find Australians' instant friendliness endearing, although it can take you aback to begin with. Mateship is a vital part of the Australian character and, in a sense, it is what makes economical travelling around Australia so pleasant. There is simply no social cachet in staying at a very upmarket hotel – Australians will still call it a pub no matter how many stars it boasts.

If you are a single passenger and you are male, when you hail a cab you sit in the front seat next to the driver so that he can bore you to death with his views on everything from cricket to politics.

Sexual and Racial Tolerance

There is no serious intolerance regarding homosexuality in Australia. The Mardi Gras parade in Sydney is held every February–March and brings crowds from all over the world. The banks and building societies sponsor floats, as do the police. It is a major attraction for what is predominantly a heterosexual crowd. Some older Australians may still exhibit intolerance, but it is rapidly disappearing.

Sadly, Australia has a long history of ethnic prejudice. The treatment of the Aboriginal peoples of Australia by the governments and the non-indigenous people has been a disgrace beyond measure and a shame that all thinking Australians feel most keenly. It is seldom discussed in social situations and you should not bring it up as a topic of conversation unless you want to start a very heated argument. Even now, with all the goodwill in the world, the situation is appalling. Australia is home to about 400,000–500,000 indigenous people.

The health of Aborigines is worrying. Alcohol is a major problem. Aboriginal and Torres Strait Islanders suffer blindness ten times more frequently than other Australians. In many communities 8–13 per cent of the people are affected by diabetes. The life expectancy for men is about 57 and for women 66. Everyone agrees that the situation is dreadful, though improving – but there is little agreement on how to tackle the problem.

Australian immigration policy was strongly weighted against non-Europeans – the so-called White Australia policy – until well into the 20th century. The White Australia policy faded away in the 1970s, and the immigration figure now stands at around 80,000 a year, the numbers depending on the level of employment on the one hand and the needs of refugees on the other. These days, most migrants come from Asia and the Middle East; New Zealand and Britain are still well represented. About one quarter of the current Australian population was born overseas. There is very little racial tension between the various groups. This is partly because there has been so much intermarriage and partly because Australians have found out that immigrants brought charm, culture and excellent food.

CLIMATE

Mainly the weather is beaut so you do not need extra clothes. It is relatively dry, with 80 per cent of the country having a mean annual rainfall of less than 600 mm. The terrible twins, El Niño and La Niña, can cause unexpected extremes: with El Niño you get drought, and the reverse for his sister. In the centre the weather does get extremely hot, with places like Marble Bar sometimes averaging 41°C, which is pretty unbearable. In the summer you can usually expect something around 28°C in most places, dropping to freezing in the alpine region in the winter. Apart from the high country, it never gets seriously cold so you don't need an overcoat. The biggest problem is the sun.

Sun Forget all other dangers. The sun, shining through very clear air, can create all sorts of problems. It is not quite the same spectrum as Europe or most parts of the United States, and it is interesting that film manufacturers often have different formulations to deal with the different light in Australia.

Australians, for reasons which are hidden deep within the collective psyche, equate suntans with physical and mental health, which is why Australia has the highest skin-cancer rates in the world. The effect the sun has on skin depends upon heredity, the length of time of exposure, and the strength of the sun's rays. It is worth remembering that sunburn is exactly that – a burning of the skin. An Australia-wide campaign with the catchy slogan 'Slip, Slop, Slap' reminds you to slip on a shirt, slop on some suncream and slap on a hat.

You need to wear **suncream** with a high protection factor whenever you are outdoors. Choose a suncream factor that suits the sensitivity of your skin – total block if necessary. Reapply after you go swimming or every two hours. Remember that you can burn under a cloudy sky, and that both sea and snow make reflective surfaces which can intensify the rays of the sun, as does water on the body.

You should never go out in the sun without a **hat**. Ever. It should shade the peaks of your ears which tend to be easily caught by the sun. Gentlemen who are thinning on top will find that sunburn of the bald bits is particularly nasty. Some school kids wear floppy hats with flaps over the neck. They look like miniature Foreign Legionnaires but it is a good idea. You must cover up.

Sunglasses are an absolute must. The stronger the sun, the darker the lenses should be. They not only stop you from squinting into the glare, they protect the tender skin around your eyes from sunburn.

If you must build up a tan, do it in the morning before the sun has built up its full power. It is better to remain pale and interesting.

CUSTOMS

Immigration and customs services at Australian airports are among the quickest and most courteous in the world. But they are very serious about certain things. They are not that worried about whether you bring in two bottles of the demon grog or one, or if you have 250 cigarettes or 300. By and large you can bring most articles into the country duty-free, provided they are for your personal use. In fact, you can make your duty-free purchases at the airport where you land, before you go through immigration.

However, customs are tigers when it comes to drugs, animal products, foodstuffs, plants and plant products. They must be declared, and if you flout the rules you are taking a serious risk. There are quarantine bins at every airport where you can dump food and other prohibited products. As for illicit drugs, sniffer dogs are used at all airports and jail sentences are almost mandatory.

Despite all rumours to the contrary, you do not go through customs when you fly from mainland Australia to Tasmania (although some Australians aver that you do). However, you will usually be checked by sniffer dogs to ensure you're not bringing in fruit that may be harmful to the state's farming industry.

DISABILITIES, TRAVELLERS WITH

In the past, facilities for travellers with disabilities in Australia have been shameful, but now a serious effort has been made to remedy this. There is much still to be done, but it is a problem of which everyone is conscious and all new facilities are, almost without exception, equipped so that they can be easily accessed by people with disabilities.

For advice and information in the UK, contact **RADAR**, 12 City Forum, 250 City Rd, London EC1V 8AF; tel: 020 7250 3222; www.radar.org.uk. In the USA, contact **SATH**, 347 5th Ave, Suite 610, New York, NY 10016; tel: (212) 447 7284; www.sath.org.

There are several organisations in Australia that provide information and guides for people with disabilities. On the internet there is **Easy Access Australia** – www.easy-access australia.com.au – which also publishes a book of that name, a complete guide to access throughout the country. The book can be obtained for $27.45 plus postage from PO Box 218, Kew 3101, Victoria. The book's author has a complete C5/6 spinal injury, and other contributions are by wheelchair users.

Other contact addresses: **ACROD NSW**, Suite 103, 1st Floor, 1–5 Commercial Rd, Kingsgrove, NSW 2208; tel: (02) 9554 3666; **ACROD ACT**, 33 Thesiger Court, Deakin, ACT 2600; tel: (02) 6282 3213; **ACROD Queensland**, Suit 15, Level 4,

Lutwyche City Shopping Centre, 543 Lutwyche Rd, Lutwyche, Qld 4030; tel: (07) 3357 4188; **ACROD Victoria**, Ground Floor, 85 Cowper St, Footscray, Vic 3011; tel: (03) 6362 0800; **ACROD NT**, 22 Albatross St, Winnellie, NT 0820; tel: (08) 8947 7070; **ACROD SA**, 246 Glen Osmond Rd, Fullarton, SA 5063; tel: (08) 8338 0733; **ACROD WA,** PO Box 1428, Osborne Park, WA 6916; tel: (08) 9242 5544; **ACROD Tasmania**, McDougall Building, Ellerslie Rd, Battery Point, Tas 7004; tel: (03) 6223 6086. **Ideas** (PO Box 786, Tumut, NSW 2720; tel: 1800 029 904) provides information on wheelchair-accessible accommodation and venues. **NICAN** (Unit 4, 2 Phipps Cl., Deakin, ACT 2600; tel: 1800 806 769) is a free service providing information on recreation, tourism, sport and the arts in Australia for people with disabilities; www.nican.com.au.

ELECTRICITY

The electrical current in Australia is 220–240 volts, AC 50Hz. The Australian three-pin power outlet is different from that in other countries, so you will need an adaptor – most hotels can supply converters, and electrical stores stock suitable equipment. Note that this does not apply to laptop computers, which are already set up to take different currents and cycles. If your appliances are 110 V, check if there is a 110/240 V switch. If not, you will need a voltage converter. Universal outlets for 240 V or 110 V shavers are usually found in leading hotels.

E-MAIL AND INTERNET ACCESS

It's a breeze getting connected in Australia, whether you're relying on 'Net cafés or lugging your own laptop. Actually, the laptop-burdened traveller has become an increasingly rare sight with the rise and rise of mobile-phone (cellphone) e-mail – not to mention all the other stuff that mobile phones can manage. A Multimedia Messaging Service (MMS) capable mobile phone is probably the only communications appliance that a young traveller needs.

If you're still relying for contact on cybercafés and a web-based e-mail service (such as Hotmail or Yahoo), you're well served in Australia. As is the case in most Western nations, cybercafés are ubiquitous in popular travellers' areas in major towns and cities; backpacker lodgings without 'Net access are as common as wet weather in Alice Springs.

Some websites (such as www.gnomon.com.au/publications/netaccess or www.do australia.com/AtoZ/INetCafeList.htm) list cybercafés, but they can get out of date pretty quickly. Checking on a big search engine like Google or Yahoo is often just as effective.

A–Z of Travel Basics

Plugging in yourself is usually no problem. There are several big ISPs (Telstra Bigpond, Optus and OzEmail are perhaps the best known); all are regular advertisers in the media and easy to find. If you're bringing a laptop to Australia, make sure you buy a universal AC adaptor (see Electricity in this section) before leaving home. Electronics chains such as Dick Smith and Tandy are the places to go if you need telephone plugs.

EMBASSIES AND CONSULATES

Most countries are represented with an embassy or consulate in Canberra, ACT. The telephone code for Canberra is 02.

Austria: 12 Talbot St, Forrest, ACT 2603; tel: 6295 1533

Belgium: 19 Arkana St, Yarralumla, ACT 2600; tel: 6273 2501

Canada: Commonwealth Ave, Yarralumla, ACT 2600; tel: 6270 4000

China: 15 Coronation Dr., Yarralumla, ACT 2600; tel: 6273 4780

Finland: 12 Darwin Ave, Yarralumla, ACT 2600; tel: 6273 3800

Germany: 119 Empire Circuit, Yarralumla, ACT 2600; tel: 6270 1911

Greece: 9 Turrana St, Yarralumla, ACT 2600; tel: 6273 3011

Netherlands: 120 Empire Circuit, Yarralumla, ACT 2600; tel: 6220 9400

New Zealand: High Commission, Commonwealth Avenue, Canberra, ACT 2600; tel: 6270 4211

Norway: 17 Hunter St, Yarralumla, ACT 2600; tel: 6273 3444

Republic of Ireland: 20 Arkana St, Yarralumla, ACT 2600; tel: 6273 3022

Singapore: High Commission, 17 Forster Cres., Yarralumla, ACT 2600; tel: 6273 3944

South Africa: High Commission, Rhodes Pl., State Circle, Yarralumla, ACT 2600; tel: 6273 2424

Spain: 15 Arkana St, Yarralumla, ACT 2600; tel: 6273 3555

Sweden: 5 Turrana St, Yarralumla, ACT 2600; tel: 6270 2700

Switzerland: 7 Melbourne Ave, Forrest, ACT 2603; tel: 6162 8400

UK: British High Commission, Commonwealth Ave, Yarralumla, ACT 2600; tel: 6270 6666

Consulate, Level 26, Waterfront Place, 1 Eagle St, Brisbane, Qld 4000; tel: (07) 3223 3200

Consulate, 17th Floor, 90 Collins Street, Melbourne, Vic 3000; tel: (03) 9652 1600

Consulate, Level 26, Allendale Square, 77 St George's Terrace, Perth, WA 6000; tel: (08) 9224 4700

Consulate, Level 16, The Gateway, 1 Macquarie Place, Sydney, NSW 2000; tel: (02) 9247 7521

USA: 21 Moonah Pl., Canberra, ACT 2600; tel: 6214 5600

Consulate General, Level 59, MLC Centre, 19–29 Martin Pl., Sydney, NSW 2000; tel: (02) 9373 9200

Consulate General, Level 6, 553 St Kilda Road, Melbourne, Vic 3004; tel: (03) 9526 5900

Consulate, 13th Floor, 16 St George's Terrace, Perth, WA 6000; tel: (08) 9202 1224

EMERGENCIES

To call the ambulance, fire and police services, dial 000. In cities help will be almost instantaneous; in the country it will depend on the distance to the nearest town.

Emergency clinics are open 24 hours a day in all the major towns, and the standard of service is excellent. There is one anomaly: a separate charge is made to everyone for using an ambulance. This is not covered by the health service.

To report loss or theft of Thomas Cook MasterCard Traveller's Cheques, tel: 1 800 127 495. To report loss of Visa traveller's cheques, tel: 1 800 127 477 (both numbers are toll free).

BITES AND STINGS (SEE ALSO WILDLIFE, P. 54)

If you are bitten by a **snake** or **spider**, follow these guidelines:

● Get away from the snake or spider – don't attempt to kill it.

● The victim should lie down and stay still and as calm as possible. Move the bitten limb as little as possible during treatment – cut away clothing rather than remove it.

● Don't wash the bite area – venom on the surface may be helpful in identifying the correct antivenom.

● Firmly bind the bite area (an elastic bandage is perfect, but strips of clothing will be fine) – make sure you don't cut off circulation.

● After covering the bite area, extend the bandage to cover as much of the bitten limb as possible.

● Immobilise the limb using splints and more bandages/clothing strips.

● If the victim is vomiting or semi-conscious, roll him/her onto his/her side (to stop inhalation of vomit).

● Get medical help as quickly as possible.

● Don't give the victim anything to eat or drink; if there is a long delay before medical help arrives, offer water only.

● Don't allow the victim to move – it's better to remain immobile and wait for evacuation than to move independently.

If stung by a **bluebottle jellyfish**, you should come ashore, sit down (lie down if you have a friend who can help) and carefully remove the tentacles still sticking to your skin. Don't try rubbing them off – more of the stinging cells will discharge their venom. If you are at a patrolled beach and uncertain about what to do, report to the lifesavers on duty. If there are any signs of a more severe reaction (such as breathlessness) to the sting, don't delay in seeking lifesaver (or medical) assistance. Once all the stinging cells have been removed, ice packs or any ointment containing a local anaesthetic may be useful in reducing pain.

FIRE BANS AND BUSHFIRES

In some areas of Australia, open camp fires are banned because of the risk of bushfires, a serious threat particularly during the summer months. Fire ban warnings are issued through newspapers, radio and television and by signs along the roads. During a total fire ban no fires may be lit in the open. Campers are always advised to carry portable stoves. It is a serious offence to light a fire on a day of total fire ban, as well as posing a grave risk to land, wildlife, property and lives.

FESTIVALS AND EVENTS

Each city in Australia has an array of festivals, from the Festival of Wine in Melbourne in April, to the Gay and Lesbian Mardi Gras in Sydney during Feb/Mar. The various state and territory tourism offices have further information on the events throughout the country. Check the following websites: www.eventwatch.com.au, www.online events.com.au or www.whatsonwhen.com. Below are a few more samples:

JANUARY	Australian Tennis Open tournament in Melbourne.
FEBRUARY/MARCH	Adelaide has two major festivals: the Adelaide Arts Festival, in even-numbered years, and the Barossa Valley Vintage Festival in odd-numbered years. The Australian Formula One Grand Prix car race takes place in Melbourne at Albert Park.
MARCH/APRIL	Bells Beach surf classic, every Easter near Torquay in south-west Victoria.
JUNE	A major event in Cape York (northern Queensland) is the Laura Aboriginal Dance and Cultural Festival, held in odd-numbered years.
AUGUST	Mt Isa Rodeo.
SEPTEMBER	Australian Football League (or Aussie Rules): grand final on the last Saturday of the month in Melbourne.
NOVEMBER	Melbourne Cup (horse race): first Tuesday in November at Flemington Racecourse.
DECEMBER	The gruelling Sydney to Hobart Yacht Race leaves on 26 Dec. Its arrival around New Year's Eve on the Hobart waterfront is cause for much liquid celebration among the sailors.

FOOD AND DRINK

In the 1960s the food in Australia, despite the quality of the produce, ranged from dire to dreadful. A balanced diet was a meat pie in each hand. Now it has been improved beyond measure by the influx of other nationalities. The country is positively alive with restaurants of every background and cuisine. Thai is probably currently leading the charge, with Vietnamese and Korean restaurants galloping up on the inside rail. But there is everything including what can only be referred to as Pacific cuisine, the style of cooking incorporating Asian ingredients which is so popular in California, Australia and, to a slightly lesser extent, New Zealand.

The food in Australia is not just totally marvellous but it is also immensely affordable. Many independent travellers will find it similar (or even cheaper) to go to some restaurants for dinner than to cook their own meal from fresh ingredients. You can still get a bad meal however. There is also a terrible tendency to make puns on restaurant names. We can cope with Thaitanic but we must draw the line at a former restaurant in Perth called Thai Me Kangaroo Down Sport.

Not only is there a plethora of superb and affordable restaurants, there is also a wondrous range of fruit. As you drive around the country you will see roadside stalls selling fruit at derisory prices. In truth, Australian apples are not in the race with British apples and some of the oranges are big on size and low on flavour, but overall there is a magnificent range and you can load up for very little expenditure. Driving around Australia with a sack of fruit on the back seat makes for very inexpensive dining.

VEGETARIAN FOOD Despite the image of steak-eating, beer-drinking macho Australians, the country is in fact gradually consuming less meat. Because of a wide range of fresh fruit and vegetables, being a vegetarian at any level – from vegan to occasional practitioner – can be fairly easy in the Australian cities. Most restaurants offer vegetarian dishes and most Asian restaurants have several vegetarian specialities. In the cities it will not be long before vegetarian dishes outweigh meat dishes. This is of great concern to Australia's farmers but is welcomed by the health authorities.

Some of the smaller towns, however, still need to catch up with the cities. Many country restaurants and takeaways offer the vegetarian little choice, making them resort to some of that wonderful fruit with a cheese sandwich.

BYO, PUBS AND LICENSING LAWS Many, but by no means all, restaurants outside the big cities are BYO, which means bring your own wine, and very few restaurants – some exceptions in Sydney and Melbourne – mind if you bring your own bottle of wine although, understandably, they charge corkage.

Where you choose to drink is invariably in a pub, whether it's the only bar in a one-dog outback town or a flashy hotel in Sydney – in Australia 'pub' is an all-embracing term. Drinking pubs can be open for almost any 12 hours in 24;

most are open until 2300 Mon–Fri, midnight on Sat and 2200 on Sun. Wine bars exist, but are still quite scarce in many of the big cities, because of determined efforts by the major hotel chains to prevent them from getting a licence. Licensed premises cannot serve liquor to anyone under the age of 18, and this rule is strictly enforced.

Breakfast, Dinner and Tea Typically, breakfast is a substantial meal, which is taken early mainly because of the coming heat of the day. As almost everywhere, the move is towards lighter, healthier breakfasts but the croissant-and-coffee continental breakfast has not, as yet, found much favour.

Dinner, rather than lunch, is the main meal of the day, and is generally served early – perhaps a relic of when pubs used to close at 1800. There is a move in the cities to later dining but while booking a table after, say, 2100 in a restaurant is not that unusual in Sydney and Melbourne it is exceptional elsewhere.

'Tea' might mean a cup of tea and a cake, but you will also hear it to describe the main evening meal.

AUSTRALIAN WINE

The wine in Australia is marvellous and relatively inexpensive. Most bars will have a bottle shop attached, stocking a range of wines which will be quite remarkable, and at reasonable prices. If you want a red which is softer on the palate, look for wines which have Merlot grape incorporated. Most of the whites will be Chardonnay but if you see a straight Semillon go for that. It will be a remarkable experience. Australia's principal wine-growing states are New South Wales, Victoria, Tasmania, Western Australia and, especially, South Australia. Each has multiple wine-growing regions, but only a few of these are producing exceptional wines. Many overseas tipplers know of the Hunter Valley (New South Wales) and Margaret River (Western Australia); Mildura (Victoria) is also gaining some attention. But they're all shadowed by South Australia's 13 wine regions, several of which – such as the Clare Valley, McLaren Vale, Coonawarra and Padthaway – are widely known. The Barossa Valley, just outside Adelaide, is far and away the most renowned of all, and Penfold's heavenly Grange Hermitage – keenly sought and wickedly expensive – is its most famous drop. For more information go to the Australian National Wine Centre's website, www.wineaustralia.com.au.

HEALTH

Not all chemists will accept all **prescriptions** issued overseas. You may need to have another issued by an Australian-registered doctor. There are 24-hour medical centres in all the major cities where this can be arranged very quickly for a small fee. Note

SMOKING

Smoking is now banned in all public buildings, airports, taxis, trams, trains, buses, restaurants, bars, nightclubs, offices, some beaches and all aircraft flying to, from and within Australia.

Cigarette advertising is banned, cigarette sponsorship is being banned, and cigarette vending machines are in the process of being totally banned. As a rough rule of thumb you can take it that, unless you are outdoors or in an area where there are signs specifically permitting you to smoke, you can't.

that not all prescription drugs are available in Australia.

Always take special precautions when travelling with **contact lenses**. It is usually best to remove them before you fly, especially if it is going to be a long journey, or if you have been wearing them excessively, or if you intend to sleep on the plane. The pressurised air of the plane has an extremely destructive drying effect on contact lenses, and the circumstances are not ideal for taking them out halfway through the flight.

When you arrive, restrict your wearing times to allow your contact-lens tolerance to be re-established, as jetlag coupled with excessive contact-lens wear can cause sore eyes. Remember to take your contact lens prescription and, if possible, a spare pair.

DRUGS

The biggest drug problem in Australia, as in almost every other Western country, is alcohol. Australian federal and state governments are working hard to ensure that alcohol is not served to intoxicated people or those under 18 years, and by targeting drink-drivers with random breath-testing. The most commonly used illicit drug in Australia is cannabis, although heroin, amphetamines, ecstasy and cocaine are also used. Those found in possession of cannabis are fined and a criminal conviction is recorded. Penalties are more severe for drug dealing. Sniffer dogs are not uncommon in Australian airports. Do not carry drugs. Long prison sentences – even life terms – are penalties for drug importation.

LANGUAGE

Old-style Australian English – now sadly declining in use – can be both hilarious and, at times, undecipherable. Here's some Aussie sayings you're likely to encounter: blowie (blowfly), bludge (laze around), cark it (die), dunny (toilet), entrée (starter in a restaurant), footpath (paved walkway beside a road), hooroo (goodbye), mozzie (mosquito), shoot through (leave), spunk (an attractive person), station (a large rural property stocked with sheep or cattle), tucker (food), bush tucker (food collected in the bush), yack (talk), hard yakka (hard work).

Be prepared for regional differences – remember that the Australian states began life as widely separated colonies. For instance, a swimming costume is referred to as 'bathers' in most parts of Australia, except New South Wales (NSW) (where it's a 'cozzie') and Queensland (Qld) ('togs'). If you're ordering an average-sized glass of beer you'll need to ask for a 'middy' in NSW; a 'pot' in Western Australia, Victoria or Queensland; a 'schooner' in South Australia; and a 'ten' in the Northern Territory.

Common Abbreviations

You'll most often see the state and territory names abbreviated thus: ACT (Australian Capital Territory), NSW (New South Wales), NT (Northern Territory), Qld (Queensland), SA (South Australia), Tas (Tasmania), Vic (Victoria), WA (Western Australia). The centre of a major city is often referred to as the CBD – central business district.

MASS MEDIA

Commercial **radio** in Australia is as bad as anything you will hear overseas. The government, in the form of the Australian Broadcasting Corporation, ABC, runs several excellent radio stations although, in the name of economy, it is cutting back.

Television is also woeful, but Australia has a lively export market for such programmes as *Neighbours* and *Home and Away*. When travelling around the country you will still find motels that you only have two television channels to choose from. They will both be dire. Make sure you have reading material.

Newspapers tend to be very provincial. There are two national newspapers – *The Australian* and *The Australian Financial Review*. All the rest devote much space to local happenings, especially sport, and can be quickly scanned.

If you want to know what is happening in the world, head for an internet café. You will find that almost every daily newspaper in the world has its own website (or try www.thepaperboy.com) so keeping in touch with the news at home is remarkably easy. If you cannot find an internet café – and almost every town now has one – head for the local library which will probably offer internet access. Again, this is a growing trend. While you are on the internet you can check your e-mail.

MONEY AND BANKS

There are several ways of taking your money with you. First, you can pay for as much as possible in advance. Secondly, to travel around Australia you need at least one good credit card. Before you leave make sure that bills will be settled monthly or that you have a reasonable credit limit. Unlike some other countries there are very few establishments in Australia which will not accept a credit card. The most widely accepted in Australia is Visa, with MasterCard following close behind. American Express has no credit limit, but some establishments won't accept Amex.

You can also use Visa and MasterCard for drawing cash almost anywhere in Australia. ATMs are everywhere and ATM cards can be used in Australia so long as they have been enabled for international access. Your ATM card must carry either the CIRRUS, PLUS or STAR international ATM mark or the Interlink or Maestro POS mark. Contact your bank at home for information on availability and service charges. Any financial organisation which has a sign in its window for either card issuer will normally advance money against the card.

Traveller's cheques are safe and can be easily replaced if you mislay them, provided you have the list of numbers kept safely somewhere else. Photocopy the list and keep it separately in your suitcase; leave the original list in your passport. If anything should happen, you can rattle off the numbers and easily get a replacement. Most shops will accept traveller's cheques in payment of goods, but the rates you get will not be favourable.

In Australia it is fairly safe to carry reasonably large amounts of **cash** – to the extent this is ever sensible. Many Australian banknotes are made of plastic and are shiny and slippery; they are not loved by most Australians.

Banks are generally open 0900–1700 Mon–Fri. The trick, especially outside major centres, is finding a branch office. Recent years have also seen a decline in the number of high-street banks and some small towns are now without a bank. However, all available banks will still handle cash advances against the right credit card.

In July 2000, the government introduced Goods & Services Tax (GST). The result is an additional 10 per cent tax added onto purchases including groceries, restaurants, clothes, tours and transport. In most cases GST has been built into the advertised prices; however, the buyer should be aware of the occasional 10 per cent that may be added on top of the price shown.

OPENING TIMES

It is impossible to generalise about opening hours in Australia as there are major differences between the big cities, tourist centres and small towns. Banks are open Mon–Fri 0930–1600; post offices 0900–1700. Traditionally, all shops and services have closed on Saturday afternoons and Sundays – a situation that still prevails in many sleepy country towns – but most major cities now have shopping and business activity at weekends too.

Shopping hours vary from state to state, but generally big department stores open 0900–1730 Mon–Fri, with late-night shopping either on Thur or Fri until 2100, and 0900–1700 on Sat. Some states have Sunday trading and major stores open 1000–1600. The biggest supermarket chains are moving towards 24-hr, 7-day trading in the large cities, and the trend is catching on elsewhere. Air-conditioned shopping at 0300 in the heat of the summer has distinct advantages.

PACKING

Because Australians are informal to a fault – Crocodile Dundee was not a caricature – wearing formal clothes becomes a nonsense. Ross Gittins, who is perhaps the best Australian writer on economics, was forced to wear a dinner jacket to a vice-regal dinner. With it he wore a pair of white trainers. In Darwin formal attire is called tropical rig, and for men means shorts and long white socks. That pretty much sums up the attitude towards formality.

So coming to Australia you need to pack your jeans, your cossie – swimming costume – some underwear and a few T-shirts. And that's your lot.

LUGGAGE DO'S AND DON'TS

● Do not bring expensive brand-name luggage. They are called 'steal-me' cases. Bring something anonymous, easily cleaned and light.

● Do not buy any luggage which has built-in or hang-on gimmicks. They invariably fail, as do combination locks.

● A suitcase with wheels is not a bad idea. Some are easy to manoeuvre, some aren't. Test before you buy. Better yet is a folding trolley which most aircrew members use.

● Clearly identify your luggage with labels and tags, preferably plastic. Paste your name, address and telephone number into the inside lid. Buy a strap-around belt in a bright colour with a difficult buckle.

● Pack with care. The experts – frequent travellers, airline cabin staff, and butlers and valets – all come up with the same advice: fold it carefully, pad it well, pack it tight.

PLANTS AND ANIMALS

FLORA Australian forest and heathlands have an astonishing floral diversity that speaks of millennia of adaptation. The most noticeable adaptation is the capacity of many Australian plants to quickly regrow after a fire. Some species, such as the banksias, actually need fire to prompt the release of their seeds; others, such as the grass tree, flower more prolifically after fire. Aboriginal people played a pivotal role in shaping the Australian bush. Through regular controlled burning, they kept the bush open, which made hunting and travelling easier and encouraged the growth of new seedlings. Arnhem Land Aboriginal people still regularly 'burn off' in their country, and land managers in some state conservation agencies have begun to do the same. It's widely thought that the destructive effects of raging busfires – such as those seen in Kosciuszko National Park in the 2003/04 summer – could be minimised by regular burn-offs.

Excluding non-vascular types – such as lichens and fungi – there are more than 15,600 known Australian native plant species. Queensland and Western Australia are the states with the greatest species diversity (more than 7000 species occur in each), while Tasmania, with fewer than 1700, has the least, although some of the most unusual native species, such as the Huon pine, are found there. The most common plant genera are the Eucalypts (usually called 'gum trees') and the Acacias (wattles). Visitors with a botanical bent should include on their list of places to see the wet tropics of Queensland, the south-western sandplains of Western Australia, Tasmania's alpine and sub-alpine regions and the old-growth forests of southern New South Wales and eastern Victoria.

FAUNA Most visitors to Australia look forward to encounters with native animals with wonder and apprehension. The nation's suite of unique furry animals has tickled their interest; its seemingly endless variety of poisonous snakes, spiders and marine animals has them worried.

AUSTRALIAN FLORAL EMBLEMS
Commonwealth of Australia: golden wattle (*Acacia pycnantha*)
Australian Capital Territory: royal bluebell (*Wahlenbergia gloriosa*)
New South Wales: waratah (*Telopea speciosissima*)
Northern Territory: Sturt's desert rose (*Gossypium sturtianum*)
Queensland: Cooktown orchid (*Dendrobium phalaenopsis*)
South Australia: Sturt's desert pea (*Swainsona formosa*)
Tasmania: Tasmanian blue gum (*Eucalyptus globulus*)
Victoria: common heath (*Epacris impressa*)
Western Australia: Mangles' kangaroo paw (*Anigozanthos manglesii*)

The furry creatures that arouse such interest are the marsupials – a group that includes kangaroos and wallabies, koalas, wombats and possums. They're distinct from the placental mammals that dominate in other parts of the world because they give birth to tiny, underdeveloped young that complete their development while attached to an external teat (which is usually – famously in the case of kangaroos and wallabies – inside a pouch).

Although they're less commonly encountered than marsupials such as kangaroos and possums, the monotremes deserve the title of greatest Australian animal oddity. The platypus (found only in Australia) and echidna (Australia and New Guinea) are the world's only egg-laying mammals. Both animals are furtive and encounters with them in the wild are rare and largely by chance – and therefore very special.

Australian birdlife can't help but catch a visitor's eye; flocks of noisy parrots, lorikeets and cockatoos are still common in urban areas, and the flightless emu – the world's second largest bird – is seen in most parts of the country. Isolated Iron Range National Park, in far north Queensland, is renowned for its diversity of resident bird species. The Top End of the Northern Territory is renowned for the sheer, staggering volume of bird populations, mostly seen near waterholes between August and October.

There's good news and bad news on the snakes and spiders front. For various reasons the vast majority of Australian snakes are venomous and more than 20 are classified as potentially deadly to humans. The best known (found in the populated south-east) are the eastern brown and common tiger snakes; both have powerful venoms, and between them have accounted for most human deaths from snakebite.

And the good news? Fortunately, snakes use their venom primarily for catching food, and no Australian venomous snakes have shown any serious interest in attempting to eat humans (or, indeed, in biting them for sport). Confronted with a human, most snakes head for cover, and fast. The vast majority of snakebites occur as the result of dumb luck: treading on a snake is one fairly certain way to prompt a bite. The same is true of the potentially dangerous spider species, such as the funnel-web and redback: they'd rather retreat from humans than bite them. Increased awareness of basic first aid, the development of antivenoms, fast-response evacuation services and intensive-care medicine have all contributed to a lessening of the risk of snake and spider bite.

The painful and/or irritating Australian critters most likely to meet visitors are the various stingers found at the seaside. The Portuguese man-o'-war jellyfish (known as a 'bluebottle' in Australia) is a frequent summer visitor, sometimes blown onto surfing beaches by onshore winds in great numbers. Its trailing tentacles contain numerous stinging cells; fortunately, a bluebottle sting is usually no worse than moderately painful, although there are cases where patients have required resuscitation. The marine stinger, or box jellyfish, of the tropical north is a far deadlier proposition, and northern Australian beaches are closed to swimmers between October and May because of them. In 2001 another tropical-waters jellyfish, the nut-sized irukandji, was responsible for the death of a British tourist, and some authorities are now suggesting that visitors to the tropics swim only in pools between December and April. If you are bitten or stung while travelling in Australia, see p. 43 for advice on treatment.

POSTAL SERVICES

Australia Post provides a domestic letter service and a range of associated postal services, handling more than 4 billion items of mail a year. Most small towns as well as city centres and suburbs have their own post offices. A standard letter within Australia costs 50 cents to mail, and will usually be delivered within two to three days. The international mail service is reliable and quick for both letters and packages – many letters from Australia make it to their destinations within the UK and the USA less than five days after posting.

PUBLIC HOLIDAYS

The major public holidays in Australia are national ones:

1 January:	New Year's Day
26 January:	Australia Day
Easter	(Good Friday, Easter Sunday, Easter Monday): some time in March/April
25 April:	Anzac Day
Early June:	Queen's Birthday
25 December:	Christmas Day
26 December:	Boxing Day

There are other holidays that vary between states, such as Melbourne Cup Day in Victoria, the annual agricultural show days in most major cities and towns, and Labour Day. On public holidays, all banks will be closed, most shops shut, and public transport services scaled down to their normal Sunday schedules. Check local newspapers for details of services, facilities and tourist activities that are open on public holidays.

READING

Referred to throughout this guide as the OTT, the *Thomas Cook Overseas Timetable* is published every two months, price £11.00 per issue. It contains timetables for all the main rail, bus and ferry services, plus details of local and suburban services, and it is available from UK branches of Thomas Cook or by mail order; tel: (01733) 416477 in the UK or visit www.thomascookpublishing.com. In North America, contact SF Travel Publications, 3959 Electric Rd, Suite 155, Roanoke, VA 24018; tel: 1 (800) 322-3834; e-mail: sales@travelbookstore.com; website: www.travelbookstore.com. A special edition of the Overseas Timetable is available from bookshops and from the outlets given above – the *Thomas Cook Overseas Timetable Independent Traveller's Edition* includes bus, rail and ferry timetables, plus additional information useful for travellers.

Please note that the OTT table numbers very occasionally change – but services may easily be located by checking the index at the front of the *Overseas Timetable*.

SAFETY

CRIME Australia is remarkably crime free. Take the worst crime – murder. If you consider murder and manslaughter together throughout the whole of Australia it works out at roughly one a day. And violence is at a similarly low rate. But for visitors the average is much lower. The vast majority of assaults happen at pubs at closing time. Avoid pubs at closing time and you will avoid almost any chance of violence.

To all intents and purposes Australia is a gun-free country – and becoming more so. Handguns are almost unheard of and it is difficult, although not impossible, for the average citizen to acquire any firearm unless working on the land or a member of a gun club. The government has recently made it illegal for most people to carry certain knives; a hefty fine is applicable if caught.

There are petty crimes against property which are committed, in the main, by drug addicts. Australia, like every other country, has a drug addiction problem, but if you take elementary precautions it is almost certain you will not be bothered.

WILDLIFE The chances of **shark** attack are remote. It rarely happens: there has been less than one a year since records were kept. Most of the sharks in Australian waters will not attack. The exception is the white pointer, but even this is not something to be over-concerned about. The white pointer is now so rare that it has been made a protected species, so if one attacks you must not fight back and harm it in any way. That is illegal.

Crocodiles are another matter. If there is a sign up saying that you should not swim because of crocodiles then take great heed. No one knows why they prefer tourists – sweeter meat? – but this appears to be the case. Paddling in shallow water is no safeguard. They can come and get paddlers.

There are over 4000 species of **snakes**, **spiders** and other things that can bite you and make you very ill, but they need not truly worry you. Just take normal precautions and the worst thing that will ever bother you is a **leech**. No one dies from leech sucks. If you are bitten, see the guidelines on p. 43.

The two most common dangerous **spiders** are the redback and the funnel-web. On ABC radio some years ago, a commentator delighted audiences by saying: 'A lady on the North Shore has been bitten on her funnel by a finger-web spider.' Sunburn (see p. 39) is a far, far greater danger.

Flies are much less of a problem than they were some years ago. The introduction of beetles that eat cow dung has cut down on the number of flies. But in the wrong season some places, Uluru (Ayers Rock) for example, have enough flies for them to be seriously annoying. In theory, insect repellent will keep them away, but after you have been sweating for a short while it loses its efficiency. Some people in the outback go to the extent of wearing veils but this is only for those who are seriously affected. However, it would be wrong not to mention that the flies are there and can be a nuisance. Always carry insect repellent.

Get on the right track for a great holiday

Travelling by rail? The best companions that global rail travellers can have are available from Thomas Cook Publishing.

OVERSEAS TIMETABLE

See the range of Thomas Cook Publishing guides at all good bookshops, or at www.thomascookpublishing.com

Thomas Cook Publishing

SIGHTSEEING

Nothing in Australia is old; or rather, nothing Europeans had anything to do with is old. Visitors from Europe will laugh at the thought that a hundred years is considered seriously old, but that is the case. As a result there is little of the great architectural heritage of other countries. Yes, there is the Opera House in Sydney, which is more wonderful than you would believe, and, yes, Canberra (designed by an American) is not so shabby.

There is some sort of town planning and there is also some protection for places of historic importance. Having said that, the local council wanted to destroy The Rocks, perhaps historically the most important centre of Sydney, and replace it with high-rise office blocks – and still defends that decision with great vigour. The project was only stopped by the unions, led by Jack Mundey, who will be remembered in history as one of the great Australians. (This is not just an Australian problem. Lord Curzon, when Viceroy of India, was actively engaged in a plan to knock down the Taj Mahal and sell it as scrap marble.)

By and large you come to Australia to see the natural attractions rather than to wonder at what man hath wrought. Australia did not have the first national park – that was Yellowstone in the United States – but it was very close behind and is still declaring new parks every year. Within spitting distance of every city there are large and numerous national parks run intelligently with a view to both preservation and access. You will find the park information offices treasure troves of useful information. Access to many national parks is free, although at the most visited of them – often those closest to the cities – there will generally be an entrance fee. Some of Australia's most beautiful and peaceful camping grounds are in national parks; usually campers pay a fee if facilities are provided.

Each state has its own national park service, the headquarters of which is invariably in the state capital. This will be the best place to get information about visiting the more isolated parks, some of which have no full-time ranger or, at best, a seasonal ranger. In the case of some outback parks, information about what to take and how to travel is critically important.

The park rangers are all willing to have a yarn and tell you what to look for and what to avoid. You could spend three years just looking at national parks and you would still not have covered half of them. As well as the parks there are forestry reserves, which are similar but easier to drive through. And throughout Australia there is more wild country than you could ever explore in one lifetime. Some of the national parks are wild and free and therefore hold dangers for the inexperienced traveller. The simple and absolute rule is – when in doubt ask a ranger. They will always err on the side of caution and safety and never let you stray into danger.

PICK OF THE NATIONAL PARKS

If your interests run to natural and cultural heritage, Australia will both delight and baffle you. There are so many national parks and conservation and wildlife reserves spread across the country (New South Wales alone has more than 100 national parks) that it's almost impossible to decide which to visit. A logical starting point is to select parks in or near the accessible Australian World Heritage Areas (WHAs). Two of the WHAs are subantarctic and definitely *not* accessible: Macquarie Island and, far to the west, Heard and McDonald Islands. All were inscribed on the World Heritage list in 1997. For more information about Australia's WHAs, go to www.deh.gov.au/heritage/worldheritage.

The **Tasmanian Wilderness WHA** is one of only three temperate wilderness areas remaining in the southern hemisphere. The 13,800 sq km area covers about 20 per cent of Tasmania and includes Cradle Mountain–Lake St Clair, Walls of Jerusalem, Franklin–Gordon Wild Rivers, Southwest and Hartz Mountains national parks. All are managed by the Tasmanian Parks and Wildlife Service, tel: (03) 6233 6191 or 1300 135 513.

The entire **Lord Howe Island Group** is World Heritage listed. Lord Howe, 700 km north-east of Sydney and accessible only by air or sea, is all that remains of a 6.4 million-year-old shield volcano. The main island includes soaring Mt Gower (875 m) and Mt Lidgbird (777 m); the group harbours about 50 plant and 5 bird species found nowhere else in the world. For information call the Lord Howe Island Visitor Centre, tel: (02) 6563 2114 or 1800 240 937.

The 2400 sq km **Willandra Lakes** region, in far south-western New South Wales, is one of four Australian World Heritage properties listed for both cultural and natural values. Up to the end of the most recent ice age, the Willandra lakes – now dry – were full of fresh water, and the crescent-shaped dunes, or lunettes, on their eastern shores have yielded extensive evidence of Aboriginal occupation dating back about 60,000 years. For information tel: (03) 5021 8900. Rainforest reserves in a number of national parks – including New England, Dorrigo and Oxley Wild Rivers – are part of the **Central Eastern Rainforest Reserves WHA**. Located on the steep eastern escarpment of New South Wales, these national parks include the world's most extensive areas of subtropical rainforest.
For information tel: (02) 6657 2309.

North of Brisbane, **Fraser Island** is the world's largest sand island, with an area of 1840 sq km. It's a singularly beautiful place, with long, uninterrupted white beaches backed by coloured sand cliffs. Inland, magnificent rainforests are dotted with freshwater lakes. Most of the island is contained in Great Sandy National Park; for information call the Queensland National Parks' Eurong office, tel: (07) 4127 9128. The **Great Barrier Reef** defies superlatives. It's the world's largest WHA, covering an area of 350,000 sq km (bigger than Italy). It protects the world's most extensive coral reef system and is one of its richest areas in terms of plant and animal diversity. The area includes the Great Barrier Reef Marine Park (for information tel: (07) 4750 0700) and most of its offshore islands are national parks managed by the

Pick of the National Parks (Cont)

Queensland Parks and Wildlife Service (Naturally Queensland Information Centre, tel: (07) 3227 8185). On shore from the Barrier Reef between Townsville and Cooktown, the 8940 sq km **Wet Tropics of Queensland WHA** includes several national parks, notably Hinchinbrook Island (tel: (07) 4066 8601) and Daintree (tel: (07) 4098 2188). Daintree preserves one of Australia's largest rainforest wilderness areas; in its Cape Tribulation region, the meeting of fringing coral reefs and rainforest coastline is a rarely seen combination.

The **Australian Fossil Mammal Sites World Heritage Property** includes two sites – Naracoorte, in South Australia, and Riversleigh, in north-western Queensland – separated by more than 2000 km. The Riversleigh site, which protects one of the world's richest fossil mammal records in the period 25–15 million years ago, is included in Lawn Hill National Park. The park's centrepiece is the remarkable sandstone Lawn Hill Gorge, which features beautiful creek scenery, a remnant vine forest and rich Aboriginal history.
For information tel: (07) 4748 5572.

Kakadu National Park, in the Northern Territory, is World Heritage listed for both its cultural and natural values. The 19,804 sq km park's key natural features are internationally important wetlands and spectacular escarpment landscape, which support diverse assemblages of plants and animals. This rich natural bounty has supported human habitation for up to 60,000 years; many Aboriginal communities still occupy the region, and the park's art sites illustrate Aboriginal interaction with the environment over tens of thousands of years. For information tel: (08) 8938 1120.

Uluru–Kata Tjuta National Park, in central Australia, was inscribed on the World Heritage List in 1987. The 1325 sq km park's main features, Uluru (Ayers Rock) and Kata Tjuta (The Olgas), are a part of an important cultural landscape and have special significance to the park's owners – the Pitjantjatjara and Yankunytjatjara Aboriginal people (known as Anangu). Various physical features of Uluru and Kata Tjuta are evidence of the work of the Anangu's creation beings (the *tjukuritja*). The travels of these ancestral beings are celebrated in Anangu religion and culture today. For information tel: (08) 8956 3138.

Isolated **Shark Bay WHA**, in Western Australia, covers 23,000 sq km at Australia's western-most point. Its waters and islands protect rare plants and animals; Shark Bay includes the 1030 sq km Wooramel Seagrass Bank, the largest structure of its type in the world. Nearby Kalbarri National Park, on the lower reaches of the Murchison River, includes spectacular gorge country and rich heathlands that bloom from winter to early summer.
For information tel: (08) 9937 1140.

The **Greater Blue Mountains Area** was inscribed on the World Heritage list in 2000. It's the closest WHA to central Sydney – just 60–180 km to the west. The 10,300 sq km area includes seven national parks – Blue Mountains, Wollemi, Yengo, Nattai, Kanangra-Boyd, Gardens of Stone and Thirlmere Lakes – and the famous Jenolan Caves Karst Conservation

PICK OF THE NATIONAL PARKS (CONT)

Reserve. It's an area of magnificent views, sheer cliffs and deep and thickly forested valleys that are rich in bird and animal life. For information tel: (02) 4787 8877.

Inscribed on the World Heritage list in 2003, **Purnululu National Park** protects the striking Bungle Bungle Range in Western Australia's remote Kimberley region. The park's main feature is beehive-shaped, striped sandstone towers. Remarkably, the area is so isolated that the Bungle Bungles were practically unknown until a film crew's visit about 25 years ago.

TELEPHONES

Australia has an extensive network of public telephones throughout the country, with most telephones accepting coins and prepaid telephone cards – although the move to prepaid telephone calls only is very noticeable. You can buy phonecards in values of $2, $5, $10, $20 and $50 at most newsagents. Interstate calls are quite expensive during business hours, cheaper in the evening and at weekends. A range of international phone cards is available from most newsagents and Thomas Cook Offices, and they are a fraction of the cost of using coins or regular Telstra phone cards.

If you are phoning Australia from overseas, dial 00 for international, followed by 61 for Australia, the area code without the first zero, then the number you want. If, for example, you were calling Sydney from Britain, you would dial 00 61 2 XXXX XXXX. Within Australia but outside Sydney you would dial (02) XXXX XXXX.

Most digital mobile (cellular) telephones will work in Australia. There is total coverage in the built-up areas and fair coverage on every main road. In the wide open spaces you will need a satellite phone to communicate. Inexpensive prepaid SIM cards are available throughout Australia; just pop them into your mobile phone and you are set to make and receive phone calls.

SOME INTERNATIONAL DIALLING CODES:

Australia	61
New Zealand	64
Republic of Ireland	353
South Africa	27
UK	44
USA and Canada	1

TIPPING

The dreaded tipping disease only exists in international hotels, where it has been brought in by Americans. You do not tip cab drivers. Indeed, you will find cab drivers who tip you. If the meter says $10.50 they may say, 'Make it ten bucks, mate.' That does not happen a lot in Manhattan.

In the service industries the unions have ensured that all employees are paid decent, living wages. They do not need, and mostly do not expect, tips as a supplement to their income. Strangely, people in the service industry are totally unimpressed by big tippers. They feel that the tippers have something to prove and are trying to make themselves look superior.

If you must tip make it small – $5 is splashing out big time. Forget 15 per cent of the bill. Just leave some small change for good service. (In Europe, Australian waiters hate to wait on Australians and New Zealanders. They know the pickings will be pitiful.)

TOILETS

Public toilets do exist, but they are few in number and not noted for their scrupulous cleanliness. However, most petrol stations have clean toilets and, although these are supposedly reserved for customers, there is no problem if you ask politely. All hotels and pubs also have clean toilets which are accessible to the public. In national parks, those supervised by the National Parks and Wildlife Service tend to be clean and usable. The slang for a toilet is 'dunny', although this is regarded as vulgar and is gradually disappearing from use. In the country and by many main roads be prepared to use composting toilets – these are often modern and well ventilated, and rely (as the name suggests) on composting to break down waste. A remarkable internet resource – the National Public Toilet Map (www.toiletmap.gov.au) – was launched in 2001. The map shows the location of more than 13,000 public toilets throughout Australia, in towns, cities and rural areas, and along major travel routes. The site provides information about each toilet, such as opening hours and access for people with a disability. Maps of specific locations can be downloaded and printed from the website.

TOURIST INFORMATION

Like most other countries, Australia invests heavily in its overseas tourist offices and is represented in many countries.

Tourism Australia www.atc.net.au and www.tourismaustralia.com.

United Kingdom	Australia Centre, Australia House, 6th Floor, Melbourne Place/Strand, London UK WC2B 4LG; tel: 020 7438 4601.
USA	6100 Center Drive, Suite 1150, Los Angeles CA 90045 USA; tel: 0310 695 3200.

State offices:

New South Wales

www.tourism.nsw.gov.au	Tourism House, 55 Harrington St, The Rocks, Sydney, NSW 2000; tel: (02) 9931 1111.
	Australia Centre, Australia House, 6th Floor, Melbourne Place/Strand, London UK WC2B 4LG; tel: 020 7887 5003.

Northern Territory

www.nttc.com.au	43 Mitchell St, Darwin, NT 0801; tel: (08) 8951 8471.
www.travelnt.com	1st Floor Beaumont House, Lambton Rd, London, SW20 0LW; tel: 020 8944 2992.

Queensland

www.tq.com.au	Tourism Queensland House, 30 Makerston St, Brisbane, QLD 4000; tel: (07) 3535 3535.
	Australia Centre, Australia House, 6th Floor, Melbourne Place/Strand, London UK WC2B 4LG; tel: 020 7438 4601.

South Australia

www.tourism.sa.gov.au	Levels 6, 8, 10 & 11, 50 Grenfell St, Adelaide, SA 5000;
www.southaustralia.com	tel: (08) 8463 4500.
	Australia Centre, Australia House, 6th Floor, Melbourne Place/Strand, London UK WC2B 4LG; tel: 020 7438 4636.

Tasmania

www.tourismtasmania.com.au	GPO Box 399, Level 2, 22 Elizabeth St, Hobart, TAS 7000;
www.discovertasmania.com	tel: (03) 6230 8235.

Victoria

www.tourismvictoria.com.au	Level 6, 55 Collins St, Melbourne, VIC 3000; tel: (03) 9653
www.visitvictoria.com	9777.
	Australia Centre, Australia House, 6th Floor, Melbourne Place/Strand, London UK WC2B 4LG; tel: 020 7438 4645.

Western Australia

www.westernaustralia.com	Level 9, 2 Mill St, Perth, WA 6000; tel: (08) 9262 1700.
	Australia Centre, Australia House, 6th Floor, Melbourne Place/Strand, London UK WC2B 4LG; tel: 020 7395 0578; e-mail: westozuk@westernaustralia.com.

It can be difficult to reach these offices by telephone – plainly, if large numbers of visitors want to visit a country it is difficult to handle all the telephone queries. In the meantime, phoning for information is not a real option. And don't hold your breath waiting for a reply to a letter or fax unless you are a travel agent. Your best bet is to go straight to the internet: the Australian Tourist Commission's official site, at www.australia.com, is massive and comprehensive.

WEIGHTS AND MEASURES

Australia has converted to the metric system. For conversion tables, see p. 514.

WORKING IN AUSTRALIA

Working holiday visas for Australia are available to 18–30-year-old single people from the United Kingdom, Canada, the Netherlands, the Republic of Ireland, Japan, the Republic of Korea, Malta, Germany, Sweden, Denmark, Norway, Finland, the Hong Kong Special Administrative Region of the People's Republic of China, Taiwan, the Republic of Cyprus, Italy, Belgium and France. Note that you can't apply for a working holiday visa once you've arrived in Australia – you have to do it abroad. (You must apply in your home country if you hold a passport from Japan, Korea, Malta, Germany, Hong Kong or Cyprus.) Owing to a shortage of unskilled labour, since November 2005 working holiday visa holders who have done seasonal work (usually fruit-picking) in regional Australia for a minimum of three months are eligible to apply for a second working holiday visa and stay for a further 12 months.

You can apply for a working holiday visa on the internet (go to www.immi.gov.au/e_visa/visit.htm), or by lodging a written application (on form 1150) at any overseas visa office (go to www.immi.gov.au/contacts/overseas.htm to find your nearest office).

There are also temporary residence programmes for people wanting to live and work in Australia for a limited period. Options include arrangements for people on exchange programmes or working with approved community groups, visiting academics, entertainers, sports people, medical practitioners, media and film staff, occupational trainees, religious workers and others. Go to www.immi.gov.au/allforms/working.htm#tempor for more information.

Temporary residents are required to pay taxes on income earned in Australia, and they don't have access to social welfare benefits or Medicare (the national public health cover). People from countries that have reciprocal health-care agreements with Australia (Finland, Ireland, Italy, Malta, the Netherlands, New Zealand, Sweden and the UK) are entitled to emergency medical insurance cover.

TIMELINE OF AUSTRALIAN HISTORY

c. 60,000 years ago –1788	Aboriginal people exclusively inhabit Australia.
1606–97	Dutch navigators reach parts of the coast of modern-day Queensland, Northern Territory, Western Australia, South Australia and Tasmania.
1770	Captain James Cook charts the east coast of Australia and claims possession for Britain.
1787	Captain Arthur Phillip and the First Fleet (11 vessels, including about 730 convicts) sail from Portsmouth, England, to establish a penal colony in New South Wales (NSW).
1788	A few days after the First Fleet reaches NSW, the British flag is raised at Sydney Cove (26 January).
1795–98	George Bass and Matthew Flinders chart the Furneaux Islands (in Bass Strait) and confirm Tasmania is an island.
1801–03	Flinders circumnavigates Australia, completes charting of the coastline and confirms Australia is a single landmass.
1803	River Derwent (southern Tasmania) settlement established (moved to site of modern-day Hobart in 1804).
1808	'Rum Rebellion' of New South Wales Corps officers deposes Governor William Bligh, famous for the *Bounty* mutiny; the corps is recalled to Britain.
1810	Lachlan Macquarie appointed governor; he encourages colonial development and exploration.
1813	Blue Mountains, west of Sydney, crossed by Blaxland, Lawson and Wentworth; George Evans finds rich pastoral country west of the mountains.
1829	Swan River Colony (later Perth, Western Australia) established.
1834–36	Port Phillip District colonies established; Melbourne established.
1836–37	South Australian colonies (Adelaide) settled.
1838	Seven Europeans hanged for 'Myall Creek Massacre' of 28 Aboriginal people.
1850s	Gold rushes in eastern colonies; Australia's population trebles in a decade.
1851	Port Phillip District separates from NSW, taking the name Victoria.
1860s–1911	Colonial (and later state) legislatures create bodies to 'protect' Aboriginal people, establishing missions and reserves.
1890	First Australian political party formed – from 1918 known as the Australian Labor Party (ALP).
1901	A federation, the Commonwealth of Australia, is created.
1902	The Commonwealth gives women full voting rights.
1914–18	World War I: 60,000 Australians die, 165,000 are wounded.
1918	The 30-year-old practice of removing children from Aboriginal mothers and placing them in foster homes or institutions is officially sanctioned; it continues to the 1950s. Those affected become known as the 'Stolen Generations'.
1927–28	Last known massacres of Aboriginal people occur.

1930s	Great Depression; unemployment exceeds 25 per cent of the workforce.
1939–45	World War II: 30,000 Australians die, 65,000 are wounded.
1942	Darwin bombed by Japanese air force.
1947–60s	Post-war immigration programme brings more than 800,000 non-British Europeans to Australia.
1949	Conservative government led by R G Menzies takes office.
1951	First Australia–New Zealand–United States (ANZUS) pact.
1951	Policy of 'assimilation' for Aboriginal people formally adopted.
1955	Southeast Asia Treaty Organization (SEATO) formed.
1967	Federal referendum overwhelmingly passed, giving Aboriginals and Torres Strait Islanders status as citizens.
1967	Prime Minister Harold Holt, Menzies' successor, disappears, presumed drowned.
1970–73	Campaign to save Lake Pedder, Tasmania, from a hydro-electric scheme sparks Australian conservation movement.
1972–75	Labor government led by E G Whitlam completes many reforms, including creation of national health scheme and abolition of university fees and national service. Department of Aboriginal Affairs established and assimilation policy replaced by one of self-determination.
1973	National Aboriginal Consultative Committee founded.
1975	Constitutional crisis sees Whitlam sacked by Governor General John Kerr; Conservative government led by Malcolm Fraser subsequently elected.
1976	Aboriginal Land Rights Act (applying to the Northern Territory) passed.
1983–90	Labor government of Bob Hawke, with Paul Keating as treasurer, deregulates banking and financial systems.
1991	Paul Keating ousts Bob Hawke as prime minister.
1992	The High Court rejects the notion of *terra nullius* (that, before British occupation, Australia belonged to no-one) and recognises that Aboriginal title existed before 1788.
1993	Native Title Act establishes a National Native Title Tribunal and sets out processes for determination of native title rights.
1996	Royalist conservative John Howard elected prime minister.
1998	National Sorry Day established in response to 1997 report on the Stolen Generations.
1999	Federal referendum on whether Australia should become a republic fails.
2000	(May) 500,000 march in Sydney in support of reconciliation with Aboriginal people; (September) Olympic Games held in Sydney.
2001	Conservative federal government re-elected.
2001–02	Summer bushfire crisis; large fires burn near Sydney and several NSW coastal towns.
2003	Australia joins US-led coalition in invasion of Iraq.
2004	Conservative federal government re-elected.

New South Wales has dusty outback, rainforests, snow-covered mountains (in season), vineyards, historic towns, some of the best beaches in Australia, and weather which, for the most part, encourages a hedonistic outdoor lifestyle.

The Great Dividing Range that runs down the eastern side of Australia rears up in the south of the state from a few insignificant hills to a series of mountains culminating in Mount Kosciuszko, at 2228 m the highest mountain in Australia. It is here that the people of New South Wales – a million or more each year – come to ski each winter.

The beaches, which stretch from near-tropical Tweed Heads in the north to Eden in the south, form an amazing 1900-km crescent of white sand, blue sky and Pacific Ocean. Yet, to the people of New South Wales, they are merely an integral part of their lives. On any weekday in summer you can drive the short distance from Sydney along the coast to Wollongong and pass at least 30 long beaches, each more perfect than the last. And most of them will be deserted. With nearly one-third of Australia's population, New South Wales may be the most populated state, but there is still room enough to spare for everyone.

The story of European settlement of the continent started in New South Wales, when in January 1788 just over 1000 people, three-quarters of them convicts, arrived on the alien shore of Port Phillip, soon to be Sydney Town. The people of Sydney do not always like to be reminded of this: 'We Australians often display a certain queasiness in recalling our founding fathers,' wrote Russell Ward in *The Australian Legend* in 1958. Transportation ended in 1840, but the effect of those early convict settlers is still to be felt. The use of cockney rhyming slang from London convicts is still prevalent in the Australian language, and an uneasy relationship between the population and the police lingers on from those days.

Those early settlers faced an uncertain future in an unexplored land, but the infant colony expanded and grew, at first along the farmlands of the Parramatta River and the flats around Windsor and Richmond. Ahead lay the seemingly insuperable barrier of the Blue Mountains. Of course, the Aboriginal people had been crossing them for millennia, but no European settler thought of asking them if they knew the way across. However, once the first party saw, in 1813, the vision of sunlit plains on the far side it was only a very short time before settlement followed: the fertile plains of Bathurst and the Central West were ripe for agricultural development.

A dozen years later the gold rushes began. The influence of gold on the formation of Australia cannot be over-emphasised, as wave upon wave of free settlers created makeshift, tented towns over-night, which rapidly increased in size and then just as quick-ly died. But this influx of optimistic prospectors made Sydney rich and filled the coffers of the New South Wales government.

After gold came coal, and later metal ores, but agricul-ture has remained one of the major props of the New South Wales economy. In a good year the gentle slopes and broad plains west of the Great Dividing Range can produce one-third of Australia's total wheat crop, and flood-prone land to the south-west has been transformed into lush pastures that produce almost all of the nation's rice, 80 per cent of the wine grapes and huge quantities of fruit and vegetables.

FEDERATION AND THE SHAPING OF NEW SOUTH WALES

The original state effectively covered half of Australia and, arguably, extended as far as Fiji. In 1856, when it was granted self-government, New South Wales was already the founding state of Australia and its destiny was clear. The northern half of the state gained its independence as Queensland in 1859 (see p. 270) but all the fledgling states were still separate parts of a British colony (there were even customs posts between New South Wales and Victoria). Then came Federation. In Sydney's Centennial Park on a very hot, windy 1 Jan 1901, Lord Hopetoun, representing Her Majesty's government, and the leaders of the States of Australia, signed the document that made Australia one nation and the states one federation.

Sydney and Melbourne, capital of Victoria, constantly vied for the leadership of the new country. Eventually a special area – the Australian Capital Territory – was set up as near equidistant as possible between the rival cities, and Canberra was declared the nation's capital (see p. 101). But New South Wales became the premier state of Australia, with Sydney the favoured entry point for the majority of tourists who started arriving from overseas. And so it remains.

Beyond all this abundant agriculture are the dry and dusty plains of the outback, where nothing grows except stunted scrub and desert grass. The only town of great signifi-cance is Broken Hill, the city in the desert that has provided enormous wealth in min-erals from the largest single body of silver–lead–zinc ore in the world. Here the land is so flat that you can see the curvature of the Earth.

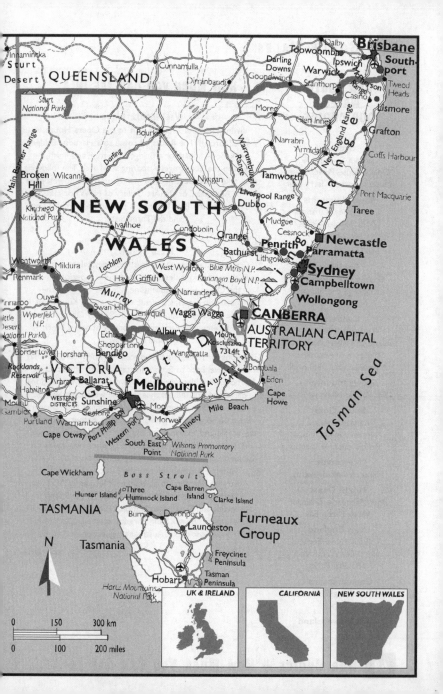

NEW SOUTH WALES: OUR CHOICE

Sydney
Harbour Bridge walk, Opera House, Powerhouse Museum, harbour ferry tour

Blue Mountains
Grose Valley, Kanangra Walls, Jenolan Caves

Bathurst
Hill End Historic Site

Far West
Broken Hill; Mutawintji, Kinchega and Mungo National Parks

Canberra
Parliament House, National Gallery, National Museum of Australia, Australian War Memorial

Snowy Mountains
Kosciuszko National Park

South Coast
Kangaroo Valley, Murramarang National Park; Montague Island

Newcastle
Hunter Valley vineyards

North Coast
Port Macquarie, Bellinger Valley, Byron Bay

New England
Armidale; New England and Oxley Wild Rivers National Parks

Coonabarabran
Warrumbungle National Park

Lord Howe Island

HOW MUCH YOU CAN SEE IN A ...

WEEKEND (2 DAYS)

Sydney harbour cruise, a visit to the Opera House, a stroll through The Rocks en route to a Harbour Bridge walk. Book ahead for a Bridgeclimb tour, and finish the day atop the 'coathanger's' soaring steel arch. The following day, take in the best of Sydney museums (the Powerhouse or Australian, or the Art Gallery of NSW) or take a day trip to the Blue Mountains to visit Katoomba, Leura and the Three Sisters.

WEEK (7 DAYS)

Consider spending three days in Sydney, taking in all the one-day attractions described above, plus a performance at the Opera House, lunchtime *yum cha* at one of the Chinatown eateries, a picnic visit to either Ku-ring-gai Chase or Royal National Parks, or Sydney Olympic Park and Bicentennial Park, and a morning at a surf beach – Bondi or Manly.

Options for remaining four days. 1. Fly north to Byron Bay and travel back to Sydney in stages (overnight at Coffs Harbour, Port Macquarie and Newcastle), taking in national parks and isolated beaches. 2. Travel west from Sydney, through the Blue Mountains (Blue Mountains and Kanangra-Boyd National Parks; Jenolan Caves) to Bathurst; spend a day at Hill End Historic Site and visit the Mudgee vineyards. 3. Travel south-west through the southern highlands to Canberra and spend two days – getting around by bicycle – visiting Parliament House, the National Gallery, the Australian War Memorial, National Museum of Australia, and other attractions. Continue on to the Snowy Mountains and Kosciuszko National Park; take the chairlift ride and (easy) walk from Thredbo to the summit of Mt Kosciuszko, Australia's highest point.

THE SUPREME HARBOUR CITY

Sydney is often criticised for being a raucous, bustling town with the rough edges showing. It pleads guilty to this, as this is what accounts for much of the city's attraction. And though Sydney can at times be honky-tonk vulgar, it is never less than beautiful. For Sydney is blessed with a position on one of the great natural harbours of the world and is, for its inhabitants, the only place on earth to live.

The location of Sydney was arrived at almost by mistake. When Captain Arthur Phillip and the First Fleet arrived in Australia on 18 January 1788, they anchored in Botany Bay. Captain Cook had landed here in 1770 and his appeared a good example to follow. But Botany Bay is shallow: Captain Phillip thought it unsuitable and instead settled at what Cook had called Port Jackson – better known today as Sydney Harbour.

MUST SEE/DO IN SYDNEY

See a performance at the Sydney Opera House

Walk across, or up, the Harbour Bridge

Take a cruise on Sydney Harbour

Stroll around The Rocks

Go interactive at the Powerhouse Museum

Get engrossed at the Australian Museum

Picnic in the Royal Botanic Gardens

Go for a surf at Bondi or Manly

Sydney was, at the beginning, mainly a convict town, although from quite early days the word was considered distasteful and many more elegant euphemisms were used. By 1815, the town had a population of 5500 (out of a total white population of Australia of about 13,000), and the new governor, Lachlan Macquarie, had expansive ideas. He engaged the services of the counterfeiter-turned-architect Francis Greenway, who was pardoned by Macquarie on the understanding that he would design great buildings. This Greenway did, and many of his creations, including Hyde Park Barracks and St James's Church, still stand.

The new town and the new country galloped along in a period of commercial expansion fired by the pastoral boom and waves of prospectors on their way to – or from – the goldfields. By 1850 Sydney had 50,000 inhabitants and in that year the New South Wales Legislative Council decided that it should have a university. This, perhaps more than anything else, set the seal of respectability on the colony.

The city's past is now being recognised and preserved – at least quite a bit of it – but it also has outstanding modern landmarks. Darling Harbour has been developed into one of the world's great convention centres, and the Opera House has reached its majority in all glory. But Sydney remains the supreme harbour city, and the harbour, so felicitously discovered by Captain Phillip, is one of the natural wonders of the world.

ARRIVAL AND DEPARTURE

Sydney Airport (Kingsford Smith airport) is probably the most centrally placed international airport in the world. It is about 9 km south of the city centre and there are shuttle links between the international and domestic terminals. Train is by far the best way to travel between the airport and the city, taking around 15 minutes. The stations are situated below the International and domestic terminals. Trains depart approximately every 10 minutes weekdays and 15 minutes at weekends between 0500–2345 (later Sat–Sun). $11; tel: 131 500; www.airportlink.com.au. By taxi the journey takes about 25 minutes and costs around $25 (passengers pay any road and airport toll charges).

There are three main routes into Sydney, each comprehensively signposted. From the south, Hwy 1 comes in from Botany Bay and alongside the airport, where it turns into a freeway called Southern Cross Drive that splits into South Dowling St and the Eastern Distributor (northbound toll $4.00). The approach through the northern suburbs brings you to the Harbour Bridge or the Harbour Tunnel (both have a $3 toll entering the city, but are free on leaving). From the west, the Blue Mountains and Melbourne the Western Motorway enters the city as Broadway and, as it passes the Central Railway, becomes George St, which runs through the heart of the city. A car is not necessarily the best way of getting around Sydney (see p. 78).

All long-distance buses come into the Sydney Coach Terminal, on the corner of Eddy Ave and Pitt St; tel: 9281 9366. The national railway station is above the Coach Terminal.

INFORMATION

TOURIST OFFICES **The Sydney Visitor Centre**, 106 George St, The Rocks; tel: 9240 8788. A cut above most visitor centres with very knowledgeable staff. It has a large range of free brochures and magazines and also a useful map of the area, $. Open daily 0930–1730. www.sydneyvisitorcentre.com, e-mail visitorinformation@shfa.nsw.gov.au. Information for wider New South Wales is also available here or tel: 13 20 77; www.visitnsw.com.au.

The Sydney Visitor Centre – Darling Harbour (behind the Imax Theatre), Darling Harbour; tel: 9240 8788. Open daily 0930–1730. Helpful staff with particular knowledge on the Darling Harbour area. www.darlingharbour.com.au.

INTERNET ACCESS As with most cities, Sydney libraries offer free internet access; however, terminals are in demand, so bookings are necessary. Some libraries, including the State Library, now block e-mail sites such as Hotmail and only allow you to use the terminals for research purposes.

The top end of George St (near Sydney Coach Terminal) has numerous internet cafés all in competition with each other – hence offering the best rates.

Almost every inexpensive hotel or hostel has internet access; most places have computers with ISDN connections.

INTERNET SITES According to Yahoo there are about 375,000 sites that deal with Sydney. The ones that follow are probably the best starting points. Yahoo rates Sydney Online at www.sydney.com.au as the best of the bunch. I think **Walkabout** by Fairfax at www.walkabout.com.au/locations/NSWSydney.shtml is somewhat superior. Almost all of them are designed for visitors on unlimited budgets, so the restaurants listed in these sites, for example, provide wonderful food but, almost without exception, fall in the $$$$ bracket.

City of Sydney: www.sydneycity.nsw.gov.au

Free Maps of Sydney: www.whereis.com.au

Sydney City Net: www.sydneycity.net

Sydney Citysearch: www.sydney.citysearch.com.au

Sydney Online: www.sydney.com.au

Sydney Restaurant Information: www.bestrestaurants.com.au

Sydney Transport Routes and Timetables: www.131500.com.au

MONEY Travelex has several foreign exchange offices which are open outside normal banking hours. In Central Sydney these are at: 175 Pitt St; tel: 9231 2523; and The Queen Victoria Building, George St; tel: 9264 1267. There are 15 locations within the international airport, tel: 9317 2100.

POST AND PHONES Australia Post has several branches in the city centre. The GPO at 1 Martin Place opens Mon–Fri 0830–1730 and Sat 1000–1400. A Post Restante facility is available at 310 George St, open Mon–Fri 0830–1730.

The telephone code for Sydney and all of NSW is 02.

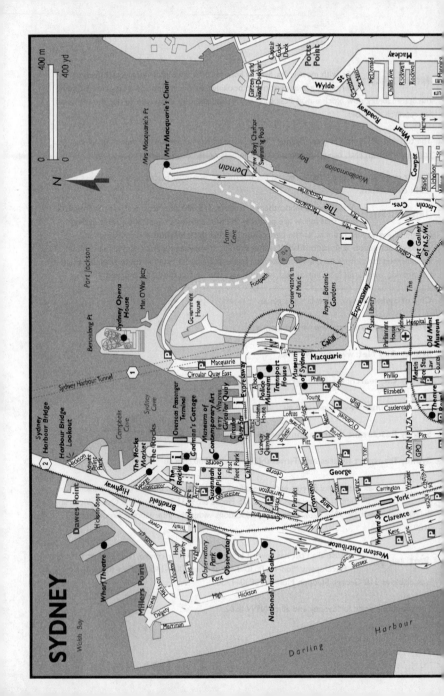

ACCOMMODATION

Staying in the city centre has its advantages, but hotels a little further out are cheaper and often the better option. Glebe is becoming increasingly popular, although it still has a lot of the alternative lifestyle about it. Kings Cross, Sydney's red-light district, is a very convenient location to the city, but is not the quietest of places. Staying in Manly can be pleasant, plus you have the bonus of the ferry ride to the city to start your day.

It is also worth checking out the major hotel chains, which are all represented in the city. They sometimes offer special deals, especially at the weekend. The Sydney Visitor Centre at Sydney Airport, tel: 9667 6050, e-mail:accombookings@tourism. nsw.gov.au, can book hotel accommodation at discounted rates.

CENTRAL SYDNEY	**Carlton Crest Hotel $$$$** 169–179 Thomas St; tel: 9281 6888.
	Castlereagh Inn $$$$ 169 Castlereagh St; tel: 9284 1000.
	Central Railway Motel $$$$ 240 Chalmers St; tel: 9319 7800.
	Grand Hotel $$$$ 30 Hunter St; tel: 9232 3755.
	Hyde Park Inn $$$$ 271 Elizabeth St; tel: 9264 6001.
	Mercantile Hotel (The Rocks) $$$$ 25 George St. Note this is a pub and can be noisy; tel: 9247 3570.
	Oaks Hyde Park Plaza $$$$+ 38 College St; tel: 9331 6933.
	Royal Garden International Hotel $$$$ 431–439 Pitt St; tel: 9281 6999.
GLEBE AND NEWTOWN	**Haven Inn $$$$** 196 Glebe Point Rd; tel: 9660 6655.
MANLY	**Manly Pacific Parkroyal $$$$+** 55 North Steyne; tel: 9977 7666.
	Manly Paradise Motel & Apartments $$$$ 54 North Steyne; tel: 9977 5799.
	Manly Seaview Motel $$$$ Cnr Malvern Ave and Pacific St; tel: 9977 1774.
	Radisson Kestrel Hotel $$$$+ 8 South Steyne; tel: 9977 8866.
OTHER	**Kirketon Hotel $$$$** 229 Darlinghurst Rd, Darlinghurst; tel: 9332 2011.
	Hampton Court Hotel $$$$ 9 Bayswater Rd, Kings Cross; tel: 9357 2711. Located in the centre of Kings Cross, good facilities.
	Olympic Hotel $$$ 308 Moore Park Rd, Paddington; tel: 9361 6315.

VERY CHEAP LODGINGS

Sydney is somewhat expensive by Australian standards; the following accommodation listings are some of the cheapest available.

Billabong Gardens Motel/Backpackers $$$$ 5–11 Egan St, Newtown; tel: 9550 3236; website: www.billabonggardens.com.au. Pool and barbecue.

Boardrider Backpacker Manly $$$–$$$$ Rear 63 The Corso; tel: 9977 6077. 15-minute jetcat ride from the city. Walk to surf beach. Website: www.boardrider.com.au.

City Central Backpackers $ 752 George St; tel: 9212 4833; www.ccbackpack.com.au. Very convenient location for the city. Dorm beds only.

Cronulla Beach YHA $$$ Level 1, 40–42 Kingsway, Cronulla; tel: 9527 7772; website www.cronullabeachyha.com. Close to the beach; trains to city.

Eva's Backpackers $$$ 6 Orwell St, Kings Cross; tel: 9358 2185. Small, hence a nice friendly atmosphere.

George Private Hotel $$$ 700A George St; tel: 9211 1800. Very clean conservative budget hotel, shared facilities, located near Town Hall.

Highfield Private Hotel $$$ 166 Victoria St, Potts Point; tel: 9326 9539. One of the cleaner and more civilised of the budget accommodations in the area. Run by a Swedish family.

Maze Backpackers CB $ 417 Pitt St; tel: 9211 5115 or 1800 813 522; website: www.mazebackpackers.com. Right in the heart of the city.

Sydney Central YHA $–$$$$ 11 Rawson Pl., cnr Pitt St and Rawson Pl.; tel: 9281 9111; website: www.yha.com.au/hostels. Located by central bus and train stations.

Sydney Glebe Point YHA $–$$$ 262–264 Glebe Point Rd; tel: 9692 8418; website: www.yha.com.au/hostels. Close to restaurants and cafés, regular buses to the city.

Y on the Park Hotel $$–$$$$ 5–11 Wentworth Ave (opposite Hyde Park); tel: 9264 2451; www.ywca-sydney.com.au. YWCA accommodation with comfortable rooms in the heart of Sydney's CBD. Price includes breakfast.

FOOD AND DRINK

In the past 20 years the Sydney restaurant scene has transformed itself. Greeks, Italians and, more recently, Thais, Japanese and Indonesians have ensured that the choice of cuisine is eclectic, interesting and reasonably priced. With the advantage of a wealth of fresh ingredients and such a mix of culinary traditions, the Pacific Rim style is, at its best, an exciting fusion of colours, aromas and tastes.

CIRCULAR QUAY

A range of new restaurants opening in the eastern side of the harbour (by the Opera House) means increased competition, hence you can have a nice meal while watching the boats come and go for a relatively good price. On the western side of the harbour (by the Harbour Bridge) the restaurants are a lot more expensive yet are well worth it if you want to treat yourself.

City Extra $$$$ Circular Quay, opposite Manly ferry terminal; tel: 9241 1422. Open 24 hours a day, extremely busy fast-paced restaurant, selling everything from stylish burgers to chow mein.

Italian Village $$$$ 7 Circular Quay West, The Rocks; tel: 9247 6111. In a recovered warehouse, three levels decorated with Italian decor and artefacts.

Sydney Cove Oyster Bar $$$$ No 1 East Circular Quay; tel: 9247 2937. Outdoor seafood restaurant, great views.

CENTRAL SYDNEY

Bodhi Vegetarian Restaurant $$ 2–4 College St; tel: 9360 2523. Good food at excellent value, open daily.

Malaya $$$ 39 Lime St, King St Wharf; tel: 9279 1170. Inexpensive Malay/Singaporean food. Try the laksa, which is brilliant.

Revolving Sydney Tower Restaurants $$$$ Centrepoint; 100 Market St; tel: 8223 3800. Expensive but well worth it. Sit in one of the two restaurants, near the top of the tallest buildings in the southern hemisphere. Open daily – bookings recommended.

Darling Harbour's Harbourside Shopping Centre and the adjacent Cockle Bay Wharf have a variety of eateries ranging from express takeaway food outlets to sophisticated restaurants. The views over Darling Harbour and the city are magnificent.

The Blackbird Café $$ Balcony Level, Cockle Bay Wharf; tel: 9283 7385. Lively café offering quality meals at reasonable prices. Open daily 0800 until late.

Zaafran $$$$ Level 2, 345 Harbourside Shopping Ctr; tel: 9211 8900. Traditional Indian cuisine with a modern presentation. Open daily for lunch and dinner.

NEWTOWN

Newtown, which has one of the more interesting high streets, was formerly something of a student-share-house, low-rent area and the prices reflect this. You'll find inexpensive eating and shopping – including many businesses with an alternative twist. Here are some of the more exotic eateries.

Eat me Sushi $$ 258 King St; tel: 9517 2012. Eat in or take away sushi bar.

Kilimanjaro African Eatery $$ 280 King St; tel: 9557 4565. A West African eatery, small and cosy, with staff in traditional West African dress. Most food is steamed in traditional clay pots.

Sling 'n' Satay $$$ 152–154 King St; tel: 9516 2817. Satay is a speciality here, prepared to a traditional Singaporean recipe. Open for dinner Tues–Sun.

Suan I San $$ 480 King St; tel: 9557 6722. Authentic Thai cuisine. Open daily from 1200–2300.

OTHER

Botanic Gardens Restaurant $$$$ Mrs Macquaries Rd; tel: 9241 2419. Have lunch surrounded by the flora and fauna of the Botanic Gardens.

South Steyne floating restaurant $$$$ Darling Harbour, by the Maritime Museum; tel: 9211 5999. Dine aboard a ship. This vessel sailed from Scotland to Australia in 1938, and now sits in Darling Harbour serving steaks, seafood and salads.

Sydney Showboats $$$$ embark/disembark King St Wharf 5; tel: 8296 7200. Dinner cruises depart every night featuring a variety of entertainment in the tradition of Moulin Rouge. Good atmosphere, booking necessary.

YUM CHA RESTAURANTS

Although not as inexpensive as you might think, but still remarkable value for money, are the *yum cha* restaurants clustered around the Haymarket in Chinatown. Literally the name means to drink tea, but it normally involves choosing the dishes you want from series of circulating trolleys or trays. The quality is as good as in Hong Kong or Taiwan; in the case of the Marigold, perhaps better.

East Ocean $$$ 421–429 Sussex St; tel: 9212 4198. Extremely busy.

Golden Harbour $$$ 31–33 Dixon St; tel: 9212 5987.

Dragon Star Seafood Restaurant $$$$ Level 3, 9 Hay St, Haymarket; tel: 9211 8988.

Marigold $$$$ 683 George St; tel: 9281 3388.

GETTING AROUND

For almost all visitors the answer is the **Sydney Pass** ($$$), which gives unlimited travel for either three, five or seven days on all the city's buses, ferries, central CityRail services, the jetcat to Manly and the high-speed RiverCat to Parramatta. It also includes return travel on AirportLink trains, with the return journey valid for two months. The only services Sydney Pass does not include are Monorail services, private bus and ferry services, and train trips beyond the Red Travel Pass zone; tel: 131500; internet www.sydneypass.info. Using the pass you can enjoy all the sights of Sydney without ever thinking of using a car.

Driving in Sydney is nowhere near as efficient as using public transport. Because of the many harbour inlets the roads tend to be narrow and parking is at a premium. All the major hire car companies are, of course, present at the airport. Cheaper, off-airport companies include:

Ascot Car Rentals, 113 William St, Kings Cross; tel: 9332 3777; www.ascotcarrental. com.au. Centrally located.

Bayswater Car Rentals, 180 William St, Kings Cross; tel: 9360 3622; www.bayswater carrental. com.au.

HIGHLIGHTS

The best way to orient yourself is to first take one of the Sydney **Explorer Buses** which circulate around the city and stop at 26 of the top tourist attractions. They follow a 28-km loop around the city. Sydney Explorer buses leave Circular Quay at 20-minute intervals from 0840. A ticket ($$$) is valid for one day; tel: 131500; internet: www.sydneypass.info.

Having obtained an overview, start walking. Sydney is a city made for walkers, with shelter from the sun and the rain provided by the awnings that line most of the streets.

Sydney ferries run morning, afternoon and evening trips from Circular Quay around the harbour with commentary, $$$; tel: 131500; internet: www.sydneyferries.info.

A nifty little visitor gadget – the 'See Sydney & Beyond Smartvisit Card' (www.seesydneycard.com; tel 1300 661 711) – offers great savings if used intelligently. For instance, the one-day card ($65) would allow you time to take a Harbour Jet jetblast ride and to visit the Sydney Aquarium, activities that combined would normally cost $85 per person. There are also two- ($119), three- ($149) and seven-day ($209) cards available.

AROUND SYDNEY COVE

Sydney's two great man-made landmarks are the Harbour Bridge and the Opera House. The water between them, an inlet of the greater harbour, is Sydney Cove. Circular Quay, at its southern end, is, of course, not circular, but the original name has stuck.

Nowadays, the **Opera House** is such a part of Sydney that it is difficult to remember the anguish that surrounded its creation. A rough sketch of the possibilities of such a building by the architectural genius Jörn Utzon, submitted to an international competition in 1956, was initially almost ignored, but was eventually selected as the plan most suited to the site's unique position on Bennelong Point.

The technology for much of what Utzon designed did not exist and had to be invented as the job went along. As a result there were staggering cost escalations, met by the Opera House lottery, and a final bill of over $100 million. In the end Utzon resigned – driven out by government philistines is a widely accepted theory, but there are two sides to every argument – and the great building was completed by others. It opened in 1973 to a fanfare of trumpets.

Today the cost is forgotten, the greatness remains. It is one of the major architectural achievements of the world. Technically, though, it is not an opera house – you cannot hold major productions there as the stages and backstage areas are too small. Billy Wentworth, Sydney MP and minister, said that the Sydney Opera House was the greatest public-relations building since the pyramids. He may well be right. You can go on a guided tour of the Opera House ($$$). These run right through the day from 0900–1700 and last up to one hour; tel: 9250 7250.

Next to the Opera House are the cafés, restaurants, cinema and shops of the East Circular Quay development, a controversial project now accepted by most residents of Sydney.

The **Harbour Bridge** is, for the people of Sydney, a reality that they know is there but hardly ever think about. The **Pylon Lookout** inside the Bridge's south-east pylon is open every day and from it you have marvellous views of Sydney Harbour; open daily 1000–1700 ($$); tel: 9240 1100.

For a different perspective on the city and the harbour, you can climb to the top of the bridge – with a **BridgeClimb** guide and a lot of safety equipment. You cannot take a camera but photos will be taken of you. You make your way over 1500 m of steel as you venture across catwalks, steep ladders and arches until you reach the top, 134 m above sea level. It is a climb of a lifetime, but does come fairly expensive, from $155. The climb operates daily (except 30th and 31st Dec) usually at ten-minute intervals from 0700 to 1900, and lasts approximately 3½ hours with preparation and a guided commentary. All twilight climbs are $225. There are also night climbs ($160 Mon–Thur; $185 Fri–Sun). Check in at 5 Cumberland St, The Rocks; tel: 8274 7777; www.bridgeclimb.com.au.

A Remarkable Prediction

In 1789 Erasmus Darwin, grandfather of Charles Darwin, wrote an epigraph to the official volume *The Voyage of Governor Phillip to Botany Bay.* At the end he makes a remarkable prediction:

'There the proud arch, Colossus-like, bestride on glittering streams, and bound the chafing tide …'

a description that uncannily fits Sydney Harbour Bridge but written 143 years before the bridge was opened.

The busy ferry terminals are on the south side of Sydney Cove, and the Overseas Passenger Terminal, opened in 1961, is regularly used by the largest liners that enter Sydney. The first wharf in Australia was built here by Robert Campbell in 1800, and his warehousing is now transmogrified into a trio of delightful restaurants.

Harbour Views

The venerable Manly ferry service – introduced in 1847 – still provides the best and cheapest views of Sydney Harbour. The 30-min, one-way journey from Circular Quay to beachside Manly costs $6.

Captain Cook Cruises operate a variety of sightseeing and dining harbour cruises, some with onboard entertainment. The Harbour Highlights Cruise is good value at $22. There are daily departures at 1100, 1245, 1430, 1600 and 1800 ($$$); No. 6 Jetty, Circular Quay; tel: 9206 1122; www.captcookcrus.com.au/sydney.

Although the **Museum of Contemporary Art** is officially in George St its front entrance is on Circular Quay, on the site of a government commissariat store built in 1812. The MCA is home to over 7000 artworks acquired since the 1960s through the J W Power Bequest. Extensive Aboriginal collections are also held in trust. The museum has an active programme of changing international exhibitions. Free guided tours run twice daily. Open daily 1000–1700; tel: 9254 2400; www.mca.com.au.

The Rocks

The area rising up to the west of Sydney Cove, loosely defined by Grosvenor St and a loop of George St to the south and the road that crosses Sydney Harbour Bridge to the west, is known as The Rocks (www.therocks.com). It was allegedly named by working parties of convicts who landed with the First Fleet and is the oldest area of Sydney.

By 1970 The Rocks away from the waterfront was in sad disarray, and developers were ready to rebuild the area as high-rise collections of offices and apartments.

Jack Mundey and the Builders Labourers Federation instituted a series of 'green bans' during the 70s to stop this havoc. If he had not done so The Rocks as we know it today would have totally disappeared. Intelligent redevelopment and restoration have created what is now one of the most interesting and attractive areas of Sydney.

There are those who would say that The Rocks has become yuppified and made into a tourist shopping area. If there is some truth in that statement, it has been executed in a style that is immensely attractive and the standard of shopping is very high. The Rocks is strong enough in both buildings and personality to survive any such minor onslaughts – it has survived almost everything else (see box on p. 82).

George Street, now the central street of Sydney, began as a track connecting the hospital (more a collection of unsanitary huts) with the main settlement. Once you pass the Regent Hotel in George St you are in The Rocks. There were stocks in George St but they were later removed because they caused an obstruction. For even in those days there were traffic problems: the narrow alleys and steps were barely wide enough for two people to pass side by side. Argyle Street, which visitors now saunter up with pleasure, was a foot track too steep for wheeled vehicles, and the Argyle Steps were hewn to make passage easier. In 1843 it was decided to make a deep cutting underneath The Rocks. The Argyle Cut was the last major work started by convicts (it was finished by labourers and the use of explosives). It is still the main east–west thoroughfare through The Rocks and an impressive engineering feat.

Although The Rocks does not cover a very large area, it is a maze of very small nooks and crannies, and a map can be most useful. The Sydney Visitor Centre in George St (see p. 70) can supply one and also publishes a wonderful booklet called *The Rocks Self-Guided Tour* ($), which pinpoints 31 places of historical interest as part of a local **heritage walk**.

Just down from the visitor centre is **Cadman's Cottage**, which was built in 1816 and is the oldest house in Sydney. It was nearly destroyed when they built the passenger terminal in 1960, but was reprieved by the Maritime Services Board. This four-room stone cottage was living quarters for the coxswain and crew of the governor's gig. At the time the back door of the cottage was less than two metres from the water's edge. The original cottage had a thatched – or perhaps tiled – roof and the galvanized roof was put on in the 1890s. Cadman, the coxswain, who had been sentenced to transportation for the term of his natural life, was later pardoned, but preferred to remain in Australia. He lived in the cottage for 29 years, ending up as Superintendent of Government Boats, and died in 1848. The cottage is now the base for the Sydney Harbour National Park Information Centre. Open weekdays 0930–1630, weekends 1000–1630. Tel: 9247 5033.

THE ROCKS IN THE EARLY DAYS

The Rocks was indeed the birthplace of Australia but for many years it was a prison camp where deported criminals were guarded by soldiers who were, in truth, not much better. There were problems with drainage, with corrupt officials, with transportation. Later, it became the refuge of prostitutes, drunks, sailors and criminals.

In The Rocks were built the first observatory in Australia, the first warehouses, the first flour mill and bakery, the first military camp, the first cemetery. Flogging was common and the hangman was often at work.

The forerunner of the formal police force began here as 12 watchmen appointed by the governor. They later covered the waterfront to prevent the escape of prisoners and the smuggling of rum. In 1817 the service came under the control of John Cadman and the watchmen were renamed constables. They were relatively disciplined and well-organised, but hardly had a chance against convicts in the maze of narrow alleys and with easy access to the sea.

The Rocks became notorious for gangs of criminals – in Australia called pushes – who fought with cut-throat razors and struck terror into the hearts of the general public. The pushes all had colourful names – the Cabbage Tree Mob, the Orange and the Green – and they defended their territories ferociously. The standard dress was tight trousers with bell-bottoms and a slouch hat set at the back of the head. (The term 'push' came into popularity again after the Second World War to describe some of the literary and bohemian sets of Sydney; the dress was not that dissimilar.)

What stopped the gangs was not the police but bubonic plague, which struck at the end of the 19th century. In an effort to contain the plague great tracts of The Rocks were burned or demolished. Much more then disappeared in the building of Sydney Harbour Bridge, which effectively split The Rocks from Millers Point, and in the construction of the Cahill Expressway.

Susannah Place, 58–64 Gloucester Street, is a museum in a working-class terrace of four brick houses built in 1844 and now incorporates a turn-of-the-20th-century corner shop. Open 1000–1700 weekends ($$); tel: 9241 1893.

George St does a left turn under the Bradfield Hwy to join Lower Fort St which leads up to Observatory Hill. Fort St was the route the troops took between the fort and the garrison church in Argyle Place. From the hilltop are views down over Millers Point and the harbour. The Observatory used to have a time ball signal which gave ships in the harbour the exact time every day at 1300. Since 1982 it has been a museum of astronomy. Open daily 1000–1700, free. 3-D Space Theatre ($$). Open Mon–Fri 1430 and 1530, weekends and NSW school holidays 1100, 1200, 1400 and 1530. Night sessions ($$$) run every evening, with a two-hour tour and chance to view the sky through telescopes. Bookings necessary; tel: 9241 3767.

MILLERS POINT AND WALSH BAY

In the 1820s some of the more respectable and richer citizens started to build large houses on the heights above The Rocks. The two most fashionable streets were Cumberland and Prince's, and some examples of these houses can be found around Argyle Place in the **Millers Point** area. The old cobbled streets remain and most of the colonial buildings have been restored to their former beauty. The Point is thought to have got its name from John Leighton, known as Jack the Miller, who ran three windmills here from 1795 to 1800. Billy Blue, a black boatman, ran his ferry service from here across the harbour to what is now known as Blues Point on the northern shore.

The old piers and warehouses of Walsh Bay, between Millers Point and Dawes Point, have been given a new lease of life. **Pier One** is a converted wharf containing a hotel. Further down on Pier Four are the headquarters of the Sydney Dance Company and Sydney Theatre Company. The Wharf Theatre has a fine restaurant which is hardly known, yet affords superb views and excellent food and wine ($$$$); tel: 9250 1761.

PUBS IN THE ROCKS

In 1810 the Judge Advocate listed some 50 licensed taverns in the Sydney area, and most of them were in The Rocks. They had splendid names – The Sheer Hulk, The Labor in Vain, The Hit or Miss, The Lord Nelson (which still exists), The Rose of Australia, The World Turned Upside Down, and The Erin Go Bragh. The drink of the time was rum – the only beer available was called Stringy Bark and was not considered a gourmet's tipple.

Here, in strict alphabetical order so that we cannot be accused of favouritism, are some of the present-day pubs of The Rocks. All of them serve, at the very least, counter meals. Eating in this way tends to be relatively inexpensive and the surroundings are always fascinating. When you are exploring Sydney Cove and Circular Quay and the Opera House these are all within walking distance.

The Australian Hotel, 100 Cumberland St, has its own brewery, brewing German-style beers. **The Brooklyn Hotel**, 225 George St. **Fortune of War**, 137 George St; another old pub with great traditions. **Glenmore Hotel**, 96 Cumberland St. **Hero of Waterloo**, 81 Lower Fort St; one of the oldest pubs in the area. **Lord Nelson**, 19 Kent St, has its own brewery on the premises and makes an excellent wheat beer which is highly spoken of by connoisseurs. **Mercantile Hotel**, 25 George St; an Irish pub which frequently has Irish bands; built in 1915. The **Observer Hotel**, 69 George St; bistro on the premises. **Orient Hotel**, 89 George St, perhaps the pub most frequented by tourists, has a first-rate restaurant. **Phillip's Foote**, 101 George St, serves barbecues in the garden.

CENTRAL SYDNEY: THE REST

South of Circular Quay, between George St and Macquarie St, lies the heart of central Sydney. Several of the streets are pedestrian malls. Down past Market St is the Town Hall. Across the road, the **Queen Victoria Building** was, a century ago, the fruit and vegetable market of Sydney but has now been restored and contains nearly 200 shops. The statue of Queen Victoria that sits outside was the result of a worldwide search – it was eventually found in Ireland.

WATERSIDE WALK

Walk along the western side of Sydney Cove until you come to the Overseas Passenger Terminal, then take an escalator to the top level and enjoy the elevated views. There are stairs down at the end or you can walk down the short street until you are back at water level. If you continue on, past the elegantly designed Park Hyatt, Hickson Rd will take you past Dawes Point and then hook smartly under Sydney Harbour Bridge and back on the other side of the peninsula, to Walsh Bay and its piers. Return via the remnant defence battery directly under the bridge deck in Dawes Point Park.

On the corner of Pitt and Market Sts, in Centrepoint, is the **Sydney Tower**. This is one of the tallest buildings in the southern hemisphere at 305 m above street level. The observation deck offers great 360° views of the city – a must for all visitors to Sydney. Open Sun–Fri 0900–2230 and Sat 0900–2330 ($$$); tel: 8251 7800.

Heading uphill to the east will bring you to **Hyde Park**, which is, as you would imagine, named after London's Hyde Park. It is one of the green lungs of Sydney and daft notions by the city council to lease out part of the park to commercial interests have been scotched. The **Hyde Park Barracks Museum** is further up Macquarie St. These barracks were designed by Francis Greenway (see p. 69) and built to house convicts, but, beautifully restored, they are now a museum of social history with many convict relics. Open daily 0930–1700 ($$); tel: 9223 8922.

The **Australian Museum** alongside the park, on the corner of William and College Sts, is Australia's oldest museum – it was founded in 1827 and opened to the public at its present location in 1857. It has Australia's largest natural history collection, and smaller but equally excellent anthropology collections if your interest is in Aboriginal Australians, and is continually putting on themed displays. The frequent special exhibitions are worth visiting. Open daily 0930–1700 ($$); tel: 9320 6000; www.amonline.net.au.

The chain of parks continues northwards with the Domain, which stretches out in front of Parliament House. Just beyond Parliament House, a little further along Macquarie St, is the **State Library of New South Wales**. This is an exemplar of what a library should be: modern, inviting and efficient. The library contains Australia's finest collection of Australian history and a superb reference collection (the Mitchell and Dixson libraries). The library also hosts a range of free exhibitions throughout the year. Open Mon–Fri 0900–2100, Sat and Sun 1100–1700; tel: 9273 1414.

On the eastern flank of the Domain is the **Art Gallery of New South Wales**. The gallery is housed in a spectacular building and consistently puts on brilliant displays of its vast collection of Australian, European, Asian and Aboriginal art. The problem is that it has nowhere near enough space to display its treasures. What it really needs is another major gallery. Free, although fees apply to visiting exhibitions. Open daily 1000–1700 (Wed 1000–2100); tel: 9225 1744; www.artgallery.nsw.gov.au.

From the art gallery you can gently stroll back to Macquarie St and make your way downhill towards the Opera House and the harbour. Near the Opera House are the **Royal Botanic Gardens**, another of the green lungs of Sydney. The gardens are situated on the edge of Farm Cove and have the sea on one side and Macquarie St on the other. Among its attractions are the field of wild flowers, the tropical glasshouse and the walk along the harbour's edge, with some of the finest views of the harbour and, of course, the Opera House. Open daily sunrise to sunset; entry is free, although there is a small charge to visit the Tropical Centre. The Botanic Gardens Visitor Centre (open daily 0930–1630) can give further details; tel: 9231 8125.

DARLING HARBOUR AND CHINATOWN

West of the central business district, Darling Harbour (www.darlingharbour.com) contains what is almost certainly the best convention centre in the southern hemisphere. Apart from the convention centre, Darling Harbour contains the **Harbourside Shopping Centre** (replete with shops, cafés and restaurants), **Sydney Aquarium**, the **Australian National Maritime Museum** and **Cockle Bay Wharf**, where there's another range of cafés and restaurants.

The **Sydney Aquarium** is one of the best of its type in the world and well worth visiting. There is a walk-through tunnel which magnifies the size of the fish; other highlights include a big collection of sharks, Great Barrier Reef display and new seal sanctuary. The aquarium, which is right on Darling Harbour, is open 0900–2200 every day; $$$; tel: 8251 7800; website: www.sydneyaquarium.com.au.

The **Australian National Maritime Museum** across the harbour from the aquarium, is excellent. There is a wide range of artefacts on display as well as several historic vessels. It is open daily 0930–1700; tel: 9298 3777. Free entry, $$ special exhibitions and historic vessels.

The **Powerhouse Museum**, an easy stroll from Darling Harbour, has modern and exciting displays of the decorative arts, science, technology and social history. Despite only a fraction of the collection being on display, it is very interactive and has a lot of 'Australian inventions' in the collection. Open daily 0930–1700 ($$); tel: 9217 0111.

It is easy to walk to **Chinatown** from Darling Harbour or from

George St a block away. The main street is Dixon which has colourful arches at the entrance. Chinatown is full of good, some great, Chinese restaurants. Adjoining Chinatown, beside Darling Harbour, is the **Chinese Garden of Friendship** ($$), well worth a visit for its peace and tranquillity. The garden's design is based on the ancient yin yang principle – creating a balancing effect. There's a range of ponds, lakes, mini forests and pavilions. Open daily 0930–1630 ($$); tel: 9281 6863.

Beaches

One of the joys of Sydney is that you are never far from a beach. While there are some complaints of pollution on some of the beaches they are magnetic attractions in the summer.

The most famous beach is **Bondi**, 8 km from the city. It is, strangely, not one of the great Sydney beaches, but it has the name, is on a pleasant part of the coast and the main street fronting the beach has some splendid cafés.

The northern beaches, starting just north of Manly and heading up to Palm Beach, are all excellent. Palm Beach is where part of the Australian soap *Home and Away* is filmed. The filming schedule is not available to the public (and filming only takes place occasionally), but as a rule go on a weekday afternoon and you're in with a chance.

SHOPPING

At the weekend the north end of George Street is closed to cars and covered with awnings, to become **The Rocks Market**. Its 150-plus stalls are open Sat–Sun from 1000–1700. The market is alive with buskers, music groups, clowns and street entertainment of all sorts. Many of the local shop owners started as traders in the market. On the corner of Hay and Thomas Sts (by Chinatown and Darling Harbour) every Thur–Sun 0900–1700 is **Paddy's Market**. Here, you can get almost anything from fruit and veg to clothes and crafts. Tel: 1300 361 589.

Done Rocks

See artist Ken Done's bright work at The Rocks Gallery, 1–5 Hickson Rd. Open daily 1000–1730; tel: 9247 2740. The nearby Done retail shop (123–125 George St) sells Done-inspired clothes, gifts and homewares.

EVENTS

Sydney hosts a range of festivals each year. The tourist offices will be happy to give you free copies of *Sydney – The Official Guide*, *This Week in Sydney*, *What's On in Sydney*, or *Where* magazines, which list events, nightlife and things to see and do in the city.

The Sydney Festival is held every year in Jan. It hosts a number of popular events and performances, including the much-loved Domain outdoor concert series where classical, opera, jazz, blues and country music are performed to huge crowds. There is also a high-quality theatre and music programme, featuring the best of Australian and overseas artists. www.sydneyfestival.org.au.

The **Gay and Lesbian Mardi Gras** each Feb/Mar is one of the most tremendous celebrations in the world, supported by institutions as straight as the police, the government and various banks. www.mardigras.org.au.

NIGHTLIFE

The best guide to shows is in Friday's *Metro* supplement of the *Sydney Morning Herald*; this gives details of every show, gig and happening.

The theatre in Sydney is good in parts. No one can accurately count how many theatres there are in Sydney because it depends on your definition. But it is somewhere between ten and twenty.

The **Sydney Opera House** (tel: 9250 7777) may not be able to stage full-scale opera but it does have a live theatre which works well enough. Major international stars touring Australia perform at the **Sydney Entertainment Centre** in Harbour St, Darling Harbour (tel: 13 61 00 for bookings; 9320 4200 for enquiries).

The **Sydney Theatre Company** at the Wharf Theatre is a true repertory company (tel: 9250 1777 for bookings; 9250 1700 for enquiries) with an excellent restaurant. The **Ensemble Theatre** on the other side of the harbour also has a good restaurant and every now and again stages a production which astounds with its excellence. It is at 78 McDougall St, Kirribilli; tel: 9929 0644.

The **Capitol** (13 Campbell St, tel: 1300 855 445 for bookings, 9320 5000 for enquiries) presents a range of musical, opera and ballet productions; the fine old theatre's future was threatened for years before extensive restoration work was undertaken in the 1990s. The **Theatre Royal** at the MLC Centre in King St has its moments and is always worth checking (tel: 9266 4800 for bookings; 9224 8444 for enquiries). The **Seymour Theatre Centre** is part of Sydney University at Chippendale (cnr City Rd and Cleveland St) and has three theatres and sometimes productions that electrify; tel: 9351 7940.

The Basement, 29 Reiby Place, Circular Quay, runs jazz evenings at which you can have a late supper and listen to some of the great jazz players of our time. It tends to be crowded late in the evening so check before turning up; tel: 9251 2797.

The only permanent comedy venue in Sydney is the **Sydney Comedy Store**, at Fox Studios, Driver Ave, Moore Park; tel: 9357 1419. It hosts original stand-up comedy and improvised comedy specials.

Sydney's pop music scene is very large, with never fewer than 70 gigs playing at the weekends: check for bands and venues in *Metro*.

The Sydney Superdome at Olympic Park, Homebush (tel: 8765 4321; www. superdome.com.au), is Australia's biggest indoor sports and entertainment centre. It was purpose-built to host the gymnastics, trampoline and basketball finals for the Sydney 2000 Olympics. It can accommodate up to 20,000 spectators and now hosts a variety of events from sporting and motocross competitions to concerts and all-night dance-party extravaganzas.

Sydney's sin centre is **Kings Cross** and, yes, you can walk around there without being mugged. The bright lights, cheap eateries and clubs make the area especially appealing to the younger traveller.

Oxford St rolls up from Hyde Park to Paddington. This is Sydney's gay capital and is colourful and stylish. There are cafés, bars and little restaurants galore and, very much later in the evening, shows that you should not take Aunt Ethel to see.

DAY TRIPS

If you visit the harbour via the bridge or the tunnel the first thing to greet you on the north shore is office blocks. Instead, take one of the many ferries from Circular Quay so that you can enjoy something of the harbour and its views, and visit some of the myriad coves, headlands and small resorts. **Manly**, a half-hour ferry ride away, has always been a holiday suburb for Sydney – reminiscent of many English seaside towns but with more charm and much more sunshine. There is a pedestrian mall, The Corso, which has restaurants and shops.

Watsons Bay, at the furthermost end of the harbour, just before the open ocean, has stunning views, pleasant small beaches and some pretty houses. But you can find those in many other places in Sydney. What you cannot find elsewhere is **Doyle's on the Beach** ($$$$), the perfect place to be on a sunny day with a bottle of chilled white wine and a feast of the best seafood Australia has to offer (11 Marine Parade; tel: 9337 2007).

The **Australian Reptile Park and Wildlife Sanctuary** at Somersby, Gosford (see p. 236), about an hour north of Sydney, makes a great day out, with crocodiles, snakes and giant tortoises on view but also cuddly koalas, kangaroos, wallabies and other uniquely Australian species. You can get there by car, coach or train; tel: 4340 1022 or visit www.reptilepark.com.au for details. Open daily 0900–1700, $$$.

The **Hawkesbury River** is a couple of hours' drive to the north of Sydney. A cruise up that most lovely river, with national parkland on both sides, takes you further away from city life than you would believe possible. The Riverboat Postman leaves the town of Brooklyn (accessible by train from Central Station) Mon–Fri at 0930 and will take you to houses only accessible by river. There are also 1330 cruises Sun–Fri (minimum eight passengers, bookings essential); tel 9985 7566 for details.

The **Blue Mountains** offer another exhilarating day trip from Sydney (see p. 90).

WHERE NEXT?

After a look at sights near Sydney (see Blue Mountains, p. 90) and an excursion to Canberra (p. 101), consider making Sydney your starting point for a grand loop of south-eastern Australia. Take the Sydney–Adelaide route (pp. 124–139) to South Australia, explore the Barossa Valley (p. 157) then travel to Melbourne (p. 178) via the coast, taking in the fabulous Great Ocean Road (pp. 201–221). Return to Sydney by following in reverse our Sydney–Melbourne coastal route (pp. 117–123).

THE BLUE MOUNTAINS

Mark Twain said of the Blue Mountains: 'It was a stunning colour, that blue. Deep, strong, rich, exquisite; towering and majestic masses of blue – a softly luminous blue, a smouldering blue, as if vaguely lit by fires within. It extinguished the blue of the sky.' More prosaically, the blue haze that gives the mountains their name is caused by vaporised gases released by the gum trees.

The Blue Mountains became a major resort for Sydney at the end of the 19th century when the opening of the railway line made it feasible to visit the area over a long weekend – or even on a day trip. Before the trains, it was an exclusive haunt for the well-to-do. The heat of the Sydney summer was quite unbearable in the thick clothes of the late Victorian era and the cool of the mountains offered a pleasant respite. Fresh mountain air was also the only known cure at the time for the killer disease tuberculosis, and sanatoriums sprang up all over the Blue Mountains. Many of the buildings are still there.

As a holiday destination, the area lost favour after World War II to Bali and Queensland, but in the past few years, the Blue Mountains have been rejoicing in a comeback. The scenery is breathtaking.

GETTING THERE

The main Western Hwy runs straight through the mountains to Katoomba, on its way to Lithgow 146 km away. En route are many lookouts and small detours, such as **Govett's Leap** and **Bridal Veil Falls**.

An interesting alternative drive from Sydney is to head for Windsor along Rte 40 and then join the Bell's Line of Road – such a splendid name – which you will find on the road to Kurrajong. This will take you through orchards to the Mt Tomah Botanical Gardens and then Mt Banks. After that, circle around via Bell and Mt Victoria so that you come back through Katoomba. The round trip is about 250 km.

[i] **Blue Mountains Information Centre**, Echo Point, Katoomba; tel: 1300 653 408; www.bluemountainstourism.org.au. Open daily. For information on Blue Mountains National Park and World Heritage Area go to Blue Mountains Heritage Centre, Govetts Leap Rd, Blackheath; tel: 4787 8877. Open daily.

[🛏] The Blue Mountains are an easy day trip from Sydney, but there are plenty of places to stay overnight in Katoomba.

[TO] Try also Leura, Blackheath and Mt Victoria, all along the main highway, for places to eat.

THE BLUE MOUNTAINS

HIGHLIGHTS

The largest place in the mountains is **Katoomba**. On one side of Katoomba is a vertical drop into the Jamison Valley and on the other side is the Grose Valley. The best way to see the town is to follow Cliff Drive, which is well signposted and starts at the railway station, goes along Lurline and Merriwa Sts and then follows around the Jamison and Megalong Valleys. Not far away is the popular lookout of **Echo Point**, which has a glorious view across to the **Three Sisters**, the **Ruined Castle** and **Mt Solitary**. It is possible to pick out many animal shapes on the mountains on the other side of the Grose valley. This is one lookout where a pair of binoculars is invaluable.

THE THREE SISTERS

The rock formation of the Three Sisters – Menehni, Wimlah and Gunnedoo – is very important in Aboriginal legend. Note that rock climbers are no longer allowed on the Sisters' well-weathered and crumbly sandstone.

For the energetic, the **Giant Stairway** of about 800 steps leads down to the floor of the Jamison Valley. An easier route, the **Prince Henry Cliff Walk**, leads left towards Leura or right towards the Scenic Railway complex. The **Scenic Railway** was originally part of a mine and the ride down to the Jamison Valley is reputed to be one of the steepest in the world, although the idea that it is not for the faint-hearted seems more publicity hype than reality.

MOUNTAINS' WORLD HERITAGE

In recognition of its outstanding natural values, in 2000 the Greater Blue Mountains area, which includes seven national parks, became the 14th Australian site inscribed on the World Heritage list.

Leura has **Leuralla** ($$), 36 Olympian Pde; tel: 4748 1169, a historic art-deco mansion containing a collection of 19th-century Australian art and a memorial museum to Dr H V Evatt. There is also a toy and railway museum. Nearby **Sublime Point** gives more views of the Three Sisters and the Jamison Valley, and **Gordons Falls Reserve** is a pleasant picnic area a gentle walk away from the **Pool of Siloam** and **Lyre Bird Dell**. A number of bushwalks start from Leura. The **Everglades** ($$), 37 Everglades Ave, is one of the great gardens of Australia, with unique drystone terraces, mature trees, native flora and a grotto pool.

WHERE NEXT?

Instead of treating the Blue Mountains as a round trip from Sydney, they could be a first point on the route to the inland destinations of Orange and Mudgee (see pp. 94 and 99).

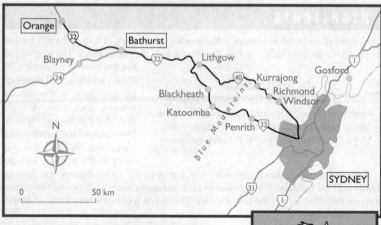

DRIVING ROUTE

The route over the Blue Mountains can either be straight up along the Western Hwy via Katoomba or along Bell's Line of Road (see p. 90 for both). After Lithgow the road undulates as it passes through interesting cultivated scenery right through to Orange (276 km).

SYDNEY — ORANGE
OTT Tables 9014/9020/9109

Service	RAIL	RAIL	RAIL	RAIL	🚌	RAIL	🚌	RAIL	🚌	🚌	RAIL	🚌
Days of operation	Ⓐ	①	Daily	Ⓐ	⑥	Ⓐ	Daily	Ⓐ	ex⑥	ex⑥	Ⓐ	ex⑦
Special notes					A			BD			C	
Sydney............d.	0400	0620	0710	0822	1100	1157	....	1432	....	1700	1716	....
Penrith............d.	0457	0706u	0755u	0908	|	1245	....	1520	....	|	|	....
Katoomba ....d.	0607	0807u	0851u	1014	1300	1355	....	1620	....	1900	1906	....
Lithgow ....a.	0655	0847u	0931u	1102	1335	1443	....	1708	....	1935	2003	....
Lithgow ....d.	0730b	0847	0931	1118b	1335	....	1500	....	1715	1935		2015
Bathurst..........d.	0820b	0957	1041	1218b	1415	....	1555	....	1815	2015		2115
Orange ....a.	0925b	1107	1156	1302b	1515	....	1640	....	1900	2115		2230

Special notes:
A–Departs 5 minutes later on Ⓒ. B–Departs 30 minutes earlier on ⑦.
C–Departs 16 minutes later on ⑥.
D–Additional trips: on Ⓐ 0657, 0957, 1529, 1559, 1800, 2003, 2203 on Ⓒ 0009, 0402 then every
    2 hours to 2202.
b–Connection by bus.

BEYOND THE BLUE MOUNTAINS

Orange is one of the most pleasant towns of inland New South Wales. It is not that large but it has immense charm; the phrase to describe it is country civilised. It is the hub of a major farming area – fruit, cattle, sheep, wheat and pigs all prosper on the red volcanic soil, and vineyards are the fastest growth industry. Banjo 'Once a jolly swagman' Paterson was born in Orange (where an obelisk commemorates the fact) and you can see exactly what he meant by 'the vision splendid, of the sunlit plains extended' as you make the steep descent from the mountains to industrial Lithgow. The road across these sunlit plains runs through the surprisingly interesting town of Bathurst.

SYDNEY

See p. 69.

BATHURST

Founded in 1815, Bathurst is Australia's oldest inland city, and possesses some superb colonial architecture in the grand style dating from the gold rush and before. It is sometimes referred to as the City of the Plains. The finest of its buildings is the Victorian Renaissance-style **courthouse** in Russell St. It has a double-storey portico, a large octagonal central dome and two wings. The wing with verandahs was built as a telegraph office; the other houses the local museum.

In Kings Parade is a statue to George Evans who was probably – there is some considerable argument – the first white person to arrive in the district. The **Boer War Memorial** has on it the name of Lt Peter Handcock, who was shot with Breaker Morant for murdering Boer prisoners. Bathurst has associations with other historic names. A plaque in Machattie Park shows that Charles Darwin visited in 1836, and Ben Chifley's Cottage in Busby St is the birthplace of a former prime minister.

Mt Panorama, on the edge of town, is home to koalas, a small **motor racing museum** ($$; open daily 0900–1630) and some epic motor racing. A few times a year, the place attracts hordes of racing enthusiasts; the circuit is actually the public road up Mt Panorama.

The **Bathurst Sheep and Cattle Drome** in Kelso, a short drive from town, allows townies to see how the country folk live. Visitors can try to milk a cow or sit back and enjoy an hour-long show of sheep shearing and wool classing. If the weather is clement you can see sheepdogs in action.

Holy Trinity Church in Kelso was completed in 1835, which makes it the oldest consecrated Anglican church in Australia. Australia's old churches go through wondrous contortions to claim to be the oldest in one sense or another, but in a country where anything built by Europeans before 1850 is very old, this is perhaps understandable.

> **GOLD TOWN**
> Bathurst grew rich from provisioning and accommodating would-be millionaires who came to make their fortune in the New South Wales gold rush of the 1850s: see p. 96.

i **Information Centre**, 28 William St; open daily; tel: 6332 1444; e-mail: visitors@bathurst.nsw.gov.au; www.bathurst.nsw.gov.au. The telephone code is 02.

🛏 **Bathurst Explorers Motel $$$** 357 Stewart St; tel: 6331 2966. Good value.
Knickerbocker Hotel Motel $$$$ cnr William & Russell Sts; tel: 6332 4500. Centrally located.

🍴 **Crowded House Café Restaurant $$$$** 1 Ribbon Gang Lane; tel: 6334 2300. Tasty à la carte.
Edinboro Hotel Bistro $$ 138 William St; tel: 6331 5020. Good-value pub food.
Ourplace Café $$ 133 George St; tel: 6334 3300. Open Mon–Sat 0730–1800. Offers internet access.

ORANGE

On reaching Orange you have arrived in a true Australian countryside town which has grown and prospered with the area. The houses on the tree-lined western approach to the town are examples of Australian country architecture at its very best.

i **Orange Visitors' Centre**, Civic Gardens, Byng St; open daily; tel: 6393 8226; e-mail: tourism@orange.nsw.gov.au; www.orange.nsw.gov.au. The telephone code is 02.

🛏 **Central Caleula Motor Lodge $$$$** 60 Summer St; tel: 6362 7699.
Downtown Motel $$$ 243 Summer St; tel: 6362 2877.
Mid-City Motor Lodge $$$$ 245 Lords Pl.; tel: 6362 1600.
Occidental Hotel Motel $$$ 174 Lords Pl.; tel: 6362 4833.
Orange Motor Lodge $$$$ 110 Bathurst Rd; tel: 6362 4600.
Oriana Motor Inn $$$ 178–184 Woodward St; tel: 6362 3066.
Templers Mill Motel $$$$ 94 Byng St; tel: 6362 5611.

🍴 There appear to be more Chinese restaurants in Orange per head of population than anywhere else in Australia.
Alfio's Pizzeria $$ 193 Lords Pl.; closed Sun; tel: 6362 6720.

All Seasons Balcony Restaurant $$$$ Metropolitan Hotel, cnr Byng and Anson Sts; tel: 6362 1353.

Canton Chinese Restaurant $$ 84 Summer St (opposite fire station); tel: 6362 6906. Fully licensed.

Diggers Brasserie $$$ Orange Ex-Services Club, Anson St; tel: 6362 2666.

Fair Dinkum Family Restaurant $$$ Bathurst Rd; tel: 6363 1580.

Golden Bowl Chinese Restaurant $$ Lords Place; closed Sun; tel: 6362 0144.

Loc Sing Chinese Restaurant $$ 293 Summer St; tel: 6362 4663.

Man Kee Chinese Restaurant $$ 116 Summer St; tel: 6362 0885.

Welcome Patmos Greek Restaurant $$$$ 87 March St; tel: 6362 5839.

HIGHLIGHTS

The local historical society has put together a brochure (available from the information centre) which describes a **walk** that takes you past over 40 places of interest. The walk takes about 1½ –2 hrs.

The **Orange Regional Gallery** in Byng St, opened in April 1986, is one of the better regional art museums in Australia. It is set in landscaped gardens in the middle of the Civic Square, and was awarded the Sulman Prize for Architectural Merit. The gallery collects Australian contemporary paintings and prints, but specialises in jewellery, ceramics and art clothes. It holds up to 30 exhibitions annually. Open Tues–Sat 1000–1700, Sun 1400–1700. Visits outside these hours can be arranged; tel: 6393 8136.

From Orange you can drive up to **Mt Canobolas** (a long-extinct volcano just southwest of the town) and then explore along the marked trails. **Lake Canobolas** – a separate park – is a recreation park built around the lake, which is popular for watersports including sailing, canoeing and fishing. Soon to open, a native wildlife sanctuary will give visitors the opportunity to see some of Australia's nocturnal animals such as sugar gliders and bandicoots on guided night walks.

The **Nangar National Park** is in the Nangar–Murga Range some 50 km west of Orange. It is an important wildlife refuge of forests and scrub in an area which has been mostly cleared

Orange's prosperity was not just built on farming. About 30 km north lie the **Ophir goldfields** – named after the goldfields in South Africa – where the first payable gold was discovered in Australia by Edward Hargraves in 1851. This was the first gold from which anyone could make money. Ophir is now a flora and fauna reserve.

GOLD!

Until a series of gold rushes in the 1850s, the Australian colonies had bumped along as an obscure backwater, with most industry struggling to gain a foothold. With the discovery of gold, the colonies' population trebled in a decade, and most of the people who had come to seek their fortune stayed – probably because most didn't find enough gold to fill a tooth. The ex-diggers provided an additional labour source in the colonies, which led to the growth of pastoralism and other industries. The increased volume of traffic to and from goldfields led to better roads and, eventually, to the construction of railways.

The first serious discoveries were made in New South Wales, at Ophir, near Bathurst, in 1851, and men flocked to the diggings. The population of the Victorian colony declined so markedly that a Gold Discovery Committee was created and offered a reward for anyone who found a profitable goldfield. Before the end of 1851, several rich fields were being worked, the best known near Ballarat and Bendigo. In December that year, the first gold-seekers from abroad arrived – leaving their ship in Melbourne although they were originally bound for Sydney and Bathurst. Victoria's population in 1851 was about 77,000; it grew by close to 100,000 the following year. Seizing the opportunity to make a few quid, colonial legislatures introduced licence fees. At Ballarat, miners' grievances over fees led to an armed clash with troops at the Eureka Stockade; about 30 miners and troopers were killed.

Rich as some were, the eastern goldfields pale beside the fabulous Golden Mile at Kalgoorlie, Western Australia, discovered in 1893. The Kalgoorlie and nearby Coolgardie goldfields did more than put Western Australia on the map – as Hill End, Ballarat and Bendigo had the eastern colonies. Gold was literally Western Australia's saviour. Colonised from 1826, the West was wild, arid and isolated and attracted little interest from prospective immigrants. Gold strikes turned the human tide. The West's population increased threefold from the mid-1880s to 1895, and had risen to nearly 240,000 by 1904. The Golden Mile's yield peaked at nearly 2.3 million ounces of gold in 1903; in the late 1990s mines in the area were still extracting about 700,000 ounces from the field each year.

WHERE NEXT?

If you've already seen the Blue Mountains (p. 90), consider travelling from Orange south via Blayney, Cowra, Boorowa and Yass (p. 125) to Canberra (p. 101). Alternatively, take a loop north and east through Wellington and Gulgong en route to Mudgee (p. 99).

Colour section
(i) Telstrar Tower, Canberra (p. 109); didgeridoo player; Parliament House, Canberra (p. 107).
(ii) Sydney Opera House and Harbour Bridge (p. 79).
(iv) Gum tree and Three Sisters, Blue Mountains (pp. 90–91).

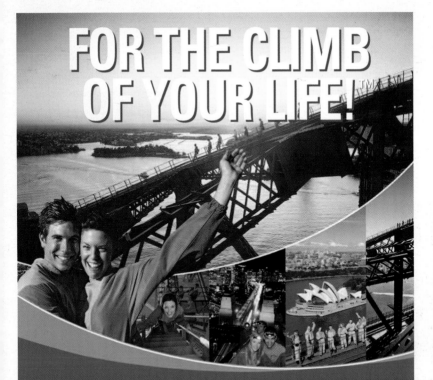

FOR THE CLIMB OF YOUR LIFE!™

Coming to Sydney? Make it an unforgettable stay by having the Climb of your Life on the Harbour Bridge. You'll make your way over catwalks, ladders and arches to the summit 134m above the water. The 360° view of the world's most beautiful harbour is waiting for you... dawn, day, twilight and at night. Call and reserve your BridgeClimb® now.

TICKET HOTLINE
+61 2 8274 7777

TICKETS ONLINE
www.bridgeclimb.com

BRIDGECLIMB
S Y D N E Y

® BridgeClimb is the Registered Trade Mark of Ottto Holdings (Aust.) Pty Ltd.

IT&P BRIDG 2051

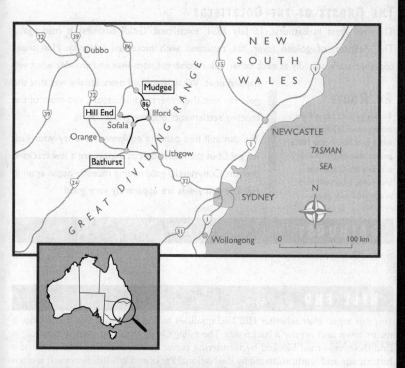

DRIVING ROUTE

Hill End is about 80 km from Bathurst, the last 30–40 km on unmade roads (make sure your insurance covers this; see pp. 28–29).

You can either drive via Sofala or via Turondale or along the old bridle track. In dry weather, this can be driven in a normal two-wheel-drive car and is very scenic, but it is a bone-shaking journey – in the wet, water running down leaves immense potholes. Most of Hill End to Mudgee is again on unsealed roads; alternatively there is a fast direct road, Rte 86, from Sydney.

THE GHOSTS OF THE GOLDFIELDS

The *Free Press* in Bathurst, 16 July 1851, exclaimed: 'Gold! Bathurst is mad again! The delirium of golden fever has returned with increased intensity. Men meet together, stare stupidly at each other, talk incoherent nonsense and wonder what will happen next.' What happened next, usually, was that the gold ran out, the miners would depart, and most of the bustling settlements became ghost towns.

EN ROUTE

Sofala gets its name from a mining town in Africa, and is much as it was in the 1860s, except that its population is only a fraction of the thousands who lived here in the gold rush years.

You can still hire panning equipment and try your luck for gold, but the most you can expect are a few traces in the pan. Commercial gold mining recently began again in Hill End and yields are apparently very good.

BATHURST

See p. 93.

HILL END

You can argue over whether Hill End qualifies as a ghost town, but it was once a major town and is now a backwater. The village is all common land so you might find the access road blocked by wandering cows. In 1967 Hill End was declared a historic site and is administered by the National Parks and Wildlife Service. It is often used as a backdrop for period movies.

In 1873 Hill End had 53 hotels and 'a mile of shops': the gold discovered in 1851 made this one of the most profitable places in Australia. It was, at the time, the largest inland centre in New South Wales and, with its sister town of Tambaroora, had a population of 20,000.

All the mining done here was alluvial because the rights had been allocated to a single company which used Cornish miners to hammer away at the reef. The Holtermann nugget was found here on 19 Oct 1872. It was 1.5 m high by 50 cm wide and weighed 236 kg. Its gold content was estimated as in excess of 3000 oz. But as is often the case, the discovery of that immense nugget marked the beginning of the end, because by 1875 miners had started to drift away.

Markers on the empty sites tell you what once stood where. One church, St Paul's, is still used but St Andrew's is now rubble. **The Royal Hotel**, which dates from 1872, still operates and is much frequented by the locals. It sells an exquisitely cold drop of beer and decent food. The hospital, built at the same date as the Royal Hotel, houses a small museum and information centre. A few shops have been restored and several of the houses are still lived in, but the old glory days have long departed.

> i **National Parks and Wildlife Service Information Centre,** Old Hospital Building, Bathurst Rd; tel: 6337 8206. Open daily 0930–1230 and 1330–1630.

MUDGEE

James Blackman was, arguably, the first European to reach the area, when in 1821 he crossed the Cudgegong River. By 1837 he had built a house, of sorts, where the town now stands. Within a few years there were 36 dwellings, including the essential three hotels, to cater for a resident population of fewer than 200 people.

With the gold rush Mudgee became important as a trading and supply centre and by 1861 there were some 1500 people living there. Today Mudgee is becoming increasingly well known for its wine.

> i **Mudgee Visitors' Centre,** 84 Market St; tel: 6372 1020. Open daily. www.mudgee-gulgong.org. The telephone code is 02.

> 🛏 **Central Motel $$** 120 Church St; tel: 6372 2268.
> **Cudgegong Valley Motel $$$** 212 Market St; tel: 6372 4322.
> **Horatio Motor Inn $$$$** 15 Horatio St; tel: 6372 7727; e-mail: motorinn@hwy.com.au. Mudgee's newest motel. Pool.
> **Winning Post Motor Inn $$$$** 101 Church St; tel: 6372 3333.
> **Mudgee Motor Inn $$$** Sydney Rd; tel: 6372 1122.

> 🍴 **Craigmoor Restaurant $$$$** Craigmoor Rd; tel: 6372 4320. Open daily 1200–1500; Fri, Sat 1830–late.
> **Eltons Café $$$** 81 Market St; tel: 6372 0772. Good food and great coffee. Open Mon 0800–1730, Tues–Sat 0800–2100 and Sun 0800–1600.
> **Golden Dragon Chinese Restaurant $$** 132 Church St; tel: 6372 1882. Open daily (no lunch Tues).
> **Rajarani Indian Restaurant $$$** Church St, cnr of Gladstone St; tel: 6372 3968. Open for lunch Thur–Fri and dinner Tues–Sun.
> **Red Heifer Grill and Carvery $$$** Lawson Park Hotel, cnr Short and Church Sts; tel: 6372 2183. Carvery with good food and local wine. Open daily for lunch and dinner.

HIGHLIGHTS

Many of Mudgee's historic buildings survive, and some of them are floodlit at night. The oldest is the **Catholic Presbytery** which was built in 1852. **St Mary's Church** was started in 1857 and has interesting stencilled decorations. The **Colonial Inn Museum** on Market St is open daily, and a **craft centre** has been built into the now non-operative railway station.

Mudgee is known for its **honey** – you can sample several varieties at The Mudgee Honey Haven, Gulgong Rd – and it is perhaps even better known for its wine. This used to be disparagingly known as Mudgee mud, because it was on the thickish side – it would come out of the bottle, but not quickly. All that has changed and now Mudgee wines are much sought after. There are about 30 wineries in the area, all of which welcome visitors for tastings and cellar sales. One produces wine without using any chemicals or fertilisers – the vineyard has the splendid notice: 'Trespassers will be composted.'

> **A TIME TO TASTE**
> Fancy a sip of Mudgee red? The annual Mudgee Wine Celebration is held in September, and is growing in popularity.

The Australian poet Henry Lawson (1867–1922) lived as a child in **Eurunderee**, north of Mudgee, where there is a **Henry Lawson memorial**. Apart from being a fine poet and short-story writer, Henry Lawson was a heroic alcoholic – claims that tales of his alcoholism are exaggerated are misguided.

> ## WHERE NEXT?
>
> *Ophir, another gold ghost town, is north of Orange (see p. 94), and to the east of Mudgee lies the scenic Wollemi National Park, an extension of the Blue Mountains (see p. 90). Historic Gulgong – famous as 'the town on the $10 note' – is a short drive north of Mudgee. Its attractions include the fascinating **Gulgong Pioneers Museum** ($); tel: 6374 1513, and the **Henry Lawson Centre** ($); tel: 6374 2049.*

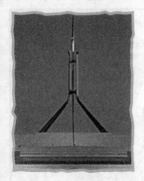

Australia's capital lies within its own enclave, the Australian Capital Territory (ACT), in the mountainous country of south-eastern New South Wales. Canberra is a new city, expressly located and designed to house the nation's government, and it arouses much contradictory opinion. Many Australians outside the ACT dislike it intensely, seeing it as soulless. But most of the other residents think it a delightful place to live and it continues to grow.

Canberra as a capital city was not even conceived until the beginning of the 20th century, but Aboriginal people, most recently the Wiradjuri, had occupied the region for millennia before that. The first European explorer to arrive here, in 1821, was Charles Throsby and he called the area Limestone Plains. Three years later the first land grant, at the foot of Black Mountain, was bought and by 1845 there was a small town with St John's Church and a school.

When the Australian colonies united as a federation in 1901, the rivalry between Sydney and Melbourne was such that neither would allow the other to be national capital. It was agreed that the seat of government would be in a federal territory of 'not less than 100 sq. miles' (259 sq. km) within NSW, and not less than 100 miles (160 km) from Sydney. The 2358 sq. km ACT was given up by NSW in 1909 and the Commonwealth took possession in 1911.

MUST SEE/DO IN CANBERRA

Take a tour of Capital Hill/Parliament House

Reflect at the Australian War Memorial

Enjoy the National Gallery of Australia

See the controversial National Museum of Australia

Stroll in the National Botanic Gardens

Cycle around Lake Burley Griffin

Walk in Tidbinbilla Nature Reserve or Namadgi National Park

Under the terms of Chapter V of the Constitution of Australia, the former colonies, which became the states, never totally relinquished their autonomy, so each state also has two houses of parliament, making Australia the nation most over-provided with politicians. The only exception used to be the ACT itself.

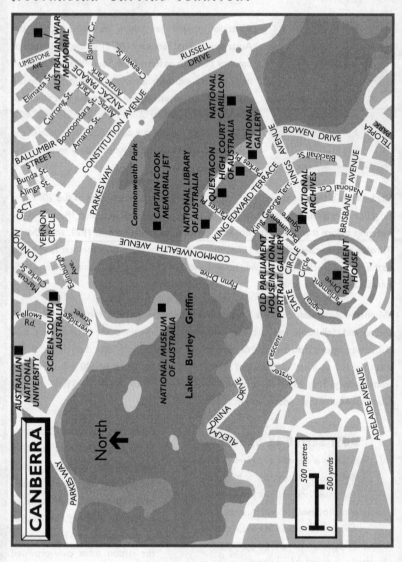

Even though the people of Canberra showed in a referendum that they were quite happy to fall under the jurisdiction of the federal government, bills passed in 1988 made the territory self-governing.

WHAT'S IN A NAME

The official story is that Canberra was named in 1913 from an Aboriginal term meaning 'meeting place'. This is very unlikely. No one knows what the Aboriginal term was precisely or how it translates, but 'hatchet to back of knee' is more probable than 'meeting place' – and, considering the usual state of Australian politics, more appropriate.

Parliament was first convened in the capital in 1927 but it was 30 years before the government of Australia seriously started to move to Canberra. The city sprang up through the 1960s, with suburbs and satellite towns to house the civil servants.

Bushfires in January 2003 destroyed about 500 homes (but, miraculously, killed only four people) in Canberra's south-western suburbs. In spite of the difficulties, many Canberrans believe the disaster strengthened their sense of community.

ARRIVAL AND DEPARTURE

For international flights, Canberra uses Sydney (see p. 70) or Melbourne (see p. 180) – Sydney is closer. There is a domestic airport 7 km east of the city centre, well served by taxis.

Canberra is 300 km from Sydney (it is 650 km from Melbourne). The quickest and easiest way from Sydney to Canberra is to take Hwy 31, turning on to Hwy 23 at Goulburn. The road is undoubtedly the best in Australia. It is also perhaps the most heavily patrolled of all main highways – speed at your peril. Long-distance buses make the journey in about 4½ hrs and come in to the Jolimont Centre, in the middle of Civic. Canberra's railway station is in Kingston, on the south side of the lake.

INFORMATION

TOURIST OFFICES **Canberra Visitors' Centre**, 330 Northbourne Ave, Dickson; tel: 6205 0044. **Travellers Maps and Guides**, Jolimont Tourist Centre, 65 Northbourne Ave; tel: 6249 6006.

MONEY **Travelex Foreign Exchange**, Shop 18–19 Ground Floor 'Canberra Centre', Bunda St; tel: 6247 9984. Open Mon–Fri 0900–1700 and Sat 0900–1300.

AUSTRALIAN CAPITAL TERRITORY

INTERNET SITES www.canberratourism.com.au, www.canberra.citysearch.com.au
Almost every national gallery and exhibition has a website.

POST AND PHONES The telephone code for Canberra is 02. Canberra City Post Office is at
53–73 Alihga St.

ACCOMMODATION

Prices in Canberra tend to fluctuate somewhat depending on whether or not parliament is sitting.

Blue and White Lodge $$$$ 524 Northbourne Ave,
Downer; tel: 6248 0498. Family-run, and price includes
breakfast; 4 km from the centre.
E-mail: blueandwhitelodge@bigpond.com.au.

Canberra Carotel Motel $$$ Federal Hwy, Watson; tel: 6241
1377. Set in 22 acres of tranquil bushland 6 km from city centre. E-mail: info@carotel.com.au.

Canberra City Accommodation $$$ 7 Akuna St; tel: 6257
3999. Situated in the heart of the city. Website: www.canberra
cityaccommodation.com.au. E-mail: info@canberracityaccom-
modation.com.au.

Canberra YHA $$$ 191 Dryandra St, O'Connor; tel: 6248
9155. In tranquil bush setting, by bus stop. E-mail:
Canberra@yhansw.org.au.

City Walk Hotel $$$ 2 Mort St; tel: 6257 0124. Geared
towards international backpackers. Maximum stay one week.

Capital Executive Apartment Hotel $$$$ 108
Northbourne Ave; tel: 6243 8333. Email mail@ceahotel.com.au.
Five-minute walk to the heart of the city. Website: www.ceaho-
tel.com.au

Greentrees Apartments $$$$ 5 Goreen St, Reid; tel: 6247
7132. Fully self-contained one- to three-bedroom apartments.
Minimum 2 nights. E-mail: info@greentrees.com.au.

Last Stop Ambledown Brook $$$$ 198 Brooklands Rd via
Hall; tel: 6230 2280. Includes breakfast, country surrounds,
walking distance to wineries. Stay in renovated 1929 Melbourne
Tram or 1935 Sydney Train Carriage. E-mail: laststopamble-
downbrook@apex.net.au.

Northbourne Lodge $$$ 522 Northbourne Ave, Downer;
tel: 6257 2599. Refurbished house.

Quality Hotel Diplomat $$$$ cnr Canberra Ave and Hely St, Griffith; tel: 6295 2277. Recently refurbished; close to Parliament House and National Gallery of Australia. E-mail: diplomat@premiergroup.com.au.

Ursula College $$$$ Australian National University, cnr Daley and Dickson Rds, Acton; tel: 6279 4300. Single rooms are subject to availability. Close to Botanical Gardens and Black Mountain Nature Park. E-mail: ursula.hall@anu.edu.au.

Victor Lodge $$$ 29 Dawes St, Kingston; tel: 6295 7777. Clean family-run lodge, all-you-can-eat breakfast included. E-mail: bookings@victorlodge.com.au.

White Ibis Holiday Park $$$ 47 Bidges Rd, Sutton, off Federal Hwy; tel: 6230 3433. On 8 ha of rural setting, 10 minutes north of Canberra; fully self-contained cabins.

FOOD AND DRINK

The food in Canberra is brilliant, possibly because politicians are fussy eaters.

Asian Café $$ Melbourne Building, West Row; tel: 6262 6233. Chinese and Malaysian cuisine, courtyard seating with roof shutters. Licensed. Open daily for lunch and dinner.

Australian Pizza Kitchen $$ lower level Bailey's Arcade, London Circuit; tel: 6257 2727. Gourmet wood-fired pizzas. Open daily for lunch and dinner.

Bookplate $$ National Library of Australia, Parkes Place, Parkes; tel: 6262 1154. Open Mon–Thur 0830–1800, Fri 0830–1600 and weekends 1100–1500. Blackboard menu, changes daily.

Café Fontaine $$ upper level Canberra Centre (nr Country Rd); tel: 6257 6978. Café food, good coffee. Licensed, open daily until 1730.

Charcoal Grill Restaurant $$$$ 61 London Circuit; tel: 6248 8015. Lunch Mon–Fri, dinner Mon–Sat. Serves steaks, salads, great Australian wine list.

Element $$$$ Shop 2, 4 Barker St, Griffith; tel: 6295 6915. Open Tues–Fri for lunch and Tues–Sat for dinner. Modern Australian cuisine. Shaded courtyard.

Flatheads Fish Café $$$ 6 Macpherson St, O'Connor; tel: 6248 0696. Open daily until around 2030. Great fish and chips. Dine in or take-away.

Foreign Affair $$$$ Upstairs, 8 Franklin St, Manuka; tel: 6239 5060. Modern Italian, licensed, upmarket. Highly regarded. Closed Sun, no lunch Mon or Sat.

Greater Indian and International Restaurant $$$ Curtin Shopping Centre, Curtin Place, Curtin; tel: 6285 3679. Lunch Mon–Fri (closed Tues), dinner daily.

Gus Café $$ Shop 8, Garema Arcade, Bunda St; tel: 6248 8118. Canberra's first outdoor café. Serves a breakfast all day in the old English good-pull-up-for-truck-drivers tradition. Open seven days until late.

Hudson's in the Garden $$ Australian National Botanical Gardens, Clunies Ross St; tel: 6248 9680. Home-made cakes, morning and afternoon tea, and lunch. Open daily.

Latin Corner $$ 5 Garema Place; tel: 6248 0840. Peruvian and Chilean cuisine. Open Mon–Sat.

Lemon Grass Thai $$$ 65 London Circuit, Melbourne Building; tel: 6247 2779. Licensed and BYO (wine), authentic Thai but calmed down a little, closed Sunday.

Mezzalira $$$–$$$$ West Row (cnr London Circuit); tel: 6230 0025. Pick of the Civic Italian places. Great pizzas and other oven treats, fine pasta, legendary tiramisu. Open Mon–Fri 1200–1430, Mon–Sat 1800–2200.

Saffron Restaurant $$$ Capitol Theatre Centre; tel: 6295 7068. Open Tues–Sun for lunch and dinner, licensed and BYO (wine) à la carte restaurant.

Tosolini's $$$ Bailey's Corner, London Circuit; tel: 6247 4317. Licensed BYO (wine), Mediterranean brasserie. Open daily. No dinner Sun or Mon.

GETTING AROUND

BY BICYCLE

Canberra boasts more than 300 km of bike tracks and hiring a bike is a great option. Row 'n' Ride ($$$; tel: 6228 1264) offers free delivery and pick up from your accommodation. The bikes are well maintained and the price includes the use of a cycleways map and a helmet. www.realfun.com.au. Mr Spokes Bike Hire is on Barrine Drive (near the Ferry Terminal), Acton Park. $$$. Tel: 02 6257 1188.

Public transport in Canberra means the Action bus – the Australian Capital Territory Internal Omnibus Network. Tel: 13 17 10; www.action.act. gov.au. However, on Sundays, fewer routes are covered. It is far better to hire a bike (there are lots of cycle paths) or, best of all, walk. There are also plenty of taxis.

A valid criticism of Canberra is that it is somewhat difficult to navigate. T A G Hungerford in *A Knockabout with a Slouch Hat* put it quite well when he wrote: 'The mad-woman's knitting of roads connecting and slicing through the enclaves was so circuitous, so confusing, that they'd become the basis of a local joke that the half of the population not employed in the Government offices consisted of touring motorists who'd despaired of ever finding their way out.' Having said that, Canberra has the best-maintained roads in the country, and parking is fairly easy.

HIGHLIGHTS

An international competition to design the nation's new capital was won in 1912 by an inspired American architect, Walter Burley Griffin. He designed Canberra from scratch and did a magnificent job. His wife, Marion Mahoney Griffin, who was also an architect, was totally involved in the project and she well deserves joint billing. Yet, despite its splendour, Canberra still has its critics – who say that its rectangles, ellipses and circles render it a city laid out by geometry rather than the natural development that most towns undergo. But it is easy to argue that it is much better for this.

To get an understanding of the way Canberra is laid out, start with the artificial but splendidly positioned **Lake Burley Griffin**. On the northern side of the lake is Civic, with shops, businesses, university and suburbs such as Reid, Braddon, Turner and Acton. To the south of the lake are parliament and other important buildings, and, further out, the suburbs of Parkes, Barton, Forrest, Deakin and Yarralumla. This last is home to the prime minister and governor general.

Exploring Canberra is a pleasure because you can walk to most places. The main attraction south of the lake must be

BOAT HIRE

A great way to spend the afternoon is to make your own way across Lake Burley Griffin on either a paddleboat or a canoe. These are available for hire daily (Sept–Apr) from 0800 until late at the Acton Ferry Terminal $$$. Tel: 6249 6861 for further information.

the newish **Parliament House**. It was opened in 1988 and sits at the top of the Parliamentary Triangle. It is actually built into the hill, and the roof has been covered with lawn so that it blends in. It is very common for Australians to make sneering remarks about this building but it is immensely impressive. And, according to the politicians who are there at least part of the year, it is a fine place to work.

On the inside it is light and airy and full of artworks by Australian artists – it is claimed that there are 3000 works on display. When parliament is not sitting, free guided tours commence daily every half hour between 0900 and 1600; tel: 6277 5399 for further details.

Australian Capital Territory

Visitors to Australia should not judge the country by the standard of political debate in the two chambers. It may well sound like an ill-informed rabble engaged in shouting each other down using terms you would not hear at Sunday school. But these are carefully selected political leaders who have dedicated their lives to finding better ways of serving the people of Australia – so if they sound like an ill-informed rabble it must be something to do with the acoustics!

Old Parliament House was used until 1988 and has now been adapted for other uses. There are guided tours through the building but you may find it more relaxing to wander around on your own. Canberra is a city of gardens, and the one at Old Parliament House is all roses which are in full bloom throughout the summer – Oct to April. King George Terrace; tel: 6270 8222; open 0900–1700 daily ($).

Also at Old Parliament House is the **National Portrait Gallery**. One of only four in the world, the gallery celebrates the achievements of the people who have helped to shape Australia. Open 0900–1700 daily ($); tel: 6270 8210. The gallery's award-winning website is also worth a look: www.portrait.gov.au.

National Displays

Carrying the label 'National' has led to something of a competition between the various venues, and as a result the quality of the many exhibitions is astonishingly high. You may not be enthralled by everything but you will not find any of the assorted National displays dull in any way. As a bonus, with a very few exceptions, you can visit everywhere free.

The **National Gallery of Australia** in Parkes Place was opened in 1982 and has a remarkable collection of indigenous Australian culture. It also has *Blue Poles* by Jackson Pollock, which created a sensation when it was bought. A pleasing addition is the outdoor sculpture garden, with 24 sculptures by Australian and overseas artists in a native garden setting. Free (fees apply for special exhibitions). Open daily: 1000–1700; tel: 6240 6502; website: www.nga.gov.au.

The **National Library of Australia**, also in Parkes Place, has some 220 km of shelving and everything that has anything to do with Australia is probably here. There is a very informative visitors' centre which gives you a splendid idea what it is all about. What's more, you can sip excellent coffee while looking out on what are reputed to be Canberra's best views of Lake Burley Griffin. Check on what is available at the website – www.nla.gov.au; tel: 6262 1111. Open Mon–Thur 0900–2100, Fri–Sat 0900–1700, Sun 1330–1700.

The **National Capital Exhibition** is just across the lake, at Regatta Point in **Commonwealth Park**. It tells the story of Canberra and has on show some of the original competition designs. Look carefully and you will understand why Walter Burley Griffin got the nod. Free. Open daily 0900–1700; tel: 6257 1068.

Anzac Parade provides a fitting approach to the **Australian War Memorial**. This was opened in 1941 and is far from morbid. Moving, yes. Morbid, no. It comprises an amazing collection of pictures and artefacts, including a series of miniature battle scenes done in exquisite detail. There are guided tours, although many people find it an emotional place to visit that needs to be taken in at a personal pace. Free. Open daily 1000 (0900 school holidays)–1700; tel: 6243 4211; website: www.awm.gov.au/.

> **OLD BUS DEPOT MARKETS**
> Every Sunday in the Old Bus Depot in Wentworth Ave on Kingston Foreshore they hold the Old Bus Depot Markets, which are mainly craft-orientated. Tel: 6292 8391.

Screen Sound Australia on the McCoy Circuit in Acton alone justifies a visit to Canberra. It is housed in a splendid art deco building but is unfortunately very tight for space – only a small fraction of the treasures is on display. But within what space is available they have created miracles. It is almost as if there were a series of small interlocking cinemas which let you see the long, long history of film in Australia. Fragments of documentaries go back to the 1880s. Most fascinating is a pre-20th-century Melbourne Cup and the signing of Federation in 1901. This is a magical place if you are at all interested in movies. Open Mon–Fri 0900–1700, Sat–Sun 1000–1700; tel: 6248 2000; website: www.screensound.gov.au. Free (small charge for special exhibitions).

Screen Sound Australia lies on the edge of the university grounds, beyond which are the **Australian National Botanic Gardens** in Clunies Ross St. It is boasted that the gardens contain the world's finest living collection of Australian plants. Open daily 0830–1700 (extended hours January), with regular guided walks; tel: 6250 9540.

Rising up from the gardens is Black Mountain, and the best views of Canberra are from the 195-m-high **Telstra Tower** on the mountain. This has both open and enclosed viewing galleries (the latter because in winter it can be bitterly cold up there). Open daily 0900–2200 ($); tel: 1800 806 718.

Fronting Lake Burley Griffin on the Acton Peninsula, the new **National Museum of Australia** in Lawson Crescent was opened in 2001, the centenary of Australian Federation. The museum features five permanent exhibitions covering the land and its people, ancient and modern. Free (charge for special exhibitions). Open daily 0900–1700; tel: 6208 5000.

OUTSIDE THE CENTRE

In the south-western suburb of Deakin is the **Royal Australian Mint**. The visitors' gallery lets you see some of the collectors' coins, medals, medallions and tokens for Australia and for a number of overseas countries that are made at the mint. The gallery also provides excellent views of the minting process, and you can make your own special $1 coin on the public coining presses. This is not an approved activity outside the Mint. Denison St; tel: 6202 6891; open Mon–Fri 0900–1600 (to see Mint in full operation), Sat–Sun 1000–1600.

Some 11 km north-west of the city is Gold Creek Village and at the corner of Gold Creek Rd and Barton Hwy there is collection of colonial-era buildings. Cockington Green, a miniaturised version of an English village is open daily 0930–1700 with the last entry at 1615 ($$$); tel: 6230 2273. It is difficult to know what all this has to do with Canberra but it appeals to children.

The **National Dinosaur Museum** in the village is in fact a private collection with replica skeletons of dinosaurs plus some real bones, including the 150-million-year-old shin bone of an apatosaurus. Open daily 1000–1700 ($$); tel: 6230 2655.

Also in the village is the **Australian Reptile Centre**, in O'Hanlon Place, where you'll find a variety of Australia's largest, most colourful and deadliest snakes, including Australia's longest snake, the scrub python of North Queensland. Open 1000–1700 daily ($$); tel: 6253 8533. The **Bird Walk**, in Federation Square, is a 1000 sq. metre walk-in aviary, where more than 500 local and exotic bird species fly freely among natural vegetation. Visitors are given a piece of apple on entry and are encouraged to feed the friendly parrots. Open daily 1000–1630 ($$); tel: 6230 2044.

The 2003 fires caused extensive damage to national parks and state forests near Canberra. One of the city's most popular attractions (and a valuable research facility), **Mt Stromlo Observatory**, was completely destroyed in the devastating firestorm of 18 January. The loss of scientific records and equipment was incalculable. The Visitor Centre and café have since reopened (Wed–Sun 1000–1700; tel: 6125 0232) and rebuilding is underway. The site offers some of the best views of Canberra and is well worth a visit.

NIGHTLIFE

Each Thursday the *Canberra Times* lists every concert and gig in the area. There is also the monthly *This Week in Canberra*, free from the visitor centre.

As throughout Australia, rock bands mainly play the pubs. Performances of classical music are held at the **Canberra Theatre Centre** (London Circuit; tel: 6275 2700) and the **Canberra School of Music** (Llewellyn Hall; tel: 6125 5771 or 6125 2527). The Theatre Centre also puts on plays and other performance arts.

DAY TRIPS

The Australian Capital Territory measures 80 km from north to south and is about 30 km wide. Canberra takes up a good deal of it and what is left over is mostly the Namadgi National Park which, in part, borders the mountainous Kosciuszko National Park in the Snowy Mountains (see p. 112). There are seven peaks over 1600 m which can make bushwalking challenging. You get to the park on the road south from Tharwa to Adaminaby. Maps and information available from the Namadgi Visitor Centre, open daily 0900–1600; tel: 6207 2900.

Beside the river near Tharwa, about 30 km south of the city, is **Lanyon Homestead**, a grand homestead completed in 1859 that has been beautifully restored. The nearby **Nolan Gallery** is home to a wonderful collection of paintings by Australia's most internationally renowned artist, Sydney Nolan. Open Tues–Sun 1000–1600 ($$); tel: 6235 5688.

The **Tidbinbilla Nature Reserve** is 27 km south-west of the city. The park was extensively damaged by the 2003 fires and in 2005 ten had reopened – entry is free. The kangaroos here are semi-tame, as are the emus. Brush-tailed rock-wallabies and the reserve's surviving koalas can be seen in an enclosure. It's best to visit on a cool day when the animals are more likely to be out and about. Open daily 0900–1800 (winter), 0900–2000 (summer). The Visitor Centre is open Mon–Fri 0900–1630 and Sat–Sun 0900–1730; tel: 6205 1233.

On the way to the nature reserve is the **Tidbinbilla Tracking Station** or, more formally, the Canberra Deep Space Communication Complex. This is a joint US–Australian venture and it has a visitors' centre with displays of spacecraft and tracking technology. Paddy's River Rd, Tourist Route 5, Tidbinbilla; website: www.cdscc.nasa.gov. Free. Open daily 0900–1700; tel: 6201 7880.

EVENTS

Canberra hosts a range of events throughout the year including **Floriade**, a spectacular exhibition of flowers and plants held in spring. The extremely popular **Royal Canberra Show** (Feb) featuring exhibits, fireworks and grand parades is also worth a visit. Find out more at www. canberra-tourism.com.au.

THE SNOWY MOUNTAINS

South of Canberra the Great Dividing Range that runs down Australia's eastern side rears up as the Snowy Mountains, the highest in Australia. Here are the headwaters of the Snowy, Murrumbidgee and Murray Rivers and the country's highest peak, Mt Kosciuszko (2228 m), and the whole area is protected within Kosciuszko National Park, the largest national park in New South Wales. The park contains much breathtaking scenery in all seasons but is known primarily for its skiing. During the winter there is skiing at Perisher, Smiggins Holes, Blue Cow and, further down the Alpine Way, at the main resort of Thredbo.

In January 2003, an extraordinary series of lightning strikes began the most severe bushfires seen in Australia's alpine regions since 1939. The huge complex of fires extended from Talbingo in NSW to Bright in Victoria – an area of about 18,000 sq km. Two-thirds of Kosciuszko National Park was burnt out, but authorities stress that far from 'destroying' the park, fire is a natural process that shapes the landscape. The next few years will be a fascinating time to visit – a period of natural regeneration and intense scientific interest in the region.

GETTING THERE AND GETTING AROUND

The gateway to the mountains is Cooma, on Hwy 23; it is about 400 km south of Sydney and 115 km from Canberra. From Cooma the Snowy Mountain Hwy snakes diagonally through the mountains, past Mt Selwyn towards Tumut and Gundagai (see p. 119). Most visitors, however, take the road to Jindabyne, 56 km further on, from which the Alpine Way leads up to Thredbo and the snowfields. Some roads are closed in winter, and you should be equipped with snow chains between May and Oct. Buses run regularly from Sydney and Canberra to Cooma, and there are extra services in the ski season.

INFORMATION

Cooma Visitors' Centre, 119 Sharp St; tel: 6450 1742. Open daily.
Snowy Region Visitor Centre, Kosciuszko Rd, Jindabyne; tel: 6450 5600. Open daily.
Thredbo Information Centre, Friday Drive; tel: 6459 4198. Open daily.
snowymountains.com.au.
The telephone code in the Snowy Mountains is 02.

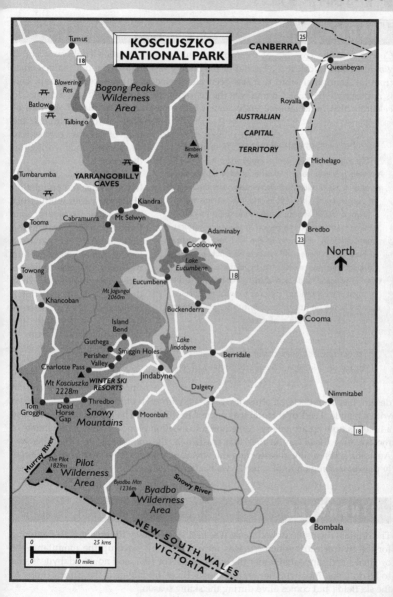

KOSCIUSZKO
NATIONAL PARK

Tumut

CANBERRA

25

Queanbeyan

18

Blowering
Res

Bogong Peaks
Wilderness
Area

Batlow

Royalla

Talbingo

AUSTRALIAN

CAPITAL

TERRITORY

Michelago

Bimberi
Peak

Tumbarumba

YARRANGOBILLY
CAVES

Kiandra

Bredbo

Tooma

Cabramurra

Mt Selwyn

Adaminaby

23

North

Cooloowye

Towong

Lake
Eucumbene

18

Eucumbene

Khancoban

Mt Jagungal
2060m

Buckenderra

Cooma

Island
Bend

Guthega

Smiggin Holes

Lake
Jindabyne

Perisher
Valley

Charlotte Pass

Berridale

Mt Kosciuzsko
2228m

WINTER SKI
RESORTS

Jindabyne

Tom
Groggin

Dead
Horse
Gap

Thredbo

Dalgety

Nimmitabel

Snowy
Mountains

Moonbah

18

Murray River

The Pilot
1829m

Pilot
Wilderness
Area

Byadbo Mtn
1236m

Snowy River

Byadbo
Wilderness
Area

NEW SOUTH WALES

VICTORIA

Bombala

| 0 | | 25 kms |
| 0 | | 10 miles |

COOMA

Cooma is at the crossing of the Monaro and Snowy Mountain Highways, and it would be fair to call it the capital of the Snowy Mountains. The odd name comes from an Aboriginal word that has been interpreted as either lake or swamp. This is appropriate because Cooma was the centre of the Snowy Mountain Scheme. To celebrate this multinational endeavour Cooma has the **International Avenue of Flags** which contains the flags of nations representing all of those that worked on the scheme.

THE SNOWY MOUNTAIN HYDROELECTRIC SCHEME

This was the largest civil engineering project that Australia has ever seen. The scheme took 25 years and more than $800 million to complete and at the height of construction – the 1950s and '60s – there were around 10,000 workers billeted in the area. The scheme transformed the region in several ways. First, it supplies 'clean' electricity to the ACT and huge areas of New South Wales and Victoria. Secondly, because the scheme was mainly built by migrants, many of them Europeans made homeless by World War II, they brought their individual cultures to what had been a country based on British food, British style and British sense of dress.

To see the scheme close up and to visit one of the power stations, contact the Snowy Scheme's Information Centre in Cooma (tel: 1800 623 776).

In the winter the population of Cooma varies wildly from day to day as skiers pour through on their way to the ski fields. At 810 m above sea level it can be chilly even in the summer, with temperatures ranging from 26°C down to 11°C. In the winter, of course, the weather is decidedly chilly and the thermometer often drops to 1°C and below.

Lambie St, which is pretty much unspoilt Victorian design, has been declared a historic precinct, with each of the 21 buildings marked with a plaque. The **Royal Hotel** was opened in 1858, and **The Lord Raglan**, once also a hotel, is now an art gallery. A memorial to aviation pioneers contains remnants of the *Southern Cloud*, an airliner that crashed in the mountains in 1931. This was Australia's first airline disaster and the wreckage was not recovered from this largely unexplored region until some 27 years after the event.

JINDABYNE

The original township of Jindabyne was beside the Snowy River, but with damming for the hydroelectric scheme it was moved piece by piece up the mountain. The original site disappeared under the water on 22 Apr 1967, and now Jindabyne is said to be on Lake Jindabyne not on the Snowy River. Jindabyne is the closest centre to the ski fields and comes alive during the skiing season.

SKIING IN THE SNOWY MOUNTAINS

Australia has relatively few mountains suitable for skiing and so downhill skiing has developed only in a few well-publicised resorts. Skiing as a seriously commercial venture did not start until 1956 when Tony Sponar, a Czech ski instructor working as a hydrographer on the Snowy Mountains Scheme, came to Thredbo and realised that the side of the steep valley would be an ideal ski resort. In 1957 the NSW state government granted a lease over Thredbo village with a view to developing a year-round alpine resort development.

Snow and skiing conditions reports in Australia have the same credibility as sightings of the Easter Bunny. To get around this, Thredbo and most other skiing resorts have installed snow-cams so that it is possible actually to see the conditions on the slopes.

THE MOUNTAINS IN OTHER SEASONS

Kosciuszko National Park has walks ranging from mild to extremely strenuous. During spring, summer and autumn the weather is ideal for walking, and in late summer the carpets of wild flowers are stunning. At Thredbo, the ski chairlift operates right around the year, allowing you the luxury of downhill-only walks in the mountains. Or you can get to the track of steel mesh (to stop serious erosion) that has been laid on most of the track to Mt Kosciuszko.

THREDBO

This is the closest ski resort to Sydney and the one that is perhaps the most professionally run (www.thredbo.com.au). It has the highest skiing and longest runs anywhere in Australia, 5.9 km from the top of Karels lift to Friday Flat, with a total vertical drop of 672 m. A must for all skiers is to ski the 3.7-km Crackenback Supertrail, starting at the highest lifted point in Australia. There are 12 lifts including four quad chairlifts, and a purpose-built beginners' area at Friday Flat has an easy quad chairlift operating on a gentle slope of only 12° inclination. There are also over 400 snow gun outlets spread over 25 km of underground tubing throughout the mountain.

Thredbo has developed into a full-blooded ski resort and the après-ski nightlife is, in a word, awesome.

By far the best bet is to go on a package tour, which every travel agent in Sydney will be delighted to sell you. This will include transport and lift passes and will work out cheaper than booking each item individually.

Many Thredbo accommodation options only take 5-day bookings (Sun–Thur) or 2-day bookings (Fri–Sat).

Bernti's Mountain Inn and Apartments $$$$ Mowamba Pl.; tel: 6457 6332.
Denman Mountain Inn $$$$ Diggings Tce; tel: 6457 6222. Bar, restaurant.
House of Ullr $$$$ Mowamba Place; tel: 6457 6210.
Lantern Lodge $$$$ Banjo Dr.; tel: 6457 6215.
Thredbo YHA $$$ 8 Jack Adams Pathway; tel: 6457 6376.

🍴 Alfresco Pizzeria $$ lower concourse, Thredbo Alpine Hotel; tel: 6457 6327. Eat in, take-away or home delivered. Open daily 1200–2030 (in winter).
Altitude 1380 $$$ Village Sq.; tel: 6457 6190. Mediterranean-style café and BYO restaurant. Open daily 0800–late.
Bernti's Café $$ 4 Mowamba Pl.; tel: 6457 6332. Open daily during the ski season from 1600 until late.
Cascades Café and Bar $$$$ Thredbo Alpine Hotel concourse; tel: 6459 4200. Spectacular mountain views. Open daily for breakfast, lunch (during ski season) and dinner.
Credo $$$$ Riverside, Diggings Terrace; tel: 6457 6844. Award-winning food, overlooking the Thredbo River. Open daily for dinner from 1800.
The Terrace $$$$ Denman Mountain Inn, Diggings Tce; tel: 6457 6222. Open for breakfast daily and dinner only during the ski season.

WHERE NEXT?

From the Snowy Mountains you can drive west via the Alpine Way and Murray Valley Highway to meet our Sydney–Melbourne inland route at Albury (p. 119). Alternatively, drive east on the Snowy Mountains Highway and meet our Sydney–Melbourne coastal route at Bega, just north of Eden (p. 123).

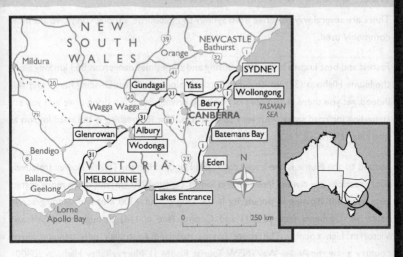

SYDNEY — MELBOURNE
OTT Tables 9014/9030/9412

Service	$\boxed{RAIL}$	🚌	$\boxed{RAIL}$	🚌	$\boxed{RAIL}$	🚌	🚌	🚌	🚌	🚌	🚌	🚌
Days of operation	Ⓐ	Ⓐ	Daily	Daily	Ⓐ	Daily	②⑤	①③④	⑥	⑦	①④	②⑤
Special notes	B		B		B		A	A	A	A		A
Sydney..............a.	0554	0730	0938	0930	1538	1515	....	....	....	....	....	....
Wollongong ....d.	0735	0930	1103	1130	1702	1718	....	....	....	....	....	....
Berry ....d.	*0859*		1209		1818		....	....	....	....	....	....
Bomaderry/Nowra ....d.	*0909*	1115	1219	1315	1828	1840	....	....	....	....	....	....
Batemans Bay.........d.	....	1300	....	1505	....	2025	0505	....	....	0630	0700	....
Eden ....d.	....	....	....	1910	....	0015	0810u	0810	0830	0935s	1025	....
Lakes Entrance..........d.	....	....	....	....	....	0305	1150s	1150s	1215s	1320	1400	1455
Bairnsdale...............d.	....	....	....	....	....	0340	1231s	1231s	1256s	1401	1430	1530
Sale ....a.	....	....	....	....	....	0510	1326	1326	1351	1456	1520	1635
Melbourne ....a.	....	....	....	....	....	0835	*1628*	*1628*	*1642*	*1803*	1900	*1930*

Special notes:
A–Connection from Sale to Melbourne is by train.
B–Additional services run throughout the day.

There are several ways to drive from Sydney to Melbourne, although only two are most commonly used.

Fastest and best known is the often boring and sometimes dangerous 863 km way along the Hume Highway (31), which runs effectively along the Great Dividing Range and will, indeed, get you there in 10 hours of non-stop driving. But it is a tiring drive and you are struggling for road space with very large trucks. Not for nothing is the road known as 'the killer Hume'.

Second to the Hume is the 'coast road', the Princes Highway (1). It's slower (relatively short sections are divided freeway) and longer (about 1050 km) but much more scenic. Less used but growing in popularity is the long (about 1300 km) and winding scenic route via Canberra (see p. 101) and Cooma (see p. 114) through the NSW and Victorian high country. The route passes mainland Australia's only genuine alpine country along the Alpine Way (NSW Tourist Route 1), Murray Valley Highway (B400), Kiewa Valley Highway (C531) and the Great Alpine Road (B500).

SYDNEY – MELBOURNE VIA HUME HIGHWAY

DRIVING ROUTE

See the Sydney–Adelaide Driving Route box, p. 125, for directions to Gundagai (371 km from Sydney) via Goulburn. Continue on Hwy 31 for 182 km to Albury, then 5 km to the Hume Freeway (still Hwy 31), which continues uninterrupted or 305 km to Melbourne.

SYDNEY

See p. 69.

YASS

See p. 126.

GUNDAGAI

There's a track winding back,
To an old-fashioned shack,
Along the road to Gundagai.

This town has a very special place in Australian folklore. It has the dog and the tuckerbox, mentions in folk songs and poems galore (see p. 128), and a replica of the altar of St Marie's Cathedral in Paris, which Frank Busconi – who did the sculpture of the dog on the tuckerbox – worked on for seven years, aided by three other masons. Over a period of 28 years he hand-turned and polished 20,948 pieces of marble. Obsessive-compulsive disorder was not, in those days, seen as a problem. Near the famous statue of the dog – 5 miles (8 km) north of Gundagai – you can see the statue of Dad and Dave and Mum and Mabel, as immortalised in the stories by Steele Rudd and the old radio serial, where the Rudds were said to live at Snake Gully. Dad and Dave are probably regarded by most older Australians as the heart of Australianism. True.

ℹ **Gundagai Tourism Centre**, Sheridan St; tel: 6944 0250; e-mail: travel@gundagai.nsw.gov.au; www.gundagai.nsw.gov.au. The telephone code is 02.

🛏 **Bushman's Retreat Motor Inn $$** cnr Mount and Cross Sts; tel: 6944 1433; e-mail: bushmans@dragnet.com.au. Fair dining room.
Garden Motor Inn $$ 101 West St; tel: 6944 1744. Licensed dining room overlooking Murrumbidgee Valley.
Gundagai Motel $$ cnr West and Sheridan Sts; tel: 6944 1066; e-mail: gundagaimotel@ bigpond.com. Clean basic rooms.

🍴 **Poet's Recall $$** cnr West and Punch Sts; tel: 6944 1777. Licensed and with a motel attached.
Niagra Café $$ Sheridan St; tel: 6944 1109. Classic country-town café.

ALBURY/WODONGA

Albury is in New South Wales and Wodonga in Victoria. Separated by the Murray River, which marks the border between the states, the twin cities have a population of around 50,000 – but over 90,000 people live within the Albury-Wodonga statistical district. This is by far the largest community along the Hume Highway and is one of the largest inland population centres in Australia. River cruises on paddle steamers are the major attraction, although the river – changed by reduced flows – is no longer as large as it was when the paddle steamers were needed in the late 19th century to move agricultural produce to the cities.

ℹ **Albury Wodonga Gateway Visitor Information Centre**, Lincoln Causeway, Wodonga; tel: 1300 796 222; e-mail: information@destinationalburywodonga.com.au; www.alburywodonga tourism.biz. The telephone code for Albury is 02, for Wodonga 03.

⊟ **Albury Backpackers $** 452 David St, Albury; tel: 6041 1822. Small and friendly; canoe tours, bike hire.

Albury Motor Village YHA $ 372 Wagga Rd, Lavington; tel: 6040 2999; e-mail: albury@yhavic. org.au. Quiet and clean.

Country Comfort Albury $$$$ cnr Dean and Elizabeth Sts, Albury; tel: 6021 5366/1300 650 464; e-mail: reservations.albury@countrycomforthotels.com. Close to town centre, restaurant on site.

Sundowner Albury Hovell Tree Inn $$$$ cnr Hume Highway and Hovell St, Albury; tel: 6042 3900/1800 654 576; e-mail: hovel@sundownermotorinns.com.au. Includes gym, swimming pool, spa and restaurant.

🔟 Dean St is Albury's eat street, with the greatest concentration of restaurants and cafés around its junction with David St. Many motels and hotels include restaurants.

Highlights

Albury Regional Museum (Australian Park Wodonga Place, tel: 6051 3450) was established by the local historical society and includes exhibits that explore the district's Aboriginal and more recent history; free. Open daily 1030–1630. **Albury Regional Art Gallery** (546 Dean St, tel: 6023 8187) occupies the old town hall and features collections of photography, works on paper and Australian artist Russell Drysdale, among others. Its photography collection is worth the visit; free. Open Mon–Fri 1030–1700, Sat–Sun 1030–1600.

En Route

Wangaratta, Victoria, has extensive facilities for travellers and beautiful parks and gardens. The aviation museum **Airworld**, 1 km east of the freeway, is one of Australia's finest. Tel: (03) 5721 8788; $$$. Open daily 1000–1700.

Go to **Noreuil Park** to see the Murray River or to swim in it (in summer). A short drive north of town, the **Ettamogah Wildlife Sanctuary** (Hume Hwy; tel: 6040 3677; $; open daily from 0900) is home to a range of Australian animals, most of which arrived injured or orphaned.

A short detour to Bright and Mount Buffalo National Park from Wangaratta is well worth the journey. Magnificent in summer and spectacular in winter, it is the gateway to the Victorian skiing area.

GLENROWAN

It was in June 1880 that bushranger Ned Kelly and his gang made their last stand at Glenrowan, which ended in Kelly being hanged in Melbourne after uttering his memorable last words – 'Such is life'. There is much argument whether he was a thug or a politically motivated defender of the poor.

⊟ **Glenrowan Kelly Country Motel $$$** 44 Gladstone St; tel: (03) 5766 2202. Simple and tidy.

Glenrowan Hotel $$ 46 Gladstone St; tel: (03) 5766 2255. This is not the Glenrowan Inn that Ned Kelly and his gang took over – the police burned it down.
Kate Kelly's Tea House $$ Gladstone St; tel: (03) 5766 2667. Named after Ned's mum.

HIGHLIGHTS

In Glenrowan, Ned Kelly is an industry. You can re-live the excitement of the siege at **Kellyland**, which shows 'Ned Kelly's Last Stand'. This theatre production combines animatronics with live actors and can seat up to 80 people at any one time. Gladstone St, tel: (03) 5766 2367; $$$. Open daily 0930–1630. Visit the **Ned Kelly Memorial Museum**, which is behind Kate's Cottage Gift and Souvenir Shop. Not only is the museum full of memorabilia but it has what it declares in Victorian terms is the 'Exact Replica of the Kelly Homestead, Kate's Cottage'. 35 Gladstone St, tel: (03) 5766 2448; $. Open daily 0930–1730.

MELBOURNE

See p. 178.

SYDNEY – MELBOURNE VIA THE PRINCES HIGHWAY

DRIVING ROUTE

Take the Princes Hwy (1) south out of Sydney and don't leave it for more than 1000 km; in Victoria it becomes first the A1, then the M1 and continues into Melbourne. Consider leaving the A1 in Sale, Victoria, and travelling via the Gippsland Hwy (A440), C445, C442, Strzelecki Hwy (B460), Bass Hwy (A420) and South Gippsland Hwy (M420) to take the scenic route through Victoria's South Gippsland.

SYDNEY

See p. 69.

ROYAL NATIONAL PARK

You might care before you get to Wollongong to divert through the Royal National Park – there is a very well signposted entrance on the left of Hwy 1. The Royal National Park was established in 1879, and is the world's second oldest national park – only Yellowstone in the USA was declared before it. With an amazing natural diversity, it offers riverside picnic areas (nearly all safe for swimming), cliff-top heathland walks and a sense of serenity.

WOLLONGONG

Australians, especially those who live in Sydney, tend to sneer at Wollongong. Yet it is a most lovely and lively destination. It has an active harbour overlooked by splendid seafood restaurants. It is cupped in a hollow surrounded on three sides by national parks and forest and, on the fourth, by the sea.

i **Wollongong Visitors Centre**, 93 Crown St, tel: (02) 4227 5545/1800 240 737; e-mail: tourism@wollongong.nsw.gov.au; www.tourismwollongong.com. The telephone code is 02.

Boat Harbour Motel $$$ cnr Campbell and Wilson Sts; tel: 4228 9166; e-mail: boatharbourmotel@bigpond.com. Near CBD but still reasonably quiet.

Normandie $$$ 30 Bourke St, North Beach; tel: 4229 4833; e-mail: normandie@ozemail.com.au. Restaurant, function centre; close to beach, parks, harbour.

Surfside 22 Motel $$ cnr Crown and Harbour Sts; tel: 4229 7288. Close to beach.

Wollongong YHA (Keiraview Accommodation) $$ 73–75 Keira St; tel: 4229 1132; e-mail: bookings@keiraviewacco.com.au. Central location.

The Beach House Seafood Restaurant $$$ Northbeach at 16 Cliff Rd; tel: 4228 5410. Fresh local seafood.

Anchorage Restaurant $$$ cnr Campbell and Wilson Sts; tel: 4228 9166. Beautiful views of Belmore Basin.

BERRY

A beautiful rural town famous for gardens, trees, arts and crafts. It is, in style, unlike most Australian towns. The best description is 'wealthy alternative lifestyle'. Berry has various buildings, most beautifully restored, protected by their National Trust classification. It is one of the oldest settlements in the area and is named after the explorer Alexander Berry, who took up land grants and became the first white settler in the Shoalhaven area.

i Visitor enquiries about Berry are handled by the **Shoalhaven Tourist Centre**, cnr Princes Hwy and Pleasant Way, Nowra; tel: 4421 0778/1300 662 808. Open daily. The area's telephone code is 02.

Woodbyne Private Hotel $$$ 4 O'Keeffes Lane, Jaspers Brush; tel: 4448 6200; e-mail: info@woodbyne.com.au. Garden setting. Country peace and quiet.

The Silos Estate Vineyard Retreat $$$ B640 Princes Highway, Jaspers Brush; tel: 4448 6082; e-mail: accommodation@thesilos.com. Vineyard with guest cottages and stunning views.

EN ROUTE

After Berry, Hwy 1 passes through Nowra, Ulladulla and Burrill Lake before winding through the forested hills north of Batemans Bay. Just north of Batemans and about 10 km off the highway is **Murramarang National Park** and **Pebbly Beach** – where resident kangaroos like to lounge by the seaside.

BATEMANS BAY

Bayside Batemans is a major holiday centre and gateway to national parks covering over 150,000 hectares of eucalypt forests and waterways. Kangaroos, wallabies, possums and parrots are guaranteed, with possible sightings of bandicoots, goannas, echidnas and wombats. The nearest coastal town to landlocked Canberra (see p. 101), Batemans is growing apace, and is especially popular with retirees.

i **Batemans Bay Information Centre**, Princes Hwy; tel: 4472 6900/1800 802 528; www.naturecoast-tourism.com. au/batemans.htm. The telephone code is 02.

Abel Tasman Motel $$$ 222 Beach Rd; tel: 4472 6511; e-mail: abeltas@acr.net.au.
Batemans Bay YHA $–$$ cnr Old Princes Hwy and South St; tel: 4472 4972; e-mail: shadywillows@bigpond.com.
Mariners Lodge on the Waterfront $$$ Orient St; tel: 4472 6222; e-mail: info@marinerslodge.com.au. Swimming pool, waterfront lawns, in-house bistro.

Batemans' restaurants and cafés are concentrated in the Orient St/Beach Rd strip, just off the highway. There's a lot to choose from and the standard is good and improving.

EN ROUTE

From Batemans Bay, Hwy 1 continues on to Moruya, Bodalla – famous for its cheese – Narooma and then Bega, another cheese-making centre. Further south you'll pass turnoffs to the popular holiday towns of Tathra, Merimbula and Pambula. Next is Eden, which was a famous whaling town and, yes, you can still see pods of whales during their annual migration.

EDEN

Eden claims to be the halfway point between Sydney and Melbourne, which is near enough. Whale-watching – through the cooler months – is one of the key tourist attractions of this picturesque and quiet town. The fishing industry is still one of the mainstays of Eden's economy and a large fleet operates out of Eden from Snug Cove.

i **Eden Tourist Information Centre**, Mitchell St; tel: 6496 1953; www.sapphirecoast.com.au. The telephone code is 02.

Australasia Hotel $–$$ 160 Imlay St; tel: 6496 1600.
Blue Marlin Motor Inn $$ 87 Princes Highway; tel: 6496 1601.
Twofold Bay Motor Inn $$ 164 Imlay St; tel: 6496 3111.
Whale Fisher Motel $$ 170 Imlay St; tel: 6496 1266.

Sea Horse Inn $$ Boydtown; tel: 6496 1361. You can also

EN ROUTE

South of Eden, the Princes Hwy passes through magnificent eucalyptus forests. About 14 km north of Genoa you cross the border into Victoria. At Genoa, consider taking a side trip to **Mallacoota**, gateway to beautiful, wild **Croajingalong National Park**. Hwy A1 continues through Orbost to Lakes Entrance.

stay here. It is the only building left standing in Boydtown and was originally built with convict labour.

Wharfside Café $ 253 Imlay St; tel 6496 1855.

Wheelhouse Restaurant $$ Eden Wharf; tel: 6496 3392.

LAKES ENTRANCE

Lakes Entrance sits next to a narrow neck of water connecting the sea to a complex of inland lakes. It enjoys a mild and pleasant climate and also has what is thought to be the largest fishing fleet in Australia. Eating fish for dinner that was caught in the morning is the norm. You can hire a boat and explore the linked system of the Gippsland Lakes. Watch for the dolphins as they come and go through the entrance.

[i] **Lakes Entrance Visitor Information Centre**, cnr Marine Parade and the Esplanade; tel: 5155 1966 or 1800 637 060; e-mail: lakesvic@egipps.vic.gov.au; www.lakesandwilderness.com.au. Open daily. The telephone code is 03.

Abel Tasman Motor Lodge $$$ 643 The Esplanade; tel: 5155 1655; e-mail info@ abeltasmanmotel.com. Close to the Lakes Entrance back beach swimming area.

Black Swan Motor Inn $$$ 679 The Esplanade; tel: 5155 1913; e-mail: info@blackswanmotel.com.

Cunningham Shore Motel $$ 639 The Esplanade; tel: 5155 2960; e-mail: info@cunninghamshore.com.

Riviera Backpackers $ 5 Clarkes Rd; tel: 5155 2444; e-mail: riviera@net-tech.com.au. East of town centre.

Café Pelican $$ 171 The Esplanade; tel: 5155 2166.

Ferryman's Floating Restaurant $$ on the Foreshore; tel: 5155 4999.

Haags Bistro $$ 567 The Esplanade; tel: 5155 1144.

Wyanga Winery Restaurant $$$ Baades Rd; tel: 5155 1508.

EN ROUTE

From Lakes Entrance it's just over 150 km through Bairnsdale and Sale to Traralgon. There, the A1 becomes motorway (the M1), which continues over the Dandenongs and all the way into central Melbourne.

WHERE NEXT?

If you're short of time, spend it all in marvellous Melbourne (p. 178). Consider day trips from Melbourne to Lorne (p. 216) or Apollo Bay (p. 214) on the Great Ocean Road; the historic Ballarat goldfields (p. 195), the Mornington Peninsula (p. 222) or the Mt Buller alpine area (p. 231)

SYDNEY — ADELAIDE

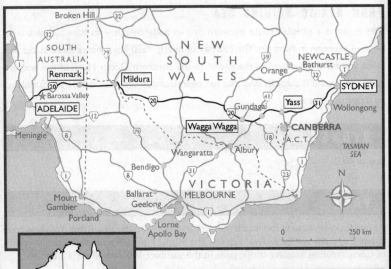

DRIVING ROUTE

Hwy 31, the Hume Highway, is a real super-highway from Liverpool through Campbelltown to Goulburn and then north of Canberra to Yass (280 km). It is tempting to speed along it, but beware: this is one of the most closely patrolled roads in the country.

SYDNEY — ADELAIDE
OTT Tables 9020/9110/9114/9330

Service	🚌	🚌	🚌	🚆RAIL	🚌
Days of operation	Daily	Daily	①③⑤	③⑥	Daily
Special notes				**AB**	
Sydney...................a.	1410	1430	....	1455	1600
Yass.......................d.	1810	2335	....	|	2205
Wagga Wagga..........d.	2035	2255	....	|	0005
Mildura...................d.	....	0820	0900	|	....
Broken Hill..........a.	....	|	1220	0645	....
Renmark.................d.	....	0940	....	|	....
Adelaide.................d.	....	1400	....	1515	....

Special notes:
A: This train conveys sleeper accommodation.
B: On ① there is a 0620 train to Broken Hill.

Gundagai is 105 km further on, and about 40 km past Gundagai turn right on the Sturt Hwy, Hwy 20, for Wagga Wagga (45 km). From here Hwy 20 runs clear across the state 560 km to Mildura, on the border between New South Wales and Victoria. (See p. 135 for a detour to Broken Hill.)

Hwy 20 shadows the northern edge of Victoria, then crosses the border into South Australia en route to Renmark (140 km), and reaches Adelaide after 255 km. The total journey is about 1425 km.

New South Wales/South Australia
From Sea to Shining Sea

This is just one possible route between Sydney and Adelaide – to have a choice is an unusual situation in Australia. The journey of nearly 1500 km crosses three states and takes you from the shores of the Pacific to the Southern Ocean. Much of the western half of the route is through land that has been transformed from desert to fruitfulness by irrigation schemes.

SYDNEY

See p. 69.

YASS

At one time, because of its situation in fertile country on the Yass River, Yass was considered as a site for the federal capital. The Hume Hwy once ran through the centre of town, creating massive traffic jams in the summer, but now there is a bypass.

The district of Yass was undiscovered by Europeans for over 30 years after the first convicts arrived, but by the 1830s settlers were arriving in a flood. Wheat production was established, then cattle raising, but it was sheep that dominated the economy, and Yass 'rode to prosperity on the sheep's back'. Its superfine wool is world-famous and most of the world-record prices have been set by the Yass clip. This is also a major wine region.

i **Yass Tourist Information Centre**, Coronation Park, Comur St; tel: 6226 2557. Open daily. The telephone code is 02.

🛏 **Australian Hotel-Motel $** 180 Comur St; tel: 6226 1744.
Colonial Lodge Motor Inn $$$$ cnr McDonald St and Yass Valley Way; tel: 6226 6221.
Hamilton Hume Motor Inn $$$ cnr Grampian and Laidlaw Sts; tel: 6226 1722.
Hi-Way Motor Inn $$$ cnr Grand Junctions Rd and Yass Valley Way; tel: 6226 1300.
Sundowner Motor Inn $$$$ cnr Castor and Laidlaw Sts; tel: 6226 3188.
Thunderbird Motel $$$$ 264 Comur St; tel: 6226 1088.
Yass Caravan Park $$ cnr Grampian and Laidlaw Sts; tel: 6226 1173.
Yass Motel $$$ 38 Laidlaw St; tel: 6226 1055.

🍴 **Café Dolcetto $$$** 129 Comur St; tel: 6226 1277. Open daily until 1700. Dinner until 2100 Thur–Sat.
Fook Lee Loy Chinese Restaurant $$$ 58 Comur St; tel: 6226 1896. Open Tues–Sun for lunch and dinner.

Galutzi $$ 93 Meehan St; tel: 6226 5261. Open daily.
Lien's Vietnamese Chinese Restaurant $$ 164 Comur St; tel: 6226 2595. Open daily for lunch (except Sun) and dinner.
Patrick's Steakhouse and Bistro $$$ Australian Hotel, Comur St; tel: 6226 1724. Open Mon–Sat for lunch and dinner.

HIGHLIGHTS

Many handsome buildings line the wide central road of Yass and some still have their hitching rails for horses. The ornate ironwork clearly shows the prosperity of this area in the 19th century.

The **Hamilton Hume Museum** in Comur St next to the TIC relates local history and development. It features a simulation shearing stand.

HAMILTON HUME

Hamilton Hume was born in Australia in 1797 and could therefore be thought of as one of the first white Australians. By 1818 he had already found Lake Bathurst and the Goulburn Plains, and three years later he crossed the Yass Plains and found the Yass River. Later he led an expedition to the Murray River and accompanied Charles Sturt on his 1828 expedition into the bush. He settled in Yass, becoming a magistrate, and lived most of the time in **Cooma Cottage** (built about 1835), 4 km from the centre on the Yass Valley Way. The cottage is listed by the National Trust and is open every day except Tues and Wed. Hume died in 1873.

The tramway that opened in 1892 became a railway line in 1917 until it closed in 1988. Now it is a **railway museum**, in Lead St, open Fri–Sun 1000–1600; tel: 6226 2169.

Several places within a 30-km radius of Yass are worth exploring. The lake of the vast **Burrinjuck Dam** snakes around west of Yass. Its 645 km of foreshore are a delight. **Wee Jasper Valley**, at the lake's southern end, has views of dramatic mountain ranges, magnificent caves, flowing streams and the lake. **Murrumbateman**, to the south, is the centre of the fast-growing wine industry. There are wine tastings in many of the numerous vineyards in the area.

Binalong, to the north-west, is famous because A B 'Banjo' Paterson is buried there. Binalong is also associated with the 'gentleman' bushranger Johnny Gilbert, known for the gallantry he displayed to his lady victims before he killed them. Legend tells that he was betrayed by his own grandfather. Visitors can see Gilbert's grave and the site where he was shot. **The Southern Cross Glass Studio** is worth visiting to observe the skill of the glass blowers and cutters.

BANJO PATERSON (1864–1941)

A B ('Banjo') Paterson was one of Australia's first great literary figures and will be remembered forever if only for writing the words of 'Waltzing Matilda'. He grew up in the Yass region and later owned a station in the Wee Jasper area. After working as a correspondent for Australian newspapers during the Boer War he returned to Sydney to become editor of the *Evening News* from 1903 to 1908. He joined the army in 1915, rising to the rank of major, but after the war resumed his career as a sports editor, journalist and freelance writer. He had begun to write verses and ballads as early as 1885, heavily influenced by his childhood years in Yass, and adopted the pen name 'Banjo' from the name of a family racehorse. Best-known among his other works are *The Man from Snowy River* and *Clancy of the Overflow*.

EN ROUTE

Gundagai is a name known to every Australian because of the lines in a folk song: 'And the dog sat on the tuckerbox/Five miles from Gundagai'. In fact, 'sat' is a politely altered version to allow schoolchildren to sing it. There is a statue of the dog, decorously sitting on the tuckerbox, at Five Mile Creek, just off the highway.

WAGGA WAGGA

The largest inland city in Australia is most commonly just called Wagga, pronounced something like 'wohguh'. In the Wiradjuri language wagga (or wahga or wahgam) means 'crow', and wagga wagga means 'crows'. The tourist office would prefer that Wagga be known as the Garden Town of the South. And, indeed, it is renowned for its gardens and parks.

Among the first European explorers was Captain Charles Sturt, on a voyage of discovery down the Murrumbidgee River in 1829. Wagga quickly developed because it was where the north–south track between NSW and Victoria crossed the river. By 1847 the village had been laid out, and the police station and court of petty sessions established. The first river-steamer to reach here was Francis Cadell's *Albury* in 1858. This was the start of a very brief period when the paddleboats navigating the inland waterways of Australia were an important form of transport. The last steamer to visit Wagga was in 1905, which means that, glorious though they were to look at, the paddle steamers were commercially important for less than 50 years.

Water, however, is still an essential part of Wagga. The city is the centre of the Riverina, an agricultural district dependent on irrigation. The Murrumbidgee runs right through the town. It even has a beach, which allows the town to boast of having Australia's only inland life-saving-club patrol. Lake Albert, formed by diverting

BUSHRANGERS BOLD AND NOTORIOUS

The area around Wagga was a haven for bushrangers. Mad Dan Morgan terrorised the area from 1863 to 1867, shooting the police magistrate. Although there was a reward on his head Morgan is said to have sat near the police magistrate at the Wagga Christmas races without being caught. He was eventually gunned down in an ambush.

In 1877 James Kelly, younger brother of the more famous Ned, was sentenced to ten years' gaol at Wagga courthouse for horse stealing. When released he dissociated himself from his family and led a respectable life, dying in 1946 aged nearly 90.

Captain Moonlite, whose real name was Andrew Scott, was the bushranger who brought most fame to Wagga. He had plenty of style and committed at least one robbery while acting as a lay preacher. His downfall came at Wantabadgery Station, east of Wagga, where he and his gang of five had taken 39 people hostage. Reports of the time are colourful in the extreme, but it is certain that he and his gang did not kill anyone. A hostage escaped and called the police, and in the ensuing shoot-out a trooper and two bushrangers (one of whom was only 15) were killed. The gang surrendered and Captain Moonlite and one accomplice were later hanged.

water from Crooked and Stringybark Creeks into a swamp, now has sailing, fishing, canoeing and waterskiing.

ℹ️ **Wagga Wagga Visitor Information**, Tarcutta St; tel: 6926 9621. Open daily. Website: www.tourismwaggawagga.com.au. e-mail: visitors@wagga.nsw.gov.au.
The telephone code is 02.

🛏️ There are two main areas for motel accommodation: along the Sturt Hwy and Tarcutta St.
Ashmont Inn Hotel Motel $$$ Tobruk St; tel: 6931 1899.
Boulevard Motor Inn $$$$ 305 Edward St; tel: 6925 5388.
Carinya Caravan Park $$ Pine Gully Rd; tel: 6933 1256.
Club Motel $$$ 73 Morgan St; tel: 6921 6966.
Country Comfort Wagga Wagga $$$$ Tarcutta St, cnr Morgan St; tel: 6921 6444.
Easts Van Park Riverview $$$ 93 Hammond Ave; tel: 6921 4287.
The Manor $$$$ 38 Morrow St; tel: 6921 5962.
Millie's Guesthouse $$$$ 199 Gurwood St; tel: (02) 6931 7638. Includes breakfast.
Red Steer Hotel Motel $$$ Olympic Way; tel: 6921 1344.
Wagga Beach Caravan Park $$$ 2 Johnston St; tel: 6931 0603.

🍴 Most of the restaurants can be found on and around Baylis St, and there are food halls in the Market Place Centre and Sturt Mall. This is a good place to taste the local wines. In Australia it is said that the irrigation wines of the Riverina have a salty taste which makes them instantly detectable.

CPM Café $$ Wagga Civic Centre, cnr Baylis and Morrow Sts; tel: 6921 1444. Open Mon–Fri 0800–1700 and Sat–Sun 0800–1600. Opposite the new Regional Art Gallery. Great outlook.
Il Corso Pizza Restaurant $$ 16–18 Baylis St; tel: 6921 9133. Open for dinner Tues–Sun and lunch Tues–Fri.
Indian Tavern Restaurant $$$$ 176 Baylis St; tel 6921 3121. Open daily from 1730.
Jasmin Village Chinese Restaurant $$ 35 Kincaid St; tel: 6921 3300.
Montezuma's Mexican Restaurant $$$ 85 Baylis St; tel: 6921 4428. Open Wed–Sat for lunch and Tues–Sun for dinner.
Tira Thai Restaurant $$$ 47 Baylis St; tel: 6921 5252. Open for dinner daily.

Highlights

The **Museum of the Riverina** is managed by the Wagga Wagga City Council. Its exhibits are spread over two sites. A changing programme of travelling exhibitions takes place in the historic Council Chambers, cnr Baylis and Morrow Sts. At the Botanic Gardens site in Baden Powell Drive, a range of exhibits that tell of the colourful history of the town is housed inside an old chapel, printery, school house and the Yallowin Hut (built 1834); free. Open Tues–Sat 1000–1700, Sun 1200–1600. Tel: 6926 9655.

The highlights among Wagga's many gardens and parks range from the **Botanic Gardens and Zoo** (about 1.5 km south of the station) to the formal **Shakespearean Garden** and **Apex Park** on the shores of Lake Albert. **Collins Park** is the oldest and features the South African War Memorial and an array of colour provided by seasonal flowers. An **Outdoor Entertainment Centre and Music Bowl**, at the Botanic Gardens, can accommodate a symphony orchestra and has seating for up to 3000 people.

Walking and Driving Tours

There are three historic walks through the city for which you can get maps and directions at the Visitor Information Centre. These take you past many of Wagga's historic buildings and start from the visitor centre. Two are very serious walks: the Wollundry Loop (10 km) circumnavigates the lagoon or, for the ultimate challenge, there is the 32-km Wiradjuri Walking Track, named after the region's traditional Aboriginal owners.

Charles Sturt University, which does much work on soil conservation, is unique in having its own **winery**. Other universities go quite green with jealousy at the thought. It is in Coolamon Rd, 9 km north of the city centre, and is an extension of Australia's leading wine science school, which focuses on combining traditional winemaking methods with state-of-the-art technology. It produces an excellent university-label wine and is open Mon–Fri 1100–1700 and Sat–Sun 1100–1600 for wine tastings and cellar door sales. There is also the **Wagga Wagga Winery** at 427 Oura Rd, open daily 1100–late.

The **Regional Art Gallery** (tel: 6926 9660; free), in the new multi-million dollar Wagga Wagga Civic Centre in Baylis St, is home to the fascinating National Art Glass Collection. Open Tues–Sat and public holidays 1000–1700 and Sun 1200–1600. The new Civic Centre – also home to the regional library – was opened by the Governor General Sir William Deane in 1999, the 150th anniversary of Wagga Wagga's proclamation as a township.

At **Junee**, 40 km north, is what is left of the railway system of New South Wales. The line runs through the centre of the town and the railway station, built in 1883, has immense presence and dignity. The Monte Cristo Homestead on a hill overlooking Junee is a two-storey Georgian mansion completed in 1884; open daily 1000–1600 ($$). The **Green Grove Organic Liquorice Factory** on Olympic Way offers tours Mon–Fri and at weekends by appointment ($); tel: 6924 3574.

MILDURA

Mildura is at the point where Victoria, New South Wales and South Australia meet, but what defines it is the Murray River.

The first white squatter arrived in 1846, and just nine years later came the epic event that was to change the fate of Mildura. In 1855 Alfred Deakin, who was later to become prime minister of Australia, managed to talk the Canadian irrigation experts, George and William Chaffey, into coming to Australia. The Chaffey brothers saw that exotic fruits would flourish in the red soil of the Mildura area, provided there was water. Accordingly, the Chaffey Agreement set aside 250,000 acres at Mildura, on which the brothers promised to spend £300,000 developing an irrigation system, using the Murray as the source. Following numerous setbacks, during which George returned home and Chaffey Bros Ltd went into liquidation, the plan became profitable after the turn of the 20th century. William, who had stayed on, established a winery, White Cliffs (now Mildara Blass), and became mayor of the town in 1920.

EN ROUTE

The Clydesdale Stud and Pioneer Farm, towards Narrandera, has antique machinery, a pioneer's hut and demonstrations of Clydesdale horses in action. Open daily except Thur.

Now Mildura is at the centre of the great Sunraysia district, the largest producer of dried vine fruits such as raisins, currants and sultanas in Australia. Around 80 per cent of Australia's total production of fruit is grown in the district, as well as a range of stone fruits and vegetables.

[i] **Mildura Tourist Information Centre**, corner of Deakin Ave and Twelfth St. The centre has an interpretative display on the main attractions and history of the region, including national and state parks, and also a small theatre and licensed restaurant; tel: 5021 4424; www.visitmildura.com.au. For further information

The Tichborne Claimant

Improbably, Wagga is involved in the story of the Tichborne Claimant. Arthur Orton was a butcher and a small-time sheep stealer. He arrived in the town in 1864 claiming to be Roger Charles Doughty Tichborne, the heir to a Hampshire baronetcy who was believed drowned when the ship in which he was travelling disappeared off South America. Orton was fat and almost illiterate. The man he impersonated was slim and fairly well educated. Yet Orton went to England and was able to persuade Lady Tichborne that he was her son.

The trustees of the Tichborne estate were not so gullible. They rejected his claim and the ensuing legal action by Orton still holds the record for being the longest in English legal history. Eventually, in 1874 Orton was sentenced to 14 years in gaol for perjury. On his deathbed he still swore he was Tichborne.

The Tichborne Claimant was one of the great melodramas of Victorian times and made Wagga so notorious that Mark Twain, on his visit to Australia, made a special detour to see the place.

on national parks call Parks Victoria (tel: 131 963) or check out the website: www.parkweb.vic. gov.au. The telephone code is 03.

🛏 Most of the motels are on Deakin Ave – all 12 km of it. You will have no trouble finding accommodation at almost any time of the year. Most of the restaurants are in the same avenue.
All Seasons Mildura Motor Inn $$$ 433 Deakin Ave; tel: 5023 3266.
Apex Park $ Cureton Ave; tel: 5023 6879.
Chaffey International Motor Inn $$$$ 244 Deakin Ave; tel: 5023 5833.
Commodore Motel $$$ Deakin Ave, cnr Seventh St; tel: 5023 0241.
Cottonwood Motel $$$ 326 Deakin Ave; tel: 5023 5166.
Early Australian Motor Inn $$$$ 453 Deakin Ave; tel: 5021 1011.
Kar Rama Motor Inn $$$ 153 Deakin Ave; tel: 5023 4221.
Mid City Plantation Motel $$$ 145 Deakin Ave; tel: 5023 0317.
Mildura Park Motel $$ Eighth St; tel: 5023 0479.
Motel Sunraysia $$$ Deakin Ave; tel: 5023 0137.
Murray View Motel $$ San Mateo Ave, cnr Seventh St; tel: 5021 1200.
The New Deakin Motor Inn $$$ 413 Deakin Ave; tel: 5023 0218.
Northaven Motor Inn $$$ 138 Deakin Ave; tel: 5023 0521.
Riverboat Bungalow $ 27 Chaffey Ave; tel: 5021 5315. Hostel dorms, fairly close to centre.
Riviera Motel $ 157 Seventh St; tel: 5023 3696.
Rosemont Holiday Guest House $$$ 154 Madden Ave; tel: 5023 1535.
Sandor's Motor Inn $$$$ 179 Deakin Ave; tel: 5023 0047.
Seventh Street Motel $$$ 153 Seventh St; tel: 5023 1796.
Three States Motel $$$ 847 Fifteenth St; tel: 5023 3735.
Vineland Motel $$$ 363 Deakin Ave; tel: 5023 4036.

Barney's Marina Restaurant $$$ 360 Deakin Ave; tel: 5021 2166.

The Bay Tree $$$ 145 Eighth St; tel: 5021 1244.

Chaffey Restaurant $$$ 244 Deakin Ave; tel: 5023 5833.

Deakin Estate $$$ Kulkyne Way, Red Cliffs; tel: 5029 1666.

Dom's Tavern Restaurant & Night Club $ 28 Langtree Ave; tel: 5021 3822.

Dragon Tower Chinese Restaurant $$ 29 Langtree Ave; tel: 5023 1925.

The Grand Bistro $$$ Seventh St; tel: 5023 0511.

Indian Tandoori Oven $$ 27 Deakin Ave; tel: 5023 6255.

Kings Palace Chinese Restaurant $$ 98 Madden Ave; tel: 5023 0994.

Lauretz of Langtree $$ 30 Langtree Ave; tel: 5022 1722.

Mildura Gateway Tavern $$ cnr 15th St and San Mateo Dr.; tel: 5021 3288.

Mildura Settlers $$ 110–114 Eighth St; tel: 5023 0474.

Regal Chinese Restaurant $$ 224 Deakin Ave; tel: 5021 3688.

Rendezvous Restaurant & Bistro $$$ 34 Langtree Ave; tel: 5023 1571.

Siam Palace Restaurant $$ 35 Langtree Ave; tel: 5023 7737.

Wirraway Bistro $$ Mildura RSL, 130 Madden Ave; tel: 5023 1750.

HIGHLIGHTS

Mildura owes much to the irrigation pioneers George and William Chaffey. The brothers were also responsible for the design of the town, which is why, following the North American pattern, avenues run north–south and have names, while streets run east–west and have numbers. The main thoroughfare is named after Alfred Deakin and runs for 12 km – the longest straight main road in Australia. Originally, the Chaffeys intended that the town would be served with trams, so the central avenue is very wide to allow for this. Mildura's many gum and palm trees were planted by William Chaffey, and the town remembers him with a statue in Deakin Ave, erected in 1929.

THE SNAKE RIVER

The Murray River flows for 2530 km, which makes it one of the longest navigable rivers in the world; its catchment area covers about 14 per cent of Australia.

The Aboriginal people have a fable to account for the presence of the river. The area was without water and had little vegetation. One day Biami, one of the most powerful ancestral beings of the Yorta Yorta community, sent a woman to dig for roots in the dry ground. As protection, he sent with her a giant snake. The snake faithfully stayed with the woman, following the line of her digging stick in the dry dusty land. Then Biami shouted out to the skies in his voice of thunder. Lightning flashed and the rain fell. The rain traced the snake's movements and developed the great, winding river we now call the Murray.

En Route

At **Lake Cullulleraine**, 58 km west of Mildura, there is boating and swimming, and a track runs for 10 km around the lake.

Mildura Wines

Some of Victoria's finest wineries are to be found in the Mildura district. Apart from **Lindemans**, the largest winery in the southern hemisphere, some local wineries include:

Mildara Blass: on the white cliffs overlooking the Murray. First established (as White Cliffs) in 1888 by William Chaffey. Open Mon–Fri 0900–1700, Sat–Sun 1000–1600.

Capogreco Winery: a small family winery in Mildura itself (Riverside Ave, between 17th and 18th Sts); produces wines in the Italian style. Open Mon–Sat 1000–1800 for tastings and cellar door sales.

Allambie Wines: south of Irymple; wine-tasting Mon–Fri 1000–1630.

William's home, **Rio Vista**, is open to the public. Completed in 1892, it is now part of the **Mildura Arts Centre** (on the corner of Chaffey and Cureton Avenues). It demonstrates the Victorian way of announcing success. It has German lead lighting, hand-painted windows imported from England, Italian floor tiles and beautifully crafted red gum fittings. Displays upstairs relate to colonial and Aboriginal history, including furniture, photos, period costumes, letters and other memorabilia. Nearby is the replica of the red gum slab homestead which was the first home in the district. Other buildings in the complex include a woolshed and stables, and there are exhibitions relating to irrigation and the town's riverboat past. Open Mon–Fri 0900–1700 and weekends 1300–1700 ($). **Rio Vista Park**, opposite, contains a number of outdoor sculptures and an amphitheatre.

The **Mildura Regional Art Gallery** has a substantial collection of traditional Australian paintings as well as one of the largest collections of contemporary sculpture in Australia.

Woodsie's Gem Shop, on the corner of Morpung and Cureton Aves, is not a promising name but this is one of Australia's largest gemstone cutting and jewellery manufacturing complexes. Open daily 0900–1730, with demonstrations of gem cutting at 1100 and 1430. On display are gems from around the world including a private collection which is quite rightly called Aladdin's Cave. Outside, a garden is set up to keep children amused and there is a small cafeteria.

The **Murray River**, of course, is an attraction in itself. There are cruises along the river and cycle paths which follow its course. **Paddle steamers** leave from Mildura Wharf at the end of Madden Ave for trips on both the Murray and Darling rivers. One of the boats, **PS *Melbourne***, is still steam-driven, making it probably one of the only two passenger ships in the world still running on coal-fired boilers (the other is the **TSS *Earnslaw*** in Queenstown, New Zealand). To book, tel: (03) 5021 4424. On the other side of the river, the **Buronga Boatman** hires out powerboats, canoes and kayaks which can be used to explore the river; tel: (03) 5023 5874.

The **Golden River Zoo** is 4 km from town along River Rd, but you can also reach it by cruise boat. There is a large aviary and a good selection of wombats and kangaroos, some of which can be patted and fed. Open daily 0900–1700 ($).

BROKEN HILL: THE SILVER CITY

Broken Hill, 300 km north of Mildura, is an artificial oasis built in the arid wastelands of the Barrier Ranges. The reason for its existence is that it stands on the richest silver–lead–zinc deposit ever discovered. The mine has so far provided minerals worth almost $2 billion and more than one-third of the silver in the world.

There were gold prospectors in the area by 1867, but it wasn't until 1883 that Charles Rasp, a watchful boundary rider at Mount Gipps station, discovered what he thought were tin deposits at the 'broken hill'. A syndicate of seven was set up to purchase the surrounding land to prevent a rush from other miners. In January 1885 they hit a body of silver–lead–zinc lodes in a continuous arch 7 km long and 220 m wide.

Charles Rasp was not just a knockabout boundary rider who got lucky. He was born Hieronymous Salvator Lopez von Pereira in Saxony, a scion of the Portuguese aristocracy. He appears to have abandoned his army career during the Franco-Prussian War – an astute move – and headed for Australia.

Within eight years of the first find Broken Hill was a major town with a population of 20,000. More than 4000 people now work directly for the mining company. What the town will do when the ore runs out or when silver is no longer needed for photography is the subject of much debate.

i **Broken Hill Tourist Information**, corner of Blende and Bromide Sts; tel: 8088 9700; www.visitbrokenhill.com.au. Open daily. The telephone code is 08.

Broken Hill City Caravan Park $$ Rakow St; tel: 8087 3841.
Day Dream Motel $$$ 77 Argent St; tel: 8088 3033.
Hill Top Motor Inn $$$$ 271 Kaolin St; tel: 8088 2999.
Lakeview Caravan Park $$ 1 Mann St; tel: 8088 2250.
Lodge Outback Motel $$$ 252 Mica St; tel: 8088 2722.
Mario's Hotel Motel $$$ 172 Beryl St; tel: 8088 5944.
Miners Lamp Motor Inn $$$ 357 Cobalt St; tel: 8088 4122.
Motor Inn Silverhaven $$$$ 577 Argent St; tel: 8087 2218.

Mulberry Vale Cabins $$$$ Menindee Rd; tel: 8088 1597.
Old Willyama Motor Inn $$$$ 30 Iodide St; tel: 8088 3355.
Ruby's Cottage $$$$ 517 Argent St; tel: 0418 464 942.

☒ **Broken Hill Musician's Club Bistro $$** 276 Crystal St; tel: 8088 1777. Open daily for lunch and dinner.

Golden Lotus Room $$ 328 Crystal St; tel: 8087 2656. Open for lunch Mon–Fri and dinner daily.

Pagoda Restaurant $$$ 357 Cobalt St; tel: 8087 3679. Open for lunch Mon–Fri and dinner daily.

Oceania Restaurant $$ 423 Argent St; tel: 8087 3695. Cantonese-style food. Open daily for dinner.

HIGHLIGHTS

Broken Hill is very much a union town – possibly the most unionised in the world – and the **Trades Hall** which was built at the turn of the 20th century was the first building in Australia to be owned by a trade union. The city also has a **mosque** which was built in 1891 by and for the Afghan camel drivers who made the development of much of the outback possible.

An ideal way to get the feel of the town is to go on one of the walking tours. These start on Mon, Wed and Fri at 1000 outside the visitors' centre. **Argent St** (all the main streets are named after chemicals) has been classified by the National Trust and includes the post office, the town hall facade, the police station, technical college and courthouse.

The **Whites Mining Museum** displays life-size replicas of current and old-time mining procedures. Wearing a miner's hat, boots and overall, you can tour **Delprat's Mine**, descending in a miner's cage to 122 m under the ground ($$$). The tour price may seem expensive but half goes in insurance. The 2-hr tours start 1030 Mon–Fri and 1400 Sat.

You may recognise **Silverton**, 25 km north-west of Broken Hill, from *Mad Max 2* or *Razorback* or any of the many other films which have been made here. Silverton was the largest town in the Barrier Ranges before the discovery of Broken Hill, but the development of Broken Hill coincided with the exhaustion of its own deposits, and by 1907 it ceased to be a municipality. Today, Silverton is a ghost town that is sort of coming to life. The gaol has been converted into a small museum (open daily 0930–1630) and there are half a dozen private art galleries. The population is at least 60.

BRUSHMEN OF THE BUSH

Although very much a mining city, Broken Hill has produced a remarkable number of artists, collectively known as Brushmen of the Bush. There are at least 20 art galleries in the town.

A further 10 km out of Silverton is the **Mundi Mundi Lookout** which offers exceptional views of the plains.

Lying 195 km east of Broken Hill, **Wilcannia** was the boom town of the 1870s. Gold, copper, silver and opals drew prospectors from far and wide, and its location on the Darling made it the third largest inland port in the country – the entire wool clip of north-west New South Wales was loaded here. By 1920 it was all over and the Queen City of the West quietly went to sleep.

If you stroll around the town you can see its past glory in the fine old buildings, most of which have been recognised by the National Trust as buildings of historic importance. A Wilcannia shower, by the way, is a dust storm.

RENMARK

Renmark, South Australia, is, in a sense, a sister city to Mildura. The town is in the heart of the Chaffey brothers' irrigation scheme (see p. 131), and is Australia's oldest irrigation settlement, begun by the brothers after they were granted 100 ha on which to test their project. The town was named by George Chaffey in 1887 and may come from an Aboriginal word said to mean 'red mud'.

The irrigation scheme still operates; it covers nearly 7000 ha of land along the Murray, and the land around Renmark produces wine and table grapes, citrus, stone and dried fruits, and vegetables for local and export markets. Renmark is a provincial centre on a beautiful bend of the river with tourism added to wheat, wool, fruit, wine and brandy production as a source of income. It is also a retirement home for some of the old paddle wheelers which ran the river trade until the railways came in and showed they could do the same thing faster and cheaper.

i **Renmark/Paringa Visitor Centre**, 84 Murray Ave; tel: 8586 6704. Open daily. The telephone code is 08.

🛏 **Citrus Valley $$$** 210 Renmark Ave; tel: 8586 6717.
Fountain Gardens Motel $$$ 282 Renmark Ave; tel: 8586 6899.
Motel Ventura $$$ 234 Renmark Ave; tel: 8586 6841.
Renmark Country Club Motel $$$$ Sturt Hwy; tel: 8595 1401.
Renmark Hotel Motel $$$ Murray Ave. Bistro, outdoor swimming pool and spa; tel: 8586 6755.
Renmark Riverfront Caravan Park $ Patey Dr. Cabins and on the river; tel: 8586 6315.
Riverbend Caravan Park of Renmark $ Sturt Hwy. Cabins but not on the river; tel: 8595 5131.

🍽 **Ashley's Restaurant $$$** 210 Renmark Ave; tel: 8586 6717.
Ginger Mick's Pizza $ 124 Murray St; tel: 8586 4066. Open until late every night except Sun.

Nanya Bistro $$ Murray Ave; tel: 8586 6755.
Riverland Golden Palace Chinese Restaurant $ 114 Renmark Ave; tel: 8586 6065. Licensed.

Highlights

Next door to the Visitor Centre, an **Interpretive Centre** tells the full story of the Murray – its history from ancient times, its geology, the story of the local Aboriginal inhabitants, the irrigation scheme and the boats that plied its waters. Open Mon–Fri 0900–1700, Sat 0900–1600, Sun 1200–1600.

The Murray's potential for transportation wasn't realised until the port of Goolwa was established at the river's mouth. Then, for the 20 years between 1880 and 1900, over 200 paddle boats and barges operated from Goolwa right up to the Victorian goldfields.

The **PS *Industry*** was built in Goolwa in 1911 for the Engineering and Water Supply Department. Its job was to go up and down the river removing snags that were a danger to navigation. Now it has been fully restored to working order and turned into a museum – one that can and does still regularly steam up and down river. Open Mon–Fri 0900–1630, Sat 0900–1530, Sun 1200–1530. The tourist office has information about cruise times and prices.

The **PS *Murray Princess***, the largest stern-paddle steamer in the southern hemisphere, takes five-day cruises out of Renmark. This old-style vessel has all modern conveniences – spa, sauna and even an electric lift.

As they did in Mildura, the Chaffey brothers had the streets of Renmark numbered in the North American style, and **Olivewood**, on 21st St, is a log cabin built in 1887 for George Chaffey. The design undoubtedly reflects the brothers' Canadian origins, but with adaptations, such as broad verandahs, made to suit its Australian location. The interior has period furniture and the house now operates as a museum telling the story of Renmark's pioneering days. The orchard has been well maintained with orange, lemon, olive and grapefruit trees. Open Thur–Mon 1000–1600, Tues 1400–1600 ($).

Community Hotel

What is reputed to be the first community hotel in the British Empire was set up here in 1897; the Renmark Hotel is still run by an elected board of management, with the profits going to community improvements.
This system exists in many towns in the area. It means they have one huge pub which makes the community a profit, but it does not lead to interesting and exciting venues.

Bredl's Wonder World of Wildlife on the corner of Sturt Hwy and 28th St is one of the largest private zoos in Australia. It reportedly has the biggest collection of reptiles, with over 200 species on display, as well as crocodiles and other animals and birds. Open daily 0900–1800. There is snake handling daily at 1100 and 1400, and you can see the snakes being fed every Sun 1400–1500.

There are several major vineyards in the area. **Renmano** was established in 1914. Mon–Fri 0900–1700, Sat 0900–1600 and Sun 1000–1400. **Angove's** was the first vineyard on the river, having started in 1886. Open Mon–Fri 0900–1700.

Renmark is surrounded by national parks and reserves, of which the most accessible is the **Murray River National Park**. It has four separate areas – Katarapko Creek, Lyrup Flats, Bulyong Island and Eckert Creek. The nearest to Renmark is Bulyong Island, which you reach by way of Renmark North. Towards Berri, southwest of Renmark, is Lyrup Flats, and beyond Berri, hanging down in a great loop towards Loxton, is Katarapko. Lyrup Flats and Eckert Creek starkly reveal the potential problems of irrigation – most of the trees have been killed either by salt or high flood levels. This is a bleak landscape but an amazing breeding and feeding ground for wild birds. Nearly 150 different species have been recorded in the park's quiet backwaters and horseshoe lagoons.

Danggali Conservation Park, 90 km north of Renmark, was created by putting together four major sheep stations. The vegetation here varies from mallee woodland to blue bush shrubland and is home to both red and grey kangaroos.

Some 50 km east of Renmark are the flood plains and wetlands of **Chowilla Game Reserve**, accessible from either Wentworth Rd or Murtho Rd. All of these form part of the **Bookmark Biosphere Reserve**; for information, tel: 8595 8010. This is rugged country with no facilities whatsoever, and should only be approached in serious expedition mode.

WHERE NEXT?

An unmissable detour from Renmark before reaching Adelaide is the Barossa Valley (see p 157), one of Australia's premier wine regions.

ADELAIDE

See p. 144.

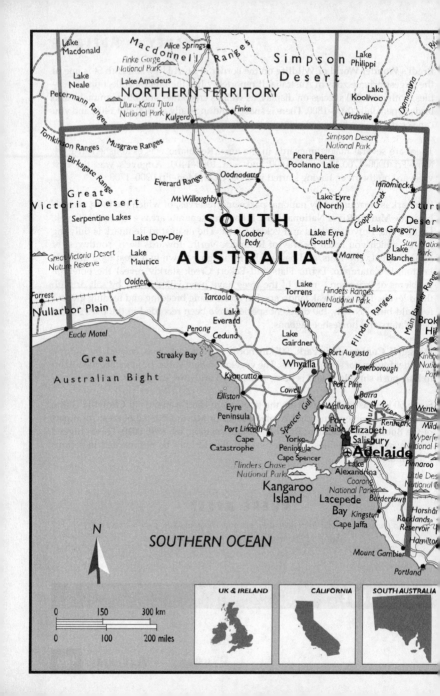

Like much of Australia west of the Great Dividing Range, South Australia is vast and empty. With an area of 984,400 sq km, it is Australia's third largest state (fourth if the Northern Territory is included) and fifth in terms of population, with close to 1.5 million people.

Except that it has no true alpine areas, South Australia rivals its south-eastern neighbours, New South Wales and Victoria, for diversity of landscape and remarkable natural attractions. Most of the state is arid land; the entire western half is dominated by the Great Victoria Desert and, reaching the Southern Ocean, the treeless (as its name would suggest) Nullarbor Plain. In the central north, Lake Eyre – Australia's largest salt lake – occasionally explodes into life after great floods in distant Queensland bring torrents of slow-moving, muddy water down the Cooper Creek and Diamantina River systems.

Nearer Adelaide, the craggy and ancient Flinders Ranges extend for about 400 km north from Port Augusta, at the tip of Spencer Gulf. Within the ranges are found about half of South Australia's 3100 plant species and more than 280 bird species. More birds – especially pelicans – await at Coorong National Park, a narrow coastal reserve that extends south-east from Lake Alexandrina, at the mouth of the Murray River. The state's human population is concentrated in a strip than runs south-east from Port Augusta through Adelaide, the state capital, to towns clustered in the vicinity of the Murray mouth.

Unlike the eastern colonies, South Australia's settlement was the result of private initiative. The colonisation theories of Edward Gibbon Wakefield – roughly, a system where the proceeds of Crown land sales would be used to fund migration of free settlers – had attracted considerable interest in London, and were applied to the establishment of South Australia in 1836–37. The colony's early days were marred by mismanagement; the work of first Surveyor-General William Light (see p. 145) in laying out graceful Adelaide was its principal triumph pre-1850. The absence of gold was South Australia's defining characteristic in the second half of the 19th century. Victorian gold rushes had South Australian settlers careering east in the 1850s; the South Australian Bullion Act succeeded in attracting many of them back with their loot to buy farm lands. By 1855 South Australia was exporting flour to the eastern goldfields and abroad. But much of the state's agricultural lands are marginal, and the latter part of the 19th century was marred by periods of rural downturn, each of which was fortuitously overcome by mineral discoveries.

SOUTH AUSTRALIA

South Australians were enthusiastic supporters of federation, although it did little at first to enhance their state's political scene: most of the ablest politicians went to the federal parliament. The state's fortunes – and those of its political masters – bumped along until 1938 when, after being particularly hard-hit by the great Depression, the conservative Thomas Playford became premier. During his record 27-year term as state leader, Playford oversaw unequalled economic expansion and a nearly 100 per cent rise in the state's population. After a few years' indecision, the South Australian electorate settled in 1970 on Don Dunstan's Australian Labor Party (ALP) government. Dunstan proved to be one of the great reformers of Australian politics, and over the next decade his government passed legislation covering Aboriginal land rights and self-determination, anti-discrimination and consumer protection.

Travel to South Australia is relatively easy, with regular air, bus and train services reaching Adelaide. Travel within the state – particularly to its fascinating desert parks – requires a four-wheel-drive vehicle. Today, South Australia is probably best known for its 13 wine regions, including the Adelaide Hills, Eden Valley, Clare Valley, McLaren Vale, the Riverland, Coonawarra and Padthaway. The Barossa Valley, just outside Adelaide, is the most renowned internationally.

SOUTH AUSTRALIA: OUR CHOICE

Adelaide
South Australian Museum, Art Gallery of South Australia, Warrawong Sanctuary

Coorong National Park

Naracoote
Naracoote Caves Conservation Park

Kangaroo Island
Flinders Chase National Park

Barossa Valley
Vineyards

Murray Bridge

Burra

Head of Bight
Whale watching

Nullarbor National Park

Quorn

Flinders Ranges National Park
Wilpena Pound

Innamincka

Oodnadatta Track
Lake Eyre

Coober Pedy
Opal mining

Witjira National Park
Dalhousie Springs

Simpson Desert Regional Reserve

HOW MUCH YOU CAN SEE IN A ...

WEEKEND (2 DAYS)

Best option is a couple of days in and near Adelaide. The various museums and galleries on North Terrace in central Adelaide could occupy a weekend on their own, as could Barossa Valley wineries; a balance between the two is ideal. If you're more interested in the bush than the city, consider spending a couple of days on Kangaroo Island, arguably the best place for seeing wildlife in this part of the world.

WEEK (7 DAYS)

Either expand on the weekend programme (with a couple of days in Adelaide and the Barossa and 2–3 on Kangaroo Island) or consider a longer journey from Adelaide, south to Coorong National Park, then north through the Barossa to Hawker and Flinders Ranges National Park. Return to Adelaide via Quorn, Port Augusta and Port Pirie.

MORE THAN A WEEK

Trips up the Oodnadatta, Birdsville or Strzelecki Tracks require four-wheel-drive vehicles and time – 2–3 weeks. A journey north into the South Australian outback is unforgettable, with Lake Eyre, the Dalhousie Springs (in Witjira National Park) and the Simpson Desert all extraordinary sights. The (sealed) Eyre Highway gives access to a narrow coastal strip to the west, where the Nullarbor cliffs form an imposing rampart against the Southern Ocean.

ADELAIDE

Adelaide is a dignified city, a place with much style and sensibility. It stands alone, serene and slightly aloof, although it is far from being a stuffy city. Adelaide has an almost European style and some Australians consider it the premier city of Australia.

The city was founded in 1836 and named after Queen Adelaide, wife of King William IV; her portrait is well known in Australia, as it appears on every bottle of Queen Adelaide wine. It is called the City of Light, partly because of its airiness and spaciousness, and punningly because much of it was designed by that remarkable pioneer, William Light. The original European explorer of the area was Captain Collett Barker in 1831, but it was Colonel Light who laid out the plan of Adelaide, 10 km inland from its port. It is impossible to overestimate Light's influence on the future style of the city, for despite huge expansion his original plan, which reserved large areas for parkland, has been maintained.

In 1841, only four years after Colonel Light presented his city plan, the town fathers had formed a council to run Adelaide's affairs. In 1842 the discovery of copper at Kapunda, followed by the Burra find in 1845, speeded up the growth of Adelaide and pushed its expansion into the outer suburbs.

The feeling prevalent in other Australian cities, that Adelaide is perhaps a little slow, a little stick-in-the-mud and overly conservative, is simply not correct. In many ways Adelaide has led the country. The University of Adelaide, which opened in 1882, admitted women as well as men from its inception, and Adelaide can claim several firsts: the Chamber of Commerce (1839) and the Chamber of Manufactures (1869) were the first institutions of their kind in the colonies; in 1856 the first

MUST SEE/DO IN ADELAIDE

Attend the Adelaide Arts Festival (even-numbered years)
Visit the Art Gallery of South Australia
Wander through the South Australian Museum
Visit Tandanya – the National Aboriginal Cultural Institute
Take in the view from Light's Vision, Montefiore Hill
Eat out in Rundle St, Gouger St or Hutt St

COLONEL LIGHT (1786–1839)

William Light fought in the Napoleonic Wars. He arrived in South Australia in 1836 as its first Surveyor-General, and began his plans for Adelaide in Jan 1837. Perhaps town planning was in his blood: his father was responsible for the layout of Georgetown on Penang, and Adelaide is now twinned with it. He resigned the post in 1838 and died from tuberculosis on 6 Oct 1839. A memorial in the form of a marble column marks his grave in Light Square, and his statue overlooks Adelaide from Montefiore Hill, but his true memorial is the City of Light itself.

state-owned steam railway in the British Empire was opened between Adelaide and Port Adelaide.

In the last three decades Adelaide has become a cultural city, a dining-out city, a sophisticated city. And yet it has managed to do this without losing any of its country town charm.

ARRIVAL AND DEPARTURE

Adelaide's airport, for both international and domestic flights, is just 6 km west, between the centre and the sea. There is an airport bus (Skylink, tel: 8332 0528) to city hotels and some hostels, which operates daily 0615–2140, running half-hourly weekday mornings and hourly afternoons and Sat and Sun, $7.50; this takes about 30 mins to Victoria Square. Hostels will pick you up or drop you off if you are staying there.

Hwy 1 passes through Adelaide on its trip around Australia's perimeter and other highways end (or begin) here: the Stuart Hwy (Rte 87), which crosses the Red Centre, and the Barrier and Sturt Hwys (Rtes 32 and 20), which link Adelaide and Sydney. Buses run directly between Adelaide and most other cities: Melbourne is about 11–12 hrs, Sydney 20–26 hrs depending on the route and Alice Springs about 25 hrs. The central bus station used by most carriers is at 101–111 Franklin St.

INFORMATION

TOURIST OFFICE **South Australian Visitor and Travel Centre**, 18 King William St; tel: 1300 655 276. Open Mon–Fri 0830–1700; Sat, Sun 0900–1400.

Port Adelaide Visitor Information Centre, 66 Commercial Rd, Port Adelaide; tel: 8405 6560; toll free 1800 629 888. Open daily 0900–1700.

INTERNET ACCESS The impressive **State Library of South Australia**, North Terrace (tel: 8207 7250), is open Mon–Fri from 0930 and weekends 1200–1700.

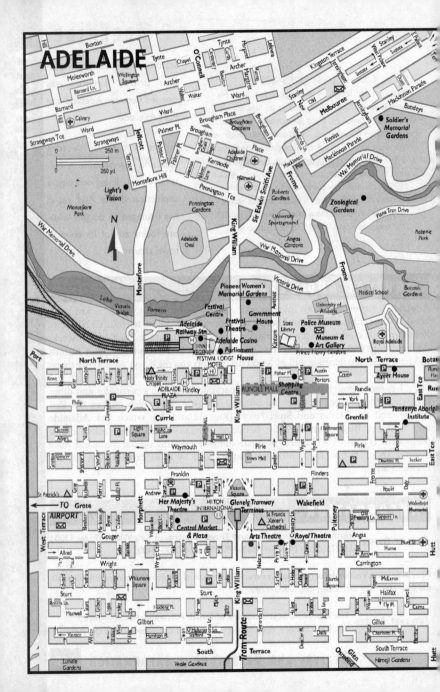

INTERNET SITES www.southaustralia.com; www.portenf.sa.gov.au; www.acta.com.au
www.adelaide.citysearch.com.au

MONEY Travelex has a foreign exchange office at 45 Grenfell St, tel: 8211 7032, and at the
international airport, James Schofield Dr., tel: 8234 3320.

POST AND PHONES The main post office is cnr King William St and Franklin St.
The phone code is 08.

ACCOMMODATION

Adelaide Backpacker's Hostel $–$$$ 257 Waymouth St; tel:
8221 5299; website: www.adelaidehostel.com.au.

Adelaide Backpackers Inn $–$$ 112 Carrington St; tel: 8223
6635. Singles and doubles in annexe.

Adelaide Central YHA $–$$$ 135 Waymouth St; tel: 8414
3010; www.yha.com.au/hostels. Centrally located, modern and
spacious. 24-hour reception, great facilities.

Adelaide City Park Motel $$$$ 471 Pulteney St; tel: 8223
1444; website: www.citypark.com.au. Rooms have balconies
overlooking parklands. Easy walk to many attractions and the
town centre.

Adelaide Meridien $$$$ 21 Melbourne St, North Adelaide;
tel: 8267 3033. Bit expensive but sauna, spa and outdoor pool.

Adelaide Paringa Motel $$$$ 15 Hindley St; tel: 8231 1000.
Heart of the Central Business District (CBD), walking distance
to Casino, Mall.

Ambassadors' Hotel $$$ 107 King William St; tel: 8231
4331. En suite. Tea making.

Austral Hotel $$ 205 Rundle St; tel: 8223 4660. Basic rooms
in music pub so check for noise.

Backpack Oz $–$$$ 144 Wakefield St, corner of Pulteney St;
tel: 8223 3551; website: www.backpackoz.com.au. Single and
double rooms.

Backpackers Glenelg Beach Resort $–$$$ 7 Moseley St,
Glenelg; tel: 1800 066 422; wwww.glenelgbeachresort.com.au.
Near beach with doubles and singles.

Blue Galah Backpackers Hostel $$$ Lvl 1, 62 King William
St; tel: 8231 9295; website: www.bluegalah.com.au. Right in the
centre of town.

City Central Motel $$$ 23 Hindley St; tel: 8231 4049.
Centrally located budget motel.

Clarice Hotel Motel $$$ 220 Hutt St; tel: 8223 3560. En suite. Car park.

Colley Motel Budget Accommodation $$$$ 22 Colley Terrace, Glenelg; tel: 8213 2500. Opposite beach. Self-contained affordable apartments.

Crown and Sceptre $$ 308 King William St; tel: 8212 4159. Centrally located budget – very inexpensive – hostel.

Director's Studios Hotel $$$$ 259 Gouger St; tel: 8213 2500. Self-catering apartments. Close to Chinatown and the Central Market.

East Park Lodge $$ 341 Angas St; tel: 8223 1228; www.eastparklodge.com.au. Single and double rooms.

Festival City Hotel/Motel $$$$ 140 North Terrace; tel: 8212 7877. Restaurant.

Flagstaff Hotel $$ 233 Franklin St; tel: 8231 4380.

Glenelg Seaway Apartments $$$ 18 Durham St, Glenelg; tel: 8295 8503. Inexpensive apartments.

Greenways Apartments $$$$ 45 King William Rd, North Adelaide; tel: 8267 5903. Self-catering units.

Grosvenor Mercure $$$$ 125 North Terrace; tel: 8407 8888. Dates from 1918 with spacious rooms, gym and sauna. Situated opposite Adelaide Casino.

Hotel 208 $$$$ 208 South Terrace; tel: 8223 2800; www.hotel208.com.

Hotel Richmond $$$$ 128 Rundle Mall; tel: 8223 4044. Restaurant and room service.

The Lodge, Mt Lofty Railway Station $$$–$$$$ 2 Sturt Valley Rd, Stirling; tel: 8339 7400. Unique tourist accommodation. Two night booking only.

Meledon Villa $$$ 268 Seaview Rd, Henley Beach; tel: 8235 0577. Seafront B&B.

Metropolitan Hotel $$ 46 Grote St; tel: 8231 5471. Old, basic but very affordable rooms.

Princes Arcade Motel $$$ 262–266 Hindley St; tel: 8231 9524. Car park. Room service.

Princes Lodge Motel $$$ 73 Lefevre Terrace, North Adelaide; tel: 8267 5566. En suite. Tea making. Price includes breakfast.

Quality Hotel Rockford $$$$ 164 Hindley St; tel: 8211 8255. Central location.

Riviera Adelaide $$$$ 31 North Terrace; tel: 8231 8000.

Strathmore Hotel $$$$ 129 North Terrace; tel: 8238 2900. Restaurant, car park, room service.

Taft Motor Inn $$$ 18 Moseley St, Glenelg; tel: 8376 1233.
Self-catering motel near the beach.

West Beach Caravan Park $$ 1 Military Rd, West Beach; tel:
8356 7230. Award-winning accommodation. On the beachfront.

FOOD AND DRINK

Adelaide claims one eatery to every 32 citizens. It seems a ridiculous ratio, but in
North Adelaide O'Connell St alone has over 40 restaurants, cafés and wine bars, and
several pubs that sell wine by the glass. Gouger St has almost as many, possibly
reflecting its nearness to Central Market and its fresh produce. Nearby is Adelaide's
Chinatown area.

Hutt St is said to be where modern Australian cuisine was born. In truth, it grew
organically in a number of places from a number of sources, but Hutt St is a
pleasant place to eat under the shade of the old broad verandahs and watch the
world go by.

Rundle St, especially the eastern end, is a lively place for street dining, and
Melbourne St gives you choices from Mexican and Japanese to Cajun, Mediterranean
and Asian. Hindley St, once rather sleazy and downmarket, has lifted its game and
has some splendid ethnic restaurants as well as a range of nightclubs.

Al Fresco Gelateria & Pasticceria $, 260 Rundle St; tel:
8223 4589. Open 0630–very late. The place to be seen and
drink superb coffee.

Austral Hotel $$ 205 Rundle St; tel: 8223 4660. A student
haunt with good-quality, reasonably priced modern Australian
cuisine. Lunch and dinner daily.

Caffe Buongiorno $, 145 The Parade, Norwood; tel: 8364
2944. Large, always lively café which reaches a crowded and
noisy crescendo on Sunday night. Serves a wide variety of
Italian food and drink. Daily 0800–0100 or later.

Cafe Miramare $$ 10 Jetty Rd, Glenelg; tel: 8295 6060.
Wood-oven pizzas. Seven days, 0800–late. Licensed.

Café Paradiso $ 150 King William Rd, Hyde Park; tel: 8272
1611. Long-established favourite; great coffee and real Italian
alfresco dining, from pasta to *osso buco*. Licensed. Daily
0830–2200.

Capriccio Restaurant $$ 10 Sussex St, Glenelg; tel: 8295
6453. Traditional Italian. Licensed. Dinner seven nights
1800–2300. Lunch Mon–Fri.

THE ADELAIDE PIE CARTS

For all Adelaide's trendy and cosmopolitan restaurant scene, its pie carts have remained very special. You can see them most easily at North Terrace but they appear in several places. The best known is Cowley's Pie Cart, which takes up its position each night at 1800 outside the post office on Franklin St and stays there until 0100 (0330 Fri and Sat). These carts have been around since 1915 and are something of an institution. The *specialité de la maison* is the floater. This is a hot meat pie with tomato sauce, sitting in a bowl of steaming green pea soup. Don't knock it until you've tried it.

Cos $$$ 18 Leigh St; tel: 8231 7611. A la carte steak and seafood. Open Mon–Fri for lunch and Mon–Sat for dinner.

D-Tox me $$$ 73a Hindley St; tel: 8410 3869. A healthy choice. Lots of vegetarian options. Open Mon–Fri 0730–late and Sat 1000–late.

East Terrace Continental $$ 6 East Terrace; tel: 8359 2255. An espresso bar with modern Australian cuisine. Open daily from 0700.

Elephant and Castle $$ 179 West Terrace; tel: 8231 9023. Good old-fashioned pub food. Lunch and dinner Mon–Sat.

Eros Ouzeri $$ 275–277 Rundle St; tel: 8223 4022. Open daily for lunch and dinner. Greek meze. Sit outside at the attached café for Greek pastries and coffee. Licensed.

Gaucho's Argentinian Restaurant $$$ 91 Gouger St; tel: 8231 2299. Not for vegetarians.

Gouger Fish Café $$ 98–100 Gouger St; tel: 8231 2320. Friendly service and excellent seafood; good wines.

Grange Jetty Kiosk $$$ cnr Jetty Rd and The Esplanade, Grange; tel: 8235 0822. Enjoy gourmet fish and chips at this chic beachside bistro.

Hawkers Corner $ cnr Wright St and West Terrace; tel: 8231 2676. Chinese, Thai, Malaysian and North Indian stalls. Tues–Sun 1700–2030, Sun 1130–2030.

House of Chow $$+ 82 Hutt St (cnr Wakefield St); tel: 8223 6181. Asian gourmet cuisine. Open for lunch Mon–Sat and dinner daily 1530–2230.

Jerusalem Sheshkebab House $ 131A–131B Hindley St; tel: 8212 6185. Lebanese for Middle Eastern dishes. Open Tues–Thur 1200–1500 and 1730 until late, Fri–Sat 1200–1600 and 1730 until late and Sun 1600 until late. BYO.

Lemongrass Thai Bistro $$$ 289 Rundle St; tel: 8223 6627. Menu includes dishes with crocodile, kangaroo and barramundi. Open Mon–Fri for lunch and dinner and Sat–Sun for dinner.

Magill Estate Restaurant $$$$, 78 Penfold Rd, Magill; tel: 8301 5551. 8 km out of town on Magill Estate Vineyard; tel: 8301 5551. Great food; greater wines. Open Tues–Sat for dinner and Fri–Sat lunch.

Manna Café $$ 12 Waymouth St, Adelaide; tel: 8231 6003. Mon–Fri 0700–1800. Good Italian pasta.

Marcellina Pizza Bar $$ 273 Hindley St; tel: 8211 7560. At the quieter western end. All-night pizza, steak and pasta bar. Open Mon–Thur 1100–0100 and Fri–Sat 1100–0500.

The Mt Lofty Summit Café Bistro $$ Summit Rd; tel: 8339 2600. 12 km from town on Adelaide's highest peak, with views over Adelaide, the Hills, and coast. Everything from a cappuccino to a three-course meal. Open seven days for breakfast, lunch and dinner Wed–Sat.

The Oyster Bar $$ 14 East Terrace; tel: 8232 5422. Open Tues–Sun 1200–late. Fresh oysters daily from the west coast.

Petaluma's Bridgewater Mill $$$$ Mt Barker Rd, Bridgewater; tel: 8339 3422, 17 km from the city beside an old watermill. The food is great but Brian Croser's Petaluma and Bridgewater Mill wines are totally wonderful. Open for lunch Thur–Mon.

Red Ochre Grill $$$$ War Memorial Dr., North Adelaide; tel: 8211 8555. Licensed. Lunch Mon–Fri, dinner Mon–Sat.

Rising Sun Inn $$$ 60 Bridge St, Kensington; tel: 8333 0721, 4 km out of town. Has won all sorts of awards. Licensed. Open lunch, dinner Mon–Sat.

Sosta $$$ 291 Rundle St; tel: 8232 6799. Argentinian restaurant. Open Mon–Fri for lunch and dinner, Sat–Sun 1800–late. Also open Sun from 0730 for a Latin breakfast.

The Balcony Restaurant (Strathmore Hotel) $$$$ 129 North Tce; tel: 8238 2900. Stonegrill cooking a speciality. Open for lunch Mon–Fri and for dinner Mon–Sat.

T Chow $$ 68 Moonta St; tel: 8410 1413. Very popular with the local Chinese population and famous for its duck dishes. Lunch and dinner daily.

Vego and Lovin' It $ 1st Floor, 240 Rundle St; tel: 8223 7411. Vegan café done with some style and very affordable.

Zuma Café $ 56 Gouger St; tel: 8231 4410. Near Central Market. Quiche is superb. Open Mon–Thur 0700–1800, Fri 0700–2200 and Sat 0700–1600.

GETTING AROUND

Getting around Adelaide is easy: it is a delightful city in which to walk, and the integrated public transport system is excellent. It is run by the Passenger Transport Board, which has an information bureau on the corner of King William St and Currie St; tel: 8210 1000.

The TransAdelaide Busway, the **O-Bahn**, provides the world's fastest suburban bus ride. The track runs between the city centre and Tea Tree Plaza, one of Adelaide's largest undercover shopping malls. The buses leave Currie and Grenfell Sts in the city at 5–10-min intervals during the week and at 15-min intervals on weekends.

The free **City Loop** service (number 99c) runs around the City stopping at many attractions including the Museum, State Library, Art Gallery and the Botanic Gardens. It also connects with services for the O-Bahn, the Glenelg Tram and the Adelaide Railway Station.

HIGHLIGHTS

Adelaide is Australia's fifth largest city, with a population of more than one million and a metropolitan area that stretches from Gawler in the north to Willunga in the south.

The best place to get an overall view of the city is **Light's Vision** on Montefiore Hill in North Adelaide. The statue of Colonel Light, a fine piece of sculpture, points across the parklands and the Torrens to the city and the Adelaide Hills which lie beyond.

For reasons which are not that easy to explain, Adelaide has always been something of the cultural centre of Australia. This is reflected in the **Art Gallery of South Australia**, which is on North Terrace. It has been in operation since 1881, only 45 years after the first European settlers arrived, and its collection of Australian colonial art is arguably the most comprehensive in Australia. Well worth searching out is the collection of Aboriginal Western Desert paintings, which are just stunning. It has its own website on www.artgallery.sa.gov.au. Open daily 1000–1700. Free.

CRICKET'S HERO

The late Sir Donald Bradman was the greatest batsman in the history of cricket, an Australian legend and international hero. When Bob Hawke was prime minister of Australia he was asked if there was anyone he would prefer to be. He answered, without hesitation, Don Bradman. Bradman's record shows that he was at least twice as good as any other cricketer that ever lived. There is a priceless personal collection of cricket memorabilia covering 1927–77, much of it provided by the great Don, housed at the State Library on North Terrace. You can worship at the shrine Mon–Fri 0930–1700, weekends 1200–1700. Free.

Another place to visit on North Terrace, Adelaide's cultural boulevard, is the **South Australian Museum**. Its internationally recognised collection of indigenous artefacts – Australia's largest and most representative – is displayed in the new Aboriginal Cultures Gallery, a top priority for every visitor. The museum's Egyptian and early Pacific ethnographic exhibits are also notable. On permanent display is the Douglas Mawson Exhibition, which unravels the fascinating Antarctic expeditions of a local hero. The museum is open daily 1000–1700. Free. Website: www.samuseum.sa.gov.au.

Further down North Terrace is **Ayers House Historic Museum** ($$). Set in the surrounds of historic Ayers House, built in 1845, it looks at life in colonial Adelaide and incorporates the history of the former home. Open Tues–Fri 1000–1600, Sat–Sun 1300–1600, closed Mon (except public holidays) ($$); tel: 8223 1234.

Just a short walk away is the historic **Adelaide Oval** cricket ground on War Memorial Drive. Tours of the Oval and Museum can be arranged; tel: 8300 3800.

A 15-minute drive from the city is **Carrick Hill** (46 Carrick Hill Dr., Springfield). Set in spectacular botanic gardens, this 1930s 'domestic castle' was left to the State with its extraordinary collection of sculpture, antiques and paintings spanning 400 years. Open Wed–Sun and public holidays 1000–1700; tel: 8379 3886.

Australia is a country of grateful migrants – of course, in the early days some of them may not have been as wholeheartedly keen on the move as later arrivals. The **Migration Museum** at 82 Kintore Ave (originally the Destitute Asylum) tells the story of the migrants, both convicts and free settlers. The museum is open Mon–Fri 1000–1700 and weekends 1300–1700; tel: 8207 7580.

The National Aboriginal Cultural Institute – **Tandanya** – in Grenfell St is the first of its size and scope in Australia. It is a multi-arts complex and includes galleries, workshops and performing areas. Tandanya is the Kaurna name for the Adelaide area. Here you can hear the didgeridoo being blown: the performers manage to keep a long continuous note by breathing in and blowing out simultaneously, which is not easy to do, as you will find out if you try. But this rotary breathing has been taken up by many other wind instrument performers, notably clarinettists, to allow the playing of far longer notes. Open daily 1000–1700 ($); tel: 8224 3200.

The foundation stone for **Holy Trinity Anglican Church** in North Terrace was laid in 1838, and Adelaide is, indeed, a city of churches: Christ Church was built in 1848–9, **St Francis Xavier's Roman Catholic Cathedral** near Victoria Square was begun in 1856 and St Peter's Anglican Cathedral was started in 1869. A mosque, finished in 1890, was paid for by the Afghans who were running camel trains into the interior. These men were absolutely vital to the building and maintenance of the Overland Telegraph from Adelaide to Darwin.

Adelaide is also a city of parks and open spaces. **Elder Park**, between the Festival Centre and south bank of the Torrens Lake, has a rotunda dating from 1882, which is one of the most identifiable sights of Adelaide. You can move elegantly and romantically along the River Torrens in a real Venetian gondola – available most days outside the Red Ochre Grill on War Memorial Drive. **Rymill Park**, in the city, has a lake with paddle boats for hire, a playground and model-boat pond. The **Adelaide Himeji Garden**, on South Terrace, is a traditional Japanese garden with a temple gate, lanterns, bridge and small lake marking a sister city link. There are many more. Like every other city in Australia, Adelaide has magnificent botanic gardens. The **Adelaide Botanic Gardens and Bicentennial Conservatory**, begun in 1855, feature the oldest glasshouse in Australia, and the conservatory contains a complete tropical rainforest. Off North Terrace; open Mon–Fri 0800–1700, weekends 0900–1700 (later in spring and summer); conservatory open 1000–1600 ($).

Adelaide Zoo, one of the oldest zoos in Australia, is in shady parklands off Frome Rd, only a short stroll from the city centre. Like all intelligent zoos it is moving away from the caged exhibit. Open daily 0930–1700 ($$$).

EVENTS

South Australia enjoys two of the country's major festivals: the biennial **Barossa Valley Vintage Festival** (held at Easter in odd-numbered years) and the **Adelaide Arts Festival** in Feb–Mar of even-numbered years. For three weeks the Arts Festival is celebrated across the city, embracing theatres, clubs and open spaces, with its epicentre the Adelaide Festival Centre in King William Rd, on the banks of the River Torrens. Book well in advance (tel: 8216 8600).

NIGHTLIFE

Adelaide has a reputation for being dead after 2000 in the evening. A browse through *The Guide* in the Thur edition of the *Adelaide Advertiser*, or *Rip It Up* (for gigs) or the *Adelaide Review* will prove otherwise.

The really big shows are at the Adelaide Entertainment Centre in Hindmarsh. The Adelaide Festival Centre has a number of performance venues – the Festival Theatre for operas, musicals and concerts, the Dunstan Playhouse for theatre and the Space for more intimate productions. Her Majesty's Theatre and the Town Hall are other major venues.

Adelaide's nightlife is mainly concentrated in Rundle St, East End, Hindley St and the West End. Many of Adelaide's pubs and nightclubs feature live bands. Some of the hottest clubs are Heaven and the Cargo Club. There is usually something happening at 'The Gov' – The Governor Hindmarsh Hotel on Port Rd. Jazz fans can dial up the Jazz Hotline (tel: 8303 3755) for gig information. Or you can try www.ripit-up.com.au.

THE FLEURIEU PENINSULA

A gentle drive down the Fleurieu Peninsula will take you to Cape Jervis and the Southern Ocean.

South of Glenelg the coast road runs along the shore to Marion, right on the edge of the Sturt Gorge Recreation Park, and then to Old Noarlunga. Turning inland here will bring you shortly to McLaren Vale.

McLaren Vale is 39 km south of Adelaide and the centre of the Southern Vales wine-growing district. Farmers grew vines here from the 1850s, mainly for their own use, but wine-making seriously began in 1873 when Thomas Hardy moved into the area. Hardy had come out on the barque *British Empire* in 1850, and drove cattle to the Victoria goldfields to make himself enough money to buy a property near Adelaide and to marry. In 1853 he grew his first crop of Shiraz and Grenache grapes. His winery increased and, in a bold stroke, in 1873 he bought the Tintara Winery in McLaren Vale for a modest sum – he was the only bidder. Today the company is one of the biggest in Australia.

Hardy's Tintara is one of more than 60 wineries in the area, many of which are open for tastings and cellar door sales. Most also offer snacks and some have high-quality restaurants; usual opening hours are 1000–1700 daily. For more information pick up a copy of the free booklet *Wine, Food and Coastal Experience* from the Visitor Information Centre, Main Rd; tel: 8323 9944. Open 1000–1700 daily. Website: www.visitorcentre.com.au.

The inland road crosses over the South Mount Lofty Ranges and reaches, 30 km further on, **Victor Harbor**, which faces the Southern Ocean and is spelled in the American way.

From there you can cut back again over the peninsula to the Gulf of St Vincent at Normanville. As the land narrows you pass through the tiny hamlet of **Second Valley**, of which Colonel Light said: 'I have hardly seen a place I like better.' The road ends at **Cape Jervis** at the very tip of the Fleurieu Peninsula, 110 km from Adelaide. Ferries cross from here to Kangaroo Island (see p. 167) and **Deep Creek Conservation Park** is just to the east.

The world's longest walking trail, the Heysen Trail, begins near Cape Jervis and ends 1200 km north in the Flinders Ranges. The trail is marked with orange triangles but parts of it require bushwalking skills. Information from Department of Environment and Heritage; tel: 8124 4792; www.environment.sa.gov.au/parks/heysen.html.

Almost every casino in Australia looks as if it were designed to dazzle rather than entertain. They all lack style, most are noisy and all the players seem never to smile. The one exception is the **Adelaide Casino** at Skycity on North Terrace, in what was the old railway station. Open Sun–Thur 1000–0400, Fri–Sat 1000–0600.

DAY TRIPS

PORT ADELAIDE Adelaide's port is about 20 mins from Victoria Square by tram and is on the Port River, a wide inlet from Gulf St Vincent. It was a serious working port in the 1880s and this has left a heritage of splendid buildings. The best way to follow how it developed is to visit the **South Australian Maritime Museum** in Lipson St; open daily 1000–1700. The museum extends over several sites: an 1850s bond store, the 1869 lighthouse, the wharf and the vessels tied alongside.

Even though you are still very close to the city you can often see dolphins here, and take a trip into a mangrove wilderness.

GLENELG Glenelg is one of Adelaide's many seaside suburbs. The tourist office likes to boast that Adelaide has the closest beaches to a city in Australia. Although this is not really true, it can boast long sweeps of magnificent beach from Semaphore past North Haven, West Lakes, Grange, Henley Beach, Glenelg, Brighton, Seacliff, Hallet Cove and southwards to the Fleurieu Peninsula.

Getting to Glenelg is easy and very pleasant if you travel on the historic tram. It runs the 10 km from Victoria Square in the heart of the city to the seaside in about half an hour.

At Patawalonga Boat Haven on Adelphi Terrace is **HMS *Buffalo***, a replica of the vessel that brought the first European settlers to South Australia. It has a restaurant as well as a small museum. Open Mon–Sat 0630–2100, Sun 1200–1400 ($).

WHERE NEXT?

Adelaide was the start of the Overland Telegraph and towns born along the line can be found all the way north to Darwin, the most famous of which is Alice Springs (see p. 366). About halfway between Adelaide and Alice Springs, the opal-mining town of Coober Pedy (p. 173) is isolated, sun-blasted and full of outback eccentrics. South Australia's great wine-producing region is the Barossa Valley (see p. 157) and a spectacular coastal route runs along the shore of the Southern Ocean from Adelaide to Melbourne (see p. 201).

BAROSSA VALLEY

It was Colonel Light, the man who designed Adelaide (see p. 144), who found what is now one of the best-known wine-producing regions in Australia. In 1837, in the course of surveying for a north-east route from Adelaide to the eastern states, he came across this broad valley and, having fought Napoleon's army in the Peninsular Wars, named (but misspelled) it Barossa after the Battle of Barrosa.

Unlike most other regions of Australia, the main influx of settlers here was neither of convicts nor of hopeful gold prospectors. George Fife Angas conceived of the idea of encouraging settlement by religious dissenters. The God-fearing Lutherans he brought in from Silesia and Prussia were not poor refugees; rather, they were successful trades-people who had fallen foul of the Kaiser.

The first group of 25 families came to South Australia in 1838, bringing with them their language, their customs and their religion. Some of the names of those early settlers – Seppelt, Henschke, Hoffmann, Gramp – are to be found in the wine industry of today.

BAROSSA VALLEY VILLAGES

Early settlements followed the German pattern of Strassendorf or Hufendorf villages. Owing to original language difficulties, these stayed small and self-contained, with households producing almost all their own food, including smoked meats, cheese and wine, and the cellars and smokehouses of the village houses still recall this self-sufficient way of life. Villages such as Krondorf and Bethany, and some of the cemeteries and churches, retain traces of their German origins, but during World War I German as a spoken language was severely frowned upon and German place names were changed by act of parliament.

It is claimed that the first vines were planted in 1847 at the Orlando vineyards, an estate which still produces wine in large quantities. However, the first wines were probably made by Johann Gramp in 1850 and were table wines for immediate use, from his small vineyard at Jacob's Creek. Others followed his example: snuff manufacturer Joseph Seppelt turned to vines after unsuccessfully trying to grow tobacco; Samuel Hoffmann, a veteran of the Prussian army who had fought at Waterloo, arrived in 1847 and started a vineyard near Tanunda. The result is that many of the wineries scattered around the Barossa Valley have a very distinct European style, a matured German manner.

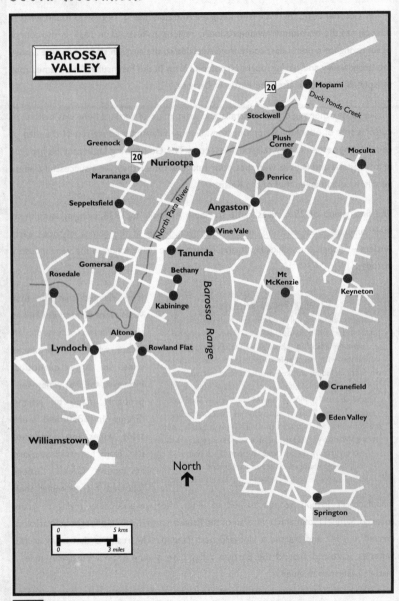

BAROSSA VALLEY

Mopami

20

Duck Ponds Creek

Stockwell

Greenock

Plush Corner

20

Moculta

Marananga

Nuriootpa

Penrice

Seppeltsfield

Angaston

North Para River

Vine Vale

Tanunda

Gomersal

Bethany

Mt McKenzie

Rosedale

Barossa Range

Keyneton

Kabininge

Altona

Lyndoch

Rowland Flat

Cranefield

Eden Valley

Williamstown

North

0   5 kms

0   3 miles

Springton

Today, the Barossa produces a very wide range of wines. It could be argued that its strength is in the dry whites and dry reds, leaving the seriously heavy reds to the Hunter Valley in New South Wales (see p. 241), but there are many exceptions to this. Although many wines on offer might be described as German-style, the closest resemblance to the soil and weather conditions of the Barossa can be found in Portugal rather than Germany. The Barossa crushes, but does not necessarily grow, about a quarter of the Australian vintage – a substantial percentage of the grapes processed here are grown elsewhere.

The Barossa Valley is not geographically distinct – it is too broad and flat for that – but this is a disappointment only if you are expecting spectacular scenery. There are about 50 wineries in the region and most welcome visitors for cellar door tastings, guided tours and cellar sales. Most of them offer light refreshments as well. The wineries are mainly between Nuriootpa and Lyndoch, which are about 20 km apart. Seppeltsfield is perhaps the most visually interesting, but all are worth a visit. Details of just a small selection are given here, but more information can be had from the information centres.

GETTING THERE AND GETTING AROUND

There are two sub-regions in this area: the Barossa Valley itself, which includes Nuriootpa, Tanunda and Lyndoch, and the Barossa Hills, with the towns of Eden Valley, Springton and Angaston.

There are several ways of exploring. You could take a coach tour or check out tours and transport operators on www.barossa-region.org; or it is a pleasant drive, about 60 km, from Adelaide. The route through Elizabeth and Gawler to Lyndoch at the south end of the valley can have a fair amount of traffic and is, perhaps, a less than interesting drive. The other and more scenic way is to come in from the other end, through Angaston and Nuriootpa.

INFORMATION

The telephone code for the area is 08.

TOURIST OFFICE **Barossa Wine and Visitor Centre,** 66 Murray St, Tanunda; tel: 8563 0600 or 1300 852 982. Open daily. There is a clever use of cylinders to tie in the history of the area with the history of Australia and, indeed, the world, and lots of information on wine and wine tasting.

SOUTH AUSTRALIA

Kies Estate, a small-scale winery on Barossa Valley Way, acts as a tourist information office as well as offering wine tastings. Open daily; tel: 8524 4110.

INTERNET SITES **Barossa Valley** www.barossa-region.org

Wine Australia, www.wineaustralia.com.au

ACCOMMODATION

ANGASTON	**Barossa Brauhaus Hotel $$$** 41 Murray St; tel: 8564 2014. Basic accommodation in a pub first licensed in 1849. Central location, breakfast available.
	Collingrove Homestead $$$$ Eden Valley Rd, 6 km from Angaston; tel: 8564 2061. National Trust-listed B&B accommodation in this beautifully restored and decorated home.
LYNDOCH	**Chateau Barossa Motor Inn $$$$** Barossa Valley Hwy; tel: 8524 4268.
	Barossa Valley Farmhouse YHA $$$ Sandy Creek Conservation Park, Sandy Creek; tel: 8414 3000. Renovated farmhouse with fantastic bush outlook. Advance bookings only – $$$ covers up to 16 people.
NURIOOTPA	**Barossa Gateway Motel & Hostel $$$** Kalimna Rd, Nuriootpa 5355; tel: 8562 1033.
	Barossa House $$$$ Barossa Valley Way, between Tanunda and Nuriootpa; tel: 8562 4022. B&B with en-suite rooms.
	Bunkhaus Travellers Hostel and Cottage $–$$ Barossa Valley Way; tel: 8562 2260. Hostel in the vineyards. Dorm beds and self-contained cottage available.
	Hotel/Motel Vine Inn $$$$ 14 Murray St; tel: 8562 2133.
	Seppeltsfield Holiday Units $$$ Seppeltsfield Rd, nr Nuriootpa; tel: 8562 8240. Log cabins overlooking the winery.
	Top of the Valley Tourist Motel $$$ 49 Murray St; tel: 8562 2111.
	Vine Inn Hotel Motel $$$ 14 Murray St; tel: 8562 2133. Modern motel. Spa and heated pool.
TANUNDA	**Barossa Junction Resort $$$$** Barossa Valley Way; tel: 8563 3400.
	Langmeil Cottages $$$$ Langmeil Rd; tel: 8563 2987. Stone cottage with cooking facilities. Heated pool.
	Langmeil Rd Caravan Park $ 70 Langmeil Rd; tel: 8563 0095.

Lawley Farm $$$$ Krondorf Rd; tel: 8563 2141. Restored stone cottages. Spa. Breakfast.

Tanunda Caravan & Tourist Park $ Barossa Valley Way; tel: 8563 2784. Parkland setting with cabins.

Tanunda Hotel $$$ 51 Murray St; tel: 8563 2030. Dates from 1845. Some rooms en suite.

Wycombe Lodge $$$$ High Wycombe Winery, Bethany Rd, Tanunda; tel: 8563 2776.

FOOD AND DRINK

Vineyards and wineries always attract good restaurants and the Barossa is no exception. Standards are remarkably high and you should make your own discoveries. However, do not miss out on tea at the Zinfandel Tea Rooms in Tanunda where, after the cakes and strudel, you will not be able to eat dinner.

ANGASTON

Barossa Bistro $$ 37 Murray St; tel: 8564 2361. Lunch and dinner daily. Has kangaroo on the menu. Licensed.

Barossa Brauhaus $$ 42 Murray St; tel: 8564 2014. Open for lunch daily, dinner Tues–Sun. First licensed in 1849.

Saltram Wine Estate Bistro $$$ Nuriootpa Rd; tel: 8564 3355. Bistro attached to a 19th-century winery. Meals lunchtime only.

Seasons of the Valley $$$ 6–8 Washington St; tel: 8564 3688. Café and gallery showing work of local artists. The café specialises in fresh seasonal produce; they even make their pasta with local duck eggs. Open daily.

Vintners Bar and Grill $$$ corner of Stockwell and Nuriootpa Rds; tel: 8564 2488. Impressive wine list; vine-covered courtyard. Tues–Sun lunch, Wed–Sat dinner.

LYNDOCH

Errigo's Cellar Restaurant $$ 23 Barossa Valley Way; tel: 8524 4015. Licensed. Open daily for lunch.

NURIOOTPA

Chinese Dragon Restaurant $$ 9 Gawler St; tel: 8562 2797. Licensed. Cantonese.

Kaesler Restaurant $$$ Barossa Valley Way; tel: 8562 2711. Open daily for lunch and dinner. Licensed. Part of the Kaesler Estate.

Nuriootpa Vine Inn $$$ 14 Murray St; tel: 8562 2133. Licensed. Open daily for lunch and dinner.

Shangri-la Thai Restaurant $$ 31 Murray St; tel: 8562 3559. Licensed.

TANUNDA

1918 Bistro and Grill $$$ 94 Murray St; tel: 8563 3408. Open daily for lunch and dinner. Licensed. Garden setting with dining on the verandah. BYO or local wines.

Bergman's $$ 66 Murray St; tel: 8563 2788.

Café Lanzerac $$$$ Main St. Trendy café. Barossa wine sold by the glass. Blackboard menu. Open daily from breakfast to dinner.

Fortune Garden $ 46 Murray St; tel: 8563 0099. Asian.

La Buona Vita $ 89a Murray St; tel: 8563 2527. Licensed. Lunch and dinner daily.

Park Restaurant/Café $ 2a Murray St; tel: 8563 3500. 1840s stone villa set in a park. South-east Asian cuisine.

Tanunda Hotel $ 51 Murray St; tel: 8563 2030. Good range of vegetarian dishes.

Zinfandel Tea Rooms $ 58 Murray St; tel: 8563 1822. Lunch and tea daily. Unbeatable strudels and cakes, not for the calorie-conscious. Open daily 0830–1800.

ANGASTON

Angaston, at the eastern end of the valley, is set in the highest reaches of the Barossa (which is not that high, at 361 m above sea level). The town is named after George Fife Angas, sponsor of many of the valley's early German settlers.

A 2.5-km **Heritage Walk** will take you around the town. Angaston has two beautiful parks, a small creek flowing through its centre and good examples of colonial architecture. It boasts two of the Barossa's oldest wineries, and a dried-fruit outlet.

Worth seeing is the **Collingrove Homestead**, 6 km from town on Eden Valley Rd (open Mon–Fri 1300–1630, Sat–Sun 1100–1630; tel: 8564 2061). Built in 1856 as a home for the second son of George Fife Angas, it remained in possession of the family until 1976, when it was given to the National Trust. It still contains many of the original furnishings and is surrounded by lush gardens. Angas also lived at nearby Lindsay Park, now the Lindsay Park Stud, Australia's leading racehorse breeding and training complex.

NURIOOTPA

This is the commercial centre of the Barossa Valley, and its largest and busiest town. Nuriootpa is possibly the most consistently mispronounced and misspelled town name in Australia – everyone bar its inhabitants tends to pronounce it incorrectly. Say 'nurreuutpa'.

In 1843 William Coulthard opened a hotel – a flattering term – called the Red Lion, to serve bullock drivers en route from Adelaide to Kapunda and Burra. This was not what you would call an upmarket trade. It is now the community-owned Vine Inn. William Coulthard's house, now a National Trust museum, was built in 1855 on the corner of Murray and Penrice Sts. It is built from local bluestone and is of an elegant Victorian design and superb workmanship. Coulthard is said to have died of thirst in 1858 while looking for new land to the north of the town.

Nuriootpa has a number of famous wineries: **Penfolds**, **Wolf Blass**, **Eldetron** and **Old Stockwell**.

Meandering through the town is the North Para River which, with the open spaces, interesting old buildings, parks and picnic spots, makes Nuriootpa a pleasant enough town to visit, although the Penfolds winery gives it something of an industrial feel.

LIGHT PASS

In this small village near Nuriootpa are two Lutheran churches and a cairn that marks the place where Colonel Light met Captain Sturt. Nearby is **Luhr's Cottage**, which was built in 1848 by the Barossa's first German schoolteacher, J H Luhrs. The house has been restored and furnished in the authentic German style. Open daily 1000–1600.

MARANANGA AND SEPPELTSFIELD

Marananga is a tiny settlement originally called Gnadenfrei – which roughly translates as 'freed by the Grace of God'. During World War I, it was given its Aboriginal name, which can be translated as 'my hands'. Marananga is minute but has a wonderful church, restored barns and cottages, and its own brass band.

From Marananga, an imposing avenue of date palms lines the route to **Seppeltsfield**, a mini-village of 19th-century stone winery buildings, the focus of the large wine-making operations of B Seppelt & Sons. Joseph Ernest Seppelt had run a liquor and snuff company in Silesia until, like other dissenting Lutherans, he was driven out by the religious intolerance of the Prussian emperor. He arrived in Australia in 1849 with his family and 13 employees and their families.

The Seppeltsfield complex offers tasting, picnicking spots and touring, while the old Seppelt family home has been restored and is available as accommodation. The beautifully maintained gardens add to the impressive buildings to make it one of the showplaces of the Barossa. The Seppelt family mausoleum sits on a hilltop which provides wonderful views over Seppeltsfield. Open Mon–Fri 0900–1700, Sat 1030–1630, Sun 1100–1600.

TANUNDA

Tanunda is one of the oldest towns in the Barossa Valley and is the heartland of German culture in South Australia.

The town was originally known as Langmeil when the first vines were planted in 1847. Two years later they built the Tabor Lutheran Church. In Tanunda, as in the rest of the Barossa, Lutheran churches are in the majority – the town has four. Pastor Auricht, who had come from Silesia with the immigrants, started a German newspaper for the town in 1855, and a printing office was built in that year. The Chateau Tanunda winery was founded in 1889, and was later bought by the Seppelt family.

Tanunda is now very much a tourist town, which you sense as soon as you enter through the Orlando archway that spans Murray St, the main street. As you wander along you will hear German music – the town got its first brass band in 1860, with a Lieder-tafel (singing society) in the year following – but you will get a better feel for the place in the smaller streets on the western side of town, towards the river. Here Goat Square is classified by the National Trust and is surrounded by century-old cottages.

The **Barossa Valley Historical Museum**, in Murray St, is housed in Tanunda's 1865 post and telegraph buildings. It specialises in Barossa German heritage, with a collection that includes wedding gowns, artefacts, books and photographs. One room has an altar and church furniture with German inscriptions. Usually open daily, but opening hours may vary; tel: 8566 0212 for current times.

Barossa Kiddypark, on the corner of Magnolia St and Menge Rd, is a truly woeful name for a splendid and well-equipped fun park which includes activities such as electric cars, dodgem cars, train rides, merry-go-round and super slide. A wildlife section has wallabies, kangaroos, emus, wombats, ponies and native birds.

The **Keg Factory** (St Hallett Rd; tel: 8563 3012; open daily) makes kegs, wine racks, barrel furniture – almost any application of the craft of coopering.

A little way out of town, on the Barossa Way at Dorien, is the Kev Rohrlach Museum. It is built on the site of the former Siegersdorf – later Hardy's – Winery, and has over 3000 exhibits in an esoteric and eclectic private collection that includes everything from space rockets to a 1902 electric car, old clothes, a Canberra bomber and a rare 19th-century maharajah's carriage used by the Duke of Edinburgh; tel: 8563 3407 for opening times.

VALLEY PANORAMA
Mengler's Hill Lookout on Mengler's Hill Rd to the east of Tanunda has panoramic views of the valley. There is a sculpture garden on the slopes below, and at night you can see the lights of Adelaide.

BETHANY

This is the valley's oldest German settlement, founded in 1842 by a group of Lutheran families – the biblical name is an indication of their devotion. They mapped out their village along Prussian lines and the cottages facing the road replicate those the settlers lived in before coming to Australia. The bell of **Herberge Christi Church** still rings each Sat at dusk to mark the working-week's end. Several houses have been restored and are open to the public as craft shops and art galleries. The village reserve where the cows used to graze is great for picnics.

LYNDOCH

Lyndoch is the southern gateway to the Barossa Valley and one of the oldest towns in South Australia. Colonel Light named it (but again misspelled it) after his friend Lord Lynedoch, who led his men to victory at the Battle of Barrosa. On seeing the site for the first time, Light reported: 'A beautiful place, good land, plenty of grass and its general appearance open with some patches of wood and many kangaroos.'

The village that began to develop in 1847 was flooded in 1854 and the move was made to higher ground. The first winery did not come here until 1896 – the focus in the early days was the watermill driven by the Para River, which was used for grinding corn. Now there are many wineries in the area, ranging from small family operations to major ones: they include **Wards**, **Yaldara**, **Cimicky**, **Burge**, **Kellermeister** and **Redgum Cellars**.

Fine examples of early dwellings survive. The **Mechanical Music Museum** has a range of 19th-century clockwork musical boxes, Edison wax cylinder machines and Berliner phonographs. Open daily 0900–1700.

Rosedale, a short distance from Lyndoch, has a quaint cemetery and an interesting herb farm.

SOUTH AUSTRALIA

The retaining wall of the Barossa Reservoir, 7 km south-east of Lyndoch off Yettie Rd, is known as the **Whispering Wall**. Its shape enables a whispered message at one end to be heard 140 m away at the other. It also provides excellent scenic views of the reservoir, and there are barbecue and picnic facilities.

WINERIES

ANGASTON

Henschke, Moculta Rd, Keyneton, south-east of Angaston, has been making wine for five generations. Open Mon–Fri 0900–1630, Sat 0900–1200.

Yalumba Wines, Eden Valley Rd, was established in 1849 and has a lovely building and gardens. Open Mon–Sat 1000–1700, Sun 1200–1700.

TANUNDA

Charles Melton, Krondorf Rd. Full-bodied reds. Tasting in a wooden shed. Open daily 1300–1700.

Grant Burge Wines, Barossa Valley Way, Jacob's Creek. New winery on an old site. Open daily 1000–1700.

Krondorf Wines, Krondorf Rd. 1860s winery and vineyard which has been updated. Open daily 1000–1700.

Langmeil Winery, Langmeil Rd. Built in the 1840s. Three reds, three whites and a tawny port. Open daily 1000–1700.

Peter Lehmann, Para Rd. Homestead with vine-entwined verandahs. The Sémillon Blanc is inexpensive but possibly the best of its type in Australia. The wine labels feature South Australian artists, whose original paintings are on display. Open Mon–Fri 0930–1700, Sat–Sun 1030–1600.

Rockford Wines, Krondorf Rd. Big, traditional wines. Tasting in an old stone barn. Open daily 1100–1700.

St Hallett Winery, Krondorf Rd. Medium-sized quality producer. Open daily 1100–1700.

BETHANY

Bethany Wines. The Schrapels have grown grapes here for five generations. Open Mon–Sat 1000–1700, Sun 1300–1700.

WHERE NEXT?

If you've time, take the opportunity to travel north to the rugged Flinders Ranges and see magnificent Wilpena Pound. Broken Hill (p. 135) is further east, in outback NSW. The Adelaide–Melbourne coastal route (pp. 201–221) runs east and south out of Adelaide.

Many visitors are surprised at the size of Kangaroo Island – at 155 km long and up to 55 km wide it is the third largest island off the coast of Australia. It sits at the mouth of Gulf St Vincent, on which Adelaide lies, and is almost totally undeveloped.

In the early 20th century evidence of stone tools and Aboriginal campsites was discovered. Subsequent dating of charcoal campfire remains indicate that Aboriginal people were living on the island at least 10,000 years ago. Why or when they abandoned Kangaroo Island is not known. The first white people to live here were sealers, escaped convicts and runaway sailors seeking refuge in the early 19th century. They lived on kangaroos and other wildlife, and traded salt plus seal, kangaroo and wallaby skins for spirits and tobacco.

The lighthouses at Cape Willoughby and Cape Borda, erected in the 1850s, were desperately needed. Kangaroo Island was a serious hazard to shipping and there are over 40 wrecks in the seas around. The lighthouse keepers and their families were the first of the legitimate European population which was later swelled by sheep farmers and, after World War II, ex-soldiers sent as part of a war service land-settlement scheme. But even to this day, the population is fairly small.

Kangaroo Island is treasured for its wildlife. More than half the island has never been cleared of vegetation, and numerous reserves and conservation parks, including five significant Wilderness Protection Areas, guarantee that it will remain wild and spectacular. These measures and the absence of foxes and rabbits combine to provide safe habitats for an extraordinary variety of wildlife, some of which have disappeared from the mainland.

ARRIVAL AND DEPARTURE

The island is a 30-min flight from Adelaide. The airport is 13 km from Kingscote, the island's principal town – transport is available, but arrangements should be made at the time of booking.

Ferries operate from Cape Jervis on the tip of the Fleurieu Peninsula to Penneshaw, on the island's eastern tip. There are coach connections between Adelaide and Cape Jervis, and between Penneshaw and Kingscote. See OTT 9055.

INFORMATION

Tourist Offices **National Parks and Wildlife**, 37 Dauncey St, Kingscote; tel: (08) 8553 2381. Open Mon–Fri.

Tourism Kangaroo Island, Howard Dr., Penneshaw; tel: (08) 8553 1185. Open daily.

The telephone code is 08.

Internet Site **Kangaroo Island Visitors' Guide** www.tourkangarooisland.com.au

National Parks www.environment.sa.gov.au/parks/kangaroo_is.html

ACCOMMODATION

Ellson's Seaview Motel $$$$ Chapman Terrace, Kingscote. Courtesy transport, licensed restaurant; tel: 8482 2030.

Flinders Chase Farm $ Flinders Chase National Park; tel: 8559 7223. Hostel accommodation and cabins.

Graydon Holiday Lodge $$$ 16 Buller St, Kingscote. Fully equipped kitchen and fridge; tel: 8553 2713.

Island Resort $$$ 4 Telegraph Rd, Kingscote. Licensed restaurant. Swimming pool; tel: 8482 2100.

Kangaroo Island Central Hostel $–$$ 19 Murray St, Kingscote; tel: 8553 2787. Tidy hostel close to shops, facilities, penguin colony, etc.

Kangaroo Island Holiday Village $$$ 9 Dauncey St. Fully equipped kitchen and fridge; tel: 8482 2225.

Kangaroo Island YHA $–$$ 33 Middle Tce, Penneshaw; tel: 8553 1344. Lovely sea views and close to ferry.

Kohinoor Holiday Units $$ 16 Buller St, Kingscote; tel: 8553 2657.

Penguin Walk Youth Hostel $ 33 Middle Terrace, Penneshaw; tel: 8553 1233.

Queenscliffe Family Hotel $$$ Dauncey St, Kingscote. Coffee shop/snack bar; tel: 8482 2254.

Tandanya Wilderness Lodge $ South Coast Highway (at the entrance to Flinders Chase National Park); tel: 8559 7275.

Timber Creek Lodge $ Timber Creek Rd (10 km east of Parndana); tel: 8559 5000.

Ulonga Lodge $$$ The Foreshore, American River; tel: 8553 7171.

Wanderers Rest Of Kangaroo Island $$$$ Bayview Rd, American River; tel: 8553 7140.

Wisteria Lodge $$$$ 7 Cygnet Rd, Kingscote. Licensed restaurant, spa, swimming pool; tel: 8482 2707.

FOOD AND DRINK

Beachcomber Restaurant $$ 7 Cygnet Rd, Penneshaw; tel: 8553 2707.

Blue Gum Café $$ Dauncey St, Kingscote; tel: 8553 2089.

Cape Willoughby Café $$ adjacent to lighthouse; tel: 8553 1333.

Cygnet Café $ Playford Highway, Cygnet River; tel: 8552 9187.

D'Estrees Bay Café $$ D'Estrees Bay Rd, D'Estrees Bay; tel: 8553 8234.

Dolphin Rock Café $$ 43 North Terrace, Penneshaw; tel: 8553 1284.

Ellsons Seaview Seafront Restaurant $$ Chapman Terrace, Penneshaw; tel: 8553 2030.

Emu's Nest $$ The Esplanade, Emu Bay; tel: 8553 5384.

Gum Creek Marron Farm $$ Gum Creek Rd; tel: 8553 5255. Café-style marron and yabbie meals (local crustaceans).

Kaiwara Food Barn $$ Seal Bay turnoff, South Coast Rd; tel: 8559 6115.

Old Post Office Restaurant $$ North Terrace, Penneshaw; tel: 8553 1063.

Ozone Family Bistro $$ The Foreshore, Penneshaw; tel: 8553 2011.

Palms Seafood Platter Restaurant $$ Telegraph Rd, Penneshaw; tel: 8553 2100.

Queenscliffe Family Hotel $ The Foreshore, Kingscote; tel: 8553 2254.

Ricks Seaview Takeaway $ 3 Kingscote Terrace, Kingscote; tel: 8553 2585.

Rockpool Café $$ North Coast Rd, Stokes Bay; tel: 8559 2277.

Sorrento Restaurant $$ 49 North Terrace, Penneshaw; tel: 8553 1028.

GETTING AROUND

There is little public transport on the island, but there are bicycles, scooters and cars for hire. If you are thinking of cycling, bear in mind that the island is 155 km long. You can bring your vehicle from the mainland, or hire cars are available from:

ROAD CONDITIONS

The major roads between Penneshaw, American River, Kingscote and Parndana are sealed, as is the road to Seal Bay and Vivonne Bay. Other roads are being upgraded but many are unsealed, and require reduced speed and caution. The road surface is ironstone, a loose floating material that tends to build up on corners, requiring careful steering and braking. Make sure that the insurance on your hire car covers you for driving on unsealed roads.

Fuel is available at Kingscote, American River, Island Beach, Penneshaw, Parndana, Vivonne Bay and Tandanya, so you should never run out.

Budget, tel: 8553 3133; **Hertz**, tel: 1800 088 296; **Wheels Over Kangaroo Island**, tel: 8553 3030; and **Penneshaw Car Rentals**, tel: 8553 1284. Four-wheel-drive vehicles are not necessary as long as you drive with care.

If you prefer someone else to do the driving, there are coach tours, or a more personalised four-wheel-drive tour can be arranged. Most tours will pick up from your accommodation or from the airport.

HIGHLIGHTS

Kingscote is the arrival and departure point for visitors to Kangaroo Island, and also the largest town. This was the first settled part of the island and makes a good base for exploration. Nearby **Brownlow Beach** has good swimming and sailing as well as fishing from the jetty. In **Hope Cottage** the National Trust has established an excellent display of photographs, family histories, china and early newspapers. Open daily 1000–1200 and 1400–1600.

One of Kangaroo Island's main tourist resorts, **American River**, is a sheltered tidal estuary between Kingscote and Penneshaw. It takes its name from the American sealers who built two 35-tonne schooners here in 1803–04. The town is on a small peninsula and shelters an inner bay, the bird sanctuary of **Pelican Lagoon**.

The island's plant catalogue lists over 850 native species, as well as approximately 250 which have been introduced from other parts of the world. The flowers are at their best during the spring months of Sept and Oct, but winter is the best time to see the wildlife. Most of the mammals are nocturnal and easily frightened. They are most successfully observed and least stressed from a distance.

The Kangaroo Island kangaroo, a sub-species of the Western grey, is smaller, darker and has longer fur than the mainland species. It shelters in the bush during the day, coming out to graze at dusk. Areas where bush and pasture adjoin make ideal places to observe them.

Tammar wallabies, with smaller and finer features than the kangaroo, are abundant on the island, whereas mainland populations are almost extinct. Wallabies are frequently seen at night along the roads, where they are easily confused by vehicle lights – drive cautiously to prevent damage to either animals or vehicles.

Of the numerous reserves and conservation areas, **Flinders Chase National Park** is the largest. It covers the western end of the island from Sanderson Bay in the south to Cape Borda in the north, and has some of the most amazing proliferation of animal and plant life in Australia. There are well-marked trails throughout the park, and in the centre there is a substantial clearing which is home for a large number of kangaroos and also Cape Barren geese. A few extremely docile kangaroos can usually be seen around the park headquarters, even though feeding is no longer allowed. **Cape du Couedic** in the south-west is a haven for about 6000 New Zealand fur seals. They breed in summer and can be seen energetically interacting in and around the natural formation of Admiral's Arch.

The other major park on the island is **Cape Gantheaume Conservation Park** along the rugged southern coast, which extends as far inland as Murray Lagoon. No vehicles are allowed but the park has much wildlife especially around the lagoon, which when full after rain can cover 2000 ha and is home to more than 200 species of bird.

> ### ITALIAN BEES
> In 1881 August Freibig brought 12 hives of bees from the province of Liguria in Italy, and established an apiary near Penneshaw. Since then no other breeds of bee have been introduced and all present-day honeybees on the island are descendants of those 12 hives. They are pure Ligurian and unique in the world.

Although Seal Bay Conservation Park on the south coast is relatively small, it is home to about 500 Australian sea lions, probably about 10 per cent of the world's population. These sea lions spend as much time on land as at sea. They can seem tame and accepting of visitors, but every now and again they get irritable and charge at humans, so the number of visitors is restricted. An Interpretative Centre (tel: 8489 4207) explains the life cycle of the sea lion. The bay is an aquatic reserve, and swimming and fishing are prohibited.

Other animals native to the island include the brushtail possum, short-beaked echidna, southern brown bandicoot, western and little pygmy possum, endemic sooty dunnart, bush and swamp rat, six bat species, six frog species, Rosenberg's sand goanna, black tiger snake and pygmy copperhead. Koalas, platypuses and ring-tailed possums were introduced and still survive here.

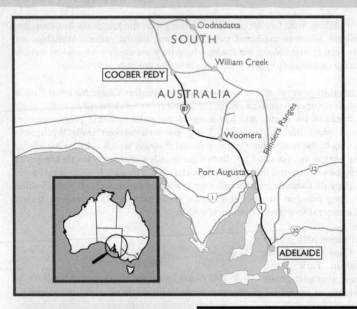

DRIVING ROUTE

Coober Pedy is about 850 km from Adelaide on the Stuart Highway. Head from Adelaide to Port Augusta on the A1 then take the Stuart Highway (A87) north. About 170 km from Port Augusta is Pimba and, just north, Woomera, once Australia's international rocket range, where accommodation and food are available. Another 113 km on past the dazzling white of the salt lakes you'll reach Glendambo, which has service stations and a hotel. Coober Pedy is about 250 km north of Glendambo.

ADELAIDE — COOBER PEDY
OTT Tables 9034/9429

Service	RAIL			
Days of operation	⑤⑦		Daily	
Special notes	**ABC**			
Adelaide ....d.	1715	....	1830	....
Port Pirie ....d.	1956	....	2110r	....
Port Augusta ....d.	2115	....	2330	....
Pimba ....d.	2334	....	0125r	....
Glendambo ....d.			0320	....
Coober Pedy ....a.	0220	....	0610	....
Alice Springs ....a.	1155	....	1400	....

A–Timings between Adelaide and Alice Springs are not guaranteed.
B–Train station is at Manguri, 47 km from Coober Pedy. Hotels will arrange transfers.
C– Additional service on ③ from May to July.

ADELAIDE

See p. 144.

COOBER PEDY

Get the name right. It is Coober Pedy, not Cooper Pedy. Coober Pedy is claimed to be an anglicised version of Aboriginal words 'kupa piti' – meaning 'white man in a hole'. The town is unusual because much of it is underground, including a restaurant, a church and a motel. Coober Pedy has a reputation for being immensely hot. In fact, this town of 3500 permanent residents has some quite reasonable weather. From April to October the semi-desert climate produces warm days – nothing over 20°C – and cold nights. But from November to March, temperatures can exceed 50°C in the shade. Add to that the almost total lack of rainfall and you have a hostile climate. Which is the reason, of course, why many of the residents have gone underground.

The opal fields were discovered in 1915 by the strangely named New Colorado Prospecting Syndicate. They were looking for gold but found opal, now the town's staple industry. If you want to get a feel for Coober Pedy before you go, hire a copy of *Mad Max III*, which was filmed in the area along with about a dozen other movies.

ARRIVAL AND DEPARTURE

Greyhound coaches run to Coober Pedy from Adelaide and from Alice Springs; www.greyhound.com.au. See OTT 9429.

Regional Express Airlines flies Adelaide–Coober Pedy six days a week. Timetable information: www.regionalexpress.com.au.

The Ghan train runs twice weekly Adelaide–Alice Springs–Darwin; an additional service runs May–July. You can alight at Manguri Station, 47 km from Coober Pedy. Transport into town has to be arranged in advance. See OTT 9034; www.gsr.com.au.

[i] **Coober Pedy Visitor Centre** is in the District Council building, Hutchison St; tel: 8672 5298. Open Mon–Fri. The telephone code is 08.
Coober Pedy – Opal Capital of the World www.opalcapitaloftheworld.com.au.

[⌂] Prices are relatively high because Coober Pedy is isolated and everything has to be freighted in. More suggestions on www.opalcapitaloftheworld.com.au.
Lookout Cave Motel $$$ McKenzie Rd (off Catacomb Rd); tel: 8672 5118. Spectacular views and amazing sunsets.
The Opal Cave (Bedrock Backpackers, Fred & Wilma's B&B, Barney & Betty's B&B) $–$$$$ Hutchison St; tel: 8672 5028; www.opalcavecooberpedy.com.au. Backpacker bunk beds for 4 people, B&B for 10, underground and over.
Radekas Dugout Motel and Backpackers $$ Hutchison St; tel: 8672 5223; website: www. radekadownunder.com. Radekas is 6.5 m underground. Offers onward booking service. Evening in underground bar is remarkable.

South Australia

Underground Motel $$ Corner of McKenzie and Catacomb Rd; tel: 8672 5324. Magnificent view of the surrounding desert from the veranda.

TO **Ampol Restaurant $** cnr Hutchison St and Malliotis Boulevard; tel: 8672 5199. Pleasant beer garden but caters for coaches.

Old Miner's Dugout Café $$ Hutchison St; tel: 8672 3552. The only licensed restaurant in town. All the others are BYO. Open seven days, lunch and dinner.

Opal Inn Chinese Restaurant $ Hutchison St; tel: 8672 5430. Australian-Chinese fusion food. Karaoke machine to drive diners mad.

Underground Café $ Stretton Rd; tel: 8672 5419. Tied to an opal showroom and shop.

Highlights

Opal seekers began arriving in numbers in Coober Pedy from about 1917. To cope with the extreme summer condition they lived underground in 'dugouts'. The underground environment has not only been maintained but extended and civilised. A Mining Permit entitles a miner to peg a claim either 50 x 50 m or 50 x 100 m. In other words, large international mining operations cannot take over large areas of land and open mines to get at the opals. The exclusion of big mining interests has done much to maintain Coober Pedy's unusual characteristics.

Opals

Opals are a mix of silica and water transformed and hardened over millions of years. Precious opal is composed of tiny, uniform, transparent silica spheres and 6–10 per cent water. Light passing through the spheres is bent and deflected, producing the rainbow colours for which opals are renowned.

Don't make the mistake of grabbing 'a bargain' from someone who sidles up to you in a pub. Extra-fine quality Australian white opals from Coober Pedy sell for $500–2000 per carat.

One of the town's main attractions is **The Big Winch**. This has a tourist shop and a town lookout. The **Oldtimers Mine** shows underground mining and some of the old equipment that was used, as well as part of an opal reef.

To get a feel of what the early explorers and miners faced, go to **Breakaways Reserve**, which is about 35 km north of Coober Pedy. This is arid scenery with mesas looking over the stony gibber desert – not somewhere to be stranded without water.

WHERE NEXT?

The logical next stop after Coober Pedy is Alice Springs (see p. 366). It's possible to travel by four-wheel-drive tour down the Oodnadatta Track via William Creek to the northern Flinders Ranges.

Australia's smallest mainland state is also its most densely populated: Victoria occupies less than 3 per cent of mainland Australia, but accounts for about 25 per cent of its population. The 5 million inhabitants, though, are spread across an area of 227,600 sq km.

Victoria has arguably the greatest variety of landscape of any Australian state, with a scenic coastline, peerless grazing and crop lands (the Western Districts), semi-arid reserves (Little Desert and Murray-Sunset National Parks, in the north-west), snow-covered mountains (in Alpine National Park) and damp forests (Errinundra National Park, in the east).

Long occupied by Aboriginal people, the area was visited by European sealers, whalers and would-be settlers throughout the early 19th century, and then settled in the late 1830s. Melbourne was surveyed and named in 1837, and most of the rich Western District grazing land had been taken up by the 1840s. Having begun life as the southern extremity of New South Wales, Victoria was proclaimed a separate colony in 1851.

The 1850s gold rushes to Ballarat, Bendigo and other points inland were the making of the colony: settlers poured into Victoria. Subsequent discontent about goldfield administration, and the resulting Eureka Stockade uprising, led to democratic reforms. For decades Victoria prospered as Australia's main financial and industrial centre.

In recent times, Victorians endured crushing economic fallout from the 1980s. A budget-minded conservative government balanced the books but also introduced reforms in education, gaming and the public sector that displeased many people. As a result, a record swing displaced the conservatives in 1999.

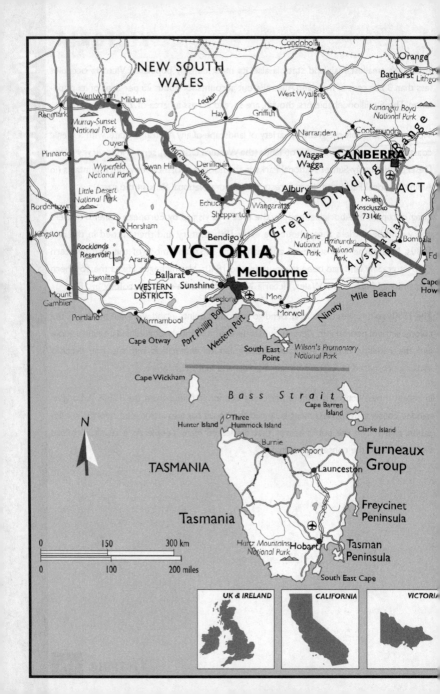

VICTORIA: OUR CHOICE

Melbourne
Restaurants, parks and gardens, Dandenong National Park

Mornington Peninsula

Great Ocean Road
Lorne, Cape Otway, the Twelve Apostles

Warrnambool
Whale watching

Grampians National Park

Alpine National Park
Victorian ski fields

Murray River country
Echuca, Swan Hill, Mildura

Wilsons Promontory National Park

Croajingolong National Park
Wilderness beaches

HOW MUCH YOU CAN SEE IN A ...

WEEKEND (2 DAYS)

Melbourne, the capital, could easily fill two days, with museums, parklands, shopping, theatre and dining out ranking high on any visitor's wish list. If visiting in winter, consider catching an Australian Football game at the Melbourne Cricket Ground – one of the great sporting spectacles in Australia's most sports-mad city. Alternatively, spend one day in Melbourne and another on a driving tour, either around Port Phillip Bay via the Mornington and Bellarine peninsulas, or westwards to the Great Ocean Road and Lorne.

WEEK (7 DAYS)

Victoria is too large to cover in a week. Any seven days in the state should include two full days in Melbourne. Beyond that, consider a loop drive to the west of Melbourne, beginning on the Great Ocean Road. After lingering in Lorne and at the Twelve Apostles, take in Warrnambool, then turn north to Grampians National Park, and finally return to Melbourne via the former gold-rush town of Ballarat. A fine driving tour east and north would begin with a visit to Wilsons Promontory National Park. From there, continue east to Lakes Entrance, then north to Omeo, Mt Hotham and the Victorian high country and on through Bright to the historic towns of Beechworth and Yackandandah. Return to Melbourne via Mansfield and Lake Eildon.

MORE THAN A WEEK

Longer stays at destination towns and extended activities – such as multi-day bushwalks or a Murray River paddle steamer journey – become an option with more time to spare. Consider a visit to Victoria's eastern extremity, where Croajingolong National Park features wild beaches (and wild weather), and friendly Mallacoota offers magnificent coastal scenery and fine fishing. If you're keen to see the mighty Murray River, head for the famed river port of Echuca, due north of Melbourne. To the north-west, the Little Desert and Murray-Sunset national parks both offer oodles of usually peaceful semi-arid reserve; to reach them, travel via Ballarat and Grampians National Park.

MELBOURNE

Victoria has the pleasure of having as its capital city Melbourne, the most civilised city in Australia. Here are the best restaurants, the best theatre, the best art galleries and the best shopping. It has been called in more than one survey the World's Most Livable City. Melbourne is a delight.

The city was named in 1837 after the British prime minister Lord Melbourne, which may not seem much of a name but is better than Bearbrass, Dutigalla and Glenelg, which were the original names of the settlement. One of the key figures in the city's history is John Batman, who in 1835 'bought' 243,000 ha on the western shore of Port Phillip from the local Aboriginal people for a few trinkets (Peter Menhuit made the same sort of deal when he bought Manhattan). On the land he had swindled, John Batman chose a site for a village which within a year had started to develop into the township that was to be Melbourne.

All of this had been done with the strong disapproval of the authorities in New South Wales, and eventually notice had to be taken of this illegal upstart. In 1837 the township was surveyed, the regular rectangular street grid laid out and a magistrate sent from Sydney to maintain law and order. Two years later Charles La Trobe was appointed Superintendent of the Port Phillip District and established a separate police force and a customs office. It was the start of the break between Melbourne and Sydney.

Through the 1840s the town grew to respectable proportions. Then came the gold rush. It is difficult to imagine the impact today, but the population left almost en masse for the tented fields of Warrandyte and Ballarat, leaving behind them a ghost town that, in 1851, was named the capital of the new colony of Victoria.

MUST SEE/DO IN MELBOURNE

Go to the creepy Old Melbourne Gaol

Be dazzled at the National Gallery of Victoria

Check out the Federation Square precinct

Visit the Melbourne Museum

Picnic in Kings Domain/Royal Botanic Gardens

Stroll by the bay at St Kilda

Eat out in Lygon St, Carlton, or Brunswick St, Fitzroy

Visit Healesville Sanctuary

The wealth the gold rush brought can be seen in the style, architecture and presence of Melbourne to this day. Money poured in from the goldfields and started an era of major civic construction – the post office, the public library, Parliament House and the Treasury were all erected in an imposing style which gave Melbourne much of its character. Over 1000 buildings were erected in 1853 alone. Melbourne Cricket Ground, a sure and certain sign of civilisation, was established that year. The first Melbourne Cup was run in 1861, and instantly became a national institution (see p. 190). The first air-mail service to Sydney began in 1914 and Essendon Airport was established in 1921.

The Age newspaper was founded in 1854 and became one of the bastions of civilisation. It is interesting that in the matter of the Eureka Stockade at Ballarat (see p. 198) *The Age* sided with Peter Lalor and the miners, while *The Sydney Morning Herald* sided with the government. The two newspapers are now owned by the same company but still offer very divergent views of the world.

The ethnic mix of Melbourne's population has always been an important influence on the city's character. Chinese and Irish diggers were attracted by gold in the 19th century and a large Chinatown grew up in the 1850s, a small area of which remains in Little Bourke St. Since World War II refugees and migrants who arrived from all over Europe (particularly Greece, Italy, Yugoslavia, Turkey and Poland), and more recently from Vietnam and Cambodia, have all contributed elements of their cultures to what could otherwise have been a conservative, passionless English society. As a direct result of these waves of migrants, eating out in Melbourne is a gourmet's dream. Name the culinary style and Melbourne has it.

MELBOURNE V. SYDNEY

It would be wrong to make too much of the rivalry between Sydney and Melbourne, but it would be wrong as well to underestimate its strength. Sydney began life nearly 50 years ahead of Melbourne – but Sydney began as a penal colony, Melbourne did not. For a while in the 19th century Melbourne was the larger and more exciting city and was known as 'Marvellous Melbourne'. Sydney now appears to have pulled ahead, in size if nothing else. Melbourne can, at times, make Sydney look like a vulgar yahoo that has just come into money.

VICTORIA

The weather in Melbourne is a constant topic of conversation and the subject of many jokes and jibes. Statistically, the climate of Melbourne is mild and sunny, but the city lies in a west-to-east air stream and the weather is, to put it politely, changeable and not easy to predict. It can change so rapidly it is possible to have all four seasons in one day – temperature changes in just a few hours can defy belief. Summers are fairly short, with really hot days confined mostly to January and February, and winters are cloudy, chilly and often windy. Melburnians dress for the weather, and do so very stylishly. You will see more elegantly dressed people in Melbourne in half an hour than you would see in Sydney in a week.

ARRIVAL AND DEPARTURE

Melbourne's international and domestic airport is 22 km north-west of the city centre at Tullamarine. When it opened the airport was a delight but it is now showing signs of fraying at the edges. The domestic terminals work very well but the international side seems somewhat sub-standard. The City Link Tullamarine Freeway makes it a fairly quick and painless trip from central Melbourne, although if travelling by car you will need to purchase a Tulla Pass ($3.60), which you can buy at the airport or, as little as 24 hours before travelling to it, by calling City Link (tel: 13 26 29). A Skybus shuttle service (tel: 9335 3066) runs every 15 mins between the airport and Spencer St Station – much cheaper at $13 (one way) and just as convenient as taking a cab.

Trains come into both Spencer St and Flinders St stations, close to the heart of the city. Flinders St Station, with its attractive dome and presence, was completed in 1899 and is a traditional meeting place for the people of Melbourne.

Greyhound Pioneer buses and other bus lines arrive at Melbourne Transit Centre, Franklin St; V/Line buses use Spencer St Bus Terminal.

INFORMATION

TOURIST OFFICE **Melbourne Visitor Centre**, Federation Sq., cnr Swanston and Flinders Sts (opposite Flinders St Station); open daily 0900–1800. There is a wide range of free brochures available. For information on Melbourne and Victoria call Tourism Victoria, tel: 13 28 42.

INTERNET SITES
Backpackers: www.backpackvictoria.com
City of Melbourne www.thatsmelbourne.com.au
CitySearch Melbourne www.melbourne.citysearch.com.au
Melbourne Online www.melbourne.com.au
Melbourne Visitors Guide www.melbournevisit.com
Only Melbourne www.onlymelbourne.com.au
Visit Melbourne www.visitmelbourne.com

INTERNET ACCESS
e55, 55 Elizabeth St, tel: 9620 3899.
Global Gossip, 440 Elizabeth St, tel: 9663 0511, open seven days 0800–late.
Offers internet access and international telephone calls at competitive rates.

MONEY
Travelex foreign exchange offices are at 261 Bourke St, tel: 9654 4222; 233 Collins St, tel: 9662 1271; and at the international airport, tel: 9335 5455.

POST AND PHONES
The main post office is in Elizabeth St, on the corner with Bourke St. The area code for Melbourne and all of Victoria is 03.

ACCOMMODATION

This list is of affordable accommodation in or near the city centre; all the major hotel chains are, of course, also in this area. In the suburbs of Melbourne there are motels aplenty well within the reach of the budget-conscious.

Chapman Gardens YHA $–$$ 76 Chapman St, North Melbourne; tel: 9328 3595; www.yha.com.au/hostels. Clean, friendly atmosphere.

Coffee Palace $–$$ 24 Grey St, St Kilda; tel: 9534 5283. Lively, popular hostel – not for those who want a peaceful night.

Elizabeth Hostel $–$$$ 490–494 Elizabeth St; tel: 9663 1685; www.elizabethhostel.com.au. Small clean hostel, excellent value.

Flinders Station Hotel Backpackers $–$$$ 35 Elizabeth St; tel: 9620 5100; www.flindersbackpackers.com.au. Large hostel, good security, fully licensed bar, close to Flinders St Station.

Friendly Backpacker $–$$$ 197 King St; tel: 9670 1111; www.friendlygroup.com.au/friendly. Excellent reputation.

Greenhouse Backpacker $–$$$ 228 Flinders Lane; tel: 9639 6400; www.friendlygroup.com.au/greenhouse. Centrally located and often recommended.

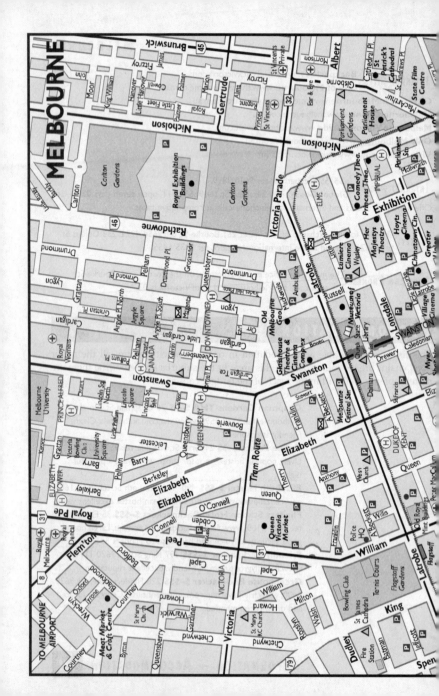

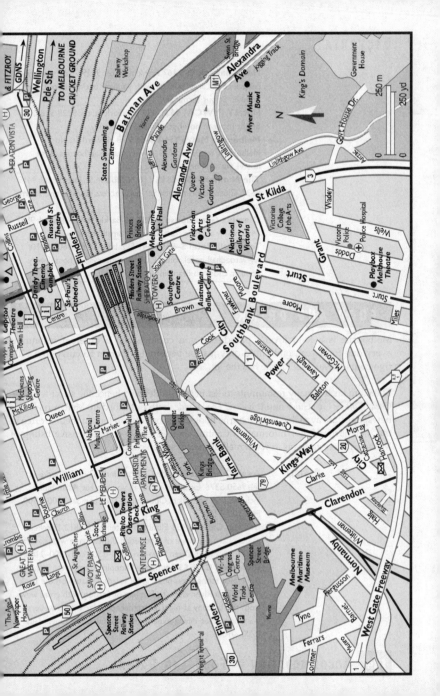

Hotel Bakpak $$$ 167 Franklin St; tel: 9329 7525; www.hotel bakpak.com. Large, popular with younger backpackers, close to Franklin St bus terminal.

Hotel Y (YWCA) $$$$ 489 Elizabeth St; tel: 9329 5188. Bright modern hotel, good value for money.

Melbourne Metro YHA $–$$$ 78 Howard St, Nth Melbourne; tel: 9329 8599; www.yha.com.au/hostels. Busy hostel, yet well organised and clean.

The Nunnery $$$–$$$$ 116 Nicholson St, Fitzroy; tel: 9419 8637. Close to Brunswick St – easy access to cafés and alternative shops.

Olembia Guesthouse $–$$$ 96 Barkly St, St Kilda; tel: 9537 1412; www.olembia.com.au. Lovely small hostel.

Toad Hall Hotel $–$$$$ 441 Elizabeth St; tel: 9600 9010; www.toadhall-hotel.com.au. Clean, conservative hostel, very popular. Close to Franklin St bus terminal.

FOOD AND DRINK

Melbourne is a food lover's paradise – you could eat at a different restaurant every day for a year, and you'd only just be beginning. From a $3 curry to a $200 five-course meal, Melbourne has the lot.

There are far too many restaurants to list in this guidebook, hence the select few. The *Cheap Eats & Café Guide* and the *Good Food Guide*, both published by Melbourne's *Age* newspaper, are available in Melbourne bookshops, or you can look at them for free in the Melbourne Visitor Information Centre. There is also a comprehensive listing of Melbourne's restaurants at www.melbourne.citysearch.com.au.

CENTRAL

Asian Gourmet $ Inside Centrepoint 283–297 Bourke St; tel: 9650 5376. Excellent value 'all you can eat' Asian buffet, includes fruit and salad. Open Mon–Thur and Sat 1100–1900, Fri 1100–2100.

Bali Inn Café $$ 433 Elizabeth St; tel: 9328 3812. Excellent value, offering a range of Indonesian dishes made with natural spices (no MSG). Open Mon–Fri 1100–1500 and 1800–2100.

Blue Train Café $$ Southgate Shopping Centre; tel: 9696 0111. Hot stone oven pizza, great salads. Situated on the bank of the Yarra River close to Flinders St Station, with great views from the balcony at night. Extremely popular with travellers wanting a great dining experience at a low price. Open daily 0700–0100.

MEALS ON WHEELS
If you insist on a totally unusual experience have dinner on the Colonial Tramcar Restaurant. It runs daily, offering dinner with two sittings and lunch on Sunday. You eat and drink as the tram glides its way through Melbourne. $$$$; tel: 9696 4000.

Café Baloo $$ 260 Russell St; tel: 9663 3226. Alternative restaurant selling dishes from around the world; great atmosphere, very popular. Open Mon–Fri 1100–2300, Sat and Sun 1600–2200.

Crossways $ 123 Swanston St; tel: 9650 2939. Unusual Hare Krishna restaurant offering extremely cheap vegetarian food, popular with all types of people – no religious pressure whatsoever (although staff will be happy to chat if asked). Open Mon–Sat 1130–1430.

Pellegrini's $$ 66 Bourke St; tel: 9662 1885. You can either sit at the long bar or round the bog-wood table in the kitchen. Basic Italian cuisine, great fun and great value. Open Mon–Sat 0800–2330, Sun 1200–2000.

Shung Feng Seafood Restaurant $$$ 276 Lonsdale St; tel: 9663 2903. Lunchtime all-you-can-eat buffet, good-quality food representing good value for money. Open for lunch Mon–Fri 1130–1430, dinner daily 1730–late.

The Waiters' Restaurant $$$ Level 1, 20 Meyers Place; tel: 9650 1508. Extremely busy eatery, has been established in Melbourne for years. Open Mon–Fri 1200–1430, Mon–Sat 1800–2315.

CHINATOWN

Practically in the city centre, **Little Bourke St** is lined with Chinese restaurants. You can find anything from fried rice to an exclusive lobster dinner.

Mask of China $$$$ 115–117 Little Bourke St; tel: 9662 2116. Cantonese seafood and Chiu Chow cuisine. Open Sun–Fri 1200–1500, daily 1800–2300.

FITZROY

Brunswick St, lined with alternative cafés, restaurants and bars, as well as ethnic restaurants, is a truly cosmopolitan experience. Whether you want an evening meal with a twist of the unusual, or just want to watch people over a coffee, this is the place to be. Some great vegetarian places. Take tram 86 from Bourke St or tram 11 from Collins St.

CARLTON

As the city goes to sleep, Carlton comes to life. **Lygon St** consists of mostly Italian restaurants. With tables on the streets and the managers standing on the door trying to entice the tourists, Lygon St is more like Rome than Australia. Tram 1 or 8 heading north from Swanston St.

Casa Malaya $$$ 118 Lygon St; tel: 9663 7068. Authentic Malaysian cuisine. Open for lunch and dinner Mon–Fri, dinner only Sat, closed Sun.

Donnini's $$$$ 320 Lygon St; tel: 9347 3128. Carlton institution for reliably good food and a cheerful, family-run atmosphere. Open daily 1200–2200.

Toto's Pizza House $$ 101 Lygon St; tel: 9347 1630. Busy Italian restaurant, large portions. Open daily 1130–late.

ST KILDA

Fitzroy St and nearby **Acland St** are lined with cafés and bars. Some great-value meals can be found here – very popular with younger independent travellers. Acland St is a cake-lover's paradise; there are several Mediterranean cake shops. A must for all stressed travellers is to sit at a table there with a slice of gateau and a cappuccino and just watch the trams and the world go by. Take tram 96 from Bourke St or any tram with St Kilda Beach displayed.

Circa, The Prince $$$$ 2 Acland St; tel: 9536 1122. Acclaimed new restaurant enjoying raves for mains, desserts and wine list. Open daily 0700–1100, 1200–1500 and 1830–2230.

RICHMOND AREA

Swan St has mainly Greek food (Richmond is one of the great Greek cities) – head here for food that is filling and inexpensive. Any tram from Swanston St to Batman Ave, then tram 70.

Victoria St has some great Vietnamese restaurants at great prices. Tram 109 from Collins St.

SOUTH MELBOURNE

Both **Toorak Road**, tram 8 from Swanston St, and **Chapel St**, tram 109 from Collins St to Victoria Parade then tram 79, offer a range of fine dining restaurants. Most are a bit on the expensive side but you can get some good, inexpensive meals.

Saigon Rose $$$ 206 Chapel St; tel: 9510 9651. Great Vietnamese food. Open Sun–Thur 1100–2200, Fri 1100–2300, Sat–Sun 1700–2300.

GETTING AROUND

Walking is the best way to see this city. It is laid out on a logical grid of broad boulevards, which makes it difficult to get lost, but lest this gets boring these are interspersed with narrow streets, alleys and lanes which create an interesting maze of thoroughfares, adding humanity to town planning.

Cycling is another excellent way to see Melbourne. Many parts of the city have specially designated cycle tracks. A recommended ride is along the banks of the Yarra River and through the Botanic Gardens. **Hire a Bike** ($$, tel: 0417 339 305) is conveniently located below Princes Bridge on the Yarra. Helmets are supplied. It is the law in Australia that all cyclists wear helmets – a fine applies if caught without.

THE MELBOURNE GREETER SERVICE

The Melbourne Greeter Service is a free service organized by the city of Melbourne. Volunteers will take you on a 2–4 hour tour around the city, including the City Circle Tram, sharing their knowledge and answering any questions you may have. This is a great way to see the city from a local's perspective. Tel: 9658 9658 for further information.

Free guides to cycling in Melbourne, complete with maps and information on history and wildlife, are available from the Melbourne Visitor Information Centre.

Public transport is an integrated system, bringing together bus, suburban railway and the trams. The city is broken down into zones, and you can get two-hour or full-day tickets at a reasonable price. The public transport system is easy to use and maps are readily available. The city circle tram runs around the city centre every 20 minutes and is free – it's clearly identified by the burgundy paintwork.

The trams add to the Melbourne style but they also give visiting car drivers some surprises. At certain intersections in the city where trams take up the centre of the road, you have to get in the left-hand lane in order to turn right. This is called a hook turn. It may seem mad, illogical and dangerous but Melburnians will explain its virtues to you at great length. No one from anywhere else in Australia has ever understood it though.

Taxis are ubiquitous and can either be phoned for or picked up at one of the many ranks. You can hail a cab on the street if its sign is illuminated. As with most cities, driving in the centre can be a nightmare. Parking is scarce and very expensive, and the fines for exceeding parking time limits are extortionate – you will get caught.

HIGHLIGHTS

The main streets within the central 'golden mile' are Collins and Bourke which run south-west/north-east and are crossed by Swanston and Elizabeth Sts. This is where Melbourne goes to shop. **Collins St** has solid Victorian business architecture – we've made a fortune and we will show it – and modern skyscrapers which manage not to be obtrusive. The eastern end is called the Parisian end and the trees make it possible, if only just, to see the resemblance. It is stylish without being snobbish. At the other end of the street lies the business centre of the city. North, the centre drifts via Flagstaff Gardens and the Queen Victoria Market to Carlton and North Melbourne. The southern border is the Yarra River.

Melbourne's Golden Mile Walking Trail, a 28-page brochure ($9), guides visitors though a 3.9-km walking trail covering most of Melbourne's historic highlights. With good maps and detailed information the trail is a must for all those wanting to see and learn more about the city.

Beside the river is the ornate **Flinders St Station**, a railway station in the grand tradition. It is the only railway station left in Australia that engenders the sense of excitement, a feeling of departing on great missions, that once all railway stations had.

Young and Jackson's, situated on the corner of Flinders St and Swanston St, is one of the world's great pubs. It's famed mainly for the painting of the young nude, Chloe, hanging in the upstairs bar.

Situated at 525 Collins St is **Rialto Towers** ($$), tel: 9629 8222. Open daily 1000–late, this is the tallest building in the southern hemisphere. At 253 metres you can catch great 360-degree views of Melbourne. Before ascending to the observation deck, visitors get to see a 20-minute sight-and-sound presentation, 'Melbourne the living city'. Well worth a visit – on clear days the views extend well beyond the city limits; those south over the bay are particularly alluring.

Melbourne Central, located between Elizabeth and Swanston Sts, is Melbourne's main shopping complex. The centre holds an excellent large food court, train station and a range of shops and department stores. Still standing inside the complex is the Coop's Shot Tower – a building once used to make bullets: melted lead was dripped from the top of the building into a deep tank of water on the ground; as the droplets fell, they cooled into lead pellets.

The building of **St Paul's Cathedral**, across Swanston St from Young and Jackson's, started in 1880 and continued until 1933. It is rigidly Anglican and Gothic. Representing, as it were, the opposition, **St Patrick's Cathedral** on the corner of Cathedral Pl. and Gisborne St is Gothic Revival architecture but, for once, done with restraint. It was designed by William Wilkinson Wardell.

At the corner of Swanston St and Latrobe St is the **State Library**. The library opened in 1856 and has an octagonal reading room – interesting, attractive and unusual. Its dome was added in 1911 and was believed then to be the largest dome in the world. Open Mon–Thur 1000–2100, Fri–Sun 1000–1800, closed public holidays; tel: 8664 7000.

Flagstaff Gardens are in the north-west corner of the central business district. This was Melbourne's first cemetery, though burials ceased in 1838. Here, on 11 Nov 1850, the news was received that Victoria had been granted its independence from New South Wales. Thirty years later it was decided to turn Flagstaff Hill into gardens, and a lake and children's playground were installed. The gardens are located at the corner of Latrobe and William Sts, one of the stops for the free City Circle tram.

The nearby **Queen Victoria Market**, 513 Elizabeth St, dates back to 1857. Originally selling fruit and veg, the market now sells almost anything from delicacies to souvenirs. Open Tues and Thur–Sun from early morning to early afternoon. Market tours ($$$), tel: 9320 5835, run most trading days and reveal more about the market than meets the eye.

To the north of the city, in Parkville, is the **Melbourne Zoo**, tel: 9285 9300. This is a fine zoo, placing a strong emphasis on recreating the animals' natural habitat. Excellent gorilla enclosure. Open daily 0900–1700 ($$$).

The Old Melbourne Gaol ($$) in Russell St is Victoria's oldest surviving prison. Learn about the infamous bushranger Ned Kelly and his notorious killings – and of course his hanging, which took place in the Gaol. Open daily 0930–1700. Night performances and tours are also available; tel: 9663 7228.

Melbourne is a city of gardens adding much to the charm of the city. Gardens played an important part in the lives of the early settlers and Melbourne's gardens go back to the mid-1800s, very early in the history of Australia.

Fitzroy Gardens are the work of Scottish landscape gardener James Sinclair. The magnificent conservatory was added in 1928. In 1934, when Melbourne celebrated its centenary, **Cook's Cottage** (in fact the home of Captain Cook's parents) was installed in the gardens. It was moved in 253 crates, brick by brick, from Great Ayton in Yorkshire, England. To make sure it was completely authentic they even shipped a cutting from the ivy that had grown on the original building. The cutting took root and today looks as though it has been there for centuries. Open daily 0900–1700 ($); tel: 9419 4677. Tram 48 or 75 from Flinders St.

SOUTH OF THE YARRA

Elspeth Huxley wrote: 'The Yarra, Melburnians will tell you, is the only river in the world that runs upside down – it looks so brown and muddy.' Despite this, the **Yarra** is one of the great attractions of Melbourne. The banks of the river have been carefully landscaped for leisure activities, with barbecues and picnic grounds, and bicycles for hire. Or you can take one of the river tour boats from Princes Walk beside Princes Bridge. There are some beautiful old bridges across the Yarra and to look down the river from one of them at night is always a magical delight.

VICTORIA

The south bank of the Yarra, not unlike London's South Bank, has been the focus of a political drive to make it work. The modern architecture of the **Victorian Arts Centre** theatre complex – what might be called modern Eiffel Tower style – is now well on the way to becoming a major landmark for Melbourne which, in truth, sorely needs one.

Running alongside the Yarra is the **Kings Domain**, home of the **Alexandra Gardens**, **Queen Victoria Gardens** and the famed **Royal Botanic Gardens**. The Botanic Gardens are widely regarded as the best in Australia, and among the top echelon in the world. Here you'll find 40 hectares of lovely interlinked gardens with lawns, lakes, trees, flower beds and birds. Open daily from 0730 until 1730. The guided **Aboriginal Heritage Walk** (tel: 9252 2429) takes visitors into the Botanic Gardens and provides an insight into the customs and rich heritage of the Bunurong and Woiwurrung people, who occupied the land before the gardens were introduced. Also within the Kings Domain is **La Trobe's Cottage**, originally the home of Charles La Trobe, the first Governor of Victoria. The cottage was originally built in England and later dismantled, packed and shipped to Melbourne, and reassembled on the site in 1839. Open Mon, Wed, Sat and Sun 1100–1600.

Apart from hosting a range of great restaurants and cake shops, **St Kilda**, tram 96 from Bourke St, is home to Luna Park (www.lunapark.com.au). This nice little amusement park was built in 1912 and boasts an extremely old, good-fun wooden roller coaster. **The Art and Craft Market** held on Sundays is well worth a visit; otherwise **St Kilda Beach**, although not the best in Australia, is close to the city centre and is fine for catching some of Australia's sunshine – don't forget to Slip, Slop, Slap!

EVENTS

Melbourne Events magazine, produced by the city of Melbourne on a monthly basis, is free and widely available, and gives comprehensive listings of current events.

Melbourne also hosts an array of sporting events year round, including the **Australian Open Grand Slam Tennis Championship** in January. **The Melbourne Cup**, one of the world's great horse races, is run on the Flemington racecourse on the first Tues in November. Only handicapped horses can race, making it more of a gamble than ever. The **Australian Formula One Grand Prix** is held in Albert Park on Labour Day weekend in March. This is the first race in the Formula One world championship calendar and it attracts a massive crowd to a four-day carnival of motor sports and public entertainment.

From the end of March to the middle of April the **Melbourne International Comedy Festival** takes place. This is the city's most popular cultural festival and it is firmly established as one of the three largest comedy festivals in the world. It presents a dynamic programme of stand-up, cabaret, visual art exhibitions, music, live radio, television and street performances. Details can be found on the website: www.comedy festival.com.au.

The **Melbourne Food and Wine Festival** in March/April showcases great food, world-class wines, stylish restaurants and bistros. You can find out more from www.melbournefoodandwine.com.au.

NIGHTLIFE

Inpress is a free weekly guide, listing nightlife and clubbing events in Melbourne and the surrounding area. The paper is available from cafés, theatres, cinemas, pubs and clubs.

Melbourne Metro Nightclub (20–30 Bourke St; tel: 9663 4288) is Melbourne's largest and most popular nightclub. **King St** also hosts a variety of clubs, and the area's reputation is gradually improving.

The recently built **Crown Casino and Entertainment Complex** along the bank of the river Yarra is large and spectacular. Apart from a huge Casino there's a 24-hour cinema, nightclubs, bars, restaurants and many designer stores. A walk alongside the river, by the water fountains and the powerful flamethrowers, is the perfect finish to a busy day.

By St Kilda Rd, the **Sidney Myer Music Bowl** in Kings Domain Gardens is Melbourne's main outdoor concert area. Tel: 9281 8000 for current events.

On the other side of St Kilda Rd the **Victorian Arts Centre** (tel: 9281 8000) consists of the **Theatres Building** where you can find the **State Theatre** and **The Playhouse**. Activities take place most nights and up-to-date listings can be obtained from the Melbourne Tourist Office.

DAY TRIPS

Melbourne is the starting point for many organized day trips. A range of tours catering for the traveller departs from Melbourne on a daily basis. They cover a wide range of possibilities, from the Mornington Peninsula to the Great Ocean Road. Details on individual tours and bookings can be obtained from most hotels and hostels, the Melbourne Tourist Office and a range of travel agents.

AUSTRALIAN RULES FOOTBALL

When the first official Australian Rules football match was played in 1858 a new religion was born. It is impossible to visit Melbourne, especially in the winter, without getting involved in the mania for Australian Rules football which grips the city. At the first recorded game, in 1858, Scotch College played Melbourne Grammar School and each side had 40 players. T W Wills, the umpire, made the rules restricting each side to a more manageable 20 players.

To get the full, fine flavour of this frenzy, here is Edward Kinglake writing in 1891: 'The colony of Victoria has a game of its own. It is supposed to be an improvement on all other species in the matter of eradicating brutality. Whether it is so is a very open question. There have been more brutal fights in Melbourne over football matches than in any other colony. It is even contended that the fact that it raises such enthusiasm, even to the point of broken heads and bloody noses, is a conclusive argument that it is the best of all games.'

Nothing has changed since he wrote those words.

The **Bellarine Peninsula** forms the western side of Port Phillip Bay. The traditional seaside resort of Queenscliff is now being restored to something of its former glory. Fort Queenscliff is a splendid example of military madness, built in the 1880s to protect Melbourne when a Russian invasion was feared.

The **Yarra Valley**, on Melbourne's north-east outskirts, is one of Australia's greatest wine-growing regions. It has more than 30 wineries producing great wines. Several are open daily and many others welcome visitors at weekends. The Melbourne Tourist Office can give further details. **Victoria Winery Tours** ($$$, tel: 9621 2089) offer day tours to the Yarra Valley, Macedon Ranges and Mornington Peninsula. Tours include wine tasting and lunch.

The **Dandenongs** and **The Ranges** are a one-hour drive north-east of Melbourne, close to the Yarra Valley, and provide some spectacular scenery and beautiful bush land. There are many wild flowers and colourful birds in the area. While here, take a ride on **Puffing Billy** ($$), Australia's oldest steam railway. Trains leave daily from Belgrave, although on days of total fire-ban steam locomotives are replaced with diesel. For up-to-date times and information, tel: 9754 6800, website: www.puffingbilly.com.au. At **Healesville Sanctuary** ($$$), Badger Creek Rd, Healesville, in the heart of the Dandenongs, you can see animals including koalas, kangaroos, wombats and platypus in a very natural setting. Open daily 0900–1700; tel: 5957 2800.

YARRA WINERIES

There is a constant argument in Australia as to the quality of wines from the Yarra region. Yarra has many admirers who believe that red wines from the Yarra are superior to those from the Hunter Valley (see p. 241). There is a very distinctive Australian taste and within that range there is a very distinctive Yarra flavour which is powerful and lingers. It is well worth experimenting with in depth. (Regional wineries website: www.yarravalleywine.com)

Among the many wineries in this area offering cellar door sales are:

Allinda Winery, Dixons Creek, tel: 5965 2450.

Oakridge Estate, Coldstream, tel: 9739 1920.

St Huberts, Coldstream, tel: 9739 1118.

Yarra Burn Winery, Yarra Junction, tel: 5967 1428.

Domaine Chandon Green Point, Coldstream, tel: 9739 1110.

Bendigo, 150 km north of Melbourne, had the greatest goldfield in Australia. It extended over 360 sq km and had about 35 gold-bearing reefs with a total output of more than 22 million ounces. The gold brought solid wealth to the town, and Bendigo is often regarded as the best-preserved example of Victorian architecture in Victoria, possibly Australia.

Bendigo has several reminders of the large community of Chinese miners who helped make Bendigo – and Melbourne – rich. The **Golden Dragon Museum** in Bridge St contains Chinese ceremonial regalia and a brilliant red Chinese joss house. It also includes the dragons Loong and Sun Loong, who are carried in the Easter Monday Chinese Procession. Open daily.

Right in the heart of Bendigo is the **Central Deborah Mineshaft** which passes through 17 levels to a depth of almost 400 m. This was the last deep-reef mine in the area to close. Now it has been fully restored and is a working exhibit for the public. Violet St; open daily ($$).

WHERE NEXT?

Victoria is relatively compact and the historic Ballarat goldfields (p. 195), Mornington Peninsula (p. 222) and Mt Buller alpine area (p. 231) are all an easy day's drive from Melbourne.

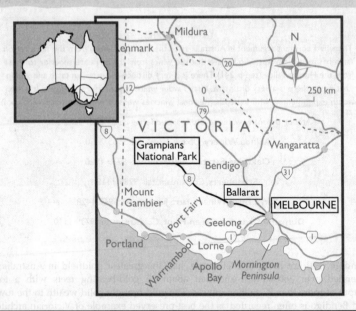

Service											
Days of operation	Ⓐ	⑥	⑦	Ⓐ	⑥	Ⓐ	⑦	Ⓐ	⑥	Ⓐ	⑦
Special notes	A	AB	AB	AB	A	A	A	A	A	A	A
Melbourne...................d.	0805	0817	0920	0938	1117	1228	1728	1745	1753	1853	1913	....
Ballarat...........................d.	0955	0949	1053	1118	1310	1420	1904	1918	1927	2040	2100	....
Stawell ....a.	1136	1120	1220	1245	1451	1600	2030	2045	2050	2216	2241	....
Halls Gap ....a.	....	1205	1305	1330	....	....	....	....	....	....	....	....

MELBOURNE to the GRAMPIANS
OTT Table 9413

Special notes:
A—Connection from Melbourne to Ballarat is by train.
B—For Halls Gap you have to change buses in Stawell.

DRIVING ROUTE

Ballarat (112 km) is the first large town and the meeting place of the Midlands Hwy from Geelong (see p. 218) and the Glenelg Hwy from Mt Gambier. From Ararat (138 km) the direct road to Horsham is 95 km, but turn onto Rte 124 (C216) for Halls Gap and the Grampians. Total journey approx. 300 km.

The Melbourne–Adelaide buses running along Rte 8 reach Adelaide in about 10½–14 hrs depending on stops. Stopping buses take 1½–2½ hrs from Melbourne to Ballarat, with Stawell a further 1–1½ hrs.

ALONG THE WESTERN HIGHWAY

Although the Western Highway (Rte 8) is the 'fast' inland route to Adelaide, as opposed to the scenic but much longer route via the Great Ocean Rd (see pp. 201–202), the only quick way between the two cities is to fly. The pleasures of this route lie in exploring the successful gold town of Ballarat – the place where independence and democracy in Australia might be said to have been born – and the rugged ranges of the Grampians, with their prolific wildlife and annual explosion of spring flowers.

BALLARAT

Ballarat – a town that was made by the gold rush – has played an important part in Australia's history.

In 1851 gold was found at Poverty Point and for the next 50 years the Ballarat fields produced more than a quarter of all Victoria's gold. At its peak it was probably the richest alluvial goldfield in the world. In 1897 Mark Twain wrote in *Following the Equator*: 'Forty five years ago the site now occupied by the City of Ballarat was a sylvan solitude as quiet as Eden and as lovely. Nobody had ever heard of it. On the 25th of August, 1851, the first great gold-strike made in Australia was made there. The news of the strike spread everywhere in a sort of instantaneous way. A celebrity so prompt and so universal has hardly been paralleled in history, perhaps.'

The mining and processing needed heavy equipment, which meant the growth in local industries such as Cowley's Eureka Iron Works and The Phoenix, companies that created the ballast of wealth on which Ballarat was built.

But it was the political action of the miners of Ballarat that made history – their armed civil uprising against the government (see p. 198) has been the only one in Australia's history.

i **Ballarat Visitor Information Centre**, 39 Sturt St; tel: 5320 5741 or 1800 446 633. The area code is 03. Open daily. **Official Visitors' Guide to Ballarat** www.ballarat.com.

Amina $$$ 209 Dufton St; tel: 0419 887 145.
Avenue Motel $$$ 1813 Sturt St, Avenue of Honor; tel: 5334 1303.
Ballarat Miners Retreat Motel $$$ 604 Eureka St; tel: 5331 6900.

Craigs Royal Hotel $$–$$$$ 10 Lydiard St South; tel: 5331 1377. Both Mark Twain and Prince Alfred once slept here.

Criterion Hotel $$ 18 Doveton St; tel: 5331 1451.

Irish Murphys $ 36 Sturt St; tel: 5331 4091. Popular with backpackers; no double rooms.

Irwins Hotel $$–$$$ 121 Lydiard St, North Ballarat; tel: 5332 1660; www.ballarat.com/irwins. Opposite the train and bus station.

**Peter Lalor Hotel $$** cnr Mair and Doveton Sts; tel 5331 1702. Inexpensive accommodation. Bistro ($$). Open daily for dinner and for lunch at weekends.

Quest Colony Motor Inn $$$$ 674 Melbourne Rd; tel: 5334 7788. Set in landscaped garden. Heated indoor swimming pool.

Robin Hood Hotel $$ Peel St; tel: 5331 3348.

Sovereign Hill Lodge (YHA) $–$$$ Magpie St; tel: 5333 3409; www.yha.com.au/hostels. Close to Sovereign Hill.

Sovereign Park Motor Inn $$$$ 221 Main Rd; tel: 5331 3955. Between Sovereign Hill and the city. Has bar and bistro.

TO Sturt St is full of restaurants of every style, shape and price. The Lydiard St historic quarter has almost as many.

Assunta's $$$ 34 Sturt St; tel: 5331 6327. Mediterranean restaurant. Open Wed–Fri 1100–1430, Mon–Sat 1700–late.

Café Bibo $$$ 205 Sturt St; tel: 5331 1255. Salads, sandwiches, cappuccinos. Open daily 0730–1800.

Café Pazani $$$$ 102 Sturt St; tel: 5331 7100. A range of international cuisine. Open Tues–Fri from 0730, Sat from 1130.

Chok Dee Thai Restaurant $$ 113 Bridge Mall; tel: 5331 7361. Large portions, good range of Australian wines. Open daily 1700–late.

Curry Delight $$ 418 Sturt St; tel: 5332 8522. Open Wed–Sun 1100–1400 and 1700–2200.

Da Vinci's $$$ 29 Sturt St; tel: 5333 4114. A unique restaurant/café designed after the famous artist. Open daily 1100–late.

Europa Café $–$$$ 411 Sturt St; tel: 5331 2486. Despite the name, actually a very cosmopolitan restaurant serving a mix of Asian and other international food. Open daily from 0845.

Frangali'a Kafeeneo $$ 313 Sturt St; tel: 5331 1312. Good range of snacks, sandwiches and main meals. Open daily 0800–2100.

La Porchetta $$ 825 Sturt St; tel: 5331 1902. Extremely busy, excellent value for money. Open daily 1100–late.
L'Espresso $$$ 417 Sturt St; tel: 5333 1789. Classy coffee shop serving good-quality food. Open daily 0745–1800, Fri–Sat 1830–late.
Mexican Terrace $$$ 71 Victoria St; tel: 5333 1435. Range of good Mexican dishes. Takeaway available. Open Tues–Sun 1800–late.
Noble Dragon Chinese Restaurant $$ 739 Sturt St; tel: 5331 3891. Eat in or takeaway. Open daily for lunch and dinner.

HIGHLIGHTS

Sovereign Hill ($$$), Bradshaw St, located on the site of the former Sovereign Quartz Mining Company, is a superb reconstruction of life on the goldfields with sights and shops being run by people in period costume. There are guided underground tours using the original tramway – not for the claustrophobic. Open daily 1000–1700; www.sovereignhill.com.au. The sound and light spectacular **Blood on the Southern Cross ($$$)** tells the story of the battle of Eureka Stockade (a great Australian legend). Shows run Mon–Sat, each lasting 80 minutes. Bookings essential. Tel: 5333 5777.

Opposite Sovereign Hill and included in the admission fee is the **Gold Museum**, with a series of galleries devoted to the lure, mining and refining of gold. Open daily 0930–1720.

Eureka Stockade Centre ($$, Eureka St; tel: 5333 1854) has a range of displays and memorabilia related to the events that took place in December 1854. Open daily 0900–1700.

Montrose Cottage ($$) in Eureka St is the last miners' bluestone cottage in Ballarat and has a collection of memorabilia from the Eureka Stockade. Open daily 0100–1700.

The **Ballarat Fine Art Gallery ($)** in the Lydiard St Historic Precinct – a place of beautiful Victorian buildings – houses what is almost certainly the original Eureka Flag, donated by a policeman's widow. Also in the gallery are a number of works by Australian artists, including Sidney Nolan, who chronicled the history of early Ballarat and Australia. Open daily 1030–1700.

The oldest theatre in Australia, **Her Majesty's**, is also in Lydiard St; for bookings and information tel: 5333 5888. Tours of the theatre are run on request; tel: 5333 5800.

The **Botanic Gardens** on the shores of man-made Lake Wendouree are magnificent. A fine collection of classical statues includes the Prime Ministers' Ave, updated with a new bust to record each incumbent. Many of the trees in the gardens are over 120

THE EUREKA STOCKADE

In 1854 the miners of Ballarat rose up against the authorities that ruled them. What were their grievances? All gold miners in Victoria had to pay for a licence. This entitled the holder to work a single 12 ft (3.6 m) square claim and cost 30 shillings a month, regardless of the amount of gold recovered. Procedures for settlement of the many claim disputes were inadequate, there were frequent licence hunts and sly grog raids, and policing was arbitrary and often brutal.

Exercising absolute authority over the diggings and the 25,000 miners was the government-appointed Resident Gold Commissioner, Robert Rede, backed by a large contingent of police and a military garrison. On Sunday 22 October, some 10,000 miners assembled and formed the Ballarat Reform League. Their attempts to negotiate with Commissioner Rede got nowhere.

At a mass meeting on Wednesday 29 November, the blue Southern Cross flag flew for the first time. The miners rallied around the old slogan 'no taxation without representation' and the meeting voted in favour of burning licences. Commissioner Rede replied the next day with yet another licence hunt. The miners, led by Peter Lalor, seized the moment. Licences were burned and the rebel flag unfurled. The next day the miners started constructing a defensive fortification at the Eureka mine. At 3 am on Sunday 3 December, a police and military force, 276 strong, approached the Eureka Stockade. Which side opened fire first is uncertain.

Those behind the stockade, probably outnumbered and certainly outgunned, were quickly routed. Peter Lalor later estimated that 22 miners died and a further 12 were wounded. On the government side were 4 dead and 12 wounded. Martial law was declared.

The groundswell of public indignation extended to Melbourne. When 13 of the rebels were tried for treason early in 1855, all were acquitted. An official inquiry was scathingly critical of the handling of the affair. The licence system was replaced by an export duty on gold and a Miner's Right, which cost a small annual fee.

Within a year, rebel leader Peter Lalor was representing Ballarat in the Legislative Council; he went on to become Speaker of the Legislative Assembly. The Southern Cross is still flown in Australia to this day. The battle of the Eureka Stockade lasted 15 minutes but saw the birth of democracy in Australia.

years old and feature on the National Trust's Register of Significant Trees. The **Ballarat Vintage Tramway** ($) runs at weekends, and school and public holidays. The short 1.3-km journey on original track takes the visitor along the lake shore.

The well-signposted **Eureka Walking Trail**, starting from the post office in Sturt St, traces the 3.5 km marched in 1854 from the government camp to the Eureka Stockade site.

There are several **wineries** in the area, producing mainly cool-climate table wines. Visit www.pyrenees.org.au or the Tourist Information Centre for more details.

Five minutes from Sovereign Hill, on the corner of Fussel and York Sts, is the **Ballarat Wildlife Park** ($$$). Its wide range of wildlife includes koalas and Tasmanian devils. Kangaroos, wallabies and emus range freely. Guided tours are conducted daily at 1100 although staff are always around to pass on information. Tel: 5333 5933.

THE GRAMPIANS

The park is renowned for its rugged mountain scenery, Aboriginal rock art and wildflower displays. **Halls Gap** is the best starting point to the park, and is accessible from Hwy 8 via Ararat and Stawell (pronounced Stawl). Stawell is the last main town before Halls Gap and is the home to the **Stawell Gift**, a world-famous foot race that takes place every Easter. The **Stawell Gift Hall of Fame**, Main St, tel: 5358 1326, pays tribute to the famous athletes who have run the race.

> *i* **Stawell and Grampians Visitor Information Centre**,
> 50–52 Western Hwy, Stawell; tel: 5358 2314 or 1800 330 080.
> The area code is 03. Can give further information on both Stawell
> and the Grampians. Open daily; www.visitgrampians.com.au.
> **Grampians and Halls Gap Visitor Information Centre**,
> Public Hall, Grampians Rd; tel: 5356 4616 or 1800 065 599. The
> main information centre for the Grampians.
> **Brambuk the National Park and Cultural Centre**, 2.5 km
> south of Halls Gap on Grampians Rd; tel: 5356 4381. Offers
> information on Grampians weather conditions and roads, as well
> as wildlife, walking tracks and best places to see. The Cultural
> Centre (tel: 5356 4452) displays information about the local
> Aboriginal people, explains the tools once used, sells Aboriginal
> merchandise and has a café ($$) selling bush tucker. There is a
> multimedia theatre ($), which focuses on Aboriginal heritage.
> Open daily; www.parkweb.vic.gov.au.

> Halls Gap is the only town within the Grampians National
> Park, and has ample accommodation.
> **Grampians Motel $$$** Dunkeld Rd; tel: 5356 4248.
> **Grampians YHA Eco-Hostel $–$$** cnr Buckler St and
> Grampians Rd; tel: 5356 4544; www.yha.com.au/hostels. Recently
> renovated.

Tim's Other Place $$ Grampians Rd; tel: 5356 4288. Small and very homely. Includes breakfast.

🆃🅾 There are a number of restaurants along Dunkeld Rd.
Halls Gap Tavern $$ lot 5, Dunkeld Rd; tel: 5356 4416. Good value daily menu, pleasant atmosphere. Open daily 0830–2100.

HIGHLIGHTS

There are over 900 different plant species in the park, but it is the wild flowers, coming into glorious bloom every spring, that attract the most attention. The prime time is Aug–Nov.

The park also has a great variety of birdlife – over 200 species have been recorded – and there are also kangaroos, emus, echidnas and koalas.

Most parts of the park are accessible by car. Halls Gap has a circular road going around into the **Wonderland Range**. This road also connects with Mt Victory Rd, which leads to points of interest in the central section of the park: **Boroka Lookout**, **McKenzie Falls**, **Lake Wartook** and **Zumstein**.

Running south from Halls Gap is the road to Dunkeld, which passes between the Serra and Mt William ranges and **Mt Abrupt**. All these roads are sealed. The park also has a wealth of secondary roads. These become a problem only after heavy rain, when they may become impassable. Check with the park information centre if in doubt.

Also in the park are more than 160 km of marked footpaths, which range from easy strolls from the visitors' centre to serious bushwalking with overnight stays (permit required). It is important to keep to the tracks to minimise soil erosion.

WHERE NEXT?

Hwy 8 continues west across the border to South Australia and Adelaide (see p. 144). From Horsham the Henty Hwy (Rte 107, or A200) runs south along the western edge of the Grampians to Hamilton and the Southern Ocean at Portland (see pp. 201–221) or north to Sunraysia and Mildura (see p. 131).

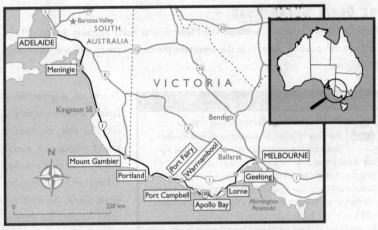

ADELAIDE — MOUNT GAMBIER
OTT Table 9420

Service	🚌	🚌	🚌		🚌		🚌	🚌
Days of operation	⑤	①–④	ex⑦	....	⑦	....	⑤	④⑤
Adelaide.................d.	0745	0815	0815	....	1445	....	1730	1730
Meningie................d.	0945	1015	|	....	1645	....	2005	|
Mount Gambier.........a.	1400	1430	1430	....	2100	....	2345	2345

MOUNT GAMBIER — WARRNAMBOOL — MELBOURNE
OTT Tables 9415/9417

Service	🚌	🚌	🚌	🚌	🚌	🚌	🚌	🚌	🚌	🚌	🚌
Days of operation Special notes	①	Ⓐ	Ⓐ	⑥	⑥	Ⓐ B		⑤ C	Ⓐ B	⑥	Ⓐ	⑦
Mount Gambier.........d.	0205	....	....	....	0330	....	....	....	....	0800	0820	1325
Portland................d.	0405	0405	....	....	0530	....	....	....	....	1005	1030	1525
Port Fairy..............d.	0500	0500	....	....	0627	....	....	....	....	1105	1125	1622
Warrnambool...........a.	0530	0530	....	....	0655	....	....	....	....	1145	1200	1655
Warrnambool...........d.	0545a	0545a	....	....	0705a	....	....	0930	....	1305a	1220a	1705a
Port Campbell..........d.	|	|	....	....	|	....	....	1045	....	|	|	|
Apollo Bay.............d.	|	|	0600	0615	|	0940	....	1230	1410	|	|	|
Lorne..................d.	|	|	0702	0715	|	1045	1350	....	1515	|	|	|
Geelong................a.	0802a	0802a	0825	0945	0914a	1220	1520	....	1641	1516a	1437a	1916a
Melbourne..............a.	0905a	0905a	0944a	1012a	1012a	1333a	1643a	....	1801a	1613a	1532a	2017a

Special notes:
a–Connections by train.
B–Additional services 0730⑦, 1445⑥, 1615⑦.   C–Also operates on ① during Jan and Dec.

THE GREAT OCEAN ROAD

The direct route between Adelaide and Melbourne is along Highway 8 (see p. 194), but if you can possibly squeeze in the time, take the coastal route, which is full of magical delights.

DRIVING ROUTE

Take Hwy 1, here called the Princes Highway, from Adelaide to Tailem Bend and stay on it as it swings south for Meningie (153 km) and the sea. The highway shadows the coast for the next 145 km and then at Kingston SE draws back from the shore as it runs to Mt Gambier (157 km). Continue on to Portland (115 km) and the sea, then round Portland Bay to Port Fairy and Warrnambool (100 km). Hwy 1 heads inland direct for Geelong, but Warrnambool is where the Great Ocean Rd now begins, winding along the coast for 300 km to Torquay. From Torquay Geelong is just 21 km inland, from where you pick up Hwy 1 for the final 74 km into Melbourne. Total journey: 1065 km.

Buses do not follow this route – they take Highway 8 (see p. 194). The inland route from Adelaide to Melbourne via Horsham takes from 9 hrs 30 mins by bus and 11 hrs 30 mins by train. See OTT tables 9035 and 9401.

There are a great many coastal drives in Australia, but this one exercises a total fascination on everyone who has ever travelled it. Even before reaching the Great Ocean Rd itself, the route includes the incredible wetlands of the Coorong, and Mt Gambier and its blue lake. After that are the prospects of whale-watching at Warrnambool, the charms of Apollo Bay, and Lorne, the preferred holiday spot for the rich of Melbourne. And the views are breathtaking – pull over at as many viewing stations and parking bays as you can along the way, so you don't miss out.

ADELAIDE

See p. 144.

MENINGIE AND THE COORONG

Meningie is on the shores of Lake Albert; the name is said to come from an Aboriginal word for mud. At the end of the 19th century travellers from Adelaide to Melbourne would have had to cross Lake Alexandrina and its smaller offshoot, Lake Albert, by paddle steamer, and Meningie was a terminus for the steamers.

Meningie is now very much a fishing town (there are 40 professional anglers here), favoured for its position at the northern end of one of Australia's greatest surviving tracts of wetlands: the Coorong.

EN ROUTE

This is the route taken by the Chinese diggers as they travelled from South Australia to Victoria in search of gold, and about 15 km past the entrance to Coorong National Park, you pass **Chinaman Well**, now restored.

> [i] **Melaleuca Tourist Information Centre**, 76 Princes Hwy; tel: 8575 1259. Open daily. As well as information, the centre has a great selection of crafts, a large nursery and a florist.
> The telephone code is 08.

> **Lake Albert Motel $$$** 38 Princes Hwy; tel: 8575 1077.
> **Meningie Lake Albert Caravan Park $** Narrung Rd; tel: 8575 1411.
> **Meningie's Waterfront Motel $$$** Princes Hwy; tel: 8575 1152.
> **Mill Park $$$$** Yumali Rd; tel: 8575 6033.

HIGHLIGHTS

The **Coorong** is a special place. The name comes from an Aboriginal word meaning 'long neck of water', an accurate description of the Coorong, which is only 2 km wide but stretches for over 100 km. The Coorong is basically a series of lagoons created by the estuary of the Murray River. As it approaches the sea the river appears to lose all its power and the flow is so depleted that bulldozers have to be used to effect an exit to the sea. Its silted waters spread slowly to Lakes Alexandrina and Albert and along the Coorong. Although in theory this is fresh water, the Coorong gets progressively saltier. The shallow lagoons are sheltered from the Southern Ocean by the Younghusband Peninsula, which is mainly sandhills occasionally bound by coastal mallee gums and bushes of golden wattle.

The **Coorong National Park** covers the Coorong along with the associated Lakes Albert and Alexandrina and has some of the most prolific birdlife in Australia. At any given time there are as many as 240 species of native birds here, some of which migrate annually to Siberia, Japan and China. Literally millions of them feed on the lagoons and fish in the Southern Ocean. This was the setting for Cohn Thiele's children's novel *Storm Boy*, which tells of a boy's friendship with a pelican; it was later made into a movie. As well as the giant pelicans, wild duck, shags, ibis, cormorants, spoonbills, black swans, gannets, plovers and terns all breed here.

The park headquarters is near Salt Creek, about 64 km from Meningie along the Princes Hwy, just opposite the Messent Conservation Area. A nature trail here explains the formation of the sand dunes and the assorted vegetation that can be found within the park.

There is car access off Princes Hwy and two crossings which span the Coorong to the ocean: **42 Mile Crossing** is accessible throughout the year, while **Tea Tree Crossing** is a summer crossing only – at other times it can be flooded up to half a metre deep.

Just 12 km to the south of Meningie is **Camp Coorong**, an Aboriginal museum and cultural centre run by the Ngarrindjeri Lands and Progress Association – tel: 8575 1557. Aboriginal guides are available to take visitors on day walks to ancient Aboriginal fish traps and introduce them to plants and shrubs which the Ngarrindjeri used as medicine.

Although Coorong is the draw, there are several other attractions around Meningie. There is windsurfing, waterskiing or boating on Lake Albert. **Poltalloch Station**, along the shores of Lake Alexandrina, was established in 1836 and its 1870s homestead is a superb example of a beautifully crafted Victorian building. Buggies and carriages are kept in the barn; the shearing shed used to be the workplace of up to 22 shearers, and the old store, carpenter's shop and blacksmith's have been converted into cottages and outbuildings. There is a 2-hr talk and tour about the station and its history. Poltalloch is 34 km from Meningie; tours by appointment, tel: 8574 0013.

MOUNT GAMBIER

Mount Gambier is a modern city built on the slopes of an extinct volcano that bears the same name, in the middle of some of the largest softwood plantations in Australia. The volcano was last active approximately 5000 years ago, and was first climbed by Europeans in 1839. Mount Gambier is sometimes referred to as the Blue Lake City, after the crater lake that is its greatest natural attraction. The ballet dancer, choreographer and actor Robert Helpmann was born here in 1909.

i **Lady Nelson Visitor and Discovery Centre**, Jubilee Hwy East; tel: 8724 9750; free call 1800 087 187; www.mount gambiertourism.com.au. The **Interpretative Centre** includes a full-size replica of the *Lady Nelson*, the brig which made the first eastward passage along the southern coast of Australia. Also in the centre are a time walk, cave walk, and geology and wetlands exhibitions. Open daily 0900–1700. The telephone code is 08.

Avalon Motel $$ 93 Gray St; tel: 8725 7200.
Blue Lake City Caravan Park $ Park Bay Rd; tel: 8725 9856.
Gambier Lodge Inn $ 92 Penola Rd; tel: 8725 1579.

EN ROUTE

Piccaninnie Ponds Conservation Park is a very large reed swamp with scenic beach areas and good bushwalking. The park is well known for its cave diving. Special diving equipment is required and permits for qualified divers are available from the Department of Environment at 11 Helen St, Mount Gambier; tel: 8735 1177. Open Mon–Fri www.environment.sa.gov.au/parks/southeast.html.

The Jail $–$$$ Old Gaol, Margaret St; tel: 8723 0032 or 1800 626 844; www.jailbackpackers.com. Rooms in a renovated 1860s lockup – great fun.

Jens Hotel $$ 40 Commercial St (east); tel: 8725 0188.

Jubilee Motor Inn $$ Jubilee Hwy (east); tel: 8725 7444.

Mac's Hotel $$$ 21 Bay Rd; tel: 8725 2402.

Motel Mount Gambier $$$ 115 Penola Rd; tel: 8725 5800.

Mount Gambier Central Caravan $ 6 Krummel St; tel: 8725 4427.

Willow Vale Camping Park $ Princes Hwy (east); tel: 8725 3631.

🍴 **Caffe Belgiorno $$** 7 Percy St; tel: 8725 4455. National Pizza Award winner.

Domenica's Restaurant $$ 175 Commercial St (east); tel: 8723 1175.

Fasta Pasta $ 102 Commercial St (west); tel: 8723 0011.

The Park Tavern $$ Commercial St (west); tel: 8725 2430.

Ric's Pizza & Pasta Bar $ 109 Commercial St (east); tel: 8725 5044.

Roma Pizza Bar $ 91 Commercial St (west); tel: 8725 5332.

Sage and Muntries Café $$ 78 Commercial Rd (west); tel: 8724 8400.

Sirroco's Restaurant $$ 118 Crouch St (north); tel: 8723 1288.

Wing Wah Chinese Restaurant $ 222 Commercial St (east); tel: 8725 0136.

HIGHLIGHTS

The mountain of Mt Gambier has four craters, of which the principal one contains the 197-m deep **Blue Lake**. About November each year, the lake turns from grey-green to an intense cobalt blue, remaining this colour until late March. It has been suggested that the onset of warm weather precipitates countless particles of calcite, which absorb all visible light except blue. When the water cools in autumn, the particles dissolve once more and the water goes back to grey-green. The lake is over 3 km in circumference and some of the cliffs which surround it are 70 m high. The lookout points give spectacular vistas of both the lake and surrounding area. The town's domestic water supply is drawn from the lake so you can go on a tour of the pumping station.

In the **Mount Gambier Courthouse**, which was in operation from 1865 to 1975, the jury box, judge's chamber and cells are open to the public, along with an exhibition of local history. Bay Rd; open daily 1200–1600.

POET'S LEAP

At the top of Mt Gambier an obelisk commemorates a mad act by a poet, Adam Lindsay Gordon, who served with the mounted police in the town from 1853 to 1855. Gordon, an exceptional horseman, took his horse to the summit and then raced it towards a post-and-rail fence, beyond which was a ledge 2 m wide and then a drop of 60 m to the rocks bordering the Blue Lake. The horse cleared the fence, turned in mid-air and landed on the very edge of the drop. It has been suggested that Gordon was world-weary and did not care whether he survived; this one jump brought him contemporary fame in Australia that he never achieved with his poetry.

One of the distinguishing features of the town is the use of local white coralline limestone for building, and there are several limestone caves. The **Cave Gardens** incorporate an open cave in the midst of rose gardens, while the **Umpherston Cave** has outside barbecue facilities and terraced gardens. The **Engelbrecht Cave** actually runs under part of the city and was used in the 19th century as a dump by a whisky distiller. This cave sometimes floods with water – as do many of the caves to be found in the area – but much of the time it is open to visitors. The tourist office has details.

PORTLAND

The first settlers here were sealers and whalers. A minimal shore-based whaling hut had been established in 1829 but the settlement grew rapidly as Portland Bay proved one of the best whale-catching areas in the world. Each year hundreds of whales were caught.

It was the arrival of the Henty family, of whom the first was Edward in 1834, that marked the beginning of serious settlement of Victoria. Ploughing started almost immediately, with the first piece of soil being turned on 6 Dec 1834 in what is now known as the Ploughed Field. The first Henty home, a hut, was somewhere in the area of the present-day Richmond Henty Hotel Motel.

The Henty clan spread inland to establish various stations; by 1839 they already owned 30,000 sheep and 500 head of cattle. When the township was surveyed and the first town lots went on sale in 1840 they commanded high prices, as Portland was in competition with Melbourne to be the premier settlement of the southern region. The major building boom that followed absorbed all available labour: by 1842 four hotels were opened, as well as four churches, and the first trading bank appeared in 1846. What finished the contest was the injection of wealth Melbourne received in the Victorian gold rush.

Having lost the contest – although the people of Portland compare their lot with those of Melbourne and are sure they won – Portland continued to develop. There are now over 200 heritage buildings in the city.

> *i* **Portland Visitor Information Centre**, Lee Breakwater Rd; tel: 5523 2671; free call (1800) 035 567. It is housed in the Maritime Discovery Centre. Open daily; www.portlandnow.net.au. The telephone code for Portland is 03.

> 🛏 **Admella Motel $$$** 5 Otway Court; tel: 5523 3347.
> **Centenary Caravan Park $$** 184 Bentinck St; tel: 5523 1487.
> **Central Portland Motel $** 66 Julia St; tel: 5523 1300.
> **Claremont Holiday Village $$** 37 Percy St; tel: 5521 7567.
> **Dutton Way Caravan Park $$** 50 Dutton Way; tel: 5523 1904.
> **Grosvenor Motel $$$** 206 Hurd St. Quiet off-highway location, all ground-floor units; tel: 5523 2888.
> **Melaleuca Motel $$$** 25 Bentinck St; tel: 5523 3397.
> **Portland Backpackers $–$$** 14 Gawler St; tel: 5523 6390. New and a bit spartan but showing potential.
> **William Dutton Motel $$$** 141 Percy St; tel: 5523 4222.

> 🍴 **Canton Palace Restaurant $$$** 7 Julia St; tel: 5523 3677. Open daily for lunch and dinner. BYO and licensed.
> **Edward's Waterfront Café/Restaurant $$** 101 Bentinck St; tel: 5523 1032. Open daily 0700 until late. Mediterranean pasta and seafood.
> **The Old Bond Store $$$** 6 Julia St; tel: 5523 7100. Open for dinner Tues–Sat. A la carte. Licensed.
> **Pino's Pizza House $$** 8 Julia St; tel: 5221 7388. Open daily for dinner (lunch and dinner Fri).
> **Ric's Pizza Bar $$** 21 Henty St; tel: 5523 5699. Open Tues–Sun from 1700. Dine in or takeaway.

HIGHLIGHTS

Portland is the only deep-water port between Melbourne and Adelaide, and its port development is huge, with much of the city's revenue deriving from the aluminium smelter (see p. 208). This does not detract from the charms of Portland; indeed, it is one of the few places where visitors can drive or walk into the heart of the wharf area. For those with an interest in the sea and sea trade, the wharf is the opportunity to take a close look at a range of vessels, from small coastal fishing boats to 80,000 d.w.t. bulk carriers.

With a self-guide map from the tourist centre you can see some of the oldest buildings in Victoria. Among them are the **Customs House** and **courthouse** in Cliff St, several old inns, Edward Henty's bluestone residence at **Burswood** on Cape Nelson Rd with its sweeping 19th-century tree-lined drive, and his brother Francis Henty's home at **Claremont**. The **Old Town Hall History House Museum and Research Centre**, off Cliff St, is open daily 1000–1200, 1300–1600. The **RSL Memorial Lookout Tower** in Wade St has great 360° views of Portland and the surrounding districts; open daily 1000–1600.

> ### SMELTER TOURS
> The **Portland Aluminium Smelter** is claimed to be Australia's single biggest export earner and is one of the most modern ever built. There are guided tours on Mon, Wed and Fri for which you need to book (tel: 5523 2671). The smelter's tree-planting programme will see over one million trees planted in and around the smelter over five years.

The original inhabitants of the area were the Kerrup-Tjmara people. There are still signs of Aboriginal presence in the area, and the **Lake Condah Mission** displays examples of their lifestyle.

Nearby there are some excellent beaches, good surfing and outstanding coastal and forest scenery. The circular track of the 250-km **Great South-West Walk** begins and ends at Portland, and winds its way through national parks and state forests to Discovery Bay and Cape Nelson. There are 17 sections of varying lengths, and 16 campsites supplied with fresh water, wood barbecues, cleared tent space and bush toilets.

PORT FAIRY

There is considerable debate as to who was the first European to visit Port Fairy and when, with claims varying from 1810 to 1828. One candidate for the first landing is Captain James Wishart, and there is no argument that the town was named in honour of Wishart's ship, the cutter *Fairy*.

By 1828, the region from Port Fairy to Portland was well known to sealers and whalers, and over the next few years buildings were established and the whalers started to settle in permanent homes. Around 1839 John Cox set up a small store on the riverbank; Cox St marks its approximate location. In the same year a Mr McNeill established an inn he called the Merrijig, which still stands today.

At one time Port Fairy was set to become a major port in Australia. What stopped it was the start of the gold rush in the mid-19th century. There are still a number of unfinished buildings which show the suddenness with which workers simply downed tools and left for the goldfields. Now over 50 of Port Fairy's small cottages and bluestone buildings have been classified by the National Trust.

> *i* **Port Fairy Visitor Information Centre**, Railway Pl., Bank St; tel: 5568 2682. Open daily. The telephone code is 03.

> 🛏 **Affordable Bed & Breakfast $$$** 21 Bank St; tel: 5568 1143.
>
> **The Boathouse $$$$** 19 Gipps St; tel: 5568 2608. Includes breakfast.
>
> **Caledonian Inn Hotel Motel $$$$** 41 Bank St. Victoria's oldest continually licensed hotel since circa 1844. Motel accommodation in adjacent units; tel: 5568 1044.
>
> **Celtic Cottage and Garden House $$$** 198 Princes Hwy. 1850s Port Fairy cottage. Secluded gardens; tel: 5568 2478. Website: www.port-fairy.com/celtic cottage; e-mail: celticcottage@port-fairy.com.
>
> **Eumeralla Backpackers $** High St, Yambuk; tel: 5568 4204; www.backpacker.faithweb.com. About 18 km west of Port Fairy.
>
> **Merrijig Inn $$$$** 1 Campbell St. The oldest hotel in town; tel: 5568 2324.
>
> **Port Fairy YHA $–$$** 8 Cox St; tel: 5568 2468; www.yha.com.au/ hostels. En suite and double rooms. Built in the 1840s by the merchant king of Port Fairy, William Rutledge.
>
> **Royal Oak Hotel $$** 9 Bank St. Built around 1857. Double rooms with shared facilities; tel: 5568 1018.
>
> **Seacombe House Motor Inn $$$$** cnr Cox and Sackville Sts. In a National Trust building in the centre of town; tel: 5568 1082.
>
> **Southcombe Park Caravan Park $$** James St; tel: 5568 2677.

> 🍽 **Caledonian Inn $$$** 41 Bank St; tel: 5568 1044. Victoria's oldest continually licensed hotel, built about 1844. Bistro with an extensive seafood and steak menu; dinner and lunch seven days a week.
>
> **Dublin House Inn $$$** 57 Bank St; tel: 5568 2022. Open for dinner. Closed Sun. Varied menu offering kangaroo, ostrich and local seafood.

Full House Chinese Restaurant $$ 79–83 Gipps St; tel: 5568 1889. Cantonese. Licensed. Open for lunch and dinner daily. Rumoured to be moving to Sackville St.

Gingernuts $$$ cnr Dank and Sackville Sts; tel: 5568 2326. Open daily from 0700 for breakfast, lunch and dinner. Café-style restaurant with weekly specials.

HIGHLIGHTS

Port Fairy marks one end of the Shipwreck Coast, which stretches east to Cape Otway. One of its attractions is the **Moyne River** which provides safe anchorage for large fishing vessels and pleasure craft. When the fleet returns with the day's catch visitors can buy fresh fish and crays from the wharf. **Pea Soup Beach** and **East Beach** are popular spots for pleasure and relaxation; East Beach runs parallel with the Moyne River and is accessible by footbridge and roadway.

> ### RETURN OF THE MUTTON BIRDS
>
> One of Port Fairy's most spectacular sights is the return of the mutton birds to Griffiths Island. Within three days of 22 Sept each year tens of thousands of these birds arrive after a 15,000-km flight across the Pacific Ocean. Each bird returns to the same nesting burrow every year and usually has the same mate for life. They all fly out to sea during the day and return again each evening. A viewing platform and walking trails on Griffiths Island, which is connected to the town by a causeway, enable visitors to observe the birds and their young. Birds inhabit the colony from late Sept to late Apr.

There are many spectacular walks to be enjoyed in Port Fairy, including the walk along Fisherman's Wharf, the Lighthouse Walk and the 22-km Mahogany Walking Track to Warrnambool. The tourist information centre has brochures.

The **Port Fairy History Centre** ($) in the old 1859 courthouse gives a good idea of the history of the whole area within an hour or so's visit. Gipps St; open Wed and weekends 1400–1700, daily during school holidays. **Emoh** at 8 Cox St is a fine example of a rich merchant's home. It was built around 1847 by William Rutledge, the merchant king of Port Fairy, and was a centre for convivial hospitality until Rutledge's firm crashed in 1862. Now it is a youth hostel.

The **Crags**, 12 km west of Port Fairy, has windswept sand dunes and panoramic views of **Lady Julia Percy Island** and the coastline. The public is not allowed on the island, 17 km from Port Fairy, but its colony of fur seals can easily be seen at close quarters from a cruise boat. (Trips are arranged in good weather; the tourist centre will advise you.) The island is also home to rookeries of mutton birds, kestrels, swamp harriers, sooty oystercatchers and blue penguins.

WARRNAMBOOL

When this town was surveyed by Lt Pickering in 1856 he gave it an Aboriginal name, taken from a hill by the Hopkins River, which has been variously translated as 'place of plenty', 'place between two waters' and 'running swamps'. You can take your pick.

Warrnambool was a whaling and sealing port in the early 1830s and was first permanently settled in 1839, but it may have been discovered by Europeans much earlier. In 1836 two shipwrecked sealers discovered an ancient wreck in the sand dunes. Called the **Mahogany Ship** because of the dark timbers used in its construction, it was last seen some time in the 1880s; it is presumed to have been buried by drifting dunes. Old Portuguese charts have since been discovered showing Australia's southern coastline as far as Armstrong's Bay, just 6 km west of Warrnambool. These suggest a Portuguese ship sailed off the coast of Australia in 1522, and some historians believe that the Mahogany Ship was a Portuguese caravel captained by Cristovão Mendonça, which was lost in the early 16th century. This theory, if proven, would rewrite the history of European discovery of Australia. Numerous searches and a reward of $250,000 offered by the government in 1992 have so far failed to solve the mystery. The 22-km **Mahogany Walking Track** runs from Warrnambool to Port Fairy, past the possible site of the mystery ship.

These were always dangerous waters and 28 ships were wrecked here between 1836 and 1908. Today, the shore is best known for the whales that come each winter to calve.

> i **Warrnambool Visitor Information Centre**, Flagstaff Hill Maritime Precinct, Merri St; tel: 1800 637 725 or 5559 4620. The telephone code is 03. Open daily.
> **Warrnambool:** www.warrnamboolinfo.com.au.

> 🛏 **Colonial Village Motel** $$$ 31 Mortlake Rd; tel: 5562 1455.
> **Downtown Motel** $$$ 620 Raglan Pde; tel: 5562 1277.
> **Elm Tree Lodge Motel** $$$ 179 Kepler St; tel: 5562 4133.
> **Flagstaff Hill Motel** $$$ 762 Raglan Pde; tel: 5562 1166.
> **Log Cabin Motel** $$$ 698 Raglan Pde; tel: 5562 4244.
> **The Stuffed Backpacker** $–$$ Kepler St; tel: 5562 2459; www.stuffed.com.au. Central, above a chocolate shop.
> **Warrnambool Beach Backpackers** $–$$ 17 Stanley St; tel: 5562 4874. Between the beach and the river. Has double rooms.
> **Western Hotel-Motel** $$ 45 Kepler St; tel: 5562 2011. Backpacker accommodation.

Whale Beach B & B $$$$ 234 Hopkins Point Rd; tel: 5562 2204; e-mail: bodycoat@datafast.net.au. Overlooks the ocean, 1 km from whale viewing platform.

🔟 **Balena's $$** Brasserie. Australian with European and Asian influences. Timor St; tel: 5562 8391. Next to Whalers Inn. Open Mon–Sat.

Beach Babylon $$$ 72 Liebig St. Open seven days a week from 1800 until late. Licensed and BYO; tel: 5562 3714.

Bojangles $$$ 61 Liebig St; tel: 5562 8751. Award-winning pasta and pizza restaurant. BYO (wine only) and licensed. Open daily for dinner.

Freshwater Café $$$ 78 Liebig St; tel: 5561 3188. Seafood. Open for dinner Mon–Sat, lunch Thur–Fri 1200–1400.

Mahogany Ship $$ Flagstaff Hill Maritime Village. Open daily. Licensed; tel: 5561 1833.

Proudfoots Boathouse $$$ 2 Simpson St. National Trust Classified building on the Hopkins River. Open for lunch and dinner; closed Sun. Licensed; tel: 5561 5055.

Restaurant Malaysia $$$ 69 Liebig St; tel: 5562 2051.

Warrnambool Dragon Inn Restaurant $$$ 219 Lava St; tel: 5562 1517. Open daily.

Whalers Inn $$ cnr Liebig and Timor Sts. Lunch. Live music at dinner time; tel: 5562 8391.

Highlights

Warrnambool is spoken of as Victoria's southern right whale nursery. Every year between June and September, southern right whale cows return to the waters off Warrnambool to calve and prepare their young for the return trip to Antarctic waters. The whales often swim within 100 m of the shore: Logan's Beach, only minutes from the town centre, is one of Australia's most popular land-based whale-viewing sites. You can watch from the beach or from a special viewing platform in the dunes, which allows a far better view.

The Southern Right Whale

Once hunted nearly to extinction, the southern right was one of the first whale species granted protection by an international agreement signed in 1935. Although it is relatively rare, with only a few thousand known, its numbers are slowly growing. The southern right has been sighted regularly along the southern coastline since 1970, with sightings and visits becoming more frequent in recent years.

One of the other major attractions of the town is the **Flagstaff Hill Maritime Museum** in Merri St. This is a life-size recreated village to give visitors a feeling of the port in the 19th century. In addition to the original lighthouse and lighthouse-keeper's cottage, there are replicas of many buildings of the time, including a sailmaker's loft, bank, town hall and chapel. The museum also tells the story of the *Loch Ard* wreck and displays the fortunate peacock. Open daily 0900–1700 ($$).

The town's **Botanic Gardens**, on the corner of Queen St and Botanic Rd, had the same great designer as the Melbourne Botanic Gardens. There are a bandstand rotunda, a fernery, and winding shaded walkways.

Award-winning **Lake Pertobe Adventure Playground** in Pertobe Rd, adjacent to the main beach, features a lake with bridges, paddle boats, a maze, flying fox, giant slides, walking tracks and bird hides. It's an ideal picnic spot.

The **Wollaston Bridge** is an early example of a suspension bridge, erected in 1890 for noted district pastoralist Sir Walter Manifold, to provide easy access to the Wollaston Estate. The cables used in its construction came from Melbourne's early cable trams.

THE GREAT OCEAN ROAD

The Great Ocean Rd runs for about 300 km between Warrnambool and Torquay. Although it is famed for its scenery, the road was built for purely practical purposes. Until it was opened there was no connection between the isolated communities along the coast of Victoria, which were cut off from the rest of the world by the Otway Range. Its construction, which began at the end of World War I, was also a form of job creation for returning servicemen, and at the same time it was thought that the road would provide a fitting memorial to all those Australians who had fallen in the war. Using, in the main, manual labour, squads of men cut the road out of the mountainsides that swept down to the sea. The road was completed in 1932.

Granny's Grave is a monument to Mrs James Raddleston, the first white woman to be buried in the Warrnambool area. She died in 1848, and the monument was erected in 1904. It is off Hickford Pde, by way of the sand dunes.

At low tide you can wade across to **Middle Island** at the mouth of the Merri River; part of the Thunder Point Coastal Reserve, it has a fairy penguin colony. There are tracks laid down so that visitors do not disturb the birds.

Along the Princes Hwy, and 12 km west of Warrnambool, is the **Tower Hill Game Reserve**. Tower Hill is believed to have been formed some 25,000 years ago in a volcanic eruption. The blast created both the funnel-shaped crater, later filled by a lake, and the islands. Noted Victorian artist Eugene von Guerard painted an exceptionally detailed picture of Tower Hill in 1855, and a re-vegetation programme based on species identified from the painting began in the late 1950s. The re-vegetation has provided new habitats for many animals – the koalas have succeeded so well that population control is being tried, including feeding them a contraceptive pill. There are boardwalks, nesting boxes and a bird hide to enable you to get close. There is open access to the reserve at all times, and the natural history centre is open daily 0900–1630.

PORT CAMPBELL

Port Campbell National Park is famous for its striking cliffs and rock formations – London Bridge, the Twelve Apostles, Loch Ard Gorge and the Arch. The **Twelve Apostles** are rock stacks which have been isolated from the coast by the sea and have become one of the most photographed natural features in Australia. This is the centre of the notorious **Shipwreck Coast**, where the slightest swell results in treacherous surf and billowing spray.

Compact and welcoming, Port Campbell township continues to grow as a tourism centre and includes a wide range of accommodation and places to eat – some of them serving pretty fair food. There are some interesting local walks and the town is the best place to get set for explorations of the national park.

> *i* **Port Campbell Visitor Information Centre**, 26 Morris St, Port Campbell; tel: 5598 6089. Open daily; www.greatoceanroad.org. The telephone code is 03.

> **Ocean House Backpackers $–$$$** Cairns St; tel: 5598 6492; www.portcampbell.nu/oceanhouse. Comfortable, opposite the beach.
> **Port Campbell YHA $–$$$** 18 Tregea St; tel: 5598 6305; www.yha.com.au/hostels. Dorms, double rooms and cabins.

APOLLO BAY

One of the most appealing features of the Great Ocean Rd is that as it winds its elegant way around the coast it passes through a series of small townships, each of which is attractive in its own right. Apollo Bay is one of them. It was once described by Rudyard Kipling as 'paradise', a fair summing up of a town which stands among cool fern gullies, rushing streams, magnificent waterfalls and rainforests, with calm waters and ocean views.

EN ROUTE

Otway National Park stretches from Cape Otway almost to Apollo Bay, and contains varied birdlife as well as swamp wallabies and ring-tailed possums.

Cape Otway was first discovered by Europeans in 1802 by Matthew Flinders, but this was ever a dangerous coast and it was not until the lighthouse was built in 1848 that it seriously attracted settlers. After World War II there was a timber boom for houses and the national park was created to protect the coast above Cape Otway and Blanket Bay.

The Great Ocean Rd runs right through the park, with Lighthouse Rd – unsealed but very well maintained – running down from the centre to the coast. You can easily explore it from Maits Rest, where there is a boardwalk. You can visit the lighthouse daily 0900–1700. Accommodation is available in the old lightkeepers' cottages; tel: 5237 9240. You can get information at the Otway National Park offices in Oak Ave, Apollo Bay; tel: 131963.

First among Europeans were whalers who worked in small boats from the shore. A whaling station was established in 1840 and stood where the golf club is today. Then in the 1850s the timber cutters came, and Apollo Bay was born.

The town depended almost totally on the sea for connection with civilisation until the Great Ocean Rd was completed in 1932. In that year the bay was the scene of a major Australian shipping disaster: as the coastal steamer *Casino* was coming into the jetty a series of freak waves turned it over and it sank. Ten lives were lost. The anchor of the ship is now at the corner of Great Ocean Rd and Nelson St.

Today Apollo Bay is a major tourist destination, but it is also a fishing port supporting a large fleet. Much of the action is centred on the jetty, and there are local markets on the foreshore on Saturdays.

The **Old Cable Station Museum** displays a photographic record of the history of the area, with interesting artefacts. The original cable station was set up to achieve telecommunications between Tasmania and the mainland. (Nowadays communication is by microwave and satellite, since there are no longer any cable-laying ships in the southern hemisphere and if something should go wrong Tasmania could be cut off for months.) The museum is open weekends 1400–1700 and during school and public holidays. Tel: 5237 7410.

The town is surrounded by interesting lookout and picnic spots including the **Barham Paradise Scenic Reserve**, the exceptionally beautiful **Barham River Valley**, **Grey River Scenic Reserve and Walk** (23 km east of Apollo Bay), **Elliot River** (10 km south-west) and the picturesque **Carisbrook Falls**. The **Marriners Falls** are on Barham River Rd, with a 2-km track running through lush forested areas. Access to **Marriners Lookout** is by a steep, narrow road, worth the effort for the superb views.

> [i] **Apollo Bay Great Ocean Rd Information Centre**, Apollo Bay Foreshore; tel: 5237 6529. Open daily; www.greatoceanroad.org. The telephone code is 03.

EN ROUTE

Cape Patton Lookout,
Kennett River and Wye River
are all perfect spots at which
to pause and be bowled over
by the stunning ocean views.

🖨 For the Christmas period, say, 15 Dec–1 Feb, every room
will have been booked some time before and the prices
adjusted upwards. Only go out of season.

Apollo Bay Backpackers $–$$$ 47 Montrose Ave; tel: 0419
340 362; www.apollobaybackpackers.com.au.

Apollo Bay Beachfront Motel $$$ 163 Great Ocean Rd; tel:
5237 6437.

Iluka Motel $$$ 65 Great Ocean Rd; tel: 5237 6531.

Kooringal Tourist Van Park $$$ 27 Cawood St; tel: 5237
7111.

Pisces Caravan Resort $$$ 311 Great Ocean Rd; tel: 5237
6749. This is probably the least expensive place to stay in
town.

Surfside Backpackers $–$$$ cnr Great Ocean Rd &
Gambier St; tel: 5237 7263. Can be a bit untidy, but friendly and
close to the beach.

Waratah Caravan Park $$$ 7 Noel St; tel: 5237 6562.

🍴 Choose the locally caught fresh fish.

Buffs Bistro $$$ 51 Great Ocean Rd; tel: 5237 6403. Open
daily for lunch and dinner. Licensed. Varied menu with
vegetarian options.

Chris's Beacon Point Restaurant $$$$ Skenes Creek Rd,
Skenes Creek. Open daily lunch and dinner. Licensed. Famous
for seafood; tel: 5237 6411.

Raj's by the Bay $$ 151 Great Ocean Rd; tel: 5237 6452.
Pizza restaurant. Eat in and takeaway. Open daily 0800–2030
(closed Tues in off-season).

Wayne's Craypot Bistro $$$ Ocean Road Hotel, 29 Great
Ocean Rd; tel: 5237 6240.

Whitecrest Restaurant $$$ 13 km east of Apollo Bay, Great
Ocean Rd; tel: 5237 0228. Open for dinner, closed Tues–Wed.
Stunning views. Accommodation available ($$$$).

LORNE

This is one of the preferred haunts of the golden people of Melbourne: over the
extended Christmas holiday period you could not force yourself in with a shoehorn.
As an idea of how full this little village can become, the field for its famous **Pier to
Pub Swim** has to be restricted to 2500 entries. At that time of the year it will be
expensive as well, so go on a weekday outside the holiday period.

The town grew around a site from which timber was shipped and until 1869 was called Loutit Bay. It became popular with pastoralists from inland areas and developed rather in the style of an English seaside resort. For years the only easy access to Lorne was by sea, but when the Great Ocean Rd opened in 1932 Lorne immediately became Melbourne's favourite playground.

EN ROUTE

Torquay, 45 km from Lorne, marks the eastern end of the Great Ocean Rd. It rejoices in the fact that it has two of the world's great surfing beaches – Bells and Jan Juc.

[i] **Lorne Visitor Information Centre**, 144 Mountjoy Pde; tel: 5289 1152. The telephone code is 03. Open daily; www.greatoceanroad.org.

[🛏] **Anchorage Motel $$$** 32 Mountjoy Pde; tel: 5289 1891.
Coachman Inn Motel $$$$ 1 Deans Marsh Rd; tel: 5289 2244.
Erskine River Backpackers $–$$$ 6 Mountjoy Pde; tel: 5289 1496. Nice views, short walk to town.
Grand Pacific Hotel $$$$ 268 Mountjoy Pde; tel: 5289 1609.
Grazi's B & B $$$ 22 Great Ocean Rd; tel: 5289 2422. Includes breakfast. Situated on the ocean front.
Great Ocean Road Backpackers YHA $–$$$ 10 Erskine Ave; tel: 5289 1809; www.yha.com.au/hostels. Lovely peaceful location.
Lorne Hotel Motel $$$$ Mountjoy Pde; tel: 5289 1409. Newly renovated.
Ocean Lodge Motel $$$$ 9 Armytage St; tel: 5289 1330.
Sandridge Motel $$$$ 128 Mountjoy Pde; tel: 5289 2180.

[🍴] **Arab Expresso Bar $$$** 94 Mountjoy Pde. Open lunch and dinner until late. BYO; tel: 5289 1435.
Chris's Restaurant $$$ Cumberland Resort; tel: 5289 2455.
Kosta's $$$$ 48 Mountjoy Pde. Open daily 0900–0100. Licensed. Greek-influenced cuisine; tel: 5289 1883.
Lorne Oven House $$$ 46a Mountjoy Pde; tel: 5289 2544. Open daily for lunch and dinner, breakfast Sat–Sun. A Mediterranean-style café specialising in wood-fired pizzas, pasta and fish.
Mark's $$$ 124 Mountjoy Pde. Open seven days for lunch and dinner. Licensed; tel: 5289 2787.
Pier Restaurant $$$ Pier Head; tel: 5289 1119.
Reif's Restaurant $$$ 84 Mountjoy Pde. Open seven days, lunch and dinner. Licensed; tel: 5289 2366.
Seaside Palace Chinese Restaurant $$$ 114 Mountjoy Pde; tel: 5289 2330. Open daily for lunch and dinner.
Tirami-Su $$$ Grove Rd; tel: 5289 1004.

Highlights

Lorne was the first town in Victoria to be declared by the state government as being of special significance and natural beauty. It is an appropriate choice. The approaches to Lorne along the Great Ocean Rd, whether from east or west, are quite spectacular, and the town is surrounded by beach, forests and the beautiful Otway Range. It has a year-round mild climate.

Two headlands sweep down to the sea either side of the white beach. The beach is patrolled and very safe, and is ideal for kids – the foreshore reserve has a children's playground, pool, amusement centre, trampolines and picnic ground. The town itself has remained relatively unspoiled. The **Lorne Historical Society** has a collection of photographs and memorabilia of the town at 59 Mountjoy Pde; open Sundays only 1300–1600.

The entrance to the **Angahook–Lorne State Park** is about a 30-min walk – go up Bay St and turn left on George St. The park stretches from Aireys Inlet to Kennett River, and in just the Lorne section there are more than 50 km of maintained walking tracks through a variety of habitats, including lush, cool-fern gullies and waterfalls. Some of the walks follow the old timber tramways built in the 19th century for the logging industry. The **Erskine Falls** are along the park's Erskine River Track, a magnificent 8-km drive or 3-hr walk along scenic forested hills (not to be attempted when the river is high). The falls, set among tree ferns and bush, drop 30 m. There are stunning views from **Teddy's Lookout**. Maps and information from the Angahook–Lorne State Park Office (tel: 5289 1732) or the Lorne visitor centre.

GEELONG

In a sense Geelong has it all. It is Victoria's second largest city, a thriving commercial centre and a quite remarkably elegant town. The surrounding countryside around Corio Bay is a paradise for walkers and nature lovers, and within the city are superb recreational areas. It emanates a feeling of metropolitan sophistication overlaid by a provincial charm.

Geelong is one of Victoria's most historically significant cities. It is in an area which was one of the first parts of Victoria discovered by Europeans; possibly the first was Lt John Murray in 1802. The land was ripe for pastoral development, and by 1841 the town had a post office and what is claimed to be Australia's oldest morning newspaper, the *Geelong Advertiser*.

Almost from the start Geelong was prosperous as a major port for wool and grain. Then, as for so many Australian cities, came gold. Geelong was a crucial link to the

Ballarat goldfields (see p. 195) and as the gold passed through some of the money stuck. The goldfields enticed many citizens to try their luck at the diggings but many others stayed to take advantage of the trade they brought. It is interesting that almost without exception towns with a strong agricultural economy benefited greatly from the trade brought about by gold, while those that grew only with gold tended to die with it.

The Aboriginals called the bay Jillong and the surrounding land Corayo, but over time the names have reversed and the bay is now Corio and the town Geelong. Jillong is said to mean either 'place of the cliff' or 'white seabird'.

i **Geelong Visitor Information Centre**, National Wool Centre, 26 Moorabool St; tel: 5222 2900. Open daily.
Geelong Net: www.greatoceanroad.org.
The telephone code is 03.

🛏 **Bay City Geelong Motel $$$$** 231 Malop St; tel: 5221 1933.
Bayview Hotel $$$ 2 Mercer St; tel: 5229 2164.
Colonial Lodge Motel $$$ 57 Fyans St; tel: 5223 2266.
Eastern Sands Motel $$$$ 1 Bellarine St; tel: 5221 5577.
Geelong Motor Inn & Serviced Apartments $$$$ Kooyong Rd, cnr Princes Hwy; tel: 5222 4777.
Innkeepers Motor Inn $$$ 9 Aberdeen St; tel: 5221 2177.
Kangaroo Motel $$$ 16 The Esplanade South; tel: 5221 4022.
National Hotel Backpackers $–$$ 191 Moorabool St; tel: 5229 1211; www.nationalhotel.com.au. Central and lively.
Rippleside Motor Inn $$$ 67 Melbourne Rd; tel: 5278 2017.
Shannon Motor Inn $$$ 285 Shannon Ave; tel: 5222 4355.

🍴 **Black Sheep Café $$$** National Wool Museum, Moorabool St; tel: 5223 2392. Open daily for lunch, dinner Fri–Sun. Varied menu. Next to Wool Museum Shop.
Elephant and Castle Pub Restaurant $$$ 158 McKillop St; tel: 5221 3707. Open daily for lunch; dinner Tues–Sat. English pub food.
Empire Grill $$$$ 66 McKillop St; tel: 5223 2132. Open lunch Mon–Fri. Dinner Mon–Sat. Licensed. Imaginative menu.
Fishermen's Pier $$$ Yarra St; tel: 5222 4100. Open daily lunch and dinner. Licensed.
Le Parisien $$$ 15 Eastern Beach Rd; tel: 5229 3110. Open daily for lunch and dinner. Licensed. French cooking.
Lord of the Isles Bistro $$$ 3 West Fyans St; tel: 5224 2522. Open seven days a week for lunch and dinner. Licensed. The name, which goes back to 1884, derives from Sir Walter Scott's poem, a favourite of the landlord at that time.

Mexican Graffiti $$ 43 Yarra St; tel: 5222 2036. Californian-style Mexican cuisine. Open seven days. Licensed.

Savvas Restaurant $$ 51 Moorabool St; tel: 5229 3703. Opposite the National Wool Centre. Medium price. Open lunch and dinner Mon–Sat and lunch Sun.

Sawyers Arms Tavern $$$ 2 Noble St, Newtown; tel: 5223 1244. Lunch Mon–Fri. Dinner Mon–Sat. Licensed.

Wharf Shed Café $$$ 15 Eastern Beach Rd (under Le Parisien); tel: 5229 3110. Open daily early to late. On the waterfront.

Zenith Brasserie and Bar $$ Mercure Hotel, Gheringhap St; tel: 5221 6844. Open daily for breakfast, lunch and dinner. Licensed.

HIGHLIGHTS

With over 200 classified Victorian buildings in its well-laid-out streets, and over 14 per cent of its area reserved for parks and sports grounds, it is difficult to remember that Geelong's principal trade is crude and refined petroleum products.

The easiest way to see how Geelong developed is to take the **Heritage Trail Walk** which starts in Moorabool St outside the Wool Museum which holds the tourist centre. The walk, which takes about an hour, lets you see most of the major sights of Geelong.

Geelong's character is defined by its remarkable historical buildings and its magnificent parks and gardens. The buildings include **Merchiston Hall** (Garden St, East Geelong), an eight-roomed stone house built in 1856 for an early settler, and **Osborne House** (Swinburne St, North Geelong), a bluestone mansion built in 1858. Within **Osborne House** is the comprehensive memorabilia of Geelong's **Naval Museum.** Two houses in Newtown are now open to the public. **The Heights**, in Aphrasia St, is a 14-roomed prefabricated timber mansion built in 1855, and **Barwon Grange** in Fernleigh St, built in the same year, is a well-maintained homestead on the banks of the Barwon River. All the rooms are furnished in the style of the times. Barwon Grange is open Wed, Sat and Sun 1100–1630 (closed in winter); tel: (03) 5221 3906, and The Heights is open Wed–Sun 1100–1630.

The old Denys Lascelles Woolstore, built in stages from 1872 on the corner of Moorabool and Brougham Sts, houses the **National Wool Museum**. Three galleries record in splendid detail Australia's wool heritage, and there are graphic sculptured displays, relics, models, photographic records, magnificent wool murals and a range of video and audio presentations. Open daily 0930–1700 ($).

The **Geelong Art Gallery** in Little Malop St has a splendid collection of over 3000 works, mainly Australian, including 'Bush Burial' by Frederick McCubbins and Eugene von Guerard's 'View of Geelong', on loan from Sir Andrew Lloyd Webber.

EVENTS AND ENTERTAINMENT

The impressive **Performing Arts Centre** in Little Malop St offers some of the best theatre and opera from around the world. Horse racing's **Geelong Cup** (tel: 5229 4414 for information) is held at the end of October, neatly tying in with the Melbourne Cup (see p. 190).

Johnstone Park, in which the gallery is set, also includes the war memorial, library, city hall, and historical records centre.

The recently restored historic semicircular promenade overlooking Corio Bay has added to the popularity of **Eastern Beach**. The beautiful **Corio Villa**, a prefabricated iron house built in 1856, is near the Eastern Beach swimming enclosure and the entrance to **Geelong Botanic Gardens**. The gardens, which include an annexe of botanical woodlands overlooking Corio Bay, were first planted in 1851 and show the far-sighted thinking of the pioneer fathers of the city. They are open daily from dawn until dusk. Teahouse open daily 1100–1600.

Buckley Falls Park, on the western outskirts of Geelong, straddles the Barwon River, which tumbles over rocks and rapids before it joins with the Moorabool River.

In the **Geelong wine district** there are properties that date back to when grapes were first planted in the area 150 years ago by Swiss immigrants. Part of Geelong's prosperity came from wool, and **Barunah Plains**, once the largest sheep station in Victoria, is still in operation; visitors are welcome. This 150-year-old estate includes a historic grazier's mansion with bluestone outbuildings and shearers' quarters. Open by appointment; tel: 5287 1234.

The **Twin Lakes**, a fauna sanctuary 19 km from Geelong, is a breeding haven for kangaroos, emus, koalas and wildfowl.

WHERE NEXT?

Melbourne (see p. 178) is about an hour away, or the Midland Hwy (Rte 149) will take you past the nature reserves and old gold towns of the Brisbane Ranges to Ballarat (see p. 195). There's a regular ferry service from Queenscliff, about 30 km east of Geelong, across the mouth of Port Phillip Bay to Sorrento (p. 225); details on www.searoad.com.au or see OTT 9056.

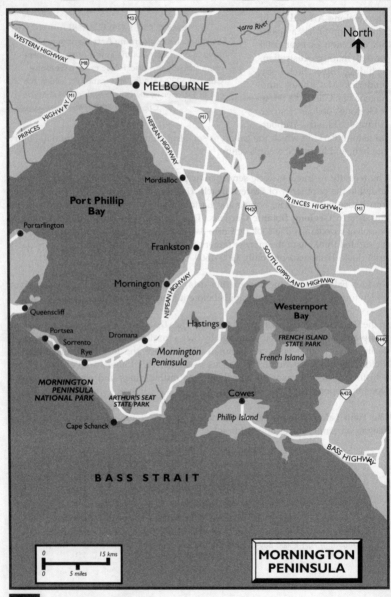

North

Yarra River

M31

WESTERN HIGHWAY

M8

MELBOURNE

PRINCES HIGHWAY

M1

NEPEAN HIGHWAY

M1

Mordialloc

M420

PRINCES HIGHWAY

M1

Port Phillip Bay

Portarlington

Frankston

SOUTH GIPPSLAND HIGHWAY

Mornington

NEPEAN HIGHWAY

Queenscliff

Hastings

Westernport Bay

Portsea

Sorrento

Dromana

FRENCH ISLAND STATE PARK

A440

Rye

Mornington Peninsula

French Island

MORNINGTON PENINSULA NATIONAL PARK

ARTHUR'S SEAT STATE PARK

Cowes

A420

Cape Schanck

Phillip Island

BASS STRAIT

BASS HIGHWAY

0		15 kms
0	5 miles	

MORNINGTON PENINSULA

THE MORNINGTON PENINSULA

The Mornington Peninsula hangs like a hook of Italy to the south of Melbourne and is, for the inhabitants of that city, a favoured weekend retreat. The peninsula has 190 km of coastline. The beaches on Port Phillip Bay are known as front beaches and those facing out to the open sea, with rougher water, are the back beaches. Swimming is excellent (and at Sorrento you can swim with seals and dolphins), but take notice of life-saver instructions: this is where a serving Australian prime minister, Harold Holt, was drowned.

GETTING THERE AND GETTING AROUND

The Nepean Hwy follows the coast of Port Phillip Bay from Mordialloc, in the southern fringes of Melbourne, through a series of almost interlinked small towns – Edithvale, Chelsea, Carrum, Seaford – to Frankston. Technically, you are still in the Melbourne greater metropolitan area but you are also at the start of the Mornington Peninsula. From here a network of roads crosses to Westernport Bay and Phillip Island on the peninsula's eastern side and reaches down to its 'toe' at Portsea. See also ferry information in Where Next? box on p. 221.

INTERNET SITES
Mornington Peninsula:
www.mornington-peninsula.com.au
www.vicnet.net.au/~morninfo

MORNINGTON

Mornington is just off the highway at Schnapper Point. Once a remote seaside village, it is now a thriving bayside area that has managed to retain its country atmosphere. Settlement began in 1840 around the harbour, its industries mainly fishing and timber. Later Mornington became a market town with a fine array of colonial buildings along the main street. Many of these are now restaurants and boutiques. Mornington's **Main Street Market** is held every Wed and is especially popular in the summer months.

The **Old Post Office**, built in 1863, is in elegant premises near the Esplanade and Main St. It is now a museum run by the local historical society, and houses local historic pieces and old telecommunications equipment. The problem is its restricted hours – a practice that seems to have infected many local museums on the peninsula and beyond. This one is only open Sun 1400–1700 and is closed mid-June–early Sept, which makes it very difficult to visit unless you are a local; tel: 5989 2219.

The **Mornington Tourist Railway**, a recently reopened historical steam train journey run by volunteers, operates between Mornington and Moorooduc on the first Sunday of the month and most public holidays ($$). Tel: 5975 3474 for times and further details.

VICTORIA

The **Mornington Peninsula Regional Gallery** ($) on the corner of Dunns and Tyabb Rds has an extensive collection of drawings, lithographs and posters as well as housing travelling exhibitions. Open Tues–Sun 1000–1700, tel: 5975 4395.

ℹ️ Mornington Community Information and Support Centre, corner of Main and Elizabeth Sts. Open Mon–Fri 0900–1700; tel: 5975 1644. The area code is 03 for the whole peninsula.

🛏️ **Brooklands of Mornington $$$$** 93–101 Tanti Ave; tel: 5975 1166. Well-furnished country-style hotel.
Mornington Caravan Park $$$ 98 Bungower Rd; tel: 5975 7373. Out of town – car necessary.
Mornington Motel $$$$ 334 Main St; tel: 5975 3711. By main shopping area.
Ranch Motel $$$ cnr Nepean Hwy and Bentons Rd; tel: 5975 4022. Swimming pool and BBQ.
Royal Hotel $$$$ 770 Esplanade; tel: 5975 5466. Overlooks the sea.

🍴 **Afghan Marco Polo $$$** 11 Main St; tel: 5975 5154. Licensed and BYO. Genuine Afghan cuisine.
Backyard Bar and Bistro $$$ 37 Main St; tel: 5975 7500. Open for lunch Wed–Fri and dinner Wed–Sat.
The Bay Hotel $$$ 62 Main St; tel: 5976 2222. Lively cosmopolitan café, bar and nightclub.
Chopsticks Inn $$ 95 Belura Hill Rd; tel: 5975 4400. Closed Mon.
Costaverde Restaurant $$ 96 Main St; tel: 5975 3085. Value Italian food. Closed Mon.
Dragon Town Chinese Restaurant $$$ 7 Main St; tel: 5975 2926. Licensed and BYO.
Garlick Kiss Café $$ 2d Empire St Mall; tel: 5976 1355. Open daily for breakfast and lunch. Stylish café serving good breakfasts, wraps and fresh juices. Friendly staff.
Julius Caesar $$$ 1002 Nepean Hwy; tel: 5975 3987. Friendly Italian restaurant, BYO and licensed. Closed Mon.
Silver Palace $$ 205 Main St; tel: 5975 2488. Good-value BYO restaurant.
Yannakis Greek Tavern 39a Main St; tel: 5976 1471. Licensed and BYO.

DROMANA

The 305-m peak **Arthurs Seat** and the outstanding views from the Old Viewing Tower on its summit have been a favourite of Melburnians for decades. There are many walks to enjoy in the area around the summit, passing local sights such as Seawinds Gardens, William Ricketts' sculptures, the Matthew Flinders Cairn, the T C McKellar Flora Reserve, Kings Falls and Waterfall Gully. The delightful Two Bays Track leads walkers down to the beach at Dromana. Bushland hereabouts harbours birdlife including kookaburras and crimson and eastern rosellas, and there's a chance of sighting wallabies, echidnas and even koalas. The access road and walking tracks are the only way up to the peak at present; the popular chairlift suffered a major equipment failure in early 2003 and its future is uncertain.

Dromana itself is a popular bayside beach resort. **The Dromana and District Historical Society** has its museum at the Old Shire Offices, 359a Point Nepean Rd. Some excellent model ships are on display, but it is only open 1400–1600 Sun and 1000–1600 first and third Tues each month. In the peak holiday period of Jan, when you do not want to visit, it is open every day.

On the slopes of Arthur's Seat is one of the oldest houses on the peninsula, the **McCrae Homestead** (11 Beverley Rd, McCrae). It was built in 1844 and is one of the few remaining examples of drop-slab construction; it is now a National Trust property. Open daily 1200–1630 ($); tel: 5981 2866.

---

i **Mornington Peninsula Visitor Information Centre**, Point Nepean Rd; tel: 5987 3078; www.visitmorningtonpeninsula.org. Open daily 0900–1700.

🛏 **Blue Dolphin Motor Lodge $$$** 21 Nepean Hwy, Safety Beach; tel: 5987 2311.
Dromana Beach Motel $$$ 91 Nepean Hwy; tel: 5987 1837.
Dromana Caravan Park $$ 131 Nepean Hwy; tel: 59810333.
Dromana Hotel $$$$ 151 Point Nepean Rd; tel: 5987 1922.
Kangerong Caravan Park $$$ 105 Point Nepean Rd; tel: 5987 2080.
Ponderosa Caravan Park $$$ 10 Ponderosa Pl.; tel: 5987 2095.

🍽 **Arthur's Peak Bistro and Restaurant $$$$** Arthur's Seat Rd; tel: 5981 4444. Bistro open daily 1000–1700. A la carte restaurant open Thur–Sun for dinner and Sat–Sun for lunch. Licensed. Very superior French cooking by Hermann Schneider, one of the great chefs of Australia. Wine bar.

SORRENTO

HOLIDAY-TOWN HISTORY

Sorrento Museum and Heritage Gallery is housed in the heritage-listed Mechanics Institute on the corner of Melbourne and Ocean Beach Rds. Exhibits depict the town's history and include memorabilia of pioneering families and models of early Sorrento trams. There's also a model sail and steamship display. Open weekends and public holidays ($). Tel: 5984 0255 (Nepean Historical Society).

It is not often that you come across a seaside resort which has been designed as one from the start. In the 1870s, entrepreneur George Coppin realised this site's holiday potential – as an ideal resort for Melburnians to escape the heat of summer in an idyllic seaside setting. He started a paddle steamer company to bring holidaymakers from Melbourne to Sorrento pier and a steam train company to take them to the rugged back beach. He also built rotundas, walkways and lookouts. And he did it without stinting, so that it was a success almost from the beginning.

Some of the original structures he created remain among the attractions of Sorrento. Fine Victorian buildings built from the local limestone give it considerable style, and the impressive hotels, excellent restaurants, open-air cafés, boutiques, galleries and other delights keep the people of Melbourne returning to the town. Sorrento has some of the most expensive real estate in Victoria outside the Melbourne central business district, and from Christmas until Easter it is both crowded and expensive.

One of the area's big attractions is **swimming with dolphins and seals**. This has become so popular that a code of practice has been put in place to ensure the animals are not frightened off. Two operators are Polperro Dolphin Swims (tel: 5988 8437) and Moonraker (tel: 5984 4211). There are two trips a day during the season (roughly, Oct–May).

🛏 **Carmel Bed & Breakfast $$$$** 142 Ocean Beach Rd; tel: 5984 3512. 100-year-old heritage building. In main street.

Sorrento YHA $$ 3 Miranda St; tel: 5984 4323; www.yha.com.au/hostels. Close to the town centre in a homely atmosphere.

Sorrento Hotel $$$$ 5–15 Hotham Rd; tel: 5984 4777. Located near the sea front, includes breakfast.

Sorrento Village Caravan Park $$$ 791 Melbourne Rd; tel: 5984 5000.

Tamasha House $$$$ 699 Melbourne Rd; tel: 5984 2413. En suite rooms, home-made food.

Whitehall $$$$ 231 Ocean Beach Rd; tel: 5984 4166. Walking distance to the shops.

🅃🄾 **Big Joe's No 1 Pizza & Bistro $$$** 77 Ocean Beach Rd; tel: 5984 3633. Busy Italian restaurant. Licensed and BYO.

Buckley's Chance $$ 174 Ocean Beach Rd; tel: 5984 2888. Named after Australian legend William Buckley, this stylish café serves burgers, steaks and pancakes. Licensed and BYO.

Palms Restaurant $$$$ 154 Ocean Beach Rd; tel: 5984 1057. Expensive, classy restaurant, excellent à la carte menu. Licensed and BYO. Open daily in summer, Thur–Sat off-season.

Saludos $$$ 3293 Nepean Hwy; tel: 5984 4255. Newly opened Mexican restaurant.

Smokehouse $$$ 182 Ocean Beach Rd; tel: 5984 1246. Licensed Italian restaurant. Open daily in summer.

SULLIVAN BAY

Sullivan Bay, 3 km south-east of Sorrento, was the site of the first white attempt to settle what was to become Victoria. Lt Governor David Collins established a camp here in 1803, consisting of 299 convicts, some free settlers, 50 royal marines, a chaplain and civil officers – in all 460 men, women and children. After seven months they gave up and moved to Van Diemen's Land (now Tasmania). A stone memorial marks the site of this short-lived settlement, and a display centre (open Sun 1300–1600) tells more of its story.

With this abortive expedition was the infamous convict William Buckley, who did a runner. He was adopted by the local Aborigines and lived with them for 32 years. When the 'wild white man' was seen again by settlers he could scarcely remember how to speak English.

PORTSEA

Sorrento is for the rich, but Portsea is for the very rich of Melbourne. Their playgrounds are **Portsea Front Beach**, on the bay by the pier, and **Shelley Beach**, which has dolphins. Portsea is more a place where you own a weekend home rather than somewhere to come and stay. Despite this, it is also one of the best skin-diving spots in the area, with excellent dives of up to 40 m off Port Phillip Heads. It is essentially a quiet seaside resort with mainly private houses and just one important hotel. The Portsea Hotel has extensive lawns which overlook the beach and are packed on summer weekends.

Although it has some impressive back beaches, your best bet is to stay with the front beach. The ocean beach can be dangerous and you should only swim where indicated by the life-savers.

🛏 **Peppers Country House Hotel $$$$** Point Nepean Rd; tel: 5984 4000.
Portsea Caravan Park $$ 70 Back Beach Rd; tel: 5984 2725.

🍴 **Punchy's Pizza $$** 3770 Point Nepean Rd; tel: 5984 0539. Pleasant pizza and pasta restaurant, fully licensed and BYO. Outdoor bar and patio in the summer months. Reduced opening times in winter.
The Starfish $$ 3756 Point Nepean Rd; tel: 5984 3631. Stylish café, only open weekends in the winter. BYO.

MORNINGTON PENINSULA NATIONAL PARK

When this park was created in 1988 it opened up the tip of the peninsula, with its fortifications, quarantine station and army base which had been banned to the public for a century. An open-topped transporter runs daily from the visitor centre (open 0900–1700) to Point Nepean at the far side of the national park (7 km). Numbers are limited and you will need to book ahead (tel: 5984 4276; $$). Most parts of the park, however, are accessible by car or on foot.

THE OCEAN SHORE

Backtracking from Portsea, the road passes through Rye, with a side road down to Rye Ocean Beach in the Mornington Peninsula National Park. A road looping round from

Rosebud on Port Phillip Bay gives access to Cape Schanck with its lighthouse, Angel Cave, neighbouring Bushranger Bay and Flinders on West Head. From here the road goes up the Westernport Bay side of the peninsula to Hastings.

PHILLIP ISLAND

At the mouth of Westernport Bay is the small, fish-shaped Phillip Island. The only land access is from the far side of Westernport Bay, across a bridge from San Remo. The island is rugged and windswept, with several small resorts, plenty of beaches and a fascinating collection of wildlife.

One of the major attractions is the **Penguin Parade®**, which takes place each evening at sundown when Little Penguins emerge from the sea and waddle up to nest. Despite being somewhat commercialised, it is well worth a visit ($$$). For those wanting to experience something a little more natural and intimate, the new **Ultimate Penguin Tour** takes small groups of visitors to a secluded beach to witness this natural phenomenon. The Penguin Parade® is managed by the **Phillip Island Nature Park**, which is also home to a unique ecotourism attraction, the **Koala Conservation Centre**, and scenic **Churchill Island**. The Nature Park is a not-for-profit organisation, so all of the revenue from visitors goes back into conservation and the environment. For more information visit www.penguins.org.au; see also photo between pp. 192–193. Bookings at Phillip Island Information Centre on the Tourist Rd at Newhaven; tel: 1300 366 422; open daily. Booking is essential in peak season.

SKIING IN VICTORIA

The Victorian Alps are to the east and north-east of Melbourne. They are much lower than alpine ranges in other parts of the world and do not have sheer escarpments and jagged peaks. They are not high enough to have a permanent cover of snow but during the winter months they can provide excellent skiing.

The snowfields of Australia may lack the regular and inevitable snow of the best European resorts. But Victoria's snow resorts are equipped with the latest lifting and snow-making equipment, they have luxurious and affordable accommodation, and they are all within relatively easy reach of Melbourne. Finally, unlike their great rivals in New Zealand, all of these snowfields have ski-in ski-out access so that there is no long drive to and from the snow each day. The skiing season officially opens on the Queen's Birthday long weekend each June and closes in October, but the weather and location control exactly how long the season lasts.

ARRIVAL AND DEPARTURE

Victoria has nine ski resorts, all within easy reach of Melbourne (Falls Creek, the furthest, is about a 5-hr drive). The three big ones are Mount Buller, Mount Hotham and Falls Creek, all reached via the Hume Hwy (M31). Come prepared with snow chains. In the ski season buses from Melbourne run to the main resorts, some with a very early start to enable you to ski and return the same day.

COSTS

There is a range of accommodation in each of the large resorts, but booking, naturally, is necessary in the high season. In every case a package tour of the snowfields will be less expensive than buying the components separately. Check on what prices include, because they can be better value than they at first appear. The best value is almost certainly one of the various midweek packages – which generally include

SNOW-MAKING

All resorts make extensive use of snow-making machines. Falls Creek, for example, has 100 ha covered by these machines, giving the certainty of snow within a defined area. The snow makers begin their task of making a good snow cover using high-tech snow guns in late May. This freezes into an excellent base which means subsequent snowfalls remain intact, creating a good early snow base which gets deeper as the season progresses.

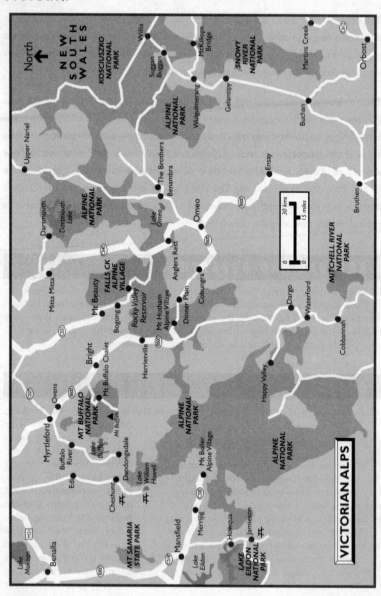

five nights' accommodation (Sun–Thur), lift passes and some meals – which can run to just over $100 per day.

INFORMATION

Victorian Tourism Information Service: tel: 13 28 42; www.legendswinehighcountry.info.

MOUNT BULLER

Mount Buller, 241 km from Melbourne via Mansfield, caters for all levels, from beginners to advanced skiers and snowboarders; equipment hire and instruction are available. At nearby **Mount Stirling** there is cross-country skiing. Most trails start at Telephone Box Junction, which has a visitor centre with public shelter, ski hire and trail maps.

ACCOMMODATION

Arlberg Hotel $$$$ 189 Summit Rd; tel: 5777 6260.

Ivor Whittaker Memorial Lodge $$$$ (includes breakfast and dinner) and **Kandahar $$$$** (self-catering) are operated by the Ski Club of Victoria and accept bookings from non-members. Book well ahead.

Mt Buller Chalet $$$$ Widely accepted as one of the finest alpine lodgings in Australia – advance bookings essential, tel: (1800) 810 200. The chalet has endless facilities.

YHA Lodge $$–$$$ tel: 5777 6181; www.yha.com.au/hostels. Very inexpensive, but gets booked up quickly. The best budget snowfield accommodation. Shared rooms only.

MOUNT HOTHAM

The 'powder snow capital' of Australia is 367 km from Melbourne via Wangaratta. Equipment hire and instruction are available, but the resort attracts experienced alpine skiers and snowboarders; there is also unlimited cross-country skiing. **Mt Buffalo**, on the way to Mt Hotham, is geared to beginners, families and cross-country skiers; features include Dingo Dell and Cresta. Dinner Plain, a new resort, is a 10-min ski-shuttle ride away from Mt Hotham.

VICTORIA

FALLS CREEK

Falls Creek, 379 km from Melbourne via Wangaratta and Wodonga, has protected runs for novices, intermediate and advanced skiers, and snowboarders; there is good cross-country skiing. There are equipment hire and instruction, and a wide range of resort facilities.

ACCOMMODATION

Alpha Ski Lodge $$ 5 Parallel St, Falls Creek; tel: 5758 3488. Self-catering.

Alpine Woodsmoke Apartments $$$$ Falls Creek Rd; tel: 5758 1188. Sheer luxury but book early.

Nelse Lodge $$$ Slalom St is also operated by the Ski Club of Victoria. Prices include breakfast, lunch and a three-course dinner. Book well ahead; tel: 5775 2893.

If you are willing to stay off the mountain and forgo the delights of ski-in ski-out there are several places where the price drops to around half. **Mount Beauty**, 32 km from Falls Creek, has several lodges and bed-and-breakfast establishments offering budget accommodation.

OTHER RESORTS

The several snowfields closer to Melbourne are at lower altitudes and are generally more susceptible to the fickle Australian winters. Check in advance on snow conditions. **Mount Donna Buang**, just 95 km from Melbourne, offers wonderful sight-seeing and limited skiing and snowboarding. **Lake Mountain**, 109 km north-east of Melbourne via Healesville, is popular with cross-country skiers. **Mount Baw Baw**, 177 km east of Melbourne via Drouin, caters for beginner skiers and snowboarders. The latter two areas provide fine cross-country skiing in perfect conditions.

WHERE NEXT?

It's about 210 km down the scenic Great Alpine Road from Mount Hotham to Lakes Entrance (p. 124), on our Sydney–Melbourne via Princes Hwy route (pp. 117–123).

LONG-DISTANCE ROUTE

This is one of the most common travel routes used by Sydneysiders going on holiday. To put it in its simplest form, you head north out of Sydney. This is Hwy 1 (see p. 235), but it goes under a number of different names: Route National 1, Route 85, Pacific Hwy ... There is an abundance of petrol stations along the way – usually only about 50 km apart. All have small shops, most sell snack food, some sell full meals. Part of Hwy 1 is multi-lane freeway (and it will, one day, become divided road all the way from Sydney to Brisbane), but in other places it is an ordinary two-lane highway. Even on the fast stretches, however, speed limits are rigorously enforced. Once you get free of Sydney, for instance, the speed limit increases for a while to 110 kph (although there is a strong movement to bring it down to 100 kph). Unlike other countries, little leeway is given and if you exceed that speed limit, eventually you will be stopped and fined by the police. Many Australian drivers who cover long distances have cruise controls fitted to their cars to help them stay on the speed limit.

Bus companies have several buses a day doing the Sydney–Brisbane run in either direction; the journey takes about 16 hours. Usually, the buses make many stops and it makes sense to break the journey or just use the bus for one leg. Sydney to Newcastle, for example, takes around 3 hours.

In the pages that follow, three routes combine to cover the 1000 km: Sydney to Newcastle, Newcastle to Coffs Harbour, and Coffs Harbour to the Gold Coast.

SYDNEY — BRISBANE
OTT Tables 9017/9091/9092

Service	🚌	🚌	🚆RAIL	🚌	🚌	🚆RAIL	🚌	🚌	🚌	🚌	🚌
Days of operation	Daily	Daily	Daily	Daily	Daily	Daily	Daily	Daily	Daily	Daily	Daily
Special notes	D		AD		B	CD	D				D
Sydney.....................d.	0700	0700	0715	1300	1315	1624	1800	1845	2045	2200	2230	....
Brisbane...................a.	2315	2320	2221	0600	0700	0630	1130	1200	1315	1450	1345	....

Special notes:
A–Train terminates at Casino, bus connection to Brisbane.
B–Operates via the inland route.
C–This train has sleeper accommodation.
D–Arrival time in Brisbane one hour earlier during NSW daylight saving (Oct–Apr).

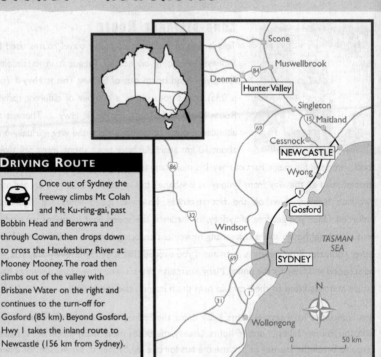

DRIVING ROUTE

Once out of Sydney the freeway climbs Mt Colah and Mt Ku-ring-gai, past Bobbin Head and Berowra and through Cowan, then drops down to cross the Hawkesbury River at Mooney Mooney. The road then climbs out of the valley with Brisbane Water on the right and continues to the turn-off for Gosford (85 km). Beyond Gosford, Hwy 1 takes the inland route to Newcastle (156 km from Sydney).

SYDNEY — NEWCASTLE
OTT Tables 9016/9017/9092

Service	🚌	🚆RAIL	🚆RAIL	🚌	🚆RAIL	🚌	🚌	🚌
Days of operation	Daily	Daily	Daily	Daily	Daily	Daily	Daily	Daily
Special notes	D	BD	A		CD		D	
Sydney....................d.	0700	0715	0816	1300	1624	1800	1830	2200
Gosford............................d.		0830u	0934		1741u	2000		
Newcastle ....a.	0945		1052	1600		2130	2110	0040
Brisbane ....a.	2320	2221	....	0600	0630	1130	1200	1450

Special notes:
A–Additional services: 0147, 0355, 0456, 0542, 0551, 0617, 0721, 0816, 0917 then at least hourly to 2317.
B–Train terminates at Casino, bus connection to Brisbane.
C–This train has sleeper accommodation.
D–Arrival time in Brisbane one hour earlier during NSW daylight saving (Oct–Apr).

THE CENTRAL COAST

About one hour's drive north of Sydney and an hour south of Newcastle, the Central Coast is a stretch of bays, national parks and seaside towns. Situated at the head of Brisbane Water National Park is Gosford, which has recently blossomed and is now a busy town with plenty of shops, restaurants and accommodation. This is very much part of the coast that is focused on family holidays. The most highly populated areas are Gosford/Narara Valley, Woy Woy Peninsula and the coastal strip along Forresters Beach to MacMasters Beach.

GETTING OUT OF SYDNEY

Cross the Harbour Bridge or drive through the Harbour Tunnel and follow the signs to Chatswood. This is a motorway with an 80-kph limit and you need to keep in one of the right three lanes. The motorway will eventually narrow down to two lanes each way; keep in the left lane for the turning to Chatswood. This brings you out onto the Pacific Hwy. This is Hwy 1 (or Route National 1 or Route 85). Drive for 13 km through suburb after suburb — Chatswood, Roseville, Gordon, Turramurra — until, just pass Wahroonga, you come to the Sydney–Newcastle Freeway, a turning on the right clearly marked to Newcastle.

EN ROUTE

The freeway swoops through **Ku-ring-gai Chase National Park**. This park can provide a real challenge to the bushwalker and yet it is only 22 km from the centre of Sydney, demonstrating how close the real bush is to the heart of the city.

Information about the park and its walking trails can be obtained from the Kalkari Visitor Centre, located between Mount Colah and Bobbin Head. The centre is open daily; tel: (02) 9457 9853.

In the pioneering period, the attractions of the Brisbane Water area were its proximity to Sydney and its wealth of timber resources. The shores of the waterways were occupied by settlers — including ex-convicts — while the timbered country on Erina and Narara Creeks was dominated by the gentry. The grave and cottage of Frederick Hely, Superintendent of Convicts in NSW, can still be seen there, beside the Pacific Hwy.

SYDNEY

See p. 69.

GOSFORD

Gosford's transformation from Sydney dormitory suburb to busy regional centre has come, not surprisingly, at the expense of its country-town feel.

Thirty years ago, access from Sydney was restricted to the rail link and a slow, winding 20-km road at the end of the (then barely begun) Sydney–Newcastle freeway.

Now, the fast road extends to within several kilometres of Gosford town centre, and many Central Coast beachside settlements are within an hour of northern Sydney. Gosford's population is now more than 130,000, and the size and style of the town and its nearby holiday havens – among them Terrigal, Avoca, Copacabana and MacMasters beaches and Killcare – have altered accordingly.

Henry Kendall's cottage ($), 27 Henry Kendall St, is where the Australian poet lived for two years from 1874. It was built as an inn in 1838 and has been restored with elegant grounds where you can picnic. Open Wed, Sat and Sun and all holidays 1000–1600; tel: (02) 4325 2270.

The **Australian Reptile Park and Wildlife Sanctuary** ($$$), Somersby (take the Gosford exit off the Newcastle Freeway and follow the signs), has one of the world's largest crocodiles in captivity. His name is Eric and he is fed every Sun at 1300. There are informative and entertaining talks on the park's critters throughout the day including the not-to-be-missed, twice-daily, reptile shows at 1130 (1100 weekends) and 1415. The park is also home to a wide range of Australian native animals including kangaroos, koalas and wombats. Open daily 0900–1700; tel: (02) 4340 1022; www.reptilepark.com.au.

Brisbane Water National Park, off the Pacific Highway just south of Gosford, covers 11,372 ha and borders the Hawkesbury River. It is especially rich in Aboriginal art. There are several walks laid out through open woodlands with occasional pockets of rainforest. Panoramic views spread from 100-m-high cliffs overlooking the Hawkesbury River at Warrah Trig and Staples Lookouts. Aboriginal art may be seen on the sandstone landscape with engravings at Bulgandry on Woy Woy Road. Displays of Christmas bells and scarlet waratah are stunning during November and December. The National Park Service regional office is at 36–38, 207 Albany St, North Gosford. Tel: (02) 4320 4299. Open Mon–Fri.

> *i* **Terrigal Visitor Information Centre**, Rotary Park, Terrigal Drive, Terrigal; tel: 4385 4430; e-mail: thecoast@cctourism.com.au. The main information centre for the Central Coast; has information on a range of walks, and also handles accommodation bookings. Open daily; Fri, Sat only in low season.
> **Gosford Visitor Information Centre**, 200 Mann St, Gosford. Open as above.

EN ROUTE

Instead of heading straight back for the freeway, you can drive to the lovely seaside town of **Terrigal** – a very popular spot with excellent surfing – and then follow the coastline north past **Wyrrabalong National Park** and through seaside resorts to **The Entrance**, which is one of the pincers that enclose the expanse of Tuggerah Lake. Among the many attractions is the **pelican feeding** that takes place at 1530 every day on the shores of Memorial Park. Take the narrow causeway between Tuggerah Lake and the sea through Norah Head and Budgewoi and then rejoin the freeway.

The Entrance Visitor Information Centre, Marine Parade, the Entrance; open daily.

Woy Woy Visitor Information Centre, 8–22 The Boulevard, Woy Woy; open daily.

Central Coast Tourism: www.visitcentralcoast.com.au. The telephone code is 02.

🛏 Gosford is a good base for exploring the Central Coast; accommodation can also be found in the surrounding towns.

Bermuda Motor Inn $$$ cnr Henry Parry Dr. and Pacific Hwy; tel: 4324 4366. BBQ, close to some good restaurants.

Galaxy Motel $$$$ 26 Pacific Hwy; tel: 4323 1711. Modern motel, part of an RSL complex.

Gosford Motor Inn $$$$ 23 Pacific Hwy; tel: 4323 1333.

Hotel Gosford $$$ Mann St; tel: 4324 1634. In town centre and near Tourist Information Office.

Terrigal Beach Lodge YHA $ 12 Campbell Cr.; tel: 4385 3330; www.yha.com.au/hostels. Beachside location several km from Gosford. Popular – book ahead.

🍽 **Crown Plaza** Pine Tree Lane, Terrigal; tel: 4384 9111. Has three restaurants: the Florida Ocean Terrace ($$$), Norfolk Brasserie ($$$) and The Conservatory ($$$$).

Gandhi at Ettalong $$ 189 Ocean View Rd, Ettalong; tel: 4341 1994. Licensed Indian restaurant. Dinner and dance weekends, and the occasional belly dancer!

Gee Kwong Restaurant $$ 197 Mann St; tel: 4325 2489. Good-value Cantonese restaurant.

Gosford Shore Line Restaurant $$$$ Masons Parade; tel: 4325 0644. Expensive, but overlooks the bay. Steak and chicken dishes available as well as seafood.

Letterbox Restaurant $$$$ 4 Ash St, Terrigal; tel: 4385 4222. Located in a heritage-listed post office building. Modern Australian cuisine. Licensed and BYO (wine only).

Monti's Ashore $ 65 Masons Parade, Gosford; tel: 4324 3366. One of the few true cheap eats in the area, a basic seafood restaurant serving good old fish and chips.

NEWCASTLE

Newcastle has a population of half a million and is the second largest city in NSW and the sixth largest city in Australia. The site was discovered when

Lt Shortland was searching for convict escapees in 1797 and discovered coal. This, together with steel, dominated life in Newcastle until the mid-1960s, and the city previously had the unenviable reputation of being one of the dirtiest, grimiest, most polluted cities in Australia. Dymphna Cusack, in her novel *Southern Steel*, describes the city during and after World War II with its 'innumerable factory chimneys' and 'the smokestacks of Southern Steel and Broken Hill Proprietary under their perpetual silver-black clouds.'

That was then. These days Newcastle is a pleasant city with some fine surfing beaches and extensive inland waterways. If you had to put a date to the time that Newcastle started to get its act together, it was 28 Dec 1989. On that day it was hit by a major earthquake with a great loss of life and many buildings destroyed. Some of the city had to be rebuilt and it was done with some style. In 1999 one of Newcastle's biggest employers, BHP Steel Works, closed down (rumour has it that a Japanese film company wants to buy it so that they can blow it up in a movie, but others want the works to be preserved for history's sake). In a need to find a new focus for the city, Newcastle has turned to tourism. With some major investments from both the government and private sectors, Newcastle has rapidly transformed itself into a city with a lovely seafront showing some intelligent modernisation, and excellent accommodation and restaurants. On top of this it is the entry point to the Hunter Valley, the greatest wine-growing area in Australia. (Please do not say that when you are in the Barossa or at Margaret River, or you will find yourself in the centre of a very heated discussion.)

> Newcastle has many safe beaches, one of which is just east of the city. These include Newcastle, Nobbys, Horseshoe, Stockton, Bar, Susan Gilmore, Merewether, Dixon Park Beach, Burwood and Dudley.

ℹ️ **Newcastle Tourism** 363 Hunter St; tel: 4974 2999. Area code 02. Open daily. E-mail: tourism@ncc.nsw.gov.au. Some good brochures and guides to some excellent walks.
Newcastle–Hunter Tourism and Accommodation Centre 1/91 Hannell St, Wickham; tel: 4927 0755; open Mon–Fri and Sat morning; e-mail: bookings@ huntertourismaccom.com.au.
Newcastle City Centre – Online www.newcastlecitycentre.com.
Newcastle Visitor Information www.newcastletourism.com.

🛏️ **Hunter on Hunter Hotel $$** 417 Hunter St; tel: 4929 3152. Budget hotel, among the central shops.
Newcastle Beach YHA $–$$$ 30 Pacific St; tel: 4925 3544; www.yha.com.au/hostels. Lively hostel in beautiful building, good location, excellent facilities, close to train station.
Newcomen Lodge B&B $$$$ 70 Newcomen St; tel: 4929 7313.

LAKE MACQUARIE
The Pacific Hwy passes through the city and if you follow it south you will come to the great expanse of Lake Macquarie. It is the largest seaboard lake in Australia and contains about four times as much water as Sydney Harbour, with 175 km of eucalyptus-lined foreshore. Lake Macquarie is a superb sailing area and there is a range of cruises. The **Lake Macquarie Tourist Information Centre**, 72 Pacific Hwy, Blacksmiths, tel: 4972 1172, has a range of brochures and information. Open daily; www.visit-lakemac.com.au.

On the eastern shore of the lake is **Belmont**. On the high ground in the town is what may have been an Aboriginal mission opened by the Rev L E Threlkeld, who also opened the first coal mine. The all-timber parish hall was built at the turn of the 20th century. In nearby Wangi Wangi is **Dobell House**, a modest place where the painter Sir William Dobell lived and worked; it is open to the public and contains a collection of his work and memorabilia.

Noah's on the Beach $$$$ cnr Zarra St and Shortland Esp; tel: 4929 5181.

Nomads Backpackers by the Beach $–$$ 34 Hunter St; tel: 4926 3472. Easygoing and friendly. Close to city centre.

West End Accommodation $$$ 775 Hunter St; tel: 4961 4446. Basic but relatively inexpensive.

🍴 **The Waterfront, Beaumont St** in Hamilton and **Derby St** in Cooks Hill are all excellent places to wander through in the evening to find the usual as well as some unusual eateries.

Bogie Hole Café $$$ cnr Pacific and Hunter Sts; tel: 4929 1790. Modern cuisine with a varied menu. Open early to late. Good breakfasts.

Brewery Restaurant $$$$ 150 Wharf Rd; tel: 4929 5792. Air-conditioned, harbourside restaurant, usually very busy. Open daily.

Café Plumbs $$ cnr Wolfe and Hunter St Mall; tel: 4929 7333. Award-winning café/restaurant in the heart of the city. Licensed.

Eliza's (Holiday Inn) $$$ Shortland Esplanade; tel: 4929 5576. Informal venue for light meals. Open daily 0615–late.

Harry's Café De Wheels $ 672 Hunter St; tel: 4926 2165. Australia's oldest takeaway, serving inexpensive food from a restored 1930s Bondi tram.

Krishnas $ 110 King St; tel 4929 6900. Inexpensive vegetarian restaurant.

Paymasters $$$ 18 Bond St; tel: 4925 2600. On what was once the site of the government employees' pay office which opened in 1879. Features artworks from local artists; has won several awards.

Scratchley's $$$$ Wharf Rd; tel: 4929 1111. Winner of numerous awards. Seafood, chicken and steak make up most of the menu. BYO.

HIGHLIGHTS

The easiest way to see the city is on board the **Newcastle Famous Tram** ($$) which leaves the railway station on the hour 1000–1400, daily. It is not a true tram, rather a bus decked up to look like a tram, but the seating is comfortable, the view excellent and the driver gives an informative running commentary. Tel: 4963 7954.

The city also has many historic 19th-century buildings, some of which have recently been restored to their former glory. The information centre offers an excellent free map of a town walk which takes in most of the sights, including **Fort Scratchley** – now housing the **Newcastle Region Maritime Museum**. Open Tues–Fri 1000–1600, weekends and public holidays 1200–1600; tel: 4929 2588. **Newcastle Regional Museum**, 787 Hunter St, is a leading Australian museum and contains Supernova, Newcastle's Science and Technology Fun Centre. Children are encouraged to touch and use the displays. Open Tues–Sun 1000–1700 (daily in school holidays); tel: 4974 1400. There are numerous other interesting walks you can do around the area. The tourist information centre has several free guides and brochures.

> ### THE FORT THAT WENT TO WAR
> Fort Scratchley on Nobbys Head, about 30 m above the entrance to the port, claims to be Australia's only fort that went to war. It was originally built in the 1880s to repel a possible Russian invasion very near the spot where Lt Shortland first landed on his search for the missing convicts. In June 1942 it was attacked by a Japanese submarine. The guns of the fort returned fire. This is almost certainly the only time in Australian history that the heavy guns of the coastal defences have been fired in deadly earnest.

The trees planted at the eastern and western edges of the large **Civic Park**, opposite City Hall, were gifts from Newcastle's sister city, Ube in Japan. The **Captain Cook Memorial Fountain** forms a backdrop and is illuminated at night.

On the waterfront, **Queen's Wharf** has been redeveloped into a modern, even trendy area with shops, restaurants, one of Australia's many mini-breweries and a watch-tower. It is a very pleasant place to walk and watch the sunset. The *William the Fourth*, a replica of the first coastal steamship built in Australia, is anchored at nearby Throsby Wharf; it offers historical cruises around the harbour. Trips only run occasionally; tel: 4974 2999 for details.

Christ Church Cathedral is situated on The Hill in Church St, overlooking the city. Its foundation stone was laid in 1892 and it was dedicated in 1902. The cathedral underwent major restorations following the 1989 earthquake, at a cost of $15 million. Up the hill to the south is the **Obelisk** which marks the site of Newcastle's first windmill. The mill, which lasted from 1820 to 1874, became a navigation mark for ships approaching the port.

WHERE NEXT?

The trail continues north towards Brisbane, but don't leave Newcastle without a taste of the wine-famous Hunter Valley (see p. 241).

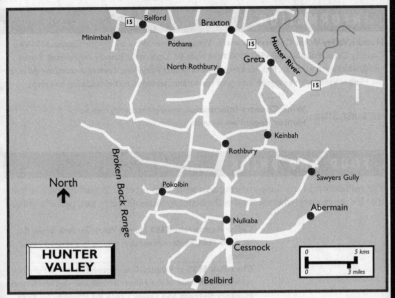

Back in the 1960s, wine from the Hunter came in bottles with hand-typed labels and was thick and strong, full of flavour and unbelievably inexpensive. Gradually the world caught on to the fact that some of the best red wines came from the red earth of the Hunter, and thus vineyards and coal mines were developed in curious juxtaposition. Most, but not all, of the mines in the Hunter Valley no longer operate, while the vineyards expand and prosper.

The valley lies an hour's drive west of Newcastle, or two hours' drive north-west of Sydney. The New England Hwy (Rte 15) will take you through Hexham, Maitland, Branxton and Singleton to Muswellbrook. To the left of Branxton, running around Cessnock and down to Wollombi, is the main wine country. To the left of Muswellbrook, down and round to Denham, are the Upper Hunter wineries. For those pushed for time and money, **Shadows Wine Country Tours** depart from Newcastle daily at 0900 and return around 1700. The buses are small and friendly; tel: 4990 7002. Other tours also run to the valley. Vintage time is normally around February when the vignerons will be at their busiest bringing in the crop.

INFORMATION

Hunter Valley Wine Country Tourism, Vintage Hunter Wine and Visitor Centre, 455 Wine Country Drive, Pokolbin; tel: 4990 0900. Area code 02. Open daily; friendly, helpful staff. E-mail: info@winecountry.com.au. Pick up a free copy of *Hunter Valley Wine Country*, a complete guide to the Hunter Valley with extensive listings of restaurants, wineries, accommodation and maps.

INTERNET SITES
Wine Country Information www.winecountry.com.au
Hunter Region www.huntertourism.com

FOOD AND DRINK

The restaurants in any wine-growing area tend to be superior in quality and this holds true for the Hunter, where several of the better restaurants are, in fact, part of a winery.

Cellar Restaurant $$$$ Hunter Valley Gardens, Broke Rd; tel: 4998 7584. Modern Australian cuisine in a relaxed casual setting.

Chez Pok $$$$ at Peppers Guesthouse, Ekerts Rd, Pokolbin; tel: 4998 7596. One of the Hunter's most awarded restaurants.

Hunters Retreat $$$ Oakey Creek Rd, Pokolbin; tel: 4990 7855. A relatively new winery with a reasonably priced restaurant. Chef Meyer, originally from Switzerland, enjoys chatting to international travellers.

WINE TOUR

This is a suggested drive that will take in most of the major vineyards. On this short-ish trip – an easy half-day's drive which could take you two weeks if you were seriously sampling wines – you come within hailing distance of over 80 vineyards, all of which encourage visits and cellar door sales.

There is no suggestion of being compelled to buy wine at any vineyard you visit or that a tasting puts any sort of obligation on the taster. On the other hand, look at it from the perspective of the vintner for a moment. A bus pulls up. Fifty people get off and taste a generous sample. One buys a single bottle and the bus moves off. If you intend to visit the vineyards try to work in the purchase of a couple of bottles of wine and/or dine at one of the many vineyard restaurants.

At Cessnock take the Allandale Rd (Rte 82). When you pass the airstrip, on the left is Broke Rd where you will find several wineries including **Lakes Folly** (tel: 4998 7507) and the **Rothbury Estate** (tel: 4998 7363), started by a syndicate led by Australia's great wine celebrity Len Evans. Further along Allandale Rd, and again on the left, is Palmers Lane, which has six small vineyards, including **Calais Estate** (tel: 4998 7654), where you can taste wines in the splendour of a convict-carved sandstone building.

Allandale Rd now continues north through Rothbury. Turn left into McDonalds Rd then right into Deasys Rd, which leads to four more vineyards. At lot 71 **Paxton-Brown Carriages** ($$$) run horse-drawn tours around the valley; tel: 4998 7362. Soon Allandale Rd reaches the New England Hwy (Rte 15) at Branxton. A quick detour right leads to the **Wyndham Estate** winery (tel: 4938 3444), which is open daily. Left is Belford and Hermitage Rd, which passes **Hardy's Hunter Ridge** winery, open daily (tel: 4998 7500), and the other end of Deasys Rd. Continue past the **Casuarina Restaurant and Country Inn** (tel: 4998 7888) to Broke Rd, which leads back to Cessnock.

Alternatively a detour to the right, away from Cessnock, will lead to wineries in the Broke area. Broke Rd passes several vineyards and restaurants, all well signposted. **Tyrrell's Wines** (tel: 4993 7000) is run by the Tyrrell family and is a splendid example of a mid-sized winery. Turn right off Broke Rd into McDonalds Rd and you'll find yourself driving towards another dozen fine vineyards. **McGuigan Cellars** (tel: 4998 7229) has gone flat out to cater for the tourist, with wine tastings, wine sales, a cheese factory, and souvenir and gift shops.

The return journey along Broke Rd passes several vineyards and restaurants, all well signposted. Broke Rd comes to a crossroads (McDonalds Rd). Turn right and you will find yourself driving towards the Pokolbin Mountain Range. In this area there are another dozen of some of the greatest vineyards in Australia. Turn back onto Broke Rd and you swing back past Lakes Folly to Cessnock.

Hunter Valley Hot Air Ballooning at Pokolbin Vineyards (tel: 4991 3566) offers trips above the valley; sunrise flights run daily (weather permitting), followed by a full cooked breakfast. Not cheap, but a great experience. For more information take a look at the website: www.huntervalleyballooning.com.au.

WHERE NEXT?

To complete the circuit, continue on Rte 15 through Singleton and up to Muswellbrook and the seven vineyards of the Upper Hunter Valley. A short drive from there you are right on the edge of the 488,060-ha Wollemi National Park. This is the largest wilderness area in New South Wales, extending from the Hunter River to Blue Mountains National Park.

DRIVING ROUTE

Beyond Newcastle, the Pacific Hwy hardly lives up to the promise of its name, as it becomes a three-lane, sometimes a two-lane road, with overtaking impossible except at designated places spaced perhaps 3–5 km apart and normally on hills.

Turn off at Raymond Terrace for Nelson Bay and the Tomaree National Park (you will have to backtrack to rejoin the highway).

From Newcastle to Taree is 150 km, and the turn-off for Port Macquarie a further 73 km. After Macksville the highway moves very close to the sea until it comes to the outskirts of Coffs Harbour, about 370 km from Newcastle without detours.

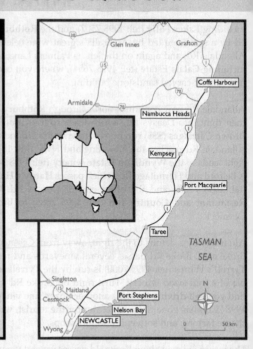

NEWCASTLE — COFFS HARBOUR
OTT Tables 9016/9017/9092

Service	🚌	🚌	🚌	RAIL	RAIL	🚌	🚌	RAIL	🚌	🚌	🚌	🚌
Days of operation	Ⓐ	Daily	Daily	Daily	Daily	Daily	Daily	Daily	Daily	Daily	Daily	Daily
Special notes	D	C	C	AC				BC		C		
Sydney............................d.	....	0700	0700	0715	1135	1300	1400	1624	1800	1845	2045	2200
Newcastle.....................d.	0705	0945				1600			2130	2110		0040
Nelson Bay...................a.	0835						1735					
Taree...............................d.	....		1210r	1236	1711	1935		2142		0015r		0330
Port Macquarie ....d.	....	1345	1330			2100	....			0110	0220	
Kempsey ....d.	....	1425	1415	1419	1855	2135	....	2327	0200	0155	0300	0445
Nambucca Heads ....d.	....	1520r	1505t	1515r	1952	2245r	....	0021r	0310r	0245r	0435r	0615r
Coffs Harbour...............d.	....	1645	1550	1554	2030	2325	....	0058	0400	0320	0515	0655
Brisbane ....a.	....	2320	2315	2221	....	0600	....	0630	1130	1200	1315	1450

Special notes:
A–Train terminates at Casino, bus connection to Brisbane.
B–This train has sleeper accommodation.
C–Arrival time in Brisbane one hour earlier during NSW daylight saving (Oct–Apr).
D–Additional services: 0825, 0935Ⓐ, 1030©, 1205Ⓐ, 1215©, 1305Ⓐ, 1400Ⓐ, 1510Ⓐ, 1515©, 1610Ⓐ, 1720, 2000Ⓐ.

All along this stretch of coastline are tourist resorts, peaceful national parks and diverting attractions, from 'the pub with no beer' to Australia's first koala hospital.

Inland, north of Port Macquarie, on the lower slopes of the Great Dividing Range are the Werrikimbe and the Oxley Wild Rivers National Parks which lead up to the heights of Armidale, where there are occasional winter snowfalls. Around here begins what is called the Holiday Coast, one of the many efforts of tourist boards around Australia to try to identify their area with a name such as Sunshine Coast, Holiday Coast, Paradise Coast and so on.

NEWCASTLE

See p. 237.

NELSON BAY AND PORT STEPHENS

Despite the closeness to Newcastle, and indeed to Sydney, Port Stephens has a totally different look and feel. The white beaches of volcanic sand contrasting with dazzling blue waters make this look like tropical Australia. The area is almost totally a holiday destination and has relatively little industry – the beaches lead back to bush with fine displays of wild flowers in the spring. The waters of the bay are home all year to bottlenose dolphins. There is a variety of dolphin and whale cruises available, one of which is **Moonshadow Cruises** (tel: 4984 9388).

On the south side of the Port Stephens inlet are dozens of marinas, all offering boats for hire, ranging from powerboats to houseboats. At the d'Albora Marina – one of the best known – **Pro Dive** offers scuba and snorkelling lessons in the clear waters of Port Stephens (tel: 4981 4331). **Big-game fishing** takes place beyond the heads, where the waters can be dangerous for an inexperienced sailor. The area is excellent for surfing and there are ocean beaches on each side which can produce excellent surfing conditions.

Oakvale Farm and Fauna World, on Nelson Bay Rd at Salt Ash, has animal feeding at 1100 and 1400 each day, and tame kangaroos wandering around the grounds. Open daily 1000–1700 (tel: 4982 6222).

SORTING OUT THE NAMES

Port Stephens is the deepwater inlet – two and a half times the size of Sydney harbour – that comes in between Yacaaba and Tomaree Heads. The main anchorage is Nelson Bay and it is here that the fishing fleet ties up in the late afternoon. Thus Port Stephens is the area, Nelson Bay the principal port.

Tomaree National Park stretches along the coast from Shoal Bay to Anna Bay. There is only one signposted walk but the

EN ROUTE

East and south-east of Bulahdelah lie **Myall Lakes National Park** and the several shallow lakes for which it's named. This is a popular holiday area for Sydneysiders, and is best avoided on summer weekends and throughout late Dec–Jan. At other times, this mid-sized park offers peace and solitude. From Bulahdelah, go right on either Bombah Point Rd or The Lakes Way to reach the park. Most of the activities centre on the water, with sailing, windsurfing and waterskiing. Houseboats for getting around and for sleeping are popular: contact **Bulahdelah Visitor Centre**, cnr Pacific Hwy and Crawford St; tel: 4997 4981 for further details. The Visitor Centre also has details on a series of walking tracks, including the Mungo Brush Rainforest Walk, the Tamboy Boardwalks (an excellent walk) and, for the healthy, a 21-km walk which links Hawks Nest to Mungo Brush. Continue the detour through **Booti Booti National Park**, between Wallis Lake and the sea, then on to **Forster**, which has golden beaches extending on each side. You then rejoin the Pacific Hwy just before Taree.

park has a series of beaches separated by rocky headlands, behind which are heaths and forests. Sometimes fairy penguins come to the headlands, and dolphins are often seen in the waves; tel: 4984 8200 for further information.

[i] Port Stephens Visitor Information Centre, Victoria Parade, Nelson Bay; tel: 4981 1579. Area code 02. Open daily. E-mail: info@portstephens.org.au.
Port Stephens: www.portstephens.org.au.

[⌂] Beaches Serviced Apartments $$$$ 12 Gowrie Ave; tel: 4984 3255. Short walk from Little and Shoal Bay Beaches.
Melaleuca Surfside Backpackers $–$$$ 33 Eucalyptus Dr., One Mile Beach; tel: 4981 9422. Bushy and peaceful location.
Port Stephens Motor Lodge $$$$ 44 Magnus St; tel: 4981 3366. Native gardens, short stroll to Nelson Bay and the town centre.
Port Stephens YHA/Samurai Beach Bungalows $–$$$$ Frost Rd, Anna Bay; tel: 4982 1921; www.yha.com.au/hostels. South of Nelson Bay; quiet and secluded.
Westbury's Marina Resort $$$$ 33 Magnus St; tel: 4981 4400. 250 metres from Nelson Bay Central Business District and Marina.

[⌷] There are several eating places around d'Albora Marina. Takeaways and cheap eats can be found around Stockton and Magnus Sts.
Chez Jules $$$ Cinema Mall, Stockton; tel: 4981 4500. Award-winning restaurant and coffee shop, menu changes every week. Open Mon–Sat for breakfast, lunch, afternoon tea and dinner.
Hogs Breath Café $$$$ d'Albora Marina; tel: 4984 2842. Hogs Breath blackened prime rib is featured on the menu, which gives the basic idea. Part of a chain of restaurants.
Ketch's Restaurant $$$$ 4th floor Westbury's Marina Resort, 33 Magnus St; tel: 4981 4400, stunning views.
Merrets $$$$ Peppers Anchorage Resort, Corlette Point Rd, Corlette; tel: 4984 2555. Short drive along the shore from Nelson Bay. Fish specialities, licensed and BYO.

TAREE

Its position on the Manning River and the fact that the nearby beaches are said to have the whitest sand in Australia – a claim made by several other places, incidentally – have made Taree a popular holiday spot. The Aboriginal word for a local fig tree is tareebit, which is probably where the name originates.

First, the bad news. Taree has got itself one of the 'Big' thingies as a tourist attraction, despite having some quite lovely buildings and parks. This time it is the seriously hideous **Big Oyster**. In contrast, Albert St has two of Taree's finest buildings. **St Paul's Church** (1869) is the oldest building in Taree; it is Gothic Revival but not as forbidding as many. On the other side of the road is the **Court House**, completed in 1897, a judicial building so well designed that it would be a pleasure to be charged there.

The **Manning Regional Art Gallery** at 12 Macquarie St is a small gallery with a strong local flavour, featuring paintings mainly from the 1850s–'60s. Open Wed–Sat 1100–1600, Sun 1300–1600; tel: 6551 0961. Free.

Taree is set back a little from the coast, but its beaches have excellent surfing as well as safe places to laze around. There are numerous riverside parks and reserves in the area and the visitor centre can give details on some excellent walks. **Manning Valley River Cruises** run a variety of cruises on the river most days; tel: 6553 2683.

[i] **Manning Valley Visitor Information Centre**, 21 Manning River Dr., Taree North; tel: 1800 801 522 or 6592 5444. Area code 02. Open daily.
Manning Valley Tourism, www.manningvalley.info.

🛏 **Arlite Motor Inn $$** 4 Pacific Hwy; tel: 6552 2433.
Caravilla Motor Inn $$$$ 33 Victoria St; tel: 6552 1822.
Fotheringham's Hotel $$ cnr Pulteney and Victoria Sts; tel: 6552 1153. In Victorian building, basic accommodation with shared facilities, but probably the cheapest in town.
Rainbow Gardens Motel $$$ 28 Crescent Ave; tel: 6551 7311.
Taree Caravan Park $$ Old Pacific Hwy; tel: 6552 1751.
The White House B&B $$$ Alban St; tel: 6551 3983.

🍴 **Hindquarter Steakhouse $$$** cnr Pulteney and Albert Sts; tel: 6552 6566. Popular steakhouse, licensed.
Il Colosseo $$$ 32 Oxley St, Chatham Plaza; tel: 6552 6289. Italian restaurant and takeaway, BYO.

EN ROUTE

Between Taree and Port Macquarie are several detours that might be treated as excursions from Taree or alternative routes north.

About 22 km north of Taree you can leave the Pacific Hwy for **Coopernook Forest Drive**, which can be rough after rain. Part-way along the drive is **Big Nellie Mountain**, a large volcanic plug rising to 560 m above sea level. There are panoramic views from the top. The climb, more a clamber, takes about 20 minutes. Looking at the view takes longer.

On the seaward side of Coopernook is **Harrington**. A breakwater provides excellent fishing and there is safe swimming on sandy beaches inside the river mouth.

Crowdy Head is 4 km from Harrington and from the headland there are spectacular views north over **Crowdy Bay National Park** ($) and Diamond Head, and to the south over the coastline through to Manning Point and Old Bar. The park, which runs between the road and the sea, has rugged, fractured sandstone cliffs with extensive banksia heaths and good coastal walks.

An alternative route is inland along Tourist Route 8. Around 15 km from Taree is **Wingham Brush**, the last remaining 10 ha of subtropical flood-plain rain forest in NSW, with Moreton Bay figs and one of Australia's largest populations of grey-headed flying foxes. Follow the route to **Ellenborough Falls** on the Bulga Plateau about 50 km north-west of Taree. This is one of the largest single-drop waterfalls in the southern hemisphere, and no matter how low the rainfall this waterfall continually flows all year. Tourist Route 8 then continues through the lush countryside of the Comboyne district to Wauchope. An alternative is to turn off at Comboyne and drive through the villages of Lorne and Kendall before rejoining the Pacific Hwy at Kew.

Plates Bistro $$$ Exchange Hotel, 154 Victoria St; tel: 6552 1160. Quality dishes at excellent value. Lunch Tues–Fri, dinner Tues–Sat.
Scenes Sidewalk Café $ cnr Manning and Albert Sts; tel: 6551 0922. Natural home-style foods, closed Sun.

PORT MACQUARIE

Port Macquarie is the main town in the Hastings region, situated close to the riverside timber town of Wauchope to the west, and the quiet seaside towns of Camden Haven to the south. Port Macquarie itself, founded in 1821 and thus the third-oldest penal settlement in Australia, is one of the most important fishing ports on the east coast. Very much a holiday town, it offers numerous attractions and activities, including some excellent beaches, museums and water sports. There is a large free-roaming koala population; you may see them gambolling along a quiet street on your travels.

i **Port Macquarie Visitor Information Centre**, cnr Clarence and Hay Sts; tel: 6581 8000; e-mail: tourism@hastings.gov.nsw.au. Open daily.
Port Macquarie: www.portmacquarieinfo.com.au.

🛏 **Anglers Rest Holiday Apartments $$$$** 15 Clarence St; tel: 6583 5032.
Aquatic Caravan Park $$ 259 Hastings River Dr.; tel: 6584 9155. Short drive out of town, by the river; pool and BBQ.
Mendip Lodge Gardens B&B $$$$ 155 North Branch Rd, via Kendall; tel: 6559 0069. About a 45-minute drive west from Port Macquarie, beautiful location off the beaten tourist-track.
Ozzie Pozzie Backpackers $–$$ 36 Waugh St; tel: 6583 8133 or 1800 620 020. Short distance to town centre and often recommended.
Port Macquarie YHA $–$$$ 40 Church St; tel: 6583 5512; www.yha.com.au/hostels. Close to the town centre.
Sandcastle Motel $$$$ 20 William St; tel: 6583 3522.

🍽 **Contasia $$** 14 Clarence St; tel: 6584 9638. Excellent value restaurant offering all-you-can-eat lunch buffets (daily), also dinner buffets Tues–Sun.

Crays $$$ Ground Floor, 74 Clarence St (by the wharf); tel: 6583 7885. Award-winning seafood restaurant, BYO.

Spinnakers Restaurant $$$ Sails Resort, Park St; tel: 6583 3999. Harbour views, light meals, sports-themed.

Toro's Mexican Cantina $$$ 22 Murray St; tel: 6583 4340. Lively restaurant, serving good fajitas.

HIGHLIGHTS

The town has all the attributes of the seaside, with camel rides on the beach (tel: 6583 7650) and a theme park called **Fantasy Glades** (tel: 6582 2506). Other activities include **Seaplane Flights** (tel: 0412 507 698) and self-guided historic **walking tours**. Pick up a leaflet at the Visitor Information Centre (tel: 6581 8000). There are numerous **River and Dolphin Cruises**, one of which is run by Port Venture (tel: 6583 3058).

St Thomas's Anglican Church, in Church St, was built between 1824 and 1828 using convict labour and handmade bricks. It is a beautiful building and a popular place of worship. **Sea Acres Rainforest Centre** ($$) on Pacific Drive, tel: 6582 3355, is open daily 0900–1630. Seventy-two acres of rainforest remain virtually unchanged since Captain Cook sailed Australia's east coast. There is a 1.3-km boardwalk taking you from the ground to 7 m up in the canopy, as well as educational displays.

DAY TRIPS

Camden Haven, the name given to communities that gather round the Camden Haven River, consists of three holiday towns at the mouth of the river – Laurietown, North Haven and Dunbogan. This is an anglers' paradise. Just outside the town, on **North Brother Mountain**, there is a lookout with panoramic views of the area.

Wauchope, pronounced 'war hope', was named after Captain Wauch who farmed there from 1841. It was, and is, a timber town, and 3 km west of the modern town is a reconstructed timber town of 1880, with steam train rides and demonstrations of working timber machinery, bullock teams and horse-drawn wagons. Free; tel: 6585 2322. South of Wauchope, there are some wonderful picnic areas and lovely views from lookouts in **Bago Bluff National Park** and nearby **State Forests**.

PORT MACQUARIE'S KOALAS

Want to see a koala? Try the Billabong Koala Breeding Centre, 61 Billabong Dr. (tel: 6585 1060), open daily 0900–1700, $$. But the best place is the Koala Hospital in Lord St. This is Australia's first koala hospital, located on the Macquarie Nature Reserve. Koala Hospital is open every day of the year 0800–1700, and visitors can view koalas up close and watch them being fed at 0800 and 1500; tel: 6584 1522.

KEMPSEY

The Macleay River wends its way down to the sea through beautiful forests and rural land to the coast where it bisects the town of Kempsey. Like almost every similar town in Australia it boasts the best year-round climate in the country, but it is true that it is always singularly pleasant here.

Country music is popular here, and every September there is a traditional music festival. Kempsey has a strong art scene, both Aboriginal and Western, with several galleries. Close to the centre of town, at Danger St, is the **Wigay Aboriginal Culture Park** ($$) where you can learn about Aboriginal food in a tour around the park and look at displays. Booking essential; tel: 6566 2332. **Wilay Bijarr Aboriginal Tours** ($$$) will take you on a half-day, full-day or overnight tour around the mid-north coast. Activities include gathering and eating bush tucker, visiting spiritual places and above all getting the chance to share culture with the Aboriginal people. Tel: 6562 5959 for details.

Situated in South Kempsey Park on the Pacific Highway, the **Kempsey Cultural Centre** has been referred to as the 'first Australian design building'. This is open to much debate but the architect, Glenn Murcutt, has given it a uniquely Australian feeling, and it houses the tourist centre and a settler's cottage. It also has a **museum** tracing the story of the Macleay Valley. Open daily 1000–1600 ($); tel: 6562 7572.

National parks and reserves protect over 80 per cent of the region's coastline, and the **beaches** are excellent and accessible, with the Arakoon State Recreation Area, the Hat Head National Park, the Goolawah Reserve and the Limeburners Creek Nature Reserve all offering clean beaches, clean water, miles of uninterrupted coast and, when the wind is in the right quarter, magnificent surfing. Crescent Head provides some of the best surfing in Australia and is the site of the annual Malibu Classic.

Scuba diving is also well catered for. The base for most diving activity is the small resort of **South West Rocks**, 35 km north of Kempsey by way of the Jerseyville Bridge. Because of the nearness of the continental shelf there are clean, warm semitropical waters to dive in for most of the year. Fish Rock Dive Centre (328–332 Gregory St, tel: 6566 6614) does a daily dive charter and offers full scuba courses, as does South West Rocks Dive Centre (5/98 Gregory St; tel: 6566 6474). For deep-sea fishing try Trial Bay Deep Sea Fishing Charters; tel: 0427 256 556.

EXPLORING THE MACLEAY VALLEY

All along the valley is a series of small villages such as Gladstone, recognised as an historically important village, Smithtown, Frederickton, Bellbrook, Willawarrin, Kinchela, Jerseyville and Kundabung. In the valley's hinterland there are over 100,000 ha of state forests, the world heritage Werrikimbe National Park, the Upper Macleay Gorges and the Oxley Wild Rivers National Park.

EN ROUTE

In the 1950s, Gordon Parson wrote a song, 'A Pub with No Beer'. It was recorded by Slim Dusty and became a hit not only in Australia but overseas. Australians doing 'The Trip' to Europe would assemble in the pubs of Earl's Court in London and make the night resound with their caterwauling of this ditty. But the pub with no beer exists (although the beer supplies have been replenished). To reach it, turn off the Pacific Hwy at Macksville South and follow the signs for about 20 km to the Taylors Arms. The pub offers lunch daily, and evening meals at weekends; there is also excellent value, newly renovated accommodation $$; tel: 6564 2100; e-mail: pubwithnobeer@tsn.cc. Do not take it as gospel that this is the pub that was written about – there is much evidence to suggest that the song was taken from a poem about a similar pub in Queensland. Most official histories try to be even-handed as to which should get the honours. This is not a subject that you bring up when drinking in the public bar at the Taylors Arms.

Trial Bay Gaol, open 0900–1700 daily, is in the Arakoon State Recreation Area. The gaol was built in 1886 but has now been transformed into a museum ($), tel: 6566 6168.

i **Kempsey Visitor Information Centre,** South Kempsey Park, Pacific Hwy; tel: 1800 642 480 or 6563 1555. In the same building as the Kempsey Historical Museum. Open daily.
Kempsey www.macleayvalleycoast.com.au.

All Nations Hallmark Inn $$$ 320 Pacific Hwy; tel: 6562 1284. Standard motel.
City Centre Motel $$$ 95 Pacific Hwy; tel: 6562 7733. Also has two licensed restaurants.
Hotel Kempsey $$$ 35 Belgrave St; tel: 6562 8588. Central hotel, with bar and bistro downstairs.
Netherby House Heritage B&B $$$$ 5 Little Rudder St, East Kempsey; tel: 6563 1777.
Sundowner Caravan Park $$ 161 Pacific Hwy; tel: 6562 1361. Close to the town.
Tall Timbers Caravan Park $ Pacific Hwy; tel: 6562 4544. Accommodation from inexpensive caravans to en-suite cabins.

Brambly Hedges Tea Shoppe $ 1/24 Clyde St; tel: 6562 6774. Cosy English-style teashop, some excellent vegetarian options.
Happy Garden Chinese Restaurant $$ New Royal Tavern, cnr York and Smith Sts; tel: 6562 2900. Pleasant restaurant offering all-you-can-eat smorgasbord.
Kempsey Chinese Restaurant $$ 54 Smith St; tel: 6563 1030.
Lou's Café Restaurant $$ 7 Belgrave St; tel: 6562 4869. Busy café with a range of dishes.

NAMBUCCA HEADS

Most of the attraction of Nambucca Heads is focused on its river. There is a range of water activities available, from boat hire to waterskiing. On the seaward side of town, **Main Beach** is patrolled in the water sports season and comes south through Beilbys Beach to Shelly Beach, protected from the sea by Cliffy Point. In the middle of the river is **Stuart Island,** which has the Nambucca Heads Island golf course.

Like most museums run by keen amateurs, the opening hours of **Headland Historical Museum**, at the end of Liston St, are somewhat eccentric – Wed, Sat, Sun 1400–1600 – but it is well organised and the area has a colourful history to recount. ($); tel: 6568 6380. Some of the first European settlers to come to the area (in 1840) were ticket-of-leave men – convicts leased on patrol to find and log cedar. The logs were originally taken overland but were later floated down the Nambucca River and transported by sailing vessels to Sydney.

Captain Cook Lookout offers excellent views of the area. Even more impressive is the view from the **Yarrahapinni Lookout** in Wellington Park, where on a clear day you can see forever. Escorted four-wheel-drive tours of the area are available from On the Wallaby 4WD Tours (tel: 6655 2171).

Urban Rainforest

Nambucca Heads boasts a rainforest reserve in the centre, virtually adjacent to the main shopping area. If you walk across Ridge St from the Nambucca Mall, you enter another world. A series of nature walks has been built through the natural bushland reserves extending to the Rotary Lookout, which overlooks the river entrance. There is a dense section of rainforest in Gordon Park.

☐ i **Nambucca Valley Information Centre** Riverside Drive; tel: 6568 6954. Open daily. E-mail: nambuct@midcoast.com.au. **Nambucca Heads**: www.nambuccatourism.com.

☐ Bowra Hotel $$ High St, Bowraville; tel: 6564 7041. Newly renovated rooms, opening onto the veranda in yesteryear hotel, includes breakfast – excellent value.
Destiny Motor Inn $$$$ Riverside Dr.; tel: 6568 8044 Pool, spa, Turkish steam bath, private courtyards to landscaped gardens.
Foreshore Caravan Park $$ Riverside Dr.; tel: 6568 6014. Good range of facilities from tent sites to four-star cabins.
Max Motel $$ 4 Fraser St; tel: 6568 6138. Close to the shops with good views.
Nambucca Backpackers Hostel $$ 3 Newman St; tel: 6568 6360. Cosy quiet hostel in bush setting.
Nambucca Resort $$$$ Pacific Hwy; tel: 6568 6899. A 28-unit family motel and licensed restaurant set in 6 ha on the Nambucca River. Salt-water pool, children's playground, spa and canoe hire.

☐ Boatshed Brasserie $$$ 1 Wellington Dr.; tel: 6568 9292. Pleasantly situated on the river. BYO and licensed.
Food Fetish $$ 47a Bowra St; tel: 6569 4676. Open Mon–Sat. Unique menu serving eclectic dishes such as prawns with banana.
Matilda's Restaurant $$$ 6 Wellington Dr.; tel: 6568 6024. BYO and licensed. Good-value three-course meals with damper and salad buffet.
Ridgy Didge Café $ 27 Bowra St; tel: 6568 7533. Excellent coffee and a range of sandwiches, smoothies and focaccia. Open daily from breakfast until late afternoon.

EN ROUTE
The Nambucca Valley is at the eastern end of the popular Waterfall Way. Heading north from Nambucca Heads, take a left onto route 78 through Bellingen and up to the New England Plateau. This brings you into waterfall country which, depending on the season, has many spectacular falls.

A TRIP BACK IN TIME
Twenty-five minutes' drive inland from Nambucca is Bowraville, where time seems to have stood still (apart from the cars!). European settlement began with the cedar-getters and their bullockies, and later the town became engaged in dairy, timber and banana industries. There is a market every Thursday, and some nice old-fashioned cafés and shops.

COFFS HARBOUR

Coffs Harbour was originally named Korff's Harbour after Captain John Korff who sheltered here in 1847 and liked the place so much he opened a store in the main street. It has retained much of that charm although the population is now over 60,000.

The major attraction of Coffs Harbour is the wide range of beaches catering for everyone from surfers to kiddies going paddling. There are even some secluded beaches used unofficially for nude bathing. Coffs Harbour is the only place where the Great Dividing Range meets the sea (just north of the town), offering some spectacular scenery and unique rainforest. This is also the centre of a tropical fruit-growing area.

i **Coffs Coast Visitor Information Centre**, cnr Mclean and Elizabeth Sts; tel: 1300 369 070 or 6652 1522. Open daily. www.coffscoast.com.au.

INTERNET ACCESS The Library, Rigby House, cnr Coff St and Duke St, offers free internet access. Tel: 6648 4900.
Happy Planet Internet Café 3/13 Park Ave; tel: 6651 7520. Open weekdays 0900–1730 and Sat 0900–1300; closed Sun.

There are plenty of motels in the area, mostly on Park Beach Rd or Ocean Parade.
Aussitel Backpackers $–$$$ 312 Harbour Dr.; tel: 6651 1871 or 1800 330 335; www.aussitel.com. Close to harbour; fun reputation.
Barracuda Backpackers $–$$ 19 Arthur St; tel: 6651 3514 or 1800 111 514; www.backpackers.coffs.tv. Reasonable proximity to Park Beach.
Coffs Harbour YHA Backpackers Resort $–$$ 110 Albany St; tel: 6652 6462; www.yha.com.au/hostels. Busy yet pleasant hostel, close to the town centre.
Park Beach Caravan Park $$ Ocean Pde; tel: 6648 4888. Close to popular surfing beach.
Toreador Motel $$$ 31 Grafton St; tel: 6652 3887.

Coffs Harbour is at the centre of the largest banana-growing area in New South Wales. There is not just a Big Banana. There is a Big Banana Leisure Park; tel: 6652 4355. All of this is some 3 km north of the town, so once you get there you have seen the last of the Big Banana. The Historical Museum ($) at 191 High St, tel: 6652 5794 (open daily 1000–1600), tells the story of how the area was developed first for cedar and gold, and then for bananas and tourists.

TO The two main groupings of restaurants are on the Pacific Hwy and High St, with the inexpensive options normally being in the latter.

Bush Turkey $$$$ 382 High St; tel: 6651 1544. Range of Australian foods, including kangaroo, emu and crocodile.

The Dragon Restaurant $$$ 108 Grafton St; tel: 6652 4187. Excellent Cantonese food in pleasant restaurant.

Fisherman's Co-op $ Marina Dr.; Coffs Jetty; tel: 6652 2811. A range of fresh fish and, of course, chips. Popular in the summer – you can expect to wait.

Iguana Beach Café $$ The Yacht Club, Marina; tel: 6652 5725. Lunch and dinner, good seafood.

Scoffs Seafood and Grill $$$$ 386 High St; tel: 6651 1516. Located in one of Coffs's oldest buildings.

Tahruah Thai Kitchen $$ 366 High St; tel: 6651 5992. Excellent Thai food at good prices.

HIGHLIGHTS

A circular drive is a useful orientation and takes in most of the attractions. Starting from **High St Mall**, drive east. After crossing a few streets you'll find Hardacre St on the left. This takes you to the **Botanic Gardens** (free, open daily 0900–1700; tel: 6648 4188). Further on, High St joins Ocean Pde. By the hospital you'll find **Beacon Hill Lookout**. Ocean Pde continues to the seafront, and a short signposted diversion lands you at **The Jetty** – several boat trips and charters depart from here. You can park your car at The Jetty and follow the **Mutton Bird Island Nature Walk**. Back on Ocean Pde, before crossing Coffs Creek, you will find the **Pet Porpoise Pool** on the left ($$$, open daily; tel: 6652 2164). From the same spot you can join the **Coffs Creek Walk**, which takes you through some places only accessible on foot. You can then continue along Ocean Pde past the Park Beach Surf Club to Pacific Hwy, which will bring you back to High St.

The Butterfly House ($$, in Strouds Rd (off Pacific Hwy south of Coffs), tel: 6653 4766) is also worth a visit. Open daily, it has one of the world's largest displays of live Australian butterflies in a rainforest setting.

WHERE NEXT?

South-west of Coffs Harbour is beautiful Bellingen, a must-see town. Further inland, up the Waterfall Way, is quiet Dorrigo and its fascinating Rainforest Centre.

DRIVING ROUTE

The Pacific Hwy – still grandiosely named Rte National I – turns inland to Grafton, skirting Yuraygir National Park and Lake Hiawatha. From there the road runs 130 km across the inlet of the Clarence River to Ballina. At Ballina you can stay on the highway or run towards the sea through Lennox Head to Byron Bay and rejoin the highway on the far side of Bangalow. After Brunswick Heads the road kinks slightly inland to Murwillumbah, on the slopes of the long-extinct volcano Mt Warning, before entering Tweed Heads, the last town in New South Wales. Traffic through town can be a problem on summer weekends, but you can use the highway and by-pass. Across the Tweed River lies Queensland. The total journey, excluding detours, is about 340 km.

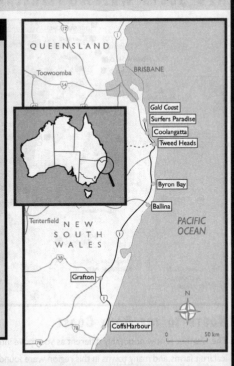

COFFS HARBOUR — SURFERS PARADISE

OTT Tables 9017/9092

Service	🚌	🚌	🚆		🚌	🚆	🚌	🚌	🚌	🚌	🚌	
Days of operation Special notes	Daily C	C	AC		C	BC	C	C	C	C	C	
Sydney ....d.	0700	0700	0715	....	1300	1624	1800	1845	2045	2200	2230	....
Coffs Harbour.............d.	1550	1645	1554	....	2325	0059	0400	0320	0515	0655	0620	....
South Grafton................d.	1655	1750	1707	....	0030	0221	0500	0420	0625	0805	0720	....
Ballina ....d.	1920	2000			....	0240	*0508*b	0715	0740	0850	1120	0945	....
Byron Bay ....d.	1955	2040	*2008*b	....	0315	*0539*b	0800	0820	0945	1215	1035	....
Coolangatta/Tweed Heads.d.	2115			*2052*b	....	0400	*0707*b	0900	0940	1110			1150	....
Surfers Paradise ....d.	2150	2205	*2159*b	....	0450	*0643*b	1000	1030	1205	1340	1225	....
Brisbane ....a.	2315	2320	*2221*b	....	0600	0630	1130	1200	1315	1450	1345	....

Special notes:
b–Connections by bus.
A–Train terminates at Casino.
B–This train has sleeper accommodation.
C–Arrival time in Brisbane one hour earlier during NSW daylight saving (Oct–Apr).

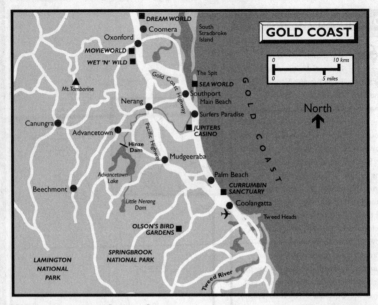

NORTH TO THE GOLD COAST

The weather is now noticeably different as you move into the subtropical zone. There are tropical fruit farms, and many towns in this region were founded on cedar logging. Much of the coast falls within national parks, and magical, laid-back Byron Bay is probably the closest you'll get (while staying on dry land) to seeing the whales migrating along the East Coast (in season).

The Gold Coast has been a holiday spot since the turn of the 20th century but has boomed since World War II. The whole strip is the most thoroughly commercialised resort in Australia, with more than 2 million visitors a year.

COFFS HARBOUR

See p. 253.

GRAFTON

Grafton is a pleasant garden town, famous for its trees – the jacarandas are a glorious sight in season. As early as 1866 the council had by-laws encouraging the planting and preservation of trees. This far-sighted action means that Grafton now has more than 6500 trees lining the streets and shading the well-maintained parks. A **Jacaranda Festival** has been held every spring – the last Sat in Oct – since 1935.

Many of the buildings in Grafton are classified by the National Trust, including **Christ Church Cathedral**, on the corner of Victoria and Duke Sts. This was designed by John Horbury Hunt in 1884 in the Gothic Revival style so popular in the Victorian era. Open daily 0830–1800; tel: 6642 2844.

Worth seeing is **Schaeffer House Museum**, at 192 Fitzroy St, which was built in 1900 by an architect as an expression of his design philosophy and has now been totally restored. Open Tues–Thur and Sun 1300–1600.

HERITAGE TRAIL
Grafton is an historical town; on almost every street in the centre you'll see a building of some significance. The Tourist Association has an excellent free guide to a Heritage Trail which takes you past not just the interesting buildings but also most of the other attractions the town has to offer.

Many of the old homesteads have been preserved; one, **Prentice House** at 158 Fitzroy St, now houses the regional art gallery. Open Tues–Sun 1000–1600; tel: 6642 3177; free.

The **Bentleg Market and Gallery** in Skinner St, South Grafton, specialises in a range of arts and crafts produced locally – there are some interesting Aboriginal artefacts on display. Open Mon–Fri 0900–1700, Sat 0900–1200; tel: 6643 2929.

Levees, built to protect the town after many floods, now form a riverside walk, which offers a range of water sports. Of the 24 parks within Grafton, perhaps the best positioned is **Memorial Park and Boulevard**, at the river end of Prince St, overlooking **Susan Island**. Great Time Cruises (tel: 6642 3456) offer cruises around the island, at one end of which is a rainforest that's home to the largest fruit-bat colony in the southern hemisphere. Seelands (tel: 6644 9381) hire out boats and canoes if you'd rather get around under your own steam.

The original town, simply known as The Settlement, developed as two separate settlements, one each side of the Clarence River, with a rowing boat the only connection. Even after the double-decker bridge (rail and road) was opened in 1932, South Grafton remained a separate community until the 1950s. Today, it is a perfect example of a 19th-century NSW river town.

> *i* **Clarence River Tourist Association**, Pacific Hwy, South Grafton; tel: 6642 4677; www.clarencetourism.com. There are many special displays, including Aboriginal art, National Parks and local products all housed in an excellent purpose-designed building. Open daily; www.tropicalnsw.com.au.

En Route

Around Grafton is a ring of national parks including, inland along Rte 38, the World Heritage park of **Washpool** and the **Gibraltar Range** and, only 40 km from Grafton, but difficult to access, **Nymboida**. Two smaller parks have combined to form **Yuraygir**, the longest stretch of undeveloped coastline in NSW. The parks comprise long sandy beaches, heathlands, paperbark swamps and lagoons. There is excellent bushwalking, surfing and fishing, as well as canoeing in the lagoons and creeks. **Bundjalung**, immediately to the north, continues the protected coastline. It covers large areas of swamp and heathland, mangrove mudflats, cypress swamps and one of the last wild coastal rivers, the Esk. Attractions include rare rainforests at Woody Head, canoeing on the rivers and lagoons, and excellent surfing and fishing. Camping is permitted at Woody Head and Black Rocks. The National Parks and Wildlife Service, Lvl 3, 49 Victoria St; tel: 6641 1500, can give further information on all of the parks.

🛏 The motels are clustered along Fitzroy and Prince Sts, which makes it easy to trawl for accommodation that suits you.

Abbey Motor Inn $$$ 59 Fitzroy St; tel: 6642 6122.

Best Western Espania Motel $$$$ Pacific Hwy, South Grafton; tel: 6642 4566. Pool and heated spa; short drive to city centre.

Clarence Motor Inn $$$$ 51 Fitzroy St; tel: 6643 3444; www.clarinn.com.au; e-mail: clarinn@nor.com.au. Has its own restaurant – Victoria's – which specialises in prawns and oysters from the river, and fish and shellfish from the sea.

Crown Hotel $$ 1 Prince St; tel: 6642 4000. Pleasant hotel, located by the town centre. Includes a backpackers' lodge.

Dovedale B&B $$$$ 3 Oliver St; tel: 6642 5706. Friendly B&B, close to the river.

Glenwood Tourist Park and Motel $$ 71 Heber St, South Grafton; tel: 6642 3466. Motel rooms, cabins, camping area, a well-maintained park.

Grafton Hotel $$ 97 Fitzroy St; tel: 6642 2000. Basic but inexpensive hotel, with a pleasant bistro.

Jacaranda Motel $$$ Pacific Hwy; tel: 6642 2833.

Seelands Homestead $$ Old Punt Road, Seelands; tel: 6644 9381. Offers canoe and boat hire and 4WD trips. Pick-up from Grafton Railway Station.

🍴 The Clarence is one of Australia's biggest seafood harvesting districts, and the seafood available in the restaurants of Grafton is outstanding. The best bet is to have it served as simply as possible. The quality of the produce needs no garnishing.

Big River Buffet $ Grafton District Service Club, Mary St; tel: 6642 2066. Good-value buffet lunch or dinner. Open daily.

Courtyard Café $$ Grafton Regional Gallery, 158 Fitzroy St; tel: 6642 6644. In pleasant courtyard setting. Light meals, good coffee. Closed Mon.

Georgies Café $$$ 230 Pound St; tel: 6642 6996. Casual relaxed dining, veranda for the pleasant days. Popular café.

New Oriental Chinese Restaurant $$ 127 Price St; tel: 6642 7888. Open daily, all-you-can-eat smorgasbord special on weekdays.

Poss' Place $$ 88 Prince St; tel: 6643 2216. Some vegetarian options; BYO.

BALLINA BY BIKE

An excellent way to see the area is by bike. Ballina has numerous designated cycle paths leading to a range of sights including the lighthouse, Maritime Museum, beaches and parks. You can hire bikes from several places, one of which is Jack Ransom Cycles at 16 Cherry St; tel: 6686 3485. The Visitor Information Centre has a free cycling guide.

BALLINA

Ballina is the sort of quiet town where everything moves at a relaxed pace in the pleasantly warm air. It is sited on the mouth of the Richmond River and the centre of the town is surrounded by water – the North Creek divides it from East Ballina and the North Creek Canal from West. Ballina has a sizeable fishing fleet and the town is surrounded by beautiful beaches – the coastline heading up to Lennox Heads has some of the best surfing beaches in NSW.

The small **Opal and Gem Museum**, open 0900–1700, has lots of souvenirs for sale made from crystal and gems. Sadly, its address is Shop 1, Big Prawn Complex, Pacific Hwy (yes, Ballina has a Big Prawn).

The lighthouse, on Beach Rd, was built in 1879 to mark the Ballina bar, which has been the doom of many ships. There are tremendous views from the **Lighthouse Hill** lookout, and in season you can see humpback whales migrating.

You can go cruising aboard MV *Richmond Princess* (tel: 0429 664 784) which has two-hour cruises ($$) every Wed and Thurs. The MV *Bennelong* (tel: 0414 664 552) also has a variety of cruises up the river, including one to Lismore. Ballina Quay Marina (tel: 6686 5450) has houseboats for rent. Just north of Ballina along the coast road is **Lake Ainsworth**, a freshwater lake which is safe for children.

The whole area inland is one of tropical fruit production. In nearby Alstonville is **Summerland House**, Wardell Rd (tel: 6628 0610), an extensive charity-owned fruit farm growing avocados, macadamia nuts, tropical stone fruit, custard apples, lychees and citrus fruits.

The **Pioneer Memorial Park** (cnr Hill St and the Serpentine), a burial ground for many sea captains and crew, contains Moreton Bay figs, white booyong, yellow-wood and bumpy ash. It was in this environment that the red cedar grew and thrived but was cut down by the early settlers as a cash crop and was, indeed, responsible for much of the European settlement of this area. On display in the park are horse-drawn vehicles and early steam-powered machines.

The **Victoria Park Nature Reserve** ($) close by, 7 km south of Alstonville on the Wardell Rd, is a remnant of the original scrubland that once covered the whole area. A boardwalk allows you to explore the last remaining rainforest giants.

LAS BALSAS EXPEDITION

An exhibition at the Ballina Naval and Maritime Museum (located behind the Visitor Centre on Regatta Ave) tells the story of the Las Balsas expedition, in which a raft with a four-man crew left Guayaquil in Ecuador in 1973 and came ashore at Ballina 178 days later. The expedition was designed to prove that South Americans could have come to Australia and New Zealand on balsa rafts, a fascinating theory which has attracted much argument over the years. The exhibition would be worth a special detour, but you will probably be going to the information centre anyway. There is also a display recording the maritime history of the Richmond River. Open daily 0900–1600; tel: 6681 1002. Free, but donations appreciated.

[i] **Ballina Information Centre**, cnr River St and Las Balsa Plaza; tel: 6686 3484; e-mail: balinfo@ballina.nsw.gov.au. Open daily.
Ballina: www.discoverballina.com.

[hotel icon] **All Seasons Motor Inn $$$$** 305 Pacific Hwy; tel: 6686 2922; e-mail: allsball@fc-hotels.com.au. Also has spa and suites at higher prices.
Almare Tourist Motel $$$ 339 River St; tel: 6686 2833. Garden area with pool, good value.
Ballina Central Caravan Park $$ 1 River St; tel: 6686 2220; www.ballina.tropicalnsw.com.au. Centrally located, peaceful environment.
Ballina Heritage Inn $$$$ 229 River St; tel: 6686 0505. In old building, pool.
Ballina Travellers Lodge YHA $–$$$$ 36–38 Tamar St; tel: 6686 6737; www.yha.com.au/hostels. Quiet location near town centre, free pickups from bus station.
Patches Beach Hideaway B&B $$$$ 10 Patches Beach Lane; tel: 6683 4473. Situated on deserted beach.
Palms Motor Inn $$$$ cnr Owen and Bentick Sts; tel: 6686 4477. Pool and BBQ area.

[food icon] **Aussie Bistro $$** The Australian Hotel, 103 River St; tel: 6686 2015. Popular bar and nightspot. Accommodation available.
Café Fresco $$$ 117 River St; tel: 6686 2411. Range of dishes from curry to octopus.
Mexican Del Rio $$$ 196 River St; tel: 6686 2775.
Paddy McGinty's $$ River St; tel: 6681 4638. Irish pub and café open daily.
Ping Sun and Mermaid Restaurant $$ 200 River St; tel: 6686 3292. Cantonese. BYO.
Shellys on the Beach $$$ Shelly Beach Rd; tel: 6686 9844. Open from 0730 daily. Cosmopolitan restaurant, bookings recommended.

BYRON BAY

Byron Bay is thought by many people to be the most attractive spot in Australia. Sydneysiders speak of it with awe and affection, and many drive or fly up here as often as they can. It is a remarkably charming place and no one ever seems to come away disappointed.

Byron Bay is defended from commercialisation by a very active and well-organised lobby – all high-rise buildings are banned and Club Med tried in vain for years to open. Despite motels and hotels galore there is no feeling of a tourist trap. Shopping is mostly tie-dyed fabrics, scented candles and handicrafts, but there is a lovely relaxed feel about the place, and people smile a lot.

Captain Cook named the town after Sir John Byron, a brave sailor who had circumnavigated the globe in HMS *Dolphin* (1764–66) and thus ventured into the Pacific before Cook himself. He was also the grandfather of the poet Lord Byron.

EN ROUTE

Bangalow, the turn-off from Rte National 1 for Byron Bay, is a small village with a rustic charm of its own, and the art, craft and antiques shops are a foretaste of Byron Bay. The **Byron Creek walking track** goes through rainforest to a picnic area. If travelling from Ballina, rather than rejoining Hwy 1, stay on River St and follow the road north, over the Missingham Bridge along the coast to Lennox Head, a seaside village with excellent surf. There are some great views, National Parks and deserted beaches along the way.

i **Byron Visitor Centre**, 80 Jonson St; tel: 6680 8558. Open daily 0900–1700. Some excellent free brochures and guides, helpful staff.
Byron Bay Information: www.visitbyronbay.com.
Byron Bay: www.byron-bay.com.

There are several places offering internet access. Many are owned by travel agents giving free access to those who book tours.

INTERNET **Backpackers World**, Shop 6, Byron St; tel: 6685 8858. Open daily. Travel agent and internet.
Global Gossip, 84 Jonson St; tel: 6680 9140. Open daily 0800–midnight. Travel agent, internet, and telephone booths.

Byron Bay is packed to overflowing in Dec and Jan, and prices shoot up accordingly.
Aquarius Backpackers Motel $$–$$$ 16 Lawson St; tel: 6685 7663 or 1800 028 909; www.aquarius-backpack.com.au. Very clean and comfortable. Good café $$.
Aussie Way Nanette's $$ 6 Julian Rocks Dr., Sunrise Beach; tel: 6685 6895. Twin/double rooms. A great personalised way of seeing Byron Bay, maximum ten guests at any time, free use of bikes.
Bay Beach Motel $$$$ 32 Lawson St; tel: 6685 6090. Located in the heart of Byron Bay opposite Main Beach.
Byron Bay Lighthouse and Clarks Beach House $$$$ tel: 6685 6552; www.byronbaypro.com.au; e-mail: byronpro@ norex.com.au. Possibly the best accommodation of its kind in Australia – located in the keepers' cottages by the lighthouse. Clarks Beach House is right on the beach. For both venues advance bookings are essential (a year in advance during the holiday season).

Getting Around
Bicycles are widely available for hire and many motels and hostels will lend you one for nothing. Earth Car Rentals offers relatively inexpensive car hire with free delivery anywhere within 5 km of Byron Bay. Tel: 6685 7472.

Nimbin

When Nimbin's dairy industry stopped in the 1970s, and land prices were cheap, the hippies moved in, turning it into a colourful hippie town. Today it is not much different and must be seen to be believed. There are Volkswagen Combis painted with flowers parked in the high street, and there is even a Hemp Museum. To reach the town you drive for about 50 km west of Byron Bay through winding country roads (a map is essential). Alternatively you can go on an inexpensive day trip from Byron Bay; there are several operators, one of which is Mick's Tours; tel: 6685 6889.

Cape Byron YHA $–$$$$ cnr Middleton and Byron Sts; tel: 6685 8788 or 1800 652 627; www.yha.com.au/hostels. Busy hostel, livelier than most YHAs, but clean and well organised. Doubles/twins available.

J's Bay YHA $–$$$$ 7 Carlyle St; tel: 6685 8853 or 1800 678 195; www.yha.com.au/hostels. The atmosphere says *relaaaaax*.

Nomads Main Beach Backpackers $–$$$ cnr Lawson and Fletcher Sts; tel: 6685 8695 or 1800 150 233. A backpacking hostel; like most in the area, it has a pool, BBQ, dorms and doubles.

🍴 Jonson St is packed end to end with cafés and restaurants; all of them are affordable and most of them are inexpensive.

Beach Café $$ Clarks Beach; tel: 6685 7598. Open daily from 0730. Get there in the early morning and you can watch the sun rise over the sea.

Byron Thai $$$ 31 Lawson St; tel: 6685 8453. Open daily, excellent Thai food, very popular.

Fundamental Food Store $ Old Post Office Building, 61 Jonson St; tel: 6685 6429. Food store with a small café serving a range of vegetarian food. Sit at the street tables and watch the world go by.

The Piggery Supernatural Food Restaurant $$ Skinners Shoot Rd; tel: 6685 5833. Open daily 1800–late. Back section of restaurant serves totally vegetarian cuisine.

Wok on the Wild Side $$ 18 Jonson St; tel: 6685 6220. Authentic Asian cuisine.

Highlights

The bay is very popular for swimming, body surfing and, a little further out to sea, skin diving. There is great surfing at **Watego's Beach** on Cape Byron, just below the lighthouse. This is considered to be one of the best surfing beaches on the east coast and is one of the few beaches in NSW with a north-westerly aspect – its long rollers are the delight of surfers. On the beach is Clarks Beach House which can be rented in the same way as the lighthouse keepers' houses (see Accommodation) – ideal if you want to sleep practically on top of the surf.

The **lighthouse**, in Cape Byron Headland Reserve, 2 km east of the town along Lighthouse Rd, was built in 1901. It is one of the most attractive in Australia and you can drive up there to the car park near the top. There is a path around the lighthouse and out to the most easterly point on the Australian mainland. The views are stunning, and between May and September it is a good place to spot migrating whales swimming past. On any day you may see dolphins swimming through the totally clear waters. When you see them perhaps you, too, will feel sadness for the dolphins that are kept cooped up in marinas for the entertainment of holidaymakers. The whiff of goat you may detect is from the descendants of the herd the keepers used to maintain for meat and milk. The Cape Byron Headland Reserve is open daily 0800–1730 (1930 in summer), although the lighthouse is not open to the public.

Running south of the lighthouse is **Tallow Beach**, 7 km of golden sand. Except for the summer holidays and weekends it is often totally deserted, and you are advised not to swim here owing to strong currents. This is not the only beach at Byron – there are over 40 km of beaches altogether so you are spoiled for choice. From Main Beach at low tide you can see bits of the wreck of the steamer *Wollongbar*, which was wrenched from its mooring by a storm in 1921.

In the bay running north towards Brunswick Heads is the **Julian Rocks Aquatic and Nature Reserve**. It is a 10-minute boat ride from the shore and is Australia's first marine sanctuary and a great place for skin diving. The tropical waters from the Coral Sea stream down to meet with the temperate southern waters and the result, as always, is a wealth of marine life. This is certainly one of the ten best dive sites in Australia, and there are several organisations which can handle dives. One is **Byron Bay Dive Centre**, 9 Marvel St; tel: 6685 8333.

Byron Bay is not a scene for formal nightclubs; however, several venues offer music and a couple of places have live performances. These are all in Jonson St, so you can start at the beach and trawl your way inland. The two best-known ones are **The Beach Hotel**, where you can sit in the beer garden and listen to the music at about the right volume, and **The Rails**, which is very much a local venue but has music every night.

Within an easy hour's drive from Byron Bay there are eight national parks and 26 nature reserves. One drive worth taking is to **Whian Whian Forest**, **Peates Mountain Lookout** and **Minyon Falls**, 20 km west of Mullumbimby. From here you're just a few minutes from Nimbin. Or walk through the rainforest at **Broken Head** to the almost total seclusion of King's and Bray's Beaches. The information centre has maps and information on all these places.

TWEED HEADS

For years this town had a substantial source of income simply because poker machines were illegal in Queensland but allowed in New South Wales. The law has now been amended but the clubs linger on – the Twin Towns Services Club, cnr Wharf and Boundary Sts, has one of the largest arrays of poker machines in Australia.

Tweed Heads is on two major lagoons that stretch inland, one of which, Terranora Lake, offers fishing and boating and is famous for its oysters. The best spot to orientate yourself with views of the area is **Razorback Lookout** at the southern edge of the town centre – it is located in a residential area, so ask the visitor centre for directions.

The coastline around Tweed Heads is, for many visitors, much more pleasant than the hustle and bustle of Surfers Paradise (see p. 268) to the north. In fact, Tweed Heads is an ideal base from which to make forays up the Gold Coast.

Point Danger's **Captain Cook Memorial and Lighthouse**, located at the top of Boundary St (half in New South Wales and half in Queensland), was opened in 1970, the bicentenary of the epic voyage undertaken by Captain Cook. The memorial consists of a capstan base made from ballast dumped from the *Endeavour*.

The Minjungbal people once inhabited the lower Tweed Valley, and on Kirkwood Rd, about 5 km south of town, is the **Minjungbal Aboriginal Centre** ($$). It is set in bushland around an old sacred ceremonial bora site and mangrove and nature walks. Open Mon–Fri 0900–1600, Sat 0900–1400, closed Sun; tel: (07) 5524 2109.

Where the Tweed River joins the Rous lies the small village of Tumbulgum – the name means meeting of the waters – which was the site of a grog shanty (an unlicensed hotel) as early as 1858. The completely restored and renovated Tumbulgum Hotel today dates from 1887 (tel: (02) (not 07) 6676 6202). From here you can explore up the two rivers in a hired boat from Tumbulgum Boat Hire, inside the General Store at 108 Riverside Dr. (tel: (02) 6676 6240). The Tumbulgum Gallery at 110 Riverside Drive (tel: (02) 6676 6234) has an excellent display of locally handmade arts and crafts for sale.

> *i* **Tweed and Coolangatta Tourism**, Tweed Mall, Wharf St; tel: (07) 5536 4244; www.tweedcoolangatta.com.au. Note: although the town is in New South Wales, Telstra insists it has the Queensland prefix of 07. Open Mon–Sat (daily during peak holiday periods).

> 🛏 As Tweed (NSW) and Coolangatta (QLD) merge together, further accommodation listings for the area can be found on p. 267. **Blue Pelican Motel $$$** 115 Wharf St; tel: (07) 5536 1777.

EN ROUTE

The World Heritage Rainforest Centre, at the corner of Pacific Hwy and Alma St in Murwillumbah (tel: 6672 1340, free) has a small theatre and exhibition covering the area's natural history – this is also a good place to go for information on the local National Parks. Open Mon–Sat 0900–1630, Sun 0930–1600. Nearby is Mount Warning. For most of the year, this is the first place where the sun hits Australia in the morning. The park entrance is at Breakfast Creek, 12 km south-west of Murwillumbah off the Kyogle Rd. There are two well-signposted tracks. One is a magnificent if steep walk leading to the summit through a range of vegetation. There are resting points along the way, and the 360-degree view from the summit is truly remarkable. The other, the Lyrebird Trail, only takes 15 mins and leads to an elevated platform within the rainforest. Beyond Mt Warning lies the World Heritage Border Ranges National Park.

Matilda Motel $$$ 108 Kennedy Dr.; tel: (07) 5536 7211. In tropical setting off the highway.

River Retreat Caravan Park $$ 8 Philp Pde, South Tweed; tel: (07) 5524 2700. Quiet location, in peaceful setting.

Tweed Billabong Holiday Park $$ Holden St, Tweed Heads South; tel: (07) 5524 2444. Saltwater billabong surrounded by cabins, with recreation facilities.

Tweed Fairways Motel $$ Cnr Pacific Hwy and Scoorley St; tel: (07) 5524 2111. The largest budget resort on the Tweed coast, with a range of accommodation from dorms to suites.

🍴 **Fisherman's Cove $$$** Calypso Resort, Griffith St; tel: (07) 5536 7073. A a carte menu specialising in BBQ fresh local seafood and grain-fed steaks.

Memory Manor $$ 106 Riverside Dr., Tumbulgum; tel: (02) 6676 6350. Open Tues–Sun, lunch only.

Mother Nature's Bush Tucker $$ 75 Upper Duroby Creek Rd, North Tumbulgum (get directions from the Tweed Visitor Centre or the Post Office, or you'll get lost); tel: (07) 5590 9826. After a walk through the surrounding bush, you can buy a kit of 20 local native bush food plants before tea and scones.

Tweed Heads Chinese Restaurant $$ 103 Wharf St; tel: (07) 5536 5077. The exterior of the building is designed like a Chinese temple.

COOLANGATTA / GOLD COAST

Coolangatta, over the border in Queensland, is the gateway to a 70-km strip of seaside gaudiness and gaiety behind which are places of natural peace and tranquillity. Surfers Paradise and the Gold Coast are together the Blackpool, the Venice Beach, the Coney Island of Australia. Seaside holiday cottages were already beginning to appear at the end of the 19th century; the railway connection in 1903 gave the place a further boost, and interest surged in the 1970s and '80s. If you like your holidays brash and booming this is the place, where the young come to celebrate leaving school and where the elderly come to wallow in the sunshine.

Coolangatta is quieter and more family-oriented than Surfers Paradise, although it too has its share of high-rise buildings and activity. The town has been called the twin of Tweed Heads, because the two towns merge together and are only divided by Boundary St. On the south side of the street is Tweed Heads in New South Wales and on the north side is Coolangatta in Queensland. Summertime gets especially confusing when New South Wales puts its clocks back an hour while Queensland remains on EST.

There are more beaches here than you could reasonably explore, 14–35 of them, and they are all protected year-round by full-time lifeguards. The Gold Coast City Council patrols more beaches than any other local authority in Australia, using helicopters, boats, jet-skis and watercraft to make the beaches safe for families.

Although Surfers Paradise (see p. 268) is the pulsating heart and unofficial capital of the Gold Coast, there is plenty of activity apart from the sand and surf, including the beautiful hinterland and several big theme parks.

Dreamworld, on the Dreamworld Pkwy, Coomera (www.dreamworld.com.au), claims the fastest, tallest ride in the world, the Tower of Terror, with other rides to make you scream. It also has a small koala sanctuary and an IMAX theatre. Open daily 1000–1700 (Main St, Plaza Restaurant and Koala Country open an hour earlier). Tel: 5588 1111.

Movie World, on the Pacific Hwy, Oxenford (www.movieworld.com.au), is run by Warner Bros, but doesn't operate as a full studio, although some movie-making does go on there. Instead, it has the country's only suspended looping coaster called … Lethal Weapon. Open daily; rides and attractions operate 1000–1700; tel: 5573 8485.

The Gold Coast airport is at Coolangatta, and from here you can enjoy flights over the area. East Coast Tourist Shuttle run regular buses to and from the airport and around the Gold Coast including the theme parks; tel: 5574 5111. The main Transit Centre is located on Beach Rd in the centre of Surfers Paradise – in the terminal there is a budget accommodation agent who will also organise a free pickup to certain accommodation.

Nearby, also on the Pacific Hwy, Oxenford, **Wet'n'Wild** offers watery excitement, including 1-m waves, slides and shoots. There are pleasant grassy areas around the assorted pools where you can picnic and barbecue. Open most days of the year from 1000–1700 (closing times vary); tel: 5573 2255; see www.wetnwild.com.au.

Exploring the country behind the Gold Coast is a delight only half an hour's drive away. Just north of the Gold Coast airport, on the Gold Coast Hwy, you will find the **Currumbin Sanctuary** ($$$), tel: 5534 1266. This parkland is full of Australian wildlife and you can explore it by miniature train. Twice a day, when they feed the lorikeets, the birds come down in massive flocks and positively submerge the spectators. Open daily 0800–1700. **The David Fleay Wildlife Park** on West Burleigh Rd, run by the Queensland Parks and Wildlife Service, is set in a beautiful natural setting and has a range of Australian animals, including platypus ($$$). Open daily 0900–1700; tel: 5576 2411.

Most of the hinterland is made up of National Parks, with some excellent walks and views. The **Queensland Parks and Wildlife Information Centre** (1711 Gold Coast Hwy, Burleigh Heads, tel: 5535 3032; open daily) has masses of information available on all the parks. **Mt Tamborine**, 30 minutes' drive north-west from Surfers Paradise, provides some breathtaking views of the Great Dividing Range. Villages with teahouses and galleries are located nearby. **Lamington National Park**, a 30-min drive south-west from Surfers Paradise, has 160 km of walking tracks leading through the park which offers some spectacular scenery and views. It is not a tough park to explore and you can select the extent of your exploration to suit your fitness and the time available.

i **Gold Coast Tourism Bureau Information Centre** Shop 14B Coolangatta Pl., cnr Warner and Griffith Sts; tel: (07) 5536 7765. Open daily, closes 1400 at weekends.
Gold Coast Bulletin: www.gcbulletin.com.au.
www.goldcoasttourism.com.au.

The Gold Coast is somewhat different from the rest of Australia. Apartments feature in a major way and are typically taken by families – or groups of young people – by the week. Resorts are not the all-encompassing types found in other countries but do include a swimming pool, restaurants, bars and other facilities within the complex.
Beach House Seaside Resort $$$$ 58 Marine Pde; tel: (07) 5536 7466. Located by the beach with good facilities.
Coolangatta Ocean View Motel $$$ cnr Clarke St and Marine Pde; tel: (07) 5536 3722. In the centre of town, opposite Twin Towns Club.
Coolangatta YHA $–$$ 230 Coolangatta Rd; tel: (07) 5536 7644; www.yha.com.au/hostels. Close to the beach.
Kirra Beach Motel $$ Marine Pde; tel: (07) 5536 3311. Standard facilities but good value for money.
Sunset Strip Budget Resort $$ 199–203 Boundary St: tel: (07) 5599 5517. Good-value resort with pool sundeck, also backpackers' accommodation, located near beaches and shops.

TO Catering for the mass tourist trade does not, by and large, lead to high culinary standards, but you will never starve – and there are dozens of places on practically every street.
The Aztec $$$ 1st Floor Food Court, Showcase Building, Marine Pde; tel: 5599 2748. Mexican restaurant with a good atmosphere, open daily.

The Castle Theatre Restaurant $$$$ 412 Coolangatta Rd;
tel: 5534 3455. Dine in medieval style, before watching a live
interactive show of comedy and special effects.
Earth 'n' Sea $$$ Marine Pde; tel: 5536 3477. Part of a small
Queensland chain of pizza and pasta restaurants. BYO.
Mr Cheung Chinese $$ 146 Griffith St; tel: 5599 5525. Offers
all-you-can-eat from 16-dish buffet. Simple; good value.

SURFERS PARADISE

Surfers Paradise boasts 300 days of sunshine a year and the sea is never too cold for swimming, the beach never too hot for sunbathing. The first Western residents were probably
two loggers, Edmund Harper and William Duncan, who lived in a hut opposite what is
now Wharf Rd. Today's Gold Coast population is somewhere around 400,000, with a large
proportion residing in Surfers Paradise, and is increasing by approximately 6 per cent each
year. In holiday times it can be unbearably overcrowded. It is brassy, brash, vibrant and,
strangely, does not feel at all Australian. Japanese tourists view it with amazement – and
have acquired a large percentage of the real estate and hotel rooms. You either love it or
hate it: for some Australians it is a place of annual pilgrimage.

The site was known to the Aboriginal people as Kurrungul (after the hardwood used to
make boomerangs), and **Cascade Gardens**, south of town by the Gold Coast Hwy, is said
to have been one of the meeting places for Aborigines from as far away as Maryborough.
In 1923, James Cavill of Brisbane paid $80 for land on which he built the Surfers Paradise
Hotel; years later the area was renamed, mainly through his efforts, Surfers Paradise.

In the 1960s and '70s large residential tracts were developed by the 'white shoe brigade' –
Queensland business people who wear white buckskin slip-ons, trendily scuffed, with no
socks so that you can admire their brown ankles. Their great belief is that every spare piece
of land should have a high-rise. Thus we have the remarkable spectacle of the beach at
Surfers Paradise, where the high-rises block out the sun during the day. The high-pressure
sales techniques used to sell these developments as summer homes took their toll when the
Asian downturn came and apartment blocks were defaulting on their mortgages. Yet there
are signs that the tide is turning. Locals are beginning to want to attract upmarket overseas
visitors, and the new message is that Surfers Paradise is more than sun, sand and sex.

Surfers Paradise was well named, and several major international championships are held
here. Most years more than 5000 competitors congregate here to fight for the national surf
life-saving titles. **Gold Coast Surfing School** (tel: 1800 787 337) is a safety-accredited surfing school, giving 2-hr lessons. Most people manage to stand on the surfboards after the
first lesson. You can see live surfing on the internet at www.coastalwatch.com.au.

One of the main attractions at **Sea World** is a waterski spectacular claimed to be Australia's longest-running live show. It is quite remarkably well done. On the other hand, Dolphin Cove may be 'the world's most environmentally friendly, natural lagoon habitat' but it doesn't really compare with the experience of seeing dolphins wild and free, as you can in many other places in Australia. In Shark Encounter, divers hand-feeding sharks, rays and giant groupers is pretty exciting and you can get very close to a variety of fish.

The park also contains a scary corkscrew ride and Australia's first monorail system (far better than the one in Sydney). Sea World is located on Sea World Dr., Main Beach; tel: 5588 2205; www.seaworld.com.au. Open daily 1000–1700 ($$$$).

> ℹ️ **Gold Coast Tourism Bureau Information Centre**
> Cavill Walk; tel: 5538 4419; www.verygc.com. Open daily, closes 1600 Sun. The telephone code is 07.

> 🛏️ **British Arms International Backpackers Resort**
> **YHA $–$$$** 70 Seaworld Dr.; tel: 5571 1776 or 1800 680 269; www.britisharms.com.au. Has its own pub on the premises. Free pickup from transit centre.
> **Candlelight Holiday Apartments $$$** 22–23 Leonard Ave; tel: 5538 1277. Budget rates.
> **Silver Sands Motel $$$** cnr Markwell Ave and Gold Coast Hwy; tel: 5538 6041. Clean motel with pool and spa.
> **Sleeping Inn Surfers Backpacking Resort and Apartments $–$$** 26 Whelan St; tel: 5592 4455; www.sleepinginn.com.au. Very clean, small resort, good value.
> **Surfers Paradise Backpackers Resort $–$$$** 2837 Gold Coast Highway; tel: 5592 4677; www.surfersparadisebackpackers. com.au. Bit outside the centre of Surfers but with great facilities.

> 🍴 **Malones $$$** Shop 306, Paradise Centre; tel: 5592 6066. Open 24 hrs serving a range of dishes from fish to pasta.
> **Melby's on the Park $$$** 46 Cavill Ave; tel: 5592 6922. Inexpensive café, popular with local people.
> **Nicolini's $$$** 3106 Gold Coast Hwy; tel: 5539 0884. Italian restaurant, licensed and BYO.

WHERE NEXT?

Surfers Paradise is a tiny and unrepresentative corner of Queensland. Beyond Brisbane *(see p. 275), Hwy 1 continues up the coast to the wilds of Cape York (see p. 351).*

Cross the border into Queensland and you could be forgiven for thinking that you were in another country. In *Australian Accent* (1958), John Douglas Pringle wrote: 'Australians themselves have a saying that when a stranger arrives in Perth, the first question he is asked is, "Where do you come from?"; in Adelaide, "What church do you belong to?"; in Melbourne, "What school were you at?"; in Sydney, "How much money have you got?"; while in Brisbane they merely say, "Come and have a drink".'

Flippant, but it contains a basic truth. Brash, self-confident, laid-back are all terms which can be applied to Queensland, but it is a huge region whose contrasts are also huge. Queensland covers more than 20 per cent of Australia and extends from the arid wastes of the Simpson Desert to lush rainforest, and from the coral cays of the Great Barrier Reef to the cosmopolitan and stylish capital, Brisbane.

Almost all the 3 million inhabitants live in the south-east corner, which leaves the rest of the state fairly empty except for the odd farming village and the occasional anomaly like the mining city of Mount Isa. But any population at all to speak of is a recent phenomenon: as late as 1845 the whole region (which was then still an extension of New South Wales) held only 1599 settlers. What changed this was timber. Sailing ships could berth quite high up the Tweed, Nerang and Coomera rivers (farming has since lowered the levels) to transport the logs of precious cedar that once grew here in abundance. Farmers followed, and Queensland has properties and stations – farms and ranches – bigger than any others in the world. There are farms as big as some European countries. Queensland's agriculture is based around beef and sugar. The cattle are continually moved around from the dry areas to the green areas, so on country roads you need to keep an eye out for the road trains which come barrelling along at ferocious speeds laden with cattle. Cane fields cover the river flats and take up most of the countryside for 1400 km from Nambour to Mossman. The sheer extent of the industry is awe-inspiring, the more so when you know that once all this cane was cut by hand.

It is not just agriculture which is on a big scale. The Selwyn Range holds one of the world's richest deposits of silver, copper, lead and zinc. To deal with this, Mount Isa, the city of the outback, was created (see p. 358).

QUEENSLAND

To get Queensland into perspective, think of it as three roughly parallel strips. That great natural wonder, the Great Barrier Reef, shadows the coastline 100 km out to sea; then there is the coastal strip itself, with its endless beaches. Inland, still running roughly parallel, is the Great Dividing Range, and on the other side of the range is the outback. The outback extends forever. In the north, towards the Gulf of Carpentaria, is the Gulf Country. This is good cattle country but in the wet season some of the smaller towns and homesteads are cut off for weeks.

The rugged challenge of the far north and the phenomenal expanse of the outback are treasured experiences, but in truth, most visitors only make short forays inland, perhaps up to the Atherton Tablelands and Kuranda (see p. 342) – the perfect beaches and the Great Barrier Reef beyond (see p. 316) are so utterly seductive.

It would be wrong to introduce Queensland without mentioning the rule of Joh Bjelke-Peterson, which ran from the early 1970s to the late 1980s. It was generally accepted in the rest of Australia that Joh was as mad as a cut snake and somewhat to the right of Genghis Khan. His government disagreed with the rest of Australia on human rights, rainforest conservation, Aboriginal land rights and censorship, but he led the state to great economic success. In 1977 his abolition of death duties led to waves of Australians – probably around a million – moving into Queensland from other states to take advantage of this new law. Queensland land developers later mounted a massive campaign for Joh to become prime minister of Australia. It failed. Joh died in April 2005, and speakers at his state funeral managed to avoid mention of the corruption allegations that finally drove him from office.

QUEENSLAND: OUR CHOICE

Surfers Paradise
Currumbin Sanctuary

Brisbane
Queensland Cultural
Centre, Lone Pine Koala
Sanctuary

Noosa

Fraser Island

Hervey Bay
Whale watching

Rockhampton
Dreamtime Cultural
Centre

Great Barrier Reef
Heron Island, sailing in the
Whitsundays, diving and
snorkelling throughout

Townsville
Reef HQ

Hinchinbrook Island

Cairns
Kuranda Scenic Railway

Atherton Tablelands

Port Douglas

Daintree National Park
Cape Tribulation

Cape York

Undara Lava Tubes

Longreach
Australian Stockman's Hall
of Fame

**Carnarvon National
Park**
Aboriginal rock art

HOW MUCH YOU CAN SEE IN A ...

WEEKEND (2 DAYS)

If arriving in Brisbane, spend a day at the Queensland Cultural Centre and a day in the Surfers Paradise area, either on quiet beaches south of the high-rise strip or at Currumbin Sanctuary.

If arriving in Cairns, one day ride the Kuranda Scenic Railway past rainforests and waterfalls to Kuranda, then spend the evening on the Cairns Esplanade and Pier. Next day, take a snorkelling trip to the Great Barrier Reef from Marlin Marina (or travel north to trendy Port Douglas and visit the reef from there). Alternatively, spend a couple of days stretched out on a beach; those on the Sunshine Coast – the best known of which is Noosa – are easily accessible.

WEEK (7 DAYS)

Select a portion of the coast, either Brisbane–Rockhampton (for visits to the Sunshine Coast, Fraser Island and Hervey Bay), or Rockhampton–Townsville (southern Barrier Reef islands, Eungella National Park, Whitsundays) or Townsville–Cairns (Hinchinbrook Island, Atherton Tablelands, Port Douglas, Daintree National Park).

MORE THAN A WEEK

With more time, you can add to coastal explorations a visit to the outback. In the subtropics, try a journey through Carnarvon National Park to Longreach. In the tropics, try overlanding to Cape York or going due west through the Gulf Country (dry season only for travel in tropical Queensland).

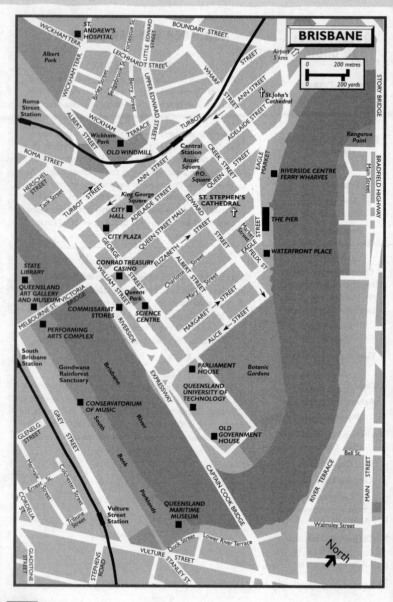

Brisbane is the third largest city in Australia but it is unlike any other. It is not big as cities go – the population is somewhere over 1.6 million – but it has the style, the presence, and the ambience of an international centre. It is possible to date exactly when this happened. Before the 1980s Brisbane was a very pleasant place but it was inward-looking, perhaps a trifle parochial. Then two events changed this for ever and for the better. In 1982 it smartened itself up for the Commonwealth Games, but then came Expo '88, and Brisbane totally reinvented itself. Buildings were refurbished, restaurants opened, and the whole South Bank, which had been an ugly warehouse and

LAND RIGHTS

As the free settlers spread out into Queensland they took by force and fraud the land belonging to the Aboriginal people. At the time Queensland probably had 100,000 Aboriginal people and they fought fiercely against this white incursion. They lost. By the turn of the century they had been run off their lands, decimated and were made to live in reserves. Only in the past few years have more enlightened policies arisen, with control of the reserves passing to the Aboriginal people. However, the government insists on hanging on to the right of prospecting or mining. The white governments of Australia have much to be ashamed of, and Queensland, perhaps, more than most.

industrial area opposite the centre of the city, was brought back to life. Brisbane became one of the most exciting cities in Australia.

All this, of course, is a far cry from its penal colony beginnings. In 1824 the governor of New South Wales sent Lt Miller to establish a penal settlement up the coast. He set it up originally at Redcliffe Point on Moreton Bay but soon moved it to a more favoured riverside position south of what is now Brisbane's business district. The settlement did not long remain a clutch of convict huts although the convicts were responsible for much of the new building work – the windmill in Wickham Terrace was built in 1828, the commissariat stores the next year. Despite these civilised additions it was still a convict town and by 1829 it was the largest penal settlement on the Australian mainland, with over 1000 convicts.

Free settlers began to arrive in numbers in 1837 and soon outnumbered the convicts. The penal settlement was abandoned in 1839 and the area was thrown open to free

QUEENSLAND

settlers in 1842. As Queensland's huge agricultural and mineral resources were developed, Brisbane grew into a prosperous city; in 1859 the state of Queensland separated from the colony of New South Wales, and Brisbane was declared its capital.

MUST SEE/DO IN BRISBANE

Check out Brisbane City Hall

Visit the Queensland Art Gallery

Explore the Queensland Museum

Cycle beside the Brisbane River

Wander through Mt Coot-tha Reserve and Brisbane Botanic Gardens

Picnic in Brisbane Forest Park

Cuddle a koala at Lone Pine Koala Sanctuary

Then everything started to happen in a hurry. In 1862 the present Government House was built and the telegraph to Sydney was connected in 1861. The city had tramways by 1875 and its first railway connection started operating in 1882. A century later the world was its oyster.

ARRIVAL AND DEPARTURE

Brisbane airport is about 15 km north-east of the city. Shuttle buses run to Brisbane's Transit Centre in Roma St approximately every 15 minutes (30 minutes after 1930), 0500–2245; tel: 3238 4700, $9 one way. The Airtrain runs between the airport and the city centre 0500–2100, $11 one way; continuing on to the Goldcoast (see p. 265), $20.

INFORMATION

TOURIST OFFICES **Brisbane Tourism Information Booth**, Queen St Mall; tel: 3006 6290. Maps, guides, tours and accommodation bookings, bus and theme-park tickets and car hire. Open daily.

Queensland Holiday Xperts, 30 Makerston St; tel: 13 88 32; www.qhx.com.au.

INTERNET ACCESS **Email Plus Internet Café,** 328 Upper Roma St; tel: 3236 0433. Close to most hostels, competitive rates. Open 0900–late daily.

Dialup Cyber Lounge, 126 Adelaide St; tel: 3211 9095. Open 1000–1800 daily.

INTERNET SITES   **Brisbane City Search:** brisbane.citysearch.com.au
Brisbane Stories: www.brisbane-stories.powerup.com.au
Brisbane Tourism: www.ourbrisbane.com

MONEY   Major branches of most banks can be found around Queen and Edward Sts. **Travelex Foreign Exchange** is located throughout the city; the most central is at Shop 56, Level E, Myer Centre, Queen St Mall; tel: 3221 9163. Open Mon–Fri 0900–1700, Sat 1000–1500.

POST AND PHONES   The main post office is at 261 Queen St. The telephone code for Brisbane and Queensland is 07.

ACCOMMODATION

Acacia Inner City Inn $$–$$$ 413 Upper Edward St; tel 3832 1663. Budget B&B accommodation, handy to city centre and attractions.

Annie's Shandon Inn $$$ 405 Upper Edward St; tel: 3831 8684. Five-minute walk to the city.

Balmoral House $$$ 33 Amelia St, Fortitude Valley; tel: 3252 1397. Close to Chinatown and restaurants.

Brisbane City Backpackers $–$$$ 380 Upper Roma St; tel: 3211 3221 or 1800 062 572; www.citybackpackers.com. Big friendly place near the YHA.

Brisbane City YHA $–$$$ 392 Upper Roma St; tel: 3236 1004; www.yha.com.au/hostels. Superb, respectable hostel catering for everyone. Within the Central Business District.

Explorers Inn $$$ 63 Turbot St; tel: 3211 3488; e-mail: explorer@powerup.com.au. Centrally located three-star hotel.

Goodearth Hotel $$$$ 345 Wickham Terrace; tel: 3831 6177; e-mail: stay@goodearth.com.au. Excellent views, stylish hotel.

Hotel George Williams Y $$$ 317–325 George St; tel: 3308 0700; e-mail: hgw@ymca.org.au. Centrally located YMCA hotel.

Kookaburra Inn $$–$$$ 41 Phillips St; tel: 3832 1303 or 1800 733 533; www.kookaburra-inn.com.au. Just outside town centre, quiet surrounds, shared facilities, good value.

Palace Backpackers $$ cnr Ann and Edward Sts; tel: 3211 2433 or 1800 676 340; www.palacebackpackers.com. Has 350 rooms, bar, restaurant and café. Big and central, popular with younger travellers.

Tourist Guest House $$–$$$ 555 Gregory Terrace, Fortitude Valley; tel: 3252 4171; www.touristguesthouse.com. Country-style building in a leafy setting. Close to pubs, clubs and restaurants.

FOOD AND DRINK

Brisbane has numerous cafés and restaurants. **Southbank** and the riverside around **Eagle St** offer several upmarket establishments, while **Chinatown** and **Fortitude Valley** offer numerous cheap eats from around the world.

Café San Marco $$ South Bank; tel: 3846 4334. Mediterranean cuisine with the stunning city skyline across the Brisbane River. Open daily for breakfast, lunch and dinner.

Govinda's Vegetarian Restaurant $ 99 Elizabeth St; tel: 3210 0255. Open for lunch Mon–Sat, dinner Fri, closed Sun. All-you-can-eat menu, excellent value.

Il Centro $$$$ 1 Eagle St Pier; tel: 3221 6090. Lunch Sun–Fri, dinner daily. Licensed. Excellent Italian cuisine, at a price.

Michael's Restaurant $$$$ Riverside Centre, 123 Eagle St; tel: 3832 5522. Owned by famous Australian chef. Licensed, probably the best in Brisbane – expensive.

Mondos Organics $$$$ 166 Hardgrave Rd, West End; tel: 3844 1132. Only organic ingredients are used to create mouth-watering dishes. Lunch and dinner Tues–Sat, brunch Sat–Sun.

Oshin $$$$ 256 Adelaide St; tel: 3229 0410. Lunch Mon–Fri, dinner Mon–Sat. Licensed. Japanese food.

Pepe's Mexican Restaurant $$$ Baroona Rd, Milton; tel: 3369 6726. Busy Mexican restaurant with Spanish/Flamenco guitar.

Plough Inn Tavern $ Stanley St, South Bank Parklands; tel: 3844 7777. Excellent-value food where you buy uncooked meat and barbecue it yourself – fun if not unusual. Open daily.

Squirrels of Newmarket $$$ 184 Enoggera Rd; tel: 3856 0966. Good-value vegetarian restaurant. Closed Mon, Tues.

Three Monkeys Coffee and Tea House $$ 58 Mollison St; tel: 3844 6045. Unusual café, with games and chessboards for you to play over your coffee and cake or light meal.

Tibetan Kitchen $$ 454 Brunswick St, New Farm; tel: 3358 5906. Decorated in vibrant colours, exciting menu.

GETTING AROUND

The compact city centre, which focuses on the pedestrianised Queen St, is built along and between the looping meanders of the Brisbane River, so exploring on foot is perfectly practical.

While there are several bridges, a more enjoyable means of getting between banks is by the ferries. The CityCat runs all the way from the University to Bretts Wharf every 30 minutes, stopping at numerous interesting places along the way. If you stay on for the whole journey, it becomes an inexpensive alternative to a formal cruise.

ON YOUR BIKE

One interesting and healthy way of touring the city is by bike. There are 350 km of bike paths in Brisbane. Your hotel/hostel can supply further details on bike hire. Valet Cycle Hire and Tours (tel: 0408 003 198) delivers bikes to you, $30 half day, $40 full day or hire by the hour from the main gate to the Botanic Gardens in Alice St.

The Loop is a free bus service that circles Brisbane's Central Business District. Stops include Central Station, Queen Street Mall, City Botanic Gardens, Riverside Centre, Queensland University of Technology and King George Square. Brisbane has several fleets of taxis; Black and White Taxis (tel: 13 10 08) are one of the largest. Brisbane City Council runs the **City Sights Bus Tour** and a $20 day-ticket allows you to take in most of the sights – you can hop on and off as you please. Buses run every 45 mins 0900–1545; tel: 13 12 30.

HIGHLIGHTS

There are innumerable interesting places to visit in the city, but an integral part of its charm is its brightness, space and sunshine. Brisbane is very much an open, accessible city, partly because of the river, which meanders with a charming lack of logic. Its sinuous curves impart a pleasing shape to the city. Some of Brisbane's individual style also comes from the unique tropical Queensland domestic architecture which still abounds. The traditional bungalow on stilts, with timber walls, lattice screens, shutters and corrugated iron roofing, is eminently functional in a warm, wet climate; it also looks great. For a while it looked as though the developers would knock every single example down and replace them with modern housing, but at last the local authorities and the people of the city have realised how perfect this architecture is for the climate and the move now is to restoration rather than demolition.

City Hall, overlooking King George Sq, Adelaide St, was built between 1920 and 1930 and contains a circular concert hall with seating for 1500. Its style is Italian

QUEENSLAND

There is a marked Heritage Trail starting from City Hall, which features colonial landmarks and scenic views. Obtain maps from Brisbane Museum gift shop.

Renaissance modified – that is, Queensland marble, granite and native timbers were used in its construction. Modern skyscrapers now surround it as if to ward off intruders, but the observation platform on the clock tower – there is a lift part of the way – still has panoramic views of the city and the countryside around. City Hall also houses the Museum of Brisbane on the ground floor. Tel: 3403 8888 for information.

The Gothic-style old **St Stephen's** on Elizabeth St was built in 1850 and is the oldest church in Brisbane. Open daily 0800–1800. There is a gift shop and a café (tel: 3224 3111). **St John's Cathedral** on Ann St is also an excellent piece of architecture.

The Old Windmill has an interesting history, and you can inspect the grounds. It was originally built by convict labour in 1828, but due to an error in design (by Captain Patrick Logan, an infamous prison warden who was later murdered but not for this error) it never worked properly. Later it became a punishment centre and convicts were used to make the mill wheels turn. A Quaker mission in 1836 complained of the cruelty of making the prisoners work 14-hour shifts on the mill without rest periods. It was later used as a fire lookout station and a meteorological observatory, and in 1934 it was used for Australia's first experimental TV broadcasts. The Old Windmill is in Wickham Terrace, just north of the city centre.

The **Commissariat Stores** at 115 William St on North Quay was one of the first permanent buildings in Brisbane. It was built by convicts in 1829 on what was the town's original wharf. Inside are three floors of displays including Aboriginal and convict relics, artefacts, costumes, furniture and paintings. It also houses the offices of the Royal Historical Society of Queensland. Open Tues–Sun 1000–1600 ($); tel: 3221 4198.

Parliament House, on the corner of George and Alice Sts, was built in 1868 in the style of the French Renaissance. There are some stunning chandeliers and magnificent coffered ceilings. Free guided tours run Mon–Fri between 0930–1600; Sat–Sun between 1000 and 1400, unless Parliament is in session. Tel: 3406 7562.

Opposite, in Alice St, are the **Botanic Gardens**, stretching alongside the river. The gardens were designed in 1855 by Walter Hill. There are free tours at 1100 and 1300 Mon–Sat, leaving from the information kiosk, but the gardens are open 24 hrs if you want to wander around solo. Tel: 3403 8888 for further details. On the edge of the gardens, among one of the Queensland University of Technology's campuses, is **Old Government House**, built in 1862 as the state governor's residence and now housing the headquarters of the National Trust. Open Mon–Fri 0830–1630; tel: 3229 1788. Queensland's first Government House, built in 1853, is now the deanery for the Anglican cathedral.

Across the Victoria Bridge is one of the landmarks of the city. The **Queensland Cultural Centre** covers two blocks on either side of Melbourne St on the south bank of the river, and contains the Queensland Art Gallery, the Queensland Museum, the State Library and a performing arts complex. Each of these is well worth investigating.

The **Queensland Art Gallery** has excellent collections of Australian art, paintings, sculpture, prints and ceramics. It also has some lesser French, European, Asian and English works, antique furniture, silver, glassware and pottery. There are also frequent travelling exhibitions to keep the place on its toes. Free, open daily 1000–1700; tel: 3840 7303. In the **Queensland Museum** is a vast range of exhibits relating to anthropology, geology, zoology, history and technology. Free (although charges apply to special exhibitions); open daily 0930–1700; tel: 3840 7555/7635.

Next to the Cultural Centre and incorporating the old South Brisbane dry dock is the **Queensland Maritime Museum**, which has some exquisitely made models showing the maritime history of the area as well as the steam tug *Forceful*. You can also take a look around the ex-warship HMAS *Diamantina*, which is moored in the outside dock. Open daily 0930–1630 ($$); tel: 3844 5361.

The **South Bank Parklands** are 17 ha of landscaped park, rainforest, and a beach facing onto the Brisbane River. The whole area is well served with cafés – well over a dozen – plus a tavern. Within the park in **Stanley Street Plaza** there is a Visitor Information Centre, tel: 3867 2051. You can take a walk through a small rainforest, or by the riverside which takes you past some interesting sights, including a **Nepalese Pagoda** and **Streets Beach** holding five Olympic swimming pools of water (patrolled by lifeguards). There is also a cinema complex.

OUTSIDE THE CENTRE

Newstead House is Brisbane's oldest surviving residence and is set in parkland on Breakfast Creek, Newstead, on the northern outskirts. The house was built in 1846 for Patrick Leslie and has been restored and appropriately furnished ($. Open Mon–Fri 1000–1600, Sun 1400–1700; tel: 3216 1846).

Lone Pine Koala Sanctuary is the oldest, the largest and perhaps the best of the Australian wildlife parks. You can see crocodiles, dingoes, Tasmanian (Tassie) devils, kookaburras, koalas and kangaroos. It is only 11 km from the city on the banks of the Brisbane River at Jesmond Rd, Fig Tree Pocket ($$$. Open daily 0730–1700; tel: 3378 1366). **Mirimar Cruises** has a vessel going to Lone Pine leaving North Quay daily at 1000; tel: 3221 0300.

Ghost Tours ($$$) run most days covering areas such as Boggo Road Gaol and Toowong Cemetery; there

---

Mt Coot-tha

Mt Coot-tha is the best place to get an overall view of the city. It is only 8 km west of the centre but on a clear day you can see across Brisbane to the islands out at sea, and the Glasshouse Mountains which lie to the north. There are well-signposted walks around Mt Coot-tha and its foothills, and at its foot are Botanic Gardens and the Sir Thomas Brisbane Planetarium, the largest in Australia $$. Tel: 3403 2578, programmes Tues–Sun.

---

are even some sleepovers in spooky places. The guides are extremely knowledgeable regarding the city's heritage – not for the faint-hearted! Tel: 3844 6606; www.ghost-tours.com.au, e-mail: enquiries@ghost-tours.com.au.

SHOPPING

Queen Street Mall runs for two blocks from Edward St to George St and is the main shopping centre of the city, with shops cheaper than those in Melbourne or Sydney. There are also numerous shopping opportunities around the inner suburbs. In **Chinatown** you will find Chinese herbalists, oriental kitchenware and oriental delicacies.

Brisbane has the climate and the style for markets, of which there are several. Perhaps the best are the arts and crafts **Brunswick Market** in Brunswick St, Fortitude Valley, on Sat–Sun 0800–1600, and **Riverside Market** in Eagle St which runs all day Sun. The **South Bank Market** runs Fri night, Sat afternoon and Sun all day. **Cleveland Bayside Markets** are open Sun 0800–1500 and are held in Bloomfield St, Cleveland, on the bay.

NIGHTLIFE

Within the Cultural Centre, the **Queensland Performing Arts Complex** has a concert hall, two theatres and an auditorium which seats 4700 people (tel: 3846 4444). Concerts are also held at the City Hall (tel: 3403 8888).

The Renaissance-style Treasury Building near Victoria Bridge on the north bank of the river houses Brisbane's 24-hr casino. There is live music daily; tel: 3306 8888 for further details. **Caxton Street Precinct**, on the eastern edge of the city, is home to several popular nightspots including Hotel LA, Casablanca and the Caxton Hotel.

DAY TRIPS

The most obvious day trips are out to the islands. At the mouth of the Brisbane River lies Moreton Bay, where there is a plethora of islands. Of these the two most important are Moreton and Stradbroke.

Moreton Island (named after James Douglas, Earl of Morton, but sadly they got his name slightly wrong) is only 40 km from Brisbane. Most of the 19,260 ha of this sand island – beaten only in size by Fraser Island (see p. 301) – is national park, and boasts what is probably the highest sand dune in the world in Mt Tempest (280 m). There is daily access from Holt St Wharf on the *Tangalooma Flyer* or *Tangalooma Jet* (a 75-minute boat ride). Do not bother taking a car. It is far better to select one of the tours of the island which start and end in Brisbane. If you decide to stay the night in the **Tangalooma Wild Dolphin Resort** ($$$$, tel: 1300 652 250) you will get the opportunity to hand-feed the wild dolphins that come to the shore each evening.

North Stradbroke Island is 20 km off the coast and so about 35 km from Brisbane. It is another sand island, and on weekdays outside the holiday period is very quiet and peaceful. A largely untouched and untouristy nature reserve, it has seven world-class surf beaches, inland lakes, rugged headlands and secluded coves. Point Lookout, at the north-east tip of the island, has some of the best beaches, and you can often see dolphins from the headland. Again, although you can take your car it is better to go there on a tour. You can get information from the Stradbroke Island Visitors' Centre which is near the ferry terminal at Dunwich; tel: 3409 9555.

There are several **National Parks** and areas of natural beauty in the vicinity. The Visitor Information Centre can supply further details. **Rob's Rainforest Tours** run excellent-value tours to a range of national parks, all of which include a walk in a rainforest and lunch; tel: 0409 496 607; e-mail: frogbus7@hotmail.com.

WHERE NEXT?

A short trip inland to Toowoomba (see p. 284) will show you a different side of southern Queensland. North lie miles of beaches and resorts and increasingly tropical towns such as Townsville and Cairns (see pp. 325 and 336), while offshore from Bundaberg is the southern tip of the wondrous Great Barrier Reef (see p. 316).

TOOWOOMBA AND THE DARLING DOWNS

Most visitors coming to Queensland rarely head into the interior. In doing this they miss much of what Queensland is about. The coast and the Great Barrier Reef are the great tourist attractions but inland lies a great agricultural state with much to offer. On the far side of the Great Dividing Range are the Darling Downs, whose rolling plains are some of the most fertile agricultural land in Australia.

Toowoomba, on the rim of the mountain range, is Queensland's largest inland city and the commercial centre for the Darling Downs. The town has a very full cultural and social life with many galleries and museums. There are also several historical buildings and sites, and the area is full of pleasant scenic drives.

ARRIVAL AND DEPARTURE

You can fly to Toowoomba, but it is only 138 km from Brisbane, about 2 hrs by car or bus. The town is some 600–800 m above sea level, and from Brisbane the route is along the Warrego Highway which makes its way up the escarpment of the Great Dividing Range.

INFORMATION

City Information Centre, 476 Ruthven St; tel: (07) 4638 7555. Open Mon–Fri.
Toowoomba Visitor Information Centre, 86 James St; tel: (07) 4639 3797 or 1800 331 155. Open daily.

ACCOMMODATION

Allan Cunningham Motel $$$ 808 Ruthven St; tel: 4635 5466.
Applegum Inn $$$ 41 Margaret St; tel: 4632 2088.
Bridge St Motor Inn $$$ 291 Bridge St; tel: 4634 3299.
Burke & Wills Toowoomba Hotel $$$$ 554 Ruthven St; tel: 4632 2433.
Coachman Motel $$$ 4 Burnage St; tel: 4639 3707.
Downs Motel $$$ 669 Ruthven St; tel: 4639 3811.
Flying Spur Motel $$$ 277 Taylor St; tel: 4634 3237.
Garden City Motor Inn $$$ 718 Ruthven St; tel: 4635 5377.
Jacaranda Place Motor Inn $$$ 794 Ruthven St; tel: 4635 3111.

Raceview Motor Inn $$$ 52 Hursley Rd; tel: 4634 6777.
YWCA Gowrie House $–$$$ 112 Mary St; tel 4632 2642.
Nice old place; both men and women welcome.

FOOD AND DRINK

Banjo's, The Great Aussie Restaurant $$$ Ruthven St
South, cnr Hanna Crt; tel: 4636 1033.

Da Vinci's Italian Restaurant $$$ 22 Hill St. BYO. Tel: 4638
4606. Licensed.

Fibber Magee $$ 153 Margaret St; tel: 4639 2702.

Golden Dragon Chinese Restaurant $$ 250 Margaret St;
tel: 4638 1258.

La Pizzaiola $$$ 173 Margaret St; tel: 4632 2997.

Mexican Cantina $$$ 164 Margaret St; tel: 4638 1888.

Mr K's Restaurant $$$ 2 Burnage St; tel: 4639 1139.

Southern Bistro $$$ 839 Ruthven St; tel: 4635 3311.

Thai Cottage $$$ 160 Margaret St. BYO. Tel: 4632 2194.

HIGHLIGHTS

Toowoomba began life in 1849 as a village near an important staging post for teamsters and travellers. To be technically accurate, the first village was where the suburb of Drayton now exists, and Drayton and Toowoomba were once two separate settlements. Toowoomba was originally known as The Swamp, but the Aboriginals called it t'wamp bah or 'place of large stinging insects', which eventually was anglicised into Toowoomba.

The **town hall**, said to be the first in Queensland, was built in 1862, and because of Toowoomba's position as, effectively, the capital of the Darling Downs area, it quickly became a relatively wealthy city. By the turn of the 20th century this was reflected in the erection of several very solid Victorian buildings and the planting of shade trees in the streets, which are now such a distinguishing mark of the city.

WINDMILLS

A large foundry was established here in 1871, its main successful products being the Southern Cross and Simplex windmills which are such a feature of the landscape. These are not windmills in the old English and Dutch sense, but modern windmills which glisten in the sun and are mainly used to pump up water from underground sources.

QUEENSLAND

At the information office you can obtain a brochure suggesting a self-conducted tour around the remarkably elegant and charming buildings in the centre of the city.

The **Cobb & Co. Museum**, 27 Lindsay St, traces the history of horse-drawn vehicles in Australia. Although Cobb & Co. was originally an American company it had much to do with the development of Australia, and this museum, part of the Queensland Museum, covers not just the activities of the company but the whole subject of horse-drawn transportation in Australia. Of its kind it is the most comprehensive museum in Australia. Open daily 1000–1600, tel: 4639 1971.

The National Trust now owns the **Royal Bull's Head Inn** in Brisbane St, Drayton. This is appropriate because this well-preserved building was not just a pub; the first religious service on Darling Downs was held here in 1848, when the Revd Benjamin Glennie held a service in one of the rooms.

ON TO THE DOWNS

There are several scenic drives from Toowoomba, such as the 48-km circuit to Spring Bluff and Murphy's Creek, and the 100-km circuit to Heifer Creek, known as the Valley of the Sun.

Open Thur–Sun 1000–1600, tel: 4630 1869.

On the eastern side of the town is **Picnic Point Lookout**, which offers splendid views down to the Lockyer Valley. The park has a number of marked walking trails.

There are over 1000 ha of parkland within the city. The principal central ones are **Lake Annand**, **Laurel Bank**, **Queens** and **Webb Park**. Next to Queens Park are the **Botanical Gardens**, which are well worth visiting.

WHERE NEXT?

If you're keen to experience Queensland's vast outback, from Toowoomba go north-west to Dalby, then take either the Balonne Hwy to Cunnamulla or the Warrego Hwy to Charleville. The Mitchell and Landsborough Hwys will lead you north to the iconic outback town of Longreach – home of the Stockman's Hall of Fame and Outback Heritage Centre (www.outbackheritage.com.au). From Longreach, take the Capricorn Hwy back to Rockhampton (p. 308) and continue on the Brisbane–Cape York route.

LONG-DISTANCE ROUTE: BRISBANE TO CAPE YORK

Driving up the east coast of Australia, the great navigator's dictum – keep Australia on your left – springs to mind. The road from Brisbane to Cairns – which is Rte 1 but also goes by the all-Australian name of the Bruce Hwy – makes you do precisely that. If you deviate to the right you come very quickly to the South Pacific Ocean. If you deviate to the left you will see looming in front of you the Great Dividing Range.

The long distances – 750 km in a day is not considered extraordinary – are relatively easy because most roads are straight and there is little traffic joining the highway. That said, the journey right the way up to the northern tip of Australia is an extremely long one: 2750 km from Brisbane, and without crossing a state border. The following chapters deal with it in several stages, and depending on your schedule, your inclinations and the time of year, it will probably make sense to fly at least certain legs. All the stopping points have airports, and there is even a jet airport out on the Great Barrier Reef, on Hamilton Island.

The first stage north from Brisbane goes to Bundaberg, the 'rum capital', with Fraser Island an unmissable detour on the way. The Great Barrier Reef roughly parallels the coast from here right the way up to Cape York and beyond. Then it's on to Townsville, Australia's largest tropical city. From Townsville to Cairns, a distance of 350 km, there is not much to detain you on the seaward side apart from access to the reef, but a number of national parks and the Atherton Tableland are worth exploring.

Cairns and beyond is truly the Far North. Across the Daintree River the going gets tough. You can drive, if you have a four-wheel-drive vehicle and an experienced driver, via the controversial Daintree/Bloomfield Road. On that run, Cairns to Cooktown is about 212 km, but this road creates serious controversy because 32 km of it was slashed virtually parallel to the coast through virgin rainforest from Cape Tribulation to Bloomfield in 1984. The road cuts nearly 200 km off the trip from Cairns to Cooktown but arouses anger among conservationists.

On the other hand, you could try coming up the coastal track which is considered by many to be the worst road in Australia. This is only to be attempted with a four-wheel-drive vehicle – and then only in the dry.

Cooktown is also served by sea and air, with regular services available from Cairns.

BRISBANE — BUNDABERG
OTT Tables 9010/9085/9086

Service	🚌	🚌	🚌	🚆RAIL	🚌	🚆RAIL	🚌	🚌	🚌	🚆RAIL	🚆RAIL	🚆RAIL
Days of operation	Ⓐ	Daily	Daily	②⑥Ⓒ	Daily	ex⑥	Daily	Daily	Daily	ex⑥	①⑤	②
Special notes	H	F	C	AB	G	AD	E			AD	A	A
Brisbane.....................d.	....	0700	0745	0855	1000	1100	1300	1430	1600	1700	1825	1825
Maroochydore ....d.	....	0840			1200		1430	1600				
Noosa Heads................d.	....	0935			1300		1515	1640	1820			
Maryborough...............d.	0525	1345	1230	1407	....	1453	1905	1935	2110	2053	2230	2306
Hervey Bay ....a.	0623	1425	1310		....	1540	1945	2025	2150	2140		
Bundaberg ....a.	....	1640	1530	1542	....	1555	....	2200	....	2150	2335	0011

A–Trains stop at Maryborough West, free bus connection to Maryborough.
B–Conveys sleepers and car transporters and on ④⑦ also conveys Queenslander Class.
C–Additional services: 1200, 1930.
D–Connection to Hervey Bay is by bus.
E–Additional service: 1300.   E–Additional service: 1400.
G–Additional services: 0800, 0900, 1100, 1200, 1400, 1600.
H–Additional services: 0625Ⓐ, 0720, 0820Ⓐ, 0930ex⑦, 1020Ⓐ, 1120Ⓐ, 1205⑥⑦, 1220Ⓐ, 1320Ⓐ,
   1350⑥, 1420Ⓐ, 1520Ⓐ, 1550⑥⑦, 1620Ⓐ, 1720Ⓐ. These services operate Maryborough–
   Hervey Bay–Maryborough, journey time 1 hr 55 mins.

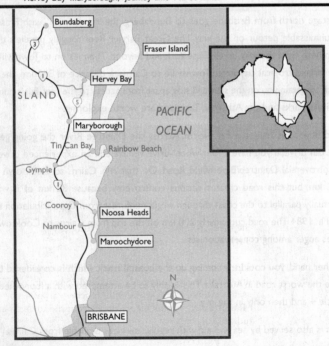

THE SUNSHINE COAST

This is where most of Australia wants to come to retire and a large percentage want to come and spend their holidays.

DRIVING ROUTE

Up to Maroochydore the highway runs through an almost totally built-up area – it is only where the highway swings slightly inland at Buderim that you get out of the busiest tourist belt. Maroochydore (100 km from Brisbane) is on a short detour which will carry you on through Bli Bli and Noosa Heads to rejoin the main highway at Cooroy. At Gympie an alternative to the direct road to Maryborough is to detour along the coast to Tin Can Bay and Rainbow Beach. From Maryborough it is a short (35 km) side route to Hervey Bay, the hopping-off point for Fraser Island, or 115 km through Childers to Bundaberg. Total journey approximately 400 km.

After the high-rise razzmatazz of the Gold Coast, the coastal scene north of Brisbane starts to calm down; by the time you get to Maroochydore things are much more civilised. Beyond the ribbon development, places such as Noosa Heads are all pastel colours and sunshine and trendy cafés, while offshore is Fraser Island, one of Australia's most amazing natural sites. Bundaberg, where Australia's rum comes from, is a lovely city with some considerable presence.

BRISBANE

See p. 274.

MAROOCHYDORE

Maroochydore caters for tourists in a serious way, but the countryside behind, the greenery and the long beaches more than make up for it. Until the tourist boom in the 1960s, Maroochydore was little more than a fly speck where paddle steamers could load up and then head off to Brisbane. A highlight in its history came in 1826 when a convict called John Graham escaped here from Moreton Bay, under the impression, allegedly, that he could row to China. He was adopted by the local Aboriginal people until 1833 when he gave himself up.

Maroochydore is lucky in its location: between the Maroochy and Mooloolah rivers, with green lushness in the hinterland, the mountains beyond and 25 km of beautiful beaches. The rivers provide safe swimming areas while the beaches can pick up an excellent surf. The **Blackall Range**, only half an hour's drive from the town, is an area full of arts and crafts studios.

The town extends into the Maroochy estuary with Pincushion Island as a pimple off the point. On the right-hand side of the peninsula Maroochydore Beach runs down to Alexandra Headland and **Mooloolaba**, 5 km to the south. The Wharf at Mooloolaba is less of a wharf and more of a shopping and restaurant centre, created in the style of a 19th-century fishing village. **Underwater World**, on Parkyn Parade, claims to be one of the largest tropical oceanariums in the southern hemisphere. Open daily 0900–1800 ($$$); tel: 5444 8488. Just outside Maroochydore, on the David Low Way (beside the Waterfront Hotel), is a replica of Captain Cook's ship the *Endeavour*. Although built to two-thirds scale, it gives a good impression of the ship in which Cook set off to explore the world. Open Sun–Thur 1000–1200 ($); tel: 5476 8391.

Cruise Maroochy $$ offers a series of different trips throughout the day along the Maroochy River; tel: 5476 5745. A few cruises also leave from the wharf in Mooloolaba, one of which is the MV *Mudjimba*; $$, tel: 5444 7477.

EN ROUTE

An appealing detour is to Kenilworth, which can be approached either from Eumundi (which has the largest outdoor market in Australia, every Sat) on the Bruce Hwy or from Nambour via Mapleton through the Obi Obi Valley – either route is picturesque. Activities include bushwalking, gem fossicking and creek fishing for freshwater mullet, bass, perch and cod. The **Ginger Factory** at Yandina is the largest ginger processing factory in the world. You are encouraged to buy samples at the end of your tour. Free; tel: 5446 7100. Maroochy Tourism and Travel can give further information on the area.

[i] **Maroochy Tourism and Travel**, cnr Sixth Ave and Melrose Pde; tel: 5479 1566; www.maroochytourism.com; e-mail: admin@maroochytourism.com. Open daily.

[accommodation] A lot of the accommodation can be found on or around Sixth Ave.
Beach Motor Inn $$$$ 61–65 Sixth Ave; tel: 5443 7044. Located near Maroochy Beach.
Maroochydore YHA Backpackers $–$$ 24 Schirmann Dr.; tel: 5443 3151; www.yha.com.au/hostels. Surrounded by leafy gardens, with pool and BBQ.
Maroochy Palms Holiday Village $$$ 319 Bradman Ave; tel: 5443 8611; e-mail: enquiries@maroochypalms.com. Four-star resort offering a range of accommodation from campsites to luxury villas.
Mooloolaba Backpackers Resort $–$$$$ 75–77 Brisbane Rd; tel; 5444 3399 or 1800 020 120; www.mooloolababackpackers.com. Dorm, double and motel-style rooms, a couple of blocks from the beach.
Wunpalm Motel and Holiday Units $$$ 137 Duporth Ave; tel: 5443 4677. Cabin-style units available – ideal for families.

[food] Maroochydore offers resort food, which means it's not a gourmet heaven. However, food is piled high and prices are acceptably low.
Café Burnett on Buderim $ 84 Burnett St; tel: 5445 3003. Breakfast and light meals, all home-made. Open Mon–Fri 0730–1500, Sat 0730–1700.

Rusty's Mexican Restaurant $$$ Sixth Ave; tel: 5443 1795.
Popular Mexican restaurant.
Summerz Café $ Shop 6, 25 Cotton Tree Pde; tel: 5479 6737.
Bright café with interesting food.
Swells Restaurant and Bar $$$ 6 Duporth Ave; tel: 5443
6401. Busy restaurant with a couple of good vegetarian options.
Valentines $$$$ cnr Maroochydore and Main Rds; tel: 5479
1388. All-you-can-eat buffet of over 120 dishes and 24 desserts.
Open daily.

NOOSA HEADS

Noosa is Australia's very own St Tropez. It has international sophistication but with
a laid-back, carefree approach to life. Hastings St is a bit like Rodeo Dr. in Los
Angeles in its number of highly attractive and highly expensive shops. These are
interspersed with restaurants, pavement bistros and beachfront apartments.

Europeans first came in 1842. Then, when the surfers discovered its north-facing
beach and perfect rollers 120 years later, tourism and the developers followed. But
Noosa made a simple rule: no building can be higher than a palm tree. Although the
rule has been broken many times the town has avoided all excess and remains
charming.

THE KABI AND THE BUNYA NUT

Prior to white settlement, the Kabi tribe inhabited this area for almost 40,000 years before the loggers arrived in the early 1800s. By nature's standard they were a rich tribe who enjoyed all the natural pleasures and abundance of the area. The Bunya festival, a celebration of the harvest of the Bunya nut (believed to be the oldest festival known to mankind), attracted tribes from as far south as northern NSW and was celebrated in the nearby Blackall Ranges.

i **Noosa Tourist Information Centre**, Hastings St
Roundabout; tel: 5447 4988; www.tourismnoosa.com.au;
e-mail: info@tourismnoosa.com.au. Open daily. Also at Noosa
Harbour, Tewantin.
Travel Bugs, Shop 3, 9 Sunshine Beach Rd; tel: 5474 8530;
e-mail: info@oztravelbugs.com. Good-value internet access.

🛏 **Chez Noosa Resort $$$–$$$$** 263 David Low Way; tel:
5447 2027. Good value by Noosa standards.
Halse Lodge Guesthouse YHA $$ 2 Halse Lane; tel: 5447
3377 or 1800 242 567; www.yha.com.au/hostels. 1880s heritage
trust guest-house, situated on 2 acres, short walk to Hastings
St and beach.
Hotel Laguna $$$$ 6 Hastings St; tel: 5447 3077; e-mail:
hotellaguna@universal.net.au. Motel-style apartments
overlooking the river or Hastings St.
Noosa Backpackers Resort $–$$$ 9–13 William St,
Noosaville; tel: 5449 8151 or 1800 626 673; www.noosaback
packers.com. Great facilities, free bus to beach and town centre.

QUEENSLAND

EN ROUTE

One of the pleasanter detours between Noosa and Gympie is to **Kin Kin**. Head first for Boreen Point, a small town on Lake Cootharaba, then on to Kin Kin and Pomona. Pomona has what is almost certainly the world's longest-running silent movie theatre, the Majestic Theatre, 3 Factory Rd, complete with a Wurlitzer pipe organ. The cinema is open Thur evenings and screens matinees at other times. Tel: 5485 2330 for further details.

Noosa Village Motel $$$$ 10 Hastings St; tel: 5447 5800; e-mail: noosavillage@bigpond.com.au. Clean bright rooms in excellent location.

Seahaven Resort $$$$ 13 Hastings St; tel: 5447 3422 or 1800 072 013. Excellent rooms, some overlooking the sea – but at a price.

Studio Apartments Sunshine Beach $$ 10 Nebula St, Sunshine Beach; tel: 5447 4129. Relatively inexpensive fully self-contained apartments; minimum stay three nights.

🍴 This is probably one of the great dining resorts of Australia. In Noosa Heads itself Hastings St alone has over 30 quality cafés and restaurants. Up the road in Noosa Junction is another great selection, and somewhat less expensive.

Beach Café $ On the Beach, Hastings St; tel: 5447 2740. Good-value café and sandwich/burger bar. Open 0700–1600.

Bistro C $$$ On the Beach, Hastings St; tel: 5447 2855. Open daily for breakfast, lunch and dinner.

Café Kokomo $$$ Shop 4, 5 Hastings St; tel: 5447 2467. Bright café with a couple of good vegetarian options.

Chilli Jam Café $$$ 195 Weyba Rd, Noosaville; tel: 5449 9755. Innovative Thai and South-East Asian cuisine. Dinner Tues–Sat from 1800.

Chinois $$$ Bay Village, Hastings St; tel: 5449 2200. Chinese and Asian food.

Cinema Paradiso $$ Noosa 5 Cinema Centre; tel: 5449 2255. Pasta, salads, cakes. Good-value movie deals.

Fusions $$$ 271 Gympie Terrace; tel: 5474 4888. Stylish café overlooking the river.

Saltwater $$$$ 8 Hastings St; tel: 5447 2234. Seafood restaurant with live lobster tanks. Open daily, licensed.

Santa Fe $$$$ Shop 4, Noosa Wharf; tel: 5474 5655. Contemporary south-western American cuisine. Closed Mon.

A Taste of Spice $$$ Thomas St, Noosaville; tel: 5474 2833. Good-value Malaysian restaurant. Closed Wed.

Tewantin-Noosa RSL $ Memorial Ave, Tewantin; tel: 5447 1766. Excellent for those on a tight budget. Open daily.

HIGHLIGHTS

The Noosa Parks Association campaigns actively towards keeping Noosa distinctly different from overdeveloped resort areas, keeping the river and its lakes the most natural in Queensland, creating a protective green belt around Noosaville and Tewantin and preserving wildlife corridors into the forests. Drive up to **Laguna Lookout** on Noosa Hill

GREAT SANDY NATIONAL PARK — COOLOOLA SECTION

This park, just north of Noosa, protects the largest intact sand dune system in the world. In addition to the coloured sand cliffs it has rainforest, open forest and heathlands, extensive beaches and peaceful lakes. Many tracks within the park are four-wheel-drive only, but there are day tours and safaris available from several sources in Noosa Heads (details from the tourist office). It is possible to take a four-wheel-drive to the North Shore and then on to Teewah Beach, view the wreck of the Cherry Venture, wrecked here when she was hit by a cyclone in 1973, and eventually end up at Rainbow Beach, gateway to the World Heritage-listed Fraser Island (see p. 301). The House of Bottles and Bottle Museum in Tewantin, 19 Myles Rd, tel: 5447 1277, is an interesting place for a browse, and sells bottles of the colourful sand from the surrounding area as souvenirs. Open daily.

(a signposted turnoff runs from Noosa Dr.) and the view will attest to their success: unspoilt green bushland, rainforest and river. These forests are one of the few places in Australia where it is possible to see a koala in the wild. Try to get there just before sunset, when koalas are most active.

There are certain walks which have almost become rituals. Stroll along Gympie Terrace and see the sun setting on the other bank of the river among the mangroves. Or take a walk along the recently constructed boardwalk from Hastings St to Noosa National Park past peaceful coves, spectacular cliffs and natural heathland to the secluded beaches of Alexandria Bay. (This is Noosa's nudist beach, where every year they hold the Nude Olympics. The mind boggles.) Continue on and make it a half-day stroll right through the park to Sunshine Beach.

Noosa National Park rejoices in the fact that it is the most visited national park in Queensland. The entrance is just a short distance from the town centre (from Hastings St follow the coast on your left for 1.5 km) and a series of tracks lets you explore rainforest, open eucalypt woodland, scrub and grasslands, and rocky headlands running right to the sea. On extremely hot summer days the rainforest tracks provide a beautiful, cool alternative to the beach.

The Noosa Harbour near Tewantin (follow River Dr.) is home to four restaurants, an art gallery, speciality shops and a Sunday market. From here you can also hire boats for the day. From Tewantin itself you can get a ferry across the river for access to the Cooloola section of the Great Sandy National Park. Tel: 5474 4462.

MARYBOROUGH

Maryborough, started as a wool port in 1847, is one of Queensland's oldest cities, and in the early days of European settlement it was second only to Sydney as an immigration port for free settlers. **The Bond Store Museum,** 101 Wharf St, houses displays featuring interesting facts on immigration history as well as on the port of Maryborough's early days. The museum has been created by the local council for tourists and is well laid out. Worth a visit ($). Open Mon–Fri 0900–1600, Sat and Sun 1000–1300; tel: 4123 1523.

The affluence that accompanied the 1867 gold rush, which centred on Gympie, brought major building to the town, and several now have heritage status. *The Walk and Drive Tours* is a free, informative brochure available from the tourist information centre, which takes you past numerous buildings of historical significance.

Brennan & Geraghty's Museum ($), at 64 Lennox St, built in 1871, is owned by the National Trust and was the centre of Martin Geraghty and Patrick Brennan's business in orchards, a preserve factory and a winery. The museum gives a detailed picture of life in the area. Open daily 1000–1500; tel: 4121 2250.

Ellena and Adelaide Sts are closed to traffic every Thur to make way for the market selling hand-crafted items, home-made food, or fruit and vegetables. It is a major attraction, full of shoppers from early morning until mid-afternoon. At 1300 on these days the time cannon is fired in the market. This is a replica of the cannon that was originally fired daily when the time signal was received from Brisbane.

> [i] **Maryborough and Fraser Island Visitor Information Centre**, South Maryborough Travel Stop, Bruce Hwy; tel: 4121 4111. Open daily; www.visitmaryborough.info.

TRAINS PAST AND PRESENT

Maryborough is a train town. Queensland's first steam locomotive, the *Mary Ann*, was built here, as are the latest tilt trains, the fastest in Australia (such as the *City of Maryborough* which runs between Brisbane and Rockhampton). A replica of the *Mary Ann* was constructed in 1999 and can be ridden every Thursday (market day) at the railway station, and on the last Sunday of the month at Queens Park – where there are also flea markets, stagecoach rides, bands, food and drink, and river cruises. The Old Maryborough Railway Station in Lennox St houses the railway museum. Free. Open Thurs 0900–1300; tel: 4123 9315.

The historic Mary Valley line is one of the great train rides of Australia. The scenic 40-km journey crosses the Mary River and its major tributaries, passing through small villages with an abundance of curves, gradients and bridges and a tunnel to its final destination, Imbil. It runs each Wed at 1000 and Sun at 1000 from Gympie, about 85 km south of Maryborough ($$$); www.thevalleyrattler.com.

More engineering marvels can be seen at the Olds Engine House and Works at 78 North St, the work of the late William Olds who was a model engineer. Open for guided tours on Thur 0930–1600 ($); tel: 4121 3649.

FLOOD

In February 1999, the Mary River rose at Maryborough to 8.75 m above its normal level. Such floods are a regular problem: during the worst, in 1893, the river peaked at over 12 m, washing away more than 100 houses, devastating farms and plantations, and destroying the sawmill. Fortunately, Maryborough now gets plenty of warning, enabling precautions to be taken. Many establishments leave their doors and windows open so that the flood water can flow through rather than damage the building.

🛏 **Arkana Motel $$$** 46 Ferry St; tel: 4121 2261. Licensed restaurant, with pool.

Carriers Arms Hotel Motel $$$ 405 Alice St; tel: 4122 2244. Newly built rooms and pool.

City Motel $$ 138–140 Ferry St; tel: 4121 2568. Pool and BBQ, under-cover parking, close to town centre.

Huntsville Caravan Park $$ 23 Gympie Rd; tel: 4121 4075. Range of accommodation from tent sites to en-suite cabins. Short drive into town.

Lamington Hotel Motel $$$ 33 Ferry St; tel: 4121 3295. One of the least expensive motels, although by a public bar.

Peppercorn Place $$$ 32 Churchill St; tel: 4121 6372. Inexpensive guesthouse, children catered for by arrangement.

🍽 This is not a gourmet city and the best bet is one of the Chinese restaurants or one of the many motel restaurants.

The Basement $$$ 389 Kent St; tel: 4123 6888. Fully licensed, range of dishes including some vegetarian.

Burgeler Bistro $$ Maryborough RSL Club, 165 Lennox St; tel: 4122 2321. As with most RSL clubs in Australia, it is open to visitors and offers excellent value for money. Lunch and dinner Thur–Sun.

Lucky Chinese Restaurant $$ 302 Kent St; tel: 4121 3645. Simple restaurant, but reasonable food at good value.

Muddy Waters $$ 71 Wharf St; tel: 4121 5011. Situated by the Mary River Marina, range of dishes from noodles to salads. Café open daily for lunch, coffee and cakes. A la carte Wed–Sat evenings, with jazz and blues.

Parkway Motel Licensed Restaurant $$$ 188 John St; tel: 4122 2888. One of numerous motel restaurants in the area offering good food at a reasonable price.

HERVEY BAY

The main reason to visit Hervey – pronounced Harvey – Bay is to arrange a trip to Fraser Island (see p. 301) or to go whale watching. Like most resort areas in Australia, Hervey Bay saw rapid growth as a holiday destination in the 1970s and is an agglomeration of what were once separate towns. It was promoted as Australia's family aquatic playground, which, oddly, it is. Protected by Fraser Island, there is no surf, and box jellyfish do not trespass here, so swimming is safe even for children. It also rejoices under the title of Whale Watch Capital of Australia. Hervey Bay promotes itself as the most accessible place in Australia, and with specially designed walkways, beach access points and accommodation, disabled travellers can undertake numerous activities.

Most of Hervey Bay's life rotates around the **Esplanade** with its restaurants, cafés, shops and bars – yet on a more relaxed, less brash scale than the resort's southern neighbours. Running alongside the Esplanade is a 14-km footpath and cycleway – there are several places to hire bikes from. Rayz Bike Hire provides a delivery and pickup service; tel: 0417 644 814.

> [i] **Hervey Bay Tourism and Development Bureau**,
> Uraween Rd (in KG Nut Factory Complex); tel: 4125 9855
> or 1800 811 728; e-mail: info@herveybaytourism.com.au.
> Open daily.
> **Hervey Bay Information:** www.herveybaytourism.com.au.

Whale Watching

Now that whaling is banned by international treaty these splendid creatures are increasing at a rate of over 10 per cent a year, and about 3000 humpback whales now migrate between Antarctica and the Great Barrier Reef. After giving birth in the warm waters of north Queensland, mothers with their calves stop in Hervey Bay to rest before completing their journey south. They can start arriving in late July and may be seen until Nov; Aug to mid-Oct is the surest period. As many as 30 whales come into the bay at the same time. It is not just their size that is so impressive – humpbacks are the most sporting of the species and they leap, roll and breach as if they, too, were on holiday. It is one of the rare and great sights of the world. They also sing and you can hear them from some of the cruise boats equipped with underwater listening devices.

The many operators who offer whale-watching cruises all work within strict restrictions as to how close they can approach. However, the current thought is that the whales have become much more comfortable with cruise vessels and there is little danger of their being frightened off. Tours (half- or full-day) all leave from Urangan boat harbour, and operators include:

MV *Islander*, tel: 1800 249 122. The largest cruise vessel, a 30-m catamaran, departs daily at 1015 and returns 1515.

MV *Volante*, tel: 1800 800 862. This 15-m fast catamaran runs dawn cruises when the whales are most active and the seas are calmest, departing at 0530 and returning 1000. Day cruises also depart at 1030, returning at 1530.

Whale Watch Safari MV *Mikat*; tel: 4125 1522. Catamaran with underwater microphone, departs daily at 0900 and returns at 1530.

All the above tours provide a pickup service and guarantee whale sightings – otherwise you get a free trip.

🛏 Hervey Bay has numerous accommodation options from campsites to four-star hotels. Most of these are located on or around the Esplanade.

Beaches Hervey Bay $–$$ 195 Torquay Tce; tel: 4124 1322 or 1800 655 501; www.beaches.com.au. Known as a party hostel.

Colonial Log Cabin Resort YHA $–$$$ 820 Boat Harbour Dr.; tel: 4125 1844 or 1800 818 280; www.yha.com.au/hostels. Located on eight acres of natural bushland, there are some friendly cockatoos, a pool, BBQ and café. A range of accommodation available from dormitories to private en-suite cabins.

Hervey Bay Caravan Park $$ Margaret St; tel: 4128 9553; e-mail: hbcaravan@net-lynx.net, www.hervey.com.au/hbcaravanpark. Close to the Botanic Gardens and the bay.

Kookaburra Backpacker Hostel $–$$ 264 Charles St, Pialba; tel: 1800 111 442. Lovely old building close to the beach, friendly atmosphere.

Lazy Acres Caravan and Camping Village $$ 91 Exeter St; tel: 4125 1840. Good value, with a range of accommodation from camping sites to deluxe cabins and units.

Tower Court Motel $$$ 460 Esplanade; tel: 4125 1322 or 1800 241 322. Excellent location; bus stop at front door.

🍴 There are numerous good restaurants along the Esplanade and around the Marina, most of them representing excellent value for money.

Blazing Saddles Bar & Grill $$$ 140 Freshwater St; tel: 4125 5466. Aussie atmosphere, good-sized portions. Open daily.

Curried Away $$ 174 Boat Harbour Dr.; tel: 4124 1577. Excellent Sri Lankan and Indian curries. Open daily from 1700.

Don Camillo Ristorante Italiano $$$ 486 Esplanade; tel: 4125 1087. Open daily from 1800.

Goody's on the Beach $$$ 54 Moreton St; tel: 4128 0227. A la carte dining and café-style lunches. Open Wed–Sun 1030–late.

Sails Brasserie and Café $$$ 433 Esplanade; tel: 4125 5170. Modern Australian-European cuisine with Asian flavours. Possibly the best restaurant in the area. Closed Sun.

Squires Restaurant $$$$ Playa Concha Resort, 475 Esplanade; tel: 4125 1544. Licensed. Open daily from 1800.

SCENIC FLIGHTS OVER FRASER ISLAND

A unique way of seeing Fraser Island is by air. Elite Airways offer scenic flights from Hervey Bay Airport; tel: 4125 3111. These represent excellent value at approximately $20 for a 15-minute flight. Longer flights also run.

BUNDABERG

Bundaberg is the southernmost access point to the Great Barrier Reef, so it must be very irritating for the citizens of Bundaberg to know that all other Australians automatically think of rum when the name of the town is mentioned. Sugar growing was established in the 19th century using Pacific Islanders who had been tricked, or 'blackburdened', into working in the cane fields. The first rum distillery was built in 1888.

But Bundaberg has much more going for it than its rum, however excellent. It is a city of parks and botanical gardens, with wide streets lined with poincianas which give a brilliant display in spring. The Burnett River adds to the charm of the place with boating and rowing at Sandy Hook, and sailing downstream near the port. Bundaberg also ranks with Cairns and Coffs Harbour as one of the three principal clearing ports for visiting yachts on the east coast.

[i] **Bundaberg Information Centre**, 271 Bourbong St; tel: 4152 2333. Open daily 0900–1700. An exceptionally well-organised information centre. Helpful staff with array of information.
Bundaberg: www.bundabergregion.info.

There are no glitzy five-star hotels in Bundaberg but numerous good-quality budget hotels, motels, hostels and bed and breakfasts. Most of the motels are located along Takalvan and Bourbong Sts.
Acacia Motor Inn $$$ 248 Bourbong St; tel: 4152 3411. Close to restaurants, with pool and BBQ.
Apollo Gardens Caravan Park $$ 83 Princess St; tel: 4152 8899. Tent and van sites as well as cabins. Short drive to town centre.
Bundaberg Backpackers & Travellers Lodge $ 2 Crofton St; tel: 4152 2080. Located close to town centre with good facilities, including garden and TV room.
Cane Village Holiday Park $$ Twyford St; tel: 4155 1022. In peaceful setting, with a range of accommodation options.
Grand Hotel $$ cnr Bourbong and Targo Sts; tel: 4151 2441. Basic, but central and inexpensive – interesting building.
Kelly's Beach Resort $–$$$$ 6 Trevors Rd; tel: 4154 7200 or 1800 246 141; www.kellysbeachresort.com.au. Excellent-value

EN ROUTE

South of the turnoff for Bundaberg, the Bruce Highway passes through the township of **Childers**. In 1902 a fire destroyed much of the town, but rebuilding has given a wide variety of architectural styles. Sadly, for some time to come, Childers will be better known for a more recent fire – the blaze at the Palace Backpackers Hostel in June 2000 in which 15 young travellers died. The Palace Backpackers re-opened in April 2004, the new $2.1 million building built around a memorial to the fire victims and featuring the restored façade of the original timber building. The Pharmaceutical Museum in Churchill St is now home to the Tourist Information Centre.

accommodation, located out of town near the beaches. On five-acre lot with pool, spa and tennis courts.

Oscar Motel $$$ 252 Bourbong St; tel: 4152 3666. With pool.

Whiston House B&B $$$ 9 Elliott Head Rd; tel: 4152 1447; e-mail: whiston@interworx.com.au. Historic Queenslander house with tropical pool.

Christina BYO Restaurant $$$ 238 Bourbong St; tel: 4153 1770. Open Mon–Sat from 1800.

Eastern Pearls Chinese Restaurant $$ 268a Bourbong St; tel: 4151 5145. Fully licensed, open daily.

Il Gambero Restaurant and Piano Bar $$$ 57 Targo St; tel: 4152 5342. Mediterranean cuisine, live entertainment. Open Tues–Sun.

Penny Lane Gardens Restaurant $$ Penny Lane; tel: 4155 2777. Bundaberg's largest restaurant, open Thur–Sun from 1100, some excellent-value meals.

Sizzler Steakhouse $$$ 222 Bourbong St; tel: 4153 3210. Part of a chain, offering good value for money.

Spinnaker Restaurant and Bar $$$ 1a Quay St; tel: 4152 8033. Located on the riverfront. A la carte dining with emphasis on seafood, live entertainment.

HIGHLIGHTS

The **Bundaberg Rum Distillery** in Avenue St runs tours for visitors and gives you the chance to taste samples. There is also a souvenir shop and rum museum. Tours run hourly between 1000 and 1500 (1400 weekends); $$. Tel: 4150 8684.

Bundaberg's parks come in many forms. **Alexandra Park**, situated along the Burnett River (accessible from Quay St), has a band rotunda dating from 1910 and a free zoo, open during daylight hours, featuring native birds and animals as well as some imported species. A great place to take children. **Baldwin Swamp** environmental park in East Bundaberg (accessible from Que Hee St) is home to many species of birds and wildlife. There are walking tracks including boardwalks which take you from tea-tree forest to dry vine shrub. In North Bundaberg is the relatively new **Botanical Garden**, on the corner of Mt Perry Rd (Gin Gin Hwy) and Young St. The gardens have a mix of native and exotic plants; the waterlily-filled lagoons are a highlight. Open daily 0600–1800.

In the centre of the botanical gardens is a curious sight. Bert Hinkler, whose role in early aviation has never been given the credit it was due, was born in Bundaberg. In 1928 he was the first man to fly solo from England to Australia, and died in 1933 in an air crash in Italy while trying for yet another world record. When his house in England, from where he had planned his pioneering flight to Australia, was scheduled for demolition, the people of Bundaberg set up a fund and brought it piece by piece from Southampton and set it up here – and yes, it does look strange to see an English suburban house translated to the Australian landscape. It is now the **Hinkler House Memorial Museum** ($, tel: 4152 0222, open daily 1000–1600). The museum commemorates aviation history and especially the intrepid Hinkler, who is said to have developed his ambition from observing the flights of ibis at the lagoons.

Bundaberg is a coastal city even though it is some 15 km from the sea. Within easy reach are over 140 km of unspoilt beaches, frequently deserted out of holiday season. Most important, the waters here are free of stingers, the big jellyfish which can make swimming dangerous (even lethal) in the wrong season as you get further north. **Bargara Beach** (accessible from the town centre by following Bourbong St, which turns into Bargara Rd) is the region's major coastal centre with numerous water activities, eateries and shops. A few minutes' drive north of Bargara Beach is **Mon Repos Beach**. Between November and March each year, after dark, loggerhead, flatback, green and leatherback turtles come ashore to lay their eggs here. Tiny hatchlings can be seen emerging from their nests from early January until the end of March. Access to the beach is limited during this time, although guided walks and tours take place from the Visitor Centre at Mon Repos Beach nightly from 1900 (Nov–Mar, $$); tel: 4159 1652.

Close to Bundaberg are **Lady Elliot Island** (see p. 324) and **Lady Musgrave Island**, the southernmost coral islands on the Great Barrier Reef.

The World Heritage Site of Fraser Island is the largest sand-massed island in the world — 125 km long and an average of 15 km wide — and a special place that imprints itself permanently in the memory of all who visit it.

The island was probably named after Mrs Eliza Fraser who was shipwrecked here when the *Stirling Castle* ran aground in 1836. It was declared a native reserve in 1860 and had an Aboriginal population of between 2000 and 3000. After a short-lived mission closed in 1904 the Aboriginal people dispersed to the mainland.

The first mineral-sands mining leases were granted in 1949. When a further application was made in 1971 the conservation lobby was up in arms: here was the largest sand island in the world and big business thought the way to deal with it was to mine it. The conservation movement fought long and hard and in 1971 the aptly named watchdog FIDO (Fraser Island Defenders Organisation) was formed. Sand-mining effectively ended in 1976.

Dili Village is the former sand-mining centre, and there are a number of smallish settlements along the coast: Eurong, Happy Valley and Cathedral Beach. The island now gets over 300,000 visitors annually, and managing them so that the least damage is done is a major task.

ARRIVAL AND DEPARTURE

Car and passenger ferries operate from River Heads to Kingfisher Bay (tel: 1800 072 555); River Heads to Wanggoolba Creek, Urangan to Moon Point (tel: 4125 4444) and Inskip Point (Rainbow Beach) to Hook Point (passenger ferry, tel: 4127 9122). You need a permit to take a vehicle across to the island; this can be obtained at a nominal price from Queensland Parks and Wildlife Service offices in Maryborough (tel: 4121 1800) or Rainbow Beach (tel: 5486 3160). Permits are also available at the River Heads Kiosk (Ariadne St) or from the Whale Watch Tourist Centre Marina Kiosk (Boat Harbour, Urangan).

GETTING AROUND

There are organised bus tours of the island. **Top Tours Ranger Guided Day Tour** for example, do a full-day tour with buffet lunch ($$$). The tour visits Eli Creek, the *Maheno* shipwreck and examples of different habitats in a four-wheel-drive coach Contact them at Great Sandy Strait Marina, Mainland Terminal; tel: 4125 3933.

The alternatives are to walk, or use a trail bike or a four-wheel-drive vehicle. The age limit for hiring four-wheel-drive seems to be only 21 here. One of the problems with such vehicles is that drivers are often inexperienced and not ecologically sensitive, and it is possible that these may one day be totally banned from the island. There are no sealed roads and driving conditions can be tricky, especially after a heavy rain. Bogging down a four-wheel-drive vehicle is distressingly easy as many, many visitors discover each year.

> ### DRIVING TIPS
> The speed limit is 35 kph on inland tracks and 60 kph on the beaches. It is desperately important that you keep to the tracks to protect the vegetation and observe vehicle-free areas. Keep four-wheel-drive constantly engaged to avoid spinning your wheels in the sand. Lowering your tyre pressures to 102–125 kPa (15–18 psi) will help you maintain traction.

INFORMATION

On the mainland: **Rainbow Beach Tourist Centre**, 8 Rainbow Beach Rd, Rainbow Beach; tel: 5486 3227; www.rainbowbeach.info. Open daily 0700–1800.

On the island: **Queensland Parks and Wildlife Service Visitor Centre**, Eurong; tel: 4127 9128; www.epa.qld.gov.au.

ACCOMMODATION

Some accommodation, from cabins to motel-style rooms, is available at reasonable cost, mostly on the east coast. There are also designated camping areas, some with showers and facilities. Contact Queensland Parks and Wildlife Service, Rainbow Beach (tel: 5486 3160) or Maryborough (tel: 4121 1800).

Eurong Beach Resort $$$$ Eurong Beach; tel: 4127 9122.
Fraser Island Retreat $$$$ Happy Valley; tel: 4127 9144.
Kingfisher Bay Resort and Village $$$$ North White Cliffs; tel: 4120 3333 or 1800 072 555.
Sailfish on Fraser $$$$ Happy Valley; tel: 4127 9494.

FOOD AND DRINK

Most of the accommodation offers buffet meals, but there are no restaurants as such. If you are camping, bring it all with you. You can buy basic supplies but they are quite expensive.

HIGHLIGHTS

The island stretches along the coast creating a massive bay on its western side, and from some angles it appears to form part of the mainland; Captain Cook certainly thought so when he saw the island in 1770.

The island has an endless variety of landscapes: long surf beaches, cliffs and gorges, dense rainforests, vast, desert-like sandblows, freshwater lakes perched high up in its dunes, winding streams and salt pans with mangrove forests. More than 230 different species of birds make it one of the largest and most varied bird communities in Australia, and there are brumbies – Australian wild horses – here, too (in Patrick White's *The Eye of the Storm* the island is fictionalised as Brumby).

THE SEA SERPENT MYSTERY

In June 1890, Miss Lovell, a schoolmistress, was taking a stroll along the beach at Sandy Cape when she saw an enormous sea creature lying partly out of the water. At first she thought that it was a giant turtle, but the tail was like the tail of a huge fish. She later wrote: 'When tired of my looking at it, it put its large neck and head into the water and swept round seaward, raising its huge dome-shaped body about five feet out of the water, and put its 12 feet of fish-like tail over the dry shore, elevating it at an angle. Then, giving its tail a half twist, it shot off like a flash of lightning. It had either teeth or serrated jaw bones. … I think it must be 30 feet in all.' In the early 1930s a book called *The Case for the Sea Serpent* came down on the side of Miss Lovell. But what was it she saw? Right along the Queensland coast people have claimed to have seen sea serpents. These creatures have been named 'Moha-Moha' – some say they were once food for the local Aborigines.

The dune systems of the Great Sandy Region, which includes Fraser Island, are the largest and oldest in the world, dating back more than 30,000 years. In **Great Sandy National Park**, the dunes rise to 200 m and the sand comes in at least 72 different colours. The dunes can be seen at their best along a 35-km stretch of ocean beach north of Happy Valley.

Happy Valley lies on Seventy Five Mile Beach, which can at times seem like a city road during rush hour. Low tide is the best time to drive on the beaches, as the sand is flat and hard-packed. Drive carefully and enjoy the scenery. When a vehicle is approaching you, signal with your indicators on which side you intend to pass. There have been sad collisions between American and Australian drivers each trying to pass on their normal sides.

From Happy Valley two signposted tracks lead inland. One goes to **Lake Garawongera** and the other to **Yidney Scrub** then past a series of lakes until, after 45 km, it returns to the beach. It is water that has given the island the ability to support vast tracts of forest, which survive on nutrients from the breakdown of other plants. Some trees are over a thousand years old, and the variety of vegetation is exceptional, ranging from mangroves to kauri forests and wallum heathlands.

Hundreds of streams flow through the forests and out into the bays. Two are exceptional. **Eli Creek**, on the eastern side of the island, is the largest of the freshwater streams flowing into the ocean. At Central Station, **Wanggoolba Creek** flows over white sand along the floor of thick rainforest, and the creek-side walkways pass through Angiopteris ferns, an ancient species boasting the largest single fronds in the world. (The many dingoes at Central Station are reputed to be Australia's purest strain; under no circumstances are they to be fed.)

There are 40 lakes on the island, formed in three ways. Window lakes occur when the ground drops below the water table and the fine white sandy base acts as a filter, giving the water exceptional clarity. Examples are **Yankee Jack**, **Ocean Lake** and **Lake Wabby**. Lake Wabby is also termed a barrage lake, which is formed by the damming action of a sandblow blocking the waters of a natural spring. Perched lakes occur above the water table. The peat-like base generally stains the water the colour of tea. Highest of them is **Lake Bowarrady**, and further south are **Lake Birrabeen** and the popular **Lake McKenzie**. **Lake Boomanjin** is the world's largest perched dune lake. Swimming in the lakes is a sybaritic delight. Wabby and McKenzie are perhaps two of the most wonderful, but all of them are glorious – much better than the sea, which in many places has a severe undertow.

DRIVING ROUTE

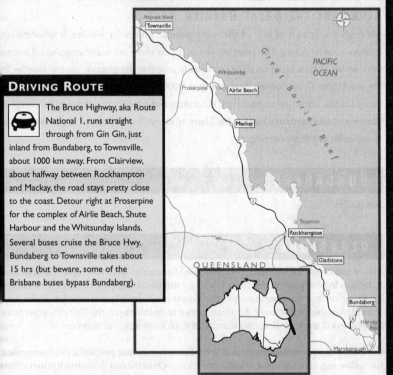

The Bruce Highway, aka Route National 1, runs straight through from Gin Gin, just inland from Bundaberg, to Townsville, about 1000 km away. From Clairview, about halfway between Rockhampton and Mackay, the road stays pretty close to the coast. Detour right at Proserpine for the complex of Airlie Beach, Shute Harbour and the Whitsunday Islands. Several buses cruise the Bruce Hwy. Bundaberg to Townsville takes about 15 hrs (but beware, some of the Brisbane buses bypass Bundaberg).

BUNDABERG — TOWNSVILLE
OTT Tables 9010/9085

Service	🚌	⟨RAIL⟩	⟨RAIL⟩	🚌	🚌	🚌	🚌	⟨RAIL⟩	⟨RAIL⟩	⟨RAIL⟩	🚌	🚌
Days of operation	Daily	②④⑥	ex⑥	Daily	Daily	Daily	Daily	①⑤	⑤⑦	②	Daily	Daily
Special notes		**AB**								**A**		
Brisbane ....d.	0745	0855	1100	1200	1430	1400	1600	1825	1700	1825	1930	....
Bundaberg ....d.	1530	1542	1555	1930	2200	2310		2335	2200	0011	0205	....
Gladstone ....d.	1810	1811	1820	2205			0215	0148	0010	0249	0520	....
Rockhampton ....d.	2010	2025	1945	2355	0250	0305	0405	0323	0135	0415	0715	....
Mackay ....d.	0040	0155	....	0425	0720	0725	0840	0755	....	....	1210	1800
Airlie Beach ....d.	0230		....	0620	0920	0935			....	....	1400	2000
Townsville ....d.	0710	0820	....	1105	1405	1400	1535	1255	....	....	1915	0020

Special notes:
A–Conveys sleepers and car transporters.
B–On ④⑦ also conveys Queenslander Class.

ALONGSIDE THE GREAT BARRIER REEF

Although this is part of one of the most popular routes for visitors, it nevertheless involves a lot of driving. The great attraction is that there are many stopping-off points from which to take boats or planes to what is probably the greatest natural wonder in the world: the Great Barrier Reef. Along its 2000 km are perhaps 900 coral cays and rocky islands, attracting scuba-divers, naturalists and tourists to marvel at its complex beauty and extraordinary marine life. There is everything here from exclusive resorts to self-sufficient bush camping.

BUNDABERG

See p. 298.

GLADSTONE

This is one of the busiest ports in Australia and since the 1960s has made a spectacular transition from a quiet coastal town to a major industrial shipping complex. One reason for this growth is the opening-up of the almost inexhaustible coal supplies in the hinterland. Another is that some 8 million tonnes of bauxite from the Gulf of Carpentaria are processed annually here into alumina, the 'halfway stage' of aluminium.

Gladstone is a hive of industry and the information centre (tel: 4972 9922) organises the following, free, one-hr guided tours: Mon – **Queensland Alumina Refinery** (the world's largest); Tues – **Gladstone Power Station** (which generates 1680 megawatts of power for the Boyne Island Smelter and the Queensland Electricity Grid); Wed – **Gladstone Port Authority** (largest tonnage port in Queensland and fifth largest coal-capacity port in the world); Fri – **QCL Group** (producing 1.6 million tonnes of clinker a year, used in cement and concrete materials).

The **Gladstone Regional Art Gallery and Museum,** on the corner of Goondoon and Bramston Sts, has three exhibition areas covering touring displays, local arts and crafts, and historical photographs of the region. Free, open Mon–Fri 1000–1700, Sat 1000–1600; tel: 4970 1242.

The **Toondoon Botanical Gardens** in Glenlyon Rd, about 8 km from the centre, specialises in local plants and those from far north Queensland. There is a signposted 3-km bush walk that takes in two lookouts. Open daily 0900–1800; tel: 4979 3326.

Gladstone is a good base to explore the southern section of the Great Barrier Reef

EN ROUTE

On the Gin Gin Hwy 25 km north of Bundaberg are 27 strange craters. They were discovered in 1971 and are at least 25 million years old, but no one is quite sure how they were caused. Theories range from a meteorite to sea action. An observation platform is open daily 0800–1700 ($); tel: 4157 7291.

for which the city has built a splendid marina. There are several trips on offer: the Information Centre has further details. **Heron Island** (80 km from Gladstone) claims some of the best diving in the world and has its own P&O resort, $$$$. Unfortunately P&O seems to have command over the helicopters and boats that visit the island, and a visit does come at a price; tel: 1800 737 678.

[i] **Gladstone Visitor Information Centre**, Marina Ferry Terminal, Bryan Jordan Dr.; tel: 4972 9000; e-mail: gapdl@gladstoneregion.org.au; www.gladstoneregion.org.au. Open Mon–Fri 0830–1700, Sat and Sun 0900–1700.

[🛏] **Auckland Hill B&B $$$$** 15 Yarroon St; tel: 4972 4907. Historical Queenslander house with country-style rooms.
Gladstone Backpackers $$ 12 Rollo St; tel: 4972 5744. Small and friendly, short walk to town centre, free bike hire.
Gladstone City Caravan Park $$ 185 Toolooa St; tel: 4979 1305. From tent sites to en-suite cabins – all good value.
Toolooa Gardens Motel $$$$ 79–83 Toolooa St; tel: 4972 2811. Good standard motel with room service.

[🍴] Most motels have restaurants offering reasonable dining. Several restaurants are located around Goondoon St.
Flinders Seafood Restaurant $$$ Flinders Pde; tel: 4972 8322. Licensed, overlooking the waterfront, indoor and outdoor eating. Open daily from 1100 for lunch and dinner.
Grand Hotel $ cnr Goondoon and Roseberry Sts; tel: 4972 2422. Basic meals at a good price. Open Mon–Sat for lunch and dinner.
Horn Bar $ cnr Goondoon St at Club 3-in-1; tel: 4972 2847. Good food at excellent value, lively atmosphere, open daily from 2000.
Kapers $$$ 124b Goondoon St; tel: 4972 7902. BYO, lively menu with items such as spicy chicken kebabs and hot pepperoni pasta. Open for dinner Mon–Sat.
Rusty Anchor Restaurant $$$ Rusty Anchor Motel, 167 Goondoon St; tel: 4972 2099. Reasonable food, licensed cocktail bar, dinner only Mon–Sat.
Swaggys $$$ 56 Goondoon St; tel: 4972 1653. Classy restaurant serving a range of dishes from vegetarian meals to crocodile, kangaroo and emu.

ROCKHAMPTON

When the cry of 'Gold!' went up at Canoona, 60 km away, Rockhampton grew almost overnight and became known as 'the town of the three S's: sin, sweat and sorrow'. The discovery of copper shortly afterwards led to further expansion, then Rocky (everyone in Australia calls it Rocky) became the centre of one of the major beef areas of the country and is known today as the Beef Capital of Australia. Rockhampton is right on the Tropic of Capricorn, and a spire in the Capricorn Information Centre marks the exact spot. It is also one of the access points for the southern islands and resorts of the Great Barrier Reef (see p. 316).

EN ROUTE

Twenty-three kilometres north of Rockhampton are **Olsen's Capricorn Caves**, probably formed from an ancient coral reef some 300 million years ago. The caves, discovered in 1882, are still privately owned. Guided tours run daily 0900–1600, $$$; tel: 4934 2883.

[i] **Capricorn Tourism Information Centre**, The Spire, Gladstone Rd; tel: 4927 2055. Regional and local information as well as booking services. Open daily.

Rockhampton Tourist Information Centre, Customs House, 208 Quay St; tel: 4922 5339 or 1800 805 865. Open Mon–Fri 0830–1630, weekends 0900–1600; e-mail: rtbi@rockhamptoninfo.com; www.rockhamptoninfo.com.

INTERNET

Rocknet Internet Café, 238 Quay St; tel: 4922 2760. Open Mon–Fri 0800–1700, Sat 0900–1200. One of several in the area.

[image] **Farm stays** are becoming increasingly popular. In some you can relax and get pampered, while at others you are expected to help with the work. The Capricorn Tourism Information Centre can give you further information and booking assistance.

Ascot Stonegrill Backpackers $ 177 Musgrave St, North Rockhampton; tel: 4922 4719; www.ascothotel.com.au. Handy to Great Keppel ferries.

Central Park Motel $$$ 224 Murray St; tel: 4927 2333. Restaurant and room service, close to shops and restaurants.

Downtown Backpackers $ cnr Denham and East Sts; tel: 4922 1837. Upstairs in Oxford Hotel, right in town centre.

Rockhampton Village Van Park $$ 810 Yaamba Rd; tel: 4936 1037. As with most caravan parks, it offers excellent-value en-suite cabins and other accommodation options.

Rockhampton YHA $–$$$ 60 MacFarlane St; tel: 4927 5288; www.yha.com.au/hostels. Short walk to town centre, range of rooms, courtesy pickup from bus and train stations.

Travellers Motor Inn $$$ 110–116 Gorge St; tel: 4927 7900. Good standard motel, reflecting good value.

PIONEER LIFE

The **Rockhampton Heritage Village**, Boundary Rd, aims to show exactly how the pioneers of this area once lived. There are some original buildings (as well as replicas), horse-drawn vehicles and agricultural machinery. Open Mon–Fri 0900–1500, Sat–Sun 1000–1600 ($); tel: 4936 1026.

🍴 There are noticeably more steakhouses in Rockhampton than other towns – for obvious reasons. However, the town does have some good eateries, and most offer good value for money.

Great Western Steakhouse $$ Great Western Hotel, 39 Stanley St; tel: 4922 1862. Menu of beef and steaks. The hotel has shows of live bull riding. Open daily.

Muddy Waters $$ Fitzroy Motor Inn, cnr Fitzroy and Campbell Sts; tel: 4922 6631. A la carte, fresh seafood daily, licensed, dinner only.

O'Dowd's Irish Pub $$ cnr William and Denison Sts; tel: 4927 0344; www.odowds.com.au. Popular with travellers, traditional Irish bar, Irish-style food, live entertainment. Also has accommodation. Open daily.

Outback Beef and Roast $$ 118 H'way George St; tel: 4921 4011. Good-value meals in Aussie-style restaurant.

Stonegrill Restaurant $$$ Ascot Hotel, 177 Musgrave St; tel: 4922 4719. Your meal is cooked at the table on a heated stone – supposed to be one of the healthiest methods of cooking, although not much for the vegetarian.

Whispers Licensed Restaurant $$$ Travellers Motor Inn, 110 George St; tel: 4927 7900. A la carte, open daily from 1800, good menu at reasonable value.

The Wild Parrot Coffee and Teahouse $$ 66 Denham St; tel: 4921 4099. A range of excellent homestyle food – excellent quiche. Open Mon–Sat 1000–late, Sun 0900–late.

HIGHLIGHTS

The best way to get a feeling for the town is to take the Heritage Walk, which takes you past most of the grand old buildings which have been lovingly preserved and restored. There is also a Heritage Drive. Both take about one hour, plus viewing time. The Information Centre in Quay St has a detailed map.

Dominating the area is the belfry and clock tower of the colonnaded **Old Post Office** on the corner of East St Mall and Denham St. The Quay St historical precinct is particularly noteworthy, and includes the copper-domed **Customs House** (now housing the Tourist Information Centre). At the Fitzroy Bridge end of Quay St the **Criterion Hotel**, with its great verandas, was built in 1890 on the site of the first hotel in the town, the 1857 Bush Inn. The Gothic-revival **St Paul's Cathedral**, on the corner of Alma and William Sts (completed 1883), is rivalled by **St Joseph's Catholic Cathedral** along William St, which has twin spires and a vaulted roof.

The **Botanical Gardens** to the south of the city (accessible from Ann St) are open daily 0600–1800. They contain one of the most extensive examples of indigenous flora in Australia, and also **Rockhampton Zoo** (free; open 0800–1700). Worth special attention is the tranquil **Japanese Garden**. The whole complex is claimed, with good reason, to be among the finest in tropical Australia. Tel: 4922 1654 for further details. The **Kershaw Gardens**, in the north of the city, off the Bruce Hwy, have colonial buildings, rainforest, waterfalls and easy walking trails. All flora and fauna are native to Australia.

> The Mount Archer Lookout gives the best view of Rockhampton and has bush trails, picnic tables and barbecues. Reach it by turning left into Dean St from Lakes Creek Rd, then right into Frenchville Rd.

The **Dreamtime Cultural Centre** is reputed to be Australia's largest Aboriginal cultural centre. It is on the Bruce Hwy, north of Rockhampton, opposite the turning for Yeppoon. The centre is built on the site where elders of the Darambal tribe made their campsite and gathered for ancient tribal meetings and burial ceremonies. It is set in natural bushland and has a sandstone cave replica, burial sites, rock art and a timber-lined billabong. Open Mon–Fri 1000–1530, with tours running regularly ($$); tel: 4936 1655.

Yeppoon, just up the coast on the shores of Keppel Bay, has developed into a quiet, low-key resort ideal for family holidays. It is wonderfully endowed with beaches and the streets are lined with pines and palms. On a headland overlooking Fisherman's Beach is an unusual and graceful **'singing ship' memorial** to Captain Cook. **Rosslyn Bay Boat Harbour** is the hopping-off point for the Keppel Islands and the Great Barrier Reef.

Cooberrie Park, 15 km north, on Woodbury Rd, is a flora and fauna reserve with a variety of animals in bushland and rainforest settings. You can hand-feed kangaroos and wallabies. Open daily 0900–1630 ($$); tel: 4939 7590. The Capricorn Coast Tourist Information Centre on Scenic Hwy, Yeppoon, offers further information on the area; tel: 4939 4888, open daily 0900–1700.

MACKAY

Mackay (M'kie) is often called the sugar capital of Australia – about a quarter of all Australia's sugar is grown in the area. Sugar and coal (Hay Point, to the south of the town, was, for a time, the world's largest coal terminal) have made Mackay prosperous, and the result is a most elegant town in the tropical Queensland style. It is also well endowed with shops, and has several weekend markets – some with live entertainment. **Queens Park**, by Goldsmith St (similar to a botanical garden), is very pleasant and has an Orchid House with some beautiful displays of flowers and foliage (open Mon–Fri 1000–1100 and 1400–1430, Sun 1400–1700). The park itself is open daily 0600–1800. Caneland Park is on the banks of the Pioneer River and also has some pleasant walks.

There are three **beaches** within the town boundaries: Town Beach, Illawong Beach and Far Beach, all side by side. There are some great views and good walks. **Harbour Beach**, a ten-minute drive north of the city, is the main beach for Mackay and has a patrolled swimming area. Adjacent to Harbour Beach is **Mackay Harbour and Marina** – a multi-million-dollar development still under construction yet worth a visit for its pleasant walks. The Historic Pine Islet Lighthouse, first commissioned in 1885 on the tiny island of pine, was dismantled and moved to Mackay in 1986 as a historic icon, and now forms part of the marina.

Ask the Tourist Information Centre for a free copy of *Mackay's Heritage Walk*. The walk focuses on the centre of the town and gives an excellent opportunity to orientate yourself and visit shops and restaurants en route. **Farleigh Mill** ($$$, on Chidlow St, off the Bruce Hwy north of Mackay) is a working sugar mill. Tours run at 1300 Mon–Fri and Wed at 1900.

PRECIOUS STONES

West of Rockhampton, in the central Highlands, lie Australia's gemfields. All the towns have wonderful names – Emerald, Rubyvale, Sapphire, Anakie. Not many overseas tourists come to these places, but they are well worth visiting. There are also six farm stays in the area.

These are the largest sapphire fields in the southern hemisphere, and fossicking licences are available. Do not get excited about making a fortune. The sapphires come out of the ground dark and dingy and are priced by the kilo. It takes a fair amount of alchemy, at which Thai jewellers are experts, to turn them into jewels. It is not generally known that most of the sapphires sold in Thailand come from Australia.

The central highlands are about 250 km along the Capricorn Hwy, but there are gems closer than this. The Mt Hay Gemstone Park, 37 km west of Rockhampton, on the Capricorn Hwy, lets you go digging for your own thundereggs. Each is guaranteed to be 120 million years old, and there are guided tours of the diggings and the gemstone processing plant. Open daily 0830–1630; tel: 4934 7183.

i **Mackay Tourism and Development Bureau,** The Mill, 320 Nebo Rd; tel: 4944 5888 or 1300 130 001; e-mail: info@mackayregion.com. Housed in an old mill, this is an organised centre with accommodation bookings, brochures and lots of general information. Open daily.

Mackay: www.mackayregion.com.

🛏 The vast majority of the motels are in Nebo Rd; prices tend to be acceptably low.

Alara Motor Inn $$$$ 52 Nebo Rd; tel: 4951 2699. Excellent facilities.

Central Tourist Park $ Malcomson St; tel: 4957 6141. Excellent-value villas, cabins and van sites, walking distance to the heart of the city.

Larrikin Lodge YHA $–$$ 32 Peel St; tel: 4951 3728; www.yha.com.au/hostels. Traditional Queenslander-style house, by town centre. Homely atmosphere, range of accommodation options.

Platypus Bush Camp $$ Finch Hatton Gorge; tel: 4958 3204. A fantastic Australian experience, set on 20 acres of rainforest near Eungella National Park. Swim in the pristine creek, spot platypus or relax by a fire. Alternative back-to-nature lifestyle. No TV, electric lights or loud music, and hardly any biting insects. The camp has an amazing hot water system, showers, sauna and hot rock tub (all heated by wood) – a truly unique experience.

Rover Holiday Units $$$ 174 Nebo Rd; tel: 4951 3711. Excellent-value self-contained accommodation, with pool and water slides, hospitable staff.

🍴 Several good eating places can be found in Victoria St and around the town centre. The new marina has a couple of upmarket restaurants and more are under development.

Banquet House $$ 68 Victoria St; tel: 4951 1003. Licensed à la carte, good-value smorgasbord dinner daily.

Cactus Jacks Bar & Grill $ 44 Victoria St; tel: 4957 8044. Busy bar and grill, good value for money.

Fratini's at the Waterfront Restaurant $$$ 8 River St; tel: 4957 8131. Italian restaurant and wine bar, located by the river; the owner is a bit of a character.

Galleons Restaurant $$$$ Ocean International Hotel, 1 Bridge Rd; tel: 1800 635 104. Award-winning restaurant.

EN ROUTE

From Mackay, follow the Mackay–Eungella Rd west (about one hour) to the **Eungella National Park**. This is Queensland's largest rainforest national park and contains Mt Dalrymple (1280 m). It is the home of the Eungella honeyeater, one of only five new bird species discovered in Australia over the past 50 years. The gastric brooding frog and the orange-sided skink also live here, and it is one of the few places in Australia where it is possible to see a duck-billed platypus in its natural environment – the viewing platform at the Broken River section of the park is the best place to look, dawn and dusk the best times. Eungella is rugged and largely inaccessible except to very serious bush walkers. Access to the easiest part is via a bitumen road through the Pioneer Valley to the ranger's offices at Broken River. Walking trails range in length and difficulty from a 1-km rainforest walk at Broken River to 16-km round trips taking in the best rainforest and mountain views. The information centre, beside the kiosk at Broken River, is open daily 0700–1700 (usually); tel: 4958 4552. There is also a chance to meet the rangers – the information centre can tell you when.

Gordies Café & Bar $$ 85 Victoria St; tel: 4951 2611. Very busy with a young atmosphere, reasonably priced food, live entertainment, karaoki, etc. Open daily.

Seafood Blues $$ cnr Nelson and Victoria Sts; tel: 4953 5453. Fresh local seafood, busy restaurant.

Taylors Hotel $ Wood St; tel: 4957 2500. Bistro offering excellent value for money. Open daily (Sun lunch only).

AIRLIE BEACH

Airlie Beach is about the same distance from the equator as Hawaii, and is the main town on the Whitsunday Coast – made up of several towns that have practically merged together. The area has developed because of its closeness to the Whitsunday Passage, and is the most popular base for visiting the nearby Whitsunday Islands. Airlie Beach has a very distinct feeling of being in the South Seas, as well as having a permanent holiday mood.

i **Queensland Parks and Wildlife Service**, cnr Shute Harbour and Mandalay Rds; tel: 4946 7022. An array of information on the local national parks, including Whitsunday Islands and the Great Barrier Reef. Open Mon–Sat; closes 1300 Sat.

The Whitsunday Information Centre, Bruce Hwy, Proserpine; tel: 4945 3711; www.whitsundaytourism.com. Unbiased information. Open daily.

In Airlie Beach's Shute Harbour Rd the numerous information centres are all privately owned and funded predominately by commissions. Nearly all offer internet access at competitive rates and sometimes good deals on selected cruises.

Most accommodation is located on Shute Harbour Rd, which runs through several towns of the Whitsunday complex. A range of accommodation – all at relatively good value.

Airlie Beach YHA $–$$ 394 Shute Harbour Rd; tel: 4946 6312 or 1800 247 251; www.yha.com.au/hostels. Busy hostel with a central location, good facilities.

Airlie Cove Resort Van Park $$ Shute Harbour Rd; tel: 4946 6727. Natural, tropical setting. Accommodation includes tent sites, cabins and villas. Plenty of facilities including a spa.

Beaches $–$$ 362 Shute Harbour Rd; tel: 4946 6244 or 1800 636 630; www.beaches.com.au. Busy backpackers' resort, located in the centre of Airlie Beach.

Backpackers by the Bay $–$$$ Hermitage Dr.; tel 4946 7276 or 1800 646 994; www.backpackersbythebay.com. Quiet, close to beach and town.

Island Gateway Holiday Resort and Caravan Park $–$$ Shute Harbour Rd; tel: 4946 6228. Peaceful location just outside Airlie Beach, range of accommodation options from tent sites to deluxe cabins. Good range of facilities.

🍴 Again the action is along Shute Harbour Rd. The majority of eating places fall into the budget-with-quantity category, but there are also some more upmarket places.

Abel's $$$$ Abel Pt Marina; tel: 4946 4344. Fine dining overlooking the marina. Open daily for lunch and dinner.

Airlie Thai $$$ Beach Plaza, The Esplanade; tel: 4946 4683. Good atmosphere, balcony overlooking the beach, excellent Thai food. Open daily.

Bayside Restaurant $$$ 44 Coral Esplanade, Cannonvale; tel: 4946 6741. Good food, overlooking the bay with indoor and outdoor eating.

Beaches Backpackers $ 356–362 Shute Harbour Rd; tel: 4946 6244. Extremely busy and noisy bar, party games. Excellent-value food and mostly huge portions. Open daily.

Chatz Bar 'n' Brasserie $$ 390 Shute Harbour Rd; tel: 4946 7223. Range of dishes including some good vegetarian options. Happy hour 1100–1930 daily. Food served 1100–2200.

Mamas Boys $$ Magnums Whitsunday Village, Shute Harbour Rd; tel: 4946 6260. Excellent-value buffets featuring food from around the world. Daily themes, such as Indian Night, Chinese Night and European Night. Open daily for lunch and dinner.

Mangrove Jacks $$ Shute Harbour Rd; tel: 4946 6233. Alfresco dining, good food, good selection of wines, open daily for lunch and dinner.

Squid Lips $$$$ Beach Plaza, Esplanade; tel: 4946 7448. Licensed seafood restaurant, good views.

HIGHLIGHTS

This is an area of beautiful beaches and you are spoiled for choice. Earlando and Dingo beaches, both a short drive north of Airlie Beach near Dryander National Park, are favourites for fishing and beachcombing, while Funnel Bay, 4 km further along Shute Harbour Rd, then left down Jasinque Drive onto Langford Rd, is one of the most picturesque spots on the coast. The final stretch of road can get very rugged in wet weather and care should be taken.

The **Barefoot Bushmans Wildlife Park** ($$$) is in nearby Cannonvale, about 8 km away, with its comprehensive collection of Australian fauna, including kangaroos and wallabies roaming around the grounds. It is in Shute Harbour Rd and open daily 0900–1630; tel: 4946 1480.

Conway National Park, accessible from Shute Harbour Rd, runs from Proserpine to south-east of Airlie Beach and extends offshore to include many of the Whitsunday Islands. It is wild country – some of the oldest surviving rainforest in the world – and is noted for a wide range of flora and fauna. There are relatively few walking tracks.

SAILING IN THE WHITSUNDAYS

The whole point of coming to this area is to have fun on boats while sailing around one of the most beautiful parts of the world – the Whitsunday Islands. Sailing options are endless but by far the most popular, and usually the best value, are the fully crewed charters. Trips last from one day to the more popular two/three days, which usually include the famous Whitehaven Beach, the Reef and a visit to a couple of islands.

There is a huge choice of vessels. Luxury cruisers, power boats (for the day trips) and white-knuckle racing yachts are a start. However, in such a beautiful area, probably the best option is a traditional boat. One of the best, *Providence V*, gives you the opportunity to climb the rigging and get fully involved in the sailing, and represents excellent value for money. Tel: 4946 5299.

Where possible book your trip when in Airlie Beach so you can check out the boats first and talk to people – you may even get a last-minute special rate directly from the skipper.

The experienced can hire a bareboat (which you skipper yourself). Once again the range of options is endless, and if there is a large group of you, it can work out at relatively good value. However, there are strict environmental guidelines you need to follow, such as where and how to anchor. You are also compelled to regularly keep in touch with base and berth by 1600.

Sailing in the Whitsundays is as good as it gets. The channels between the islands are deep, so you are unlikely to get stranded on a reef, and most of the islands are within line of sight of one another so it is almost impossible to get lost. Of the 74 islands, 66 are National Parks so there is always something to explore. Pages 319–320 discuss the Whitsunday Islands in further detail.

TOWNSVILLE

See p. 325.

GREAT BARRIER REEF

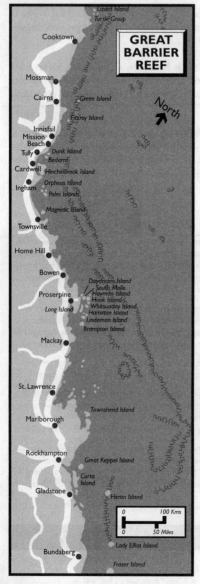

The Barrier Reef is so massive, so astounding, that you just run out of superlatives. It is the most extensive coral reef system in the world and the largest structure made completely by living organisms – its total coverage is greater than the states of Victoria and Tasmania combined.

The reef, which is not a single reef but features more than 2900 individual reefs and 900 islands, stretches from the Tropic of Capricorn, parallel with Rockhampton, to beyond the tip of Queensland, almost to Papua New Guinea. In the north the reef comes in close to the land, while further south it runs parallel to the coast at a distance of about 100 km.

Average water temperatures on the reef range from around 22°C in July to around 27°C in January, making it perfect for diving all year round. The reef is also the breeding area for a number of rare and endangered species. Humpback whales swim up from the Antarctic to give birth to their young in the warm waters, six of the world's seven species of sea turtle breed here, and dugongs make their home among the sheltered seagrass beds.

One of the problems is keeping the reef in its wondrous natural state, because everyone wants to come and see it. In the 1950s and '60s it used to be the haunt of skin-divers, and even in the 1980s there were only about 150,000 visitors a year on the reef. Now it is approaching 2 million and commercial operators run about 1.3 million scuba-dives per annum. Tourism brings in over $1 billion a year. Most of the reef's tourism is concentrated in two tiny areas – offshore from Cairns and the Whitsundays.

ARRIVAL AND DEPARTURE

Where you arrive on the reef will depend on which part of the mainland you leave from. Main departure points are Rockhampton or Gladstone for the southern islands (see pp. 308 and 306), Airlie Beach for the Whitsundays (see p. 319) and Townsville or Cairns for the northern groups (see pp. 325 and 336). You can fly in and land on the reef itself from any major airport in Australia – there is a full-scale jet airport on Hamilton – or you can helicopter in from almost any Queensland resort.

INFORMATION

Queensland Holiday Xperts, 30 Makerston St, Brisbane; tel: 13 88 33.

INTERNET SITES
Great Barrier Reef Discovery Coast: www.barrierreef.net
Great Barrier Reef in Queensland: www.queenslandholidays.com.au
Great Barrier Reef Marine Park Authority: www.gbrmpa.gov.au

ACCOMMODATION

A basic problem for any tourist on a budget is that staying at many of the resort islands is totally out of the question – some charge thousands of dollars a week. To preserve their exclusivity they also make it quite difficult to get there unless you have access to a charter boat.

There is justification for the prices charged. Everything, including all rubbish, has to be either shipped or flown in and out. Keeping staff is also a problem. Although it is like living in paradise, they are cut off from any serious social life and most last on average three months before heading back to the mainland.

There are, however, resorts with budget prices. Especially outside of the holiday season it is well worth enquiring about special rates. Details under individual islands include some expensive resorts, where they are worth the money if you can possibly afford it.

If you are going to camp you need to be totally self-sufficient. Fresh water is almost non-existent and you must bring everything with you. Camping permits are available from the Queensland Parks and Wildlife Service (tel: 4066 8601 Northern Islands, or 4946 7022 Whitsundays), which also provides guidelines to camping on the islands.

THE CORAL

Visitors tend to comment that the coral is not as colourful as they expect from seeing it on television. The problem is that underwater colours are filtered at different depths. Red and yellow disappear first, leaving the reef with a predominantly blue/green appearance which increases with depth. Video taken using lights shows the true colours of the reef. The colours are there – you just need light to see them. To view them at their very best you should try night diving, when the colours are dazzling.

Most of the reef is some way off the coast because coral cannot stand fresh water or the nutrients normally carried in the run-off from the mainland, so the major growth is out at sea away from such conditions. Some corals are more tolerant than others.

Trying to identify particular species of coral is very difficult. Indeed, unless you are a marine biologist, it is almost impossible except by form: plate, branching and so on. Every year over a third of the reef's species of coral reproduce sexually during a mass spawning event. For the majority of inner reefs this is around November, with the outer reefs later in December. Spawning always takes place at night, any time up to six days after the full moon, when eggs and sperm are released into the water in a massive cloud.

Fishing is not allowed in green national park zones, pink preservation zones and orange scientific zones. In other zones there is a fairly strict set of rules and some animals are, of course, totally protected. Take it that, generally, fishing, and coral- and shell-collecting are totally barred everywhere on the reef and you will not go far wrong.

THE REEF ISLANDS

There are islands the length of the Great Barrier Reef, although no one can say precisely how many. Some are small, bare, sand cays, others permanently vegetated cays or continental, i.e. rock not coral, islands. Wildlife includes goannas, possums, rock wallabies and 156 species of birds. There are vine forests, hoop pines, eucalypts and acacias inland.

THE WHITSUNDAYS

The 70-odd islands of the Whitsunday group, off Airlie Beach, are far and away the most popular part of the Great Barrier Reef, but

JELLYFISH

When box jellyfish congregate in these coastal waters during the summer (Oct–Mar) you really don't want to go swimming except in protective swimming enclosures or wearing a wet suit. This only applies near the coast – the jellyfish are not found out on the reef – but they can sometimes be found around islands close to the mainland. Other stingers sometimes encountered here include the irukandji and bluebottle. Both can cause a nasty sting. Vinegar can be used on both box jellyfish and irukandji stings but not on bluebottle stings; for these use cold water and ice.

bear in mind that some of the finest resorts lie elsewhere. Captain Cook, the first European in the area, achieved an amazing feat in navigating the narrow passage through these islands on a Whitsunday – hence the name. All the islands in the group are continental, and most are national parks, with the rules regarding parks strictly imposed.

BRAMPTON Most of this relatively hilly island is forested and was used as a nursery for palm trees. There are clearly marked walking tracks, and wildlife on the island includes cockatoos and grey kangaroos.

The only commercial access is via Macair Airlines from Mackay Airport, which makes it somewhat exclusive unless you are in a charter boat. This is done mainly to discourage day trippers. The Brampton Holiday Resort at Sandy Point, opened in 1933, is one of the oldest resorts on the Reef. It is low-key and has its own train to take guests from the jetty to the resort. Tel: 1800 737 678. At low tide you can walk across to the undeveloped island of Carlisle.

DAYDREAM This is the closest Whitsunday island to the mainland (easily accessible for day trips) and covers less than 2 sq km. It is covered with dense bush with a beach running the whole of the east side.

The resort ($$$$) was closed for a time; now it is thriving once again and is one of the largest in the group. It offers excellent facilities with most normal activities and non-powered water sports free. It is designed for families, and has safe beaches and makes a major effort to keep children occupied. Tel: 1800 075 040; e-mail: reservations@daydream.net.au.

HAMILTON ISLAND There are those who consider the development of Hamilton a lesson in how not to develop islands and ecologically sensitive places. It has been called the Gold Coast of the reef islands and is run as a town rather than as a small island resort, with a wide range of accommodation and entertainments not all connected with the Great Barrier Reef (unless you consider a Polynesian floor show an essential part of reef life). Prices tend to be high and it would perhaps be worth considering less obtrusive and pretentious places.

The east side of the island is relatively undeveloped, and there is a walk around the coastline at Catseye Beach and up to the summit of Passage Peak, with views north to Whitsunday Island.

HAYMAN ISLAND Hayman is nearer to the outer reef than most other islands in the group. It has bushwalking and snorkelling, and is close to good diving sites. It is also one of the most luxurious and expensive resorts. You fly to Hamilton and then take a 55-min boat transfer. The resort ($$$$) has the style of a 5-star international hotel rather than an island resort, which somehow feels out of place in this setting. Men must wear a jacket in the main dining room in the evening. Tel: 4940 1234.

HOOK ISLAND Hook is a true wilderness island and Hook Peak (459 m) is the highest mountain in the islands. There are few walking tracks but excellent beaches and superb diving. The snorkelling at the north end of the island is some of the finest in the area – the coral is in fair condition, the water is normally very clear and the aquatic life spectacular. Nearby is an underwater observatory where you can observe the fish and the coral from 10 m down. There are several campsites, and two fiord-type inlets at the southern end – Nara and Macona – provide safe and scenic anchorage. Ferries run once daily from Shute Harbour.

LINDEMAN Lindeman was the very first resort island in the Whitsundays. A camp for visitors was established in 1923 and this small beginning grew from strength to strength until, in 1992, the resort was taken over by Club Med. Despite the organisation's reputation of sun, sex and compulsory games, Lindeman Island Club Med ($$$$) is ideal for a family holiday, in that children are taken care of from dawn to dusk. Everything is included in the price and most packages are for five days. Tel: 3229 3155; e-mail via website: www.clubmed.com. The excellent beaches are all easily accessible and there are 20 km of marked walking tracks, including a 4-km walk to the top of Mt Oldfield (210 m). Most visitors fly first to Hamilton and then cross by launch on a 30-min trip.

SOUTH MOLLE

This is the largest of the Molle group and to all intents and purposes is joined to Mid Molle and North Molle – no matter what the state of the tide you can paddle to Mid Molle. West Molle is now Daydream (see p. 319).

South Molle is a hilly island with grasslands and patches of rainforest, and is still recovering from overgrazing a century ago. It is 4 km by about 2 km, and has 12 km of sand and coral shorelines. Local Aborigines appear to have come here from the mainland to get the hard stone from which they made their weapons. It is ideal for fairly strenuous walking, with well-signposted tracks leading around the island and up Mt Jeffreys.

Getting there takes about 20 mins from Shute Harbour or half an hour from Hamilton Island (see p. 320). The resort is to the north of the island, by the ferry terminus. It has yet to suffer the indignities of massive refurbishment and is affordable, especially for family holidays ($$$$ including as-much-as-you-can-eat buffets and most sports). Tel: 4946 9433.

NORTHERN ISLANDS

DUNK AND BEDARRA ISLANDS Dunk, part of the Family Group, is 6 km long, 2 km wide and one of only three rainforest islands on the reef, a lush home to native flora and fauna. The island is about 4 km off Mission Beach from which there are regular water-taxi services. It also has its own airstrip for access from Cairns or Townsville. There is an area set aside for campers and one resort ($$$), in the northwest of the island overlooking Brammo Bay. Tel: 1 800 737 678.

Bedarra, south of Dunk Island, houses the small, exclusive and expensive 5-star Bedarra Island Resort run by P&O Australian Resorts (16 villas). Most people get there by water taxi from Dunk. The charges are very high ($$$$) but cover everything, including the bar and the champagne. Tel: 1 800 737 678.

FITZROY ISLAND Almost ignored and much underrated, Fitzroy is less than an hour by high-speed catamaran from Cairns. It is a true continental island – once part of the mainland – and covered in rainforest surrounding a peak which rises to 271 m. The island is almost completely surrounded by coral reef and has a good safe anchorage. There are excellent tracks, splendid beaches and snorkelling, and affordable accommodation catering for everything from backpackers to families.

Fitzroy Island Resort ($$$$) is one of the few resorts that caters to the economy end of the market. It's a jewel of a place which is often overlooked. Tel: 4051 9588; e-mail: res@fitzroyislandresort.com.au.

FRANKLAND ISLAND This beautiful, uninhabited national park is situated directly off the coast from Russell Heads, 40 km south of Cairns.

GREEN ISLAND Green Island is a true coral cay surrounded by reef, with white sandy beaches and safe swimming. This was where Joe Harman took Jean Paget for an innocent holiday before the romance took a turn for the better in Nevil Shute's novel *A Town Like Alice*.

It is popular for day trips from Cairns – a fast catamaran takes 50 mins. Serious attempts have been made to maintain as much of the natural charm as possible. The island itself is fairly small – 15 ha – and you can stroll around it easily in less than half an hour. The interior is rainforest fringed by a mixture of compacted coral and sandy beaches.

Accommodation in the Japanese-owned resort ($$$$) has recently gone through a $500 million refurbishment. Tel: 4031 3300.

HINCHINBROOK ISLAND Hinchinbrook is separated from the mainland only by a narrow but deep and mangrove-fringed channel. The main access point is at Cardwell, roughly halfway between Cairns and Townsville.

The island is 52 km long and 10 km wide, with mainly mountainous rainforest soaring on Mount Bowen to 1121 m. Much is barely touched wilderness, and the only visitors are experienced bushwalkers. The 3- to 4-day coastal walk along the island's eastern side is the finest on any of the reef islands. There are some great expanses of beach, and wildlife such as wallabies, goannas, echidnas, bats, turtles and interesting birds. The small Hinchinbrook Island Resort ($$$$) offers all-inclusive accommodation and is specially suited to serious nature lovers. Tel: 4066 8585. There are also campsites, and bush camping is permitted everywhere except near the resort.

LIZARD ISLAND This national park paradise has abundant wildlife, such as the huge lizards which gave the island its name, five species of snakes, a small colony of bats and more than 40 species of birds. It offers some of the best scuba-diving, snorkelling and game-fishing in the world (it's only 15 km from the outer edge of the reef) and you do not need to be able to skin-dive; snorkelling is quite enough. At times you will have to push the fish to one side to proceed. There are 23 superb beaches and many fine walks. Captain Cook slept at the base of what is now called Cook's Look, climbing before dawn so that he could see clearly at first light a passage through the Barrier Reef.

Lizard is far to the north: 93 km from Cooktown. The Lizard Island Lodge ($$$$) is expensive but worth every cent. Tel: 4060 3999; e-mail: lizard.island@poaustralia.com;

website: www.poresorts.com. There is also a research station and a camping site. Campers must be entirely self-sufficient as the resort does not particularly welcome non-tariff-paying visitors. Most visitors fly in to the small airstrip, or are divers or anglers on charter boats. There is also a possibility of being dropped off from one of the island cruises out of Cairns.

ORPHEUS ISLAND   Orpheus – just 11 km long and about 1 km wide – is a nature wonderland: 100 species of fish and 340 of the 350 known species of reef coral can be found in the underwater gardens of its sheltered bays. Reefs around the island have been zoned 'A' (limited fishing only) and 'B' (look but don't touch), and the Parks Service go to some trouble to ensure that visitors do not damage the coral in any way.

Orpheus Island Resort ($$$$) is one of the few remaining privately owned Australian island resorts, and is the longest established on the Great Barrier Reef. It has only 31 rooms which will handle, at most, 74 guests at a time. They do not welcome day trippers or cater for under-15s. Tel: 4777 7377; website: www.orpheus.com.au; e-mail: orpheus@t140.aone.net.au. There are also little-publicised camping sites at Yankee and Pioneer bays.

Orpheus lies 20 km east of Ingham, 80 km north-east of Townsville and 190 km south of Cairns. Most visitors arrive by the Orpheus Seaplane which operates a daily 1-hr flight from Cairns and a twice-daily 30-min service from Townsville. Transport from Taylor's Beach, 25 km from Ingham, may also be possible.

SOUTHERN ISLANDS

GREAT KEPPEL ISLAND   Keppel, only 15 km from the coast and 55 km from Rockhampton, is an easy day trip – you can get there by boat from Rosslyn Bay or fly in from Rockhampton. It has 17 magnificent beaches and despite being some way from the reef there is plenty of coral to explore. Both the diving and snorkelling are good, and there are well-signposted walking trails through the thick forest.

Great Keppel has some good budget accommodation options – a feature not shared with many Barrier Reef islands – and it remains popular with younger travellers. **YHA Backpackers Village Great Keppel Island** ($–$$$; tel: 4927 5288 or 4933 6416; www.yha.com.au/hostels) has a range of accommodation and a bar and bistro that serves some affordable meals. There are other places to stay of varying quality and price; the Contiki-run **Great Keppel Island Resort** ($$$$+; tel: 1300 305 005) is perhaps the best known.

HERON ISLAND This tiny coral cay, 100 km from Rockhampton and 80 km out from Gladstone, rises only 3 m above sea level. Its great attraction is the 24 sq km of reef which is all within wading distance – the coral itself is less than stunning but the aquatic life is amazing. It has great diving, which must be done from a boat, not the beach. At the end of each year the Heron Island Underwater Festival attracts divers from all over Australia. Visits can be arranged to the Heron Island Research Centre, which works on numerous reef-related projects.

There has been a resort here since 1932, literally on the edge of a reef. Although many activities are on offer here, the emphasis is on snorkelling and skin-diving ($$$$). Tel: 4972 9055. Camping is not allowed.

LADY ELLIOT ISLAND This small island lies 90 km east of Bundaberg, a 25-min flight. It is very popular with divers because of the numerous shipwrecks in the area – there have probably been more wrecks off Lady Elliot than any other piece of coastline in Australia. Scuba-divers can dive straight off the beach, the underwater visibility is good and the coral is excellent. The island boasts more than 57 varieties of birds – it was originally mined for guano – and more than 200,000 of them nest here in the summer. Sea turtles also nest on Lady Elliot.

Feral goats stripped the island of vegetation before a new owner arrived in 1969. He killed them off to give the vegetation a chance and built an airstrip to take light aircraft. The island still looks comparatively bare, but marine life and the immediate access to the surrounding reef make up for this. The no-frills resort ($$$$) has safari-style tents with shared facilities or motel-type units. Tel: 4125 5344; e-mail: reservations@lady elliot.com.au.

CORAL BLEACHING

Global warming and rising sea temperatures are a huge threat to the Great Barrier Reef's (GBR) corals. A sea temperature just 1°C above the long-term monthly summer average is sufficient to cause coral bleaching, a stress condition that prompts corals to expel the single-celled algae (zooxanthellae) that give them food for growth and colour.

Zooxanthellae create the colours seen in most corals, and their loss reveals the bright whites of coral skeletons – hence 'bleaching'. If warmer conditions last long enough, bleached corals will die.

The GBR suffered widespread coral bleaching in the summers of 1998 and 2002; the latter year was the GBR's worst-ever bleaching event. A small but significant number of GBR reefs were severely damaged in 1998 and 2002, and they will take many years, or decades, to recover.

Townsville is Australia's largest tropical city and the business and cultural centre of North Queensland. It is named after Sydney businessman Captain Robert Towns, who was the major financial backer of John Melton Black, the founder of the settlement started in 1864. Towns only visited the place once, but his name lives on.

Townsville was originally used for shipping tallow and it is now a major port for minerals, sugar and meat. World War II saw the region transformed into a garrison for the tens of thousands of American, Australian and other allied service personnel who used it as a forward base for the war in the Pacific. Today it remains strategically important and home to Australia's largest defence establishment.

Townsville is wholly in the tropics. Three-quarters of its annual rainfall comes thundering down between Oct and Mar. Despite this, the area falls into the dry tropics zone, and warm sunny weather is one of Townsville's greatest assets, with more sunshine hours than any other North Queensland coastal centre.

Two World Heritage Areas – the Great Barrier Reef and the Wet Tropics World Heritage Area – are within easy reach, and Townsville boasts one of the best scuba-diving sites in Australia, the *Yongala* wreck. The town is also the headquarters of the Great Barrier Reef Marine Park Authority and several reef research institutes. Nearby Magnetic Island (see p. 329) is a mecca for budget travellers, with its extensive national park lands, glorious beaches, long walks and many backpacker resorts.

ARRIVAL AND DEPARTURE

The airport is just to the north-west of the city and for half the price of a taxi fare you can catch one of the shuttles that meet main flights. Tel: 4775 5544 for current timetable and bookings. All buses come into the Transit Centre at the corner of Palmer and Plume Sts, just outside the town centre, on the south side of Ross Creek.

INFORMATION

TOURIST OFFICES **Flinders Mall Information Centre**, Flinders Mall; tel: 4721 3660. Open daily, closed 1300 Sat–Sun. **Highway Information Centre**, Bruce Hwy on the southern approach to Townsville; tel: 4778 3555. Open daily.

Reef and National Parks Information Centre, Cape Pallarenda; tel: 4721 2399; e-mail: tsv.info centre@epa.qld.gov.au. Information on all the state's national parks. Open Mon–Fri 1000–1600.

INTERNET SITES **Townsville Information:** www.townsvilleonline.com.au
Several places along Flinders St offer internet access at competitive rates.
The Internet Den, 265 Flinders Mall; tel: 4721 4500. Open daily 0800–2200.

ACCOMMODATION

EN ROUTE

About 60 km north of Proserpine, along the Bruce Hwy, is the shire of Bowen. Hailed the Climate Capital of Australia, temperatures here remain fairly constant year-round. There are some beautiful beaches, of which one of the best is Horse Shoe Bay. Bowen is the oldest town in Northern Queensland and several museums display its history.

Adventurers Resort $–$$$ 79 Palmer St; tel: 4721 1522 or 1800 211 522; www.adventurersresort.com. Big, modern and with good facilities; close to town centre.

Beach House Motel $$$ 66 The Strand; tel: 4721 1333. Standard motel, located on the seafront.

Civic Guest House $–$$$ 262 Walker St; tel: 4771 5381 or 1800 211 522; www.backpackersinn.com.au. Central and popular, renowned for laid-back atmosphere.

Coral Lodge B&B $$$ 32 Hale St; tel: 4771 5512. Well-equipped rooms, small and quiet.

Downtown Motel $$$ 121 Flinders St; tel: 4771 5000. Close to main shops, cafés and bars, backpackers' accommodation available, usual facilities.

The Lakes Holiday Park $$$ cnr Hugh and Woolcock Sts; tel: 4725 1577. Range of accommodation options, close to town centre. Adjoins 18-acre lake.

Reef Lodge Budget Accommodation $–$$ 6 Wickham St; tel: 4721 1112. One minute from Reef HQ, excellent-value accommodation, basic facilities.

The Rocks Historic Guesthouse $$$$ 20 Cleveland Terrace; tel: 4771 5700. In beautiful building with period furniture. Close to town centre.

Sun City Caravan Park $$ 119 Bowen Rd; tel: 4775 7733. Range of accommodation options, good facilities.

FOOD AND DRINK

Flinders St, in the centre of town, and **Palmer St**, a newly developed area on the south side of the creek, are the two best options. **The Strand** also has several eating places including a few more upmarket establishments.

Allen Hotel $$ cnr Gregory and Eyre Sts, North Ward; tel: 4771 5656. Open daily for breakfast, lunch and dinner. Self-service buffet with every main meal.

EN ROUTE

Further along the Bruce Hwy, 28 km south of Townsville, is the turn-off for Bowling Green Bay National Park. This is the largest national park between Bowen and Townsville and includes the rugged Mount Elliot. There are some good swimming holes and a fine 17-km walk to Alligator Falls.

Australian Hotel $$$ 11 Palmer St; tel: 4771 4339. Aussie pub, in old Aussie building serving good-value Aussie food!

Covers Restaurant, Café and Wine Bar $$$$ 209 Flinders St; tel: 4721 4630. Expensive but popular restaurant. Menu features Australian game, as well as the more traditional steak. Licensed.

Gauguin $$$ Gregory St Headland, The Strand; tel: 4724 5488. Pleasant restaurant serving Spanish, French and Polynesian food. Open daily.

La Met $$ Metropole Hotel, 81 Palmer St; tel: 4771 4285. Dine alfresco in the beer garden or indoors in air-conditioned comfort. Varied menu includes salads, vegetarian options, pasta dishes and value burgers. Open daily for lunch and dinner.

Scirocco $$$ 61 Palmer St; tel: 4724 4508. East meets west Asian/Mediterranean cuisine. Indoor and outdoor dining. Closed Sun evening and Mon.

Tim's Surf 'n' Turf $$ Fisherman's Wharf, Ogden St; tel: 4721 4861. Busy seafood restaurant offering excellent value for money. Can get very busy – popular with travellers.

Zollies $$ 114 Flinders St; tel: 4721 2222. Busy pizzeria, good-value food, very popular with travellers.

HIGHLIGHTS

The easiest way to orientate yourself is to climb **Castle Hill** at Mt Cutheringa. This 286m pink granite monolith gives a 360-degree panorama and shows the layout of Townsville perfectly. It is possible to drive up, or to walk via a track that starts at the top of Blackwood St. The rock face is floodlit at night, making orientation very simple.

The city is remarkably easy to get around. At the centre is **Flinders Mall**, a shaded, palm-fringed and tropically landscaped shopping and pedestrian way. The popular Cotters Market is held here every Sunday 0800–1300. Meandering through the town is Ross Creek, an offshoot of Ross River, which is deep enough to provide anchorage for pleasure craft and trawlers. It is from here that fast catamarans run to Magnetic Island (see p. 329), and cruises go to other islands and the Great Barrier Reef (see p. 316). The newly developed **Strand Boulevard** stretches for 2.2 km along the seafront. On one side are hotels and restaurants. In the centre is a long footpath made interesting with coloured lighting, displays of art, newly planted trees and grassy areas. On the far side are the marina, beaches (with several stinger enclosures for safe swimming in the summer) and some good views of Magnetic Island.

Flinders St East, with its restored early 20th-century buildings, leads to **Reef HQ**. This is the world's largest living coral-reef aquarium and has a 20-m-long walk-through tunnel. All fish, plants and corals on display come from parts of the Great Barrier Reef. Guided tours, covering various topics, run throughout the day and are included in the admission price ($$$). Open daily 0900–1700; tel: 4750 0800.

Next door to the Great Barrier Reef Wonderland is the **Museum of Tropical Queensland**. The newly opened museum features displays on the wreck of *Pandora*, the ship that chased the *Bounty* mutineers. After hitting the reef in 1791, the wreck lay undiscovered until 1977. The museum is also a centre of maritime archaeology and has further displays on numerous other maritime subjects ($$). Open daily 0900–1700; tel: 4726 0606.

ACCESSIBLE WILDLIFE

The deceptively named **Town Common** is a short 5-min drive from the centre of the city, along Cape Pallarenda Rd. It is in fact a wetland sanctuary fed by the Bohle River and is a remnant of the Townsville-Burdekin wetlands. You may drive through the park on a 7-km-long road and there are bird-hides and walking tracks along the way. The best times to visit are early morning or late afternoon. It is estimated that some 260 different species of birds gather here to nest or stop over on their migratory routes. You also have a good chance of seeing wallabies and possibly some dingoes. Open daily 0630–1830; tel: 4722 5385 or 4774 1382.

The **Billabong Sanctuary**, 17 km south of the city on the Bruce Hwy, is a native Australian wildlife sanctuary. It has a 2-ha billabong with saltwater crocodiles, cassowary and waterfowl, and in the grounds are koalas, wombats, dingoes and parrots ($$$). Open daily 0800–1700; tel: 4778 8344.

NIGHTLIFE

When it comes to nightlife, **Flinders St** (for clubs and standard bars), **Palmer St** (for cosmopolitan cafés and bars) and **The Strand** (for the more upmarket establishments) are your best bets. For the more cultural evening the 1000-seat **Civic Centre**, at 41 Boundary St (tel: 4727 9797), and the 5000-seat **Entertainment Centre**, Entertainment Dr. (tel: 4771 4000), have regular performances, and bring plays, artists, groups and assorted entertainment to the city every month.

Colour section
(i) Mural at Byron Bay (pp. 260–263); Tropical Queensland beach; marina at Port Douglas (pp. 345–347).
(ii) Daintree River ferry, en route to Cape Tribulation (pp. 348–349); mangrove boardwalk; snorkelling on the Great Barrier Reef (pp. 316–324).
(iii) Billabong in Kakadu (pp. 399–405).
(iv) Australian wildlife: koala; estuarine crocodile; grey kangaroo; sea lion.

MAGNETIC ISLAND

If there was any destination in Australia almost specifically designed for the budget traveller it is **Magnetic Island**. The granite island, only 8 km off the coast, has around 40 km of dramatic coastline, much of it studded with magnificent hoop pines, 23 beaches and endless opportunities for swimming, diving, walking and lotus-eating. Much of it is a national park and its highest point is Mt Cook (497 m).

Captain Cook gave the island its name when the compass aboard his ship, the *Endeavour*, swung wildly as it sailed past the island. No one has ever been able to repeat that anomaly, which still causes much speculation.

The island is partly developed in that there are four settlements and there is vehicular traffic – indeed it has approximately 2000 permanent residents, many of whom commute to Townsville to work. But nearly two-thirds of the island is a national park, which restricts further development and allows the island to retain its appeal. Getting there is easy: Sunferries high-speed catamarans run regularly (15 times a day) from Townsville to Picnic Bay. The trip takes 20 minutes and is inexpensive at approximately $15 return; tel: 4771 3855. Slower car ferries also run daily to Geoffrey Bay in Arcadia; tel: 4772 5422.

ORIENTATION

The island is a rough upside-down triangle with the main centre of **Picnic Bay** at its southern point. This is where the passenger ferries arrive. The right side of the triangle, the east side, is where most of the development has taken place. Following the island's only main road, you first come to **Rocky Bay**, which has an excellent beach, and then **Nelly Bay**. Beyond **Geoffrey Bay** is **Arcadia** and, back from the road, the **Alma Bay Lookout**. The road then splits with the left fork taking you to **Horseshoe Bay** and the right to **Radical Bay Lookout** (hire cars are not allowed down this road, but it is more pleasant to walk).

TRAVELLING AROUND

It is possible to ferry a vehicle across but this is expensive and uneconomic for a short stay. Bicycles, motorcycles and cars are available for hire, but probably the most fun are the Mini-Mokes – Moke Magnetic, on the Esplanade at Picnic Bay (tel: 4778 5377), claims to have the largest fleet of Mokes for hire in the world and prices are extremely reasonable at just $65 a day (with unlimited km). The Magnetic Island Bus Service (tel: 4778 5130) offers 1-, 2-, and 5-day pass tickets (1–2-day passes also available from the Information Office) and has two guided tours of the island every day (bookings essential). Several of the larger backpacker resorts have a free bus service (for guests) running through the four towns of the island several times a day.

WHAT TO DO

This is a low-pressure sort of place and the weather is ever pleasant: typically 1°C below that of the mainland and in a rain shadow that ensures 320 sunny days a year. Most of the people who come here on holiday are regulars. The only time to avoid is possibly during the Christmas break.

Apart from the numerous beautiful beaches, there are plenty of other things to do. For **birdwatchers**, over 100 species of birds have been sighted on the island, including blue-wing kookaburras, sulphur-crested cockatoos and black cockatoos. An 8-km walk from Picnic Bay to West Point offers the chance to sight wading birds, mudskippers, fiddler crabs and mangrove snails that inhabit these wetlands, particularly in the Cockle Bay area.

There is plenty of **bushwalking**. An excellent leaflet/map produced by the national parks (available at the tourist office) shows all the many walks on the island. These will take you to most places in the national park area, through a variety of flora and fauna. The hillsides are strewn with boulders and covered with mostly open eucalypt woodland of bloodwoods, stringybark and grey ironbarks. There are also small pockets of rainforest in the gullies. You will certainly see rock wallabies and perhaps koalas – this is the most northerly point in Australia to have large free-ranging colonies.

For those not willing to make the trek there is the **Koala and Wildlife Park**. It is always full of visitors being photographed with the koalas; there are also kangaroos, lorikeets, wallabies, emus, cockatoos and wombats. The lorikeets come in for a feed at 1130 each day. The sanctuary is on Pacific Dr., Horseshoe Bay ($$). Open daily 0900–1700; tel: 4778 5260.

Tropicana Tours (tel: 4758 1800) run the most unusual trips. The stretched jeep will take you on a range of island tours lasting from a few hours to a full day. All trips are informative, fun and friendly, and most get you close to the natural environment – and have a real element of adventure.

WATER SPORTS

The fringing reef is wonderful for snorkelling. Beaches range from wildly popular to almost totally deserted. Some, such as Balding Bay, are so secluded they can be reached only by foot or by boat. Easier to reach is Arthur Bay, which has some of the best snorkelling, as well as interesting caves. The largest, noisiest and busiest bay on the island is Horseshoe, where almost every watercraft imaginable is available for hire. Bluey's Bush and Beach Rides (38 Gifford St, tel: 4778 5109) take you around the bay and you can experience swimming on horseback; if that is too tame for you, try para-ailing. The waters are part of the Great Barrier Reef Marine Park, which means that certain activities may be restricted in some zones part of the time. Get details of what is and what is not allowed from the Great Barrier Reef Marine Park Authority or the Department of Environment and Heritage in Townsville.

INFORMATION

For information on Magnetic Island, visit the tourist information centres in Townsville (see pp. 325–326).

Magnetic Island:

INTERNET SITES www.magneticisland.info
www.magnetic-island.com.au

Courtyard Cyber Café, The Courtyard, Picnic Bay; tel: 4778 5407. Open daily 0830–1730.

Pleasure Divers is just metres from some of the best dive sites in Geoffrey and Alma Bays. It teaches everything from resort diving to full PADI certification, and runs Outer Barrier Reef trips and dive trips to the famous *Yongala* wreck. Shop 2, Arcadia Resort, Arcadia; tel: 4778 5788; e-mail: pleasure.divers@ultra.net.au.

ACCOMMODATION

No other island in Australia has such a wide range of affordable accommodation. You can stay within easy access of a perfect beach for less than at anywhere else remotely comparable. There are several large backpacker resorts on the island, but be warned, most of them revolve around alcohol and partying: if it's peace and quiet you want then look elsewhere.

Beaches B&B $$$ 39 Marine Pde, Arcadia; tel: 4778 5303; e-mail: beaches@tpgi.com.au. Pleasant timber cottage on Geoffrey Bay.

Centaur House $$ 27 Marine Pde, Arcadia; tel: 4778 5668; e-mail: centaurhouse@email.com. Small, pleasant and quiet hostel. Free activities take place most nights, including barbecues and games.

Dandaloo Gardens $$$ 40 Hayles Ave; tel: 4778 5174. Set among towering paper barktrees. Pleasant, fully self-contained units available.

Dunoon Beachfront Apartments $$$$ The Esplanade, on the beach at Picnic Bay; tel: 4778 5161. Tropical Gardens, two pools, spa. Newly renovated.

Geoff's Place – YHA $–$$$ 40 Horseshoe Bay Rd, Horseshoe Bay; tel: 4778 5577; www.yha.com.au/hostels. This is not your typical YHA; drinking and partying occurs every night. Good facilities; camping sites available.

Hideaway Budget Resort $$ 32 Picnic St, Picnic Bay; tel: 4778 5166. Just 120 metres from the island's passenger ferry terminal.

Island Palms Resort $$$$ 13 The Esplanade, Nelly Bay; tel: 4778 5571. On the beachfront. Quality accommodation, can work out good value for several people staying a few weeks.

Maggies Beach House $–$$$ Pacific Drive, Horseshoe Bay; tel: 4778 5144 or 1800 001 544; www.maggiesbeachhouse.com.au Fairly new and very comfortable hostel.

Magnetic Island Tropical Resort $$$ 26–56 Yates St, Nelly Bay; tel: 4778 5955; e-mail: tropres@byte-tsv.nat.au. Set in 16 acres, 200 metres from beach, winner of 13 major tourism awards. Slightly more expensive than most backpacker resorts, but a lot quieter and more civilised. Excellent bistro.

Marshall's B&B $$$ 3–5 Endeavour Rd, Arcadia; tel: 4778 5112. Pleasant homestay with free pickup from ferry terminal, located in quiet area.

Traveller Backpackers Resort $$ 1 The Esplanade, Picnic Bay; tel: 4778 5166. For backpackers, with three bars and a nightclub. Closest accommodation to the ferry terminal.

Food and Drink

Restaurants are dotted around the four main towns. The island caters well for vegetarians and food is relatively inexpensive, although this is not a gastronomic destination.

Alma Beach Trattoria $$$ Alma Bay, Arcadia; tel: 4778 5757. Mediterranean cuisine, alfresco dining overlooking the bay. BYO. Closed Mon and Tues.

Blue Water Gallery Restaurant $$$ Shop 2–3, 5 Bright Ave, Arcadia; tel: 4778 5645. Varied menu with blackboard specials. Open Tues–Sun for dinner, Sat–Sun also for breakfast and lunch.

Crusoe's Magnetic Island Restaurant $ 5a Picnic Bay; tel: 4778 5480. Pleasant café serving crêpes, omelettes, burgers, fish and chips, and excellent lentil burgers! Open daily.

Magnetic Island Chinese Restaurant $$ 9 The Esplanade, Picnic Bay; tel: 4778 5706. Standard Chinese restaurant.

Mexican Munchies $$ 37 Warboys St, Nelly Bay; tel: 4778 5658. Dining in a tropical setting. Some good-value options. Dinner only, closed Wed.

Possum's Café $ Nelly Bay shopping Plaza, Nelly Bay; tel: 4778 5409. Basic but delicious home-made food. Open daily.

WHERE NEXT?

North lies Cairns, capital of the 'Far North' (see p. 336), or for a very different side of Australia, the Flinders Hwy heads inland for Alice Springs and Uluru (Ayers Rock) (see pp. 366 and 374).

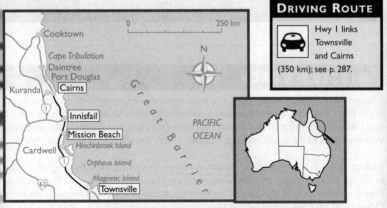

DRIVING ROUTE

Hwy 1 links Townsville and Cairns (350 km); see p. 287.

Note
Trains do not stop at Mission Beach.

TOWNSVILLE — CAIRNS
OTT Tables 9010/9085

Service	🚌	🚆	🚌	🚌	🚌	🚌	🚆	🚌
Days of operation Special notes	Daily	②④⑦ **AB**	Daily	Daily	Daily	Daily	①⑤ **B**	Daily
Brisbane ....d.	0745	0855	1200	1430	1400	1600	1825	1930
Rockhampton ....d.	2010	2025	2355	0250	0305	0405	0323	0715
Townsville......................d.	0710	0820	1105	1405	1400	1535	1305	1915
Mission Beach................d.	1055			1455	1745	1720	1920			
Innisfail..............................d.	1145	1357	1545	1835	1815	2010	1720	2345
Cairns..............................a.	1255	1600	1700	1955	1930	2125	1920	0050

Special notes:
A–Conveys sleepers, car transporters and on ④⑦ Queenslander Class.
B–Days of operation are from Brisbane.

Captain Cook, on his momentous voyage in 1770, was the first European to discover this region, known as the Cassowary Coast. He did not land, as his previous attempts had met with a hostile reception. The first European to explore the countryside was Edmund Kennedy, who had undertaken to investigate the country between the coast and the Great Dividing Range up to Cape York. His journey showed that successful settlement of the district's coast would require regular sea communication due to the difficulty and cost of building roads through the dense tropical terrain. The discovery of gold and other metals on and beyond the Atherton Tableland made the government keen to open up the tropical North Coast. Cardwell was the first settlement, followed by Port Douglas, Cairns and Geraldton – renamed Innisfail in 1910.

TOWNSVILLE

See p. 325.

MISSION BEACH

Mission Beach today is a quiet area, made up of six small communities stretching 14 km north from Tam O'Shanter Point through South Mission, Wongaling, Mission Beach and Clump Point to Bingil Bay. The area is more laid-back than Cairns to the north and various towns to the south, making it popular with travellers wishing to unwind.

Mission Beach is surrounded by rainforest – home to Australia's highest concentration of the endangered cassowary. There are many excellent walks; the **Tam O'Shanter State Forest** contains one of the largest tracts of coastal rainforest remaining in northern Queensland and has a trail taking you through cassowary habitat. The forest can be reached via the Mission Beach–Tully road.

Some of the **beaches** here come close to paradise. In the north, towards Bingil Bay, there are several secluded coves, fringed with coconut palms and backed by rainforest. At the southern end the beaches are more open. Offshore from Mission Beach is **Dunk Island**; see p. 321.

ⓘ **Mission Beach Visitor Centre**, Porters Promenade; tel: 4068 7099; e-mail: info@mission beachtourism.com.au; www.missionbeachtourism.com.au. Open daily 0900–1700.
C4 Environment Centre and Wet Tropics Visitor Information Centre, Porters Promenade; tel: 4068 7197; e-mail: C4@qldnet.com.au; www.cassowaryconservation.asn.au. Open daily 1000–1700.

🛏 **Mission Beach Retreat $–$$** 49 Porters Promenade; tel: 4088 6229 or 1800 001 056; www.missionbeachretreat.com.au. Small, pleasant and welcoming.
Sanctuary Retreat $$ 72 Holt Rd, Bingal Bay; tel: 4088 6064. Excellent-value lodge, situated on a hill in rainforest overlooking the sea. There is a small bar, café and pool, natural yet stylish.
Scotty's Beach House $–$$$ 167 Reid Rd; tel: 4068 8676 or 1800 665 567; www.scottys beachhouse.com.au. Renowned good-time hostel.
Treehouse YHA $–$$ Bingil Bay Rd; tel: 4068 7137; www.yha.com.au/hostels. Natural wooden lodge, set in rainforest. Relaxed, easy-going atmosphere, free-roaming animals. Occasional BBQ evenings.

🍴 **Café Coconutz $$** The Village Green; tel: 4068 7397. Bright orange café, serving a range of drinks and juices as well as food with an Asian twist.
Early Birds Coffee Shop $ The Hub Shopping Centre, Porters Promenade; tel: 4068 7299. Basic food – burgers, salads and sandwiches all at good value.

Friends $$ Porters Promenade; tel: 4068 7107. Wooden furnishings, alternative atmosphere. Range of seafood, steak and traditional foods. Closed Sun.
Piccolo Paradiso $$ David St; tel: 4068 7008. Italian restaurant; good pizzas and pasta.

INNISFAIL

Innisfail is the largest town on the Cassowary Coast. It gives the genuine feel of a Queensland country town serving the needs of the surrounding countryside, mainly the sugar and banana plantations and the small fishing fleet. It is not a tourist town – there is no Big Sugar Cube – but it has a lot of charm.

The town's Italian community was established in 1880 when the Catholic Bishop of Brisbane and 11 Carmelite nuns bought and cleared 10,000 ha of jungle for sugar planting. The marble **Pioneers Monument** at the end of the main street was given to the town by the local Italians. It shows a cane-cutter at work – a reminder that sugar could never have initially been harvested without their unrelenting physical labour in extreme conditions. Asian immigrants also came to work the sugar fields, and their influence is still apparent. There is even a Joss House, on Owen St, built in the 1940s after an earlier one was destroyed in a hurricane. A small **museum**, housed in the old School of Arts building on Edith St, and run by volunteers ($), is open Mon–Fri 0900–1200 and 1300–1500.

This is crocodile country: take a safe look at the **Johnstone River Crocodile Farm** ($$$, Flying Fish Pont Rd; tel: 4061 1121, open daily 0830–1630). There are over 2000 crocodiles here, mostly estuarine. Guided tours run throughout the day from 0900.

⓵ **Innisfail Visitors Centre**, Bruce Hwy; tel: 4063 2655; e-mail: innisfailinfocentre@znet. net.au; www.innisfailtourism.com.au. Open daily. (May vary in low season.)
Queensland National Parks and Wildlife Service, 19 Flyingfish Point Rd; tel: 4061 5900. Open Mon–Fri.

🛏 **Backpackers Paradise $–$$** 73 Rankin St; tel: 4061 2284. Basic accommodation, but inexpensive and close to town centre.
Codge Lodge $–$$ 63 Rankin St; tel: 4061 8055. Pool. Cable TV. Views of the river.
Mango Tree Van Park $$ Couche St; tel: 4061 1656. On the banks of the Johnstone River.

🍴 **Gumloon Restaurant $$** 96 Edith St; tel: 4061 1164. Basic restaurant/café.
Innisfail Fish Depot $ Fitzgerald Esplanade; tel: 4061 1579. Raw seafood fresh off the boats.
Roscoe's Pizza Place $$ 3B Ernest St; tel: 4061 6888. Standard, good-value pizza bar.
Seafood and Eat It $ Central Arcade, Rankin St; tel: 4061 8477. Inexpensive home-made seafood meals. Closed Sun.

CAIRNS

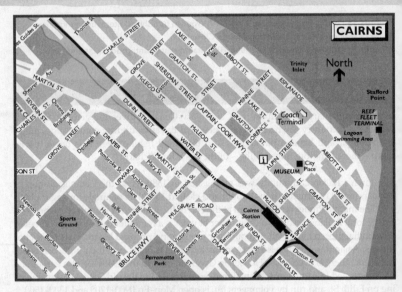

Cairns creates a feeling that it was planned specifically for the tropics. There is an esplanade running right along the edge of the city centre by the foreshore; parks and gardens appear to be perpetually ablaze with exotic flowers and trees. It is perfectly sited for both relaxing and adventurous exploration, with the Great Barrier Reef to the east, the refreshing green plains of the Atherton Tableland to the west, palm-fringed beaches north and south and, just up the track, the wonders of the Daintree rainforest and Cape Tribulation.

Cairns has a sense that it is just coming into its own, that its prospects are pleasing. Indeed, Cairns is very pleasing, except that it had a distressing tendency until recently to pull down the last beautiful examples of Far North Queensland wooden architecture; only now are the last ones being preserved.

Captain Cook sailed the *Endeavour* into Trinity Bay on Trinity Sunday 1770, but it was 1873 before the first pioneers came to settle what was then called Thornton. When gold was found in the area it remained a sleepy backwater, while Cooktown (see p. 349) boomed. In 1876 the township was renamed in honour of the Governor of Queensland, Sir William Cairns, and declared the port of entry and customs points. Tremendous trading rivalry arose and continued for many years between Cairns and Port Douglas, just to the north, until the railway line from Brisbane was only extended as far as Cairns and Port Douglas lapsed into tropical somnolence.

Today, tourism is a major factor in the prosperity of Cairns – every day over 600 land, sea and air tours depart from here, taking visitors from around the globe on journeys to experience nearby natural attractions.

ARRIVAL AND DEPARTURE

Both domestic and international flights come into Cairns International Airport on the northern outskirts of the city. The inexpensive airport shuttle bus runs regularly between the airport and most accommodation; tel: 4048 8355.

Cairns is the end of the line for bus routes up the east coast; the ride from Townsville, 350 km south, takes 4½ to 6 hours depending on the number of stops. The terminus is at Trinity Wharf Centre in Wharf St. The railway station is nearby.

INFORMATION

TOURIST OFFICE **Tourism Tropical North Queensland Gateway Discovery Centre**, 51 The Esplanade; tel: 4051 3588. Open daily 0830–1830; www.tropical-australia.com.au. Information on Cairns and the surrounding area. Most of the other information centres in Cairns are privately owned and funded by commission.

INTERNET ACCESS **Inbox Café**, 119 Abbott St; tel: 4041 4677. There are numerous internet and call centres around the city all offering competitive rates – although exact prices fluctuate depending on the season.

Cairns Visitor Information: www.cairnsweb.com.au
Tourism Tropical North Queensland: www.tropicalaustralia.com.au

MONEY **Travelex** has several foreign exchange offices throughout the city, including 13 Shield St (tel: 4041 0644) and at the domestic and international terminals at Cairns airport.

ACCOMMODATION

There is no shortage of budget accommodation in Cairns. There is an array of motels on the approach from the south, hostels are interspersed around the town centre, and most hotels are strung along the Esplanade. Many travellers use Cairns as a stopping place after travelling the east coast.

Acacia Court Hotel $$$$ 223–227 The Esplanade; tel: 4051 5011. One of a string of mid-range hotels along the Esplanade. Prices can fluctuate from good value to expensive depending on the season.

Cairns Central YHA $–$$$ 20–24 McLeod St; tel: 4051 0772; www.yha.com.au/hostels. Lively youth hostel, close to bus and train station. Pool area.

Cairns Coconut Caravan Resort $$ cnr Bruce Hwy and Anderson Rd; tel: 4054 6644; e-mail: coco@coconut.com.au. High-standard resort offering a wide range of accommodation, including tent sites.

Calypso Inn Backpackers $–$$ 5–9 Digger St; tel: 1800 815 628; www.calypsobackpackers.com.au. Smaller and quieter than some other hostels.

Caravella Backpackers & Backpackers 77 $–$$$ 149 & 77–81 Esplanade; tel: 4051 2431 & 4051 2159; www.caravella.com.au. Big, central and long open.

Central Plaza Apartments $$$$ 255–259 Lake St; tel: 4031 0333; e-mail: centralplaza@internetnorth.com.au. New, fully self-contained apartments at good-value prices.

Dreamtime Travellers Rest $ 4 Terminus St; tel; 4031 6753; e-mail: dreamtime@dreamtimetravel.com.au. Small, quiet hostel close to central Cairns.

Half Moon Bay Resort $$$$ 101–103 Wattle St, Yorkeys Knob; tel: 4055 8059; e-mail: info@halfmoonbayresort.com.au. Set on a beautiful beach 19 km north of Cairns.

Nutmeg Grove B&B $$$$ 7 Woodridge Close; tel: 4039 1226; e-mail: stay@nutmeggrove.com.au. Set in 3 acres of rainforest.

YHA on the Esplanade $–$$ 93 The Esplanade; tel: 4031 1919; www.yha.com.au/hostels. Rainforest courtyard; like most hostels in the area, has a lively atmosphere.

FOOD AND DRINK

There are numerous eating places in Cairns; every appetite and budget is catered for.

Pattaya Thai Restaurant $$$ 62 Spence St; tel: 4051 3135.
Busy Thai restaurant, licensed. Open daily 1800–late.

Charlie's $$$ 223–227 The Esplanade; tel: 4051 5011. Part of
the Acacia Court Hotel. Seafood restaurant, also has all-you-
can-eat smorgasbord – starve yourself all day and it's excellent
value for money! Open daily.

Cock & Bull $$ cnr Grove and Digger Sts; tel: 4031 1160.
Open daily for lunch and dinner, breakfast Sun. Traditional
British-style pub serving food and beer.

Damari's $$$ 171 Lake St; tel: 4031 2155. Closed for lunch at
weekends. Pleasant Italian dining indoors or on the patio.

Dundee's $$$ 29 Spence St; tel: 4051 0399. Busy restaurant
with informal atmosphere, serving traditional steaks, seafood
and pasta, as well as the more outrageous bush tucker such as
crocodile and kangaroo. Open daily from 1730.

Kani's $$$ 59 The Esplanade; tel: 4051 1550. Excellent seafood,
overlooking the waterfront. Dinner only.

Rattle 'N' Hum $$$ 67 The Esplanade; tel: 4031 3011.
Good value pub-style meals. Casual atmosphere. Open daily
1130–late.

Red Ochre Grill $$$$ 43 Shields St; tel: 4051 0100. Original
restaurant creating dishes from native Australian ingredients –
there are some unusual and interesting options. Open daily for
lunch (except Sun) and dinner.

Taj $$$ 61 Spence St; tel: 4051 2228. Award-winning, traditional
Indian restaurant. Open for dinner daily.

Taste of China $$$ 36 Abbott St; tel: 4031 3668. Yum cha
lunch, specialises in seafood.

The Woolshed $ 24 Shields St; tel: 4031 6304. Very much for
the 'wilder' traveller. Open every night till 0300, inexpensive
meals, Aussie woolshed decor, dancing on tables, loud music
and outrageous party games.

HIGHLIGHTS

The **Esplanade** runs for almost 2 km and is a chance to get Cairns into perspective.
There is a walkway along the Esplanade's landscaped parkland, which fringes a

strip of restaurants on one side and the sea on the other. At the southern end you'll find the pier complex, good for shopping and dining. You'll also see the wharves around Trinity Inlet, which originally accounted for the city's prosperity. At the northern end of the Esplanade there are mid-range hotels lining the street offering some good bars and restaurants.

> Cairns Tropical Zoo $$$ on the Captain Cook Hwy, Palm Cove, has over 100 freshwater and saltwater crocodiles as well as other native animals. Open daily 0830–1700; tel: 4055 3669.

Almost everything is within easy walking distance, including two big shopping centres: **The Pier**, at the southern end of the Esplanade, and **Cairns Central**, on the block between Bunda and McLeod Sts. In fact, shopping is a major part of the city-centre attractions, and there are a range of duty-free, fashion and souvenir shops.

If you're looking for a fun, educational evening where you can learn some amazing facts about the Great Barrier Reef, **Reef Teach** is a must. Presentations ($$$) take place Mon–Sat from 1815: Irish marine biologist Paddy Colwell is a little eccentric but very knowledgeable. Located at 14 Spence St; tel: 4031 7794.

The **Cairns Museum** ($) is housed in what was the school of art at the corner of Lake and Shields Streets. Among its delights it has the contents of a joss house that stood until recently in Grafton Streets. It also shows the construction of the rail link between Cairns and Kuranda. One major section is devoted to the history of the Aboriginal people in the area – essential if you are to understand how Cairns, a late developer as a town, is the result of a series of conflicting pressures. Open Mon–Sat 1000–1600; tel: 4051 5582.

Boardwalks are very popular in Cairns. The **Foreshore Promenade** boardwalk is popular with locals and tourists alike. It allows pedestrian access over the mudflats that line the Cairns coastline. There are viewpoints along the way for birdwatching. **The Jack Barnes Bicentennial Mangrove Boardwalk**, on Airport Ave, the road to the airport, is a series of educational walks through the complex ecosystem of a mangrove swamp. Hides let you see the life of the mangrove swamps up close. Spray yourself well with insect repellent before you set out for either.

The **Flecker Botanical Gardens** on Collins Ave (off Sheridan St) are open daily and cover 300 ha up the slopes of Mount Whitfield Conservation Park. Instead of trying to recreate European vegetation, as several parks in the south of Australia do, the plants here reflect the wide range of local habitats.

At the **Royal Flying Doctor Base** ($), 1 Junction St, Edge Hill, near the gardens, you can see how this organisation, unique to Australia, has operated in the outback since 1928. Open to the public Mon–Sat 0900–1630; tel: 4053 5687.

EXCURSIONS TO THE GREAT BARRIER REEF

Cairns is a good starting point for a cruise out to the reef. The range of options is endless: you can choose from one-day sea-cat cruises to five-day diving courses. Prices are not cheap, although there is a range of options to suit most budgets.

Below is just a selection of the numerous operators. A good site for further information on reef trips is www.tnq.org.au; for dive operators, travel and bookings have a look at http://diversionOZ.com.

Cairns Dive Centre, 121 Abbott St; tel: 4051 0294. Runs a range of dive courses, and also operates day and overnight trips for experienced divers and snorkellers to the outer reef.

Down Under Cruise and Dive, 287 Draper St; tel: 4052 8300. Runs several different trips including half- and full-day reef cruises on a super cat; two-day diving, snorkelling and relaxing trips on a sailing boat; and fully certified dive courses.

Prodive, cnr Abbott and Shields Sts; tel: 4031 5255 (shop) or 116 Spence St; tel: 4031 5255 (training centre). PADI five-star dive school, offering a range of certificates for three-, four- and five-day courses. Also runs one-day trips to the reef.

Sunlover Cruises, Trinity Wharf; tel: 4050 1333. Runs daily cruises from Cairns to the outer reef on high-speed catamarans. Having moored at the reef you can take either a guided snorkelling tour or a trip on a glass-bottom boat.

Compass; tel: 4051 5777. Runs inexpensive day trips to the outer reef, where you get the chance to try out snorkelling, diving (at extra cost), and go on a glass-bottom boat. Departs Marlin Jetty daily at 0800.

BEACH AND SEA LIFE

The foreshore boasts an incredible 4800 sq. m, man-made swimming lagoon, which offers year-round safe swimming but in a 26-km sweep up towards Port Douglas are some of the best beaches in Australia. Closest to the city are **Machans**, **Holloways**, **Yorkey's Knob** and **Trinity Beach**. In the summer the box jellyfish can inflict a grievous, even deadly sting, but some of the northern beaches have stinger enclosures, offering safe swimming all year. Most of the beaches are backed with lush rainforest and have a range of water activities, and several also have a strip of accommodation, restaurants and bars nearby.

The Reef Fleet Terminal at the end of Spence Street is where most of the sports-fishing charter boats are based, as well as an array of boats that run to the islands and the reef. From here you can take a cruise to Green Island, a small island with good beaches, national park, snorkelling and a five-star resort; tel: 4051 0444 or 4044 9944. Cairns Habitat Cruises do a three-hour calm water cruise on Trinity Inlet, which includes a tour of the Cairns Crocodile Farm; tel: 4031 4007.

NIGHTLIFE

Cairns, like every other city in Australia, has a casino. The Reef Hotel Casino in Wharf St is built around and is part of the old Customs House. The casino is topped with a four-storey conservatory in a delicate glass dome which is open to the non-gambling public; tel: 4030 8888. The **Night Market**, on the Esplanade, is open 1700–2300 daily and has a range of stalls selling arts and crafts; there is also a food court.

Cairns is well known for its night scene and nearly all the hotels have bars and clubs. Further bars can be found along the Esplanade and around the city centre, and the Cairns nightlife can offer something for everyone, from the raving backpacker to those wanting a quiet evening drink.

DAY TRIPS

One of the great delights of Cairns is its closeness to one of the most pleasant areas of country in Australia. The **Atherton Tablelands** stretching out to the west contain rainforest, waterfalls and wonderful wildlife, and have a different style and feel.

Atherton itself is 85 km south-west of Cairns on the Kennedy Hwy and more than 760 m above sea level. It can be argued that the climate up on the Tablelands is the best in Australia. Certainly it seems close to perfect all year – if it is a little too hot and moist for you in Cairns you merely escape by driving up to Atherton.

The Tablelands are rich in national parks – seven in all – with lush tropical rainforest, waterfalls and lakes to explore. Many tourists coming through north Queensland skip Atherton and the Tablelands thinking, perhaps, that they do not compare with the splendours of the Daintree further north. But the Atherton Tablelands have a quiet, elegant charm all of their own and, if time allows, you should spend at least a day up there looking at the splendid scenery and enjoying the weather.

You can get to **Kuranda**, up on the Tablelands, in three different ways. To drive is interesting and pleasant but the alternatives are so much better. The train runs on what is arguably the finest stretch of scenic railway line in Australia. One section actually runs across the face of the Stony Creek Falls and the views are nothing short of amazing. Trains depart Cairns daily 0830 and 0930 and return 1400 and 1530; $$$. Tel: 4031 3636. See OTT 9000.

THE TJAPUKAI ABORIGINAL CULTURAL PARK

This is a rare opportunity to experience Aboriginal culture, in this case the society of the Djabugay and Yirrgandyji peoples. So-called 'cultural shows' are often dreadful. The Tjapukai Aboriginal Theatre is the exception: remarkably entertaining, informative and moving. Each dancer explains a particular aspect of Aboriginal life ranging from the boomerang to the didgeridoo, songsticks, spears and clothing – blended with dancing and singing using quite modern and stunning techniques. The theme which comes across time and time again is 'Proud to be an Aborigine'. Unmissable. $$$+ Kamarunga Rd, Smithfield; tel: 4042 9999.

When the Skyrail to Kuranda was first proposed there was much opposition from environmentalists, but it has worked very well, is not intrusive and does not appear to have damaged the rainforest. You travel for 7.5 km, the world's longest cable-car trip, over rainforest up to the top of the escarpment. It is a most wonderful journey. There are stops at the Barron Falls Station for a staggering view of the Barron Gorge, and at Red Peak Station, where you can inspect the rainforest from a wooden walkway. The Skyrail terminal is by the Captain Cook Hwy, a short drive north of Cairns. Tel: 4038 1555.

Kuranda is pretty, fits neatly into the mountains, and is in a 1960s time warp. At the **Kuranda Heritage Market**, open daily 0900–1500, you can have your fortune told and purchase arts and crafts, and home-made jams and cakes. There are several other reasons to visit the town, including the excellent rainforest walks, an aviary and a nature park.

There is also the **Australian Butterfly Sanctuary** ($$, Rob Veivers Dr., tel: 4093 7575, open daily 1000–1600), with up to 2000 butterflies, covering 35 indigenous and protected species, in a rainforest enclosed by a massive walk-through flight aviary. **The Kuranda Visitor Information Centre** in Centenary Park has further details; tel: 4093 9311; www.kuranda.org.

WHERE NEXT?

Cairns is the Far North, but the tip of Australia is still over 1000 km away. Take a tour up to Port Douglas, Cooktown and the Cape York Peninsula (see pp. 344–352). Alternatively, make the journey on board a working cargo vessel up to Thursday Island and back again; www.seaswift.com.au. Or spend time on the northern section of the Great Barrier Reef (see p. 316).

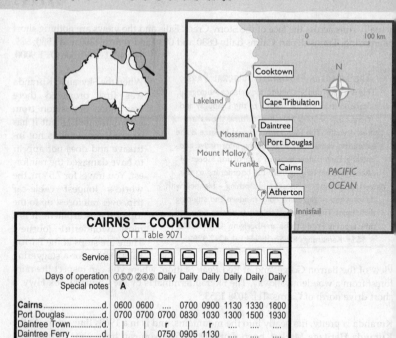

CAIRNS — COOKTOWN
OTT Table 9071

Service								
Days of operation Special notes	①⑤⑦ A	②④⑥	Daily	Daily	Daily	Daily	Daily	Daily
Cairns..............................d.	0600	0600	....	0700	0900	1130	1330	1800
Port Douglas..................d.	0700	0700	0700	0830	1030	1300	1500	1930
Daintree Town................d.	|	|	r	|	r	....	....	....
Daintree Ferry................d.	|	|	0750	0905	1130	....	....	....
Cape Tribulation............d.	|	0845	0900	1000	1300	....	....	....
Cooktown........................d.	1115	1200	....	....	....	....	....	....

Special notes:
A–This service operates via Lakeland.

DRIVING ROUTE

The 75 km north to Port Douglas and Mossman are regular highway. After Mossman it continues in a series of zigzags either north to Daintree or inland to Mount Molloy and then north on the inland road towards Lakeland. But there is a total transformation. Roads which were sealed become intermittently sealed and then just graded dirt. Bulldust, ultra-fine powder, is everywhere, choking engine filters which have to be cleaned every day. In the Wet many of the roads to the north, sealed or not, are impassable; in the Dry they can be a challenge. With a conventional vehicle you could, in the Dry, drive as far as Cooktown if you head first for Lakeland (220 km from Cairns) and then turn east for the last 82 km of the journey. Despite being risky, in the dry season it is usually possible to make it to Cooktown, by following the road up from Daintree. But only attempt this in an old banger that won't suffer too much from driving through the creeks and potholes.

Port Douglas, just an hour from Cairns, is a laid-back tropical resort, while the village of Daintree, on the banks of the Daintree River, is the gateway to the Daintree National Park and the starting point for a rough ride up to Cooktown, where the great navigator and 'discoverer' of Australia is commemorated. Driving on the Cape York Peninsula is like embarking on an expedition.

CAIRNS

See p. 336.

PORT DOUGLAS

Port Douglas is, in some ways, an upmarket extension of Cairns. They are only 70 km apart and the airport services both. Port Douglas was first established in 1877 when Christie Palmerston (in full, Cristofero Palmerston Carandini, a remarkable man from a theatrical family but with a great talent for trailblazing) cut a road through the rainforest and down the mountain range. The town rose rapidly with the gold rush, but when Cairns won the battle for major port in the area, Port Douglas went into dormancy.

Then Christopher Skase came along. Skase was one of a handful of overambitious entrepreneurs in Australia in the 1970s and '80s. He took a total backwater and changed it into an international resort. Then his companies – the lead company was called Quintex – crashed resoundingly. If, in his ambition, he had not tried to buy an American film studio he might have weathered the storm and he would now be praised for his foresight in creating one of Australia's foremost resorts.

> [*i*] There are no government-funded information centres in Port Douglas; however, there are several privately owned operations – all of them are helpful.
> **Port Douglas Tourist Information Centre**, 23 Macrossan St; tel: 4099 5599. Open daily.
> **BTS Tours and Information Centre**, 49 Macrossan St; tel: 4099 5665; e-mail: info@btstours.com.au. Open daily 0800–1800.
> **Cyberworld Internet Café**, 38 Macrossan St (at the back of Cactus Bar Restaurant); tel: 4099 5661. Open daily.
> **Port Douglas Daintree Tourism Association:** www.pddt.com.au.

EN ROUTE

During the 1930s, Depression job-creation labourers built a dirt road from Cairns to Port Douglas. A man known as Pop Evans established a roadhouse at Hartley's Creek about halfway between the two towns, and to entertain visitors performed shows featuring local wildlife. In 1934 he acquired Charlie the crocodile. Charlie died in 2000 at the estimated age of between 70 and 80 years old; he holds the record for the crocodile held longest in captivity. Now **Hartley's Creek Crocodile Farm** (tel: 4055 3576) is not only home to hundreds of crocodiles (both freshwater and saltwater), but also koalas, kangaroos, cassowaries, dingoes, snakes and other native animals. Tours, shows and activities take place throughout the day. $$$ Open daily 0830–1700.

🛏 Although Port Douglas does attract the very rich – and some of the prices charged at the top end would choke a horse – there is a range of affordable accommodation.

Archipelago Studio Apartments $$$$ 72 Macrossan St; tel 4099 5387; e-mail: info@archipelago.com.au. Beach and sea views from all balconies, excellent location.

Dougies Backpackers Resort $–$$$ 111 Davidson St; tel: 1 800 996 200; www.dougiesbackpackers.com. Close to the beach, short walk to town centre.

Port O'Call Lodge YHA $–$$$$ Port St; tel: 4099 5422; www.yha.com.au/hostels. Small dorms, doubles and twins – all en suite. Excellent facilities. Good value bar and bistro.

Tropic Breeze Van Village $$ 24 Davidson St; tel: 4099 5299. Range of good-value accommodation including camping sites.

🍽 Restaurants here tend to be upmarket and expensive or very noisy, but it is easy to stroll along Macrossan, Port and Wharf Sts peering into the cafés and ethnic restaurants to see if you like the place and the prices. Most places cater well for vegetarians.

Café Macrossan $$ 42 Macrossan St; tel: 4099 4372. Casual, street-side alfresco dining. Open daily till late.

Courthouse Hotel Bistro $$ cnr Wharf and Macrossan Sts; tel: 4099 5181. Beer-garden setting, live music, can get very busy and noisy. Open daily.

Jade Inn Chinese Restaurant $$$ 39 Macrossan St; tel: 4099 5974. Affordable Chinese food in pleasant surrounds. Open daily 1200–1430 and 1700–2200.

Salsa Bar and Grill $$$ 26 Wharf St; tel: 4099 4922. Popular, lively restaurant with a cosmopolitan menu; award winner.

HIGHLIGHTS

Port Douglas lies on a long low spit of land and one of its charms is that all of the main roads are lined with palm trees.

Rainforest Habitat has won awards galore. You can explore it on your own, but the experience is massively heightened if you go on one of the guided tours. There are 140 species of birds, koalas, kangaroos and crocodiles in their natural environment, which you view from elevated walkways. You can even have breakfast with the birds. Located on Port Douglas Rd, just off the Captain Cook Hwy ($$$); tel: 4099 3235; open daily 0800–1730 (last entry 1630).

The activities available in and around Port Douglas are very varied. There are, for example, a couple of world-class golf courses which are also world-class expensive. Much more affordable is **Four Mile Beach**, on the eastern side of the town (there are some safe swimming enclosures here). **Cycling** around the town and further afield – there are fine opportunities for cycle touring in the region — is inexpensive and there are some good places to explore (bikes can be hired throughout the town). Walk up **Flagstaff Hill** for some excellent views – follow Wharf St to Island Point Rd, which takes you to the top. You can take the **Bally Hooley Railway** ($, tel: 4099 5051) from the station at the Marina (departs 1030, 1130, 1330, 1430, 1530 and 1700). This open-carriage train potters along for 15 minutes through a few resorts to St Crispins Station. From here, you can catch the paddle wheeler *Lady Douglas* ($$$) which makes her stately way up the Dickinson Inlet. There are two departures daily (not Sun); tel: 4099 5051.

Port Douglas is the closest mainland resort to the Great Barrier Reef, but it is never emphasised that the reef is a fair way out and you need to go by very fast boat to get the most out of it. There is a wide range of day cruises to choose from – all fairly expensive. **Quicksilver Connections** runs two boats, carrying 300 and 400 passengers, and includes a stop at an underwater viewing platform; tel: 4087 2100. Alternatively, **Aristocat** runs smaller tours (a maximum of 40 passengers) and includes a guided snorkelling tour; tel: 4099 4727. Both are around $170 for the day.

Much closer in are the **coral gardens of the Low Isles**. Visit them aboard *Shaolin*, a charming wooden boat that cruised the South China Sea for 16 years before retiring on the Great Barrier Reef; tel: 4099 1231. Less expensive is *Sailaway*, which also offers an excellent day trip; tel: 4099 5599.

Closer to Mossman but easily reached from Port Douglas, the 400-seat **Karnak Playhouse and Rainforest Sanctuary** (tel: 4098 8144) borders Daintree National Park and features world-class productions. The Kubirri Restaurant and bar is open when plays are in season.

DAINTREE NATIONAL PARK

The Daintree forms part of the World Heritage-listed wet tropics area. This area is particularly unusual owing to its being left undisturbed for 100 million years from both environmental changes and human impact – it contains the most prolific and complex plant communities on earth. There are giant palms 3000 years old, interesting flora, and an array of kangaroos, wallabies, possums, birds, snakes, crocodiles and other reptiles. The Daintree is partly accessible by conventional car; however, many people visit this area and never appreciate its significance – much better is to do one of the numerous **guided tours** from either Port Douglas or Cairns. Alternatively you can join one of

LEARN TO SCUBA

The Great Barrier Reef is one place where scuba-diving is not essential – you can see more aquatic life in a day with snorkel and fins then you would see in a lifetime of scuba-diving elsewhere. But because the water is so warm and the scenery so magnificent it is a good place to get at least a resort certificate, which will let you dive with a qualified diver. Calypso (tel: 4099 3377; 0413 388 444), Discover Dive School (tel: 4099 6333), and Quicksilver (tel: 4099 5050) all offer a range of diving courses and day trips.

several expeditions organ ised by the accommodatio around Cape Tribulation (se below).

Daintree Village, a relaxed old-fashioned little town with a population of less than 250 was originally settled by the red cedar timber cutters. The Timber Museum, in Stuar St, where there are also cafés and souvenir shops, is well worth a visit. Free. Open daily 1000–1630; tel: 4098 6166.

The Daintree River, just north of the village, is an excellent place to see wildlife. A range of river cruises run from various points along the river. You'll find numerous booking agents around Daintree Village. One of the most interesting cruises is the *Spirit of Daintree*, which is basically an eco-friendly string of floating carriages attached to an engine; tel: 4090 7676.

CAPE TRIBULATION

To reach Cape Tribulation you need to take the ferry, which runs constantly 0600–2400 every day, across the Daintree River. The short journey is expensive, at approximately $16 per vehicle each way, but is the only means of getting across – swimming is not a safe option! Ten kilometres north of the river ferry is the **Daintree Rainforest Environmental Centre** ($$, tel: 4098 9171, open daily 0830–1700), where you can climb a tower for some excellent views of the rainforest and follow a boardwalk at ground level. There is also a display centre, theatres and a shop.

STINGERS AND SNAPPERS

In the summer months, Nov–Apr, sea swimming outside swimming enclosures is highly dangerous. Among other nasty jellyfish, such as the sea wasps, box jellyfish are around and their stings can be fatal. These are not known to inhabit the Outer Reef, and generally only exist within 1–2 km of mainland beaches. Fully protected swimming enclosures are provided at Port Douglas, Palm Cove and Mission Beach.

Crocodiles are a protected species. Both **freshwater** and (extremely dangerous) **saltwater, or estuarine, crocodiles** live in this area. The warning signs are not some tourist attraction – if you swim near a croc warning sign your chances of being attacked are around 50 per cent. And for reasons not fully understood, they prefer the flavour of tourists!

he **Cape Tribulation Section of the Daintree National Park** is the only place where he Great Barrier Reef actually meets the rainforest, but before you dive in with snorkel nd mask, seek safety advice regarding crocodiles and box jellyfish. The rest of the park ffers excellent bushwalks with flora and fauna that only the Daintree can provide.

eyond Cape Tribulation the unsealed road takes you towards Cooktown. You are est taking a four-wheel-drive (as signs advise), although in the dry season if you ave your own banger (so it doesn't matter if the car gets the odd bang) you have a ood chance of making it in a two-wheel-drive. En route you'll pass a turning for **loomfield Falls** – these are quite impressive. You can also drive inland to ooktown, on better roads, via Mount Molloy and Lakeland.

COOK'S CAPE

ape Tribulation is the most unlikely name for an achingly eautiful place, and James Cook is the man responsible or it. The reef his ship *Endeavour* struck on 11 June 770 is just north of the ape, which Cook named as he place where his 'tribula- ions' began.

🖃 There are several accommodation options in Cape Tribulation, most of them in the budget category.
Crocodylus Village YHA $–$$$ Lot 5, Buchanan Creek Rd, Cow Bay; tel: 4098 9166; www.yha.com.au/hostels. Several km north of the Daintree ferry.
Jungle Treehouse B&B & Farmstay $$$$ tel: 4098 0090 or 4099 5651. In the heart of the national park – transfers arranged when booking.
PK's Jungle Village $–$$$ On the main road, Cape Tribulation; tel: 4098 0040. Budget resort offering a range of accommodation. Extremely popular with backpackers.

🍴 There are a few eating places in the area, which can be found simply by following the main road.
Café on the Sea $$ Esplanade, Thornton Beach; tel: 4098 9118. Fourteen steps from the beach, this elegant café is good value and has light meals. Open daily for lunch.

COOKTOWN

aptain Cook beached the *Endeavour* on the shores of the river here (which he named the ndeavour) in June 1770 to repair the damage created by running onto the reef. A mon- ument by Charlotte St marks the spot. Cook and his crew stayed about six weeks, the ongest time they spent on land anywhere in Australia. This little town, today with a pop- ulation of about 1800, is steeped in history, not only because of its significance regarding he discovery of Australia, but also owing to the gold rush that began in 1873 (and the irth of the town) with its influx of miners from around the world.

What used to be the town's convent, on the corner of Helen and Furneaux Sts, is now he **James Cook Museum ($$)**. The story of the fixing of the hole in the *Endeavour* is recorded here, and among many other exhibits are Cook's cannon and anchor, jettisoned in the efforts to get the *Endeavour* off the reef. The museum has recently been renovated. Open daily 0930–1600 (closed Feb and most of Mar); tel: 4069 5386.

The Cemetery, on McIvor River Rd, represents the hardships of the early settlement and there are many unmarked graves here. You will also see the grave of the remarkable Mrs Mary Watson. She escaped with a servant and her baby from Lizard Island in 1882 after an attack by Aborigines, but eventually died of thirst. There is also a Chinese shrine dedicated to the 18,000 Chinese who came to the region during the gold rush.

The best view of the town is on **Grassy Hill Lookout** (follow Hope St right to the top) which has an old lighthouse and a memorial to Captain Cook, who used this vantage point to plot a course through the Reef. **The Black Mountains National Park**, 28 km south of Cooktown, on the main road, gets its name from the blue-green algae that grows on the boulders giving a black appearance. The site is the subject of Aboriginal legend and you can only see the mountain from the viewing point. In the past people have disappeared here, while others have heard moaning and groaning sounds. Have people got lost in the caves, or is it the wind …?

i **Nature's PowerHouse Visitor Information and Environment Centre**, Finch Bay Rd (in the Botanic Gardens); tel: 4069 6004; info line: 1800 174 895; e-mail: keep@fni.aunz.com; website: www.naturespowerhouse.info. Has a bookstore, gallery and café. Open daily.

Alamanada Inn $$$ Hope St; tel: 4069 5203. Guest house, motel and self-contained units. Standard facilities.
Cooktown Orchid Travellers Park $$ cnr Charlotte and Walker Sts; tel: 4069 6400. Range of budget options, including camping spots. Reasonable facilities.
Hillcrest B&B $$$ Hope St; tel: 4069 5305. An 1890 building in a beautiful setting.
Pam's Place Budget Resort YHA $$ cnr Charlotte and Boundary Sts; tel: 4069 5166; www.cooktownhostel.com. Pleasant hostel with pool and courtyard.

TO There are few eating places here, none a gastronomic delight nor particularly good value – owing to difficulty in getting supplies to the town. Most are located along Charlotte St.
Diggers Inn $$ Cooktown RSL Memorial Club, Charlotte St; tel: 4069 5780. Open daily for lunch and dinner.
Sovereign Hotel $$$$ cnr Charlotte and Green Sts; tel: 4069 5400. Part of a small resort, good food, but not that good value.

CAPE YORK PENINSULA

This northern finger of the continent contains some of the most spectacular and rugged country in Australia and one of the world's last rainforest wildernesses, with thousands of species of tropical birds, beautiful waterfalls and crocodiles. The rainforest near the road which runs up the spine of Cape York often demonstrates a curious phenomenon: it can be thundering down rain on the road but in the rainforest there is just a gentle mist. The tree canopy is so dense that it acts as an effective umbrella.

Safari tours are available from Cairns and take about 10–14 days for a round trip with visits to Thursday Island off the tip of Cape York (see also Where Next? box on p. 343). The recommended time for travelling is during the dry season (June–Sept) as the rivers swell during the wet season, often closing roads.

In theory, in the Dry, you could drive along the Peninsula Developmental Road as far as Weipa. This is true frontier country. It is best to have a four-wheel-drive, especially if you intend to explore off the main road, and you must carry enough supplies, especially water and petrol, to get you from place to place with a safe reserve. Having said that, the first vehicle to make the journey all the way to the tip of Cape York was a 1927 Austin 7, and many other two-wheel-drive vehicles have made the journey in the Dry, although their condition was not enhanced by the journey.

The Quinkan Reserve near Laura contains hundreds of Aboriginal cave paintings, and guided tours are available. The reserve is at the southern end of Lakefield National Park, the state's second-largest national park. Lakefield has a wide range of birdlife and other native animals in its rainforest, woodlands, grassy plains and coastal mudflats along Princess Charlotte Bay. On Flinders and Stanley Islands, in Princess Charlotte Bay, are spectacular Aboriginal galleries of marine life – stingrays, crabs, flying fish, turtles and the rare dugongs. Lakefield is a major crocodile habitat, and is for serious bushwalkers only.

Mungkan Kandju National Park covers drier woodlands between McIlwraith Range and the Archer River. The Archer and Coen rivers commonly spread over the flood plains in summer, and the lagoons and swamps which remain into the dry season attract an abundance of bird life. The park is accessible only in the dry season. Iron Range National Park is a wilderness area containing the largest remaining tract of lowland tropical rainforest in Australia. It has quite spectacular coastal scenery and unusual wildlife. In the very north of the peninsula, Jardine River National Park is a tropical wilderness in the catchment of the Jardine River, Queensland's largest perennial stream. There are swamps and heathlands, with tropical vegetation which includes many varieties of New Guinea origin, again accessible only in the dry season. Before setting off you should notify somebody that you are leaving and get them to call for help if you do not return or notify them by an agreed date. It is also wise to contact the Queensland Parks and Wildlife Services' Far North Queensland Centre (tel: 4053 4533) prior to leaving to check the latest conditions of the roads, creeks, etc.

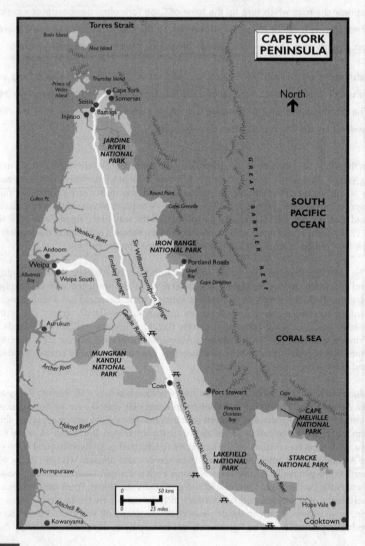

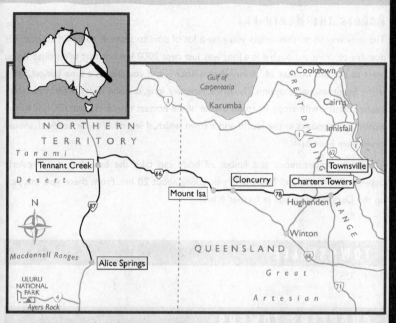

TOWNSVILLE — ALICE SPRINGS
OTT Tables 9001/9075/9428

Service			RAIL	RAIL	
Days of operation	Daily	Daily	④	③⑦	④⑤⑦
Special notes		AB	A	C	
Townsville .... a.	0705	....	....	1530	1930
Charters Towers .... d.	0840	....	....	1833	2110
Cloncurry .... d.	1725	....	....	0820	0600
Mount Isa .... d.	1920	....	....	1235	0725
Tennant Creek .... d.	0300	0335	0427	....	....
Alice Springs .... a.	....	0930	0920	....	....

Special notes:
A–These services starts at Darwin.
B– Additional trip 2245.
C–This train conveys sleeper class.

DRIVING ROUTE

There's not a lot of tricky navigating to be done, as the Flinders Hwy (Hwy 78) runs all the way from Townsville to Mount Isa, from where the Barkly Hwy (Hwy 66) continues through to Tennant Creek to meet the north–south transcontinental Hwy 87, the Stuart Hwy. Be prepared for a lot of long, boring road and take sensible precautions.

Queensland/Northern Territory

Across the North-east

The only way to do this, unless you have a lot of time to spare, is to fly. Of course, it is possible to drive, although it is a long way, just over 2000 km, but that takes time. If you want to see the wonder of Uluru – Ayers Rock – and you are on a time budget, flying is the only reasonable option. The drive, however long, dry and dusty, is through interesting country, with stops en route at one of the hottest towns in Australia, one of the richest ore deposits in the world and a town which, if legend is to be believed, should never have been built.

The young, impecunious and limber of body can take the bus: they run regularly between Townsville and Tennant Creek, taking about 20 hrs. From there you can pick up the Darwin–Alice bus (a further 6 hrs).

TOWNSVILLE

See p. 325.

CHARTERS TOWERS

In this hot, dry region, many consider Charters Towers to be the most attractive town in Queensland. It lies to the east of the Great Dividing Range, and it still has much of the opulence that was given it by the gold rush, although now the main industry in the surrounding country is cattle-raising.

The story, almost certainly apocryphal, is that the first gold here was found by a young Aboriginal boy named Jupiter, who was with a party of prospectors, including Hugh Mosman. Jupiter went out to look for horses that had bolted in a thunderstorm. As he bent down to drink from the local creek he saw gold-bearing quartz below the surface. Mosman registered the claim, was rewarded by the government, adopted Jupiter and brought him up as his son. Statues of Mosman and Jupiter commemorating this event are in Centenary Park.

Charters Towers once had a population of 30,000, more than three times what it is today. In the 40 years from 1871 some 7 million oz of gold were extracted from the region, and during the boom there were about 100 gold mines in the area, and possibly even more pubs. In the 1890s the residents called Charters Towers, with little modesty, The World. It was enough of the world to get Dame Nellie Melba to come and perform at the Theatre Royal.

To get the town into perspective, **Rotary Lookout** (follow the signs from Mosman St) gives a panoramic view of the town. At ground level you can clearly see the prosperity that came with the gold in the classical Australian Victorian architecture decorated with verandas and lacework. The town has more National Trust properties than any other place in Queensland. Bankers thought the gold would last forever, and many of the most imposing buildings in town were once banks, for example the **library** and the **World Theatre**, both in Gill St. **City Hall** and the Post Office in Gill St are in the same Victorian we-will-last-forever style.

Charters Towers also boasted Australia's first regional **stock exchange**, opened in 1890. This magnificent heritage building, in Mosman St, has been fully restored and now houses the National Trust, a mining museum ($) and some shops. In 1912, the town started to run downhill quickly as the gold came to an end. By the start of World War I it was pretty much all over, and the exchange closed in 1916.

On the Milchester Rd, about 5 km from the centre, is the old **Venus Gold Battery** ($, well-signposted). In 1872 this was the first permanent gold-ore battery to be erected in the area and was used commercially for exactly a century. Open daily 0900–1500, with guided tours at 1000 and 1400 which show how it all worked. When running, the noise is beyond belief. At the height of its fortune Charters Towers boasted 29 of these monsters.

---

[i] **Charters Towers Tourist Information Centre**, 74 Mosman St; tel: 4752 0314; www.charterstowers.qld.gov.au. Open daily.

[≘] **Cattleman's Rest Motor Inn $$$** Plant St, cnr Bridge St; tel: 4787 3555.
Charters Towers Caravan Park $ 37 Mt Leyshon Rd; tel: 4787 7944. Two km from the centre of town.
Dalrymple Caravan Park $$ Lynd Hwy; tel: 4787 1121.
Enterprise Hotel Motel $$$ 217 Gill St; tel: 4787 2404.
Mexican Tourist Park $ cnr Church and Tower Sts; tel: 4787 1161.
Park Motel $$$ Deane St, cnr Mosman St; tel: 4787 1022.

Plain Creek Cattle Station $$$$ tel: 4983 5228; website: www.charterstowers.qld.gov.au/plaincreek; e-mail: plaincrk@cqhinet.net.au. 180 km south of Charters Towers. Experience life in the outback on a 30,000-ha working cattle-station. Good hospitality. Comfortable cottages. Swimming pool.

Rix Hotel Motel $$$ 69 Mosman St; tel: 4787 1605.

🍴 **Crown Hotel Bistro $$** 119 Mosman St; tel: 4787 2471.

Enterprise Hotel Steakhouse $$$ 217 Gill Street; tel: 4787 2404.

Gold City Chinese Restaurant $$ 18 Gill St; tel: 4787 2414.

Gold Mine Chinese Restaurant $ 10 Mosman St; tel: 4787 7609.

The Stock Exchange Café $$ Mosman St; tel: 4787 7954.

CLONCURRY

Cloncurry currently holds the record for the hottest temperature in Australia a 129.07°F or 53.9°C – and is a typical outback Queensland town right in the heart o the Great North-East. The town was built on its mining riches and it very much look as if it is being revived through mining. Four major mines – Ernest Henry, Selwyn Osborne and Cannington – are now in operation and there are other major project in the pipeline. You can see the style of the original mining in the **Great Australian Mine** and treatment plant 3 km out of town. This was established by the prospecto Ernest Henry, who discovered rich deposits of copper in 1867.

ℹ️ **Cloncurry Information Centre and Mary Kathleen Memorial Parks & Museum**, McIlwraith St; tel: 4742 1361. Open daily (closed Fri–Sat Oct–Mar).

🛏️ **Cloncurry Caravan Park Oasis $** McIlwraith St; tel: 4742 1313.

Cloncurry Motel $$$ Daintree St, cnr Sheaffe St; tel: 4742 1268.

Gidgee Inn $$$$ Matilda Hwy; tel: 4742 2429; e-mail: gidgeeinn@bigpond.com.au. Luxurious outback motel, built of red earth, with sweeping verandas in traditional colonial style.

Gilbert Park Cabins $$$ Matilda Hwy; tel: 4742 2300.

Leichhardt Hotel/Motel $$$ 5 Scarr St; tel: 4742 1389.

Oasis Hotel/Motel $$$ Ramsay St; tel: 4742 1366.

Wagon Wheel Motel $$$ 54 Ramsay St; tel: 4742 1866. The Prince of Wales Inn is part of the premises, the oldest remaining licensed premises in North-West Queensland. The licence was granted in the 1880s.

🍴 **Gidgee Grill $$$$** Matilda Hwy; tel: 4742 2429. The restaurant is part of the motel which is of quite remarkable and appropriate outback design.

The Prince of Wales Inn $$$ 54 Ramsay St; tel: 4742 1866. Now part of a motel but still a part of the history of the town.

Highlights

If you fly into Cloncurry you will see Qantas's original name at the airport – **Queensland and Northern Territory Aerial Service**. The first paying passenger on Qantas went from Charleville to Cloncurry in November 1922. Sadly Qantas no longer flies here, so you will have come in on Flight West or Macair Airlines.

In the **cemetery** in Henry St are the graves of what were called Afghan camel drivers – in fact, they were nearly all Pakistanis. Only one is named; the others are just numbers in a foreign land.

Possibly the most comprehensive mineral collection in Australia is in the **Mary Kathleen Memorial Park and Museum** at the eastern entrance to Cloncurry, with more than 18,000 exhibits. The park displays some of the buildings which once stood in the ghost town of Mary Kathleen, dedicated to the mining of uranium. Open weekdays 0700–1600, weekends during the season 0900–1500. Tel: 4742 1361.

The Flying Doctor Service

It is difficult to overstate the place that the Flying Doctor Service has in the minds and make-up of Australia. Here is where it all started, pushed along by the sheer guts and energy and vision of the Revd John Flynn. Working with primitive aircraft and small transmitting and receiving sets which, when he conceived of them, were only theoretically possible, he set out to provide the outback with a doctor with wings and wireless communication. In 1927 the *Victory*, a single-engined DH50 aircraft, took off with a doctor on board for its first mission, to Julia Creek.

In the **Flying Doctor Complex** in John Flynn Pl., Daintree St, is a one-third-size model of the *Victory*, together with equipment used in the early days of the service, set into realistic displays. It includes the pedal generator, part of the transceiver equipment which was very important to the early progression of the service, and the first Traegar Pedal Wireless which for many years was the only means of distant communication for many people living in the outback. The complex also houses the Fred McKay Art Gallery, Alfred Traegar Cultural Centre, the Allan Vickers Outdoor Theatre and the Cloncurry Gardens. Open weekdays 0700–1600, weekends 0900–1500. Tel: 4742 1251.

MOUNT ISA

Mount Isa exists for the **Mount Isa Mine**, one of the largest mines in the world and the biggest underground mine in Australia. It directly employs about 3500 people, nearly 20 per cent of the total population, which makes it very much a one-company town. The mine is the world's biggest single producer of silver and lead, and is among the top ten producers of copper and zinc.

EN ROUTE

At the junction of the Barkly and Stuart highways stands a memorial to the famous missionary and pioneer Flying Doctor of the outback, the Revd John Flynn.

Near the remains of the telegraph station at Barrow Creek are the graves of John Franks and James L. Stapleton. The two telegraphers were killed in 1874 by members of the local Kayteje tribe, possibly over an enclosure that denied the Aboriginal people access to a freshwater spring. The telegraphist sent a message for help to the Central Telegraph Office in Adelaide, and as John Stapleton lay mortally wounded he tapped out a last message to his wife: 'God bless you and the children.'

---

i **Mount Isa Tourist Information**, Outback at Isa Centre, 19 Marian St; tel: 4749 1555; e-mail: info@outbackatisa.com.au; www.outbackatisa.com.au. Open daily. The Riversleigh Fossil Centre is also located here.

🛏 **Barkly Hotel Motel** $$$ 55 Barkly Hwy; tel: 4743 2988.
Boyd Hotel $$ 20 West St; tel: 4743 3000. Basic old-style accommodation.
Copper City Caravan Park $$ 185 West St; tel: 4743 4676.
Fourth Ave Motor Inn $$$ 20 Fourth Ave; tel: 4743 3477.
Inland Oasis Motel $$$ 195 Barkly Hwy; tel: 4743 3433.
Mercure Inn, Burke & Wills $$$$ Camooweal St, cnr Grace St; tel: 4743 8000.
Mercure Outback Motor Inn $$$$ 45 West St; tel: 4743 2311.
Moondarra Caravan Park $$$ Lake Moondarra Rd; tel: 4743 9780.
Mt Isa Caravan Park $$ 112 Marian St; tel: 4743 3252.
Silver Star Motel $$$ Doughan Terrace, cnr Marian St; tel: 4743 3466.
Travellers Haven Backpackers Hostel cnr Spence and Pamela Sts; tel: 4743 0313; users.bigpond.net.au/travellershaven. Clean and quiet.
Verona Motel $$ Camooweal St, cnr Marian St; tel: 4743 3024.

🍴 **Carpentaria Buffalo Club** $$$ cnr Grace and Simpson Sts; tel: 4743 2365. Open daily for lunch and dinner.
Keanes Bistro and Buffet $$$ Irish Club, cnr 19th and Buckley Aves; tel: 4743 2577. Open daily for lunch and dinner.
Los Toros $$$ 79 Camooweal St; tel: 4743 7718.
Maxim Chinese Restaurant $$ 24 West St; tel: 4743 6567.
Overlander Restaurant $$$ Marian St; tel: 4743 5011.
Raffles Riverside $$$$ 17 Barkly Hwy; tel: 4743 3219. Open for dinner Mon–Sat, lunch Fri.
Red Lantern Chinese Restaurant $$$ 1 Simpson St; tel: 4743 4070.

HIGHLIGHTS

Mount Isa is quite aware of public relations and encourages tours of the mines, but these are popular and frequently fully booked, so it is important that you give as much advance warning as possible. Either tel: 4749 1555 or, for surface tours, tel: 4743 2006.

In 1927, to accommodate the mineworkers, the company built a low-cost town consisting of 200 tents protected by a permanent roof structure. An example of these unique tent houses is now owned and displayed by the National Trust. To appreciate the spread and integration of mine and town, climb the **City Lookout** opposite the tourist centre. The view at night is infinitely more attractive as the illumination highlights the good points and darkness disguises the rest, so it is worth visiting the lookout twice.

The **Royal Flying Doctor Service** (open Mon–Fri 0900–1700) is still a vital service in this isolated area, as is **Distance Education** (the School of the Air, tours at 0900 and 1000 during school term; to check on school terms, tel: 4744 9100). From this centre teachers broadcast to more than 220 children on 150 cattle and sheep properties throughout the north-west every school day.

The World Heritage-listed Riversleigh fossil site does what possibly only a couple of places on the planet can do: it provides a snapshot of a whole rainforest environment dating back 20 million years. At Riversleigh almost an entire ecosystem has been preserved in fossilised form and the **Riversleigh Fossils and Interpretive Centre** in Marian St lets you see, in some considerable comfort, what all the fuss was about. The centre has recreated limestone caves, a video documentary, a palaeontology display and collections of actual fossils from Riversleigh. The fossilised animals bear a slight, but only a slight, resemblance to the animals of today. Open daily 0930–1600.

TENNANT CREEK

If only the story were true, but perhaps it is. A wagon, loaded with beer and building supplies for a hotel to be built at the Overland Telegraph Station, broke its axle 10 km short of its destination. In true Australian style the problem was solved by building the hotel were the axle had broken. A town slowly grew around the hotel and before anyone knew it Tennant Creek had been born.

In 1930 gold was discovered in payable quantities, which led two years later to what has been referred to as Australia's 'last genuine gold rush'. More gold was found in 1934 at Noble's Nob. The find – and this is true – was made by one-eyed John Noble and his partner, William Weaber, who was blind. Noble's Nob closed only in 1985 and was beyond doubt Australia's richest gold mine.

Tennant Creek likes to think of itself as being the 'golden heart' of the Red Centre. It is the largest town between Katherine and Alice Springs.

> ℹ️ **Tennant Creek Regional Tourist Association,**
> Information Centre, Battery Hill, Peko Rd; tel: (08) 8962 3388
> or 1800 500 879; www.barklytourism.com.au. Open daily.
> The telephone area code for Tennant Creek is 08.

> 🏨 **Bluestone Motor Inn $$$$** Paterson St; tel: 8962 2617.
> Licensed restaurant.
> **Desert Sands Serviced Apartments $$$** Paterson St; tel:
> 8962 1346.
> **Goldfields Hotel Motel $$$** Paterson St; tel: 8962 2030.
> Licensed restaurant.
> **Safari Backpackers YHA $–$$** 12 Davidson St; tel: 8962
> 2207; www.yha.com.au/hostels. Air conditioned and
> comfortable.
> **Tennant Creek Caravan Park**, Paterson St; tel: 8962 2325.
> Bunkhouse rooms $; Cabins $$; en-suite cabins $$$. Pool, BBQ,
> kitchen and laundry facilities.
> **Tourist's Rest VIP Tennant Creek Youth Hostel $–$$** cnr
> Windley and Leichhardt Sts; tel: 8962 2719. Neat, tidy and austere.

> 🍽️ **Eldorado Restaurant $$$** Paterson St; tel: 8962 2402.
> **Fernanda's $$$** 1 Noble St; 8962 3999.
> **Goldfield's Hotel Chinese Restaurant $$$** Paterson St; tel:
> 8962 3347.
> **Margo Miles Steakhouse $$$** 146 Paterson St; tel: 8962 2227.
> **Memories Restaurant $$$** Memorial Club, Memorial Dr.; tel:
> 8962 2474.

Highlights

Tennant Creek's history is explored at the **National Trust Museum**, in the Tuxworth Fullwood House in Schmidt St (open daily 1500–1700 May–Sept, or by appointment). Originally a WWII army hospital ward, it has six rooms of local memorabilia and reconstructed mining scenes. You can also discover historic sites from the gold-rush days and interesting features of the area by taking a town **Heritage Walk** using the Discovering Tennant Creek brochures (available from the information centre). The Jurnkurakurr Aboriginal Mural on Paterson St, telling the story of the local

Warumungu people, is one of the many community paintings along the Mural Drive. **Tennant Creek Art Gallery** is situated on Peko Rd.

En Route

The massive granite rocks of The Devil's Marbles (not to be confused with the Devil's Pebbles just north of Tennant Creek) can be seen from Hwy 96 to the south of Tennant Creek.

If you're interested in the region's mining history and processes, it is perhaps better to take a conducted tour of a gold mine than try to find your own way around. The gold in this area is mainly trapped in ironstone and has to be crushed and treated in a complex process. You can take an underground mine tour (May–Sept 1100 and 1530; Sept–Apr 1100 only) and see the original Stamp Battery gold-ore crushing plant in action at the **Battery Hill Mining Centre**, 1.5 km from the town centre on Peko Rd (next to the information centre). Gold panning is also available (May–Sept) or you can visit the museum or follow the nature walk. If you have the equipment, public fossicking is possible 65 km north-west of Tennant Creek. Permits can be arranged at the information centre.

Bill Allen Lookout, just past the Battery, has a breathtaking 360-degree view, and plaques showing where the mines were dug and other local points of interest. The **Overland Telegraph Station**, 12 km north of town and built on Tennant Creek, is one of only four remaining stations built when Australia's first international telegraph line was built in 1872. The historic buildings have interpretive signs.

If you don't have a vehicle you can walk or hire a bicycle in town to reach the **Mary Ann Recreational Lake**, north of the town off the Stuart Hwy, via the Ted Ryko Path. This takes you through the picturesque Honeymoon Ranges, so-called because two miners brought their new brides to live here. The lake offers swimming, picnicking and bushwalking, or boating if you have your own vessel.

The Devil's Pebbles, 17 km north-west of town off the Stuart Hwy, is a collection of huge, randomly stacked granite boulders, and is an Aboriginal women's Dreaming site known as Kundjarra. Best time for viewing is at sunset, when the rocks glow in the dying sun's rays.

In the first weekend in May (an NT public holiday) Tennant Creek hosts the **Australian Street Circuit Go-Kart Grand Prix**. More than 100 go-karts from all over the country scream around the public streets. For a quieter time, consider the week-long **Desert Harmony Festival of Arts and Culture** in September, which features art and craft exhibitions as well as dance, musical and cultural nights.

ALICE SPRINGS

See p. 366.

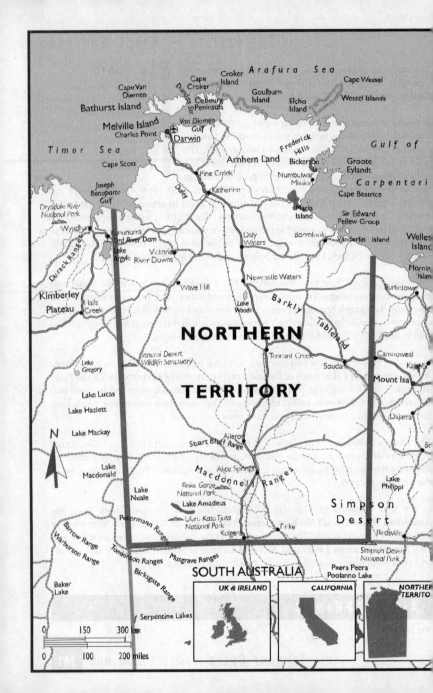

THE NORTHERN TERRITORY

The Northern Territory covers one-sixth of Australia. It is six times the size of Great Britain and twice the size of Texas, and has a population of fewer than 200,000. Alaska has nearly three times as many people.

Until 1911 the whole area was ruled from Adelaide as part of South Australia's Northern Territory. (Adelaide's jurisdiction covered an area larger than any European country.) The Federal Government took over for a while, and then from 1926 to 1931 it was divided into two self-governing districts – Northern Australia centred on Darwin and Central Australia centred on Alice Springs. But this proved costly and inefficient and the Northern Territory again came under Federal control from Canberra. Not until 1978 was the Northern Territory granted self-government.

This is traditionally the province of large-scale pastoralists and miners, although in the 20th century, war and the defence industry impinged on some areas. As a strategic route north, the Stuart Hwy from Alice Springs was sealed during World War II, and Japanese bombing of Darwin changed both the face and people's perception of this northern city. In 1967 a joint US–Australian defence and space research facility was established at Pine Gap, close to Alice Springs; its exact functions have never been made clear to an apprehensive public.

The landscape is one of extremes. The Red Centre, around Alice Springs in the south, is a land of sandhills and featureless plains, where the vegetation – acacia scrub, hardy semi-desert grasses and stunted eucalypts – has adapted to the aridity and the heat. Northwards, deeply eroded scarps, mountain ranges and broad pastures characterize the high tablelands that fall away to the low-lying coast, washed by the Timor and Arafura seas and the Gulf of Carpentaria. This is Australia's Top End. The contrast between lazing in a flat-bottomed boat as you drift through the Katherine Gorge and the harshness of the land around Alice is immense. But such contrasts are the heart and soul of the Northern Territory.

IN THE WET

The local Aborigines distinguish six seasons throughout the year, but for most visitors it is either the Wet, with up to 1600 mm of torrential rainfall between December and March, or the Dry, an almost complete drought. Territorians speak of the build-up to the Wet (Oct–Dec) as a distinct season. Days and nights grow hotter and more humid; trying to get to sleep can be a trial. The 'piccaninny dawn' hours (before sunrise) are often punctuated by spectacular thunder and lightning storms. The first rains come and the country turns green. Many animals are active, feeding or giving birth; the buzz of cicadas is, at times, deafening. There's a tremendous sense of crescendo – and then the Wet arrives.

The Northern Territory in the Wet is wonderful; Territorians seem to prefer the Wet. They speak of the tremendous storms with awe and affection. If there is anything in the theory of positive and negative ions it can be easily tested by being at the top end of Australia immediately after a storm. As one Darwinian said, 'That's when you come alive.'

The rain comes down in a Niagara of water, solid beyond comprehension. And such rain. Rain in solid sheets of water. Rain that overwhelms. And then, like a miracle, you are back again in brilliant sunshine and the air is fresh and sparkling and your spirit sings.

INDEPENDENT TRAVELLERS

PASSPORT TO
SAFER TRAVEL
By Mark Hodson · 3rd edition

Foreword by Simon Calder

The Suzy Lamplugh Trust
Ideal for gap year students and
first time travellers

We'll guide you
to a safer holiday
everywhere
under the sun

See the range of Thomas Cook Publishing
guides at all good bookshops, or at
www.thomascookpublishing.com

Thomas Cook
Publishing

NORTHERN TERRITORY: OUR CHOICE

Darwin
Museum and Art Gallery of the Northern Territory

Kakadu National Park
Wildlife, Aboriginal rock art, Jim Jim Falls and Twin Falls

Arnhem Land
Aboriginal culture

Nitmiluk National Park
Katherine Gorge

Alice Springs
Museum of Central Australia, Strehlow Research Centre, Alice Springs Desert Park

West MacDonnell National Park
Standley Chasm

Finke Gorge National Park

Watarrka National Park
Kings Canyon

Uluru–Kata Tjuta National Park
Ayers Rock and The Olgas

HOW MUCH YOU CAN SEE IN A ...

WEEKEND (2 DAYS)

Choose either the north, or Alice Springs and around, or Uluru–Kata Tjuta National Park. In the north, opt for an exploration of Darwin or a two-day tour to Kakadu. A weekend in Alice Springs and West MacDonnell National Park will allow just enough time for an overview, and the same is true of Uluru–Kata Tjuta National Park.

WEEK (7 DAYS)

Concentrate either on the north (Darwin and Kakadu National Park) or the south (Alice Springs and Uluru–Kata Tjuta National Park).

A week in the north will allow you just enough time to enjoy Darwin, get more than an overview of Kakadu (perhaps venture into Arnhem Land) and take in a visit to Nitmiluk National Park (Katherine Gorge). In a few days, you can take in the main sights and activities in the Alice Springs region, although you'll only touch on West MacDonnell National Park. Uluru (Ayers Rock) is Australia's best-known natural icon and a 3–4-day visit here is easy to fill, with walks around Uluru and Kata Tjuta (The Olgas), Aboriginal culture and secular whitefella pleasures at Yulara, Uluru's 'resort' town.

MORE THAN A WEEK

A driving trip north–south (or vice versa) gives the best perspective on the NT's size. With the right equipment (and permits), extended journeys through seldom-seen country (such as the Tanami Desert) are possible.

ALICE SPRINGS

Alice Springs, set in the MacDonnell Ranges, is often considered the geographical centre of Australia, which it is not. But for many it is the definitive outback town, made famous by Nevil Shute's novel *A Town Like Alice* and the subsequent films and television series. The road north, considered a strategic route in World War II, has been sealed since 1943, and in 1987 the old road south to Port Augusta and Adelaide was finally replaced by a new, shorter and fully sealed highway. In 2004, the new Alice Springs–Darwin rail line opened, further easing access. With these connections both north and south, the influx of tourism has eradicated much of the old Alice Springs and there is little of the noble outback experience that literature would lead you to expect.

Many visitors find the city has yet to come completely to terms with tourism; others find it immensely attractive. This is not a new phenomenon. Fred Blakely, who cycled 3500 km through central Australia in 1908, recalled in *Hard Liberty* the intensity of the light and the healthy atmosphere; he called the Alice a perfect winter resort. Winter days are warm but the temperature drops like a stone at sunset. In summer the mercury on occasion climbs to 45°C.

The town grew up around a telegraph repeater station built in 1871–1872 at a water-hole in the dry bed of the Todd River. The station was one of a series in the overhead telegraph line which ran from Adelaide to Darwin, where it connected with the undersea line to Indonesia and put Australia in direct contact with Europe for the first time.

Alice Springs, always spoken of as 'the Alice', is not so much a town as a pleasant idea (and the gender of the idea is feminine). The country in the immediate vicinity is not particularly interesting, but there is spectacular mountain and desert scenery within a day's journey.

HOW ALICE GOT HER NAME

The major force driving the construction of the telegraph line, and after whom the river was named, was Sir Charles Todd, superintendent of telegraphs. There had been great difficulty in finding a way through the MacDonnell Ranges, but in 1871 one of the surveyors wrote to Sir Charles Todd that he had discovered a pass which had 'numerous water-holes and springs, the principal of which is the Alice Spring which I had the honour of naming after Mrs Todd.' Despite this, the town was officially named Stuart (after the explorer John McDouall Stuart) when it was surveyed in 1888. But public opinion won out – they insisted on calling it Alice Springs or the Alice, and in 1933 this was formally recognised.

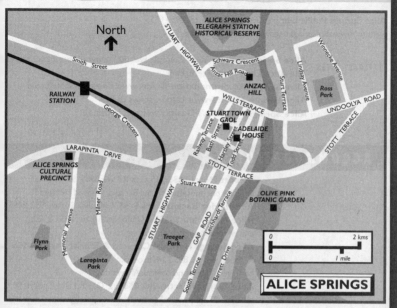

ARRIVAL AND DEPARTURE

The airport, about 15 km south of Alice Springs, has a shuttle bus link to the centre.

Alice Springs is roughly halfway along the Stuart Hwy linking Adelaide and Darwin. The journey from either city takes around 20 hours.

INFORMATION

TOURIST OFFICE **Central Australian Tourism Visitor Information Centre**, Gregory Terrace; tel: 8952 5800 or 1800 645 199; website: www.centralaustralian-tourism.com.main.php. Open daily.
Northern Territory Holiday Centre; tel: 13 61 10 or 1800 808 666; website: www.travelnt.com.

INTERNET ACCESS **Internet Outpost**, 94 Todd St; tel: 8952 8730; e-mail: alicesprings3@internet-outpost.com.
Outback Travel Shop, 2a Gregory Terrace; tel: 8955 5288; website: www.outbacktravelshop.com.au; e-mail: online@outbacktravelshop.com.au.

NORTHERN TERRITORY

Alice Springs Public Library, Gregory Terrace; tel: 8950 0555;
website: www.alicesprings.nt.gov.au/community/library.

INTERNET SITES   **Alice Springs Online** (Town Council's website): www.alicesprings.nt.gov.au
The Alice Link: www.alice.au.com
Alice Springs Accommodation Guide: www.alicespringshotels.com
Alice Springs News: www.alicespringsnews.com.au
Alice Springs, Australia's Oasis: www.thealice.com.au

ACCOMMODATION

Airport Motel $$$$ 115 Gap Rd; tel: 8952 6611; e-mail:
info@airportmotelas.com.au. Bar and licensed restaurant.

Alice Lodge Backpackers $–$$ 4 Mueller St; tel: 8952 8855.

Alice Motor Inn $$$$ 27 Undoolya Rd; tel: 8952 2322;
e-mail: reception@alicemotorinn.com.au.

Alice Springs Heritage Caravan & Tourist Park $$–$$$
Ragonesi Rd; tel: 8953 1418; e-mail:
heritagecp@bigpond.com.au. Allows dogs.

Alice Tourist Apartments $$$ cnr Gap Rd and Gnoilya St;
tel: 8952 2788; e-mail: alicetouristapartments@hotmail.com.

Annie's Place $$ 4 Traeger Ave; tel: 8952 1545 or 1800 359 089;
www.anniesplace.com.au.

Aurora Alice Springs $$$$ Leichardt Tce;
tel: 8950 6666; e-mail: asp@aas.auroraresorts.com.au.

Desert Palms Resort $$$$ 74 Barrett Dr.; tel: 8952 5977;
e-mail: desertpalms@desertpalms.com.au.

Desert Rose Inn $$$–$$$$ 15 Railway Terrace; tel: 8952
1411. Pool and licensed restaurant.

Elkes Backpacker Resort $–$$$ 39 Gap Rd; tel: 8952 8422
or 1800 633 354; www.elkesbackpackers.com.au/alice. Well
appointed and convenient.

Melanka Motel ($–$$$$) and Backpackers ($–$$$) 94 Todd
St; tel: 8952 2233.

Mercure Inn Diplomat $$$$ Gregory Terrace, cnr Hartley
St; tel: 8952 8977; e-mail: reservations.diplomat@bigpond.com.

Mercure Inn Oasis $$$$ 10 Gap Rd; tel: 8952 1444; e-mail:
h3113-reo1@accor.com.

Ossie's Homestead Backpackers $$ 18 Warburton St; tel:
8952 2308; e-mail: ossie@ossieshomestead.com.au.

Pioneer YHA $–$$$ cnr Parsons St and Leichhardt Terrace; tel: 8952 8855; www.yha.com.au/hostels; e-mail: alicepioneer@yhant.org.au.

Sienna on Todd $$$$ 13 South Terrace; tel: 8952 3888. Self-contained apartments.

Stuart Caravan Park $$–$$$ Larapinta Dr.; tel: 8952 2547; e-mail: info@stuartcaravanpark.com.au.

The Swagman's Rest $$$$ 67 Gap Rd; tel: 8953 1333 or 1800 089 612; e-mail: book@theswagmansrest.com.au.

Toddy's Backpacker Resort $–$$$ 41 Gap Rd; tel: 8952 1322; www.toddys.com.au.

FOOD AND DRINK

Alfresco Café Restaurant $$$ Cinema Complex, Todd Mall; tel: 8953 4944.

Alice Springs Memorial Club $$ Todd St; tel: 8952 2166. Classic bargain-priced club fare. Bistro open Mon–Sat 1200–1400, Mon–Wed 1800–2030, Thur–Sat 1800–2100.

Bar Doppio $$ Shop 2, Fan Arcade, Todd Mall; tel: 8952 6525. Open daily 0800–1700 (Sun 1000–1600). Caters for vegetarians.

Barra on Todd $$$$ 34 Stott Tce; tel: 8952 3523. Seafood specialists, situated in the Alice Springs Resort. Open 0600–1000, 1100–1800, 1830–2130.

Bluegrass Restaurant $$$ 95 Todd St (cnr Todd St and Stott Terrace); tel: 8955 5188. In heritage-listed former CWA Hall. Asian/European cuisine.

Bojangle's Saloon & Restaurant $$$ 80 Todd St; tel: 8952 2873. Serves barramundi, kangaroo, buffalo, NT beef and camel. Live Australian music and entertainment seven nights a week.

Golden Inn Chinese Restaurant $$$ 9 Undoolya Rd; tel: 8952 6910. Open Mon–Fri 1200–1400, daily 1700–2230.

Keller's Restaurant $$$$ Diplomat Hotel, 20 Gregory Tce; tel: 8952 3188. Swiss and Indian cuisines, Australian flavours. Popular with visitors.

The Lane $$ 58 Todd Mall; tel: 8952 5522. Mediterranean-style bistro, highly recommended. Open daily 1200–1500, 1800–late.

Oriental Gourmet Restaurant $$$ 80 Hartley St; tel: 8953 0888.

Overlanders Steakhouse $$$$ 72 Hartley St; tel: 8952 2159. Dedicated meat-lovers should strap on their serviettes for the 'Drovers Blowout'. Not a place for vegetarians.

BOAT RACES

In early October, Alice Springs holds the Henley-on-Todd regatta when boats are raced along the river bed despite the fact that there is no water. The boats are all bottomless and the crews run the course.

There is also the peculiar but genuine anomaly of the Alice Springs Yacht Club of Central Australia. (You can join for a small sum.) The most isolated yacht club in the world, and the furthest from the sea, it was formed in 1993 mainly to enter the Sydney to Hobart Yacht Race (see p. 488). It quickly collected over 200 members and has taken part in most of the races since; in 1996 Alice's *Neata Glass* won division F.

Pinky's Pizza $$$ Shop 57/485 Stuart Hwy; tel: 8955 5021.
Pulver's Café Restaurant $$$ Ross Hwy (over John Blakeman's Bridge, off Stuart Hwy); tel: 8953 3533. Great setting – watch the sun go down over the ranges.
Red Ochre Grill $$$ Todd Mall; tel: 8952 9614. Haute cuisine bush tucker.

HIGHLIGHTS

Alice Springs is easy to get around, as it is basically a square, with the dry Todd River on one side and the Stuart Hwy on the other. Anzac Hill to the north offers good views over the town, and at the south end is Stuart Terrace. Most of the shopping, restaurants and many of the hotels are within this rectangle. Todd St for part of its length is a pedestrian precinct; in truth, it could be anywhere in any tourist resort. Although the Alice is in a desert area, it does occasionally rain and the normally dry Todd River can flood, cutting off parts of the town.

Designed by Royal Flying Doctor Service founder, John Flynn (see p. 357), **Adelaide House** in Todd Mall opened in 1926 as the Alice's first hospital. Today it has photographs of the early days in Alice Springs and outback settlements, and the Radio

LASSETER'S REEF

One day in 1897 Harold Bell Lasseter was found unconscious by an Afghan camel driver. When he recovered he told of a rich reef of gold that he had discovered beyond the Petermann Ranges, but refused to disclose its exact location. In July 1930, subscribers put up £5000 and an expedition started off from Alice Springs. After incredible hardships the expedition was abandoned but Lasseter went on alone. His body was found by Aboriginal trackers and buried near where he died. In June 1958 he was reburied in the Alice Springs cemetery. There are still many Australians who believe the reef exists and that one day someone will strike it lucky and find Lasseter's Reef.

Hut was where Flynn and Alfred Traeger broadcast their first radio transmission. The Royal Flying Doctor Service's visitor centre is on Stuart Terrace.

The CBD's oldest building, the **Old Stuart Town Gaol** (1909), in Parsons St, is close to two 1920s heritage-listed buildings. The Residency ('The Palace in the Alice') is where HM Queen Elizabeth II and HRH the Duke of Edinburgh stayed in 1963; opposite is the Old Courthouse, now the **National Pioneer Women's Hall of Fame** (open daily 1000–1700), housing an inspirational tribute to Australia's pioneering women. Billed as the 'World's largest classroom', the uniquely Australian Alice Springs School of the Air was the first of its type. The Visitor Centre (80 Head St; $–$$) is open daily although it's best on a weekday during school terms, when lessons in progress via HF radio can be observed.

Paintings by Albert Namatjira are on public display within the **Alice Springs Cultural Precinct** (Larapinta Dr.; open daily 1000–1700; $$). The grave of this great Aboriginal artist is nearby in the Memorial Cemetery (Memorial Dr.) along with that of Harold Lasseter. The Precinct also incorporates the Museum of Central Australia and Strehlow Research Centre, which contains Australia's most comprehensive and controversial collection of Aboriginal spirit items, entrusted to Professor Strehlow by the local Arrernte Aboriginal people. There is a photographic display on Strehlow's work but the bulk of the treasures are only accessible to accredited researchers (who must be male). The Aviation Museum, on the site of the Alice's first landing ground, is also within the Precinct.

Alice Springs Desert Park, 10 km along Larapinta Dr. (open daily 0730–1800, $$$), displays the ecology of Australia's deserts and explains their traditional use by Aboriginal people. Desert Park Transfers operates a bus service (tel: 8952 4667).

The **Old Telegraph Station** (N Stuart Hwy), near the original springs, continued to operate until 1932. It has been restored to represent the pioneering lifestyle in central Australia (open 0800–1700, picnic grounds till 2100).

Through Heavitree Gap on Palm Circuit is Australia's first date garden. In the same direction, 8 km south-east of town on the Ross Hwy, is the **Frontier Camel Farm** (tel: 8953 0444). Here you can take a short, somewhat rolling ride (1000–noon; $$) or book a longer ride along the Todd River ($$$). For many years camels were the main form of transport in the interior. The farm museum (open 0900–1700) explains the importance of the camel trains and their 'Afghan' drivers (really Pakistani) in opening up the outback.

The Afghans are commemorated in the name of another famous outback feature: the legendary **Ghan train**. A modern version runs 2–3 times a week between Adelaide, Alice Springs and Darwin. At the MacDonnell Siding, about 10 km south of Alice Springs, the Ghan Preservation Society (tel: 8955 5047) has restored some locomotives and carriages; a museum is housed in a replica of the old station. Train trips are sometimes conducted.

DAY TRIPS

The number of attractions that can be visited in one- or two-day trips from Alice Springs can hardly be counted for this is an area full of national parks. Most of the roads are unsealed and a four-wheel-drive vehicle may be essential depending on the state of the roads. But in the right season some of the countryside around Alice Springs is among the most remarkable in Australia. What follows is a sampling.

SIMPSONS GAP Simpsons Gap, on the western outskirts of Alice Springs, is an excellent place to gain a brief taste of the MacDonnell Ranges. A pleasant way of getting there (during the cooler months or early in the morning) is via the Simpson's Gap bicycle path. Hire a bike in town (several hotels have their own bikes, or go to the Pioneer YHA or Melanka Backpackers) and ride out to John Flynn's grave along Larapinta Dr. (7 km) where you turn off onto the 17-km sealed bike path. There is always a good display of wild flowers after the winter rains. The eastern wall of Simpson's Gap rises 250 m above the sandy bed of Roe Creek.

ELLERY CREEK BIG HOLE Ellery Creek Big Hole, about 93 km west of Alice Springs, along Namatjira Dr., is a colourful small gorge with river gums standing out against dark-red rock cliff walls. Depending on the season, there is a large pool in the gorge.

> **ALBERT NAMATJIRA**
> The first Aboriginal painter to be recognised by Europeans was born here in 1902. His memorial here is inscribed: 'This is the landscape which inspired the artist.'

Namatjira Dr. is sealed as far as Glen Helen, but is unsurfaced from there on. Near Glen Helen and 130 km from Alice Springs is one of central Australia's most spectacular canyons, **Ormiston Gorge**. The lower cliffs are deep reds and purples, in the river bed are white bars of rock, and on the high rim are ridges of quartzite which reflect a dozen different colours. Go down through the gorge and you come to **Ormiston Pound**, a basin valley 10 km across, with a small, episodic stream. Yet it was the power of this river which in ancient times breached the end of the pound and slashed through, leaving the gorge which is the main attraction of the park.

REDBANK GORGE PARK Redbank Gorge Park is about 30 km beyond Glen Helen, along an unsealed road. A long narrow cleft carved through the rock by the Redbank Creek has resulted in a series of deep rock pools in a narrow chasm. Swimming can be dangerous, for the water is ice-cold and the handholds are few. The recommended way of progressing through the gorge is on an air mattress.

HERMANNSBURG Hermannsburg is 125 km west of Alice Springs along the fully sealed Larapinta Dr. Its missionary buildings are up to 100 years old and house a collection of memorabilia of early Lutheran Missionary/Aboriginal contact (the town is named after the place in Germany where the missionaries trained). Lutheran missionaries took nearly two years to make the overland trek with livestock from Bethany, South Australia. The first Aboriginal school was established here in 1879 and a grammar book and dictionary of the Arrernte language was compiled in 1891. Freehold title in the land was given to the local Aborigines in 1982.

Hermannsburg is close to **Finke Gorge National Park**. There are walks along the gorge with views of incredible rock formations, which contrast with the greenery and rock pools of nearby **Palm Valley**.

Just east of Alice Springs, **Emily and Jessie Gaps Nature Park** encloses two semi-permanent waterholes. Emily Gap – the word gap is used here to mean short gorge – has one wall decorated with Aboriginal paintings with tall caterpillar-like figures. The gaps were created by a tributary of the Todd River flowing south through a jagged ridge of the MacDonnell Ranges. There is sparse vegetation on the ridge, but gums grow along the river bed, some of them very large. The best time to visit is between June and September when there is often a blaze of wild flowers.

Trephina Gorge, about 70 km further east, was formed in the same way. In places its dark red cliffs are up to 100 m high, and along the river bed are many large eucalypts. In the west of Trephina National Park the John Hayes Rock Hole is pleasant and shady. This deep pool retains water well after the summer rains have passed, but sadly it is very attractive to feral cattle and is often polluted.

Close by, near Ross River, is the **N'Dhala Gorge**, which has Aboriginal petroglyphs thought to be 30,000 years old. A four-wheel-drive is essential.

At **Arltunga**, 37 km further east, explorer David Lindsay reported the discovery of 'rubies' – they turned out to be garnets – in 1887. The report of rubies drew miners who discovered gold, and mining continued on and off until 1916. The area is now a historical reserve, with a few miners' huts and the ruins of the government battery and police station. For a true outback experience, get a beer at the Arltunga Bush Hotel, one of the most isolated pubs in Australia.

WHERE NEXT?

About 450 km south-west of Alice Springs is perhaps Australia's most famous natural attraction: Uluru or Ayers Rock (see p. 374). Almost 1500 km north along the Stuart Hwy lies Darwin, capital of the Northern Territory (see p. 390).

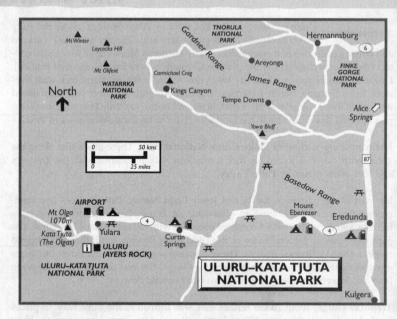

ULURU AND KATA TJUTA (AYERS ROCK AND THE OLGAS)

The great red monolith of Uluru (Ayers Rock) is Australia's most powerful and awesome sight. For millennia it and the neighbouring great rocks of Kata Tjuta (The Olgas) have been a place of magic and sanctity for the Aboriginal people, and a visit here can be a deeply moving experience.

It was in 1872 that the first European, the explorer Ernest Giles, set eyes on Uluru. He did not climb it. A year later, on 17 July 1873, William Gosse, another explorer, climbed this 'immense pebble rising abruptly from the plain' and named it Ayers Rock after his uncle, Sir Henry Ayers, then governor of South Australia. It was also Ernest Giles who, in October 1872, reached the northern shore of Lake Amadeus and saw, about 80 km to the south, Kata Tjuta rising from the plains. Seeing them as one mountain, he named them Olga after the Grand Duchess of Russia who married the King of Greece. An odd choice.

This was the very start of the white settlement of Australia's Red Centre. With it came the relocation of the traditional owners, the Anangu, from the lands around Uluru, and a severe depletion of the delicate desert environment by grazing stock. At the time, no one knew any better. Now we do.

> More and more these two amazing manifestations of nature are being referred to by their Aboriginal names. As they belong to the local Aboriginal people and we only go there as their guests it seems more appropriate to use the correct names. Uluru and Kata Tjuta also seem names far more in tune with the feeling of the area and the wonder of its sights.

In 1958 the area was declared a national park and in 1985 control was returned to the original owners, the Anangu. They lease the park back to the Australian Nature Conservation Agency but have kept a strong interest and involvement so that the park has developed without affecting the traditional relationship of the Anangu with their land. Many areas sacred to Pitjantjatjara and Yangkunytjatjara Aboriginal groups and associated with legends of the Dreamtime are closed to the public.

ARRIVAL AND DEPARTURE

From Alice Springs, Yulara is 200 km south along the Stuart Hwy (Hwy 87) to Erldunda, and then west on the Lasseter Hwy for another 250 km. In a reasonable car the journey will take 4–5 hrs.

There are daily coaches from Alice Springs, and some tour companies offer round-trip day tours. These are long and tiring but as you are not driving you may be able to sleep for part of the way.

It is far easier but more expensive to fly. Qantas has direct flights to Yulara from Sydney, Alice Springs, Cairns and Perth; there is a courtesy shuttle service to the resort. Often visitors arrive in Sydney with Ayers Rock – they are not quite yet used to using Uluru – penciled into their itinerary as a day trip. Unless you are chartering a private jet plane that is simply not possible.

INFORMATION

Ayers Rock Resort Visitors and Information Centre, Yulara; tel: 8957 7377. Open daily 0800–2030 with all possible information and informative displays on the geology, nature and Anangu connections with Uluru. There is also the Cultural Centre (tel: 8956 3138) within the park, on the access road to the Rock. Both are staffed by well-informed, enthusiastic and helpful people. The rangers within the park are quite willing to give the answer to any question you might care to ask.

INTERNET SITES **Department of Environment and Heritage: Uluru National Park:** www.deh.gov.au/parks/uluru

Australian Tourism Net: Uluru: www.atn.com.au/nt/south/nt-e.htm

Ayers Rock Resort: www.ayersrockresort.com.au

ACCOMMODATION AND FOOD AND DRINK

To see both Uluru and Kata Tjuta you stay at Yulara, on the edge of the park. The resort has a variety of accommodation, places to eat and support services, such as a bank and shops.

Desert Gardens Hotel $$$$ Yulara Dr.; tel: 8957 7888 or 1300 134 044.
Emu Walk Apartments $$$$ Yulara Dr.; tel: 8957 7888 or 1300 134 044.
The Lost Camel $$$$ Yulara Dr.; tel: 8957 7888 or 1300 134 044.
Outback Pioneer Hotel & YHA Lodge $$–$$$$ Yulara Dr.; tel: 8957 7888 or 1300 134 044; www.yha.com.au/hostels.
Sails in the Desert Hotel $$$$ Yulara Dr.; tel: 8957 7888 or 1300 134 044.
For an unforgettable experience there is the **Sounds of Silence** restaurant (see p. 379); tel: 8957 7514.

GETTING AROUND

Uluru is 20 km from Yulara, and Kata Tjuta a further 30 km from Uluru. Excellent roads connect the two and circumnavigate them.

Because of a 'remote surcharge', a saloon car will cost something around 50 per cent more than elsewhere in Australia. As is true in most locations in Australia, you can hire a four-wheel-drive vehicle, but there is an excess charge of $5000 and, as this is an eco-logically sensitive area, protecting over 500 species of plants, 24 native mammals and no fewer than 72 species of reptiles, you are not allowed to drive off the track.

Yulara has a ring road and well-signposted, well-kept roads, although everything within the resort is in walking distance. Special tours out to Uluru and Kata Tjuta include pickup and drop-off.

ULURU (AYERS ROCK)

Uluru rises 348 m above the flat plain, and its circumference around the base is nearly 10 km. The rock moves through an incredible range of colours as you watch, especially at sunrise and sunset, as if it were some sort of supernatural light show.

Uluru is one of the few natural landmarks that lives up, completely, to its prior billing. As you get closer to the Rock there starts a series of magic transformations. People flock to see the rock changing colour at sunset, but it also changes colour during the day. A cloud crosses the sun and the rock changes instantly from red ochre to a deep purple and then back to a complex red. The single-shaded colour seen from a distance becomes a subtlety of hues with greys and blacks and reds glinting through the ochre. Right up to the rock and the immensity overwhelms you and the colours change as you move your head. See it a dozen times and you will always find a new view, a new dimension. And is the Rock truly red? Indeed it is. It is not just the reflections from the sun when it is rising and setting. The iron oxide on the rock reacts with the atmosphere and oxidises, producing that deep rusty colour. Underneath, the Rock is a dull grey.

> **HIGHLIGHTS**
>
> Uluru and Kata Tjuta are embraced by the Uluru–Kata Tjuta National Park. The entry fee to the park (\$\$\$) lasts for three consecutive days.

Viewing areas have been set up to take advantage of the sunset and sunrise colours, which can vary from a bright orange/red to the deep brown of the main body of rock to a solid and moody purple. A spectacular sight comes after rain on the rock, when it takes on a silver sheen. At Yulara there is also the Imalung Lookout and, nearby, the Observatory, which offers a chance to view the desert stars.

To understand the impact of Uluru you need to get clear in your mind that this is a single piece of rock. It has very few cracks which can be affected by weathering, and the hard grain sandstone protects the rock from erosion. In some places, where the surface of the rock has been worn away, it has resulted in caves and spectacular formations such as the fluting effect along the south-east and north-west flanks of the rock. After a storm, waterfalls crash down these flutes for a short but spectacular lifetime.

If you are in a car you can make a slow and careful perambulation of its base – several times. This way you will see the Rock in air-conditioned comfort and, in the summer, without the flies. Or walk around the Rock and feel its solidity with the earth.

CLIMBING ULURU

Visitors are often tempted to climb Uluru, but most experienced people recommend that you don't, for two reasons. It is an ascent of 1.6 km and very steep in parts, and it is sadly common for elderly visitors to find that it is slightly more than their heart can take, resulting in park rangers having to lower them down with stretchers. There have been deaths on Uluru. Most years there are several rescues, with climbers suffering from vertigo, torn muscles, broken limbs and worse.

More importantly, the local Pitjantjatjara (see p. 381) have always regarded the Rock as a special place and they find the idea of tourists climbing all over it distasteful. You should not read too much into this. The Rock is not as important a site to the local people as, say, Kata Tjuta, where you are simply not allowed to climb. But the local people do not climb the Rock, they see it as inappropriate, and would prefer it if you didn't. So perhaps you shouldn't, certainly not without giving it much thought and consideration beforehand.

Climbing Uluru is not forbidden, but definitely not recommended (see box). You will almost certainly find that a walking tour around its base, with or without a guide, is less physically taxing and also more spiritually rewarding. The 9-km **Base Walk** around the Rock takes about three hours. Take plenty of water with you, for the sun strikes hard and dehydration is ever lurking. There are warning notices to keep you away from the sacred sites. This walk allows you to experience the Rock in a quite remarkable way. Even if there are people around you will feel there are only two spirits in the area: you and the Rock. The feeling is quite eerie but has been experienced by far too many visitors to be written off as pure imagination.

KATA TJUTA (THE OLGAS)

Kata Tjuta (the Olgas) are 50 km from Yulara, and seem at first to be overshadowed by Uluru. This is an illusion. The tallest peak on Kata Tjuta, Mt Olga, is more than 200 m higher than Uluru. The distinctive domes and striated, weathered surfaces of Kata Tjuta match Uluru in colour, and some visitors prefer its subtleties and hidden pleasures.

It is probable that Kata Tjuta was originally larger than the Rock, but, whereas Uluru has effectively resisted erosion, Kata Tjuta (meaning 'many heads') has been weathered over the aeons into a group of 36 of what the explorer Giles called 'monstrous domes'.

Climbing the Olgas is forbidden, but there are two exploratory walks. The **Olga Gorge Walk** is an easy stroll through the chasm for about 1 km. Much more satisfying is the

Valley of the Winds Walk, which is a 6-km loop that takes about three hours. Dehydration is a serious potential problem and you must take enough water with you. Most people tend to visit Uluru in the morning and Kata Tjuta in the afternoon. Reverse the order and you will be very much on your own.

The **Sounds of Silence** restaurant does not have walls. It is out in the open air, staged in a clearing in the sand dunes a few km from the resort. Over a pre-dinner drink you can watch the setting sun, both reflecting in the western face of Uluru and, to the west, painting the sky over Kata Tjuta a series of vivid colours, for at the Sounds of Silence you have a 360-degree view and you can get the best of the sunset from any angle.

> Typical central Australian weather has warm to hot days with mild nights in summer, and warm days with cool to cold nights in winter. What must be mentioned are the flies. In the summer they are a serious nuisance and you often see people wearing veils to avoid them. An industrial-strength insect repellent is an absolute essential.

Tables are lit by gas lantern and the meal is a buffet of Northern Territory specialities such as kangaroo, barramundi and emu from the barbecue, and Australian native fruits and berries. After dinner the lanterns are extinguished and the conversation hushed by the sudden and absolute darkness. For some people, this will be the first time that they have ever truly heard the sound of silence. As eyes become adjusted to the dark, slowly the canopy of stars in all their brilliance is revealed. Because it is in the desert this is one of the clearest skies in the world. An astronomer invites guests to look at some of the better-known planets through a powerful telescope, and tells the tales of ancient mythologies and the Aboriginal stories of creation, and how they are played out in the sky. Magic.

YULARA

The Ayers Rock Resort was designed by Philip Cox, who has much to be proud of. It was recognised as far back as 1965 that a hotel was needed for the park, but the problems were immense: the inhospitable environment, the huge temperature fluctuations, the lack of any existing infrastructure or services such as power, water or sewage. In addition, the site had to be acceptable to the traditional owners who, after all, have been around for over 22,000 years, and located where it was possible to maintain the environment of the area. Nothing happened for another 20 years.

The resort had to start from base zero, developing its own water and power supplies and bringing in everything from scratch. From the beginning, a concerted effort was made to train all members of staff in environmental awareness and to build up a close and consultative working relationship with the local Aboriginal community and the National Park headquarters and local staff.

The buildings have been positioned and constructed to take advantage of widely varying temperatures. Extensive use has been made of double roofs to provide insulating air space which reduces the need for air-conditioning, and one of the resort's most striking features is the immense white sails which act as air-conditioners. The fabric collects heat and filters out all ultraviolet radiation. Rooftop solar panels provide about 70 per cent of domestic hot-water and air-conditioning requirements which reduces the demand on the power station. The resort has its own water treatment plant, which can produce up to 41,000 litres of drinking water an hour as well as 135,000 kg of ice. The water is pumped from underground wells and then purified. Waste treatment plants make sure that as much water as possible is returned to the land.

Running the resort in such an ecologically sensitive area means that if it imports a chocolate bar it has to provide for the silver wrapper to be shipped out afterwards. Not an easy task, so visitors, too, must be eco-sensitive. Leaving litter around in a national park, especially a national park such as this, is a serious sin. If you bring it with you, take it back. This is a most remarkable place. Everyone needs to focus most seriously on keeping it that way.

The **Cultural Centre** contains an information desk, the Walkatjara Art Centre and Gallery Shop (mainly ceramics; open 0830–1730), the Ininti Café and souvenir kiosk (open 0700–1715) and the **Maruku Arts and Crafts Centre** (tel: 8956 2558) which was established in 1984 to cater for a growing demand for the work of Aboriginal crafts people. It started when nine vehicles containing artists and their work made the journey from Amata, 300 km away. In two weeks they sold more to visitors to Uluru than they did in a whole year in the Amata community. The word quickly spread about the success of this expedition and many communities got together to establish a regional arts centre. Today, in addition to its sales at the centre, Maruku exports unique and original arts to international markets. It is based in the Cultural Centre at the foot of Uluru and provides a service to about 800 Aboriginal craftspeople from 20 or more communities. Open daily 0830–1730 (Apr–Sept); 0800–1730 (Oct–Mar).

The Cultural Centre itself has been widely accepted as one of Australia's more remarkable interpretive centres since it opened in late October 1995. The design evolved from sand sketches and paintings by the traditional owners, and the complex comprises two main buildings in the shape of snakes: Kumniya, the female python, and Liru, the poisonous snake. The buildings are constructed with mud-brick walls, with massive timber trunks supporting the roof and the veranda and a roof of copper and shingles which suggest a snake's scales.

The centre offers visitors a basic understanding of Tjukurpa, the creative view of life that forms the foundation of Aboriginal living. The relationship the local people have with the area is relayed through paintings which have been directly applied to the walls, audio recordings of senior members of the Anangu, descriptive panels, displays and videos. Most of the exhibits are interactive so that pushing a button brings the display to life with the words of the people and the distinctive sounds of the desert. The Cultural Centre is on the way to Uluru from the resort and entry is free. Open 0700–1800 (Information desk 0800–1700); tel: 8956 3138.

Camels have long been associated with the outback. In the early days they were the only means of getting

The Aboriginal Peoples and Tjukurpa

Uluru is in the area that has traditionally been the territory of the Pitjantjatjara and the Yankunytjatjara people. In the 1966 census there appeared to be 948 Aboriginal people living in Pitjantjatjara country, but as they are a very mobile people, this is probably an underestimation. It is also probable that the population is increasing through improved healthcare.

These are Western Desert peoples and they are all connected, either directly or indirectly, by the religious traditions of the Tjukurpa. Tjukurpa is a most sophisticated and complex relationship between the people and the land. It is, among other things, the law, lore, moral code and religion, defining people's exact relationships and obligations to each other. It includes the code for managing the land and its animals, and it sets out the proper way that things should be done. At Uluru these rules are most often seen in terms of access and appropriate behaviour, such as being quiet in Kantju Gorge or not climbing Uluru. The Tjukurpa is memorised and transmitted by ceremony, its layers or chapters maintained by various members of the community. It is stored in the rituals of dance, and represented in sacred objects that non-Anangu, never mind *pirampa* – non-indigenous visitors – must never see.

goods and material around the deserts of the Red Centre, and played an important part in opening up the Australian outback. **Frontier Camel Tours** offer camel tours of the desert (they run a similar and very successful operation in Alice Springs – see p. 371). They neatly avoid the heat of the day by operating very early in the morning and late in the evening, with 'Camel to Sunrise' and 'Camel to Sunset'. Riding a camel is not as difficult as riding a horse as you are securely held in the saddle and the camels do not trot – at least not on these tours. On the other hand, there is a certain amount of lurching around and it is not a recommended experience for someone suffering from a serious hangover.

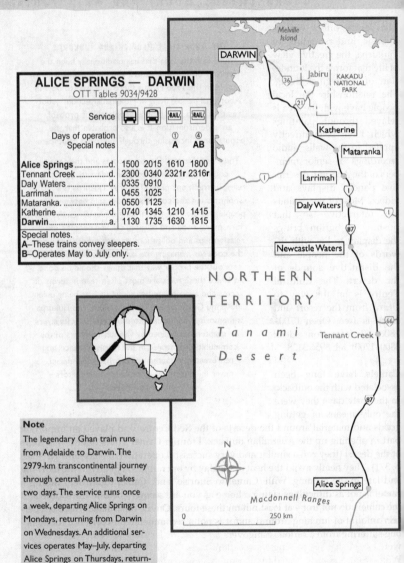

ALICE SPRINGS — DARWIN
OTT Tables 9034/9428

Service	🚌	🚌	🚆 RAIL	🚆 RAIL
Days of operation			①	④
Special notes			A	AB
Alice Springs ....d.	1500	2015	1610	1800
Tennant Creek ....d.	2300	0340	2321r	2316r
Daly Waters ....d.	0335	0910	│	│
Larrimah ....d.	0455	1025	│	│
Mataranka ....d.	0550	1125	│	│
Katherine ....d.	0740	1345	1210	1415
Darwin ....a.	1130	1735	1630	1815

Special notes.
A–These trains convey sleepers.
B–Operates May to July only.

Note

The legendary Ghan train runs from Adelaide to Darwin. The 2979-km transcontinental journey through central Australia takes two days. The service runs once a week, departing Alice Springs on Mondays, returning from Darwin on Wednesdays. An additional services operates May–July, departing Alice Springs on Thursdays, returning from Darwin on Saturdays. OTT table 9034; www.gsr.com.au.

CROSSING THE NORTHERN TERRITORY

From the arid scrubland of the Red Centre, this route stretches into the torrid tropic zone, crossing the land of the great cattle drives to reach the frontier city of Darwin. Of course, if time is at a premium you can fly direct from Alice Springs to Darwin, but you will be missing much of interest that lies between.

> ### DRIVING ROUTE
>
>
>
> It is tough country but there is an excellent sealed highway all the way – although despite its name, the Stuart Hwy is mostly two lanes only. The traffic is light except for the cattle trains – trucks with several trailers – and you would be wise to give them a wide berth. But otherwise this is a perfectly acceptable drive and it takes you to such interesting places. See pp. 31–33 for advice on long-distance driving. By bus the 1530-km journey takes about 20 hrs.

ALICE SPRINGS

See p. 366.

NEWCASTLE WATERS

Newcastle Waters, accessible only by car, sits at the intersection of the Barkly and Murranji stock routes. The Murranji, one of the most famous stock routes in the country, was opened in 1886 and cut nearly two-thirds of the distance off the conventional route through Katherine and the Roper River area. The route passed through rich pastoral land owned by some of the wealthiest Territory landowners of the day, and as many as 75,000 cattle travelled along the track annually.

The waterholes were named after the Duke of Newcastle, who was Secretary of State for the Colonies at the time that John McDouall Stuart came upon the area in 1861.

In the 1920s Newcastle Waters was a depot for construction gangs working on watering facilities for the east–west stock route. When government bores provided reliable water points after 1930, a fledgling township grew up, the stores and a hotel relying almost entirely on the stockmen for its livelihood. As motorised road trains began to replace the stock drives in the early 1960s, alternative transport routes were established, bypassing Newcastle Waters. When the owners of the Newcastle Waters Station found a need for accommodation for married workers and their families, the town's deserted buildings were renovated. Today, there is a teacher and basic facilities in the town, catering for the small population. **Jones Store**, known as George Man Fong's house, is one of the oldest buildings, constructed in 1934. It originally sold provisions to drovers and was later used as a butchery, bakery and as a saddlery. The property is managed by the National Trust and has a fine display of memorabilia.

DALY WATERS

Daly Waters is a minute settlement near where the Carpentaria Hwy joins the Stuart Hwy, on an area of land that traditionally belonged to the Jangman people. It has two claims to fame: the oldest pub in the Territory, licensed in 1893, and the first international airfield in Australia.

Daly Waters was chosen as a site for one of the repeater stations of the Overland Telegraph. Like other stations at the time, it was pretty basic, consisting primarily of an office, sleeping quarters and a meat house. Mail and supplies came in once a year, carried by camels and packhorses which had travelled for four or five months. As a result, there was always a chronic shortage of basic necessities. The railway never quite made it from Darwin, but then W T Pearce and his wife arrived to set up a store: the **Daly Waters Pub**. Originally built for the cattle drovers on the months-long overland routes, the low stone building now serves the same need for drivers of the huge road trains conveying cattle to the railheads. It is also a police station, post office, bank and museum, and the main source of employment. There are all sorts of odd paraphernalia on display: saddles, Morse receivers, even a non-operational set of traffic lights.

Daly Waters is also a footnote in aviation history. It was one of the stop-off points in the 1926 London–Sydney air race, and in 1930 Amy Johnson landed nearby on her historic flight from London. In the 1930s it was chosen as a Qantas refuelling stop, and the establishment of the aerodrome created the incentive to expand the pub business to look after the needs of the incoming thirsty and hungry passengers. During World War II, bombers and fighters refuelled here before heading north. Although the airstrip is now closed, the **Daly Waters Hangar** has been restored by the National Trust and is an interesting information source with both text and photos on the history of aviation in the area. Open daily 0800–0900, 1500–1600.

🏨 **Daly Waters Pub** $$ Stuart Hwy; tel: 8975 9927.
Hi-Way Inn Roadhouse $$$ Stuart Hwy; tel: 8975 9925.

LARRIMAH

The road from Daly Waters is flat but winding, passing through scrub grassland with ghost gums, salmon gums and patches of pink and white hibiscus to Larrimah. Another town that started life mainly because of the Overland Telegraph line, Larrimah later became a railhead on the now-defunct service from Darwin. At one time 3000 men were stationed here during World War II.

The narrow-gauge line of the North Australia Railway originally ended at Birdum, 8 km south, but was moved closer to the town because of problems with flooding. The train often had trouble pulling her passenger compartments along, and stopped frequently to raise steam or to undergo mechanical adjustments. The train was given the affectionate nickname of 'Leaping Lena', and its slowness was the subject of innumerable outback yarns. But it provided an essential connection with the Top End: in the 1930s passengers could fly from Queensland to Camooweal, connect by air to Daly Waters, continue by pony to Birdum and then take the train to Darwin. All that is left is relics: the Gorrie airstrip a few km out of town, the abandoned railway siding and the building that was the officers' mess and is now the town pub.

MATARANKA

Mataranka is known as the capital of Never Never country. The area came to prominence after the publication of Jeannie Gunn's *We of the Never Never*.

The town was the brainchild of J A Gilruth, who was Administrator in the early part of the 20th century. He believed that there was great potential for the surrounding land; indeed, he was in favour of establishing Mataranka as the Territory's inland capital city, replacing Darwin. Gilruth knew that growth and development meant attracting settlers and investors, and he set about trying to prove the quality of the land by establishing the Mataranka Horse and Sheep Experimental Farm in 1913.

In 1928 the railway arrived. There were great expectations for the town, but only 22 out of the 60 blocks offered at auction were actually taken up. A peanut-growing scheme that started in 1930 to help the unemployment situation in Darwin collapsed because of crop failure and a poor market for peanuts, and effectively the town was abandoned. Gilruth's plans for Mataranka were finished.

i **Ranger Station** Stuart Hwy, Mataranka; tel: 8975 4560; www.nt.gov.au/ipe/pwcnt. Open daily in the dry season.

Mataranka Roadhouse $$$ Roper Terrace; tel: 8975 4571.

Old Elsey Wayside Inn $$$ 13 Roper Terrace; tel: 8975 4512.
Territory Manor $$$$ Martins Rd; tel: 8975 4516.

Highlights

The **Mataranka Home-stead**, which dates back to 1916, is where Dr Gilruth set up his experimental station for sheep and horses. The homestead is within **Elsey National Park**, which has numerous walking tracks, waterfalls and rainforest. The park entrance is 10 km east of Mataranka near the junction of the Stuart and Roper highways. The best time to visit is in the dry season (May–Sept). A highlight is the **Mataranka Thermal Springs**, a clear thermal pool surrounded by weeping palms, pandanus, cabbage tree palms, paperbarks and yellow passionfruit in a pocket of rainforest. The waters are reputed to cure whatever ails you, but it can get a bit crowded in high season.

Near the springs is the replica of the **Elsey Homestead**, which was built in 1982 for the film of *We of the Never Never*. Inside are various displays relating to the people and early days of the area. Open daily 0700–1500. The site of the original building is near the present-day Elsey Graves, some 20 km south of Mataranka.

We of the Never Never

Jeannie Taylor Gunn, a teacher, travelled in the region with her husband Aeneas, a Melbourne librarian, whom she had married in 1901. After less than 15 months of marriage he died from malarial dysentery. Jeannie Gunn left the outback but her book, *We of the Never Never*, was to introduce people to how tough it can be in the outback. The book was rejected by five publishers, but finally published in 1908. It sold nearly one million copies. The story is told that the outback is called the 'never never' because Mrs Gunn wrote that she 'never, never' wanted to leave. This seems doubtful. The grave of Aeneas Gunn is in the Elsey Homestead cemetery. Jeannie Gunn lived to be 91 and is buried in Melbourne.

En Route

The Cutta Cutta and Tindal Caves are limestone rock formations that lie about 15 m below the surface. There are well-marked and signposted walking tracks, and tours are conducted daily (hourly 0900–1500). Open all year except in the height of the Wet, when they can be inundated.

KATHERINE

At Katherine the Stuart Hwy, the Victoria Hwy, the North Australia Railway and the old Overland Telegraph converge, and thus it is a meeting place for the outback. The River Katherine – the locals pronounce it to rhyme with wine – was named in 1862 by John McDouall Stuart after the daughter of one of his sponsors.

The river is important because it is the first permanent water north of Alice Springs. The town is traditionally a cattle centre, but adding much to the economy is a local air force base (off limits). The beautiful Katherine Gorge National Park was established in 1963 and has had much effect on the growth of tourism in the town.

i **Katherine Region Tourist Association**, cnr Stuart Hwy and Lindsay St; tel: 8972 2650; www.krta.com.au. Open daily (closes 1400 weekends Dec–Mar).

🛏 **Beagle Motor Inn $$$** Lindsay St, cnr Fourth St; tel: 8972 3998.

Crossways Hotel Motel $$$ Katherine Terrace; tel: 8972 1022.

Edith Falls Kiosk & Campground $ Edith Falls Rd (in Nitmiluk National Park); tel: 8975 4869.

Katherine Hotel Motel $$ Katherine Terrace; tel: 8972 1622.

Kookaburra Backpackers Lodge $–$$ cnr Lindsay and Third Sts; tel: 8971 0257 or 1800 808 211; www.kookaburra backpackers.com.au. Comfortable, sometimes busy.

Palm Court YHA $–$$ Third St, cnr Giles St; tel: 8972 2722; www.yha.com.au/hostels.

Riverview Motel & Caravan Park $$$ Victoria Hwy; tel: 8972 1011.

Springvale Homestead Tourist Park $$$ Shadforth Rd; 8972 1355 or 1800 089 103; e-mail: info@travelnorth.com.au.

Victoria Lodge $–$$ 21 Victoria Hwy; tel: 8972 3464.

🍴 **Buchanan's $$$** cnr O'Shea Terrace and First St; tel: 8972 2644. Part of Paraway Motel. Licensed.

Kirby's Restaurant $$$ Katherine Terrace; tel: 8972 1622. Part of Katherine Hotel Motel. Also Aussie's Bistro $$ for lunch.

Last Chance Bistro $$ 23 Katherine Terrace; tel: 8972 1022. Part of Crossways Hotel Motel.

Nitmiluk Visitors' Centre, Nitmiluk National Park, has an à la carte restaurant; tel: 8972 1253. Breakfast from 0700.

Olympia Café & Restaurant $$$ 7 Victoria Hwy; tel: 8971 0422. Wood-fired pizzas, Greek and Italian cuisine, fish and chips and takeaway.

Pedro's Bistro $$ O'Shea Terrace; tel: 8972 1250. Part of Katherine RSL Club. Open for lunch (except Tues) and dinner (except Mon and Sun).

The Pines Restaurant $$$ 3 Third St; tel: 8972 2533. Part of the Pine Tree Motel.

Seasons Restaurant $$$ cnr Cyprus St and Stuart Hwy; tel: 8972 1744. Part of Mercure Inn Katherine. Also Rusty's Bar.
Steakhouse Plus on Third $$$ Shop 1/15 Third St; tel: 8972 1909.
Terrace Café $$ Oasis Shopping Centre, Katherine Terrace; tel: 8972 2728. Fast food takeaway.

HIGHLIGHTS

What attracts visitors to Katherine is the gorge, but the town itself has a few places worth visiting while you are here.

The easiest way to find out about the history of the area is to go to the **Katherine Museum** in Gorge Rd (open daily, reduced hours at weekends and during summer) and the **Katherine Railway Museum and Gallery**, Railway Terrace. This old railway station, built in 1926, is now the local headquarters for the National Trust. There is a considerable display of railway memorabilia as well as more information on the history of Katherine. Open Mon–Fri 1300–1500.

EN ROUTE

Pine Creek, 92 km north-west of Katherine, is the gateway to Arnhem Land. The Miners Park tells the history of gold and uranium mining in the area, and old mining machinery is on show. There are still a few buildings left from that time, including a tin pub and a tin lock-up, and Ah Toy's General Store is a last reminder of the 2000 Chinese who worked Pine Creek's gold mines.

The **Katherine School of the Air** (tel: 8972 1833) claims to be the largest classroom in the world. It broadcasts daily to children over a distance of 800,000 sq km. During term time you can see it in operation at its headquarters in Giles St and see how the sheer size of the outback has, to a certain extent, been conquered by this early form of distance learning. It is open to the public Mon–Fri, from mid-Mar to mid-Dec, five tours daily.

Just west of the town is **Katherine Low Level Nature Park**. This park covers the full width of the river valley with paperbarks and pandanus lining the river banks. You can swim there in shallow water during the dry season but in the Wet the whole area will probably be flooded. Above all Katherine is the gateway to the **Katherine Gorge**, which is 30 km away in the **Nitmiluk National Park**. The Nitmiluk Visitors' Centre (tel: 8972 1253) is at the end of the sealed road off the highway. The park is rich in Aboriginal art, with rock paintings representing the spiritual 'dreaming' of the Jawoyn people, the traditional owners of the land. More than 100 km of walking tracks meander through the park, including some that merit serious bushwalking expeditions. It is essential that you register with the park ranger before setting out on any of the major walks. There is a camping area (tel: 8972 3150) at the entrance to the park, and accommodation is available at Katherine.

Near to town are some delightful hot springs. Go along the Victoria Hwy for 3 km, turn off just before the Riverview Caravan Park and you come to Katherine Hot Springs. While no medicinal benefits are claimed, these hot springs on the banks of the Katherine River make for pleasant swimming.

Springvale Homestead is the oldest homestead still standing in the Territory. It is 8 km from Katherine via Zimmin Dr. or Victoria Hwy, then Shadforth Rd (tel: 8972 1355). It offers two tours daily of the old homestead (1000 and 1500, Apr–Oct), and crocodile-spotting tours. There is a swimming pool, motel and camping.

KATHERINE GORGE

The name 'gorge' is misleading, for this is a series of 13 canyons of stunning beauty, rich in flora and fauna, including freshwater crocodiles. It is arguably the most colourful and grandly proportioned river canyon in inland Australia, with walls that tower over the slow-moving water in the dry season and are dotted with Aboriginal murals and paintings.

Formation of the gorges began 23 million years ago as torrents of water poured along tiny cracks in the earth. The Katherine River, which eroded the canyons, rises in Arnhem Land and further downstream becomes the Daly River before it runs into the Timor Sea.

There is a big seasonal difference in the water levels and the behaviour of the river. During the Dry, the gorge and its waters are calm and majestic but in the Wet, between Nov and Mar, the river can storm through the gorge with torrential waters that reach up to 6 m above the normal level.

For most of its length the 12-km-long gorge is filled wall to wall with deep water which reflects the coloured cliffs on either side, and the blue sky above. Experiencing the gorge can be done in several ways. From the Visitors' Centre you can walk about 200 m to the jetty and go on one of a range of cruises. A two-hour cruise shows you the first two gorges, a four-hour cruise makes it three gorges, and the full-day, nine-hour cruise will take you through five gorges.

If you are fit and adventurous (and it is not the height of the Wet) you can hire a canoe (Nitmiluk tours at the Nitmiluk Park Visitors' Centre; tel: 8872 1253), take your time and explore all the gorges. There are also, for experienced bushwalkers, walking tracks that follow the clifftops along the gorge. There is much wildlife, including freshwater crocodiles and rock wallabies.

DARWIN

See p. 390.

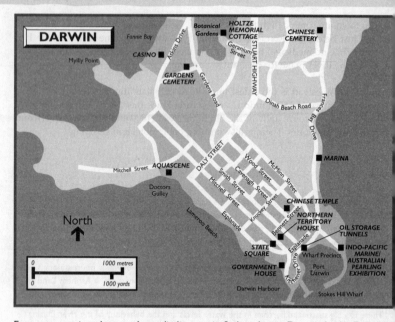

For many tourists the true Australia lies not in Sydney, but in Darwin. In the European dream all Australian men are tall, thin, sunburned, laconic, casual, drink ice-cold beer and speak with a strong accent. All Australian women are brave, resourceful, beautiful in an outdoors style and capable of swimming a flooded creek, breaking a recalcitrant horse or fighting bushfires. Darwin is the town that most fits this European dream.

The city was named after Charles Darwin, but not by him. Possibly the first European to visit the area was John Stokes, when he landed in the *Beagle* in 1839. He named the site after the English naturalist who had travelled with him on a previous voyage of discovery on the same ship.

MUST SEE/DO IN DARWIN

Visit the Museum & Art Gallery of the Northern Territory

Picnic in Darwin Botanical Gardens

See the fish feed at Aquascene

Go to Mindil Beach Sunset Market (Thurs & Sun in Dry Season)

Cycle from central Darwin to Casuarina Beach

Visit Territory Wildlife Park

ohn McDouall Stuart's expedition arrived overland in 1862 and the Northern Territory was made part of South Australia, which was uncertain what to do with its new acquisition. Finally, South Australia's surveyor-general himself visited it, and within a month of his party making camp in the harbour, he reported that he had chosen the principal site for settlement, and a town plan for Palmerston – the original name for Darwin – had already been prepared (basically the design of Adelaide with minor changes).

> ### CYCLONE TRACY
>
> Cyclone Tracy hit the city on Christmas Day 1974. It flattened 85 per cent of the city's buildings and left 48 people dead. No one knows exactly what strength the cyclone winds achieved (the anemometer broke after recording a gust of 217 kph) but a guess is that at one point gusts of 270 kph hit the city. Somewhere between $500 million and $1 billion worth of damage was done, making it Australia's most costly natural disaster until it was exceeded by, of all things, a monster hailstorm in Sydney in 1999.

This was the northern terminus of the Overland Telegraph, so vital to communication across the continent and with Europe, and within five years Palmerston had a population of 600 Europeans and 180 Chinese. There was little in the way of building materials and for the first 20 years of its existence the town had the appearance of a shanty. Administration of the territory passed to Commonwealth control in 1911 and with it came the name change from Palmerston to Darwin.

The first Japanese attack on Australia during World War II was a bombing raid on Darwin Harbour on 19 Feb 1942, during which a jetty was destroyed, eight ships sunk and at least 240 people killed. There were 63 air attacks on Darwin during 1942 and 1943. The bombing was to change the relative importance of the city, which was now seen as Australia's northern frontier. In 1951 travel writer Ernestine Hill wrote: 'In its glorious setting Darwin was unloved and unlovely. Apart from a few old faithfuls, there were only two classes – those paid to stay there and those with no money to go.' Times have changed.

GETTING THERE AND GETTING AROUND

Darwin's airport (tel: 8920 1811), which serves both international and domestic flights, is close to the city. The new Darwin railway terminal is at East Arm, south-east of the city.

All highways heading north eventually flow into Darwin, but the distances are very great. By bus it's about 20 hrs from Alice Springs, over 40 hrs from Cairns (one bus a week) and nearly 2½ days from Perth.

INFORMATION

The telephone code for Darwin and the Northern Territory is 08.

TOURIST OFFICE   **Tourism Top End**, Beagle House, cnr Knuckey and Mitchell Sts; tel: 8936 2499; www.tourismtopend.com.au. Open daily.

INTERNET SITES   www.northernterritory.com; www.ntholidays.com

MONEY   **Travelex Foreign Exchange** office is at the airport, Henry Wrigley Dr.; tel: 8945 2966 or at Shop 1a, Star Village, Smith St Mall; tel: 8981 6183.

ACCOMMODATION

Air Raid City Lodge $$$ 35 Cavenagh St; tel: 8981 9214; e-mail: dscwong@octa4.net.au. Right in town centre. Communal kitchen.

Banyan View Lodge $$–$$$ 119 Mitchell St; 8981 8644; e-mail: bvl@ywcaofdarwin.org.au.

Chilli's Backpackers $$ 69a Mitchell St; tel: 8941 9722; website: www.chillis.com.au.

Comfort Inn Asti Darwin $$$$ 7 Packard Pl., cnr Smith St; tel: 8981 8200; e-mail: asti@iinet.net.au. Large motel with spa, restaurant and pool.

Capricornia Motel $$$ 44 East Point Rd, Fannie Bay; tel: 8981 4055; 3 km from town centre.

The Cavenagh $$$ 12 Cavenagh St; tel: 8981 5311; e-mail: sales@thecavenagh.com.au. Has pool and BBQ area.

City Gardens Apartments $$$$ 93 Woods St; tel: 8941 2888; e-mail: citygardens@ozemail.com.au. Two-bedroom family units in a tropical setting; 2 mins from park, 5 mins from city.

CWA Hostel $$–$$$ 3 Packard Pl.; tel: 8941 3305. Small, shady house in its own grounds for women, couples and families only (no single men).

Darwin International YHA $$ 69 Mitchell St; tel: 8981 3995; www.yha.com.au/hostels.

Elke's Inner City Backpackers $–$$$ 112 Mitchell St; tel: 8981 8399; e-mail: elkes@dayworld.net.au.

Frogshollow Backpackers $–$$$ 27 Lindsay St; tel: 8941 2600 or 1800 068 686; www.frogs-hollow.com.au. Clean and excellent reputation.

Gecko Lodge $–$$$ 146 Mitchell St; tel: 8981 5569 or 1800 811 250; www.geckolodge.com.au. Small hostel with pool, 10-min walk to Mindil Beach.

Globetrotters Backpackers Lodge $–$$$ 97 Mitchell St; tel: 8981 5385; www.globetrotters.com.au.

Melaleuca on Mitchell Backpackers $$$ 52 Mitchell St; tel: 8941 7800; e-mail: info@momdarwin.com.au.

Top End Hotel $$$$ cnr Daly and Mitchell Sts; tel: 8981 6511. Attractively designed low-rise with large pool.

Value Inn $$$ 50 Mitchell St; tel: 8981 4733; e-mail: reservations@valueinn.com.au. Very central, no-frills motel but with good facilities.

Wilderness Lodge $–$$$ 88 Mitchell St; tel: 8981 8363 or 1800 068 886; www.wildlodge.com.au. Small hostel in tropical garden with possums living in the frangipani tree. Reputedly the best pool in the street.

FOOD AND DRINK

Asian Gateway $$$ 58 Aralia St, Nightcliff; tel: 8948 1131. If you're serious about Thai food this is the place to go, but you'll need to take a taxi.

Moorish Café $$$ 37 Knuckey St; tel: 8981 0010. Breakfast, lunch, dinner available.

Charlie's Restaurant $$ 29a Austin Lane; tel: 8981 3298. Authentic Italian cuisine. Open Mon–Sat for lunch and dinner.

Cornucopia $$$ within the Museum & Art Gallery of the NT, Conacher St; tel: 8981 1002. Perfect on the terrace at sunset. Australian–Pacific Rim cuisine. Lunch daily, dinner Fri, Sat only, booking essential.

Crustaceans on the Wharf $$$$ Stokes Hill Wharf; tel: 8981 8658. Fresh seafood but also serves steak, chicken and lamb dishes.

Giuseppe's Italian Restaurant Pizzeria $$$ 64 Smith St; tel: 8941 3110.

Mindil Beach Sunset Markets $+ (see p. 395) boast almost 60 food stalls from more than 30 different countries. Enjoy fabulous food and watch the sunset.

Nirvana $$$ Smith St; tel: 8981 2025. Indian, Thai, Malay, seafood. Open daily 1830–late. Live blues and jazz Tues, Thur–Sat.

Pee Wee's At the Point $$$$ Alec Fong Lim Drive, East Point; tel: 8981 6868. Located in East Point Nature Reserve at Fannie Bay. Open daily 1800–late.

Rorke's Drift Bar Café $$$ 46 Mitchell St; tel: 8941 7171. Traditional British fare including fish (barramundi) and chips.

Salvatores $$ cnr Smith and Knuckey Sts; tel: 8941 9823. Reputedly the best coffee in Darwin.

Shenannigan's Irish Pub and Restaurant $$ 69 Mitchell St; tel: 8981 2100.

Twilight on Lindsay $$$ 2 Lindsay St; tel: 8981 8631. Garden restaurant. Asian influences on cooking. Dinner daily, lunch Fri–Sun.

Yum Cha $$–$$$ Shop 9, 21 Cavenagh St; tel: 8981 0781. Open for lunch Tues–Fri and Dinner Tues–Sun. Yum Cha served Sat–Sun.

HIGHLIGHTS

The city centre runs south-east from Daly St; the main city-centre shopping area, Smith St and its mall, is about 0.5 km further on. It is all within such a small compass that it is very easy to stroll from one end to the other. There is a **historic trail** but as most of the city was flattened by Cyclone Tracy you find yourself often looking at a site where a building used to be, which is less than enthralling.

One building that rode out the cyclone was **Government House** on the Esplanade. It was built in 1883 to replace the timber version of 1870 which had been zapped by ants. There are lovely gardens but you cannot go inside. Just up the road is the **Old Courthouse and Police Station**, built in 1884 and used until Cyclone Tracy. Now the buildings house the offices of the Northern Territory Administrator.

TOUR TUB

The easiest way to see Darwin is to take the Tour Tub (tel: 8985 6322). It runs from the Mall and passes ten of the city's main attractions, from East Point Reserve and Fannie Bay Gaol to the Aquascene and Botanical Gardens. You can hop on and off all day as you please for a flat fee ($$$). www.citysightstours darwin.com.au.

DARWIN'S MARKETS

Darwin is a city with many markets. The **Big Flea Market** is at Rapid Creek every Sun 0800–1400. The **Palmerston Night Market** runs every Fri from about 1700. **Mindil Beach Market** is arguably the most popular. It's open 1700–2200 on Thur and 1600–2200 on Sun (in the dry season, April–October).

The **tunnels** on Kitchener Dr. were constructed for safe oil storage during World War II. One was used as an air-raid shelter and is now a sort of museum which you can tour ($). Open daily 0900–1700 (May–Oct); Tues–Fri 1000–1400 and Sat–Sun 1000–1600 (Nov–Mar); closed December. Across Port Darwin, the Wharf Precinct has a number of interesting places to visit. The **Pearling Exhibition** in the precinct records the pearling industry which started in 1884 when the first pearl was found in the Darwin area. The exhibition does not try to gloss over the desperate danger to the pearl divers who often died or got the bends. Open daily 1000–1700; tel: 8999 6573. Tropical fish and living coral reefs can be seen at the **Indo-Pacific Marine** – a great way to find out about the reef. Open daily 1000–1600 ($$$); tel: 8981 1294 to check times. Night tours Wed, Fri and Sun.

More fish can be seen at **Aquascene**, at 28 Doctors Gully Rd. Every day hundreds of fish arrive for hand-feeding sessions, depending on the times of the tides (check timing by phoning 8981 7837).

The **Fannie Bay Gaol Museum** is on East Point Road (tel: 8999 8290). It is full of stories of the desperates who were its past prisoners. It operated as a prison between 1883 and 1979. Open daily 1000–1630; free. Nearby at the East Point Reserve is the **Military Museum**, especially interesting for its thorough coverage of the Japanese bombing of the city in 1942; tel: 8981 9702. Open daily 0930–1700 ($$).

The **Museum and Art Gallery of the Northern Territory** is on Conacher St in Fannie Bay. Although small, it is wonderfully well laid out, with five permanent galleries and lots of touring exhibitions; the section on Aboriginal art shows how it should be done. Open Mon–Fri 0900–1700, weekends 1000–1700; tel: 8999 8201. Fees may apply for travelling exhibitions.

Almost every city in Australia has amazing botanical gardens. **Darwin Botanic Gardens** are no exception: they contain the southern hemisphere's largest array of tropical palms – over 400 species – an orchid farm, a

BOX JELLYFISH

Darwin has plenty of beaches but from Oct to May do not swim because of the box jellyfish. Take the advice of locals on the subject – they are not joking. The sting is dreadful and can be fatal.

rainforest, waterfalls and wetland flora. The gardens were established in 1879 in Fannie Bay by Dr Maurice Holtze, who had worked in the Imperial Gardens in Russia. He migrated to Australia, and with his son Nicholas, who followed him as curator, he started experiments to see what crops would grow in the Northern Territory. In 1866 many of the trees were dug up and moved to their present site, some of these original plantings are now magnificent mature specimens. In the 20th century the gardens were hit by fire, cyclones and bombs – Cyclone Tracy destroyed some 80 per cent of the buildings, trees and shrubs – but they retain their international importance with regard to tropical flora. Entrance in Geranium St off the Stuart Hwy or Gardens Rd off Gilruth Ave. Open daily 0730–1800 (from 0830 Sun).

Along the Stuart Hwy at Winnellie is Darwin's **Aviation Heritage Centre**. On display is a B52 bomber and the wreckage of a Zero fighter shot down in the first air raid on Darwin during World War II. You can either wander through the exhibits at your own pace or join a guided tour. Open daily 0900–1700; tel: 8947 2145.

NIGHTLIFE

For an odd night out try the **Deckchair Cinema** at Frances Bay near Stokes Hill Wharf on Darwin Harbour, which during the dry season – it is closed Nov–Mar – shows movies which you never quite got round to seeing. Check what is showing tel: 8981 0700.

It would be wrong to write about Darwin without mentioning the demon grog. Partly because of the heat and the humidity the people of Darwin can sink more beer than is believable. The last major set of statistics suggests that beer consumption was around 230 litres per year per head of population. If you take account of children and a few teetotallers, you have a beer consumption that is at least 50 per cent higher than anywhere else in Australia. Realising the health hazard, the government has been pushing the advantages of lite beer, but it is not yet known how effective this campaign will be. Many of the pubs in Darwin have been transformed from swill palaces into slightly more sophisticated bars, but many are still rough as guts and not safe for an unaccompanied woman. There are plenty of bars where you can enjoy a quiet drink, but you need to pick with care.

DAY TRIPS

The **Territory Wildlife Park** is bushland with open-plan natural habitats for the animals and is a great place to visit. It has a walk-through aviary and an excellent aquarium with a walk-through tunnel. There is an astounding display of eagles hawks and other birds of prey soaring and feeding every day at 1000 and 1500. Finally there is the Nocturnal House where you can see the bilby, water rats, barn owls and ghost bats, none of which you would normally even glimpse. Take the open motorised train or get some exercise and follow the walking trails. On Cox Peninsula Rd, 45 km south of Darwin; open 0830–1800 with last admissions around 1600 ($$); tel: 8988 7200.

Noonamah is 44 km from Darwin along the Stuart Hwy. The town developed during World War II as a service depot. Today, Noonamah offers basic facilities – a hotel with a beer garden and a filling station – but its major attraction is the **Crocodile Farm**. There are 8000 crocodiles on display. Many of the animals have been relocated here from local rivers and waterways where they have posed a threat to human life. You can try eating farm-raised crocodile meat, which is not bad, and there is a gift shop with a selection of crocodile leather products. There are guided tours at 1200 and after the big feed at 1400, when you realise that you never want to swim in crocodile-infested waters; tel: 8988 1491.

At **Howard Springs Nature Park** there is a spring-fed swimming pool surrounded by monsoon rainforest – ideal for swimming and bush walking. A weir crossing the pool was constructed in the 1940s, when World War II troops swelled the local population and Howard Springs was required to supplement Darwin's water supply. The crossing lets you look down on the fish, several of which are large barramundi, although fishing is not permitted. A signposted trail will take you on a 45-min walk through the forest. The park is just off the Stuart Hwy 25 km south of Darwin (sealed roads allow access all year). Open 0800–2000; tel: 8983 1001.

Casuarina Coastal Reserve can be accessed by way of Trower Rd and Lee Point Rd. It has expanses of golden sand stretching from the mouth of Rapid Creek northward to Lee Point. Against a backdrop of cliffs and casuarina trees are pockets of monsoon forest and an attractive picnic area. There is also a nude bathing beach. Visitors who use the nudist beach must remain within the signposted boundaries and put their clothing back on before leaving the area so as not to shock the locals.

The major attraction to the east is Kakadu National Park (see p. 399), which should not be treated as a day trip. However, the drive from Darwin to Kakadu can be an adventure in its own right. Along the way you will pass many attractive places to stop and visit, at which you can either dally en route or treat as trips out from Darwin.

The Arnhem Hwy, which turns east off the Stuart Hwy for Kakadu, is virtually a causeway running through, almost atop, the **Mary River wetlands**. These wetlands are alive with wildlife and driving through you will see more species of birds than anywhere else in Australia outside a zoo. In the Wet this road can be flooded – sometimes for many kilometres at a time – but it is sealed all the way to Kakadu and is hardly ever impassable. Even when it is flooded, if you motor at a steady speed you are unlikely to get into trouble. If your car does break down, do not worry about the lack of garages. The next vehicle along will certainly stop and help you get out of trouble. People in the Northern Territory all appear to belong to a mutual help society.

Humpty Doo, about 11 km after the turning onto the Arnhem Hwy, was the scene of one of the greatest agricultural investment disasters in Australia. This was to be the centre of one of the world's largest rice-growing areas and many millions of dollars were invested before the whole scheme was aborted.

Next comes **Fogg Dam**. This was established in the 1950s as a water source for one of the doomed rice-growing projects, and the surrounding wetlands are now home to spectacular numbers of waterbirds – pied geese, brolgas, ducks, herons, egrets, ibis, corellas, cockatoos and many, many more. The best time to view the birds is at dawn and dusk but at any time it is worthwhile. You can view them from purpose-built vantage points complete with informative signs along the low dam wall. There is also a signposted 3.5-km walk through the pockets of monsoon rainforest, for which you will need your industrial-strength insect repellent. The best time to visit is during the dry season (May–Oct), although the water plants in the dam flower spectacularly in the Wet.

At the **Adelaide River Bridge**, 64 km from Darwin, you will come across a wonderful sight. When you explain it later you will not be believed unless you have photographs to support your claim – and not even then. Cruises on the *Adelaide River Queen* leave here along the river in search of – honestly – leaping crocodiles. There are normally four cruises a day, but check for times as these vary with the seasons; tel: 8988 8144. The crew members put out meat bait and the crocodiles leap vertically out of the water as high as 2 m to take it. Sometimes sea eagles swoop in to try and snatch it from their jaws.

Next is the **Leaning Tree Lagoon**, 90 km from Darwin, which is a picnic spot as well as a site for birdwatching. You come off the bitumen and in the Wet it is possible for a two-wheel-drive vehicle to get bogged down, so take care.

Off the highway and 170 km from Darwin are the **Wildman** and **Shady Camp Reserves**, which incorporate a large part of the Mary River flood plain. Within the reserves the Rockhole Billabong and Shady Camp is renowned as the definitive spot to catch the Top End's barramundi. Information can be obtained at the Ranger Information Station at the corner of Point Stuart and the Rockhole Rds.

n 1898 A B ('Banjo') Paterson wrote in *Visiting the Park*: 'Far in the north of Australia lies a little-known land, a vast half-finished sort of region, wherein Nature has been apparently practising how to make better places. This is the Northern Territory of South Australia. The decline and fall of the British Empire will date from the day that Britannia starts to monkey with the Northern Territory.' Well, as the Empire has fallen, he might better have forecast some other cataclysmic event, but the general feeling is correct, especially regarding Kakadu National Park.

For many, Kakadu is the prime reason for venturing into the Top End of Australia, and few are disappointed. This huge, untamed wilderness – a world of craggy escarpments, lagoons, billabongs and birdlife – is a most amazing place. It is a UNESCO World Heritage Site and shares with Uluru (Ayers Rock) the title of most visited natural site in Australia. This was where they filmed *Crocodile Dundee*, a movie that helped define Australia colourfully if not accurately. Its history as a park is relatively short. Its history as a homeland of the Aboriginal people stretches back to the Dreamtime. The name Kakadu comes from the Gagudju language group of Aborigines who are among the area's traditional custodians.

About 15 per cent of the world's known reserves of uranium are in this area, and the decision to allow mining, reached in 1978 when the Northern Lands Council agreed to give royalties to the local Aboriginal people, was one of the most contentious issues in Australia. The forces of conservation opposed it absolutely on the grounds that it would irreparably damage one of the last great wildernesses of the world.

In the end the conservationists both lost and won. They lost because the processing plant was built in 1981. They won, because the storm of controversy had much to do with the designation of 6000 sq km of the region as a national park in 1979. In 1984 the size of the park was nearly doubled. Its status made the miners very conscious of the cost of putting a foot wrong, and a lot has been done to minimise the effect of the mine on the town of Jabiru and the park. Avoiding the argument about whether uranium mining should be allowed anywhere in the world, let alone in one of the great national parks, the results are, on the evidence available, successful. The Gagudju Association now manages the park in close co-operation with the Australian National Conservation Agency and receives about $10 million a year from the mine.

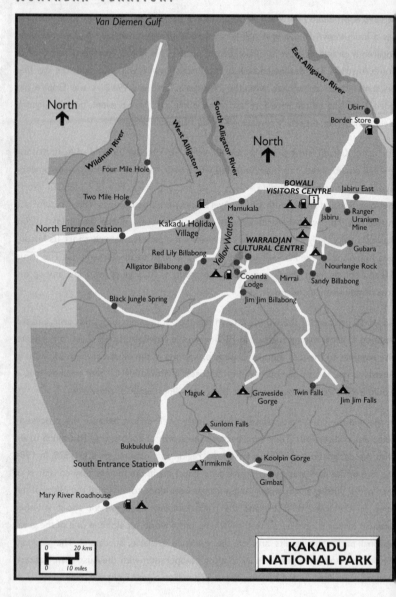

There are many ways of seeing Kakadu. You can roll up in an air-conditioned bus, stay at the air-conditioned Gagudju Crocodile Hotel, see the Aboriginal art at Ubirr and Nourlangie Rock and visit the Jim Jim Falls all in civilised comfort. Or you can go on a four-wheel-drive safari, camp out in the bush, drink tea from a billy, and pretend you are John McDouall Stuart in 1862 seeing the wonders of the wild.

If you travel with care and intelligent forethought and take heed of the advice of the rangers, you will see Kakadu, the soul if not the heart of Australia, at its very best.

GETTING THERE

The route from Darwin is south on the Stuart Hwy, then 10 km after Howard Springs, left along the Arnhem Hwy (Rte 36). The highway enters the park about 40 km after the Bark Hut Inn. Continue for nearly 140 km to the park headquarters near Jabiru. Greyhound Pioneer run a seasonal daily services to Kakadu from Darwin, OTT table 9432.

In theory it is possible to visit Kakadu on a day trip from Darwin, but that is rather like doing Rome on a Tuesday. Kakadu deserves more time.

INFORMATION

TOURIST OFFICE   **Jabiru Tourist Centre**, 6 Tasman Plaza; tel: (08) 8979 2548. Open daily.
Kakadu National Park Bowali Visitor Centre, Kakadu Hwy, Kakadu National Park; tel: (08) 8938 1120; e-mail: kakadunationalpark@deh.gov.au. Open daily.

Make sure you get a copy of the *Visitor Guide to Kakadu National Park*, which neatly spells out all the options. Also get a copy of the schedule of ranger-guided walks and talks. Time spent with a tour guide or ranger means that while exploring art sites you learn about Aboriginal Dreamtime and culture. When you are taken on a bushwalk your enjoyment is enhanced by the expert commentary and observations of the guides.

INTERNET SITES   **Kakadu World Heritage site:** www.unesco.org/kakadu
Kakadu National Park: www.deh.gov.au/parks/kakadu
Northern Territory Visitors Centre Kakadu pages: www.northernterritory.com

ACCOMMODATION

Bark Hut Inn and Caravan Park $$ Arnhem Hwy,
Annaburroo; tel: (08) 8978 8988. Historic building, great base to
explore Mary River wetlands and Kakadu.

Gagudju Crocodile Holiday Inn $$$$+ Flinders St, Jabiru;
tel: (08) 8979 2800. The crocodile-shaped hotel. International
standard.

Gagudju Lodge YHA $–$$$ off Kakadu Hwy, Kakadu;
tel: (08) 8979 0111; www.yha.com.au/hostels. Near Yellow
Waters and Warradjan Cultural Centre. Budget-style accommodation with communal kitchen.

Kakadu Lodge and Caravan Park $$–$$$$ Jabiru Hwy,
close to Park HQ, Jabiru; tel: (08) 8979 2422. Caravan park,
camping and plain, backpacker four-bed, air-conditioned rooms
and cabins with shared facilities.

Kakadu Resort $$$$ Jabiru Dr., Arnhem Hwy, 2.5 km west
of South Alligator Bridge; tel: (08) 8979 0166; e-mail:
kresort@aurora-resorts.com.au. Resort with café and
restaurant but somewhat isolated if you do not have your
own transport.

Mary River YHA $ Arnhem Hwy, Mary River; tel: (08) 8978
8877; www.maryriverpark.com.au. Restaurant. Crocodile cruis-
es; wetland and wildlife tours.

Point Stuart Wilderness Lodge $$$$ Point Stuart Rd
via Arnhem Hwy; tel: (08) 8978 8914;
e-mail: pswl@ntadventuretours.com.au.

Wildman River Wilderness Lodge $$$$ off Point Stuart
Rd, Wildman River; tel: (08) 8978 8912.

FOOD AND DRINK

Almost all the eating places are in the motels, hotels and lodges listed above.
Others are:

Bowali Café $ (at Bowali Visitor Centre) Kakadu Hwy; tel:
(08) 8979 2600. Open daily 0900–1700.

Jabiru Plaza Café $ Shopping Plaza; tel: (08) 8979 2570. Open
Mon–Fri 0830–1600; Sat 0900–1300. Café and takeaway.

ABOUT THE PARK

o get Kakadu into perspective you need to accept that it will not be what you xpect. The film *Crocodile Dundee* has raised expectations of a green paradise with ocky outcrops and billabongs where the sheila can appear in a thong bikini and get ttacked by a croc. It isn't quite like that. In the Dry it is large tracts of undifferen-ated flat terrain with scrubby vegetation. There will be green spots and swamps ut they do not form the greater part of the park. In the Wet it is somewhat differ-nt but then progress becomes somewhat more difficult.

akadu divides into five distinct regions: the sandstone plateau of Arnhemland nd the escarpment walls (which extend for 600 km) so well shown in *Crocodile Dundee*; the vast lowland plain; the flood plain north of the plateau, which in the Vet is almost a lake and in the Dry a series of billabongs; the tidal flats, which re mangrove wastelands that have formed because the salt water allows little else o grow; and finally the hills and basins in the southernmost part of the park near isher Creek.

ou will not be able to explore all of the park on a single visit. At any season access o the various parts of the park is limited. There is also danger from crocodiles, vhich keeps you away from some of the wetlands. Some parts of the park are acred Aboriginal sites vhere you are not wel-ome. Finally, this is ough country and get-ing around the harsh errain is not that easy. ut it all together and ou realise that Kakadu an be properly seen nly with a series of vis-ts. Depending on the ength of your visit and he time of the year, you eed to prioritise. For a hort visit, top of the list vould probably be Ubirr nd the Nourlangie Rock. You should also ake a cruise at Yellow Vaters.

WHEN TO GO

Most visitors go in the Dry when humidity and temperatures are down. But a strong case can be made for visiting the park at other times of the year. Kakadu in the Dry is wonderful; in the Wet it is magnificent, a sublime experience. With the rains the flood plains become inland seas. Some, but never all, of the attractions of Kakadu may be closed, but this seems to many to be a small trade-off for the extra wildlife that can be seen at that time.

In the Wet the road to Kakadu runs like a gangplank across flooded water plains. On both sides the view extends forever with birdlife you would never see at other times of the year, or in any other place on earth. The vegetation is a verdant green, the countryside alive.

JABIRU

Jabiru is both a mining town and the base for travellers to Kakadu. It has a sma
supermarket (open Mon–Fri 0900–1730, Sat 0900–1300 and Sun 1000–1200), a take
away, bakery, post office and Westpac bank in the shopping plaza. There is also
health and dental clinic, an Olympic-sized swimming pool, an artificial lake and th
international-class Gagudju Holiday Inn, in the shape of a crocodile – a desig
approved by the Gagudju people, whose totem is the crocodile. The hotel is owne
by the Gagudju.

You can go on a tour of the Ranger Uranium mine although it is, in the main, a pub
lic relations exercise to let you know that uranium is good for you. A walk-throug
exhibition takes you through a condensed version of Kakadu which sort of sets yo
up for the coming experience.

HIGHLIGHTS

Almost everywhere you want to go can be reached from the Kakadu Hwy, whic
runs south-west from Jabiru out of the park. Most attractions within the park ar
accessible by sealed roads. The exceptions are Jim Jim, Twin Falls and Maguk, whic
are accessible only by four-wheel-drive. One way to deal with this is to use a two
wheel-drive conventional vehicle to get to the park, then, if you want to venture int
four-wheel-drive territory, take a guided tour and let someone else do the driving
Getting stuck is horribly easy.

Nourlangie Rock is one of the most visited sites in the park, mainly because it i
so easily accessible (31 km south of the park headquarters). It contains an amazin
collection of Aboriginal rock paintings. A couple of these have been repainted with
in recent history, a rare habit of the Aboriginal people. There is a lookout here whic
gives terrific views over the Arnhemland escarpment. You can view Nourlangi
Rock from **Nawulandja Lookout**. Down below is the Anbangbang Billabong, whic
you may recognise from *Crocodile Dundee*.

BUSHWALKING IN KAKADU

There are very few marked long-distance bushwalks
within the park, although this is being remedied. If you
are venturing on a serious expedition you must register
with the park rangers before you leave.

Also in the Nourlangi
Rock area is **Nanguluwu**
another art site at the end of
1.7 km walk. It is very wel
signposted.

Ubirr is 43 km north of th
park headquarters and ha

KAKADU WILDLIFE

The varied habitats of the park result in an incredible diversity of plants, birds and animals. There are probably over 1300 different plants – the number keeps increasing as biologists discover new varieties – more than 10,000 species of insect, about a quarter of the varieties of Australia's freshwater fish and over 120 different reptiles. One-third of all Australia's birds are represented in Kakadu (300 species), including the Jabiru stork, and among the 50 native mammals are kangaroos, wallabies, walleroos, 26 bat species, and dingoes. There is also the water buffalo, which was brought in from Indonesia early in the 19th century and went feral. It became so prevalent that it was damaging the environment, but an eradication programme found that some weeds increased as a result, creating a life-choking mat over the water. Keeping the ecology in fine balance is no easy task in a place like Kakadu.

amazing Aboriginal rock art. From the lookout here you can see across the East Alligator River to the rocky outcrops of Arnhemland. In the Dry, you can take the **Guluyambi Cruise** along the East Alligator River from Ubirr (about 1½ hrs).

Yellow Water is an inland lagoon formed by Jim Jim Creek, some 50 km south-west of Jabiru, near the Cooinda resort. There are six daily cruises but it is best to take the very first or last of the day, when the air is cooler and the wildlife at its best. For bookings tel: (08) 8979 0145.

The 12-km corrugated track from the Kakadu Hwy to **Maguk (Barramundi Gorge)**, 57 km south-west of Cooinda, is perfectly negotiable in an ordinary vehicle in the late Dry. From the car park there is a 2-km return walk to a swimming hole and waterfall.

Gunlom, located on Waterfall Creek, is on an unsealed road 36 km off the Kakadu Hwy near the south-western exit of the park. In the Dry you will probably not see any falls at all but there is a most pleasant swimming hole. Access may be difficult in the Wet.

Jim Jim Falls and **Twin Falls** are 100 km south of the park headquarters and can only be reached with a four-wheel-drive vehicle. Jim Jim Falls drop 215 m over the edge of the escarpment. Seeing them requires some neat timing – in much of the Wet the road is closed, but in the middle of the Dry the falls dwindle to almost nothing. The ideal time is just as the Wet is ending and the road is passable – by someone else, not you.

Warradjan Aboriginal Cultural Centre is 4.5 km off the Kakadu Hwy. Its displays portray the creation era as interpreted by the Binij people. Open daily 0900–1700.

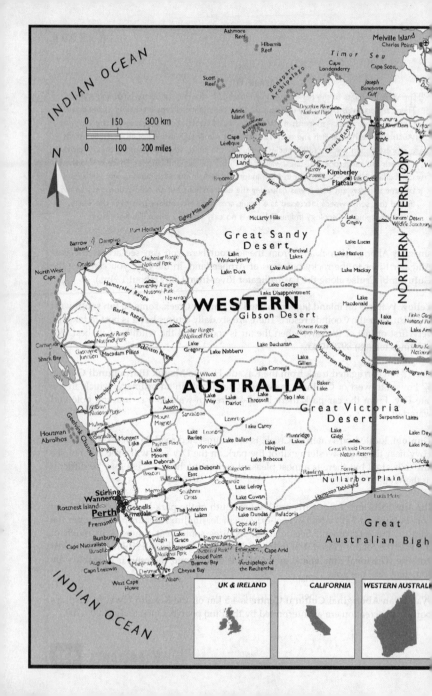

It is almost impossible to comprehend the size and emptiness of Western Australia. The state covers one-third of Australia but only contains about a tenth of the population. It considers itself a state apart. Indeed, there has been a movement for secession on and off for many years. In 1933 there was a referendum on the subject and the vote for secession was passed by almost two to one. No one in the federal government took much notice but the idea pops up every now and again.

Western Australia has 5000 km of coastline and at its longest point the state stretches nearly 2400 km. Within this vast area – 2.5 million sq km – more than two-thirds of the population lives in Perth, the capital, or its immediate area. The number of people spread out among the rest of the state is therefore very thin indeed. Much of the state is simply not inhabited in any significant way: the Gibson Desert, the Great Sandy Desert, the Great Victoria Desert and the Nullarbor Plain are to all intents and purposes empty, and the roads running across are unsealed.

Perth is the civilised centre of this vast expanse of nothing, and can claim to be the most isolated city on earth. It is as near to another capital city as, say, Athens is to Copenhagen. In Europe between those two cities lie countries, people, cities, towns, villages without number. In Western Australia there is almost nothing. Empty space.

Think of Western Australia as the Great Plateau. Hanging on to the edge by their fingernails are the coastal plains, separated from the emptiness of the Great Plateau by scarplands. This is forbidding country. It is very probable, but by no means certain, that the first European to sight the place was Willem de Vlamingh aboard the *Geelvinck*. In 1696 he found Rottnest Island off the mouth of the Swan River. It is not a very solid claim because there are records which show other sightings from earlier that century. But de Vlamingh sailed back to the Dutch colony in Indonesia and told the Dutch government in Batavia – now Jakarta – that it was not worth further effort.

Well over a century was to elapse before there was another serious effort, when the British came to deny the French, who were sniffing around the area, the chance of forming a new colony. Major Edmund Lockyer, with a party of 44 convicts and soldiers, landed in December 1826 at what is now Albany and took possession of

WESTERN AUSTRALIA

Western Australia in the name of the Crown. The following year Captain James Stirling explored the Swan River and selected a town site, and the colonists came out to this new land. The place nearly collapsed because of its isolation and the aridity of the region: what saved it was gold (see p. 96).

THE WILD FLOWER STATE

Western Australia calls itself the 'wild flower state'. This is a well-deserved title. Because it is isolated by the sea on three sides and an inhospitable desert on the fourth, Western Australia has developed a range of plants unique to the state. There are about 10,000 varieties of flowering plant to be found, most of them unique to Australia, some of them unique to the state. The jarrah forests in the south-west alone have over 3000 species. The Australian spring is the best time to see this amazing variety of wild flowers. The flower season is at its best between Aug and Nov, but at each end of the state the season is considerably extended, starting in late winter in the north and going strong well into the summer months down on the south coast.

There are tours to take you to view the wild flowers but, in truth, they are almost everywhere and the display in Kings Park in the heart of Perth itself is world-class. Close to Perth they can be found in profusion in the Nambung, John Forrest and Walyunga National Parks. Then there are wild-flower routes through the Midlands and Geraldton, and along the Brand and the Great Southern highways.

WESTERN AUSTRALIA: OUR CHOICE

Perth
Perth Cultural Centre, Kings Park

Rottnest Island

Bunbury
Dolphin Discovery Centre

Margaret River
Wine tasting, Leeuwin–Naturaliste Caves

Shannon National Park
Great Forest Trees Drive

Walpole-Nornalup National Park
Valley of the Giants

Kalgoorlie
Museum of the Goldfields

Nambung National Park
Pinnacles Desert

Geraldton
Houtman Abrolhos Islands

Kalbarri National Park
Murchison Gorge

Shark Bay
Monkey Mia dolphins

Ningaloo Marine Park

Karijini National Park

Broome

Bungle Bungle (Purnululu) National Park

Wolfe Creek Meteorite Crater

Lake Argyle

HOW MUCH YOU CAN SEE IN A ...

WEEKEND (2 DAYS)

Best options are either a temperate experience (around Perth) or a tropical one (in Broome). In Perth, visit the Perth Cultural Centre, get down to Fremantle (for a cold beer and a warm sunset) and, next day, visit the quokkas at Rottnest Island. Broome's Cable Beach is about as good as it gets for a swimming holiday; there's plenty of accommodation and decent places to eat in town.

WEEK (7 DAYS)

Aim for either the north or south. From Perth, travel to the south-west forests and see giant karri and jarrah trees, take in the Margaret River wine-growing region and loop down to Albany; this itinerary involves a lot of travel. From Broome, relax on the beach and explore some of the rugged Kimberley region. Plan ahead to make the return journey to Purnululu National Park, to see the Bungle Bungle Ranges.

MORE THAN A WEEK

More time in WA will allow a classic up-the-coast journey, beginning in Perth and ending in either Broome or Kununurra, taking in such sights as Kalbarri National Park, Shark Bay, Karijini National Park, Ningaloo Reef and the Kimberley.

PERTH

Perth and its adjunct, Fremantle, are said to enjoy the best weather in Australia, and the city is lush, green and verdant. Perth is thought by many Europeans, especially the British, to be the most attractive city in Australia. Probably as a result of this it has, as a percentage, more Britons than any other state, and the largest group of migrants still comes mainly from England. The attraction is obvious. Here is a city with the weather of the French Riviera during the Riviera's better months, where the language spoken is English and where the style of living is, in the best sense of the word, hedonistic. And the government tends to be to the right of the British Conservative party.

Perth extends over three parallel land strips. The first is a heavily eroded coastal reef and dune region about 6 km wide. Next comes a coastal plain, dunes, low sandhills and swamps extending about 16 km, and finally the lower slopes of the Darling Escarpment.

One aspect of Perth that has kept the city immensely attractive through all the phases of its development has been the Swan River. The foreshore south of the central business district has been reserved as park and recreational land and carefully cultivated and improved over the years.

MUST SEE/DO IN PERTH

Check out the museum, gallery and library at Perth Cultural Centre

Visit a winery or restaurant in the Swan Valley

Sip a cool drink and watch sunset over the beach at the Cottesloe Hotel

Picnic in Kings Park

Bargain hunt at Fremantle Markets, then grab a beer at the Sail and Anchor pub

Take a ferry to Rottnest Island

ARRIVAL AND DEPARTURE

Perth's international terminal is about 16 km east of the city, and the domestic terminal about 3 km to the west. From both there are shuttle buses into the city for less than the cost of a taxi. Expect to pay $20–25 in a taxi.

Transwa country buses and the Prospector train arrive at the Westrail Centre, West Parade, East Perth. Trains to Bunbury (the Australind) and Greyhound buses arrive at Wellington St.

Urban rail services connect Perth to East Perth.

Regular free Central Area Transit (CAT) buses serve Perth central business district; for details, see www.transperth.wa.gov.au.

INFORMATION

TOURIST OFFICE   **Western Australian Visitor Centre**, Ground Floor, Albert Facey House, Forrest Place, cnr Wellington St; tel: 1300 361 351. Open Mon–Sat.

INTERNET ACCESS   **The Travellers Club Tour and Information Centre**, 533 William St, is inexpensive and quick; tel: 9226 0660. **Exclusive Backpackers** (158 Adelaide Terrace, Perth; tel: 9221 9991) has competitive rates. $1 will buy you about 15 minutes at **Lonestar City Backpackers** (13–21 Palmerston St, Northbridge, Perth; tel: 9328 6667).

INTERNET SITE   www.westernaustralia.com is WA's official tourism website. www.countrywide.com.au has a fund of information about Perth and Fremantle.

MONEY   There are **Travelex** foreign exchange bureaux at Perth International Airport, Horrie-Miller Dr., New Burn, tel: 9477 1477; and Ground Floor, 760 Hay St, tel: 9321 7811.

TELEPHONE CODES

The area code for Western Australia is 08. If you are calling Western Australia from elsewhere in Australia you use 08. If you are calling from overseas you drop the 0 and just dial 8 as a prefix. So, from Britain you would dial 00 61 8 and then the 8-digit number you want.

ACCOMMODATION

Adelphi Hotel Apartments $$$$ 130a Mounts Bay Rd; tel: 9322 4666. One-bedroom serviced apartments. Close to city, river and parks.

Britannia International YHA $$–$$$$ 253 William St, Northbridge; tel: 9328 6121; www.yha.com.au. Six to eight share dorms, single and private rooms, free sheets.

Chifley on the Terrace $$$$ 185 St Georges Tce; tel: 9226 3355. Boutique hotel with great restaurant.

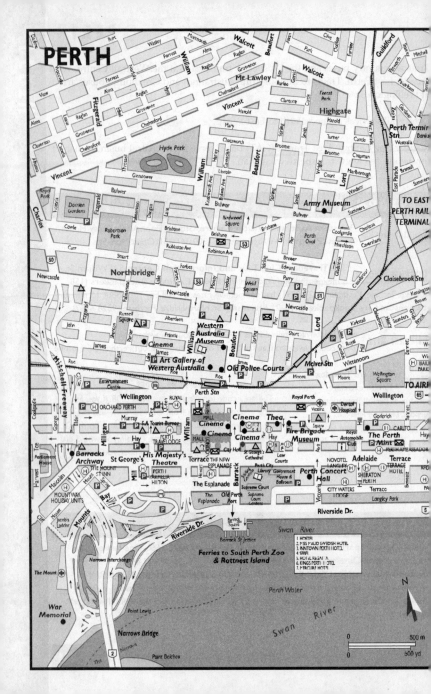

Djaril-Mari YHA $–$$$ Mundaring Weir Rd, Mundaring (in the hills 45 mins from Perth city); tel: 9295 1809; e-mail: perthillsyha@aol.com.

Florina Lodge $$$ 6 Kintail Rd, Applecross; tel: 9364 5322. One-, two- and three-bedroomed self-contained apartments within five minutes of the city.

Hay Street Backpackers $$ 266–268 Hay St; tel: 9221 9880. Good value, close to central Perth.

Hotel Ibis $$$ 334 Murray St; tel: 9322 2844.

Miss Maud Swedish Private Hotel $$$$ 97 Murray St; tel: 9325 3900.

Mountway Holiday Apartments $$ 36 Mount St; tel: 9321 8307. Fully serviced apartments five minutes' walk from the city.

Perth City Hotel $$$$ 200 Hay St; tel: 9220 7000. Within walking distance of the city shopping area

Regency Motel $$$ 61 Great Eastern Hwy, Rivervale; tel: 9362 3000. Restaurant, café, pool, spa, gym, tennis, videos, 24-hour room service, courtesy airport transfers.

Underground Backpackers $$–$$$ 268 Newcastle St, Northbridge; tel: 9228 3755 or 1800 033 089; www.undergroundbackpackers.com.au. New hostel with swimming pool.

FOOD AND DRINK

Almost all restaurants are BYO – bring your own bottle – but only wine, not spirits and rarely beer. This applies to most licensed restaurants as well.

Annalakshmi $$$ 2/12 The Esplanade, Perth; tel: 9221 3003. Delicious vegetarian Indian buffet with a huge range of dishes. Excellent value.

Belgian Beer Café $$$ 347 Murray St, Perth; tel: 9321 4094. Wonderfully tasty range of food and beer. Very busy on Friday nights!

Chantarelle@Jessica's $$$$ 1/99 Adelaide Tce; tel: 9325 2511. Claims to be Perth's finest seafood restaurant, overlooks the Swan River.

Coco's Restaurant $$$$ South Shore Centre, 85 The Esplanade, South Perth; tel: 9474 3030. Seafood and steak restaurant located on the South Perth foreshore.

Dusit Thai $$$ 249 James St, Northbridge; tel: 9328 7647. Award-winning Thai cuisine.

Emperor's Court $$$$ 66 Lake St, Northbridge; tel: 9328 1628. Good Cantonese food and a fine choice for Yum Cha.

Laguna Restaurant $$$ 20 Roe St, Northbridge; tel: 9328 7888. Said to specialise in Japanese, Malaysian, Chinese, Thai, Singaporean and Indonesian, which doesn't leave much out in Asian food. Open daily.

Mamma Maria's $$ cnr Aberdeen and Lake Sts, Northbridge; tel: 9328 4532.

Moon & Sixpence $$$ 300 Murray St; tel: 9481 0727. Bustling pub with decent food and an ace beer garden.

Simon's Seafood Restaurant $$$ 73 Francis St, Northbridge; tel: 9227 9055.

Stephenies at Steve's Hotel $$$ 171 Broadway, Nedlands; tel: 9386 3336. Good food, next to the Swan River.

Viet Hoa $$ 349 William St, Northbridge; tel: 9328 2127. Good range of cheap tasty Vietnamese and Chinese dishes. Fast service.
Yen Do Asian Restaurant $$ 416 William St, Northbridge; tel: 9227 8833.

GETTING AROUND

For the most part you can walk around the centre easily, although cycling is very popular. Important: wearing a bicycle helmet is compulsory. For information on cycling or walking in Perth contact the Department of Planning on 9216 8558 (cycling) or 9216 8737 (walking). For public transport information, contact the Public Transport Authority on 9326 2000.

The Transperth train system (tel: 13 62 13) provides a quick and easy way to get around. Travel is free on any Transperth bus or train as long as you board and alight within the Perth city centre, an area which covers all major shopping streets in Perth and Northbridge. You can travel from Perth to

THE PERTH TRAM

This is not a true tram, but a bus made to look like one of the trams that operated in Perth in 1899. Visits Kings Park, the Casino, Old Perth Port at the Barrack St Jetty and the city shopping areas. A full tour takes 1½ hours, with an interesting commentary by knowledgeable drivers. You can break your journey at any point and rejoin later. Tickets are available on board. Tel: 9322 2006.

Fremantle (or the other way) in around 30 minutes, stopping at all the stops. All services originate from Perth station, starting at 0523 and finishing at 2355. Tickets are purchased on the platforms from ticket dispensers which take coins only but give change. There are note-changing machines at Perth station.

There is also a special free bus service, the Central Area Transit (CAT) system, which operates three routes around central Perth. Red and yellow buses travel in an east–west loop of the central business district. Blue CAT buses travel in a north–south loop, south to the Busport and north into Northbridge.

Transwa operates a daily rail service to Bunbury, *The Australind*, which also leaves from the city station. The Kalgoorlie train *The Prospector* runs every day and leaves from the Transwa Centre, West Parade, East Perth. For more information and bookings on these country trains, call 1300 662 205.

Perth is well served by meter-operated taxi cabs. There are taxi ranks throughout the Perth central business district and Fremantle, or taxis can be ordered by telephoning the major operators: Swan Taxis (tel: 13 13 30) or Black & White Taxis (tel: 13 10 08).

The Royal Automobile Club of WA (RAC) is at 228 Adelaide Terrace, Perth (tel: 13 17 03), and there are other metropolitan and country branches. The RAC Roadside Assistance operates at all hours (tel: 13 11 11). If you are a member of an affiliated interstate or overseas auto club, you should receive reciprocal membership.

HIGHLIGHTS

Perth is neatly marked out and therefore easy to explore. The Swan River sweeps through the city centre westwards towards the sea at Fremantle. The main shopping area is along the Hay St and Murray St malls and the arcades between. The northern boundary of the city centre is marked by the railway line and to the north is Northbridge, a popular restaurant and entertainment area. The western end of Perth slopes up to Kings Park, which overlooks the city and the Swan River. Further to the west, suburbs extend as far as Perth's superb Indian Ocean beaches.

The arts are well catered for in Perth. The **Art Gallery of Western Australia** is at the Perth Cultural Centre, James St, Northbridge. This is Western Australia's principal public art gallery and the collection of Aboriginal art is one of the finest in Australia. Open daily 1000–1700. Also in the Cultural Centre precinct is the **Perth Institute of Contemporary Arts**. Entry is free. Open Tues–Sun 1100–1800.

Just around the corner, in Francis St, the **Western Australian Museum** is a complex rather than a single building. It is home to some of Perth's oldest buildings including the original Old Gaol and an early settler's cottage. Well worth a visit. Admission is free. Open daily 0930–1700.

London Court, an 18th-century-style arcade running between Hay St and St George's Terrace, appears in all the tourist photographs. It was actually built in 1936 and its fakery somehow jars. At one end of this shopping court St George and his dragon appear above the clock each quarter of an hour, while at the other end knights joust on horseback – useful if you want a backdrop for a photograph. Also in St George's Terrace is **St George's Cathedral**, in English Victorian Gothic Revival-style, and consecrated in 1888. You either like it or you don't.

Just off St George's Terrace, at the corner of Barrack St and on your way towards the river, is the Law Centre in Stirling Gardens. This contains the **Old Courthouse**, the oldest building in the city, dating from 1836. Guided tours and arrangements may also be made for groups to take part in mock trials and visit the Supreme Court to view court proceedings. Open Mon, Wed–Fri 1030–1400; tel: 9325 4787.

The **Perth Mint**, at 310 Hay St on the corner of Hill St, was very active during the gold rush. Daily demonstrations show pure gold bars being poured and moulded. There is an excellent viewing gallery and Perth Mint's bullion and proof issue coins are produced today ($). Open Mon–Fri 0900–1600, Sat–Sun 0900–1300; tel: 9421 7223.

Ten minutes' walk from the city centre is Barrack Sq., a relatively new complex of cafés, shops and attractions known as **Old Perth Port**. It houses the glass spire of the **Swan Bells Tower**, built as a Millennium Project, which offers wonderful views of the city, river and surrounds. The 12 bells rang in the New Year in London's Trafalgar Square for over 275 years and have celebrated every British monarch's coronation since George II in 1727. The pre-14th-century bells are some of the largest musical instruments on Earth. Open 1000–1700 daily, $$; www.swanbells.com.au. The South Perth ferry, which will take you across the river and to the zoo, departs from here. There are also cruise boats which go downriver to Fremantle or on to Rottnest Island (see p. 418), or you can take a trip upstream to visit assorted wineries.

KINGS PARK

Kings Park covers 4 sq km on the western edge of the city and has been in existence since 1872, when 172 ha of native bushland on the summit of Mt Eliza was set aside as public open space. Two-thirds of the park still comprises natural bushland and is one of the most beautiful recreation areas in Australia. Much of it bursts into bloom during the WA spring wild-flower season (Sept and Oct), when the display is superb.

Have breakfast at **Fraser's Restaurant/Café** ($$$$) and watch the city come to life – an expensive but gorgeous way to start the day. This park is truly a magical spot and is certainly the most attractive inner-city park in Australia.

ACROSS THE RIVER

One of the earliest buildings in the Swan River Colony was the **Old Mill** on Mill Point Rd, on the southern side of the Narrows Bridge. The foundation stone was laid in 1835 by the first Governor, James Stirling, for the designer-owner, William Shenton. The mill, adjacent miller's cottage and grounds have all been restored and are furnished with relics of the pioneer days. Open daily 1000–1600.

Perth Zoo is at 20 Labouchere Rd, South Perth, which is only minutes from the city.

On a per capita basis this is the most popular zoo in Australia. It is set in spectacular gardens with walkways, an Australian wildlife park and a Nocturnal House. ($$$); open daily 0900–1700; tel: 9474 0444.

BEYOND THE INNER CITY

In Whiteman Park is the **Motor Museum** ($$; open daily 1000–1600; tel: 9249 9457). There are normally about 85 historic cars and 25 motorbikes on show. They are privately owned and the display seems to change completely about four times a year.

Discover the wonders of WA's plentiful marine life at **Aqwa**, a huge aquarium at 91 Southside Dr., Hillary's Boat Harbour. Stroll through and observe the wonders through the safety of glass, or 'dive' in the main aquarium tunnel with the sharks and fish ($$$). Open daily 1000–1700; tel: 9447 7500.

The **Scitech Discovery Centre**, on the corner of Railway Pde and Sutherland St, West Perth (tel: 9481 6295; open daily 1000–1700), has well over 160 exhibits which all promote the learning of scientific principles – and are as enjoyable as any funfair arcade ($$).

And for something totally different there is the **Cameleer Park Camel Farm**, 300 Neaves Rd, Wanneroo, on the northern outskirts of the city and an easy drive from the centre. Take a short ride before booking anything more ambitious.Rides depart daily at 1000, 1400 and 1630; $$$; tel: 9405 3558.

Western Australia's first marine park was **Marmion**, which extends along the northern metropolitan coastline from Trigg Island to Burns Rock and about 5 km offshore.

THE BEACHES

Perth residents claim that their home town has the best beaches and surf of any Australian city. There are 19 beaches in the city area, and there is truly a beach for everyone.

There are calm beaches on the Swan River at Crawley, Peppermint Grove and Como. And there are many patrolled surf beaches on the Indian Ocean coast, including the nude beach at Swanbourne. Some of the other surf beaches include Cottesloe, Port and Scarborough. Most metropolitan beaches are patrolled at weekends and public holidays during the summer season, which runs Oct–Mar.

NIGHTLIFE

Perth has a most amazing music scene which is separate from, and different from, that in the rest of Australia. One of the main band venues for mainstream entertainment is the **Perth Entertainment Centre**, a building that, from a distance, resembles a giant hamburger. The main nightclub area in Perth is Northbridge, which boasts some twenty nightclubs, ten pubs, and a hundred or more restaurants.

The influences on the music scene are mainly European and Asian. The only way to see what is happening – the scene changes every day with new groups coming out of the woodwork – is to grab a free copy of *Xpress* magazine, which has a gig guide, from a music shop.

DAY TRIPS

At Armadale, 27 km south-east of Perth, **Pioneer Village** has a working model of a 19th-century village, with shops, public buildings, goldfield operations and everything from a cinema to antique shops. Tel: 9399 2050.

The **Swan Valley vineyards** run along the river from Guildford right up to the Upper Swan. The valley may be overshadowed by the Margaret River when it comes to wine in WA, but it is only 16 km, or 20 minutes' drive, east of the city, and the valley certainly rivals Margaret River for scenic beauty, particularly in the greener winter months. Many vineyards are open for tastings and cellar sales, including two of WA's biggest producers – Sandalford and Houghton. The Houghton Winery produced the region's first commercial vintage – in 1842 – although Olive Farm Winery was established earlier. The wineries of the valley are well signposted once you get to Guildford, itself an easy one-road-all-the-way trip from Perth via Guildford Rd.

A good way to experience the valley is on one of the river cruises that ply the waters of the Swan River. Several companies offer trips with stops for lunch and tastings. These wine cruises are a great way to spend a day, but you do usually only get to see and taste at one of the larger vineyards. Contact: Oceanic Cruises (tel: 9325 1191), Captain Cook Cruises (tel: 9325 3341) and Boat Torque 2000 (tel: 9221 5844).

Then there's **Rottnest Island**, which has a lifestyle that attracts all of Perth during the annual holidays – avoid it, if you can, during Dec and Jan. In 1925, in a novel called *Black Swans*, Mollie Skinner wrote about Rottnest, 'It was the cleanest, sweetest, most delightful place in all the universe – the sandy, salt-like place where the air is ndescribably exhilaratingly crisp and clear. Amongst that everlasting green shrub the wallaby abounded and over the lakes the ducks abounded, and off the rocks to seaward the fish abounded.' Mollie Skinner was not one of the great literary talents of Australia.

Rottnest is only 21 km north-north-west of Fremantle, opposite the mouth of the Swan River. It is about 11 km long, less than half that across, and is low-lying and mostly sand with five shallow salt lakes. The beaches and bays are mainly protected by offshore reefs that make them very safe. The waters and beaches are perfect for swimming, snorkelling, windsurfing, skin diving, sunbathing, surfing, boating and fishing.

There are no cars. Bring a bicycle across from the mainland or hire one on the island and don't forget your helmet). There is a hop-on hop-off round-island bus (tickets are valid all day) and a two-hour guided tour ($$$). There is also an island railway, called Rotto Rail – not a selling name – which once hauled guns and ammunition for the Army. Now it carries tourists. Tickets from the Visitors' Centre at the end of the jetty.

Getting to Rottnest is easy. Ferries leave from the Barrack St Jetty (Old Perth Port, see p. 416) and from Northport in North Fremantle or Hillary's Boat Harbour, OTT 9050. Flights leave from Perth Airport.

Penguin Island has other charms. It is not a rival to Rottnest for it is very different. It is situated in the Shoalwater Islands Marine Park, some 45 km from Perth, and boasts spectacular coastal scenery and diverse wildlife. It is home to the largest colony of little penguins on the west coast, as well as more than 30 species of birds, and is managed by the Department of Conservation and Land Management. The penguins are nocturnal on land, coming ashore in small flocks after sunset. Noisy courtship activities signal the start of the breeding season. Both parents will incubate the eggs, which are laid any time between mid-April and mid-October. Rescued and rehabilitated penguins are housed in a viewing enclosure in the Island Discovery Centre within the park.

Nearby **Seal Island**, another magic spot, is home to a group of protected rare Australian sea lions and often attracts groups of visiting dolphins. A range of ferry cruises is run by Penguin & Seal Island Cruises; tel: 9528 2004, or e-mail: rst@pengos.com.au.

Further afield, near the small town of Hyden, is remarkable **Wave Rock** (www.wave rock.com.au), one of the many granite outcrops that dot Western Australia's main wheat-growing region. As its name suggests, the 100-m-long rock bears an uncanny resemblance to a giant wave poised on the point of breaking. It's an impressive feature, although most photographs fail to reveal the remarkably ugly concrete-block wall above the 'wave's' lip – built in the 1950s to collect rainwater.

A short drive from Wave Rock, **Mulka's Cave** contains Aboriginal rock art, particu-larly hand stencils. In Aboriginal lore, the cave was the home of Mulka, a tall, strong man who was unable to hunt successfully because he was cross-eyed. He turned to eating local children, killed his own mother when she remonstrated with him and eventually fled south, where he was caught and killed. The Wave Rock Wildflower Shoppe (tel: 9880 5182) is the local information centre for Wave Rock and Mulka's Cave. Food and accommodation are available in Hyden, which is about 340 km south-east of Perth and too distant for a day trip if you're planning to drive alone.

WHERE NEXT?

Fremantle, just downriver, is a delightful port town, and could be first stop on a tour of the south-western corner of WA (see p. 421). Strike east to the goldfields of Kalgoorlie (see p. 444), or follow the coastline north beside the Indian Ocean for Geraldton (see p. 453) and Shark Bay (see p. 458).

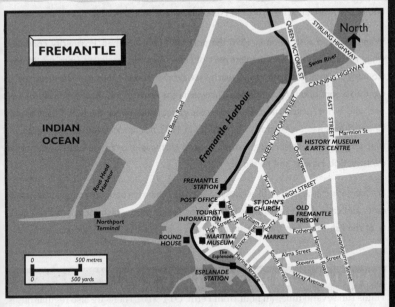

FREMANTLE

INDIAN
OCEAN

Fremantle Harbour

Rous Head Harbour

Port Beach Road

QUEEN VICTORIA ST

STIRLING HIGHWAY

North

Swan River

CANNING HIGHWAY

QUEEN VICTORIA STREET

EAST STREET

Marmion St

HISTORY MUSEUM
& ARTS CENTRE

Ord Street

Perry St

HIGH STREET

FREMANTLE
STATION

POST OFFICE

ST JOHN'S
CHURCH

OLD
FREMANTLE
PRISON

TOURIST
INFORMATION

Market St

William Street

Parry St

Fothergill St

Swanbourne Street

Northport
Terminal

High Street

Essex Street

South Terrace

Alma Street

Hampton Road

Street

ROUND
HOUSE

MARITIME
MUSEUM

MARKET

Stevens

Street

The
Esplanade

Marine Terrace

Wray Avenue

ESPLANADE
STATION

0   500 metres
0   500 yards

Although it is effectively a suburb of Perth, Fremantle has a style of its own. It is not a big place, with a population around 25,000, but it is very distinctive.

The name Fremantle comes from the captain of the *Challenger*, one of the trio of ships which, in 1829, brought the first European settlers to Western Australia. Captain Fremantle was 28 at the time and formally took possession of Western Australia in the name of Britain shortly after arriving. So Freo, as the town is called by locals who insist on using the Australian diminutive, was proclaimed by what, in Australian European colonisation terms, is very early indeed. The following year Advocate-General George Fletcher Moore wrote: 'A bare, barren-looking district of sandy coast; the shrubs cut down for firewood, the herbage trodden bare, a few houses, many rugged-looking tents and contrivances for habitation … a few cheerless, dissatisfied people with gloomy looks, plodding their way through the sand from hut to hut.' And yet, within two years the port was enjoying considerable prosperity and by 1832 it became the port for the colony in Western Australia. The designer and builder of the port was C Y O'Connor, one of the more amazing figures in West Australia, who is buried in the local cemetery.

When the gold rush came in 1890 the port and town boomed. Prosperity continued while Fremantle remained the first port of call in Australia for liners from the 'Mother Country', Britain, but with the advent of jet aircraft in the 1960s the town started to slip into a sort of tatty somnolence. Then came the America's Cup. It is difficult for anyone who is not Australian to understand the effect that winning the Auld Mug from the United States had on Australia. On that day in 1983, not an occasion any Australian will ever forget, wildly celebrating crowds poured champagne over the head of the prime minister, Bob Hawke, and he did not mind.

Fremantle is characterised by its busy sailing and fishing harbour surrounded by restaurants and cafés. And Fremantle is still a major fishing port, which means that the quality of the fish served in the restaurants is very high, even by Australian standards.

ARRIVAL AND DEPARTURE

Trains run several times an hour from Perth, OTT 9037. There are also regular buses. Cruises (ferries with a commentary) operate from Barrack St Jetty. Free CAT buses serve Fremantle CBD and tourist precinct; they run every 10 minutes. Details can be found on www.transperth.wa.gov.au.

INFORMATION

Tourist Information Office, Fremantle Town Hall, Kings Square; tel: 9431 7878. Open Mon–Fri 0900–1700, Sat 1000–1500, Sun 1130–1430.

INTERNET ACCESS   **The Travel Lounge**, 16 Market St; tel: 9335 4822.

INTERNET SITES   **Fremantle Tourist Bureau**: holiday-wa.net/freotour.htm
www.fremantlewa.com.au

ACCOMMODATION

ALN House $$ 39 Scott St, South Fremantle; tel: 9437 5780; www.alnhouse.com. Immaculate, light and spacious three-bedroom cottage with open-plan living/dining/kitchen area and out-

ON THE GHOST TRAIL
Worth experiencing, if
you are that way
inclined, are the Arts
Centre's ghost walks,
which take you on a
lamplit tour through
the darkened corridors
of one of Australia's
most haunted buildings.

door courtyard. Five-minute stroll to South Beach and central
Fremantle. TV, laundry facilities, fully furnished.

Barbara's Cottage $$$$ 26 Holdsworth St; tel: 9430 8051;
website: www.iinet.net.au/~barbaras/. An 1886 original Victorian
cottage classified by the National Estate and the National Trust.
Near old Fremantle Prison and the Fremantle Markets in the
Fremantle Heritage District.

Esplanade Hotel $$$$ Essex St, cnr Marine Terrace; tel: 9430
4000.

Fremantle Colonial Accommodation $$$$ 215 High St;
tel: 9430 6568. An 1897 terrace house about 200m from the
Town Hall. Also has three old two-bedroom, 1850 cottages
located at the Historical Fremantle Prison.

Fremantle Village & Chalet Centre $$$$ Lot 1, Cockburn
Rd; tel: 9430 4866; website: www.fremantlevillage.com.au. Offers
chalets, caravans and cabins.

Ocean View Lodge $$ 100 Hampton Rd; tel: 9336 2962.

Old Firestation Backpackers $–$$ 18 Phillimore St; tel:
9430 5454 or 0419 966 066; www.old-firestation.net. Formerly
Fremantle Backpackers.

Pirate Backpackers $–$$$ 11 Essex St; tel: 9335 6635;
www.austliquor.com.au. Small and friendly.

Sundancer Backpackers Resort $–$$$ 80 High St; tel: 9336
6080; www.sundancer-resort.com.au. Heritage building, clean
and comfortable.

FOOD AND DRINK

Eating out has been a stylish experience in Fremantle since the earliest days. In 1841
Edward Wilson Landor arrived and, as he recounted in *The Bushman: or Life in a New
Country*, 'We dined and slept at Francisco's Hotel, where we were served with
French dishes in first-rate style, and drank good luck to ourselves in excellent claret.'
Francisco's has, alas, gone but you can still eat in first-rate style and drink excellent
claret. Here are some suggestions.

The Cedar Tree Lebanese Restaurant $$ Unit 1, 36
SouthTce, Fremantle; tel: 9336 7669.

Clancys Fish Pub $$ 51 Cantonment St; tel: 9335 1351. Fresh
fish, casual atmosphere, beer garden.

Esplanade Hotel $ cnr Essex St and Marine Terrace; tel: 9432
4000.

Gino's Café $ 1–5 South Terrace; tel: 9336 1464; website: www.ginoscafe.com.au. Claims the best coffee in Australia. Supports local artists with a wide range of paintings on the wall for sale. Some of them stunning. Open from 0600 until late.

Granita's Café Restaurant $$ 330 South Terrace; tel: 9336 4660.

Jade Court Chinese Restaurant $$$ 569 Stirling Hwy; tel: 9383 3431.

Joy Kitchen $$ 17 Point St, Fremantle; tel: 9336 6868.

Kailis Fish Market Café $$ Fishing Boat Harbour, Mews Rd; tel: 9335 7755. Multi-award-winning seafood restaurant.

The Left Bank Café Bar Restaurant $$ 12 Riverside Dr.; tel: 9319 1116. Lovely outdoor seating with fine Swan River views. Good value in the café; more expensive fare in the restaurant.

Little Creatures $$ 40 Mews Rd, Fremantle; tel: 9430 5555. Pub, restaurant and brewery.

Maya Indian Restaurant $$ 75 Market St; tel: 9335 2796.

Mexican Kitchen $ 19 South Terrace; tel: 9335 1394.

Overseas Chinese Restaurant $$ 62 High St; tel: 9430 4032.

Pizza Bella Roma $$$ 14 South Terrace; tel: 9335 1554.

Red Herring River Restaurant $$$$ 26 Riverside Rd; tel: 9339 1611.

Sail & Anchor $$$ 64 South Terrace; tel: 9335 8433. Has its own brewery.

Sails Seafood Restaurant $$$$ 1st Floor, 47 Mews Rd; tel: 9430 5050. Very upmarket, but worth the money. Lively, cosmopolitan crowd. Open daily.

Sandrino Café $$$$ 95 Market St; tel: 9430 6126.

Song Tam Vietnamese Restaurant $$ 211 South Tce; tel: 9335 2659.

HIGHLIGHTS

In a few square kilometres, it would be hard to find a greater variety of sights, sounds and experiences. It can be argued that Fremantle is one of the best-preserved 19th-century seaports in the world and it has over 150 buildings classified by the National Trust. Since the restoration for the America's Cup challenge, it has become a visual delight.

Exploring Fremantle is easy. You can walk most places, or even better, hire a bicycle – Fremantle is a great place for cycling. Perhaps a tour should begin, mid-morning, with a coffee or a locally brewed beer on South Terrace, called the Cappuccino Strip

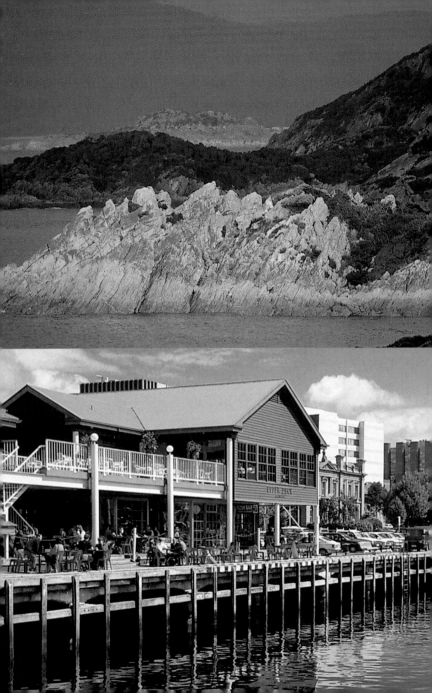

by locals for its outdoor-café atmosphere. On Fridays, Saturdays and Sundays (and public holidays) a stroll through the venerable **Fremantle Markets**, also on South Terrace, will give you a strong feeling for the place and produce anything from potted shrimp to a 78 record or a busker wearing a boater. The buildings where the markets are held (from about 1000–late) are classified by the National Trust.

With its maritime tradition, Fremantle is a good place for pubs. The beautifully restored **Norfolk Hotel**, on the corner of South Terrace and Norfolk St, has a congenial courtyard area. Opposite the markets on the other side of the Henderson St mall, the **Sail & Anchor** brews its own beers on the premises. The most famous of these is India Pale Ale which is powerfully alcoholic and flavourful, and should be sipped as if it were wine. Never drink a second glass – instead, have one of the wood-fired pizzas which are available in the pub's garden.

The port area is rich in maritime history. The **Western Australia Maritime Museum** has three sites – the Shipwreck Galleries (1 Cliff St, tel: 9431 8444; open 0930–1700), the Submarine Ovens and the New Maritime Museum (both on Victoria Quay, tel: 9431 8335; open 0930–1700). The New Maritime Museum has seven galleries showing *Australia II*, *Endeavour* and the story of Fremantle Harbour and the Swan River. Built in the 1860s in Gothic Revival architecture style, the Shipwreck Galleries exhibit a section of the *Batavia* and relics from three other early Dutch ships.

Fremantle Arts Centre, at 1 Finnerty St, is housed in a picturesque colonial Gothic Revival building built by convicts. This is perhaps the port's most distinguished building. It was mentioned by Anthony Trollope on his visit in March 1872 (he plainly did not like the town, for he described it as 'a hot, white, ugly town with a very large prison, a lunatic asylum and a hospital for ancient worn-out convicts'). The Arts Centre is in the old asylum, and now mainly holds works by Western Australian artists. There is free live music in the courtyard on Sunday afternoons from September to April. Open daily 1000–1700.

Another building of consequence is the **Round House**, at 10 Arthur Head. Completed in 1831 as a prison, it is the State's oldest public building and arguably the oldest building in Western Australia. The grounds are still attractive and the building itself is interesting. There is a tunnel that runs from the grounds which is where the whalers carried their supplies down to Bathers Beach. Open daily 1030–1530.

WHERE NEXT?

If Fremantle has been your first port of call in Western Australia, then Perth is the obvious next stop (see p. 410). South lies the beautiful Margaret River region and the south coast (see p. 426). See pp. 450 and 452 for routes into the sparser regions of WA.

PERTH — ALBANY

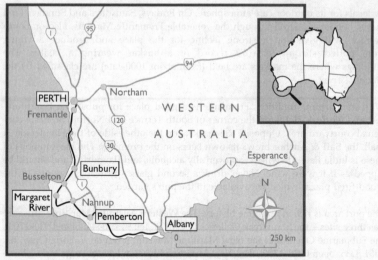

PERTH — ALBANY
OTT Tables 9036/9438/9447/9448

Service	🚌	🚌	🚆	🚌	🚌	🚌	🚌	🚌	🚌	🚌	🚌	🚌
Days of operation	②③⑤	①④⑦	Daily	③⑤	ex③⑤	ex⑥	①③	②④⑦	ex⑥	⑤	⑦	⑤
Special notes		**A**	**B**									
Perth...........................d.	0800	0800	0930	....	....	0830	1220	1220	1220	1220	1530	1700
Bunbury........................d.	|	|	1155	1200	1200	1205	1545	1545	1545	1545	1850	2020
Margaret River...............d.	|	|	....	|	1405	|	1745	1745	|	|	2214
Pemberton.....................d.	|	|	....	|	1421	....	1800	2020	....	1816	2100	....
Albany.........................a.	|	*1145*	....	1730	1805	....	....	....	....	2140	....	....
Esperance ....a.	1800	1815	....	....	....	....	....	....	....	....	....	....

Special notes:
A–Bus from Albany connects with Perth–Esperance service at Ravensthorpe on ①④ only.
B–Additional service: 1755.

Note: It is also possible to go from Perth to Albany via an inland route.

DRIVING ROUTE

Take the coast road, Hwy 1, south to Bunbury (198 km). Continue on Hwy 10 (called the Bussell Hwy) through Busselton to Margaret River (108 km). Take Hwy 10 inland to Nannup and Pemberton (182 km). Rejoin Hwy 1 at Pemberton through Shannon National Park and along the south coast to Denmark and Albany (244 km). Total: 732 km.

EXPLORING THE SOUTHWEST

The drive around the coast south from Perth to Albany will show you one of the most favoured parts of the country. Bunbury is a large town noted for its cosmopolitan attractions as well as its beaches, while the beautiful valley of the Margaret River is famed for its wines. The country along the southern coast is very different from further north, with karri forests of some of the tallest trees in the world, amazing wild flowers, and the opportunity to go whale watching.

PERTH

See p. 410.

BUNBURY

Bunbury is the second-largest town (in area) in Western Australia and lies on the junction of the Collie and Preston rivers. It was named after Lt H W St Pierre Bunbury. Governor Stirling, Western Australia's first governor, requested Lieutenant Bunbury to pioneer land exploration in the south-west in 1836. Bunbury was favourably impressed with the area on his overland trek from Pinjarra to the Vasse River. In his journal, *Early Days in Western Australia*, he wrote: 'A township has been … laid down on the maps, comprising the southern promontory and part of the north beach of Port Leschenault Inlet which the Governor named "Bunbury" in compliment of me.'

In 1841 Louisa Clifton, the wife of the Commissioner, wrote, 'Friends in England should be made acquainted with the dangers of this Australian coast in this season. A fatal grievance prevails on the point and I feel horrified to think of people coming out at any time of the year, to be exposed to such awful weather as this.' She did not last long in Australia and would plainly never have found a job with the tourist board.

In contrast to Mrs Clifton's experience, CSIRO – the Australian government scientific research body – has identified Bunbury as the centre of an area with the most comfortable climatic environment for human existence. And there is much to see. Bunbury is only two hours from Perth and is famous for its white sandy beaches, great fishing and cosmopolitan lifestyle.

EN ROUTE

Australind, just north of Bunbury, gets its strange name from an amalgamation of 'Australia' and 'India'. The idea was that the Western Australian Land Company, which purchased land in the area, would breed horses for sale to the British Army in India. Before that happened, however, the company went bust and most of the original settlers, who had arrived in 1841, left. The town is on the edge of an estuary which provides sheltered waters for sailing.

i **Bunbury Visitor Information Centre**, Old Railway Station, Carmody Place; tel: 9721 7922 or 1800 286 287; e-mail: welcome@bunbury.wa.gov.au; www.justsouth.com.au. Open daily.
Internet Access: Old Station Coffee Lounge (in the old station next to the Tourist Bureau); tel: 9791 1254.

Admiral Motor Inn $$$$ 56 Spencer St; tel: 9721 7322.
Bunbury Caravan & Chalet Villa $$$$ Bussell Hwy; tel: 9795 7100.
Bunbury Glade Caravan Park $$$ Timperley Rd; tel: 9721 3800; website: www.glade.com.au
Burlington Hotel Motel $$ 51 Victoria St; tel: 9721 2075.
Bussell Motor Hotel $$ Bussell Hwy; tel: 9721 1022.
The Clifton $$$$ cnr Clifton and Molloy Sts; tel: 9721 4300.
Dolphin Retreat Bunbury YHA $–$$ 14 Wellington St; tel: 9792 4690; www.yha.com.au/hostels. Short walk to town centre and beach.
Lighthouse Beach Resort $$$$ Carey St; tel: 9721 1311. Great views.
Ocean Drive Motel $$$ 121 Ocean Dr.; tel: 9721 2033.
Wander Inn Backpackers $–$$$ 16 Clifton St; tel: 9721 3242. Clean and friendly.
Welcome Inn $$$ Ocean Dr.; tel: 9721 3100.

Alexanders Bistro $$ 20 Symmons St; tel: 9721 9966.
Burlington Hotel Restaurant $$$ 51 Victoria St; tel: 9721 2075.
Cazenoas $$$ 10 Victoria St; tel: 9721 3866.
China City Garden Restaurant $$ 47 Victoria St; tel: 9721 1711.
Jacaranda Diner $ 123 Victoria St; tel: 9791 2104.
Kebab Company $ 43 Victoria St; tel: 9791 1523.
L'Amour De La Femme $$$ 18 Wittenoom St; tel: 9791 3504.
Lord Forrest Hotel $$$$ 20 Symmons St; tel: 9721 9966.
Louisa's Restaurant $$$ 15 Clifton St; tel: 9721 9959.
Mancini's Café Restaurant $$$ 66 Victoria St; tel: 9721 9944.
Nicola's $$$ 30 Victoria St; tel: 9791 3926.
Sibs $$$ 52 Victoria St; tel: 9791 5886.
Top Of The Town Garden Restaurant $$$ 91 Victoria St; tel: 9721 2202.

Uncle Vinnie's Italian Restaurant $$$ 113 Spencer St; tel: 9721 7247.

White Elephant Chinese Restaurant $$$ 38 Victoria St; tel: 9721 6522.

HIGHLIGHTS

The fastest way to orient yourself in Bunbury – not a simple town to navigate – is to go first to the **Old Railway Station**, which was the terminus for the railway line from Perth until the service was discontinued in 1985. Now it is the local bus depot and Tourist Bureau. The Tourist Bureau has *Walk About* and *Browse Around* brochures which give you self-guided tours to the town. The most important of these is the Heritage Trail which combines driving and walking, and takes you to some 50 sites of interest.

The city has several attractive heritage buildings dating from around the 18th century and many have been totally restored. **The Bunbury Arts Complex** is housed in what was the Convent of Mercy, blessed and opened in 1897, which in turn stands on the site of the original Catholic Chapel, built in the late 1860s. Within the arts complex, the **Bunbury City and Regional Galleries** are open daily 1000–1600.

St Patrick's Cathedral dominates several of the views, being positioned at the top of Bury Hill on Parkfield St. It was supposedly completed in 1921, except that there was not enough money for the steeple. That 18.3-m addition came along 46 years later but it all looks very integrated. It's worth viewing the interior to see what can be done with the local wood, jarrah, when you have an inspired carpenter.

At the north end of the beach stands a checkered lighthouse dating from 1959. A short walk from the light up to Marlston Hill provides an excellent view over Koombana Bay and the breakwater from the Rotary Lookout Tower. Lookout visitors sometimes see dolphins frolicking in the bay – call the Visitor Centre (tel: 9721 7922) for details.

Boulter's Height is the town's most popular lookout. The view is of the city, the port, the north shore and the Leschenault Estuary. Reach it on foot from the junction of Wittenoom and Stirling Sts, at the base of the 26-m waterfall constructed in Mar 1966 to tie in with a visit by the Queen Mother. When it is switched on, the water tumbles down the eastern face of the heights.

King Cottage Museum, 77 Forest Ave, was built around 1870 – there is some debate about the exact date. The owner, Henry King, and his four sons built it with bricks made from clay found on the property. The Bunbury Historical Society opened it as a museum in 1968 and has furnished it with items from the 1870–1920 period. It's open by appointment, tel: 9721 1586, and Sat–Sun, school holidays and public holidays 1400–1600, $.

Incidentally, the Kings are buried in the grounds of St Mark's.

The **Leschenault Inlet** abounds with birdlife – pelicans, ducks, black swans, magpies, wagtails, parrots and many others. In the area are also kangaroos, wallabies and possums, but its true wealth lies, perhaps, in the abundance of flora – the wild flowers which have made Western Australia famous.

The **Bunbury Entertainment Centre**, on the shores of the inlet, was opened in 1990 and contains the largest entertainment venue in regional Western Australia. A state-of-the-art, multifunctional complex, it can cater for straight theatre, concerts, films, conferences and exhibitions; tel: 9791 1133.

> ## THE STORY OF ST MARK'S
>
> St Mark's Anglican church in the nearby hamlet of Picton is claimed to be the oldest church in the state. The church is testament to one man's faith. In 1840, the *Samuel Wright*, an American whaling ship, was wrecked in Koombana Bay. Captain Coffin, the sadly named master of the ship, turned adversity to his own ends and used salvaged timber from the wreck to build a cottage in Picton. Two years later he sold the cottage to the Revd John Ramsden Wollaston, who had come there to be chaplain of Australind and arrived to find the place collapsing under debt. Wollaston decided that God was testing his faith. Enlisting the help of some of the locals, he built his own very primitive church. In 1942 the building was extensively restored, but you can still get a feeling of the effort that went into building it from scratch with no money and very little support from the Anglican church. The church is on the corner of Flynn and Charterhouse Close – it's not easy to find so ask for a map and directions at the tourist office.

Koombana Bay has a **Dolphin Education Centre** ($), and if you arrive early in the morning on most days you will be greeted by dolphins. They apparently enjoy swimming with humans, but it is advised that you do not touch them.

Big Swamp Wetlands and Boardwalk has a 100-m elevated boardwalk from which you can look for some 70 different kinds of birds as well as the long-necked turtle. The Wildlife Park features kangaroos, wallabies, snakes, fruit bats, koalas and a large walk-in aviary containing a variety of birds. Open daily 1000–1700. The Park is on Prince Phillip Dr., 3 km from the city centre.

MARGARET RIVER

Margaret River was originally a dairy town – it still is to a certain extent – but over the past few years it has been gaining fame as the centre of a major wine-growing region and as a tourist destination in its own right. The town and its name now appear to have a built-in magical appeal. The town, 10 km inland from where the river flows into the Indian Ocean, developed slowly between 1910 and 1920. The railway arrived in 1927, and closed 30 years later. Then, in the early 1970s, wine growing was successfully attempted and since then the district has boomed.

EN ROUTE

Busselton is in a beautiful site. John Garett Bussell, after whom the town was named, certainly thought so when he first saw the place in about 1830: 'Here was a spot that the creative fancy of a Greek would have peopled with Dryad and Naiad and all the beautiful phantoms and wild imagery of his sylvan mythology. Wide waving lawns were sloping down to the water's edge. Trees thick and tangled were stooping to the banks.' Yes, it is purple prose, but the area around Busselton is still like that and inspires writers today. **St Mary's Church** in Busselton, on Geographe Bay, is the oldest stone church in the state. (St Mark's in Picton is said to be the oldest church in Western Australia; see p. 430.)

i **Tourist Information Bureau**, cnr Tunbridge Rd and Bussell Hwy; tel: 9757 2911; www.margaretriverwa.com. Open daily.

Adamsons Riverside Accommodation $$$$ 71 Bussell Hwy; tel: 9757 2013.
Captain Freycinet Inn $$$$ Tunbridge St, cnr Bussell Hwy; tel: 9757 2033. Despite the name, a modern motel.
Colonial Motel $$$$ Wallcliffe Rd; tel: 9757 2633.
Inne Town Backpackers $–$$ 93 Bussell Hwy; tel: 9757 3698 or 1800 244 115. Town centre, opposite the Margaret River tourist office.
Margaret River Lodge YHA $–$$$ 220 Railway Tce; tel: 9757 9532; www.yha.com.au/hostels. Just outside town, quiet and interesting.
Prevelly Park Beach Resort $$$ 99 Mitchell Dr.; tel: 9757 2374.

1885 Inn & Restaurant $$$$ Farrelly St, next to St Thomas More Church; tel: 9757 3177. Built as a country house in 1888, this is the ideal place to sample one of the 150-odd Margaret River wines in the cellar.
Arc of Iris $$$ 151 Bussell Hwy; tel: 9757 3112.
Eats Diner $$ Shops 6 and 7, Town Sq., Bussell Hwy; tel: 9757 3155.
Goodfellas Café $$$ 97 Bussell Hwy; tel: 9757 3184.
Mama's Oriental $$ Bussell Hwy; tel: 9757 2622.
Spaghetti Bowl $$ 117 Bussell Hwy; tel: 9757 2999.

HIGHLIGHTS

As you come into the town from the north you first see **Rotary Park**, where a steam engine is on display. The engine was built in England in 1889, shipped to Margaret River the following year and used for log hauling until 1909. After working elsewhere it came back to Margaret River in 1964 to stand as a memorial.

The **Old Settlement Historical Museum** is privately owned and is well worth visiting, for it is light years better than most of the amateur efforts around Australia. It is a living museum and you can happily spend an afternoon exploring the site. Open daily 1000–1600.

Ellensbrook House is the Bussell family homestead. It was built in the 1850s with what was available, a tough way to construct a house. The ridge beam is a mast found as driftwood. A framework of bush poles and paper bark, gathered from the banks of the Margaret River with the help of the local Aboriginal people, has been sealed with plaster made by burning limestone from nearby dunes. Hand-hewn slabs were used for later weatherboard additions. The house has changed little over the years, but is now a National Trust-listed property and has recently had a major refurbishment and restoration. Open daily 1000–1600 ($). The house is a longish walk from the road – vehicle access is promised – but it is well worth the effort.

THE BUSSELL FAMILY

Bussell is a recurrent name in the history of the area. In 1834 the family settled along the Vasse valley; their homestead, Ellensbrook, was named by Alfred Bussell after his wife. Their name was given, against their wishes, to Busselton, and Margaret River was named after Margaret Wicher, a family friend. At Margaret River, Alfred tried to emulate a grand English country house by building Wallcliffe in 1865.

In 1876, 16-year-old Grace Bussell and Sam Isaacs, an Aborigine, rode 12 km on horseback to go to the rescue of survivors from the *Georgette*, shipwrecked on a reef off Calgardup Beach. They ferried survivors to shore and a monument at Calgardup Beach commemorates their bravery.

About 500 m away from the house is the **Meekadarribee waterfall** – the moon's bathing place. It is surrounded by tall peppermint trees which arch over a limestone cave behind the falls.

One of the most remarkable attractions in this remarkably attractive town is **Eagles Heritage**. It opened in January 1988 to care for birds of prey that were taken there injured, orphaned or displaced. The centre now boasts the largest collection of raptors in Australia, including eagles, hawks, falcons and owls. You can see 21 of the 24 diurnal species and 5 of the 8 species of owl here.

The centre is situated on 12 ha of bushland and visitors can enjoy a 1-km walk which takes approximately 30–40 minutes and features an abundance of wild flowers and orchids (in season). All the aviaries are built of natural bush poles and nylon netting which saves the birds from injury. A major feature is the enormous free-fly cage where the injured birds can learn to fly again before being released back into their own environment. The centre is a few minutes' drive south of Margaret River along Boodjidup Rd. Open daily 1000–1700 ($), with free-flight displays at 1100 and 1330.

EN ROUTE
Beedelup National Park, off Vasse Hwy, contains the Underwood Tree which is 400 years old and has a 3- by 4-metre hole cut into it, hacked out using a chainsaw. This took ten hours. You can stand in the hole with over 151 tonnes of tree above you. Also in the park are Beedelup Cascades and Falls, which drop over a steep gorge 107 m high in two sections. They are set in beautiful forest surroundings and feature a short walk crossing Beedelup Brook on a footbridge built from a karri log.

Four spectacular **caves** are within easy reach of Margaret River – Lake, Mammoth, Jewel and Moondyne. All have conducted tours and are well lit so that you can see the stalactites and stalagmites.

Bellview Shell Museum at Witchcliffe, 8 km south of Margaret River, has one of the best shell collections in Australia. Open daily (except Thur) 0900–1700 ($).

Of the many **wineries** you can visit in the area, try:
Cape Mentelle, Wallcliffe Rd; tel: 9757 3266; open daily 1000–1600.
Chateau Xanadu, Terry Rd; tel: 9757 2581; open daily 1000–1700.
Evans and Tate, Caves Rd and Metricup Rd; tel: 9755 6244; open for tastings daily 1030–1630.
Leeuwin Estate, Stevens Rd; tel: 9757 6253; open daily for lunch. Saturday evenings for dinner. Wine tasting and winery tours daily, 1000–1630.
Redgate Wines, Boodjidup Rd; tel: 9757 6208; open daily 1000–1700.
Vasse Felix, Caves Rd and Harmon South Rd; tel: 9755 5242. Cellar open daily 1000–1700; restaurant open daily 1100–1500.

PEMBERTON

Pemberton is a successful logging town surrounded by vast areas of national park and state forest, mainly karri trees. Some of the tallest hardwood trees in the world grow in this area. The tallest tree felled here was 104 m high.

The first European to settle in the area was Edward Brockman, son of Perth's first mayor. He arrived in 1861, bred horses for the Indian market and established a homestead, Warren House, in 1863. It still stands where the Pemberton–Northcliffe road crosses the Warren River. Pemberton Walcott, the man who gave the town its name, arrived in 1862 but his farming enterprise failed and he left the area just two years later. A road linking Vasse (now Busselton) to Pemberton was built – by convicts – in 1866.

The town is only 25 km from the Southern Ocean and even in summer the nights can be cool, while winters are cool and wet with heavy dews and forest mists. As a result, most accommodation in the area has wood fires.

EN ROUTE

On a detour to the coast, there are sandy beaches and good fishing at Windy Harbour. The road to Albany is along the splendidly named Pacific Hwy Rte 1 that circumnavigates mainland Australia. Sadly, the name is all that is splendid about the highway.

i **Pemberton Tourist Centre**, Old School Building, Brockman St; tel: 9776 1133; www.pembertontourist.com.au. Open daily.
Internet access: Pemberton Telecentre, 29 Brockman St; tel: 9776 1745; e-mail pembytc@wn.com.au. Open Mon–Fri and Sat morning.

Forest Lodge and Motel $$$ Vasse Hwy; tel: 9776 1113.
Gloucester Motel $$$ Ellis St; tel: 9776 1266. Beautiful view of the forest. Restaurant.
Karri Valley Resort $$$$ Vasse Hwy; tel: 9776 2020. Self-contained chalets with secluded forest views.
**Pemberton Backpackers YHA $–$$** 7 Brockman St; tel: 9776 1105; www.yha.com.au/hostels. Lounge with TV and video, 200 m from shops, walking maps available, mountain bikes for hire ($$).
Pemberton Caravan Park $$$ Pumphill Rd; tel: 9776 1300. Next to the Pemberton Pool.

Gourmet Coffee Shop $ 246 Dickinson St; tel: 9776 1159.
Pemberton Chinese Restaurant $ 3 Dean St; tel: 9776 1514.
Salitage Wines $$$ Vasse Hwy; tel: 9776 1711.
Shamrock Restaurant $$$ Brockman St; tel: 9776 1186.
Silver Birch Restaurant $$$ Widdeson St; tel: 9776 1019.

HIGHLIGHTS

This is a timber town, and all else is secondary. In 1913, Pemberton mills supplied half a million sleepers for the rail line across the Nullarbor Plain. The World Forestry Commission visited the district in 1928 and judged karri second only to Californian redwood as a timber tree; the Pemberton National Parks Board was formed two years later to administer Pemberton, Warren and Beedelup national parks.

For an idea of working life in the forest before the turn of the 20th century, the **Brockman sawpit** on the Pemberton–Northcliffe road has been restored to its original state of around 1865. In those days, lengths of timber were cut by hand with a cross-saw. The sawmill is no longer in use, but can be viewed.

The **Gloucester Tree** is 2.4 km east of the town, named after a visit by the Duke of Gloucester. This great karri tree houses the world's highest fire lookout, built in

1946. It is possible to climb up its 153 rungs of alternate wooden karri pegs and steel spikes for 61 m. This is only for the very fit and should not be attempted if there is any sort of a wind. The whole thing sways and can make a climber feel seasick.

On the **Pemberton Tramway** you can ride in a 1907 replica tram through towering karri and marri forests along one of the most scenic rail lines in Australia, crossing rivers and streams on rustic wooden bridges to enjoy the quiet beauty of the forest. Departs daily at 1045 and 1400 – the trip takes 1¾ hrs and the turnaround point is the Warren River. On Tues, Thur and Sat there is a 5½-hr trip – this includes 1½ hrs in Northcliffe – which leaves at 1015; tel: 9776 1322.

For those to whom steam trains provide the ultimate thrill, a **steam train service** operates May–Nov between Pemberton and Lyall (10 km south of Manjimup). This historic section of railway was originally a State Saw Mills line, completed in early 1914. Everything imaginable was transported on this railway. There was even a payroll robbery in 1925 between Collins Siding and Barrenhurst. The return trip takes just under 3 hrs and travels through beautiful forest and pasture. Departs Pemberton railway station, Sun 1030.

If you're more adventurous or a genuine enthusiast, consider taking a Driving Experience course, and have a go driving a steam locomotive and train. After an hour's instruction you can drive one of the passenger service trains, under the supervision of an experienced driver; tel: 9776 1322 for more information.

The **Pemberton swimming pool** is a mountain pool formed by the damming of the Lefroy Brook in 1929. You can catch your own rainbow trout at the **King Trout Farm** just 7 km out of town. It supplies brown and rainbow trout fingerlings (little fish, a finger long) to stock dams and rivers all over Western Australia. Open 0930–1730 daily; tel: 9776 1352.

Other attractions include the **Big Brook Arboretum**, with 32 different species of tree, and the **One-Hundred-Year Forest**, which consists of trees of roughly the same age. It is so-named because it was cleared for wheat-growing in the early days. When the area was abandoned, natural regeneration from a fire-induced seed fall from the surrounding areas and the karri forest was started. It was recognised and dedicated as a state forest 31 years later.

Warren National Park has some of the very little virgin karri forest remaining in Western Australia, with trees over 80 m high. The 18-km Rainbow Trail recalls where, in the 1920s, the steam locomotives used to haul giant karri logs along a bush tramway to the Pemberton sawmill.

WESTERN AUSTRALIA

Pemberton is a new wine-growing region. The main varieties planted are Pinot Noir, Chardonnay and Cabernet Sauvignon. Several wines have already won major awards. Most of the **wineries** offer cellar sales and some also have a café or restaurant. Bus tours of the wineries are available. These are a few that welcome visitors.

Gloucester Ridge, 100 m from the Gloucester Tree. Open daily 1000–1600.

Salitage Winery, on the Vasse Hwy, uses only estate-grown fruit.

Warren Vineyard, on Conte Rd, 3 km west of the post office, was established in 1985 and produces mainly fine reds.

ALBANY

Albany has been called both the Gem of the Southern Ocean and Queen of the Southlands. One suspects these names came from the fertile imaginations of the tourist office, but a view from the top of Mt Clarence (and a steep but safe drive) offers panoramas which show that the names may be only slightly over the top.

The name Albany is very English but it could have been different – this was the proposed site for a French settlement. There are many such places around the coasts of Australia and New Zealand, but in every case the British got there first or came with more people.

You could consider Albany the capital for the Great Southern Region. The area has a Mediterranean-type climate; the rain tends to be concentrated in the winter months but there is no truly dry season. The most popular time to visit is from Aug–Oct, when the wild flowers are in bloom and the whales pass during their annual migration.

i **Albany Visitor Centre**, Old Railway Station, Proudlove Parade; tel 9841 1088; www.albanytourist.com.au. Open daily.

Motels line the highway coming into town. You can sort one out with the Vacancy sign showing but try to get the furthest unit from the road.
Ace Motor Inn $$$ 314 Albany Hwy; tel: 9841 2911.
Albany Backpackers $–$$ cnr Stirling Terrace and Spencer St; tel: 9841 8848; website: www.albanybackpackers.com.au. Breakfast included.

Not all visitors to the town have had a happy time. Anthony Trollope was outraged that he had to take a signed certificate from a policeman in Albany to prove to other Australian states that he had 'not been a lag'. Visitors are no longer required to do this.

Albany Happy Days Caravan Park $$ 21 Millbrook Rd; tel: 9844 3267.

Balneaire Seaside Resort $$$$ 27 Adelaide Crest, 3.5 km from the centre of town; tel: 9842 2877; website: www.balneaire.com.au

Bayview YHA $–$$ 49 Duke St; tel: 9841 3949; www.yha.com.au/hostels.

Discovery Inn $$$ 9 Middleton Rd, 3.5 km out of town, one street back from Middleton Beach; tel: 9842 5535; e-mail: mra@iinet.net.au

Dolphin Lodge Albany $$$ 32 Adelaide Cres.; tel: 9841 6600.

Flinders Park Lodge $$$$ cnr Lower King and Harbour Rd; tel: 9844 7062; website: www.parklodge.com.au/. Eight guest rooms, most overlooking acres of land with views to Oyster Harbour, the hills beyond and the lights of Emu Point.

Middleton Beach Bed & Breakfast $$ 7 Griffiths St, 100 m from the beach; tel: 9844 1135; e-mail: bbysea@iinet.net.au. Not for smokers.

Ryan's Premier Hotel/Motel $$$ 208 York St; tel: 9841 1544.

The Terrace $$$$ 36 Marine Terrace; tel: 9842 9901. Luxurious colonial-style bed and breakfast 3 km from the centre of Albany and three minutes' walk from Middleton Beach.

🍴 Adelaides Restaurant $$$ Forts Rd; tel: 9842 1090.

Al Fornetto Ristorante & Pizzeria $$$ 132 York St; tel: 9842 1060.

Argyles $$$ 42 Stirling Terrace; tel: 9842 9696.

Beachside Middleton Beach $$$$ 1 Flinders Pde; tel: 9841 7733.

Café on the Terrace $ 134 Stirling Terrace; tel: 9842 1012.

Earl of Spencer Historic Inn $$$ Earl St and Spencer St; tel: 9841 1322.

Esplanade Hotel $$$ Flinders Pde; tel: 9842 1711. Open daily 1030–late.

Kooka's Restaurant $$$$ 204 Stirling Terrace; tel: 9841 5889.

Rustler's Steakhouse $$$ 63 Frederick St; tel: 9842 2454.

Three Plenties Palace $$$ 148 York St; tel: 9841 4121.

Whalers Galley $$ Whaling Station; tel: 9844 4347.

WESTERN AUSTRALIA

HIGHLIGHTS

The first recorded European sighting of this area was probably in 1627, by François Thyssen and Peter Noyts (it was outlined on a Dutch East India chart of 1628). The huge natural harbour of King George Sound, on which Albany is sited, was discovered, charted and named in 1792 by Captain George Vancouver, who served with Captain Cook and after whom Vancouver, in Canada, is named. In a second voyage to the area, Vancouver sent a party ashore, which climbed Mt Clarence and sighted Princess Royal Harbour to the north. The French explorer Bruny d'Entrecasteaux came by the same year, and Matthew Flinders landed here in 1801. Within a few years King George Sound was a regular stopping place for ships, including sealers and whalers.

In late 1826, Major Edmund Lockyer arrived in the brig *Amity* with troops and convicts to establish a penal colony, but this lasted only until 1831. In 1976, for the town's 150th anniversary, the people of Albany decided to reconstruct the *Amity*; it is moored only 200 m from the landing place of the original vessel.

Lockyer, unaware of Vancouver's previous visit, had named the village Frederickstown in honour of Frederick, Duke of Albany. The name was never popular and in 1832 it was formally changed to Albany. With one of the greatest natural harbours in the world, it became a major port of call for warships in the Indian Ocean and mail steamers on the Australian run. However, when Fremantle was established as a port in 1900 Albany declined. It regained some popularity when it was discovered as a tourist resort.

Albany was an important whaling station, and since the international ban on whaling, the whales are starting to come back. If you can't be there when they migrate you can still visit what is claimed to be the world's largest whale museum and Australia's last whaling station. **Whaleworld** (Frenchman's Bay Rd), created from an operational whaling station, was the Cheynes Beach Whaling Company until 1978. In its time the station's chasers took up to 850 whales per season. Today the restored *Cheynes IV* whale chaser is the centrepiece of Whaleworld. Open daily 0900–1700, with 45-minute tours starting every hour.

Albany has a number of interesting old buildings reflecting its early history. **St John's Church of England,**

WHALE WATCHING

Southern right whales can be seen from July–Nov calving in the calm waters of sheltered bays in the Bremer Bay area. They can be observed from many vantage points along the coastline, at times as close as only 6 m from shore. Occasionally humpback whales can be seen from a distance, as well as other marine mammals such as dolphins and seals.

Church St, dates from 1846. It was the first church consecrated in Western Australia and has beautiful stained-glass windows and an imposing tower.

The **Old Gaol**, just back from the harbour, was built in 1851 as the convict hiring department and became the district gaol in 1872. After it had stood empty for many years, the Albany Historical Society began its restoration in 1968. The museum contains a fascinating collection of social and historical artefacts. Visitors can shut themselves in the black hole – not recommended for the claustrophobic – or ramble through the numerous small rooms and cells. There is an audio-visual display of its history. Open daily 1000–1600.

The **Albany Residency**, nearby, was built in the early 1850s, and in 1975 it became the first branch of the Western Australian Museum outside the Perth area. It is a focal point for both the social and natural history of the Albany region.

The **Old Forts** on top of Mt Adelaide offer a fascinating look at bygone days, with memorabilia from World War I including exhibits from the Light Horse Brigade, gun turrets from old ships and historic photographs. There's a great view from the top of the hill, and having a good stroll around is recommended. The Old Forts are open daily 0930–1600 except Mondays. There's a tearoom on site providing light refreshments.

> **Dog Rock** in Middleton Rd is Albany's unofficial mascot and, after Gundagai, the most photographed 'dog' in Australia. It is, in fact, a granite outcrop that looks like the enormous head of a bloodhound sniffing the breeze.

Patrick Taylor Cottage, on the corner of Stirling Terrace and Parade St, was built in 1832 of wattle and daub. It has been restored as much as possible to its former state and is now a museum containing clothes of the period, household goods, old clocks and silverware.

The **Old Farm**, off Middleton Rd, Strawberry Hill, was the site of the government farm for the settlement of Albany. It was developed from 1827 to 1830 and then bought by Sir Richard Spencer for 15 guineas. The two-storey stone building was built for him in 1836 and is one of the oldest in Western Australia. It has been maintained by the National Trust since 1964 and has splendid gardens.

Torndirrup National Park is on the coast south of Albany and Princess Royal Harbour and includes some of the most spectacular scenery in Australia. The Gap is a 24-m drop to the sea. When a heavy swell is running, the thunder of the ocean and the drifting spray are an awesome experience. The Natural Bridge, like a huge, granite suspension bridge, is an awe-inspiring sight in rough seas. Visitors are asked to be wary of king waves that have been known to surge up 9 m and have taken lives.

Nearby is the 4639-ha Two Peoples Bay Nature Reserve, the sanctuary of the noisy scrub bird, thought for many years to be extinct. The bird is a brilliant mimic and several pairs are thought still to exist.

WILD FLOWER TOURS

More than 3500 varieties of wild flower have been listed within a 48-km radius of Albany. For botanists this is paradise. A botanical illustrator wrote in 1893: 'In one place I sat down and without moving I could pick twenty five different flowers within the reach of my hand. The banksias were quite marvellous, their huge bushy flowers a foot in length, and so full of honey that the natives were said to get tipsy sucking them.' (This idea that you can get tipsy from banksia is incorrect!)

The two favourite places to visit for wild flowers are the nearby national parks. The flowers can change quite rapidly, and the tourist office will be able to advise you. It's well worth making the effort.

Stirling Range National Park was named after the first governor of Western Australia. The park covers 115,671 ha and there are many tracks providing easy access to wildlife and flowers. The western access via Tourist Drive No. 253 from Cranbrook takes travellers along the Salt River Rd, Red Gum Springs Rd and into the heart of the park. Picnic areas with barbecue facilities are located throughout the park. The ecology is delicately balanced, and to ensure the flora and fauna are preserved, camping and fires are permitted only where facilities are provided. Five of the peaks within the park rise to over 1000 m and are often shrouded in mist.

Porongurup National Park has some of the oldest rock in the world and covers 2401 ha. Easy walking tracks lead to most of the peaks, giving spectacular views. In the Porongurups 'climbing' is a bit of a misnomer. The walks are all relatively easy and not over-long.

Both of these national parks are about 40 km from Albany and offer magnificent climbs, spectacular views and beautiful wild flowers. There are said to be almost 1000 species of wild flowers in these ranges, more than 100 unique to the area.

WHERE NEXT?

Hwy 30 will take you back to Perth along a direct inland route (450 km). About the same distance east along Hwy 1 will bring you to the beaches and clear waters of Esperance and the Bay of Isles (see p. 441). There are buses from Albany to Esperance on Mondays and Thursdays (change at Ravensthorpe); journey time 6 hrs 15 mins (OTT table 9448).

Although Esperance is a small town with a population of something under 9000, it has some considerable importance in the area. It is a service centre for the surrounding agricultural area – this is one of the oldest apple-growing areas in Western Australia and is now starting to be seen as a holiday destination of high potential. It has everything that a holidaymaker needs although, like so many places in Western Australia, it suffers from the tyranny of distance – it's a long way from major centres of population (Perth, for example, is over 725 km away).

INFORMATION

Esperance Visitor Centre, Museum Village, Dempster St; tel: 9071 2330. www.visitesperance.com. Open daily; closes 1400 Sat and 1200 Sun.

ACCOMMODATION

Most of the motels – standard Australian model – are along The Esplanade. If you have not booked, drive along it looking for Vacancies signs and then choose the one you like.

A SMALL CLAIM TO FAME

In 1979 Esperance town council, totally unintimidated by the potential wrath of the United States, served the crashdown team at NASA with an infringement notice for littering.

Blue Waters Lodge YHA $–$$ 299 Goldfields Rd; tel: 9071 1040; www.yha.com.au/hostels.

Esperance Backpackers $–$$ 14 Emily St; tel: 9071 4724. Central location.

Esperance Bayview Motel $$$ 31 Dempster St; tel: 9071 1533.

Esperance Motor Hotel $$$ 14 Andrew St; tel: 9071 1555.

Esperance Seafront Caravan Park $ Goldfields Rd; tel: 9071 1251. Caravan and tent sites; grassy, shady.

Esperance Travellers Inn $$$ Goldfields Rd; tel: 9071 1677.

Hospitality Inn $$$$ The Esplanade; tel 9071 1999.

Jetty Motel $$$ 1 The Esplanade; tel: 9071 5978.

Old Hospital Motel $$$ 1a William St; tel: 9071 3587. Nine self-contained units, central, TV, video, microwave.

Pier Hotel $$$ The Esplanade; tel: 9071 1777.

FOOD AND DRINK

You do not come to Esperance for a great culinary experience, but there are plenty of restaurants that cater to the economy-minded traveller. The main restaurant thoroughfare is Dempster St.

Emperor's Garden Chinese Restaurant $ 123 Dempster St; tel: 9071 2866.

Golden Orient Chinese Restaurant $ 49 Dempster St; tel: 9071 3744.

Gray Starling Restaurant $$$ 126 Dempster St; tel: 9071 5880. BYO.

Ocean Blues $ 19 The Esplanade; tel: 9071 7107. Open daily from 0600.

Pizza Kitchen Esperance $ 85 Dempster St; tel: 9071 4666

HIGHLIGHTS

The beaches and waters around Esperance have been described as some of the finest and clearest in the world. The Esperance archipelago contains over 100 islands and has a wealth of maritime life, including seals, sea lions and dolphins. And, like all of the other towns along this coast, it is an ideal spot to watch the migrations of the whales – the southern right whales come here July–Nov to calve in the warm and sheltered waters. Known as the Bay of Isles, this is another of the fisherman's paradises on the Western Australia coastline – virtually any point off the Esperance coast will produce a good catch.

One of the biggest attractions is a cruise out around some of the islands. These cruises have full commentaries and last for 3½ hours. Visitors can see sea eagles being hand fed, dolphins at play and colonies of sea lions and seals, plus a host of other marine life and seabirds. **Esperance Diving and Fishing** has a purpose-built cruise vessel which can carry up to ten passengers and offers whale watching, fishing and scuba-diving. It is at 72 The Esplanade, directly opposite the Taylor St Jetty; tel: 9071 1511; website: www.gei.net.au/~espdive.

The history of Esperance is recorded in the **Esperance Municipal Museum** (open daily 1330–1630, cnr James and Dempster Sts).

DAY TRIPS

As a town from which to explore national parks, Esperance has few equals: there are four national parks within striking distance. Most importantly, all are accessible by sealed road.

Only 56 km from Esperance, **Cape Le Grand National Park** is probably the most spectacular and beautiful area on the west coast. It has a wide range of bays with white sand and clear water, among them Hellfire Bay, Thistle Cove and Lucky Bay. The view across the bay and the national park from Frenchman's Peak is worth the journey alone. About 6 km east of Cape Le Grand is Mississippi Hill and Rossiter Bay. It was here in 1841 that English explorers Eyre and Wylie met Captain Rossiter of the French whaler *Mississippi* at the end of their long and arduous expedition from Adelaide. There is camping (in designated areas only) here; take your own water and supplies.

Further east along the coast, 120 km from Esperance and just past Duke of Orleans Bay, comes **Cape Arid National Park**. The park stretches over nearly 20,000 ha of sandplains and heathlands, but is better known for its sweeping beaches, clear blue seas and Precambrian granite headlands.

On the coast to the west of Esperance is **Stokes National Park**, which covers an area of 10,667 ha and has the historic Moir Homestead. The coastal scenery is beautiful and there is ocean fishing and sandy beaches good for swimming. You will see copious birdlife (over 40 species have been recorded), grey kangaroos and probably the occasional seal. Access to the park is on good gravel roads from the main highway to camping bays close to the inlet. There are caravan pads and borehole toilets at the sites, but no water. Other roads within the park are four-wheel-drive tracks only (caravans are restricted to the gravel roads).

About halfway between Esperance and Albany (see p. 436) is the huge **Fitzgerald River National Park**. Like all these national parks, it has almost deserted beaches and clear blue waters and an over-abundance of maritime life.

WHERE NEXT?
Buses run from Esperance to Kalgoorlie on Tues, Fri and Sun, and take 5 hrs 15 mins; OTT table 9444.

KALGOORLIE

Kalgoorlie has always had a certain reputation in Australia. When the country was mor
strictly run by wowsers – meaning anyone who disapproves of sex – Kalgoorlie was th
only city in Australia that had brothels which operated under both city and polic
tolerance. And it was the only city in Australia where the pubs stayed open night an
day – this at a time when all of the pubs in the rest of the country had to close a
1800 (thus creating that awful spectacle, the Six O'Clock Swill).

Today, licensing hours throughout Australia are relaxed, and Melbourne, of all place
boasts in the Daily Planet the largest and most luxurious brothel in the country. Bu
original sin started with Kalgoorlie, and there is still a sort of hint of a leer associate
with it. The name Kalgoorlie comes from an Aboriginal word said to mean 'silky pear
On the other hand, a British magazine described it as the 'mad bastard capital c
Australia', which is unkind but accurate enough to sting.

The reason Kalgoorlie attracted so much attention from ladies of the night is becaus
for a long time it was the richest square mile in the world. And the source of that wealt
was gold. Kalgoorlie is unusual in that it is a gold-mining town that has avoided becom
ing a ghost town. The surrounding countryside, stripped of its vegetation by the earl
miners, is forbiddingly ugly and the summers are extremely hot. Don't go there i
December or January because the heat will be a foretaste of hell and you will find tha
the local population has rather smartly gone elsewhere for its holidays. During the res
of the year, however, the town is a major tourist attraction where there is much to se

GETTING THERE AND GETTING AROUND

There are two flights a day from Perth to Kalgoorlie airport, south of the town.

Kalgoorlie is 595 km east of Perth, along the long, straight road of Hwy 94. By bu
the journey takes 5½–8 hours. The Perth Goldfields Express covers the route, OT
9439 (it is also included on Greyhound Pioneer's Perth–Adelaide route, OTT 9430)

Transwa runs a daily service to Kalgoorlie from East Perth Station, OTT 9033. Thi
service, known as the Prospector, runs Australia's most modern railcars which cam
into service in 2004.

INFORMATION

algoorlie-Boulder Tourist Centre, 250 Hannan St; tel: 9021 1966;
-mail: visitors@kalgoorlie.com. Open daily.

INTERNET SITE **Kalgoorlie-Boulder Virtual Tourism:** www.kalgoorlie.com/tourism

ACCOMMODATION

Gold Dust Backpackers $–$$ 192 Hay St; tel: 9091 3737.
Good facilities.

Goldfields Backpackers $–$$ 164 Hay St; tel: 9091 1482.

Midas Motel $$$$ 409 Hannan St; tel: 9021 3088.

Old Australian Hotel $$$$ 138 Hannan St; tel: 9021 1320.

Palace Hotel $$$ Hannan St, cnr Maritana St; tel: 9021 2788.

Star & Garter Hotel/Motel $$$$ 497 Hannan St; tel: 9026
3399.

Tower Hotel $$$$ Maritana St; tel: 9021 3211.

FOOD AND DRINK

Amalfi Restaurant $$$ 409 Hannan St; tel: 9021 3088.

Amy's Restaurant $$$ 1 Macdonald St; tel: 9021 1749. Open
Tues–Sat 1800–late. Continental and Australian.

Basil's on Hannan $$$ 268 Hannan St; tel: 9021 7832. Open
Fri–Wed 0730–1700, Thur 0730–2000. Pasta, Italian and
Continental.

Crock Pot Restaurant $$$ Hannan's Boulevard; tel: 9021
2997.

Kadees Bistro $$$ 6 Maritana St; tel: 9021 7235. Open
Mon–Sat 1830–late. Continental, Italian.

New Hong Kong Chinese Restaurant $$ 248 St Barbara
Sq., Hannan St; tel: 9021 1336. Open daily. Lunch and
dinner.

Pizza Cantina $$$ 211 Hannan St; tel: 9021 4870.

Star & Garter Restaurant $$$ 497 Hannan St; tel: 9026
3399.

Top End Thai Restaurant $$$ 71 Hannan St; tel: 9091 4027;
website: www.thai.net.au/. Open daily 1800–2100. BYO.

HIGHLIGHTS

Technically, the town is Kalgoorlie-Boulder, for in 1989 the two towns amalgamated. The main street of Boulder, Burt St, lies 5 km from the main street of Kalgoorlie, Hannan St. Boulder was named after the Great Boulder Mine, the first mine to be established on the Golden Mile.

Kalgoorlie was originally known as Hannans, after the prospector Paddy Hannan. Gold had been found in Coolgardie (see p. 448) and in 1893, Patrick Hannan, Tom Flanagan and Daniel Shea were prospecting to the east. One of their horses cast a shoe near Mt Charlotte and the group had to camp for the night. They were lying on a fortune – in a few days they collected 100 oz of nuggets. **Paddy Hannan's Tree**, which marks the site where Hannan, Flanagan and Shea struck lucky, is in Outridge Terrace.

The easily won alluvial gold was worked out in a year or so but when the seam was found under the Golden Mile the bigger companies moved in. The town was surveyed and proclaimed in 1895, and the first local newspaper, the *Western Argus*, was established the same year. Many buildings from those early boom years survive. After that, the goldfield's prosperity came and went in cycles. In disputes in 1897 over the distinction between alluvial and other mining claims, an effigy of the minister for mines was hanged and burned.

> The Top End Thai Restaurant is almost a tourist destination in its own right. It is in one of the town's oldest buildings (1897) which originally housed one of Kalgoorlie's numerous pubs – Tattersal's Hotel, and later The Savoy. The name Top End comes from its situation at the eastern end of Hannan St, in what is referred to as the Top End Block (Hannan St has a noticeable slope), near the Mt Charlotte gold mine. The food is very authentic, and its sister restaurant in Perth has won a swag of awards for the same cuisine.

Gold production peaked in 1903 but the mines started up again in 1931 when gold increased in price. Other declines followed in 1942, the 1950s and then 1963, when many mines on the eastern goldfields were closed. Gold was replaced in importance by a nickel boom in the 1970s. Nickel was first discoverd in 1966 and two years later Kalgoorlie had the only commercial nickel smelter in Australia and the second of its kind in the world. But the Kalgoorlie Goldfields are the largest in Western Australia and the Golden Mile still managed to produce 632,034 oz of gold as recently as 1995/96.

The town is still all about gold mining. From early on it was seen that the way to get the gold was reef,

> At the turn of the 20th century when more than 8000 people were riding bicycles in the district, the machine was known locally as 'the ship of the desert'.

pen-cut and deep-shaft mining, which is the way it has been mined to this day. The pen-cut mine, which is currently at a depth of 260 m, is expected to increase to a epth of 575 m, 2 km in width and almost 5 km in length. **Hannans North** in roadarrow Rd allows you to go underground, under the care of an experienced uide, to the original mine workings and witness the life of miners at the turn of the)th century. For safety reasons you will need to wear proper shoes when you are nderground. Once you are back on the surface you can ride the railway around the -ha site with its restored historic buildings and mining machinery. There is also a egular gold-pouring demonstration. Open daily 0930–1630, with tours on demand llow 3 hrs); tel: 9091 4074.

1 the **School of Mines Museum** in Cassidy St (open Mon–Fri 0830–1230, except)ec–Jan when it's too hot) there are replicas of the giant nuggets found in the region. he **Museum of the Goldfields**, at the end of Hannan St, has a 400-oz gold bar on isplay in the underground vault, along with the Western Australian State Gold Collection. It also houses many other exhibits relating to life in the goldfields since ne beginning of the 20th century.

our the surrounds of the Golden Mile on the **Loopline Tourist Railway**, which once arried hundreds of miners to work every day. The journey lasts an hour and has an nteresting audio commentary about the history of the miners and the area. The train eparts from the Boulder Railway Station on Burt St daily at 1000 ($$).

1 Sutherland St are the **Mt Charlotte Reservoir** and Lookout. The reservoir, one of ne greatest hydraulic engineering works in the world, is the remarkable design of harles Yelverton O'Connor, the state's water engineer. Water was scarcer than gold 1 Kalgoorlie in the early 20th century, and O'Connor's brilliant but seemingly npossible plan was to pipe water across the desert from Mundaring, near Perth, vhere the Helena River had been dammed. Despite ongoing criticism, enormous bstacles and five years of construction, on 22 Jan 1903 water gushed from pipes on 1t Charlotte to fill the reservoir. The water had travelled for ten days through eight umping stations and a 340-m climb – a journey of 560 km. Water has flowed ever ince. Distressed by the criticism of the experts who said it would never work, owever, O'Connor committed suicide only days before his amazing scheme was ut into operation.

ou can't go to Kalgoorlie without at least seeing a game of two-up (coin-tossing). t is illegal almost everywhere else except in casinos and on The One Day of the 'ear (Anzac Day). In Kalgoorlie the law is more liberally interpreted, and there s a permanent floating Bush Two-Up School. This is held in a corrugated-iron ing in the bush every afternoon from 1715. The tourist office will give you the urrent details.

TOURS

To the north of Kalgoorlie lies a series of **ghost towns** such as Bonnievale, Grant Patch, Broad Arrow and Ora Banda. If you would like to try your own luck, Roger Alter (tel: 0419 915 670) organises gold-detecting tours. A full-day tour ($$$+) needs a minimum of four people; you'll spend an hour gold detecting, and the rest visiting old towns. Roger's half-day tour ($$$+) is spent gold detecting only, and needs a minimum of two people. On the three-hour tour ($$$) at Hannan's North Tourist Mine, visitors go underground for an hour, watch gold pouring for an hour and pan for gold for the last hour.

DAY TRIPS

In the bush around Kalgoorlie there are over 60 species of eucalyptus to be found, including many flowering varieties. The wild flowers are outstanding July–Oct. **Goongarrie National Park** covers nearly 50,000 ha, including large areas of mulga, an arid habitat of rough, sparse grassland. The park can be reached by travelling north towards Menzies and turning east on the signed gravel road (reasonable standard). Spring is the best time to visit.

Tourist brochures like to refer to **Coolgardie** as the best-known ghost town in Australia, but a town with 690 inhabitants can hardly be said to have given up the ghost. Mind you, the town is not what it was at its peak in 1896, when the gold rush meant there were 23 hotels, eight newspapers, two stock exchanges and six banks to service a population of some 20,000 within the town, and probably half as many again in the surrounding area. At the time it was the third-largest town in Western Australia and regarded as civilisation, while Kalgoorlie, then known as Hannans, was the wild frontier.

Everything you go to see in Coolgardie revolves around gold. Discoveries started in 1892 when Arthur Bayley and William Ford found alluvial gold on Fly Flat. Then Paddy Hannan registered the Kalgoorlie claim and the gold rush was on. It was relatively short-lived; by 1902 the gold was starting to run out. The wild days were over and the town started to slide into oblivion, as did the prospectors. Arthur Bayley may have struck it rich, but he died by the time he was 31.

The most imposing building in town, solid Victorian architecture at its best, is the **Warden's Court** in Bayley St, built in 1898 using local stone. It contains the tourist office, the Mining Registrar's office and the courthouse. One good way of getting an understanding of the town is by way of the Goldfields Exhibition, staged here by the Tourist Bureau. It is open 0900–1700 daily and is much better than most efforts of this kind. Among the fascinating photographs is one showing Herbert Hoover, who spent time out here before going back to the United States and becoming president.

The **railway station** in Woodward St was built in 1876 and closed in 1971 when the standard-gauge railway was relocated north of the town. It is now a museum, open daily 0900–1600 (except Wed), and has a dramatic account of the Modesto Varischetti rescue from a flooded gold mine in 1907.

> The broad main street is still wide enough to turn a camel train. The early goldfields were supplied by camels and you can repeat that experience at the Camel Farm, 3 km to the west and open daily 0900–1700.

Another memento of early goldfield life is **Warden Finnerty's residence** in Hunt St. This dates from 1894 and it was here that John Michael Finnerty, warden and resident magistrate of the Coolgardie goldfields, lived and meted out justice. The house has now been restored by the National Trust. Next door is the **gaol tree**, to which prisoners who were awaiting trial were chained – it makes for a good photograph and is open daily (except Thur) 0900–1600 ($).

[i] **Coolgardie Tourist Bureau**, Warden's Court, Bayley St; tel: 9026 6090. Open daily.

🛏 **Coolgardie Caltex Motel** $$ 110 Bayley St; tel: 9026 6049.
Coolgardie Motel $$$ 53 Bayley St; tel: 9026 6080. Also has an à la carte restaurant.
Coolgardie Motor Inn $$$ 10 Bayley St; tel: 9026 6002.
Coolgardie Tourist Village $$ 99 Bayley St; tel: 9026 6009.
Railway Lodge $$ 75 Bayley St; tel: 9026 6238.

WHERE NEXT?

South lie the Southern Ocean, Esperance and the coastal national parks (see pp. 426–443). Halfway to Esperance is Norseman and the turnoff to the Eyre Hwy (1), which crosses the Nullarbor Plain and eventually leads to Adelaide (p. 144). Formerly one of the most testing drives in Australia, the Nullarbor crossing has been tamed by better (sealed) roads, but it's still a classic. If you have a reliable car and time on your hands, consider making your way to the eastern states via this route. Westwards is the state capital, Perth (p. 410) and its neighbour Fremantle (p. 421).

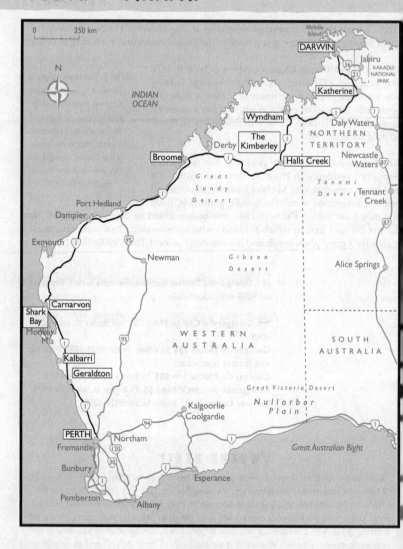

In discussing the journey from Perth to Darwin you need to consider the distance involved. On the quickest route it is over 4000 km. Yes, it can be done, but it is time intensive and it is definitely not recommended if you are on a time budget.

PERTH — DARWIN OTT Table 9431			
Service	🚌	🚌	
Days of operation Special notes	Daily	Daily A	
Perth............................d.	....	0845	....	....
Geraldton ....d.	....	1610	....	....
Overlander......................d.	....	2015	....	....
Carnarvon ....d.	....	2220	....	....
Broome ....d.	....	1915	1930	....
Halls Creek......................d.	....	....	0510	....
Wyndham........................d.	....	....	0920t	....
Katherine.........................d.	....	....	1850	....
Darwin ....a.	....	....	2240	....

Special notes:
A–This service is subject to delays in wet weather.

You could drive as far north as Carnarvon (see p. 463), and then fly from there to Darwin. Or drive to Carnarvon and come back by the inland route which passes through Gascoyne, Meeberrie, Billabalong, Mullewa (just inland from Geraldton), Morawa, Perenjori, Wubin, Northam and then into Perth. None of those towns listed after Gascoyne consists of much more than two houses, a pub, a petrol station and a dog asleep in the middle of the road, but it is a taste of the outback and it is very different from the coastal route.

If you continue to drive all the way to Darwin you must realise that you will be traversing large expanses of nothing followed by much of the same. Along the way you will visit Broome (see p. 468) and Halls Creek, but it is, as they say, a long way between drinks. Combining driving with flying is the way to go.

DRIVING ROUTE

The main route simply follows Hwy 1 on this section of its route around Australia. From Perth to Geraldton is 423 km, and Carnarvon a further 481 km. Two highlights, however, are major detours from the highway: the turn-off to Kalbarri is 100 km north of Geraldton, while a further 179 km along Hwy 1 is Overlander Roadhouse and the turn-off for Denham and Monkey Mia (130 km from Hwy 1 to Denham). Total: approx 1300 km, excluding local explorations.

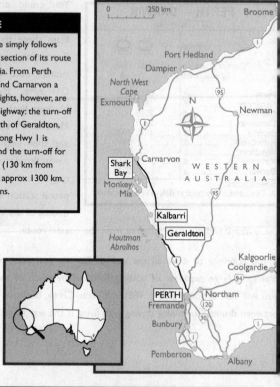

PERTH — SHARK BAY
OTT Tables 9431/9435

Service	🚌	🚌	🚌	🚌	🚌	🚌	🚌	🚌	🚌	🚌	🚌	🚌
Days of operation Special notes	①	②④⑥	①③⑤	Daily	①③⑤	①③⑤	②④	⑦ A	⑤	④⑦	②④⑦	①③⑤
Perth ....d.	0715	0830	0830	0845	....	....	0930	1300	1730	1930	1945	....
Geraldton ....d.	1551	1430	1440	1610	....	....	1630	1740	2330	0110	0245	....
Binnu ....d.	....	....	|	1730t	1745t	....	....	....	....	....	0240	|	....
Kalbarri ....d.	....	....	1700	|	1845	....	....	....	....	....	|	....
Overlander ....a.	....	....	....	2015	....	2100	....	....	....	0450	0725	0900
Denham ....d.	....	....	....	....	....	2230	....	....	....	....	....	1030
Monkey Mia ....a.	....	....	....	....	2300	....	....	....	....	....	....	1100

Special notes:
A–Additional services: 0930⑦, 1145⑦, 1700⑤,

THE INDIAN OCEAN AND DOLPHINS

The coastline north of Perth is barely known compared with its Queensland counterpart on the east coast, but it has some of the finest marine attractions in the world – from diving on old shipwrecks and excellent surfing to the thrill of feeding wild dolphins. The area around Geraldton is scenic and appealing, while Shark Bay is a World Heritage Site with some truly unique habitats.

PERTH

See p. 410.

GERALDTON

Geraldton, a popular holiday location, is 424 km north of Perth and 481 km south of Carnarvon, which in Western Australia are not considered formidable distances. It calls itself Sun City, and as it boasts an average of eight hours of sunshine a day, this is a fair claim. It also has good beaches, good fishing, splendid scenery, many restaurants and lots of accommodation.

> The first official airmail service in Australia was established in 1921 between Geraldton and Derby.

In 1846 the Gregory brothers led an expedition to open up vast areas in the district. This was the start of a long period of determined Aboriginal resistance to European settlement, a conflict which, in truth, is not yet totally resolved.

The best way to get an idea of the town is to follow the **Geraldton Heritage Trail**, a 30-km driving tour of both the natural and cultural heritage of Geraldton. There are 30 points of interest included and by the time you have finished you will have a good overall feel for the place.

Geraldton has had a fairly exciting history. Three major vessels were wrecked on these coasts: the *Batavia* (1629), the *Zuydorp* (1712) and the *Zeewijk* (1727) from the Dutch East India Company mariners pioneering Indian Ocean sea routes. The new **Western Australian Museum Geraldton**, on the marina, houses some fascinating relics from these and other wrecks, as well as items recovered from campsites set up by the survivors. Costing just under $8 million to build, the museum has some excellent natural and cultural displays, and is well worth a visit. Entry is free; open daily 1000–1600; guided tours can be arranged by appointment (tel: 9921 5080).

The **Residency** was built by convict labour in 1861 for the Government Resident of the town – a sort of governor appointed by direct authority of the British government. This residence, splendid in comparison to the rest of the town's buildings, became a hospital in 1924 and later a community centre.

Inland, along Cathedral Dr., is the truly wonderful **St Francis Xavier Cathedral**, probably the best example of the work of the architect-turned-priest Monsignor John Hawes. He began the design before he came to Geraldton in 1915 and work started the following year. Progress was hampered by the sparseness of the population and religious politics, and the cathedral was finally completed in 1938. It is most odd, yet charming, in that it seems to have borrowed its styles from other cathedrals with both a Catholic style and Catholic abandon. It is one of the most interesting religious buildings in Australia and is just as fascinating on the inside as it is on the outside. There is a John Hawes Heritage Trail where you can trace his other works, and the tourist office will provide you with a map.

LOBSTER CAPITAL OF THE WORLD

Geraldton is famous for cray fishing. It calls itself the lobster capital of the world and claims the largest lobster fleet on the west coast, but the crustaceans caught in the area in such numbers lack nippers, so technically 'lobster' is incorrect – these are crayfish. The market for them boomed in the 1970s, particularly due to American demand. They were renamed rock lobsters so that the American market would not confuse them with the crawfish, native to the rivers and bayous of the southern states.

FAMOUS NAMES IN GERALDTON

Edith Cowan was born in Geraldton in 1861 and was, in 1921, elected to the Western Australia Legislative Assembly as Australia's first woman member of parliament.

The **Revd C G Nicolay**, who arrived as Anglican chaplain in 1870, was an English eccentric in the grand manner. He tried, but failed, to establish a coffee plantation and then became editor of the *Western Australian Times* in Perth. He wrote the *Handbook of Western Australia* in 1876 and was responsible for the creation of an Aboriginal reserve of 20,235 ha in the Upper Murchison district in 1878. He also founded Western Australia's first public museum.

Novelist **Randolph Stow** was born in Geraldton in 1935, and his novel *The Merry-Go-Round in the Sea* is set in the town.

Out to the west of the town, the **Port Moore Lighthouse** was built in 1878 and stands 34 m high (an earlier lighthouse – Bluff Point – was destroyed by fire in 1952). The **Lighthouse Keeper's Cottage** in Chapman Rd was built in 1876 and is now the headquarters of the Geraldton Historical Society. Open Thur only.

Geraldton has some excellent surfing. In the summer it needs a strong breeze to build up the waves, but in winter the waves are up to 2–3 m at spots such as Flat Rocks, Greenough, Coronation, Pipeline and Back Beach.

ⓘ **Tourist Bureau,** Bill Sewell Complex, Chapman Rd; tel: 9921 3999. Sited in what was the Old Victoria District Hospital, built in 1884. Open daily.
Geraldton Tourist Bureau: www.geraldtontourist.com.au.

🛏 **Abrolhos Reef Lodge $$$** 126 Brand Highway; tel: 9921 3811.
Batavia Backpackers $–$$ cnr Chapman Rd and Bayly St; tel: 9964 3001. Small and central.
Batavia Motor Inn $$$ 54 Fitzgerald St; tel: 9921 3500.
Drummond Cove Holiday Park $$$ NW Coastal Highway; tel: 9938 2524; e-mail: dcovehp@bigpond.com.
Foreshore Backpackers YHA $–$$ 172 Marine Tce; tel: 9921 3275; www.yha.com.au/hostels. Nice old place with good facilities.
Geraldton Goodwood Lodge $$$ Durlacher St (cnr Brand Hwy); tel: 9921 5666. Eighteen self-catering suites with ocean views.
Hacienda Motel $$$ Durlacher St; tel: 9921 2155.
Mariner Hotel Motel $$$ 298 Chapman Rd; tel: 9921 2544.
Sun City Resort $$$ 137 Cathedral Ave; tel: 9921 6111.

🍽 **Beach Break Bar & Grill $$$** 166 Chapman Rd; tel: 9964 3382.
Boatshed Seafood Restaurant $$$$ 357 Marine Terrace; tel: 9921 5500. Open Tues–Sun. Not lunch. Licensed.
Colonial Hotel $$$ Fitzgerald St; tel: 9921 4444.
Cruisers Restaurant $$ 6 Armstrong St; tel: 9964 1666.
Cuisine Connection $$ 56 Durlacher St; tel: 9964 2289.
Flintstone Pizzas $$$ 357 Marine Terrace; tel: 9921 2255.
Hardy's Restaurant and Coffee Shop $$ Chapman Rd; tel: 9964 2660.
Huckleberry's Bar & Grill $$$ 298 Chapman Rd; tel: 9921 2544.
Jade House Chinese Restaurant $$ 57 Marine Terrace; tel: 9964 1222.
La Mexita $$$ 56 Durlacher St; tel: 9921 8110.
Lemon Grass Restaurant $$$ 18 Snowdon St; tel: 9964 1172.
Reflection Restaurant $$ Foreshore Dr.; tel: 9921 2921.

Rose Chinese Restaurant $$ 9 Forrest St; tel: 9921 5645.
Skeetas Garden Restaurant $$$ 9 George Rd; tel: 9964 1619.
Tanti's Restaurant $$$ 174 Marine Terrace; tel: 9964 2311.

DAY TRIPS

Geraldton is in the centre of one of the richest native flora regions in the world, which makes it a perfect base for **wild-flower walking** or **driving tours** throughout the year, although July and Oct are the favourite months. The Tourist Bureau has maps, information, brochures and booklets on all wild-flower sites and can provide last-minute information.

Surrounding the town to the north, east and south is the **Shire of Greenough**, named after the scenic river which winds through it. Its next-door neighbour is the equally beautiful Chapman Valley. The areas known as the Front and Back Flats were once vast lagoons that were gradually cut off from the sea and then filled with alluvial soil brought down by the meandering and frequently flooding river, resulting in an extremely fertile land.

Greenough is famous for its leaning trees (*Eucalyptus camaldulensis*) which bend themselves into fascinating shapes to escape the salt blown in from the sea. Their shape comes not from constant wind but their sensitivity to the salt content of the wind.

The **Greenough Hamlet**, with its 11 original buildings, including the police station and courthouse, store, cottage, churches, presbytery, convent and schoolhouses, is the only such collection of original buildings to be found in Australia.

The **Greenough Walkway Heritage Trail**, a distance of 57 km, begins at the Pioneer Museum and ends at the picturesque Ellendale Pool, a favourite picnic spot for locals and travellers alike.

The **Houtman Abrolhos Islands**, 80 km west of Geraldton, is an extraordinary series of about 100 small islands on the edge of the continental shelf. They run from North Island to the Pelsaert group. None of the islands rises more than 14 m above sea level, and their treacherous reefs have wrecked many ships.

The Abrolhos is where survivors of the wreck of the *Batavia* came ashore – some of them managed to get to Jakarta by ship's boat, a most remarkable achievement – and thus it is probably the site of the first white settlement in Australia. Sadly, it was also the scene of murder most foul when some of the survivors turned on the others. Later, a Dutch expedition returned and hanged some of those remaining and marooned two of the mutineers, Wouter Loos and Jan Pelgrom, on the mainland at

Kalbarri. Although no one knows exactly what became of them, there is genetic evidence that they integrated with the local Aboriginal people.

The islands boast sea eagles, turtles, myriad fish, bronze whaler sharks, dolphins and lots of crayfish. In the crystal-clear water around the islands there is clear visibility down to 92 m (50 fathoms).

No visitor is allowed to stay the night on the islands, but there are day tours for skin diving, fishing, surfing or just sightseeing – the tourist office has details.

KALBARRI

Kalbarri is on the coast, 66 km from the turn-off on Hwy 1 and the setting-off point for **Kalbarri National Park**. This park covers 186,000 ha and is divided by the 100-km-long Murchison River which has cut spectacular gorges through the rock – The Loop, Z Bend, Ross Graham Lookout and Hawks Head. All these gorges are well signposted and access is via well-maintained gravel roads and well-marked trails. During the wild-flower season the park puts on an amazing display – more than 850 varieties have been discovered here.

The road south of town leads past Jakes Corner, a renowned surfing spot, to a series of cliff formations including Red Bluff, Eagle Gorge and the Striking Natural Bridge. At Wittecarra Gully there's a cairn to mark the site of the first permanent landing of Europeans.

In Kalbarri itself, the pelicans are fed on the river bank along Grey St every morning at 0845. Local volunteers give a brief account of these birds as they feed them fish. Another species of bird is to be found along Red Bluff Rd. **Rainbow Jungle** (open daily 0900–1700) is a parrot breeding centre and has a successful pro-gramme for breeding Australia's endangered species.

Cruise up the Murchison River on the **Kalbarri River Queen** (tel: 9937 1104) or propel yourself in a hired canoe from **Kalbarri Canoe Safaris** (tel: 9937 1245).

> [i] **Kalbarri Visitor Centre**, Allen Community Centre, Grey St; tel: 9937 1104 or 1800 639 468; www.kalbarriwa.info. Open daily.

> 🛏 **Kalbarri Backpackers YHA $–$$** 51 Mortimer St; tel: 9937 1430; www.yha.com.au/hostels. Good value, well appoint-ed and fun.
> **Kalbarri Beach Resort $$$$** cnr Clotworthy and Grey Sts; tel: 9937 1061. Big and centrally located.

Black Rock Café $$$ 96 Grey St; tel: 9937 1062.
Pleasant for breakfast, good quality and value for lunches and dinners.
Lure 'n' Line Café $$$ 29 Grey St; tel: 9937 1122. Open late seven nights. Pleasant outlook.

SHARK BAY

Shark Bay is a series of islands and semi-enclosed gulfs divided by the Peron Peninsula. With 1500 km of coastline and covering 30,000 sq km, it is half land and half sea, and has been declared a World Heritage Site.

Aboriginal people inhabited the bay area for thousands of years and evidence of their presence can still be seen in numerous cave shelters and shell middens around the peninsula. They were probably among the first Australian Aboriginals who had contact with Europeans. The first Europeans came here in Oct 1616, when Dutchman Captain Dirk Hartog landed at Cape Inscription and left behind an inscribed pewter plate to record the fact. Then, in 1627, the Dutch ship *Gulden Zeepaard*, en route to Indonesia, ran too far south and travelled along 1700 km of Australia's coastline. That was an accident, but the discovery was carefully recorded on Dutch maps of the day. Dirk Hartog was followed 81 years later by another Dutch explorer, Captain William de Vlamingh, who replaced the original pewter plate with one of his own. (The Hartog pewter plate is in the Rikjsmuseum in Amsterdam, while that of de Vlamingh is on show at the Western Australia Maritime Museum, see p. 425.) Shark Bay was given its name by English navigator William Dampier in 1699 after he caught a 3.4-m shark there.

The nomenclature in this area gets a little complicated. It is generally known as the Gascoyne area and extends up the coast past Carnarvon to the Ningaloo Reef. But this is not enough for those trying to market tourism and now we are told this is the Outback Coast. The problem is, none of the locals knows what you are talking about when you mention the name.

As Shark Bay is at the northern extreme of the southern wild-flower varieties and at the southern extreme of the northern varieties, it has the longest wild-flower season of any part of Western Australia, with over 700 species of flowering plants, of which many are exclusive to the World Heritage Site.

Denham, on the west side of the Peron Peninsula, is the westernmost town in Australia. It is a good base from which to explore the area, including the miracle of

An alternative to driving is to fly: Western Airlines and Skywest Airlines offer regular air services to Denham–Shark Bay from Perth.

Monkey Mia. To reach Denham, and thus Shark Bay, turn off Hwy 1 opposite the Overlander Roadhouse: this brings you to two peninsulas that run parallel to the coast. The first, Peron, runs out past the Hamelin Pool and Shell Beach to Denham, Monkey Mia and finally the lighthouse. The seaward peninsula is somewhat longer and eventually ends up as Dirk Hartog Island.

i **Denham Shark Bay Tourist Centre**, 71 Knight Terrace, Denham; tel: 9948 1253; www.sharkbay-wa.gov.au. Open daily.
Department of Conservation and Land Management (CALM), 89 Knight Terrace, Denham; tel: 9948 1208. Open Mon–Fri. CALM is responsible for managing François Peron National Park, Hamelin Pool Marine Nature Reserve, Shark Bay Marine Park and the numerous island nature reserves in the bay. Contact them for information before you visit: www.naturebase.net/national_parks.
Shark Bay Tourist Association: www.sharkbay.asn.au.
Monkey Mia Dolphin Resort: www.monkeymia.com.au.

Bay Lodge YHA $–$$$ 95 Knight Terrace, Denham; tel: 9948 1278; www.yha.com.au/hostels. Beachfront accommodation made from shell brick. Free daily shuttle to Monkey Mia.
Blue Dolphin Caravan Park $$ 5 Hamelin Rd, Denham; tel: 9948 1385. On-site vans, many with en-suite facilities, some with air-conditioning.
Denham Seaside Caravan Park $$$ Knight Terrace, Denham beachfront; tel: 9948 1242.
Denham Villas $$$$ 4 Durlacher St, Denham; tel: 9948 1264. Each villa is fully self-contained.
Heritage Resort Hotel Shark Bay $$$$ Durlacher St, cnr Knight Terrace, Denham; tel: 9948 1133. Views over Shark Bay. Close to shops, cafés and the jetty.
Monkey Mia Dolphin Resort YHA $–$$ Monkey Mia Rd, Monkey Mia; tel: 9948 1320 or 1800 653 611; www.yha.com.au/hostels.
Shark Bay Caravan Park $$$ 119 Spaven Way, Denham; tel: 9948 1387.
Shark Bay Holiday Cottages $$$ 13 Knight Terrace, Denham; tel: 9948 1206.

Tradewinds Holiday Village $$$ 3 Knight Terrace, Denham; tel: 9948 1222. New waterfront apartments.
YHA of WA $$ Monkey Mia Bay Lodge; tel: 9948 1278.

🍴 **Bay Café and Takeaway $$$** 69 Knight Terrace, Denham; tel: 9948 1308. Locally caught snapper and whiting, and great ocean views from a shady pergola.
Bough Shed $$$ The Monkey Mia Dolphin Resort; tel: 9948 1171. Open daily, breakfast, lunch and dinner. Licensed.
Old Pearlers Restaurant $$$ Knight Terrace; tel: 9948 1373. The only restaurant in the world built entirely from coquina shells carved from Shell Beach. Fresh local seafood with crabs and crayfish in season.

HIGHLIGHTS

About 30 km after turning off Hwy 1 is the Hamelin Pool Telegraph Station, originally built in 1884 and now a visitors' centre for **Hamelin Pool Marine Nature Reserve**. Evidence of the beginnings of life on earth can be found in these saline waters. Hamelin Pool is one of only two places in the world where living marine stromatolites are known to occur, and it is the only place where they can easily be seen from shore.

Microscopic organisms – invisible to the human eye – concentrate and recycle nutrients which combine with sedimentary grains to form domes of rock-like materials known as stromatolites. Stromatolites first colonised the shallow waters of Hamelin Pool only 2000–3000 years ago, but the organisms that built them were the earliest forms of life on earth, with a lineage dating back 3500 million years. A wooden boardwalk with informative panels lets you view the stromatolites without damaging them. They may be the first expression of life on earth but they are not enthralling to look at.

Shell Beach, on the Hamelin–Denham road, has been formed by countless tiny white shells of the burrowing bivalve *Fragum erugafum*. Some of the shell deposits are up to 10 m deep, and the beach, depending how you measure it, runs for nearly 100 km.

Nanga Station, 50 km before Denham, was built from shell blocks cut from a nearby quarry. The half-million-acre sheep station also has a bottle-shop licence and restaurant. At **West Australian Ocean Park** (9 km towards Denham) visitors can feed sharks, stingrays and fish in a holding pond, check the park's breeding tanks and learn about the history and biology of Shark Bay. Open daily ($); tel: 9948 1765.

THE DOLPHINS OF MONKEY MIA

For almost 30 years wild bottlenosed dolphins have made a ritual of visiting Monkey Mia, which has become one of the most important dolphin research centres in the world. It started back in the 1960s when a visitor out fishing began feeding one of the dolphins from a boat. Other dolphins soon joined in and over three generations have become so adapted that they now swim right into the beach to be fed. They truly appear to enjoy and understand this relationship with humans.

Most mornings, small groups of dolphins visit the beach to interact with visitors, who can walk among them in the shallows and feed them under the supervision of the park rangers. They are fed only freshly caught local fish and never more than one-third of their daily requirement, to ensure that they do not become dependent on human handouts. Dolphins quite often offer visitors fish which they themselves have caught in return. Many have developed a technique of carrying a sponge on their beak; this is thought to be used as a tool for fossicking among the seagrass beds for food.

A separate section of the beach is set aside where visitors can swim with the dolphins and observe their antics. The dolphins show a marked attraction towards heavily pregnant women.

It is important to remember that Monkey Mia's dolphins are wild animals and must support themselves in an environment that can be hostile and dangerous. The young calves must learn natural behaviour from their mother, to ensure that they know how to survive in the wild. Too much feeding and long periods at the beach would significantly reduce these vital lessons.

Since 1984, over a dozen scientists from Australia, North America and Europe have been involved in research here. Most of the research focuses on the offshore population of over 400 animals, but with particular emphasis on the 100-plus dolphins who frequent the beach. Researchers investigate different aspects of dolphin ecology, reproduction and behaviour, including male and mother–calf relationships, juvenile social development, ranging patterns, community structure, habitat and diet. A catalogue of fin pictures helps identify each animal.

Monkey Mia is 27 km north-east of Denham. There is a small entrance charge, and the place to start is at the Dolphin Information Centre on the beach (run by the National Park and Wildlife Service and not a commercial organisation). A leaflet outlines the way in which you should approach and feed these most attractive of animals. There are problems looming with the massive increase of visitors and it is likely that some sort of rationing control and book-ing system will be introduced. Check before you go.

Denham was once a thriving pearling town, boasting the only street in the world to be paved in pearl shell. Several buildings, including St Andrew's Church and the Old Pearler Restaurant on Knight Terrace, have been built of local shell blocks. Denham has become the centre of Shark Bay's tourism and fishing industries.

Manta rays, turtles and other aquatic life are all easy to view in Shark Bay because of the clarity of the waters. The bay is home to some of the world's near-extinct or endangered marine life, including over 10,000 dugong, the most secure colony of these ungainly but endearing mammals left on earth. The dugong (a Malay name) is one of two surviving sirenians, or sea cows, the other being the manatee. They live for some 70 years, measure about 2.7 m and weigh up to 400 kg. It is possible the dugong is the origin of the mermaid myth.

Dugongs spend much of their time grazing on the soft and delicate seagrasses. Females do not calve until they are at least ten years old; then they bear a single calf every three to seven years after a gestation of 13 months. Mothers are attentive and care for their young for up to two years, communicating with them through bird-like chirps and high-pitched squeaks and squeals. Calves never venture far from their mothers and frequently ride on their back, particularly when danger threatens. At Monkey Mia there is the rare chance to go on a dugong-watching cruise, travelling aboard a specially equipped sailing catamaran that brings you close to dugongs in the wild. This cruise operates every day from the Monkey Mia Dolphin Resort jetty.

Between Denham and Monkey Mia is the **François Peron National Park**, for which you need a four-wheel-drive vehicle if you wish to explore it properly. Several tours operate out of Denham, which is the way to see the park with the least fuss. The park is 52,500 ha of true wilderness, with salt lakes and arid scenery.

WHERE NEXT?

Carnarvon is the base from which to set off for two of Australia's most incredible, yet least-known natural wonders: Ningaloo Reef and Mt Augustus (p. 466).

Carnarvon is pretty much a long way from anywhere. The Tourist Board tries its best by referring to the town as 'the sun's winter home' which is romantic but not inaccurate.

The Dutch navigator Dirk Hartog was probably the first European to examine the coast, in 1686. William Dampier, explorer and part-time pirate – not an uncommon combination of trades – followed in 1699 and reported that the country seemed barren and useless. He was the first whingeing Pom and thus set a tradition which persists to this day.

No settlers came until sheep stations were established in the 1870s, and in 1883 the township of Carnarvon was named after Lord Carnarvon, British Secretary of State for the Colonies from 1866 to 1874.

Today, Carnarvon is the centre of a high-tech area; it is the satellite tracking station of the Overseas Telecommunications Commission and the base of Radio Australia, and was a space-vehicle tracking station operated by NASA for ten years until 1974. These are located in the Brown Range, 12 km behind the town. The huge satellite tracking station – locally called the Big Dish (it is 29.6 m across) – dominates the skyline and is in the process of becoming something of a historical monument because it was here that Australia received its first satellite broadcast.

Carnarvon is a prosperous town partly due to the influx of technicians, partly to the prawning industry and partly to the success of the irrigated fruit and vegetable farms near the mouth of the Gascoyne River. It does attract visitors but that is not a primary source of revenue. A whaling station continued operations until 1962, by which time the disappearance of the whales had made it uneconomic. However, now the whales are coming back, and Carnarvon has made a small industry out of watching them as they make their annual stately progression to and from their breeding grounds.

INFORMATION

Carnarvon Tourist Bureau, 11 Robinson St; tel: (08) 9941 1146. Open daily (hours may vary out of season).

ACCOMMODATION

Carnarvon Backpackers $–$$ 97–99 Olivia Terrace; tel: 9941 1095. Not great – only if there's no alternative.

Carnarvon Caravan Park $$$ Robinson St; tel: 9941 8101.

Carnarvon Hotel Motel $$$ 28 Olivia Terrace; tel: 9941 1181.

Carnarvon Tourist Centre Caravan Park $$ 90 Robinson St; tel: 9941 1438. Self-contained park cabins.

Fascine Lodge $$$$ 34 David Brand Dr.; tel: 9941 2411. Swimming pool.

Gascoyne Hotel Motel $$ 88 Olivia Terrace; tel: 9941 1412.

Gateway Motel $$$$ 309 Robinson St; tel: 9941 1532.

Hospitality Inn $$$$ 6 West St; tel: 9941 1600.

FOOD AND DRINK

This is not a gourmet destination. But there is more fresh fruit on sale than you would believe.

Dragon Pearl Chinese Restaurant $$$ 18 Francis St; tel: 9941 1941.

Kingsford Restaurant (at Fascine Lodge) $$$ 34 David Brand Dr.; tel: 9941 2411. Licensed; à la carte.

Schnappers (at Gateway Motel) $$$ 309 Robinson St; tel: 9941 1532. Licensed; à la carte.

HIGHLIGHTS

Carnarvon's grassy waterfront goes by the strange name of The Fascine. 'Fascine' is from a Latin word for a bundle of sticks, and in the early days these were used along the foreshore to stop erosion when the Gascoyne River was in full spate. Now it flows gently and is lined with palms, and in the evening it is the most pleasant place in town.

The original port of Carnarvon is part of the Carnarvon Heritage Precinct, which consists of One-Mile Jetty, Lighthouse Keeper's Cottage Museum, the Carnarvon Tramway and a memorial to Australia's worst naval disaster, the sinking of HMAS *Sydney*. The precinct is a continuing project run by amateurs who give up immense amounts of time to it; you can check progress on www.wn.com.au/carnarvonheritage/news.htm.

One-Mile Jetty – almost 1500 m long – has a toy train running its length, giving a rather bumpy ride. The idea is that eventually – Real Soon Now – you will be able to take the train all the way from town to the jetty, which is on Babbage Island, 3.5 km out of town (take the turning at the Caltex petrol station and on past the lighthouse). The jetty was built in 1897, lengthened in 1904 and widened in 1912. It stopped being used by ships in 1966, fell into disrepair and was burnt by vandals in 1985. However, the locals set up a fund and rebuilt the jetty.

THE BIG BANANA

Carnarvon's Big Banana is what many might consider a visitor-repellent. The tourist board says: 'There is an exclusive list of Australian rural towns that feature a landmark "Big Something", whether it be the Big Pineapple, Big Crocodile, or Giant Ram. Carnarvon is among them with its vertically positioned Big Banana ... You won't miss it!' If you have any sort of luck, you will. Avert the gaze.

The lighthouse on Babbage Island, named after English mathematician Charles Babbage, the father of computing, is a modern replacement of an original erected in 1897. **Lighthouse Keeper's Cottage** was built around 1900 and was used by the keeper and his family until the lighthouse was electrified in the 1970s. Community effort has seen to the preservation of the cottage, which is open daily 1400–1600 (tel: 9941 4309 to check times).

Tours of the fully operational **Munro's Banana Plantation** (tel: 9941 8104), one of the first banana plantations established in Carnarvon, take place twice daily. A tour ($) gives hands-on information about planting techniques, growing and harvesting. Tours run at 1100 Sun–Fri (Nov–May); and 1100 and 1400 June–Oct. Munro's is on South River Rd about 5 km from town.

Pelican Point, 5 km south-west, is a popular swimming and picnic spot. To get there, follow the Babbage Island road, ignoring the turn-off to the jetty near the lighthouse.

DAY TRIPS

The **Blowholes** were discovered in 1911 and are some 70 km north of Carnarvon. Powerful jets of water are forced up with enormous pressure through the holes in the rock sometimes to a height of 20 m. These can be immensely dangerous and people can get killed when a rogue wave hits – you must observe all the warning signs and act with prudence. You get there by way of the North West Coastal Hwy, or the Bibbawura Bore tracks. About 1 km south of the Blowholes lies a small reef adjacent to the island which contains tropical fish and shells.

Red Bluff is 71 km north of the Blowholes via a limestone coastal road. It has become a popular surfing spot, with waves ranging from 1 m to 6 m depending on the time of year.

There are two breathtaking natural phenomena in this corner of Western Australia, each very different but equally remarkable. They are not a casual day trip but well worth the effort.

Mount Augustus is 480 km east of Carnarvon and an incredible sight. It's the world's largest monad rock, twice the size of Uluru (Ayers Rock), yet it is almost unknown to tourists. There are several tours to Mount Augustus, both from Perth – a trip of several days – and from Carnarvon. If you are driving there yourself head first to Gascoyne Junction (173 km). Gascoyne Junction has one small pub which is genuine outback Australia and is also the general store. Not to be missed, as this is the last place you can get a cold beer. There is a 47-km track around Mount Augustus; it is an unsealed track but fine with a two-wheel-drive vehicle provided the insurance covers you.

The North West Cape extends into the Indian Ocean to the north of Carnarvon, and running for 260 km off its western side is the **Ningaloo Reef**. If the Great Barrier Reef didn't exist this would be considered one of the great natural wonders of Australia. This reef, which the majority of tourists know nothing about, is not only the largest fringing coral reef in Australia, but also the largest reef in the world to be found so close to a continental landmass. It is about 20 m offshore at its nearest point and less than 7 km at its furthest. There are lots of safe deserted swimming beaches of white sand.

Take Hwy 1 (the North West Coastal Hwy) for 118 km until you get to the Minilya Road House. Turn left along Learmonth Minilya Road to the small resort of Coral Bay – 78 km – and then about the same distance on to Exmouth. These two towns are the main centres serving Ningaloo Reef Marine Park visitors. Coral Bay is smaller, prettier and closer to the reef, with snorkellers able to view corals after a short wim from the beach. The Ningaloo Reef Resort (tel: 9942 5934) has accommodation ($$$) right on the beach, a lively pub and a restaurant ($$$). Fin's café, in the Peoples Park shopping centre, serves fine seafood dinners ($$$$).

Ningaloo is home to approximately 250 species of coral and 520 species of fish, and is an amazing place to see dugong, greenback turtles and whale sharks. Whale sharks, the world's largest fish, visit the reef Mar–late May to feed on the spawn released by the coral. This is the only place in the world where they are known to appear regularly in any numbers far enough inshore to be easily accessible to observers. In June–July and Oct–Nov you can watch the humpback whales as they make their stately progression to and from their breeding grounds. One of the companies that offers cruises and diving on the reef is **Exmouth Ningaloo Deep**, PO Box 757, Exmouth; tel: 9949 1663; website: www.ningaloodeep.com.au.

WHERE NEXT?

This is another point where the decision should be made whether to fly, drive on or turn back. To drive even to Broome (see p. 468) will take three days minimum and perhaps a week depending on how you push along. Unless you have time and enough to spare then you should consider flying. If you're in for the long haul, many natural treasures lie between Carnarvon and Broome. The corals at Ningaloo Reef Marine Park have the added attraction of nearby Cape Range National Park. Further north in the iron-ore-rich Pilbara region, Millstream-Chichester National Park and Karijini National Park are among WA's finest.

BROOME

Broome, at the southern tip of the Kimberley region, and once the pearling capital of the world, is both a very upmarket resort and, in a sense, an alternative destination. It is also a long way from anywhere: 2230 km north of Perth and 1885 km south of Darwin.

The first inhabitants of the Broome area were a tribe of Aborigines called the Djugan and it is also very probable that the area was visited by Asian seafarers. In 1644 Dutch navigator Abel Tasman sighted the Australian coast near Broome, and in 1699 English navigator William Dampier landed somewhere near the town. His report on the area was so damning that other sailors stayed well clear until the beginning of the 19th century.

Then came the discovery of rich pearling grounds off the coast. Despite the fact that it was dangerous and that cyclones ravaged the area, by 1925, the peak of the trade, some 350 luggers with 3000 men were working out of Broome. Often the divers went down to more than 27 m and there was an appalling death rate. Most of the good divers were Japanese and the number of Japanese graves in the cemeteries show how the divers suffered.

Plastics and artificial pearls almost totally killed the trade – by the late 1950s it was pretty much all over and Broome was almost deserted. The industry never quite died out, however; there are still some luggers fishing for young pearl oysters to supply stock for the cultured pearl farms at Kuri Bay and Cygnet, where a Japanese–Australian consortium has been operating since 1954.

You can see reminders of Broome's pearling past all over the town: in the houses built for the pearlers, in Chinatown, which was once home to 3000 Asians and is now the small commercial centre of the town, and in the Japanese cemetery.

ARRIVAL AND DEPARTURE

The airport handles scheduled domestic flights by Qantas. **Broome Aviation** provides scheduled regular public transport services between Broome and Fitzroy Crossing, Halls Creek and Kununurra. **Skippers Aviation** provides scheduled regular public transport services between Broome and Derby, connecting with main line services into and out of Broome. Broome is trying to upgrade itself by having an international airport. So far it has the name, and customs, immigration and quarantine facilities in place. It has its own website at www.broomeair.com.au/html/flight.htm. International flights are still limited to private charters, with a commercial service expected in the future.

There is a daily bus service to Broome from Perth, journey time 32 hrs.

INFORMATION

TOURIST OFFICE **Broome Tourist Bureau**, Gt Northern Hwy and Bagot St; tel: 9192 2222. Open daily.

INTERNET SITE **Broome:** www.broomevisitorcentre.com.au

ACCOMMODATION

Broome Apartments Park Court $$$ 7 Haas St; tel: 1800 801 225; e-mail: andrea@parkcourt.net. Air-conditioned units at moderate rates. Quiet central location opposite library and Roebuck Bay. Weekly and off-season rates.

Broome Bird Observatory $$ Crab Creek Rd, Roebuck Bay, 25 km from Broome; tel: 9193 5600; e-mail: bbo@tpgi.com.au. Bird research centre with camping and accommodation. Opportunities for guest participation, plus regular interpretive tours.

Broome's Last Resort YHA $–$$$ 2 Bagot St; tel: 9193 5000 or 1800 801 918; www.yha.com.au/hostels. Pool and nice facilities.

Cable Beach Backpackers $–$$$ 33–37 Lullfitz Dr., Cable Beach; tel: 9193 5511 or 1800 655 011. Close to Cable Beach.

Kimberley Klub $–$$$$ 62 Frederick St; tel: 9192 3233 or 1800 345 400; www.kimberleyklub.com. Prize-winning establishment.

Mangrove Hotel $$$$ 120 Carnarvon St; tel: 1800 094 818; e-mail: reservations@mangrovehotel.com.au. Two restaurants.

Ocean Lodge $$$ Cable Beach Rd; tel: 9193 7700. Opposite the Broome Sport and Recreation Centre, between Chinatown and Cable Beach.

Palms Resort $$$$ 1 Hopton St (PO Box 77); tel: 9192 1898; e-mail: palmsresort@wn.com.au. Set in tropical gardens.

Roebuck Bay Backpackers $–$$$ cnr Carnarvon St and Napier Terrace; tel: 9192 1183. Right in Chinatown.

Roebuck Bay Hotel $$$$ Carnarvon St; tel: 1800 098 824. I Chinatown on Roebuck Bay.

FOOD AND DRINK

Beer & Satay Hut $$ Palms Resort, Walcott St; tel: 9192 1898. Burgers, seafood, pizza in outdoor setting.

Bloom's Café $$$ Shop 2/31 Carnarvon St, Chinatown; tel: 9193 6366. Open daily for breakfast, lunch and dinner. Tapas menu, freshly squeezed juices. BYO.

Cable Beach Tearooms $$$ Cable Beach Rd; tel: 9193 5090. Open daily for breakfast, lunch and dinner. On Cable Beach; great views and ambience.

Charters Restaurant $$$$ Mangrove Hotel, 120 Carnarvon St; tel: 9192 1303. Magnificent view of Roebuck Bay.

Matso's Café & Gallery $$$ 60 Hamersley St; tel: 9193 5811 Licensed. Open daily.

Noodlefish $$ Hamersley St; tel: 9192 5529. Thai food. Open seven nights.

The Old Zoo Café $$$ 2 Challenor Dr.; tel: 9193 6200. Oper daily for breakfast, lunch and dinner. In the old Pearl Coast Zoological Gardens.

Town Beach Café $$$ Town Beach, Robinson St; tel: 9193 5585. Lunch and dinner alfresco.

HIGHLIGHTS

Broome is a multicultural town because of the Japanese, Filipino and Malay pearl divers who were an essential part of its history. Chinatown, with its unique mixture of occidental and oriental buildings, has been restored, and even the street signs are in five languages.

MOVIES WITH A DIFFERENCE

Nightlife in Broome is not great but what there is, is unique. *Sun Pictures* in Chinatown is not a picture theatre – it is a picture garden. Opened in 1916, it claims to be the world's oldest theatre of its type. As it was the only entertainment in the area it was immensely popular and often enjoyed Saturday night crowds of over 600. You can still see movies under the stars and even bring a picnic dinner with you.

The **Broome Historical Society Museum** is housed in the old Customs House in Robinson St. It is very small but extremely well done, without the over-ordered structure which is so off-putting in some museums – a real highlight of the town. Features include a display of pearling and many old photographs and files which piece together the town's fascinating history. Open 1000–1300; tel: 9192 2075.

Captain Gregory's House was built in 1917 for the man who operated one of Broome's most successful pearling businesses. This fine example of early Broome architecture has now been converted to an art gallery, the Monsoon Gallery. It is on the corner of Hamersley and Carnarvon Sts in the same grounds as Matso's Gallery and Broome Brewery.

Flying boat wrecks sunk by the Japanese air raid on Broome during World War II are about 1 km offshore from Town Beach and visible only on very low tides. Check with the Tourist Bureau for tide times and viewing information.

The **court house** in Hamersley St was originally a cable station, the terminus of the cable across the Timor Sea from Java, opened in 1889. Its presence in the town, however, is a complete accident: the teak building had been shipped from England the year before, but was intended for Kimberley, South Africa, not the Kimberley, Australia! Markets are held in the court house grounds Sat 0700–1300.

Cable Beach, where the cable terminated, has talc-white sand and runs for 22 km. The beach is unusual in that the sea will recede as much as 500 m at low tide. About 6 km from Broome rise the craggy red cliffs of **Gantheaume Point**. At low spring tide you can examine the dinosaurs' tracks embedded in the sandstone at the base of the cliffs – they are believed to date back about 130 million years. Nearby is **Anastasia's Pool**, a small pool blasted from the sandstone by a pearler named Patrick Percy, who decided to make a safe bathing place for his arthritic wife.

During the 1980s, the 624 km of road from Port Hedland across the fringes of the Great Sandy Desert was sealed, sparking a minor tourist boom and occasioning the creation of the **Cable Beach Club** by Lord MacAlpine. A few kilometres outside Broome, this five-star resort (tel: 1800 199 099) offers tropical rustic life with service to international standards. Lord MacAlpine eventually sold all his Australian interests, but the style and the ambience remain.

Broome is popular with birdwatchers, with the **Broome Bird Observatory** on Roebuck Bay rating as one of Australia's top non-breeding grounds for migrant Arctic waders from Siberia. Nearly 250 different types of birds are to be found in the area, and there are self-interpretative walks.

If you want to see how pearls are harvested the **Willie Creek Pearl Farm** in Lullfitz Dr., 35 km from Broome, has demonstrations of how it produces south-sea cultured pearls from the silver-lipped oyster. Shell displays and curios may be seen in several places around the town, including Shell House in Guy Street and Paspaley Pearling Company in Short St.

DAY TRIPS

Broome is the gateway to the vast Kimberley region (see p. 473). Exploring it by car is almost always beyond the scope of most visitors, but there are plenty of easier trips.

To the south of Broome is **Eighty Mile Beach**. Unique among features named in this way, it is indeed 80 miles long (137 km, to be precise). This is where the Great Sandy Desert meets the Indian Ocean.

Beagle Bay is 118 km north of Broome – considered a short step in this part of the country. Beagle Bay church was built by Pallotine monks with raw materials from the area and completed in 1918. Its altar is beautifully decorated with shell pearl.

Beyond the Beagle Bay Reserve, the **Dampier Peninsula** has red pindan cliffs, azure waters and a wonderful variety of flora and fauna. Several Aboriginal communities offer bush-tucker walks and mud-crabbing tours. Access is by four-wheel-drive only but there is a variety of day tours available from Broome. The Tourist Bureau has details.

Rowley Shoals, 260 km offshore, is on the edge of the continental shelf. This is one of the best diving areas in the world with magnificent coral gardens, where giant clams and large reef fish astound visitors. The Broome Tourist Bureau has a list of operators.

WHERE NEXT?

North of Broome you're practically off the map. The town of Derby is just north of Hwy 1 and its tour and charter operators provide access to some remote and remarkable Kimberley country. Derby is also gateway to the legendary Gibb River Road, the nearly 700 km 'back road' to Wyndham (p. 477). The Gibb River Road is impassable during the Wet and only suitable for well-equipped four-wheel-drives, touring motorcyclists and mountain bikes – it's popular with adventurous bicycle tourers – during the Dry.

The Kimberley is unimaginably large, almost unknown to tourists and contains some of the best cattle country (and some of the biggest cattle stations) in the world. There are diamonds near Lake Argyle and gold at Halls Creek, rugged ranges, broad tidal flats, rainforest pockets, gorges and waterfalls. The Kimberley has them all. Yes, it is a tough trip to make. Yes, it is only for the truly adventurous. Yes, it is well worth the effort.

If you are going to this remote area, the best time is Apr–Sept, in the Dry. Temperatures are mild and the humidity low, you can almost guarantee there will be no rain and the skies are a bright clear blue much of the time. The night skies are superb for stargazing and offer great viewing of any comets or other objects that may be passing. The area is at its busiest during the coolest months of June and July, but there are those who believe that the Kimberley is at its very best just after The Big Wet: in early March it can be a green and verdant land. In the summer, outside temperatures can reach 52°C. If you have never experienced that sort of heat, and very few people have, breathing becomes difficult and anything but very lethargic movement utterly impossible. Dec–Feb is also the Wet and this is not a time to go exploring. Most of the rain comes thundering down over a period of 25 days in Jan–Feb, the roads are flooded and impassable, and the main town, Halls Creek, is totally cut off.

GETTING THERE

Qantas flies to Kununurra direct from Darwin and via Broome from Perth. Northwest services Halls Creek from Kununurra and Broome. Driving yourself is the other option, but there is a daily bus service between Darwin and Broome along Hwy 1 (OTT table 9431), which is known on this remote stretch as the Great Northern Highway.

HALLS CREEK

Halls Creek lies on the northern edge of the Tanami Desert. It is roughly 2800 km from Perth and 1200 km from Darwin, and the closest large regional centre is Kununurra, 360 km to the north-east. It is indeed in the Never Never. It is one of the most isolated towns in Western Australia, and if you can say you have explored Halls Creek you are not only rare among tourists but rare among all Australians. Although the town is on Hwy 1 it is used mainly as an overnight stop by travellers, rarely as a destination in itself.

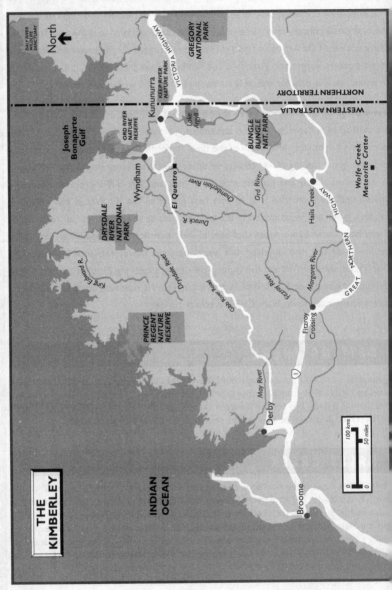

THE
KIMBERLEY

INDIAN
OCEAN

GOLD FEVER

Halls Creek came about, of course, because of gold. In 1872, the state government offered a reward of £5000 to anyone finding gold which produced 10,000 oz within two years of the discovery.

There were several expeditions and one led by Charles Hall found payable gold near the head of the Elvire River in July 1885. The first gold rush in Western Australia was on in earnest. The reward was, of course, never paid: Halls Creek produced enough gold to satisfy the reward requirements but much of it was taken across the border to avoid paying tax at the customs stations on the coast. In the end Charles Hall received £500 and this only after a bitter legal battle.

As with so many settlements in this area there is an old town and a new town. The new town was established in 1955, 15 km from the old site. The old town no longer exists except for a few foundations and a lot of empty bottles.

Halls Creek has a frontier atmosphere and it is a real part of the wild west – attending a rodeo here is another experience altogether. Although it is basically a Kimberley cattle town, Halls Creek is a base from which to see some rare distinctions and attractions. Nearest is **China Wall** which looks as though it was constructed like the Great Wall of China but is, in fact, a freak of nature. The weathered white quartz is set in the stone as if it were mortar, with the appearance of a wall running for many kilometres across country. It is 5 km east of the town and then about 1.5 km off the road.

i **Halls Creek Information Centre**, Community Resource Centre, entrance from Town Park; tel: 9168 6262. Open daily Apr–Oct, 0800–1600. Out of season, information can be obtained from the council offices behind the resource centre; tel: 9168 6007. Also has information on trips into the Kimberley to sights such as Wolf Creek Crater and the Bungle Bungles.
Internet Access: Halls Creek Telecentre, Community Resource Centre, Lot 71 Thomas St; tel: 9168 5230.

Halls Creek Caravan Park $$ Roberta Ave; tel: 9168 6169; e-mail: lanus@bigpond.com.au. The only caravan park in town.
Halls Creek Lodge $$ Cummins St, off Duncan Rd; tel: 9168 8999. At the site of Old Halls Creek, 15 km from town on Duncan Rd. The Lodge includes a restaurant and there are some good swimming spots nearby.
Halls Creek Motel $$$$ 194 Great Northern Hwy; tel: 9168 6001. Pool and fully licensed restaurant.
**Kimberley Hotel Motel $$$$** Roberta Ave; tel: 9168 6101; e-mail: kimberleyhotel@bigpond.com.au. Swimming pool and restaurant. Budget accommodation is also available ($).

📞 **Gabys Restaurant $$$** Roberta Ave; tel: 9168 6101.
Halls Creek Lodge $$ 15 km from town on Duncan Rd; tel: 9168 8999.

WOLF CREEK CRATER

Wolf Creek Crater is claimed to be the second-largest meteorite crater on earth, having a diameter of 853 m and a depth of 61 m. It was probably formed about 2 million years ago, but Europeans did not 'discover' it until 1947.

The crater is located 151 km due south of Halls Creek. Access is along a dirt road and you will need a four-wheel-drive vehicle, so it is best to go on one of the many tours available (enquire at Halls Creek Information Centre). The road is normally only open May–Nov.

PURNULULU (BUNGLE BUNGLE) NATIONAL PARK

Known to Europeans only since 1983, the Bungle Bungles are mind-blowing, one of the finest natural sights in Australia. They are a series of massive rock towers in a sort of beehive shape, with tiger stripes in the form of horizontal banding produced by black lichens and orange silica. There is Aboriginal art here, too, and dramatic gorges and caves, within a park covering 280,000 ha.

The Bungle Bungles are pretty inaccessible. The first part of the journey is fine, 109 km north from Halls Creek, but then you have to turn east on the Spring Creek Track. This track is one of the worst in Australia – a country that specialises in desperate tracks – and although it is only 55 km long, it takes well over two hours to navigate it safely. You can only make it Apr–Oct. It is best to go on a guided tour with someone who knows the area very well (ask for information in Halls Creek). The Bungle Bungles make the trip well worth while.

EL QUESTRO AND EMMA GORGE

El Questro was developed in 1991 as a truly Australian holiday destination designed to show visitors one of the world's last unspoilt frontiers. It is on the eastern perimeter of the Kimberley and runs for approximately 80 km into the heart of the region. In old measurements the property covers a million acres.

ATTRACTIONS BETWEEN EL QUESTRO AND WYNDHAM

There are many **Aboriginal rock paintings** in the area. There is also a **prison tree**, a hollow tree in which Aboriginal prisoners were locked up en route to court. The **Grotto**, a rock-edged waterhole near Wyndham, is a shaded, cool oasis.

The prices charged at El Questro are astronomical and intended for the jet set who will undoubtedly fly in. But there is affordable accommodation at El Questro's Emma Gorge Resort. The resort entrance is 2 km off the Gibb River Rd.

Accommodation consists of tented cabins set in a landscaped area. The cabins each have two single beds and their raised roofs allow the tropical sounds and scents to filter through. They all have 240 V power and fans for the warmer nights. This is a way of exploring part of the Kimberley without desperately, seriously, roughing it. Tel: 9169 1777; four-wheel-drive vehicle recommended for exploring the property.

WYNDHAM

Wyndham, on the Cambridge Gulf, which runs into the Timor Sea, is the most northerly town and port in Western Australia. It is the terminus of the Great Northern Hwy.

Wyndham started as a port to service the Kimberley goldfields. It was also the point through which the telegraph line from Perth passed, and the Flying Doctor base for the region was established here in 1935. Wyndham was attacked by Japanese aircraft in 1942, but there were no casualties.

The summer climate is excessively hot and humid, and locals boast the highest per capita beer consumption in Australia. But Wyndham has its elusive charms. Arthur Upfield got it right when, in *Cake in the Hatbox* (1955), he wrote: 'For ten miles the track was almost level as it crossed the flats south of Wyndham, a ship sailing on a sea of grass, and yellow and as tall as ripe wheat. Thereafter it proceeded up an ever narrowing valley between flat-topped ranges sparsely covered with stunted scrub and armoured with red and grey granite.'

The original town is now known as Wyndham Port, while a new town opened up 6 km away on the road to Kununurra. This second town is sometimes known as Wyndham Three Mile and sometimes as Wyndham East. The population of both towns together is well under 2000.

Until 1985 the meatworks was Wyndham's main industry. Since this closed down the town has operated as a service centre for the pastoral industry, mining and tourism. The port also serves some large mango and banana plantations. It's a very quiet town. There is a **Heritage Trail** around the buildings in the old port area, and the Mobil service station or Boab Gallery, in the port, can provide a printed guide.

Isolated though it is from the mainstream, Wyndham has still fallen for the 'Big' syndrome that so afflicts Australian tourism. Near the entrance to the new town is the 20-m-long Big Crocodile. It's better to visit **Wyndham Crocodile Farm**, established to breed estuarine and saltwater crocodiles commercially for their hides and meat. Set in scenic grounds, the farm is open to visitors (0830–1600, Mar–Oct) and there's a daily guided tour (1100).

Near the farm is the **Afghan cemetery**. This area was once totally dependent for supplies on camel trains operated by what were called Afghans. They were, in fact, nothing of the sort, coming mainly from Pakistan, but it is woven permanently into Australian folklore that they were Afghans and nothing is going to change it.

The **Five Rivers Lookout** to the east of the town is clearly signposted. It offers staggering views of the Kimberley over the five rivers (the Durack, King, Pentecost, Forrest and Ord) and the vast mudflats which run forever as far as the eye can see.

i **Kimberley Motors** (Shell service station), 6 Great Northern Hwy; tel: 9161 1281. Open daily.

Gulf Breeze Guest House $$–$$$ 6 O'Donnell St; tel: 9161 1401.
Three Mile Caravan Park $ Baker St; tel: 9161 1064.
Wyndham Town Hotel $$ O'Donnell St; tel: 9161 1003.

Wyndham Community Club $$$ Great Northern Hwy; tel: 9161 1130.

WHERE NEXT?

The nearest points of civilisation either side of the Kimberley are Broome to the west (see p. 468) and Darwin to the north-east (see p. 390). About 600 km east along Hwy 1 is Katherine. From here it is 300 km north to Darwin or a mere 1175 km south to Alice Springs (for the Alice–Darwin route, see p. 382).

Tasmania is Australia's smallest and most southerly state (see map on p. 481). But size is relative: including its 20 or so offshore islands, it is not far off the size of the Republic of Ireland or West Virginia, is on a par with Sri Lanka and is twice the size of the Netherlands. Nearly half a million people live on the island, mostly in Hobart, the capital, and Launceston in the north, the only other city. It has better preserved historical monuments than any other states and nowhere is more than 115 km from the sea, which makes it a most delightful place to visit. It is extremely easy to explore by car.

Tasmania is shaped like a triangle with two dots at the top, one on each side. These dots, which are King Island and the Furneaux Group, lie in the Bass Strait which separates Tasmania from the rest of Australia. Until something like 12,000 years ago they were part of a land bridge that connected mainland Australia and Tasmania. At the pointed end of the triangle, which faces south, halfway between Tasmania and the Antarctic continent, is Macquarie Island which has, among other things, elephant seals and 4 million penguins.

Tasmania is named after the Dutch navigator Abel Janszoon Tasman, but he himself named it Van Diemen's Land, a name it kept until 1856. As commander of the ships *Heemskirk* and *Zeehan*, Tasman had been sent to discover the mysterious Southern Land by Antony Van Diemen, Governor General of the Dutch East India Company. In Nov 1642 Tasman sighted the island's west coast. He landed just east of the Forestier Peninsula, at Blackmans Bay. One hundred and fifty years later the British came to make this a convict settlement and one of the furthest reaches of the British Empire.

At the time of the establishment of the first white settlement there were reckoned to be about 5000 Aboriginal people in Tasmania. Flocks were set to graze on prime Aboriginal hunting land, and when hunting parties began to take sheep, whites indiscriminately killed Aborigines in retaliation. In about 1826 a group of Aboriginal men, seeking revenge for the rape of their women, speared a shepherd and killed 100 sheep. In return, a group of 30 unarmed Aborigines was killed by shepherds, and their bodies thrown over a cliff which is now misleadingly called Suicide Cove. In 1828 Governor Arthur declared martial law, expelling all Aboriginal people from the settled districts and, in practice, giving settlers a licence to shoot on sight. The British government, alarmed by these events, planned to round up the remaining Aborigines and confine

TIGERS AND DEVILS

Because of its millennia of separation, Tasmania has a wildlife and flora uniquely its own. As well as its own indigenous kangaroo, it has the fearsome Tasmanian devil and that mystery animal, the marsupial Tasmanian tiger or thylacine.

Tasmanian tigers were still common at the beginning of the 20th century but were hunted extensively because they were alleged to have threatened sheep. They have been extinct since 1936 when the last one died in Hobart's Beaumaris Zoo. That is the official story but the number of sightings since have rivalled sightings of flying saucers.

The thylacine was about 1.5 m long, and had light brown fur with dark stripes across its lower back and what are thought to be the widest opening jaws of any mammal. In Jan 1995 an officer of the Parks and Wildlife Service, normally a most phlegmatic and cool-headed bunch, observed a tiger in the eastern Pyengana region. The government launched an investigation to confirm its existence. It is rare to meet a Tasmanian who truly believes the tiger is extinct – that it is not still out there in impenetrable bush. Tiger skins and a preserved tiger can be seen in Hobart Museum.

The Tasmanian devil is appropriately named. It is an ugly, mostly black, dog-like animal with large jaws and strong teeth. It has a ferocious nature, and is not the sort of animal you can pick up for a cuddle.

them to Bruny Island. In 1830 a militia of 3000 settlers formed an armed human barrier, the Black Line, to sweep across the island, clearing Aborigines before them in preparation for 'resettlement'. The line failed, and in the end only 135 Aboriginal people were found to be moved to a makeshift settlement on Flinders Island. Within four years, most had died: a dreadful record.

Today this grim history is largely swallowed by Tasmania's breathtaking natural attractions. The Tasmanian Wilderness World Heritage Area's 13,838 sq. km – about one-fifth of the state – contains one of only three remaining temperate wilderness areas in the Southern Hemisphere. It's one of the most popular destinations in Australia for a variety of adventurers – rafters, kayakers, walkers and rock-climbers – who come to savour wild and isolated coastlines, tracts of cool-climate rainforest barely touched by humans, untamed rivers such as the Franklin and craggy peaks including Mt Ossa, Cradle Mountain and Frenchmans Cap.

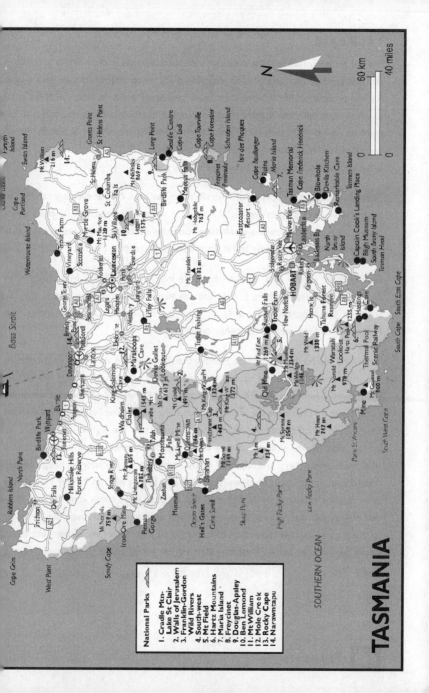

TASMANIA

National Parks ⬧

1. Cradle Mtn-
   Lake St Clair
2. Walls of Jerusalem
3. Franklin-Gordon
   Wild Rivers
4. South-west
5. Mt Field
6. Hartz Mountains
7. Maria Island
8. Freycinet
9. Douglas-Apsley
10. Ben Lomond
11. Mt William
12. Mole Creek
13. Rocky Cape
14. Narawntapu

TASMANIA

It is not generally realised that the most impenetrable jungle in the world is in Tasmania, nor that parts of the state are still unexplored – it is too difficult to hack your way in. A good proportion of the state is set aside in national parks or reserved areas, some of which have been the subject of enormous and heartfelt antagonisms, still not fully resolved (see p. 493): they give Tasmania unrivalled regions of wild beauty. Tasmania's central plateau has an average height above sea level of 1000 m in the south and is scattered with some 3000 lakes of assorted sizes.

Tasmania escapes the excesses of Australia's summer heat. Winter evenings can be a bit nippy and warmer clothes are useful no matter what the season. But Tasmania is not, despite what many Australians would have you believe, a cold-climate country. It is closer to the equator than Rome and is warmer, on average, than Madrid.

Getting there is very easy because there are frequent daily flights from every other Australian state (see Hobart, p. 484). You can also take the car ferry across the Bass Strait to Devonport (see p. 504), or take the high-speed Devil Cat ferry from Melbourne to Georgetown (Dec–Apr only).

The island has four major towns. Hobart, the capital, in the south and Launceston in the north are rated as cities although Hobart has a population of roughly 200,000 and Launceston fewer than 100,000. The port towns of Burnie and Devonport are on the north coast. All the towns are joined by what are grandly called National Highways and what would be called country roads in other countries. The highways are sealed and are of good quality although they are, like most Australian roads, fairly narrow. In wilderness areas there are unsealed roads which can quite often be navigated by normal car, but care must be taken (see conditions for car hire, pp. 27–29). Four-wheel-drive vehicles must stay on marked tracks and roads. Unlike roads in most parts of the rest of Australia, the roads of Tasmania twist and turn their way through the landscape so the average journey time tends to be longer by a margin of say 25 per cent than it would be in other states. Despite claims by the locals, traffic jams do not exist in Tasmania.

TASMANIA: OUR CHOICE

Hobart
Tasmanian Museum and Art Gallery, Salamanca Markets, Mt Wellington

Bruny Island

Mt Field National Park
Russell Falls

Tasman Peninsula
Port Arthur, Tasman National Park

Maria Island National Park

Freycinet National Park
Wineglass Bay

St Columba Falls

The Blue Tier

Bay of Fires

Mount William National Park
Wildlife

Ben Lomond National Park

Launceston
Cataract Gorge, Queen Victoria Museum and Art Gallery

Devonport
Tasmanian Aboriginal Culture and Art Centre, Don River Railway

Rocky Cape National Park

Stanley
The Nut, Highfield House

HOW MUCH YOU CAN SEE IN A ...

WEEKEND (2 DAYS)

In the south, a quick spin around the Hobart waterfront and museums and a day visiting any of several nearby sights. Port Arthur is probably the most popular option for day trips from Hobart; for natural attractions, try Hartz Mountains National Park, the portion of the Tasmanian Wilderness World Heritage Area nearest Hobart. In the north, two days could easily be filled in Launceston and the Tamar Valley. A weekend would also allow enough time to travel the length of the Midlands ('Heritage') Highway, which links Hobart and Launceston via several historic inland towns.

WEEK (7 DAYS)

With Hobart and Launceston as start/finish points, aim to see the best of either the east (Port Arthur; Mount William, Ben Lomond, Freycinet and Maria Island National Parks) or west and centre (Strahan and Queenstown, Cradle Mountain–Lake St Clair and Franklin–Gordon Wild Rivers National Parks). Stops for walks in national parks will consume a lot of time but are well worth while. It is possible to circle Tasmania in a week, although you would have to skip some of the better national park walks.

MORE THAN A WEEK

Tasmania's national parks offer some of Australia's best multi-day adventure-tour options. Long walking trails include the Overland, South Coast and Port Davey tracks; other options include 14-day rafting journeys down the Franklin River.

Preminghana
Aboriginal rock engravings

Mole Creek Karst National Park

Great Western Tiers

Cradle Mountain–Lake St Clair National Park

HOBART

Hobart has always had a singular advantage because of its siting. The city is on the west bank of the Derwent River estuary with, rising behind it, the forest-clad slopes of Mt Wellington, which may be snow-capped in winter. In such a beautiful setting it would be difficult for a city to be ugly. But Hobart is also one of the most beautiful cities in Australia, possibly because for a long time it escaped the ravages of developers.

The village of tents and wattle-and-daub huts that sprang up here in 1804 was named after Robert Hobart, fourth Earl of Buckinghamshire and Secretary of State for the Colonies. When Governor Lachlan Macquarie visited in 1811, the straggle of makeshift huts offended his Scottish sense of order and good discipline, so he ordered a survey and had building regulations instituted. The town started to grow: in 1813 it became the administrative centre for all of Van Diemen's Land and in 1825 the colonial capital of Van Diemen's Land. It was by now a solid, well-to-do town hardly less important than Sydney, with a population of 5000.

Today Hobart explodes at its once-a-year party that is the Sydney to Hobart Yacht Race (see p. 488), but throughout the year the city operates with an immense amount of style.

MUST SEE/DO IN HOBART

Visit the Tasmanian Museum & Art Gallery
Visit the Allport Library & Museum of Fine Arts
Stroll around Battery Point
See Salamanca Place (and markets)
Take a cruise on the Derwent River
Hike up Mt Wellington

GETTING THERE AND GETTING AROUND

Hobart airport is 26 km east of the city. The Airporter shuttle service (tel: 0419 38 240) is much cheaper than a taxi.

Ferries from the mainland arrive not in Hobart but in Devonport (see p. 504), on the north coast of the island about 280 km from Hobart.

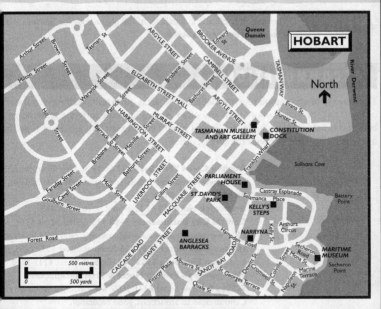

Hobart is quite compact and the easiest way to see it is to walk. Alternatively you can buy multiple tickets for the excellent public bus system, called the Hobart Metro (tel: 13 22 01). The eastern bank of the Derwent is connected to the rest of the city by the Tasman Bridge (rebuilt after being rammed by a ship in 1975) and Bowen Bridge, and also a daily ferry service from Pier One (tel: 6223 1914).

For exploring further afield, the best way is by hired car. All the major car hire companies are there but also some which are less expensive. Worth checking are Europcar Rentals (call 1300 131 390); Bargain Cars, 173 Harrington St (tel: 6234 6959); or Lo-Cost Auto Rentals, 105 Murray St in Hobart (tel: 6231 0300).

INFORMATION

Tasmanian Travel and Information Centre, 20 Davey St; tel: 6230 8233. Open daily.

INTERNET SITES
Hobart City Council: www.hobartcity.com.au
Hobart service directory: www.streetsofhobart.com.au
Tourism Tasmania: www.discovertasmania.com.au

POST AND PHONES The main post office is in Elizabeth St. The phone code for Tasmania is 03 (confusingly, the same as Victoria).

ACCOMMODATION

The amount of accommodation available in Hobart is quite remarkable given the siz of the town. Tasmania, more than any other Australian state, offers a wide range c bed and breakfast establishments. If you intend staying for any length of time the are worth checking out with the tourist office.

Adelphi Court YHA $–$$$ 17 Stoke St, New Town; tel: 6228 4829; www.yha.com.au/hostels. Large and with good facilities, 2½ km from city centre.

Brunswick Hotel $$ 67 Liverpool St; tel: 6234 4981.

Central City Backpackers $–$$ 138 Collins St; tel: 6224 2404; www.centralbackpackers.com.au. Big, central, 24-hr access

Hobart Vista Hotel $$$$ 156 Bathurst St; tel: 6232 6255.

Lodge on Elizabeth $$$$ 249 Elizabeth St; tel: 6231 3830.

Montgomery's Private Hotel & YHA Backpackers $–$$$$ 9 Argyle St; tel: 6231 2660; www.montgomerys.com.au. Central, close to attractions, good reputation.

Narrara Backpackers $–$$ 88 Goulbourn St; tel: 6231 319 Shared facilities, recently renovated.

The Old Woolstore $$$$ Macquarie St; tel: 6235 5355 or 1800 814 676. Big apartments and hotel rooms.

FOOD AND DRINK

Eating out in Tasmania has improved out of sight in recent years and is no noticeably more expensive than in the rest of Australia. Much of the dining action i Hobart takes place within strolling distance of Salamanca Place.

Amigo's $$ 329 Elizabeth St; tel: 6234 6115. Mexican, BYO. Open daily.

Amulet $$$$ 333 Elizabeth St, North Hobart; tel: 6234 8113. Innovative modern cuisine, BYO. Lunch and dinner seven days.

Annapurna Indian Cuisine $$$ 305 Elizabeth St, North Hobart; tel: 6236 9500. Excellent value Indian food, recommended for vegetarians. Open Mon–Fri 1200–1500, seven days 1730–2200.

Drunken Admiral $$$ 17–19 Hunter St; tel: 6234 1903. In an early waterfront warehouse. Seafood, licensed.

Jackman & McRoss $$ 57–59 Hampden Rd; tel: 6223 3186. Best bakery in town. Open daily 0730–1800 (1700 Sat, Sun).

Le Provencal $$$$ 417 Macquarie St; tel: 6224 2526. Open for dinner Tues–Sat. French provincial cooking.

Maldini Café Restaurant $$$–$$$$ 47 Salamanca Pl.; tel: 6223 4460. Italian, licensed. Open seven days for coffee, lunch and dinner.

Meehan's Restaurant $$$$ 1 Davey St; tel: 6235 4535. Dinner Tues–Sat. Wonderful views of the waterfront with the food nearly as good. Well-prepared food, specialising in the use of Tasmanian ingredients.

Mezethes Restaurant $$$ Salamanca Arts Centre; tel: 6224 4601. Traditional Greek food and good wine list. Open daily.

Mikaku Japanese Restaurant $$$ Salamanca Pl.; tel: 6224 0882. Japanese, licensed. Open daily. Be warned, they have karaoke parties upstairs.

Mure's Upper Deck Restaurant $$$$ Victoria Dock; tel: 6231 2121. Seafood, licensed. Open daily for lunch and dinner.

Prosser's on the Beach $$$$ Long Beach Rd, Sandy Bay; tel: 6225 2275. Award-winning seafood, licensed. Open Wed–Fri for lunch, Mon–Sat for dinner.

Rockerfellers $$$ 11 Morrison St; tel: 6234 3490. Lunch and dinner seven days.

Salamanca's Food Fair & Café $$$ 55 Salamanca Pl.; tel: 6224 3667. Licensed café. Open seven days. Good for light snacks and a glass of wine.

Sisco's Restaurant $$ Murray St Pier; tel: 6223 2059. Spanish, licensed, BYO. Open Mon–Sat.

T42 $$$ Elizabeth Pier; tel: 6224 7742. Popular café/bar/restaurant in prime waterfront location. Tasty Modern Australian cuisine. Open Mon–Fri 0730–late, Sat–Sun 0830–late.

HIGHLIGHTS

t is easy to find your way around Hobart. In the centre the streets are arranged round the Elizabeth St Mall, which runs down to the waterfront wharves. alamanca Place runs along the south side of the waterfront towards the well-reserved early colonial district of Battery Point. Follow the river around from attery Point and you come to Sandy Bay. Here stand the University of Tasmania nd Wrest Point Casino, one of Hobart's landmarks. To the north of the centre is the

TASMANIA

THE SYDNEY TO HOBART YACHT RACE

One of the world's great sailing events began shortly after World War II as a suggested post-Christmas cruise out from Sydney; it escalated into a race to Hobart. Of the nine yachts competing only one completed it – *Rani*, skippered by Captain John Illingworth RN, a guest of the Sydney Cruising Yacht Club. The race, which takes place between Christmas and the New Year, is unremittingly tough – in 1993, for example, only 38 of the 104 yachts finished. At the end await Constitution Dock and the celebration of The Quiet Little Drink, a party where the quantity of beer drunk per head of crew is not printable lest it cast a doubt on all the other statistics. It defies belief.

Domain, a recreation are that includes the Roya Botanic Gardens and abu the Derwent River.

Hobart is defined by its posi tion on the Derwent estuar and its deep-water port one of the ten deepest city ports in the world. Th waterfront has strenuousl resisted modernisation an still shows its rich historica associations and unique, pie turesque charm. The centra Franklin Wharf bound **Constitution Dock**, wher the annual Sydney to Hobart Yacht Race ends, and nearby is Hunter St, which has row of fine Georgian warehouses that have not been tarted up.

A warehouse behind Constitution Dock, built in 1808 and so probably the olde building in central Hobart, now contains the **Tasmanian Museum and Art Galler** (40 Macquarie St; open daily 1000–1700). It includes the Commissariat Store (1808 which issued the supplies for the people and the new colony; the Bond Store (1824 and the Cottage, built originally as a private store or stable before 1810 and conver ed into a residence for the Governor's secretary in 1828. Among the exhibits are som splendid photographs of the allegedly extinct Tasmanian tiger.

The **Allport Library and Museum of Fine Arts** at 91 Murray St is one of the fou collections of the State Library Service. The Allport family settled in Van Diemen Land in 1831. Henry Allport, a Hobart solicitor, died in 1965 and gave to the people of Tasmania his collection of 18th- and 19th-century furniture, colonial paintings, silver, objets d'art, fine china and rare and antique books. It is housed on the ground floor of the State Library. Open Mon–Fri 0930–1700.

SALAMANCA MARKET

The market began in 1972 with ten stalls occupying a small section of Salamanca Place; it has now become something of an institution. The 'Winter' market operates 0830–1400 and the 'Summer' market 0830–1500. There are some 300 stalls and the place has a tremendous buzz and a rather alternative feel. As you shop you are serenaded by musicians, calmed by incense and delighted by the variety and quality of produce.

he heart of the old city is **Salamanca Place**, one of the more elegant courtyards f Australia. The square is surrounded by sandstone warehouses constructed in e early 1830s, a prime example of Australian colonial architecture. They were the entre of Hobart Town's trade and commerce, catering in large part for the whaling ade. Today they contain galleries, restaurants, nightspots and shops. Every Sat orning a popular open-air craft market is held here.

arliament House is at the north end of Salamanca Place opposite the law courts. It as built by convicts between 1835 and 1840, initially as Hobart's first customs ouse and bond store, and was converted to parliamentary use when the colony ecame self-governing in 1856. Now the lower ground floor has become a museum f historical archives and is open to the public on weekdays. The oak plantation you ee as you approach was planted while the building was under construction.

longside is **St David's Park**, which was built on the site of the first cemetery. Some f the tombstones have been moved and set into sandstone walls as a reminder of e early days of Hobart and of the difficulties the earliest settlers faced.

he extraordinary number of buildings that survive from Georgian- and Victorian- ra Australia is one of Hobart's defining features. The streets nearest St David's Park Davey and Macquarie Sts – contain about 60 of the 90-or-so Hobart buildings clas- ified by the National Trust. One of the Trust's prized properties, the 1831 enitentiary Chapel and Criminal Courts building (open seven days 1000–1400; $$) s further north, on the corner of Brisbane and Campbell Sts.

rom Salamanca Place it is only a short walk – up Kelly's steps at the end of the quare and follow the signs – to **Battery Point**. This was named after the battery of uns placed here when the British government was seriously concerned that the ussian fleet would invade outposts of the British Empire. That this was a total onsense was shown a little later when the Russian fleet was effectively destroyed y the Japanese. But, at the time, it was believed that the Russians might invade ustralia and New Zealand, and you will find such batteries all around the coast- ines. The battery still has the **Anglesea Barracks** which date from 1814, making hem the oldest military establishment in Australia.

attery Point's pubs, churches, houses and narrow winding streets have all been pre- erved and the National Trust has listed many of the buildings. To see its full charm walk to **Arthur Circus** where a group of Georgian cottages built in 1847–52 forms ne of the most charming urban landscapes in Australia.

utting through this area is Hampden Rd, which has antique shops, coffee houses nd colonial cottages. One of them, no. 103, is **Narryna**, a mansion which now

houses a **Folk Museum**. The furnishings are in keeping with its age and in th
grounds there are a smithy and a collection of horse-drawn vehicles. Open Mon–F
1000–1700, Sat–Sun 1400–1700.

The new **Maritime Museum** – formerly on Secheron St – is on the corner of Argy
and Davey streets in the city. Its exhibits cover early exploration, whaling, ship
building and the history of shipping in Hobart from the days of sail. Tel: 6234 142
Open seven days 1000–1700; $$.

On the sloping banks of the Derwent just north of the city centre is the Queen
Domain. At the base of the hill are Hobart's **Royal Botanical Gardens** (open dail
from 0800; check for closing times), which have some superb formal gardens. On
interesting piece of early scientific endeavour here is a wall built in 1829 by convict
It is connected to Government House and could be heated by means of intern
fireplaces to provide an appropriate environment for exotic plants.

Many Australians are willing to swear that the **Cascade Brewery** produce
Australia's finest drop. There are tours of the brewery in Woodstock Gdns, south
west of the city centre, at 0930 and 1300 Mon–Fri. You have to book (tel: 6221 830
and there is a small charge ($$) for the tour. But you get to sample the product.

BEYOND THE CENTRE

Mt Wellington (1270 m) provides a wonderful backdrop for the city and is only
22-km drive away, with an observation and information centre on the summit. On
clear day you can see, if not forever, about 100 km inland. The road to the summit i
somewhat tortuous and is sometimes closed due to snow in the winter, when th
strength of the wind up there could blow a dog off its chain – take care getting ou
of the car. Luckily, there is a sheltered lookout.

The **Taroona Shot Tower** is 10 km south of Hobart, along the shores of the Derwen
The 48m high tower, which is open to visitors (0900–1730; $), was in use until jus
before World War II. From the top there are wonderful views of the Derwent estu
ary. From here you can stroll down to Taroona Beach and then wander the 3 km t
Kingston Beach, admiring the scenery as you go.

Just south of Kingston is the **Australian Antarctic Headquarters** (tel: 6232 320
which has an exhibition, open weekdays 0900–1700. Kingston is the gateway to th
Tinderbox Peninsula. A blowhole at **Blackmans Bay** gives spectacular displays i
stormy weather and from **Pierson Point** at the tip of the peninsula are tremendou
views of Bruny Island.

DAY TRIPS

Tasmania is often referred to within Australia as the Apple Isle and **Huonville** is the centre of the largest apple-producing area in the state. Although it is only 37 km south-west of Hobart it has a very different style and pace. In Hobart people walk more briskly than they do in Huonville. You can take a jet-boat ride on the Huon River or hire pedal boats and aqua-bikes.

Enclosing the eastern side of Storm Bay is the **Tasman Peninsula**, which has superb scenery, many bushwalks and a most beautiful and complicated coastline. **Tasman Arch** is a natural arch between two cliffs cut by wave action. At the **Devil's Kitchen** the waves roar onto the rocks hundreds of feet below. The sea rushes in under the rock and shoots into the air at the **Blowhole**. These are all near Eaglehawk Neck, site of the notorious dog barrier that guarded the entrance to the peninsula and to **Port Arthur**, Australia's most infamous convict prison. Nowadays it is one of Tasmania's most visited sites.

HUONVILLE AND HUON PINE

The name of the town comes from the huon pine, whose wood is prized for being clean, relatively free of knots and slow to rot. The trees, which are unique to Tasmania, favour swampy conditions and are the second-oldest living things on earth after the bristlecone pines of North America. The timber was used extensively in shipbuilding and in the construction of some of the pioneer aircraft.

Demand was such that the forests were eventually commercially exhausted, and what is left is protected. You will find many craftspeople offering small objects in huon, carved from sunken logs that have been hauled from the rivers. These are noteworthy because huon timber is now so rare; for decorative purposes the wood is fairly plain as it has little figuring and an almost plastic finish.

PORT ARTHUR

A sad and emotional place, Port Arthur is an essential destination for visitors. From 1830 until 1877 this was the most infamous convict settlement of Australia. Over 12,000 convicts were sentenced to spend time there – it has been suggested that the figure may have been as high as 30,000. Many of them never left.

In 1830 Lieutenant-Governor George Arthur chose the Tasman Peninsula as the place to confine those he termed the 'worst of the worst'. This meant convicts who, while in custody, had committed further crimes. The reason this awful, and awesome, place was chosen was that it offered only one land escape route, at Eaglehawk Neck – and the Neck, only 100 m across, was manned by guards who ran a chain from one side to the other with, tethered to it, between 9 and 18 savage dogs.

In *The Escape of the Notorious Sir William Heans* (1919), William Gosse Hay saw the Tasman Peninsula as a pear and Eaglehawk Neck its stalk. He wrote: 'A few celebrated escapes were accomplished along the Hobart Road from the flower to the stalk, the prisoner swimming over, braving the dogs, soldiers and sharks which watched it. Except by the stalk, how could anyone escape from the pear?'

One of the most astounding facts about Port Arthur is that flogging was not widely used as a punishment. Instead, offenders were sentenced to solitary confinement. This meant, for example, they were allowed to go to church but sat in individual pews so that no contact was possible and the only thing in view was the prison chaplain. When they exercised they wore masks to prevent them speaking to anyone. After a spell of this treatment many convicts went mad, and the madness often led to death.

It would be wrong to think of Port Arthur as just a penal settlement. It had many industries, such as timber milling, shipbuilding, coal mining and brick manufacturing. In the 1830s a primitive railway running for 7 km was laid between Taranna and Deep Bay. But there were no steam engines involved – convicts pushed the trains.

The penal settlement lasted 37 years, and continued for 14 years after transportation ceased. In recent times a terrible footnote was added to the bitter memories of this place. In April 1996 Port Arthur hit the world's headlines when a gun-crazed lunatic massacred 35 innocent visitors here.

In 1979 Port Arthur's national significance as a historic site was recognised when the Tasmanian and Federal governments committed $9 million to a seven-year conservation and development programme. Now, despite its harrowing history, Port Arthur is a beautiful and tranquil site with green lawns and huge English trees, and it feels more like parkland than prison.

> [i] **Visitor Information Office**, Historic Site, Arthur Hwy;
> tel: 6251 2300; e-mail: bookings@portarthur.org.au;
> www.portarthur.org.au. Open daily.
> **Port Arthur and the Tasman Peninsula:**
> www.portarthur-region.com.au.

WHERE NEXT?

The quaint oast houses of New Norfolk (see p. 496) and the moonscape around Queenstown (see p. 509) are an introduction to some of the contrasting faces of Tasmania, while the island's 'northern capital', Launceston, is just 200 km away (see p. 499).

There have been protected natural areas in Tasmania in one form or another for well over a century. In 1863 land was first set aside as 'reserves for scenic purposes'. These reservations were made under the Waste Lands Act of 1863 and subsequently under the Crown Lands Act. By 1899 Tasmania had 12 reserves. In 1915 the government established the Scenery Preservation Board and in 1971 the National Parks and Wildlife Service started in Tasmania.

National parks now cover over 20 per cent of the island, but have been the subject of a series of long and bitter struggles between the Tasmanian government, supported by the majority of the population of the states on the one side, and the conservationists on the other. Towns, families and friends were split in their support, and it would be fair to say that the struggle has not ended to this day.

The government of Tasmania has not always been conservation-conscious, as can be judged by the devastated landscape of Queenstown (see p. 509). Then, in 1972, the government flooded Lake Pedder for a hydroelectric scheme. In response the Wilderness Society was formed, which started a war – campaign is too soft a term – against the Hydro-Electricity Commission's next plan, the damming of the Franklin. This was Tasmania's last wild river. The protests ran for nearly ten years. In 1981 the whole south-west area was proposed as a World Heritage Area, but the government ignored this and continued with its plans. The Franklin Blockade, organised by the Wilderness Society, began on 14 December 1982 and continued for two months, with protesters lying down in front of the bulldozers. In all 1200 protesters made the journey upriver from Strahan. Eventually the Labour government of Bob Hawke was voted in and in March 1983 the Federal government forbade further work on the hydroelectric scheme. This created immense bitterness among Tasmanians who supported the dam. They believed that they were being denied employment by mainlanders who rarely visited the state.

The Wilderness Society still exists, and still campaigns, but some of the tensions are starting to ease as Tasmanians find that the wealth of national parks is attracting more and more tourists, and that tourism is now a substantial industry.

THE EASTERN PARKS

On the far north-eastern coast, above St Helens, is the **Mt William National Par** which is a native animal sanctuary. Tasmania's only native kangaroo, the Foreste Bennett's wallaby and the Tasmanian devil all live here. **Ben Lomond Nation** **Park** is 50 km east of Launceston and is also a major winter ski resort. Closer to th sea is **Douglas-Apsley National Park**, created in 1989, which can be traversed nort to south in a three-day hike. The peninsula of the **Freycinet National Park**, whic lies further south, has white sands, black swans and granite peaks. Within this par is Schouten Island, 1 km off-shore. Further down the coast still is **Maria Island**, where no vehicles are allowed and there are con-vict ruins, easy walks and a wealth of wildlife, including a marine reserve. Access is by ferry from Louisville or Triabunna.

OTHER PROTECTED AREAS

Tasmania has numerous other regions designated as conservation areas, protected areas, state reserves etc.
The first **marine reserves** were established at Governor Island, Maria Island, Tinderbox and Ninepins Point, and much of the north-west shore is covered by **coastal reserves**.

THE NORTH COAST PARKS

To the east of Burnie is **Rocky Cape National Park** and to the east of Devonport th similarly sized **Narawntapu National Park** (see p. 506). Offshore, the southern en of Flinders Island, in the Furneaux Group, is protected by **Strzelecki National Par** which has campsites and walking trails.

THE WESTERN PARKS

Due south of Devonport is the latest addition to Tasmania's national parks system the karst caves of **Mole Creek**. From here a grand sweep of parks starts in the nort

EXPLORING THE PARKS

Daily or holiday passes are available ($$$). For details, tel: 1300 135 513 or see www.parks.tas.gov.au

with the superlatively beautiful **Cradle Mountain Lake St Clair**, with its Overland Track and Tasmania' highest mountain, Mt Ossa (1617 m). The mountai that gives the park its name is probably one c Tasmania's most recognised natural features. Abuttin it is the **Walls of Jerusalem National Park**, which ha forests of pencil pines and many lakes and tarn Access is by foot only.

djoining Cradle Mountain to the south is the **Franklin–Gordon Wild Rivers ational Park** – the park, created in 1980, that resulted from the Franklin Blockade rotests. This park is virtually inaccessible, You can fly over it, or explore the edges y cruising the Gordon River (see p. 513) or, if you are adventurous, you can go on raft down the Franklin – but only between December and March and not always en, for this is by far the most dangerous rafting river in Australia. The full trip kes 8–14 days. By and large the area remains unvisited.

uth again, the **Southwest National Park** is equally remote and half as large again Franklin-Gordon. Almost adjoining its eastern border is **Mt Field National Park** ee p. 498). Finally, on the south-eastern fringes and only 80 km from Hobart, is the artz Mountain National Park. This is a rugged but accessible region, with hiking warded by tremendous views.

1982 this great mass of contiguous parks, together with other adjoining protected eas, was declared a World Heritage Area covering 1.38 million ha.

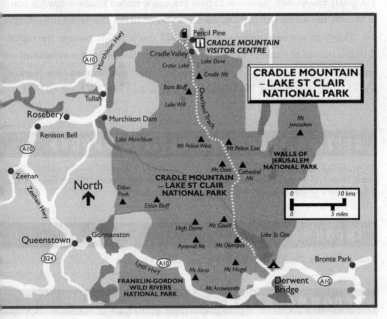

NEW NORFOLK

New Norfolk, upriver from Hobart, is at the heart of what was Tasmania's hop-growin country. Although it would be an exaggeration to say that Australia ran on beer for hundred years, the first experimental crops in the mid-19th century grew into th largest hop farm in the southern hemisphere. Styles in beer have changed and hops a no longer the important agricultural crop they once were, but the area is full of th conical oast houses in which the hops were dried.

The first European to sight the area was probably Lt John Hayes, who first sailed up th Derwent in 1793. The first serious group of settlers to arrive were from the abandone colony of Norfolk Island. A vanguard of 34 islanders arrived in 1807 and within a yea 544 Norfolk Islanders – convicts and free settlers – had been transplanted. They wer guaranteed free rations for a year and each was given 4 acres of land to cultivate.

The young town, which Governor Lachlan Macquarie named Elizabeth Town in honou of his wife, thrived so well that the executive council of Van Diemen's Land (effective the colony's government) recommended in 1825 that it should become the capital Tasmania instead of Hobart. Nothing came of the plan because of the expense of shif ing civil servants from Hobart. Two years later the town was renamed New Norfolk, i honour of its early settlers. The whole town is registered with the National Trust.

GETTING THERE AND GETTING AROUND

New Norfolk is 37 km north-west of Hobart, and connected to the capital by th Lyell Hwy (A10). Buses run regularly between the two towns during the week, bu infrequently at weekends.

INFORMATION

Council Offices, Circle St; tel: 6261 3700. Open daily.

ACCOMMODATION

Amaroo Motel $$$ Lyell Hwy, cnr Pioneer Ave; tel: 6261 2000.

Bush Inn $$$ 49–51 Montagu St; tel: 6261 2011.

Glen Derwent Cottages $$$$ Lyell Hwy; tel: 6261 3244. Non-smoking.

New Norfolk Caravan Park $$ The Esplanade; tel: 6261 1268. Holiday cabins.

New Norfolk Hotel $$$ 79 High St; tel: 6261 2166.

Rosie's Inn $$$$ 5 Oast St; tel: 6261 1171.

FOOD AND DRINK

Chats Restaurant $$ 47A High St; tel: 6261 2924. Open Mon–Fri 0730–1700, Sat 0900–1200.

Martin Cash Pizza Restaurant $$ 15 Stephen St; tel: 6261 2150. Italian, BYO. Closed Mon. Dinner only.

Ponds Restaurant $$$ Salmon Ponds Rd, Plenty; tel: 6261 1614. What else but fish? Licensed.

Shanghai Restaurant $$ 50 High St; tel: 6261 2866. Chinese. Licensed. Open daily.

Tynwald $$$ Willow Bend Estate, Hobart Hwy; tel: 6261 2667. Specialises in game. The mansion, named after the parliament on the Isle of Man, is 170 years old and you can dine on local produce in a candle-lit dining room. Open daily for dinner.

HIGHLIGHTS

St Matthew's Anglican Church, facing Arthur Sq., was built in 1823 and is Tasmania's oldest existing church, although only the original walls and the flagged floor of the nave remain. The modifications to the church were almost a continuous process: it was substantially extended in 1833; in 1870 a tower was added; and in 1994 the church was given a chancel and a makeover of the windows, roof and transepts. It is well worth a visit to see if you can spot the original bits and to view the splendid stained-glass windows.

The **Bush Inn** at 49 Montagu St is claimed to be the oldest continuously licensed hotel in Australia, the licence having been given to Mrs Ann Bridger in Sept 1825. Many other pubs have made the same claim but it is very probable that the Bush Inn does hold the record. It has been considerably extended and altered from the original and, in the process, lost much of its original charm. There is a story, which may well be true, that in the 1920s Dame Nellie Melba stood on the balcony and sang opera selections to the assembled populace. As her motto was 'Give 'em muck' this may not have been quite as enthralling an experience as it sounds.

The **Old Colony Inn** further down Montagu St was built in 1835 and contains fine antiques and a collection of items dating back to the penal era. It also has a restaurant attached.

Willow Court is now part of the Royal Derwent Hospital and is the only, and reputedly the earliest, mental hospital in Tasmania. It was originally designed and built in 1830 as a military hospital. The name comes from a willow in the courtyard, and the building has much style and presence.

> **FROM CONVICT TO CONSTABLE**
>
> One of New Norfolk's most remarkable inhabitants was Denis McCarty, a Fenian rebel who had been transported. He became the town's constable and built the first house in the district. He also built the road between Hobart and New Norfolk.

Just off the Lyell Hwy is the **Oast House**, which is both a unique museum devoted to the history of the hop industry and a tearoom. The building has been classified by the National Trust. It was built in the 1820s and converted into a kiln for drying hops in 1867. Open Sat, Sun 1000–1600 ($).

Other industries have grown up to take the place of hops. Chief among them is paper manufacture, but trout farming is also important and long-established. At **Salmon Ponds** in Plenty, only 9 km away, the first rainbow and brown trout in the southern hemisphere were bred in 1864. It is now run by the Inland Fisheries Commission as a historic site and you can visit the farm on Lower Bushy Park Rd any day of the week; tel: 6261 1076. How did they get the trout here back in 1864? The eggs were carried in an ice chest on the sloop *Norfolk* to Melbourne, from there to Hobart on a steamship, then by river-steamer, horses and finally messengers to the farm, where their descendants, some of them over half a metre long, live to this day.

DAY TRIPS

Only an hour's drive away is **Mt Field National Park**. Mt Field was one of Tasmania's first national parks, and the area within the park around Russell Falls, near the entrance, was made into a reserve in 1885. This is one of the major refuges for the Tasmanian devil. Some of the eucalypt trees in the park are over 400 years old, 90 m high and 20 m around the base.

Launceston is named after the English town in Cornwall, and sits on the Tamar River, another Cornish echo. Indeed, there are many British reminders in this attractive town. A great description came from Elspeth Huxley, when she wrote in *Their Shining Eldorado*: Victoriana is everywhere. Buildings in alternate layers of cream and liver-red like a Neapolitan ice, their waywardly pitched roofs flounced with ornament and filled with scrolls; balconies also full of scroll-work; tortured brick, unexpected turrets, multi-coloured tiles, heavy colonnades, thick vaulted doorways, potted palms in dark lobbies; an overgrown English country town. The narrowish streets are packed with people, the women mostly wearing gloves.' They have stopped wearing gloves but the rest remains true.

The first European to explore the Tamar up to the site of present-day Launceston was William Collins who made the journey in 1804. The following year Lieutenant-Colonel William Paterson arrived with a group of settlers and almost immediately the township became the headquarters for northern Tasmania. The town originally rejoiced under the name of Patersonia, but was renamed in honour of the birthplace of Governor King. The town hall was built in 1864, just in time to take care of the expansion that followed a mining boom in north-eastern Tasmania in the 1870s and '80s. It was this mining boom that prompted the railway connection to Hobart in 1876.

Launceston is bounded by the North Esk and South Esk rivers as they meet to form the Tamar, and one of its most famous attractions is the breathtaking gorge on the South Esk.

GETTING THERE AND GETTING AROUND

Launceston is 200 km along the Midland Hwy (Rte 1) from Hobart, and 80 km from Devonport where the car ferry docks (see p. 504). Buses travel the routes three or four times a day. You can also fly into Launceston from the mainland, principally Melbourne, and Redline (www.redlinecoaches.com.au) provides a shuttle service from Hobart for less than half the taxi fare. For shuttle services from Launceston airport into town, tel: (05) 0051 2009.

Getting around Launceston is easy. Everything is within walking distance, and the centre is arranged in a grid pattern, so you should never get lost.

Tasmania

INFORMATION

Tasmanian Travel Centre, cnr St John and Cimitiere Sts; tel: 6336 3133; www.discoverlaunceston.com. Open daily.

Despite having been in existence since 1824, the *Launceston Examiner* has shown other country papers how to embrace the internet. Its website is exemplary: www.examiner.com.au.

ACCOMMODATION

Batman Fawkner Inn $$$ 35 Cameron St; tel: 6331 7222.
Centennial Hotel $$$ Balfour St; tel: 6331 4957.
Launceston Backpackers $–$$ 103 Canning St; tel: 6334 2327; www.launcestonbackpackers.com.au. Lovely old building and helpful staff.
Metro Backpackers YHA $–$$ 16 Brisbane St; tel: 6334 4505; www.backpackersmetro.com.au. New and well appointed.
Motel Maldon $$$$ 32 Brisbane St; tel: 6331 3211.
Parklane Motel $$$ 9 Brisbane St; tel: 6331 4233.

FOOD AND DRINK

Arpar's Thai Restaurant $$$ cnr Charles and Paterson Sts; tel: 6331 2786. Open daily for dinner, lunch Fri. Licensed. BYO.
Bailey's Restaurant $$$$ 150 George St; tel: 6334 2343. Holds murder-mystery nights – not an impediment to digestion Open Tues–Sat for dinner.
Calabrisella $$$ 56 Wellington St; tel: 6331 1958. Italian, BYO. Dinner only. Closed Tues.
Franco's Restaurant $$$ 197 Charles St; tel: 6331 8648. Italian, BYO. Closed Mon.
Gorge Restaurant $$$–$$$$ Cataract Gorge; tel: 6331 3330 Game. Closed Mon.
Hallams Waterfront Restaurant $$–$$$ 13 Park St; tel: 6334 0554. Tasmanian farmed and 'free-range' seafood; good-value fish and chips. Open seven days.
Kai-Zen Tepanyaki $$$ 32 Brisbane St; tel: 6333 0888. Japanese cuisine; licensed and BYO (wine only).
La Cantina $$$ 63 George St; tel: 6331 7835. Italian. Open daily, licensed.

Montezuma's $$$–$$$$ 63 Brisbane St; tel: 6331 8999. Open for lunch Mon–Fri, dinner daily. Mexican food.

Original Pizza Pub $$ 111 Wellington St; tel: 6331 4280. Pizza, licensed. Open daily.

Pierre's Coffee House & Restaurant $$$ 88 George St; tel: 6331 6835. Open Mon–Sat. Casual dining. Tasmanian wines by the glass.

Postreos Café-Restaurant $$$ 68 Cameron St; tel: 6331 9962. World food. Licensed and BYO.

Quigleys $$$$ 96 Balfour St; tel: 6331 6971. Specialises in game and seafood. Open for lunch Tues–Fri, dinner Mon–Fri.

Satay House $$$ Innocent St, Kings Meadows; tel: 6344 5955. Tasmania's first and very authentic Indonesian restaurant. Dinner Mon–Sat from 1830. BYO.

Stillwater $$$–$$$$ Paterson St; tel: 6331 4153. Casual dining in the old mill. Open daily.

Vegie Mania $$$ 64 George St; tel: 6331 2535. One hundred per cent vegetarian. Open daily.

Victoria's on the Park $$ cnr Cimitiere and Tamar Sts; tel: 6331 7433. A la carte, licensed. Speciality seafood dishes. Open daily.

Woofies $$ Macquarie House, Civic Sq.; tel: 6334 0695. A la carte, licensed. Closed Sun.

HIGHLIGHTS

Central to the city is Brisbane St Mall, between Charles and St John Sts. To the east is Yorktown Square, a charming area of restored buildings.

The **Community History Museum**, on the corner of Cimitiere and St John Sts, is in the old Johnstone and Wilmot store, which was built in 1842 and is still maintained in its original condition. Open Tues, Wed 1000–1600. **Macquarie House** in Civic Square was built in 1830 and is now part of the Queen Victoria Museum (see p. 502).

The **Old Umbrella Shop**, classified by the National Trust, was built in the 1860s and was owned by three generations of the Shott family. The interior is lined with Tasmanian blackwood timber. It is at 60 George St and open Mon–Fri 0900–1700, Sat 0900–1200.

Launceston has many beautiful public squares, parks and reserves. The **City Park** has an elegant fountain and a bandstand, and **Princes Square** has a bronze fountain bought at the 1858 Paris Exhibition.

In **Royal Park**, near the junction of the Esk and Tamar rivers, is the **Queen Victoria Museum and Art Gallery**. Built in the Victorian era, it displays its imperial splendour both inside and out. It has a unique collection of Tasmanian artefacts, relics and colonial paintings. It also has a Chinese joss house built in the 1870s by Chinese labourers who were brought to work the tin mines. Open Mon–Sat 0900–1700, Sun 1400–1700. Launceston Planetarium is housed in the museum and has shows Tues–Fri 1500, Sat 1400 and 1500 ($). It is one of only four in Australia.

A gentle 10-min walk from the city centre is the nature reserve of **Cataract Gorge**. The South Esk River cuts a deep canyon through the hills near its junction with the Tamar, and as it enters and becomes the Tamar the rivers are constricted into a gorge by almost vertical cliffs. When there has been heavy rain in the highlands this can result in spectacular rapids.

There are two walking tracks, one on either side of the gorge. These lead up to First Basin, filled with water from the South Esk River. There is a chairlift ride – at something just short of 500 m the longest single-span chairlift in the world – across the basin to the reserve on the other side, which takes about 6 mins. It operates daily 0900–1700, but weekends only mid-June to first week of Aug. You can also cross by the suspension bridge, although this is called 'the Swinging Bridge' by the locals and does feel rather less than solid. Either route takes you to the **Cliff Grounds** which are elegant gardens with a rotunda.

Penny Royal World (open daily 1000–1600, $$$), near the bottom of the gorge, claims to take you back to a 'world of yesteryear'. It started as a collection of buildings situated at Barton, which was moved to Launceston. Exhibits include working 19th-century watermills and windmills, gunpowder mills and model boats. You can take a ride on a barge or cruise up the gorge on the PS *Lady Stelfox*. The mill complex is linked by a restored tramway to the Penny Royal Gunpowder Mill at the old Cataract Quarry site. It also includes modern accommodation, restaurants and a tavern.

> **TROUT FISHING**
>
> Launceston Lakes is a private company that has the fishing rights to five lakes with 5 km of shoreline, all within 20 mins of the city; 1166 Ecclestone Rd; tel: 6396 6100. You do not need a licence and lessons are given on fly-fishing if required.

Further upstream along the South Esk is the **Trevallyn Dam** and hydroelectric power station. The station is close to Duck Reach, the site of Australia's first, and one

f the world's earliest, hydroelectric projects. In 1895 Launceston became the first
ity in the southern hemisphere to be lit by electricity generated by water power,
nd the plant was in continuous operation for 60 years. The original buildings and
uspension bridge across the river are still standing.

One of Launceston's major historic attractions is **Franklin House**, 6 km south of the
ity at 413 Hobart Rd. It is a fine example of a Georgian-style house and was built by
onvicts in 1838 for Britton Jones, an early Launceston brewer and innkeeper. By
842 it had changed hands and, for the next 40 years, it was the W K Hawkes School
or Boys. It now belongs to the National Trust, which first opened it to the public in
961 – in fact the National Trust was established in Tasmania in 1960 specifically to
urchase the building. Open daily 0900–1700; closes 1600 June–Aug.

DAY TRIPS

North of Launceston, the **Tamar Valley** is Tasmania's premier winemaking region,
where most of the vineyards are small and family-run. The tourist office has a
brochure detailing a well-signed Wine Route, which will lead you deep into the
valley and to the vineyards.

WHERE NEXT?

*The north-eastern corner of Tasmania is rich farming and forest country. The main town is
Scottsdale, 65 km north-east of Launceston. West of the mouth of the Tamar, on the Bass
Strait, lie the north-coast towns of Devonport and Burnie (see pp. 504–508).*

DEVONPORT AND THE NORTH COAST

This is where the ferries from the mainland arrive, and Devonport is often labelled 'the gateway to Tasmania'. It is an ideal base for exploring the northern part of the island, and the chief attractions in the town itself are the Aboriginal carvings and the restored railway.

The first European settler arrived in 1826, but was killed by local Aborigines three years later, which had a discouraging effect on settlement. Devonport developed as a shipping port, but a major boost came in 1959, when the ferry terminal for Bass Strait vehicular ferries from Melbourne was established. Although Devonport was named after the English coastal town in Devon, it stands at the mouth of the River Mersey, and visitors from Merseyside will find it fitting that one of the two townships amalgamated to form Devonport was called Formby.

The industrial port of Burnie is worth a short visit for its links to Tasmania's historically important commerce in timber and copper, and for the wild country that lies beyond.

GETTING THERE AND GETTING AROUND

Overnight services on the *Spirit of Tasmania I* and *Spirit of Tasmania II* depart nightly from Melbourne and Devonport at 2100 and arrive 0700. There are also day sailings, on variable schedules. For information, tel: 1 800 634 906, www.spiritoftasmania. com.au. See OTT 9062.

The 429-km journey takes about 10 hrs, crossing what can be one of the world's roughest stretches of water. The ferries dock at the Esplanade, on the eastern side of the Mersey, and a Redline bus runs to the town centre.

You can also fly from Melbourne and Hobart, or sail from (and back to) Sydney on the *Spirit of Tasmania* service (which sails between one and three times weekly, depending on season: tel: 1800 634 906; www.spiritoftasmania.com.au). Devonport is linked to most Tasmanian towns by bus.

INFORMATION

Tasmanian Travel and Information Centre, 92 Formby Rd; tel: 6424 4466.

INTERNET ACCESS   **Devonport Online Access Centre**, Devonport Library Building, 21 Oldaker St; tel: 6424 9413; e-mail: devonport@tco.asn.au.

Devonport Council: www.dcc.tas.gov.au

Guide to Devonport: www.devonporttasmania.com

ACCOMMODATION

Abel Tasman Tourist Park $$$ 6 Wright St; tel: 6427 8794.

MacWright House (Devonport YHA) $ 115 Middle Rd; tel: 6424 5696; www.yha.com.au/hostels.

Molly Malone's Irish Pub $–$$$ 34 Best St; tel: 6424 1898. Dorm beds and basic doubles upstairs from a pub. Central.

Tasman House Backpackers $–$$ 114 Tasman St; tel: 6423 2335; www.tasmanhouse.com. Good facilities.

FOOD AND DRINK

Accents $$ 140 North Fenton St; tel: 6424 8411. BYO. European with good vegetarian dishes. Open Mon–Sat.

Alexander Hotel $$ 58 Formby Rd; tel: 6424 2252. Dining room open daily.

Autographs on the Beach $$$ Mersey Bluff; tel: 6424 2204. Seafood. Open daily.

Chinese Chef $$ 4b Kempling St; tel: 6424 7306. Cantonese. BYO. Open daily.

New Mandarin Inn $$ 156 Williams St; tel: 6424 4398. Cantonese. BYO. Open daily for dinner; lunch Mon–Sat.

Old Rectory $$$ 71 Wright St; tel: 6427 8037. BYO. Dinner only. Non-smoking.

Rialto Gallery Restaurant $$$ 159 Rooke St; tel: 6424 6793. Italian. BYO. Dinner Mon–Sun.

Taco Villa $$ Kempling St; tel: 6424 6762. Mexican. Closed Mon. BYO.

HIGHLIGHTS

The **Tasmanian Maritime and Folk Museum** is on Victoria Pde and tells graphically of the rich history of passenger and cargo shipping, whalers, sealers, and fishing fleets dating back to the first white settlement. Open daily (except Mon) 1000–1630 summer, 1000–1600 winter ($).

The former home of Sir Joseph Lyons, the only premier of Tasmania to become prime minister of Australia (in the 1930s), is at **Home Hill**, 77 Middle Rd. It has been made a National Trust property and is open Tues, Wed, Thur, Sat and Sun; $$.

In 1929 Aboriginal rock carvings were discovered on Mersey Bluff, on the northern edge of town. The site was declared protected, and the **Tiagarra Tasmanian Aboriginal Culture and Art Centre** was established there in 1972. You can see the carvings themselves just outside the centre, and inside are dioramas showing the lifestyle of the Aboriginal people of the region. Open daily 0900–1700 ($); closed July. The lighthouse on the bluff was built in 1889 and is said to be visible 27 km out at sea.

A 7-km cycle and walking track extends around the picturesque foreshore from the city past the Olympic swimming pool to the historic Don River Railway. The railway from Launceston arrived in 1885 and the port grew rapidly in the 1890s; then in 1916 a railway was installed to haul limestone from the Broken Hill Proprietary quarries. This was closed in 1963, but local enthusiasts have restored 3.5 km of the original track as the **Don River Tourist Railway**. It starts at Don Recreation Ground, 4 km out of town on the Bass Hwy, and runs along the Don River to Coles Beach, hourly 1000–1600; $$. On Sun and public holidays steam locomotives are used; the diesel used the rest of the time may offend purists but is perfectly acceptable to everyone else. Associated with the railway is a museum which has the largest collection of locomotive carriages and traction engines in Australia.

Nearby **Braddons Lookout**, close to Forth, has a panoramic view of the coastline. Forth's spring of pure water is claimed to have medicinal qualities.

At Port Sorell, 20 km east of Devonport, the wildlife reserve of the **Narawntapu National Park** stretches out along the coast. It has several marked trails, the best of which is the hour-long Springlawn Nature Walk.

The Bass Hwy runs along the northern shore, dipping inland only to terminate at the remote north-western coastal township of Marrawah. The principal town along the way is Burnie, 50 km west on Emu Bay.

BURNIE

Burnie grew to service the enormously rich tin mine at Mt Bischoff, inland near Waratah, which came into production in the early 1870s. In 1890 the breakwater was built to improve the safety of the harbour, and the Emu Bay Railway, the only privately owned rail company in the state, was extended ten years later so that it could serve mines in the Zeehan–Rosebery area.

When Associated Pulp and Paper Mills opened a factory in 1938 it quickly became the biggest paper producer in Australia, owning private forest and cutting rights over all land within 24 km of the Emu Bay Railway. This was a cartel monopoly on a grand scale and the company still effectively controls the production of almost all paper in Australia.

Despite being primarily an industrial port, Burnie has tremendous natural charm. Being in a major timber area, most of the houses are made of wood and rise in tiers up the hillsides with views out over the beach and the bay. It also has some excellent gardens and reserves, including **Emu Valley Rhododendron Gardens**, which has one of Australia's finest displays of wild and hybrid rhododendrons around its lakes.

Since Burnie is older than, say, Melbourne it is appropriate that it has a **Pioneer Village Museum**. This is a reconstruction of Burnie's small shops at the turn of the century and is housed in the Civic Centre Precinct in Little Alexander St ($$). Open Mon–Fri 0900–1700, Sat, Sun 1330–1630.

Burnie Inn, the oldest remaining building, is a single-storey timber cottage built in the late 1840s by shipwright John Wiseman and has been re-erected in Burnie Park. The most impressive building in the town is the **police station** in Wilson St which was built in 1907 as a house and surgery for a dentist. It is Federation finery at its finest.

> **THE BURNIE FOOTRACE**
> Once a year the boardwalk is jammed with competitors in the **Burnie Ten Footrace**, one of the richest in Australia. The race draws hundreds of athletes and crowds of spectators every autumn.

The art of the region is well displayed at the **Burnie Regional Art Gallery** in Civic Centre Precinct. It has a permanent collection of regional art but also has touring and local exhibitions. Open Tues–Fri 1030–1700, Sat, Sun 1330–1630.

Burnie's busy shopping district leads directly to a boardwalk on the beach.

Round Hill, just outside the town, has panoramic views of the district. **Ridgley**, 11 km south, has picnic grounds and views of five waterfalls, the largest of which is the Guide Falls. There are well-marked and interesting bushwalks.

> *i* **Tasmanian Travel and Information Centre**, Civic Square Precinct, off Little Alexander St; tel: 6434 6111. Open daily.

> **Beach Hotel $$$** I Wilson St; tel: 6431 2333.

Duck House $$$$ 26 Queen St; tel: 6431 1712.

Glen Osborne House $$$$ 9 Aileen Cres.; tel: 6431 9866.

Top of the Town Hotel-Motel $$$ 195 Mount St; tel: 6431 4444.

Weller's Inn $$$$ 36 Queen St; tel: 6431 1088.

🍴 **Fortuna Garden $$** 66 Wilson St; tel: 6431 9035. Cantonese and Szechuan dishes; open daily. BYO and licensed.

Gianni's European Food $$$ 104 Wilson St; tel: 6431 9393. Open Tues–Sat for dinner.

Hodgy's Restaurant and Wine Bar $$$ 8 Alexander St; tel: 6431 3947. A la carte. Licensed. Open daily for lunch and dinner.

Li Yin Chinese Restaurant $$ 28 Ladbrooke St; tel: 6431 5413. All-you-can-eat specials. Open daily, BYO.

Mallee Grill (in the Regent Hotel) $$$ 26 North Terrace; tel: 6431 1933. Open daily for lunch and dinner.

Mandarin Palace $$ 63 Wilson St; tel: 6431 5413. Cantonese. BYO.

Partners Restaurant $$$ 104 Wilson St; tel: 6431 9393.

Rialto Gallery Restaurant $$$ 46 Wilmot St; tel: 6431 7718. Venetian cuisine – Italian with frills. Licensed and BYO. Open daily for lunch and dinner.

WHERE NEXT?

Devonport is 1½ hrs away from Tasmania's most famous natural sight: Cradle Mountain (see p. 494). A regular bus service operates from the Tasmanian Travel and Information Centre at Devonport and there are several Cradle Mountain day tours (take a look at www.tasredline.com.au and www.tigerline.com.au). Burnie is the gateway to Tasmania's scenic and historic north-west.

Do you go to visit a place where the local flora and fauna have been destroyed by mining and the countryside has been left looking like the landscape of the moon? This is something for the individual to decide.

Queenstown, the major town on the west coast, was established as a result of the discovery of gold and other minerals at nearby Mt Lyell, and mining has been continuous in this area since 1888. The gold ran out in 1891 and its place was taken by copper. The copper smelters started in 1895, and all the timber in the area was used to fire the furnaces. This process, until relatively recently, gave off sulphur fumes which prevented regeneration of the vegetation. To add to this, heavy rain washed away the exposed topsoil and the minerals stained the skeletal rocks purple, grey and pink – the town is surrounded and overshadowed by brightly stained, naked hills.

In 1922 a change in processing eliminated many of the fumes and, little by little, there has been a very slow regeneration of plant cover. There are now two schools of thought. One is that the colours of this industrially created wasteland are, in themselves, a tourist attraction. The other is that the landscape should be restored as quickly as possible to some semblance of normality. As it stands there are impressive – or depressive – mountain views from the town centre, and the first 3 km of the Lyell Hwy as it climbs steeply out of Queenstown is spectacular.

Strahan, the one-time port for Queenstown, has its own memorials to the heyday of mining, and is the access point for Tasmania's great south-western wilderness.

GETTING THERE AND GETTING AROUND

Queenstown is 270 km from Hobart along the Lyell Hwy. Buses run between the two towns, but not every day (OTT 9520).

INFORMATION

Galley Museum, cnr Driffield and Stitch Sts; tel: 6471 1483. Open daily.

ACCOMMODATION

Bayview Cottages and Strahan Wilderness Lodge $$$
Ocean Beach Rd, Strahan; tel: 6471 7142.

Commercial Hotel $$ 35–39 Driffield St, Queenstown;
tel: 6471 1511.

Gold Rush Motor Inn $$$$ 65 Batchelor St, Queenstown;
tel: 6471 1005.

Mountain View Holiday Lodge $–$$$ 1 Penghana Rd,
Queenstown; tel: 6471 1163.

Mt Lyell Motor Inn $$ 1 Orr St, Queenstown; tel: 6471 1888.
In 1898 this used to be the stock exchange.

Queenstown Cabin $ 19 Grafton St, Queenstown;
tel: 6471 1332.

Queenstown Motor Lodge Motel $$$ 54–58 Orr St,
Queenstown; tel: 6471 1866.

Strahan Backpackers $–$$$ 43 Harvey St; tel: 6471 7255 or
1800 444 442. Nice bushy setting, basic but clean facilities.

Westcoaster Motor Inn $$$$ Batchelor St, Queenstown;
tel: 6471 1033.

FOOD AND DRINK

Strahan's reputation as a gourmet town continues to grow – fresh Southern Ocean
seafood is the meal of choice. Expect to find simpler fare in Queenstown eateries.

Franklin Manor $$$ The Esplanade, Strahan; tel: 6471 7311.
Open daily for dinner. Seafood.

Hamers Restaurant $$$ The Esplanade, Strahan; tel: 6471
7191. Open daily for dinner. Seafood.

Milan's Pizza Bar Restaurant $ 109 Port Rd, Strahan; tel:
6447 2102.

Vic's Bistro Restaurant $$ 1 Penghana Rd, Queenstown; tel:
6471 1163. BYO.

HIGHLIGHTS

Because of the ugliness of the surrounding countryside, Queenstown is listed as a his-
toric town. You can see some of the reasons in the **Eric Thomas Galley Museum**. This
was the Imperial Hotel, the first brick hotel in the town, and now 21 of its rooms house

MINING GHOST TOWNS

A 30-min drive from Queenstown is **Zeehan**. A century ago this was Tasmania's third-largest town, with 26 hotels and a population of 10,000. One tin mine still operates and many of the town's historic buildings have survived, including the Gaiety Theatre, at one time the largest theatre in Australia.

Gormanston, near Mt Lyell, was set up in 1881 as the original mining settlement with the discovery of Iron Blow. At the beginning of the 20th century it was quite a prosperous mining town but, now home to less than a dozen families, its glory days are well past – as they are also for **Linda**, 8 km from Queenstown, which is a ghost town in more than one sense. In 1912 Linda was the site of the area's last major mining disaster, when a fire killed 42 miners.

a photographic collection of mining life in the area ($); corner of Driffield and Stitch Sts; open Mon–Fri 1000–1630, Sat, Sun 1300–1630.

The refinery closed in 1964, the smelters in 1969 and the West Lyell mine in 1972, but mining, albeit on a much smaller scale, still continues. There are daily tours of the **Mount Lyell Mine** (departures from the Western Arts and Crafts Centre at 1 Driffield St). Surface tours, which last an hour, begin at 0915 and 1630, and an underground tour lasts $2^1/2$ hrs or eternity depending on your endurance. During the holiday months you should book in advance; tel: 6471 2388.

Because of a decided absence of grass Queenstown has the only gravel sports oval in Australia – football and cricket are played on it regularly.

One way of getting an overall view of the area is to ride the **chairlift**, which rises to 150 m. The ropeway was originally constructed in 1895 and is run by Queenstown Ropeways (tel: 6471 2338) from Penghana Rd, on the north side of the town. The chairlift runs seven days a week, no matter what the weather, and the views from the top are extensive if not sublime. The return journey takes about 15 mins.

North of Queenstown, in the Yolande River Valley, is the **Lake Margaret Power Station** which is Australia's second-oldest working hydroelectricity station. It was completed in 1914 and much of the original machinery is still working.

DAY TRIPS

There are extensive nature walks on the **Mullens and Franklin River Nature Trail**, and one of the great attractions of the Franklin River is white-water rafting. To the west is the old port of **Strahan** and access to part of the **Franklin–Gordon Wild Rivers National Park**.

STRAHAN

Strahan is the only town on the somewhat bleak and surf-swept west coast of Tasmania. In 1899 the Mount Lyell Mining Company constructed 35 km of railway to bring copper and passengers here. It crossed difficult country and needed 48 bridges, and in some sections was so steep that rack and pinion were needed to help the two steam engines haul the train up the slopes. The effort was worthwhile for access to **Macquarie Harbour**, the second largest in the southern hemisphere after Sydney. But it was never a port where ships could easily and safely enter. The mouth of the harbour is only 80 m across and rightly called Hell's Gates. A formidable bar limits the port to ships of shallow draft and they have a very tough time in the rough weather which is prevalent in the area. The first recorded entry into the practically landlocked harbour was made in 1815 by explorer James Kelly.

SALUTE TO THE MINERS

The men who mined the ore are well remembered at **Miners Siding**. First, there is the splendid **Mount Lyell No. 3 Abt Locomotive**. Built and commissioned in Queenstown in 1898, it travelled almost one million miles during its working life. From 1896 to 1932 the railway was the only transport link between Queenstown and the outside world. The old Abt railway line is being restored, and the aptly named Abt Wilderness Railway (Driffield St, Queenstown; tel: 6471 1700) will eventually take visitors on a 35-km journey from Queenstown to Strahan through magnificent west-coast forests. Currently the railway's steam locos and heritage carriages run as far as Rinadeena, a 22-km return journey from Queenstown; $$$.

Also at Miners Siding is **Miners Sunday**, a tableau in bronze and huon pine by sculptor Stephen Walker.

Finally, 11 bronze historical plaques, entitled **Ten Decades of Man and Mining**, depict 21 facets of the evolution of the Lyell district and, again, are the work of the sculptor Stephen Walker.

In 1821 two ships with 74 convicts were sent to establish a penal colony. It was a tough post. The prison settlement on **Sarah Island** hardly lasted a decade because it was far too difficult to keep supplied with the necessities of life; it became known as the worst prison for convicts in Australia. The convicts lived in appalling conditions and worked upriver for 12 hours a day, often wearing leg-irons. Sarah Island inmates were subsequently moved to Port Arthur (see p. 491).

The arrival of the timber men turned the town into a milling centre for huon pine, which grows well in this wet region. Then, during the mining boom, Strahan became a busy port shipping the copper out. Now the harbour caters mainly to abalone and cray fishermen.

Buildings such as the post office and the Union Steamship Company building are reminders of past prosperity. The Customs House, next door to the post office, houses the tourist office and has details of the **Strahan Historic Foreshore Walkway**, which links West Strahan Beach, the town centre and the old Regatta Point railway station.

Strahan's 30-km-long **Ocean Beach** is the longest in Tasmania, but visitors mainly come to Strahan for the **Gordon River** and a taste of true wilderness.

This is the wettest part of Australia after the tropical lowlands of north Queensland. It has rugged coastlines, wild rivers, open plains, thick rainforest and spectacular peaks. Tough and unforgiving country, it is virtually inaccessible to all but very experienced and well-equipped bushwalkers. It is also precious and has been declared a World Heritage Site, in the teeth of bitter opposition (see p. 493).

The easiest way to see at least some of this wild country is by cruising upriver. A number of companies (enquire at the tourist office) will take you by launch, cutting through spectacular mountain country covered by rainforest. The river's deep-brown colour is caused by the tannin from the buttongrass plains and does not mean it is polluted in any way; it is perfectly drinkable. At Heritage Landing there is a boardwalk that takes you above the rainforest floor.

> *i* **Strahan Visitor Centre**, The Esplanade; tel: 6471 7622; e-mail: strahan@tasvisinfo.com.au. Open daily (reduced hours during winter). See also: www.westcoasttourism.com.au/strahan.

WHERE NEXT?

To follow the route taken by the mined ores, take the Murchison Hwy to Burnie on the north coast (see p. 506).

CONVERSION TABLES

DISTANCES (approximate conversions)
1 kilometre (km) = 1000 metres (m) 1 metre = 100 centimetres (cm)

Metric	Imperial/US	Metric	Imperial/US	Metric	Imperial/US
1 cm	⅜ in	10 m	33 ft (11 yd)	3 km	2 miles
50 cm	20 in	20 m	66 ft (22 yd)	4 km	2½ miles
1 m	3 ft 3 in	50 m	164 ft (54 yd)	5 km	3 miles
2 m	6 ft 6 in	100 m	330 ft (110 yd)	10 km	6 miles
3 m	10 ft	200 m	660 ft (220 yd)	20 km	12½ miles
4 m	13 ft	250 m	820 ft (275 yd)	25 km	15½ miles
5 m	16 ft 6 in	300 m	984 ft (330 yd)	30 km	18½ miles
6 m	19 ft 6 in	500 m	1640 ft (550 yd)	40 km	25 miles
7 m	23 ft	750 m	½ mile	50 km	31 miles
8 m	26 ft	1 km	⅝ mile	75 km	46 miles
9 m	29 ft (10 yd)	2 km	1½ miles	100 km	62 miles

24-HOUR CLOCK
(examples)

0000 = Midnight	1300 = 1 pm
0600 = 6 am	1415 = 2.15 pm
0715 = 7.15 am	2000 = 8 pm
1200 = Noon	2345 = 11.45 pm

TEMPERATURE
Conversion formula: (°C x 9) ÷ 5 + 32 = °F

°C	°F	°C	°F	°C	°F	°C	°F
-20	-4	-5	23	10	50	25	77
-15	5	0	32	15	59	30	86
-10	14	5	41	20	68	35	95

WEIGHT
1 kg = 1000 g 100 g = 3oz

kg	lb	kg	lb	kg	lb
1	2¼	5	11	25	55
2	4½	10	22	50	110
3	6½	15	33	75	165
4	9	20	45	100	220

FLUID MEASURES
1 ltr (l) = 0.88 Imp quarts = 1.06 US quarts

ltr	Imp gal	US gal	ltr	Imp gal	US gal
5	1.1	1.3	30	6.6	7.8
10	2.2	2.6	35	7.7	9.1
15	3.3	3.9	40	8.8	10.4
20	4.4	5.2	45	9.9	11.7
25	5.5	6.5	50	11.0	13.0

MEN'S SHIRTS

Aus/UK	Europe	US
14	36	14
15	38	15
15½	39	15½
16	41	16
16½	42	16½
17	43	17

LADIES' CLOTHES

Aus/UK	France	Italy	Rest of Europe	US
10	36	38	34	8
12	38	40	36	10
14	40	42	38	12
16	42	44	40	14
18	44	46	42	16
20	46	48	44	18

MEN'S CLOTHES

Aus/UK	Europe	US
36	46	36
38	48	38
40	50	40
42	52	42
44	54	44
46	56	46

AREAS
1 hectare = 2.471 acres
1 hectare = 10,000 sq m
1 acre = 0.4 hectares

INDEX

Independent Travellers Australia

Feedback Form

Please help us improve future editions by taking part in our reader survey. Just take a few minutes to complete and return this form to us, or even better, e-mail your feedback to *books@thomascook.com* or visit *www.thomascookpublishing.com*.

We'd also be glad to hear of your comments, updates or recommendations on places we cover or you think that we ought to cover.

1. Why is this your preferred choice of budget travel guide?

(Please tick as many as appropriate)

a) the price ☐

b) the cover ☐

c) the content ☐

d) other _____

2. What do you think of:

a) the cover design _____

b) the design and layout styles within the book _____

_____

c) the content _____

_____

d) the maps _____

3. Please tell us about any features that in your opinion could be changed, improved or added in future editions of the book, or any other comments you would like to make concerning this book _____

_____

_____

_____

_____

4. What is the single most useful/helpful aspect of this book? _____

_____

cut along the dotted line

5. Have you purchased other *Independent Travellers* Guides in the series?

a) yes ☐

b) no ☐

If Yes, please specify which titles _____

6. Would you purchase other *Independent Travellers* Guides?

a) yes ☐

b) no ☐

If No, please specify why not _____

7. What other titles would you like to see in this series?

_____

_____

Your age category: ☐ under 21 ☐ 21–30 ☐ 31–40 ☐ 41–50 ☐ 51+

Mr/Mrs/Miss/Ms/Other

Surname_____ Initials _____

Full address: (Please include postal or zip code) _____

_____

_____

Daytime telephone number: _____

E-mail address: _____

Please detach this page and send it to: The Series Editor,
Independent Travellers **Guides, Thomas Cook Publishing, PO Box 227,**
The Thomas Cook Business Park, Units 15–16, Coningsby Road,
Peterborough PE3 8SB, United Kingdom.

Alternatively, you can e-mail us at: *books@thomascook.com*